TAKING SIDES

Clashing Views in

World Politics

FOURTEENTH EDITION, EXPANDED

Selected, Edited, and with Introductions by

John T. Rourke
University of Connecticut

McGraw Hill

Connect
Learn
Succeed™

TAKING SIDES: CLASHING VIEWS IN WORLD POLITICS,
FOURTEENTH EDITION, EXPANDED

Published by McGraw-Hill, a business unit of The McGraw-Hill Companies, Inc., 1221 Avenue
of the Americas, New York, NY 10020. Copyright © 2010 by The McGraw-Hill Companies, Inc.
All rights reserved. Previous edition(s) 2009 and 2008. No part of this publication may be
reproduced or distributed in any form or by any means, or stored in a database or retrieval
system, without the prior written consent of The McGraw-Hill Companies, Inc., including, but not
limited to, in any network or other electronic storage or transmission, or broadcast for distance
learning.

Some ancillaries, including electronic and print components, may not be available to customers
outside the United States.

Taking Sides® is a registered trademark of The McGraw-Hill Companies, Inc.
Taking Sides is published by the **Contemporary Learning Series** group within the McGraw-Hill
Higher Education division.

1 2 3 4 5 6 7 8 9 0 DOC/DOC 1 0 9 8 7 6 5 4 3 2 1 0

MHID: 0-07-804993-8
ISBN: 978-0-07-804993-4
ISSN: 1094-754X

Managing Editor: *Larry Loeppke*
Senior Managing Editor: *Faye Schilling*
Senior Developmental Editor: *Jill Meloy*
Editorial Coordinator: *Mary Foust*
Editorial Assistant: *Nancy Meissner*
Production Service Assistant: *Rita Hingtgen*
Permissions Coordinator: *Shirley Lanners*
Senior Marketing Manager: *Julie Keck*
Marketing Communications Specialist: *Mary Klein*
Marketing Coordinator: *Alice Link*
Senior Project Manager: *Erin Melloy*
Design Specialist: *Tara McDermott*
Cover Graphics: *Rick D. Noel*

Compositor: MPS Limited, A Macmillan Company
Cover Image: © Corbis/RF (background globe), with insets: US AID (displaced persons in Darfur,
Africa), © Photodisc/Getty Images/RF (UN flag), © Creatas/PunchStock (smoke stack), Digital
Vision/Getty Images/RF (soldiers), Erica Simone Leeds, 2007 (Coke truck in India), © 1997
IMS Communications, Ltd/Capstone Design (All Rights Reserved) (shipping dock), © The
McGraw-Hill Companies (President Obama), © Getty Images/RF (stock market), © Creatas/
PunchStock/RF (oil drill)

Library of Congress Cataloging-in-Publication Data

Main entry under title:
 Taking sides: clashing views in world politics/selected, edited, and with introductions
 by John T. Rourke—14th ed., expanded

 Includes bibliographical references.
 1. World Politics—1989-. I. Rourke, John T., *comp.*
909.82

www.mhhe.com

Editors/Academic Advisory Board

Members of the Academic Advisory Board are instrumental in the final selection of articles for each edition of TAKING SIDES. Their review of articles for content, level, and appropriateness provides critical direction to the editors and staff. We think that you will find their careful consideration well reflected in this volume.

TAKING SIDES: Clashing Views in WORLD POLITICS
Fourteenth Edition, Expanded

EDITOR

John T. Rourke
University of Connecticut

ACADEMIC ADVISORY BOARD MEMBERS

Preface

In the first edition of *Taking Sides: Clashing Views in World Politics,* I wrote of my belief in informed argument: [A] book that debates vital issues is valuable and necessary. . . . [It is important] to recognize that world politics is usually not a subject of absolute rights and absolute wrongs and of easy policy choices. We all have a responsibility to study the issues thoughtfully, and we should be careful to understand all sides of the debates.

It is gratifying to discover, as indicated by the success of *Taking Sides* over 13 editions, that so many of my colleagues share this belief in the value of a debate-format text.

The format of this edition follows a formula that has proved successful in acquainting students with the global issues that we face and in generating discussion of those issues and the policy choices that address them. This book addresses 21 issues on a wide range of topics in international relations. Each issue has two readings, one pro and one con. Each is also accompanied by an issue *introduction,* which sets the stage for the debate, provides some background information on each author, and generally puts the issue into its political context. Each issue concludes with a *postscript* that summarizes the debate, gives the reader paths for further investigation, and suggests additional readings that might be helpful. I have also provided relevant Internet site addresses (URLs) in each postscript and on the *Internet References* page that accompanies each part opener. At the back of the book is a listing of all the *contributors to this volume,* which will give you information on the political scientists and other commentators whose views are debated here.

I have continued to emphasize issues that are currently being debated in the policy sphere. The authors of the selections are a mix of practitioners, scholars, and noted political commentators.

Changes to this edition   The dynamic, constantly changing nature of the world political system and the many helpful comments from reviewers have brought about significant changes to this edition. More than a third of the issues are new. They are: Does Capitalism Undermine Democracy? (Issue 3); Should the United States Substantially Limit Its Global Involvement? (Issue 4); Is a Military Intervention in Darfur Justified? (Issue 10); Do Sovereign Wealth Funds Threaten Economic Sovereignty? (Issue 12); Should U.S. Development of a Missile Defense System Continue? (Issue 15); Is UN Peacekeeping Seriously Flawed? (Issue 16); and Has the U.S. Detention and Trial of Accused Foreign Terrorists Been Legally Unsound? (Issue 18). All these use readings new to this edition, and because of the kaleidoscopic dynamism of the international system most of the issues that have been carried over also have new readings. The eight issues (42 percent) that were included in the last edition but have one or more new readings are: Is Economic Globalization a Positive Trend?

(Issue 1); Does Globalization Threaten Cultural Diversity? (Issue 3); Will China Soon Become a Threatening Superpower? (Issue 6); Should All Foreign Troop Soon Leave Iraq? (Issue 8); Does Hugo Chávez Threaten Hemispheric Stability and Democracy? (Issue 9); Is Patient Diplomacy the Best Approach to Iran's Nuclear Program? (Issue 14); Is U.S. Refusal to Join the International Criminal Court Wise? (Issue 17); Has the U.S. Detention and Trial of Accused Foreign Terrorists Been Legally Unsound? (Issue 18); and Are Warnings about Global Warming Unduly Alarmist? (Issue 19). In all, 31 of the 42 readings in this edition are new. Additionally, new does not just mean new to this edition. The articles are also "fresh," with 71 percent authored in 2007 or 2008, and another 24 percent from 2005 and 2006.

It is important to note that the changes to this edition from the last should not disguise the fact that most of the issues address enduring human concerns, such as global political organization, arms and arms control, justice, development, and the environment. Also important is the fact that many of the issues have both a specific and a larger topic. For instance, Issue 16 is about the specific topic of the performance of United Nations peacekeeping, but it is also about more general topics. These include the proper role of international organizations in the global system and the degree to which countries should subordinate their sovereignty to them.

A word to the instructor An *Instructor's Manual with Test Questions* (multiple-choice and essay) is available through the publisher for instructors using *Taking Sides* in the classroom. A general guidebook, *Using Taking Sides in the Classroom,* which discusses methods and techniques for integrating the pro-con approach into any classroom setting, is also available. An online version of *Using Taking Sides in the Classroom* and a correspondence service for *Taking Sides* adopters can be found at http://www.mhhe.com/cls. *Taking Sides: Clashing Views in World Politics* is only one title in the *Taking Sides* series. If you are interested in seeing the table of contents for any of the other titles, please visit the *Taking Sides* Web site at http://www.mhhe.com/cls.

A note especially for the student reader You will find that the debates in this book are not one-sided. Each author strongly believes in his or her position. And if you read the debates without prejudging them, you will see that each author makes cogent points. An author may not be "right," but the arguments made in an essay should not be dismissed out of hand, and you should work to remain tolerant of those who hold beliefs that are different from your own. There is an additional consideration to keep in mind as you pursue this debate approach to world politics. To consider divergent views objectively does not mean that you have to remain forever neutral. In fact, once you are informed, you ought to form convictions. More important, you should try to influence international policy to conform better with your beliefs. Write letters to policymakers; donate to causes you support; work for candidates who agree with your views; join an activist organization. *Do* something, whichever side of an issue you are on!

Acknowledgments I received many helpful comments and suggestions from colleagues and readers across the United States and Canada. Their suggestions have markedly enhanced the quality of this edition of *Taking Sides*. If as you read this book you are reminded of a selection or an issue that could be included in a future edition, please write to me in care of McGraw-Hill/ Contemporary Learning Series with your recommendations or e-mail them to me at john.rourke@uconn.edu.

My thanks go to those who responded with suggestions for the 14th edition. I would also like to thank Jill Meloy, my editor for this volume, for her help in refining this edition.

John T. Rourke
University of Connecticut

For my son and friend—John Michael

Contents In Brief

Contents

Staff members of the International Monetary Fund conclude on the basis of experiences across the world that unhindered international economic interchange, the core principle of globalization, seems to underpin greater prosperity. Nancy Birdsall, founding president of the Center for Global Development, argues that globalization is not benefiting all and that a major challenge of the twenty-first century will be to address persistent and unjust inequality, which global markets alone cannot resolve.

Julia Galeota of McLean, Virginia, who was seventeen years old when she wrote her essay that won first place for her age category in the 2004 *Humanist* Essay Contest for Young Women and Men of North America, contends that many cultures around the world are gradually disappearing due to the overwhelming influence of corporate and cultural America. Philippe Legrain, chief economist of Britain in Europe, an organization supporting the adoption by Great Britain of the euro as its currency, counters that it is a myth that globalization involves the imposition of Americanized uniformity, rather than an explosion of cultural exchange.

Robert B. Reich, professor of public policy at the University of California, Berkeley, and former U.S. secretary of labor, writes that capitalism leaves democratic societies unable to address the tradeoffs between economic growth and social problems. Taking the opposite point of view, Anthony B. Kim, a policy analyst at the Heritage Foundation's Center for International Trade and Economics, contends that economic progress through advancing economic freedom has allowed more people to discuss and adopt different views more candidly, ultimately leading societies to be more open and inclusive.

UNIT 2 REGIONAL AND COUNTRY ISSUES 59

Ivan Eland, senior fellow at the Independent Institute, a libertarian think tank in Oakland, California and Washington, DC, contends that neither the Republican nor the Democratic Party in the United States has shown any inclination to follow the wise counsel of the country's founders such as George Washington and practice restraint in the country's overseas involvement. By contrast, Barack Obama, then a Democratic U.S. senator from Illinois and the 2008 nominee of the Democratic Party for president, sharply criticizes the foreign policy of President George W. Bush for undercutting American leadership of the world and argues that it is time to reclaim that leadership through a new approach.

Tucker Herbert and Diane Raub, both of whom are on the staff of the *Stanford Review,* an independent, student-run newspaper at Stanford University, argue that under President Vladimir Putin, Russia has fallen from the ranks of democracies and is engaged in a foreign policy that pits U.S. interests against those of Russia. Eugene B. Rumer, a senior research fellow at the National Defense University's Institute for National Strategic Studies in Washington, DC, recognizes that Russian democracy falls short of full scale and that Russian policy sometimes clashes with that of the United States, but argues that compared with the history of Russian democracy, which was zero before the 1990s, the country is not doing poorly and that Russia's pursuit of its own interests should not be construed as necessarily antagonistic.

position Michael Eisenstadt, a senior fellow and director of The Washington Institute's Military and Security Studies Program, contends that there is no doubt that the surge of U.S. forces into Iraq in 2007 has dramatically improved the security environment in Iraq, and that too rapid a withdrawal would reverse the gains that have been made.

Issue 9. Does Hugo Chávez Threaten Hemispheric Stability and Democracy? 146

Norman A. Bailey, a senior fellow at the Potomac Foundation, a conservative think tank in Vienna, Virginia, and formerly senior director of international economic affairs for the National Security Council, argues that Venezuela's President Hugo Chávez is ruining the country economically, destroying its democracy, and undertaking foreign policies, including supporting terrorism, which threaten hemispheric stability. Taking a more sympathetic viewpoint toward Venezuela, Jennifer McCoy, professor of political science, Georgia State University and director of The Americas Program at The Carter Center, argues that the reforms Hugo Chávez has instituted in Venezuela are very popular there, that the charges that he supports terrorism are overdrawn, and that the best course for U.S. foreign policy is to start with positive signals and focus on pragmatic concerns of interest to both countries.

Issue 10. Is Military Intervention in Darfur Justified? 163

Susan E. Rice, a senior fellow in foreign policy and global economics and development at the Brooking Institution, formerly U.S. assistant secretary of state for African affairs and nominated to be U.S. Ambassador to the UN in January 2009, says that using military force is long overdue to halt what she portrays as an ongoing genocide in Darfur. Alex de Waal, program director at the Social Science Research Council, a research organization in New York City, contends that inserting a military force into a very unstable situation would not likely bring success and that using diplomacy to create a situation where all sides want peace is a better strategy for now.

for addressing a growing threat in an uncertain world. Taking the opposite side, Philip E. Coyle, III, senior advisor at the Center for Defense Information, a liberal think tank in Washington, DC, and former U.S. assistant secretary of defense, takes the view that trying to build a missile defense system will be very expensive, is unlikely to work, and will reignite a destabilizing nuclear arms race.

Kate Martin, director of the Center for National Security Studies, criticizes what she describes as extraordinary and unsupportable claims by the executive branch that the president is free to ignore statutory law and violate civil rights in order to conduct the war against terror. She also notes that the president's stand has been repeatedly rejected by the courts. Rebutting this point of view, David B. Rivkin, a partner in the law firm of Baker & Hostetler and former deputy director of the Office of Policy Development, U.S. Department of Justice, contends that while some aspects of the treatment of accused foreign terrorists in U.S. custody have not met the civil liberties standards normally enjoyed by Americans, the Bush administration's policies have been indispensable in protecting Americans during the war on terrorism and that the administration's legal positions have generally been upheld by the courts.

UNIT 6   THE ENVIRONMENT   363

James Inhofe, a Republican member of the U.S. Senate from Oklahoma, tells the Senate that objective, evidence-based science is beginning to show that the predictions of catastrophic humanmade global warming are overwought. Rejecting Senator Inhofe's contentions, Barbara Boxer, a Democratic member of the U.S. Senate from California, responds that Senator Inhofe's is one of the very few isolated and lonely voices that keeps on saying we do not have to worry about global warming, while, in reality, it is a major problem that demands a prompt response.

Harold Hongju Koh, the Gerard C. and Bernice Latrobe Smith Professor
of International Law at Yale University and former U.S. assistant secretary
of state contends that the United States cannot champion progress for
women's human rights around the world unless it is also a party to the
global women's treaty. Grace Smith Melton, an associate for social issues
at the United Nations with the Richard and Helen DeVos Center for
Religion and Civil Society at The Heritage Foundation, contends that
ratifying would neither advance women's equality nor serve American
foreign policy interests, including the security and advancement of women
around the globe.

Issue 21.   Is President Barack Obama's Strategic Nuclear Arms Control Policy Sound?   408

William J. Perry, former U.S. secretary of defense, reviews and generally
supports the statements and early policy moves of the Obama
administration with regard to strategic nuclear weapons. Keith B. Payne,
professor in and head of the Department of Defense and Strategic Studies
at Missouri State University, outlines "six major concerns" he has with the
apparent early direction of the Obama administration's efforts to re-
establish strategic arms control as a centerpiece of U.S.-Russian
engagement.

Correlation Guide

The *Taking Sides* series presents current issues in a debate-style format designed to stimulate student interest and develop critical thinking skills. Each issue is thoughtfully framed with an issue summary, an issue introduction, and a postscript. The pro and con essays—selected for their liveliness and substance—represent the arguments of leading scholars and commentators in their fields.

Taking Sides: Clashing Views in World Politics, 14/e, Expanded is an easy-to-use reader that presents issues on important topics such as *globalization, economics, armaments and violence, the environment,* and *international law.* For more information on *Taking Sides* and other *McGraw-Hill Contemporary Learning Series* titles, visit www.mhcls.com.

This convenient guide matches the issues in **Taking Sides: World Politics, 14/e, Expanded** with the corresponding chapters in two of our best-selling McGraw-Hill Political Science textbooks by Rourke and Boyer.

Taking Sides: World Politics, 14/e, Expanded	International Politics on the World Stage, 12/e by Rourke	International Politics on the World Stage, Brief, 8/e by Rourke/Boyer
Issue 1: Is Economic Globalization a Positive Trend?	**Chapter 5:** Globalism: The Alternative Orientation	**Chapter 5:** Globalization and Transnationalism: The Alternative Orientation **Chapter 10:** Globalization in the World Economy
Issue 2: Does Globalization Threaten Cultural Diversity?	**Chapter 5:** Globalism: The Alternative Orientation	**Chapter 5:** Globalization and Transnationalism: The Alternative Orientation
Issue 3: Does Capitalism Undermine Democracy?	**Chapter 12:** National Economic Competition: The Traditional Road	
Issue 4: Should the United States Substantially Limit Its Global Involvement?	**Chapter 5:** Globalism: The Alternative Orientation	**Chapter 5:** Globalization and Transnationalism: The Alternative Orientation
Issue 5: Has Russia Become Undemocratic and Antagonistic?	**Chapter 6:** National States: The Traditional Structure	**Chapter 6:** Power and the National States: The Traditional Structure
Issue 6: Will China Soon Become a Threatening Superpower?	**Chapter 8:** National Power and Statecraft: The Traditional Approach	**Chapter 6:** Power and the National States: The Traditional Structure
Issue 7: Would It Be an Error to Establish a Palestinian State?	**Chapter 4:** Nationalism: The Traditional Orientation **Chapter 6:** National States: The Traditional Structure	**Chapter 7:** International Organization: An Alternative Structure
Issue 8: Should All Foreign Troops Soon Leave Iraq?	**Chapter 3:** Levels of Analysis and Foreign Policy **Chapter 5:** Globalism: The Alternative Orientation **Chapter 6:** National States: The Traditional Structure	**Chapter 9:** Pursuing Security

Taking Sides: World Politics, 14/e, Expanded	International Politics on the World Stage, 12/e by Rourke	International Politics on the World Stage, Brief, 8/e by Rourke/Boyer
Issue 9: Does Hugo Chavez Threaten Hemispheric Stability and Democracy?	**Chapter 2:** The Evolution of World Politics **Chapter 6:** National States: The Traditional Structure **Chapter 12:** National Economic Competition: The Traditional Road **Chapter 13:** International Economic Cooperation: The Alternative Road	**Chapter 6:** Power and the National States: The Traditional Structure
Issue 10: Is Military Intervention in Darfur Justified?	**Chapter 11:** International Security: The Alternative Road	**Chapter 9:** Pursuing Security
Issue 11: Is World Trade Organization Membership Beneficial?	**Chapter 13:** International Economic Cooperation: The Alternative Road	**Chapter 10:** Globalization in the World Economy
Issue 12: Do Sovereign Wealth Funds Threaten Economic Sovereignty?	**Chapter 13:** International Economic Cooperation: The Alternative Road	**Chapter 10:** Globalization in the World Economy
Issue 13: Is Immigration an Economic Benefit to the Host Country?	**Chapter 4:** Nationalism: The Traditional Orientation	**Chapter 11:** Global Economic Competition and Cooperation
Issue 14: Is Patient Diplomacy the Best Approach to Iran's Nuclear Program?	**Chapter 3:** Levels of Analysis and Foreign Policy **Chapter 12:** National Economic Competition: The Traditional Road	**Chapter 9:** Pursuing Security
Issue 15: Should U.S. Development of a Missile Defense System Continue?	**Chapter 8:** National Power and Statecraft: the Traditional Approach	**Chapter 9:** Pursuing Security
Issue 16: Is UN Peacekeeping Seriously Flawed?	**Chapter 11:** International Security: The Alternative Road	**Chapter 9:** Pursuing Security
Issue 17: Is U.S. Refusal to Join the International Criminal Court Wise?	**Chapter 9:** International Law and Justice: An Alternative Approach	**Chapter 8:** International Law and Human Rights: An Alternative Approach
Issue 18: Has the U.S. Detention and Trial of Accused Foreign Terrorists Been Legally Unsound?	**Chapter 10:** National Security: The Traditional Road	**Chapter 8:** International Law and Human Rights: An Alternative Approach
Issue 19: Are Warnings about Global Warming Unduly Alarmist?	**Chapter 15:** Preserving and Enhancing the Biosphere	**Chapter 12:** Preserving and Enhancing the Global Commons
Issue 20: Should the United States Ratify the Convention to Eliminate All Forms of Discrimination Against Women?	**Chapter 14:** Prospective Human Rights	**Chapter 8:** International Law and Human Rights
Issue 21: Is President Barack Obama's Strategic Nuclear Arms Control Policy Sound?		

Introduction

World Politics and the Voice of Justice

John T. Rourke

Some years ago, the Rolling Stones recorded "Sympathy with the Devil." If you have never heard it, go find a copy. It is worth listening to. The theme of the song is echoed in a wonderful essay by Marshall Berman, "Have Sympathy for the Devil" (*New American Review,* 1973). The common theme of the Stones' and Berman's works is based on Johann Goethe's *Faust.* In that classic drama, the protagonist, Dr. Faust, trades his soul to gain great power. He attempts to do good, but in the end he commits evil by, in contemporary paraphrase, "doing the wrong things for the right reasons." Does that make Faust evil, the personification of the devil Mephistopheles among us? Or is the good doctor merely misguided in his effort to make the world better as he saw it and imagined it might be? The point that the Stones and Berman make is that it is important to avoid falling prey to the trap of many zealots who are so convinced of the truth of their own views that they feel righteously at liberty to condemn those who disagree with them as stupid or even diabolical.

It is to the principle of rational discourse, of tolerant debate, that this reader is dedicated. There are many issues in this volume that appropriately excite passion—for example, Issue 7 on whether or not Israel should agree to an independent Palestinian state, or Issue 18 which examines whether or not those accused of terrorism should have legal protections similar to those given prisoners of war. If not, then the question is what are the boundaries? Can such prisoners be held without trial? Can interrogators use torture?

As you will see, each of the authors in all the debates strongly believes in his or her position. If you read these debates objectively, you will find that each side makes cogent points. They may or may not be right, but they should not be dismissed out of hand. It is important to repeat that the debate format does not imply that you should remain forever neutral. In fact, once you are informed, you *ought* to form convictions, and you should try to act on those convictions and try to influence international policy to conform better with your beliefs. Ponder the similarities in the views of two very different leaders, a very young president in a relatively young democracy and a very old emperor in a very old country: In 1963 President John F. Kennedy, in recalling the words of the author of the epic poem *The Divine Comedy* (1321), told a West German audience, "Dante once said that the hottest places in hell are reserved for those who in a period of moral crisis maintain their neutrality." That very same year, while speaking to the United Nations, Ethiopia's emperor Haile Selassie (1892–1975) said, "Throughout history it has been the inaction of those who could have acted, the indifference of those who should have known better, the silence of the voice of justice when it mattered most that made it possible for evil to triumph."

The point is: Become Informed. Then *do* something! Write letters to policymakers, donate money to causes you support, work for candidates with whom you agree, join an activist organization, or any of the many other things that you can do to make a difference. What you do is less important than that you do it.

Approaches to Studying International Politics

As will become evident as you read this volume, there are many approaches to the study of international politics. Some political scientists and most practitioners specialize in *substantive topics,* and this reader is organized along topical lines. Unit 1 (Issues 1 through 3) features debates on the evolution of the international system in the direction of greater globalization. In Issue 1, members of the staff of the International Monetary Fund and Nancy Birdsall, president of the Center for Global Development, debate the general topic of economic globalization. The IMF staff members argue that economic globalization has generally brought prosperity. Birdsall counters that globalization is not benefiting all and that the process needs to be regulated in order to alleviate persistent and unjust inequality. Issue 2 addresses the accompanying phenomenon of cultural globalization. American student Julia Galeota fears that American culture is wiping away cultural diversity in the world, while British analyst Philippe Legrain rejects these charges and points to the positive aspects of cultural diversity. The current norm of economic globalization presses countries to adopt a capitalist system, and in Issue 3, Professor Robert B. Reich and policy analyst Anthony B. Kim differ on whether capitalism and democracy are compatible.

Unit 2 (Issues 4 through 10) focuses on regional and country-specific issues, including the U.S. positions in the world trends in Russian domestic and foreign policy, whether China should be considered a growing threat, the possibility of a Palestinian state, whether U.S. and other foreign troops should withdraw quickly from Iraq or stay for an extended time to try to stabilize and democratize the country, and the role of Venezuela in the Western Hemisphere.

Unit 3 (Issues 11 through 13) deals with specific concerns of the international economy, a topic introduced more generally in Issue 1. Issue 11 takes up the general topic of free trade and the more specific topic of whether membership in the World Trade Organization is beneficial or not. Monetary relations are another aspect of economic globalization. Issue 11 takes up the related issue of international investment, with a specific focus on sovereignty wealth funds, investment organization that are owned or controlled by a government. Former U.S. Assistant Secretary of Commerce Patrick Mulloy and former Under Secretary of State Stuart E. Eizenstat differ over whether sovereign wealth funds present economic and national security problems for the country. In Issue 13, the debate turns to the impact of immigration on host countries. The flow of both legal and illegal immigration is a contentious topic in many countries, and here the debate focuses on the United States as an example of the controversy.

Unit 4 (Issues 14 and 15) examines violence and the attempts to limit it in the international system. The past few decades have witnessed a rising concern about the spread of nuclear weapons among countries and the capability to deliver the weapons over long range by ballistic missiles. Issue 14 takes up the specific case of Iran's nuclear and missile programs, and Issue 15 addresses whether the United States is being wise in its recent concerted efforts to develop and deploy a system to defend against attacking ballistic missiles.

Unit 5 (Issues 16 through 18) addresses controversies related to international law and organizations. The ability of the United Nations to deploy effective peacekeeping forces is severely constrained by a number of factors, and in Issue 16, Brett D. Schaefer and William J. Durch, analysts from two private research and advocacy organizations (think tanks), debate whether UN peacekeeping is fundamentally flawed or is on the way to overcoming its internal problems and deserved renewed and increased global support. Issue 17 evaluates the wisdom of establishing a permanent international criminal court to punish those who violate the law of war. It is easy to advocate such a court as long as it is trying and sometimes punishing alleged war criminals from other countries. But one has to understand that one day a citizen of one's own country could be put on trial. The third debate in Unit 5 takes up the treatment of terrorist combatants, such as the al-Qaeda fighters captured by U.S. forces in Afghanistan, with countervailing arguments about whether a series of recent Supreme Court cases including *Boumediene v. Bush* (2008) mean that the Bush administrations treatment of such prisoners has been basically unjust.

Unit 6, which consists of Issue 19, addresses the environment. Over the past few decades there has been a growing concern about global warming. Many people believe that it is mostly being caused by human activities, especially the burning of petroleum and other fossil fuels that discharges carbon dioxide into the atmosphere. There is also widespread belief that global warming will bring increasingly catastrophic results and that strong measures should be quickly taken to greatly reduce the emission of carbon dioxide and similar gases. U.S. Senator James Inhofe rejects this view in the first reading, and his view is directly contested in the second reading by U.S. Senator Barbara Boxer.

Political scientists also approach their subject from differing *methodological perspectives*. You will see, for example, that world politics can be studied from different *levels of analysis*. The question is, What is the basic source of the forces that shape the conduct of politics? Possible answers are world forces, the individual political processes of the specific countries, or the personal attributes of a country's leaders and decision makers. Various readings will illustrate all three levels.

Another way for students and practitioners of world politics to approach their subject is to focus on what is called the realist versus the idealist (or liberal) debate. Realists tend to assume that the world is permanently flawed and therefore advocate following policies in their country's narrow self-interests. Idealists take the approach that the world condition can be improved substantially by following policies that, at least in the short term, call for some risk or self-sacrifice. This divergence is an element of many of the debates in this book. Issue 17 is one example. In the first reading, State Department official John Bolton says that if the United States adheres to the treaty establishing the International Court of Justice, Americans will be sacrificing their national sovereignty and putting U.S. troops and officials at risk of being arrested and tried on politically motivated charges of having committed war crimes. Jonathan Fanton, head of one of the world's largest foundations promoting world peace, disagrees, arguing that the ICC is a major step toward a more just world and does not pose any threat to the United States.

Dynamics of World Politics

The action on the global stage today is vastly different from what it was a few decades ago, or even a few years ago. *Technology* is one of the causes of this change. Technology has changed communications, manufacturing, health care, and many other aspects of the human condition. Technology has given humans the ability to create biological, chemical, and nuclear compounds and other material that in relatively small amounts have the ability to kill and injure huge numbers of people. Another negative by-product of technology may be the vastly increased consumption of petroleum and other natural resources and the global environmental degradation that has been caused by discharges of waste products, deforestation, and a host of other technology-enhanced human activities.

Another dynamic aspect of world politics involves the *changing axes* of the world system. For about 40 years after World War II ended in 1945, a bipolar system existed, the primary axis of which was the *East-West* conflict, which pitted the United States and its allies against the Soviet Union and its allies. Now that the Cold War is over, one broad debate is over what role the United States should play. In Issue 4 libertarian analyst Ivan Eland argues that the United States should substantially cut back on its level of international involvement. This view is disputed by U.S. then presidential candidate Barack Obama. Some believe that the old East-West axis might return, and Issue 5 looks at Russia, the last rival to the U.S. super power status before the Soviet Union's collapse in 1991, and assesses whether Moscow is once again becoming undemocratic and hostile. Then Issue 6 deals with China. Some people believe that China is the next superpower and that it will pose a threat to U.S. security and interests. Others do not see China as a threat, but believe that treating it as one could become a self-fulfilling prophecy.

Technological changes and the shifting axes of international politics also highlight the *increased role of economics* in world politics. Economics have always played a role, but traditionally the main focus has been on strategic-political questions—especially military power. This concern still strongly exists, but now it shares the international spotlight with economic issues. One important change in recent decades has been the rapid growth of regional and global markets and the promotion of free trade and other forms of international economic interchange. As Issue 1 on economic interdependence indicates, many people support these efforts and see them as the wave of the future. But there are others who believe that free economic globalization and interdependence undermine sovereignty and the ability of governments to control their destinies. In part because of the dominance of the United States, capitalism is the prevailing economic globalization model for domestic economic systems, and in Issue 3 former Secretary of Labor Robert Reich argues there is a tension between capitalism and democracy; a contention that is rejected by policy analyst Anthony Kim. Yet another related topic is taken up in Issue 11, which addresses free trade and its oversight body, the World Trade Organization, are making a positive contribution to the world as a whole. Discussions on trade lead to discussions on international investment, and the benefits or harms accompany a relatively new phenomenon, sovereign wealth groups, which is the topic in Issue 12.

Another change in the world system has to do with the main *international* actors. At one time states (countries) were practically the only international actors on the world stage. Now, and increasingly so, there are other actors. Some actors are regional. Others, such as the United Nations, are global actors. Turning to the most notable international organization, Issue 16 examines the UN peacekeeping and, by extension, the role of that world organization and the proper approach of member countries to it and to global cooperation. Issue 17 focuses on whether or not a supranational criminal court should be established to take over the prosecution and punishment of war criminals from the domestic courts and ad hoc tribunals that have sometimes dealt with such cases in the past.

Perceptions Versus Reality

In addition to addressing the general changes in the world system outlined above, the debates in this reader explore the controversies that exist over many of the fundamental issues that face the world.

One key to these debates is the differing *perceptions* that protagonists bring to them. There may be a reality in world politics, but very often that reality is obscured. Many observers, for example, are alarmed by the seeming rise in radical actions by Islamic fundamentalists. However, the image of Islamic radicalism is not a fact but a perception; perhaps correct, perhaps not. In cases such as this, though, it is often the perception, not the reality, that is more important because policy is formulated on what decision makers *think,* not necessarily on what *is.* Thus, perception becomes the operating guide, or *operational reality,* whether it is true or not. Perceptions result from many actors. One factor is the information that decision makers receive. For a variety of reasons, the facts and analyses that are given to leaders are often inaccurate or represent only part of the picture. The conflicting perceptions of Israelis and Palestinians, for example, make the achievement of peace in Israel very difficult. Many Israelis and Palestinians fervently believe that the conflict that has occurred in the region over the past 50 years is the responsibility of the other. Both sides also believe in the righteousness of their own policies. Even if both sides are well-meaning, the perceptions of hostility that each holds means that the operational reality often has to be violence. These differing perceptions are a key element in the debate in Issue 7.

A related aspect of perception is the tendency to see oneself differently than some others do. Specifically, the tendency is to see oneself as benevolent and to perceive rivals as sinister. This reverse image is partly at issue in the debate over Iran's nuclear program. Many Americans and others see Iran as a rogue nation intent on developing nuclear weapons to use to threaten or attack other countries. But Iran claims that its intentions are only to develop nuclear energy plants, as many other countries have, and that even if it does choose to develop nuclear weapons, they would only for defense against such hostile nuclear powers as the United States and Israel. Which view is the reality and which is the perception? Perceptions, then, are crucial to understanding international politics. It is important to understand objective reality, but it is also necessary to comprehend subjective reality in order to be able to predict and analyze another country's actions.

Levels of Analysis

Political scientists approach the study of international politics from different levels of analysis. The most macroscopic view is *system-level analysis*. This is a top-down approach that maintains that world factors virtually compel countries to follow certain foreign policies. Governing factors include the number of powerful actors, geographic relationships, economic needs, and technology. System analysts hold that a country's internal political system and its leaders do not have a major impact on policy. As such, political scientists who work from this perspective are interested in exploring the governing factors, how they cause policy, and how and why systems change.

After the end of World War II, the world was structured as a *bipolar* system, dominated by the United States and the Soviet Union. Furthermore, each superpower was supported by a tightly organized and dependent group of allies. For a variety of reasons, including changing economics and the nuclear standoff, the bipolar system has faded. Some political scientists argue that the bipolar system is being replaced by a *multipolar* system. In such a configuration, those who favor *balance-of-power* politics maintain that it is unwise to ignore power considerations. Or it may be that something like at least a limited one-power (unipolar) system exists, with the United States as that power. Whatever exists, its future will depend in part on the willingness of the United States to take an actively global role, a topic taken up in Issue 3.

State-level analysis is the middle and most common level of analysis. Social scientists who study world politics from this perspective focus on how countries, singly or comparatively, make foreign policy. In other words, this perspective is concerned with internal political dynamics, such as the roles of and interactions between the executive and legislative branches of government, the impact of bureaucracy, the role of interest groups, and the effect of public opinion. This level of analysis is very much in evidence in Issue 13 and the debate over immigration to the United States, a topic that has cultural, as well as economic, ramifications. The dangers to the global environment, which are debated in Issue 19, extend beyond rarified scientific controversy to important issues of public policy. For example, should the United States and other industrialized countries adopt policies that are costly in terms of economics and lifestyle to significantly reduce the emission of carbon dioxide and other harmful gases? This debate pits interest groups against one another as they try to get the governments of their respective countries to support or reject the steps necessary to reduce the consumption of resources and the emission of waste products.

A third level of analysis, which is the most microscopic, is *human-level analysis*. This approach focuses, in part, on the role of individual decision makers. This technique is applied under the assumption that individuals make decisions and that the nature of those decisions is determined by the decision makers' perceptions, predilections, and strengths and weaknesses. A great deal of Issue 9 on whether Venezuela threatens hemispheric stability is based on the debate over whether its president, Hugo Chavez, is a dynamic champion of his people or dangerously unstable.

The Political and Ecological Future

Future *world alternatives* are discussed in many of the issues in this volume. Abraham Lincoln once said, "A house divided against itself cannot stand." One suspects that the sixteenth president might say something similar about the world today if he were with us. Issue 1, for example, debates whether growing globalization is a positive or negative trend. The world has responded to globalization by creating and strengthening the UN, the IMF, the World Bank, the World Trade Organization, and many other international organizations to try to regulate the increasing number of international interactions. There can be little doubt that the role of global governance is growing, and this reality is the spark behind specific debates about the future that are taken up in many of the selections. Far-reaching alternatives to a state-centric system based on sovereign countries include international organizations' (Issue 16) taking over some (or all) of the sovereign responsibilities of national governments, such as the prosecution of international war criminals (Issue 17). The global future also involves the ability of the world to prosper economically while not denuding itself of its natural resources or destroying the environment. This is the focus of Issue 19 on the environment.

Increased Role of Economics

Economics have always played a part in international relations, but the traditional focus has been on strategic political affairs, especially questions of military power. Now, however, political scientists are increasingly focusing on the international political economy, or the economic dimensions of world politics. International trade, for instance, has increased dramatically, expanding from an annual world export total of $20 billion in 1933 to $15 trillion in 2006. The impact has been profound. The domestic economic health of most countries is heavily affected by trade and other aspects of international economics. Since

World War II there has been an emphasis on expanding free trade by decreasing tariffs and other barriers to international commerce. In recent years, however, a downturn in the economies of many of the industrialized countries has increased calls for more protectionism. Yet restrictions on trade and other economic activity can also be used as diplomatic weapons. The intertwining of economies and the creation of organizations to regulate them, such as the World Trade Organization, is raising issues of sovereignty and other concerns. This is a central matter in the debate in Issue 1 over whether or not the trend toward global economic integration is desirable, in Issue 3 on the impact of capitalism on democracy, in Issue 11 on the benefits of free trade, and in Issue 12 on international investment through sovereign wealth funds. Many of the other issues have at least some economic component. For example, petroleum plays a role in the events related to resurgent Russia (Issue 5), crucial Iraq (Issue 8), assertive Venezuela (Issue 9), and war-torn Darfur (Issue 10).

Conclusion

Having discussed many of the various dimensions and approaches to the study of world politics, it is incumbent on this editor to advise against your becoming too structured by them. Issues of focus and methodology are important both to studying international relations and to understanding how others are analyzing global conduct. However, they are also partially pedagogical. In the final analysis, world politics is a highly interrelated, perhaps seamless, subject. No one level of analysis, for instance, can fully explain the events on the world stage. Instead, using each of the levels to analyze events and trends will bring the greatest understanding.

   Similarly, the realist-idealist division is less precise in practice than it may appear. As some of the debates indicate, each side often stresses its own standards of morality. Which is more moral: defeating a dictatorship or sparing the sword and saving lives that would almost inevitably be lost in the dictator's overthrow? Furthermore, realists usually do not reject moral considerations. Rather, they contend that morality is but one of the factors that a country's decision makers must consider. Realists are also apt to argue that standards of morality differ when dealing with a country as opposed to an individual. By the same token, most idealists do not completely ignore the often dangerous nature of the world. Nor do they argue that a country must totally sacrifice its short-term interests to promote the betterment of the current and future world. Thus, realism and idealism can be seen most accurately as the ends of a continuum—with most political scientists and practitioners falling somewhere between, rather than at, the extremes. The best advice, then, is this: think broadly about international politics. The subject is very complex, and the more creative and expansive you are in selecting your foci and methodologies, the more insight you will gain. To end where we began, with Dr. Faust, I offer his last words in Goethe's drama, *"Mehr licht,"* . . . More light! That is the goal of this book.

Internet References . . .

The Ultimate Political Science Links Page

Under the editorship of Professor P. S. Ruckman, Jr., at Rock Valley College in Rockford, Illinois, this site provides a gateway to the academic study of not just world politics but all of political science. It includes links to journals, news, publishers, and other relevant resources.

http://www.rvc.cc.il.us/faclink/pruckman/PSLinks.htm

Poly-Cy: Internet Resources for Political Science

This is a worthwhile gateway to a broad range of political science resources, including some on international relations. It is maintained by Robert D. Duval, director of graduate studies at West Virginia University.

http://www.polsci.wvu.edu/polycy/

The WWW Virtual Library: International Affairs Resources

Maintained by Wayne A. Selcher, professor of international studies at Elizabethtown College in Elizabethtown, Pennsylvania, this site contains approximately 2,000 annotated links relating to a broad spectrum of international affairs. The sites listed are those that the Webmaster believes have long-term value and that are cost-free, and many have further links to help in extended research.

http://www.etown.edu/vl/

The Globalization Web Site

The goals of this site are to shed light on the process of globalization and contribute to discussions of its consequences, to clarify the meaning of globalization and the debates that surround it, and to serve as a guide to available sources on globalization.

http://www.sociology.emory.EDU/globalization/

UNIT 1

Globalization and the International System

*T*he most significant change that the international system is experiencing is the trend toward globalization. Countries are becoming interdependent, the number of international organizations and their power are increasing, and global communications have become widespread and almost instantaneous. As reflected in the issues that make up this part, these changes and others have led to considerable debate about the value of globalization and what it will mean with regard to human governance.

- Is Economic Globalization a Positive Trend?
- Does Globalization Threaten Cultural Diversity?
- Does Capitalism Undermine Democracy?

ISSUE 1

Is Economic Globalization a Positive Trend?

YES: International Monetary Fund Staff, from "Globalization: A Brief Overview," *Issues Brief* (May 2008)

NO: Nancy Birdsall, from "The World Is not Flat: Inequality and Injustice in Our Global Economy," WIDER Annual Lecture 9, United Nations University, World Institute for Development Economics Research (October 31, 2005)

ISSUE SUMMARY

YES: Staff members of the International Monetary Fund conclude on the basis of experiences across the world that unhindered international economic interchange, the core principle of globalization, seems to underpin greater prosperity.

NO: Nancy Birdsall, founding president of the Center for Global Development, argues that globalization is not benefiting all and that a major challenge of the twenty-first century will be to address persistent and unjust inequality, which global markets alone cannot resolve.

Globalization is a process that is diminishing many of the factors that divide the world. Advances in travel and communication have made geographical distances less important, people around the world increasingly resemble one another culturally, and the United Nations and other international organizations have increased the level of global governance. Another aspect, economic integration, is the most advanced of any of the strands of globalization. Tariffs and other barriers to trade have decreased significantly since the end of World War II. As a result, all aspects of international economic exchange have grown rapidly. For example, global trade, measured in the value of exported goods and services, has grown about 2,000 percent since the mid-twentieth century and now comes to over $14 trillion annually. International investment in real estate and stocks and bonds in other countries, and in total, now exceeds $25 trillion. The flow of currencies is so massive that there is no accurate measure, but it certainly is more than $1.5 trillion a day.

In this liberalized atmosphere, huge multinational corporations (MNCs) have come to dominate global commerce. Just the top 500 MNCs have combined annual sales of over $15 trillion. The impact of all these changes is that the economic prosperity of almost all countries and the individuals within them is heavily dependent on what they import and export, the flow of investment in and out of each country, and the exchange rates of the currency of each country against the currencies of other countries.

The issue here is whether this economic globalization and integration is a positive or negative trend. For about 60 years, the United States has been at the center of the drive to open international commerce. The push to reduce trade barriers that occurred during and after World War II was designed to prevent a recurrence of the global economic collapse of the 1930s and the war of the 1940s. Policymakers believed that protectionism caused the Great Depression, that the ensuing human desperation provided fertile ground for the rise of dictators who blamed scapegoats for what had occurred and who promised national salvation, and that these fascist dictators had set off World War II. In sum, policymakers thought that protectionism caused economic depression, which caused dictators, which caused war. They believed that free trade, by contrast, would promote prosperity, democracy, and peace.

Based on these political and economic theories, American policymakers took the lead in establishing a new international economic system, including helping to found such leading global economic organizations as the International Monetary Fund (IMF), the World Bank, and the World Trade Organization (WTO). During the entire latter half of the twentieth century, the movement toward economic globalization was strong, and there were few influential voices opposing it.

In the following selection, members of the IMF staff contend that there is substantial evidence, from countries of different sizes and with different regions, which suggests that as nations globalize, their citizens benefit because they gain "access to a wider variety of goods and services, lower prices, more and more better-paying jobs, improved health, and higher overall living standards." Not everyone agrees, though, and in recent years the idea that globalization is necessarily beneficial has come under increasing scrutiny and has met with increasing resistance. Within countries, globalization has benefited some, while others have lost jobs to imports and suffered other negative consequences. Similarly, some countries, notably those in sub-Saharan Africa, have not prospered. Reflecting this uneven impact, one line of criticism of globalization comes from those who believe that the way global politics work is a function of how the world is organized economically. These critics contend that people within countries are divided into "haves" and "have-nots" and that the world is similarly divided into have and have-not countries. Moreover, these critics believe that, both domestically and internationally, the wealthy haves are using globalization to keep the have-nots weak and poor in order to exploit them. Representing this view, Nancy Birdsall argues in the second selection that global markets are inherently "disequalizing" and that important reforms are needed to ensure that economic globalization benefits most people and countries.

YES

Globalization: A Brief Overview

A perennial challenge facing all of the world's countries, regardless of their level of economic development, is achieving financial stability, economic growth, and higher living standards. There are many different paths that can be taken to achieve these objectives, and every country's path will be different given the distinctive nature of national economies and political systems. The ingredients contributing to China's high growth rate over the past two decades have, for example, been very different from those that have contributed to high growth in countries as varied as Malaysia and Malta.

Yet, based on experiences throughout the world, several basic principles seem to underpin greater prosperity. These include investment (particularly foreign direct investment) [owning foreign companies or real estate], the spread of technology, strong institutions, sound macroeconomic policies, an educated workforce, and the existence of a market economy. Furthermore, a common denominator which appears to link nearly all high-growth countries together is their participation in, and integration with, the global economy.

There is substantial evidence, from countries of different sizes and different regions, that as countries "globalize" their citizens benefit, in the form of access to a wider variety of goods and services, lower prices, more and better-paying jobs, improved health, and higher overall living standards. It is probably no mere coincidence that over the past 20 years, as a number of countries have become more open to global economic forces, the percentage of the developing world living in extreme poverty—defined as living on less than $1 per day—has been cut in half.

As much as has been achieved in connection with globalization, there is much more to be done. Regional disparities persist: while poverty fell in East and South Asia, it actually rose in sub-Saharan Africa. The UN's Human Development Report notes there are still around 1 billion people surviving on less than $1 per day—with 2.6 billion living on less than $2 per day. Proponents of globalization argue that this is not because of too much globalization, but rather too little. And the biggest threat to continuing to raise living standards throughout the world is not that globalization will succeed but that it will fail. It is the people of developing economies who have the greatest need for globalization, as it provides them with the opportunities that come with being part of the world economy.

These opportunities are not without risks—such as those arising from volatile capital movements. The International Monetary Fund works to help

From *IMF Issues Brief*, May 2008. Copyright © 2008 by International Monetary Fund. Reprinted by permission.

economies manage or reduce these risks, through economic analysis and policy advice and through technical assistance in areas such as macroeconomic policy, financial sector sustainability, and the exchange-rate system.

The risks are not a reason to reverse direction, but for all concerned—in developing and advanced countries, among both investors and recipients—to embrace policy changes to build strong economies and a stronger world financial system that will produce more rapid growth and ensure that poverty is reduced.

The following is a brief overview to help guide anyone interested in gaining a better understanding of the many issues associated with globalization.

What Is Globalization?

Economic "globalization" is a historical process, the result of human innovation and technological progress. It refers to the increasing integration of economies around the world, particularly through the movement of goods, services, and capital across borders. The term sometimes also refers to the movement of people (labor) and knowledge (technology) across international borders. There are also broader cultural, political, and environmental dimensions of globalization.

The term "globalization" began to be used more commonly in the 1980s, reflecting technological advances that made it easier and quicker to complete international transactions—both trade and financial flows. It refers to an extension beyond national borders of the same market forces that have operated for centuries at all levels of human economic activity—village markets, urban industries, or financial centers.

There are countless indicators that illustrate how goods, capital, and people have become more globalized.

- The value of trade (goods and services) as a percentage of world GDP [gross domestic product: the value of all goods and services produced within an economic unit] increased from 42.1 percent in 1980 to 62.1 percent in 2007.
- Foreign direct investment increased from 6.5 percent of world GDP in 1980 to 31.8 percent in 2006.
- The stock of international claims (primarily bank loans), as a percentage of world GDP, increased from roughly 10 percent in 1980 to 48 percent in 2006.
- The number of minutes spent on cross-border telephone calls, on a per-capita basis, increased from 7.3 in 1991 to 28.8 in 2006.
- The number of foreign workers has increased from 78 million people (2.4 percent of the world population) in 1965 to 191 million people (3.0 percent of the world population) in 2005.

The growth in global markets has helped to promote efficiency through competition and the division of labor—the specialization that allows people and economies to focus on what they do best. Global markets also offer greater opportunity for people to tap into more diversified and larger markets around the world. It means that they can have access to more capital, technology, cheaper imports, and larger export markets. But markets do not necessarily ensure that the benefits of increased efficiency are shared by all. Countries must be prepared to embrace the policies needed, and, in the case of the poorest countries, may need the support of the international community as they do so. The broad reach of globalization easily extends to daily choices of personal, economic, and political life. For example, greater access to modern technologies, in the world of health care, could make the difference between life and death. In the world of communications, it would facilitate commerce and education, and allow access to independent media. Globalization can also create a framework for cooperation among nations on a range of non-economic issues that have cross-border implications, such as immigration, the environment, and legal issues. At the same time, the influx of foreign goods, services, and capital into a country can create incentives and demands for strengthening the education system, as a country's citizens recognize the competitive challenge before them.

Perhaps more importantly, globalization implies that information and knowledge get dispersed and shared.

Innovators—be they in business or government—can draw on ideas that have been successfully implemented in one jurisdiction and tailor them to suit their own jurisdiction. Just as important, they can avoid the ideas that have a clear track record of failure. Joseph Stiglitz, a Nobel laureate and frequent critic of globalization, has nonetheless observed that globalization "has reduced the sense of isolation felt in much of the developing world and has given many people in the developing world access to knowledge well beyond the reach of even the wealthiest in any country a century ago."

International Trade

A core element of globalization is the expansion of world trade through the elimination or reduction of trade barriers, such as import tariffs. Greater imports offer consumers a wider variety of goods at lower prices, while providing strong incentives for domestic industries to remain competitive. Exports, often a source of economic growth for developing nations, stimulate job creation as industries sell beyond their borders. More generally, trade enhances national competitiveness by driving workers to focus on those vocations where they, and their country, have a competitive advantage. Trade promotes economic resilience and flexibility, as higher imports help to offset adverse domestic supply shocks. Greater openness can also stimulate foreign investment, which would be a source of employment for the local workforce and could bring along new technologies—thus promoting higher productivity.

Restricting international trade—that is, engaging in protectionism—generates adverse consequences for a country that undertakes such a policy. For example, tariffs raise the prices of imported goods, harming consumers, many of which may be poor. Protectionism also tends to reward concentrated, well-organized and politically-connected groups, at the expense of those whose interests may be more diffuse (such as consumers). It also reduces the variety of goods available and generates inefficiency by reducing competition and encouraging resources to flow into protected sectors.

Developing countries can benefit from an expansion in international trade. Ernesto Zedillo, the former president of Mexico, has observed that, "In every case where a poor nation has significantly overcome its poverty, this has been achieved while engaging in production for export markets and opening itself to the influx of foreign goods, investment, and technology."

And the trend is clear. In the late 1980s, many developing countries began to dismantle their barriers to international trade, as a result of poor economic performance under protectionist polices and various economic crises. In the 1990s, many former Eastern bloc countries integrated into the global trading system and developing Asia—one of the most closed regions to trade in 1980—progressively dismantled barriers to trade. Overall, while the average tariff rate applied by developing countries is higher than that applied by advanced countries, it has declined significantly over the last several decades.

The Implications of Globalized Financial Markets

The world's financial markets have experienced a dramatic increase in globalization in recent years. Global capital flows fluctuated between 2 and 6 percent of world GDP during the period 1980–95, but since then they have risen to 14.8 percent of GDP, and in 2006 they totaled $7.2 trillion, more than tripling since 1995. The most rapid increase has been experienced by advanced economies, but emerging markets and developing countries have also become more financially integrated. As countries have strengthened their capital markets they have attracted more investment capital, which can enable a broader entrepreneurial class to develop, facilitate a more efficient allocation of capital, encourage international risk sharing, and foster economic growth. Yet there is an energetic debate underway, among leading academics and policy experts, on the precise impact of financial globalization. Some see it as a catalyst for economic growth and stability. Others see it as injecting dangerous—and often costly—volatility into the economies of growing middle-income countries.

A recent paper by the IMF's Research Department takes stock of what is known about the effects of financial globalization. The analysis of the past 30 years of data reveals two main lessons for countries to consider.

First, the findings support the view that countries must carefully weigh the risks and benefits of unfettered capital flows. The evidence points to largely unambiguous gains from financial integration for advanced economies. In emerging and developing countries, certain factors are likely to influence the effect of financial globalization on economic volatility and growth: countries with well-developed financial sectors, strong institutions, sound macroeconomic policies, and substantial trade openness are more likely to gain from financial liberalization and less likely to risk increased macroeconomic volatility and to experience financial crises. For example, well-developed financial markets help moderate boom-bust cycles that can be triggered by surges and sudden stops in international capital flows, while strong domestic institutions and sound macroeconomic policies help attract "good" capital, such as portfolio equity flows and FDI.

The second lesson to be drawn from the study is that there are also costs associated with being overly cautious about opening to capital flows. These costs include lower international trade, higher investment costs for firms, poorer economic incentives, and additional administrative/monitoring costs. Opening up to foreign investment may encourage changes in the domestic economy that eliminate these distortions and help foster growth.

Looking forward, the main policy lesson that can be drawn from these results is that capital account liberalization should be pursued as part of a broader reform package encompassing a country's macroeconomic policy framework, domestic financial system, and prudential regulation. Moreover, long-term, non-debt-creating flows, such as FDI, should be liberalized before short-term, debt-creating inflows. Countries should still weigh the possible risks involved in opening up to capital flows against the efficiency costs associated with controls, but under certain conditions (such as good institutions, sound domestic and foreign policies, and developed financial markets) the benefits from financial globalization are likely to outweigh the risks.

Globalization, Income Inequality, and Poverty

As some countries have embraced globalization, and experienced significant income increases, other countries that have rejected globalization, or embraced it only tepidly, have fallen behind. A similar phenomenon is at work within countries—some people have, inevitably, been bigger beneficiaries of globalization than others.

Over the past two decades, income inequality has risen in most regions and countries. At the same time, per capita incomes have risen across virtually all regions for even the poorest segments of populations, indicating that the poor are better off in an absolute sense during this phase of globalization, although incomes for the relatively well off have increased at a faster pace. Consumption data from groups of developing countries reveal the striking inequality that exists between the richest and the poorest in populations across different regions.

As discussed in the October 2007 issue of the *World Economic Outlook,* one must keep in mind that there are many sources of inequality. Contrary to popular belief, increased trade globalization is associated with a decline in inequality. The spread of technological advances and increased financial globalization—and foreign direct investment in particular—have instead contributed more to the recent rise in inequality by raising the demand for skilled labor and increasing the returns to skills in both developed and developing countries. Hence, while everyone benefits, those with skills benefit more.

It is important to ensure that the gains from globalization are more broadly shared across the population. To this effect, reforms to strengthen education and training would help ensure that workers have the appropriate skills for the evolving global economy. Policies that broaden the access of finance to the poor would also help, as would further trade liberalization that boosts agricultural exports from developing countries. Additional programs may include providing adequate income support to cushion, but not obstruct, the process of change, and also making health care less dependent on continued employment and increasing the portability of pension benefits in some countries.

Equally important, globalization should not be rejected because its impact has left some people unemployed. The dislocation may be a function of forces that have little to do with globalization and more to do with inevitable technological progress. And, the number of people who "lose" under globalization is likely to be outweighed by the number of people who "win."

Martin Wolf, the *Financial Times* columnist, highlights one of the fundamental contradictions inherent in those who bemoan inequality, pointing out that this charge amounts to arguing "that it would be better for everybody to be equally poor than for some to become significantly better off, even if, in the long run, this will almost certainly lead to advances for everybody."

Indeed, globalization has helped to deliver extraordinary progress for people living in developing nations. One of the most authoritative studies of the subject has been carried out by World Bank economists David Dollar and Aart Kraay. They concluded that since 1980, globalization has contributed to a reduction in poverty as well as a reduction in global income inequality. They found that in "globalizing" countries in the developing world, income per person grew three-and-a-half times faster than in "non-globalizing" countries, during the 1990s. In general, they noted, "higher growth rates in globalizing developing countries have translated into higher incomes for the poor." Dollar and Kraay also found that in virtually all events in which a country experienced growth at a rate of two percent or more, the income of the poor rose.

Critics point to those parts of the world that have achieved few gains during this period and highlight it as a failure of globalization. But that is to misdiagnose the problem. While serving as Secretary-General of the United Nations, Kofi Annan pointed out that "the main losers in today's very unequal world are not those who are too much exposed to globalization. They are those who have been left out."

A recent BBC World Service poll found that on average 64 percent of those polled—in 27 out of 34 countries—held the view that the benefits and burdens of "the economic developments of the last few years" have not been shared fairly. In developed countries, those who have this view of unfairness are more likely to say that globalization is growing too quickly. In contrast, in some developing countries, those who perceive such unfairness are more likely to say globalization is proceeding too slowly. As individuals and institutions work to raise living standards throughout the world, it will be critically important to create a climate that enables these countries to realize maximum benefits from globalization. That means focusing on macroeconomic stability, transparency in government, a sound legal system, modern infrastructure, quality education, and a deregulated economy.

Myths about Globalization

No discussion of globalization would be complete without dispelling some of the myths that have been built up around it.

Downward pressure on wages: Globalization is rarely the primary factor that fosters wage moderation in low-skilled work conducted in developed countries. As discussed in a recent issue of the *World Economic Outlook,* a more significant factor is technology. As more work can be mechanized, and as fewer people are needed to do a given job than in the past, the demand for that labor will fall, and as a result the prevailing wages for that labor will be affected as well.

The "race to the bottom": Globalization has not caused the world's multi-national corporations to simply scour the globe in search of the lowest-paid laborers. There are numerous factors that enter into corporate decisions on where to source products, including the supply of skilled labor, economic and political stability, the local infrastructure, the quality of institutions, and the overall business climate. In an open global market, while jurisdictions do compete with each other to attract investment, this competition incorporates factors well beyond just the hourly wage rate.

According to the UN Information Service, the developed world hosts two-thirds of the world's inward foreign direct investment. The 49 least developed countries—the poorest of the developing countries—account for around 2 percent of the total inward FDI stock of developing countries. Nor is it true that multinational corporations make a consistent practice of operating sweatshops in low-wage countries, with poor working conditions and substandard wages. While isolated examples of this can surely be uncovered, it is well established that multinationals, on average, pay higher wages than what is standard in developing nations, and offer higher labor standards.

Globalization is irreversible: In the long run, globalization is likely to be an unrelenting phenomenon. But for significant periods of time, its momentum can be hindered by a variety of factors, ranging from political will to availability of infrastructure. Indeed, the world was thought to be on an irreversible path toward peace and prosperity in the early 20th century, until the outbreak of Word War I. That war, coupled with the Great Depression, and then World War II, dramatically set back global economic integration. And in many ways, we are still trying to recover the momentum we lost over the past 90 years or so.

That fragility of nearly a century ago still exists today—as we saw in the aftermath of September 11th, when U.S. air travel came to a halt, financial markets shut down, and the economy weakened. The current turmoil in financial markets also poses great difficulty for the stability and reliability of those markets, as well as for the global economy. Credit market strains have intensified and spread across asset classes and banks, precipitating a financial shock that many have characterized as the most serious since the 1930s.

These episodes are reminders that a breakdown in globalization—meaning a slowdown in the global flows of goods, services, capital, and people—can have extremely adverse consequences.

Openness to globalization will, on its own, deliver economic growth: Integrating with the global economy is, as economists like to say, a necessary, but not sufficient, condition for economic growth. For globalization to be able to work, a country cannot be saddled with problems endemic to many developing countries, from a corrupt political class, to poor infrastructure, and macroeconomic instability.

The shrinking state: Technologies that facilitate communication and commerce have curbed the power of some despots throughout the world, but in a globalized world governments take on new importance in one critical respect, namely, setting, and enforcing, rules with respect to contracts and property rights. The potential of globalization can never be realized unless there are rules and regulations in place, and individuals to enforce them. This gives economic actors confidence to engage in business transactions. Further undermining the idea of globalization shrinking states is that states are not, in fact, shrinking. Public expenditures are, on average, as high or higher today as they have been at any point in recent memory. And among OECD [Organization of Economic Cooperation and Development is composed of 30 mostly high-income countries] countries, government tax revenue as a percentage of GDP increased from 25.5 percent in 1965 to 36.6 percent in 2006.

The Future of Globalization

Like a snowball rolling down a steep mountain, globalization seems to be gathering more and more momentum. And the question frequently asked about globalization is not whether it will continue, but at what pace.

A disparate set of factors will dictate the future direction of globalization, but one important entity—sovereign governments—should not be overlooked. They still have the power to erect significant obstacles to globalization, ranging from tariffs to immigration restrictions to military hostilities.

Nearly a century ago, the global economy operated in a very open environment, with goods, services, and people able to move across borders with little if any difficulty. That openness began to wither away with the onset of World War I in 1914, and recovering what was lost is a process that is still underway. Along the process, governments recognized the importance of international cooperation and coordination, which led to the emergence of numerous international organizations and financial institutions (among which the IMF and the World Bank, in 1944).

Indeed, the lessons included avoiding fragmentation and the breakdown of cooperation among nations. The world is still made up of nation states and a global marketplace. We need to get the right rules in place so the global system is more resilient, more beneficial, and more legitimate. International institutions have a difficult but indispensable role in helping to bring more of globalization's benefits to more people throughout the world. By helping to break down barriers—ranging from the regulatory to the cultural—more countries can be integrated into the global economy, and more people can seize more of the benefits of globalization.

Nancy Birdsall  **NO**

The World Is not Flat: Inequality and Injustice in Our Global Economy

Introduction

. . . The title of this lecture is an allusion to Thomas Friedman's 2005 book entitled *The World Is Flat: A Brief History of the Twenty-first Century*. Friedman argues that in today's highly integrated and competitive global economy, the US and other advanced economies can no longer count on the past comforts and advantages of the mountaintop. But focusing on the flattening process (between the US and China, for example) overlooks (literally and figuratively) half the world's population—those countries and people within countries in ruts and craters beneath the surface. What are the implications of global economic integration for those countries and those people in this highly 'not-flat', unequal world? And in particular, what is the challenge that this inequality poses for the development process itself in the developing world?

In Part I, I address the question of whether and how money inequality (hills and craters) matters to people, and what it has to do with the broader issue of injustice. That is a question best addressed at the country level. There is a rich literature on country inequality and for many people the country in which they live constitutes a key reference group. I then turn in Part II to a fundamental problem of globalization: that it tends to benefit more those already ahead. . . . In the conclusion I briefly suggest what can be done about the resulting challenge to global security, stability, shared prosperity, and most fundamentally to global social justice: how to reconcile the reality that we have a global economy but not an effective global polity.

A word on definitions and on regional patterns. Inequality is, of course, a relative concept, and except where I specify otherwise I am referring to money inequality, that is, inequality of income, consumption, or wealth (the latter is everywhere more concentrated but less often measured). By poverty I refer to the condition of people who are poor in absolute terms, using the World Bank standard of US$2 a day (in 1985 dollars), and for extreme poverty of US$1 a day. Across countries there is at best a weak association between absolute poverty and inequality. I use the term equity, or social equity, as in an 'equitable'

From *WIDER Annual Lecture #9*, October 31, 2005 (excerpts). Copyright © 2006 by UNU–WIDER, UN University/World Institute for Development Economics Research. Reprinted by permission.

society, to refer to the idea of justice or fairness in the processes that lead to outcomes such as income, and in contrast to outcomes or income per se. A society with relatively high income inequality might be an equitable society if the observed inequality were the outcome of an entirely fair process—in which some worked harder or took more economic risks with resultant greater economic gains than others. Equity is sensibly thought of as equality of opportunity and is a more satisfactory concept from a normative point of view; but it is harder to measure. I argue that in developing countries high money inequality is likely to be a sign of processes that are not equitable.

. . . Inequality is lower in the advanced economies than in developing country regions. . . . Within regions, and more so within countries, inequality does change over time. . . . [I]n many countries there has been a marked trend of increasing inequality since the early 1980s [because, some scholars believe, of] the trend to the increasing recourse to markets without sufficient intervention by governments to ensure that the poor are not left behind. Other scholars look at wage inequality in manufacturing and attribute the trend to the virtually worldwide acceptance of the priority of stabilization over employment generation in the last two decades, and the resulting emphasis on fiscal and monetary restraint since the 1980s. Growing inequality appears to be the case in many industrialized countries including the US, the UK, Japan, Ireland, and New Zealand, in many developing countries including China and India, and in most of the transitional, post-Communist economies of the former Soviet Union and Central and Eastern Europe.

Part I—Inequality within Countries: Why It Matters for Development

For the most part, mainstream economists have not been concerned with the apparent trend of rising inequality. The assumption of textbook economics is that inequality is likely to enhance growth by concentrating income among the rich, who save and invest more, and by creating a necessary incentive for individuals to work hard. . . .

For development economists, inequality has not been the central policy issue, but rather the reduction of absolute poverty. . . . Only beginning in the 1990s, once the fall of the Berlin Wall had liberated the mainstream from the taboo of Marxian thought, did inequality begin to be viewed as a possible cause of low growth, and thus as a phenomenon that mattered, at least for understanding growth itself. In the past 15 years there has finally been more theoretical and empirical work on inequality and development. . . .

Still there is no agreement among economists, and no particular attention among development practitioners, to the likelihood that inequality matters—for growth itself or for poverty reduction, or for any larger definition of development or of individual well-being.

Yet if people care about their relative income status then ipso facto inequality matters. That they do, to some extent, has long been remarked; consider Adam Smith, who noted that for a man to retain his dignity, he may in one society need enough income to buy a linen shirt. . . . Because it is relative and not absolute income that matters . . . , economic growth and subsequent increases in a country's average income do not seem to increase the average level of happiness in a country. What matters for people is their relative not their absolute income. [Surveys show, for example, that] people in Nigeria are as happy as people in France despite the huge discrepancy in per capita income.

In short, inequality of absolute income seems to matter: more obviously to people at the low end, who may resent the better-off, but probably to some at the high end too, who may enjoy their own affluence less if others are visibly worse off. Inequality is probably most bothersome (to the rich as well as the poor) when low income is persistent for identifiable groups of people and thus most obviously unjust—rooted in racial or other discrimination, for example, or in inadequate access to education for low-income children. Reducing inequality may therefore be an end in itself for some people and in some societies.

There are also, however, instrumental reasons why inequality matters. . . .

1.1   Inequality Can Stall Growth

The assumption of textbook economics is that a tradeoff exists between augmenting growth and reducing inequality. . . . [One argument] is that a high level of saving, and resulting investment, is a prerequisite of rapid growth, so that income must be concentrated in the hands of the rich, whose marginal propensity to save is relatively high compared to that of the poor. . . . [A second argument] is that inequality provides an incentive for individual effort—for hard work, innovation, and productive risk-taking—which ultimately ensures higher output and increasing productivity, and thus higher average income and rates of growth. . . .

That inequality creates positive incentive effects at the microlevel implies that inequality is 'constructive', that is, that it reflects differences in individuals' responses to equal opportunities and is therefore consistent with efficient allocation of resources in an economy. Let us define 'destructive inequality' as that inequality which reflects privileges for the already rich and blocks potential for productive contributions of the currently less rich, and therefore contributes to economic inefficiency and reducing rather than enhancing the potential for growth. . . . It follows that a sensible interpretation of destructive inequality is that it reflects mostly inequality of opportunity. . . .

There are no internationally comparable measures of opportunity . . . [but] inequality matters, especially in developing countries, . . . because the evidence is that it has a large 'destructive' component, that is, it is associated with unequal opportunities and contributes to lower growth than otherwise might be possible.

. . . [I]nequality matters especially in developing countries, because by definition (in the nature of being 'developing') those countries' markets are relatively weak and their governments less effective in compensating through public policy for the weakness of their markets and the fundamental failures of markets (that prevail everywhere). Inequality may be constructive in the rich countries, in the classic sense of motivating individuals to work hard, innovate, and take productive risks. But in developing countries it is more likely to be destructive. . . .

If inequality in one form or another reduces growth, then it is implicated in reduced poverty reduction—since growth is necessary if not sufficient for reducing poverty, and since whatever growth occurs will help the poor less in an accounting sense the less equal the distribution of income. There may also be a more substantive link of inequality to the persistence of poverty when some growth occurs. [Research indicates] that across countries, greater land and education inequality reduces the income growth of the poorest quintile about twice as much as they reduce average income growth for all quintiles. In the extreme, unequal distribution of land may cut off altogether the usual effect (in East Asia and elsewhere) of growth in agriculture on reduction of rural poverty. Some evidence suggests that agricultural growth in Latin America in the 1970s and 1980s failed to reduce poverty at all, as large landowners captured most of the benefits. In contrast, in Indonesia, where small farmers provide the bulk of agricultural production, growth was good for the rural poor. . . .

In short, in the real world beyond the textbook, inequality may inhibit growth—and especially so in developing countries where markets are not as competitive and governments are not as effective. Inequality matters because it tends to reduce growth in those very countries where the bulk of the world's poor—who would benefit from growth—live.

1.2   Inequality Tends to Undermine Good Public Policy

Behind the evidence that inequality inhibits growth is the likelihood that concentration of income and assets at the top not only interacts with market failures to reduce growth, but also leads to government failure. Public-choice models attribute poor public policy to government regimes in which bureaucrats and insiders face no real checks on the pursuit of their own interests. If the rich favour public policy that preserves privileges even at the cost of growth, inequality not only inhibits growth given government failure, but contributes itself to government failure. The problem seems especially great when the concentration of income at the top is combined with substantial poverty at the bottom, and there is no large middle class to demand accountability from government. . . .

It is possible for income inequality to contribute to poor policy even where there is little or no absolute poverty. If large differences in income and wealth lead some people to 'feel inferiority and shame at the way they must live', then these people are likely to feel and be less politically active. . . .

In many other settings where there is little absolute poverty (including most, if not all, advanced economies), relatively low income is combined with racial or ethnic minority status (in part reflecting past if not current discrimination), and with a weak political voice. Though it is not clear whether minority status or relatively low income is the real culprit, income inequality probably compounds, if not causes, political weakness.

In the extreme, the political weakness of the relatively poor may mean that the advantaged exercise sufficient control over others to constitute an 'abridgement of liberty'. Sometimes that control occurs as a result of financial contributions to political campaigns, access to the media, or less benign exercises of political influence such as bribes and extortion. If these kinds of influence in turn affect job availability, workplace safety, or local environmental conditions, then large inequalities can be said to matter because of their political repercussions.

There may also be bad political outcomes when those who feel disadvantaged do have political voice. Because people care about inequality, inequality raises the likelihood of perverse policy responses—economic policies that make inequality worse while also inhibiting growth. Put another way, high inequality may generate not only inadequate social policy through perverse effects on political participation; it may also lead to positively perverse economic policies. . . .

It would be silly to blame all bad policy on income inequality, but it would also be foolish to ignore the risks of inequality to sound policy and the frustrations it produces. The reality, or the perception, of a growing gap between the middle and the rich is particularly fertile ground for the perverse choices mentioned above. The evidence is that the gap tends to be greater in developing compared to developed countries, and has grown in the last decade in the former socialist economies of Eastern Europe and Russia.

1.3   Inequality Tends to Inhibit Effective Collective Decisionmaking

[One scholar] places considerable emphasis on individuals' 'capability' to participate in the life of the community. Participation in the life of the community suggests there are assets that are held not individually but only in relation to others; [another scholar] defines the asset of social capital in terms of trusts, norms, and networks that can improve the efficiency of society, 'facilitating coordinating actions'. Social capital has economic value because it is likely to reduce the cost of transactions and of contract enforcement and reduce resistance of the losing groups to political compromises.

There is good evidence from microeconomic analyses that income inequality adversely affects some of the inputs or correlates of social capital. . . .

Finally there is . . . evidence from studies of crime and violence . . . [that i]ncome inequality . . . had a significant and positive effect on homicide rates. . . . Ratios of income of contiguous quintiles . . . exacerbate crime, and at an increasing rate. In other words, it was neither poverty nor inequality at the bottom that explained crime, but the disparity between the middle strata and their richer counterparts. It was not absolute but relative income that mattered.

Part II—Globalization Is Disequalizing

A fundamental challenge posed by the increasing reach of global markets ('globalization') is that global markets are inherently disequalizing, making rising inequality within developing countries more rather than less likely. To the extent inequality reduces growth prospects of developing countries, given capital market failures and given its potential perverse effects on policymaking and social capital, a disequalizing effect of globalization within developing countries is a development issue. Before elaborating on why and how globalization is inherently disequalizing, I review what we know about changes in inequality over the last two decades.

2.1 Recent Trends of Global Inequality

Global inequality measured across countries and across individuals irrespective of where they live (that is, just lining up all individuals in the world from poorest to richest) is extraordinarily high—higher than measured inequality within Brazil and South Africa, the highest inequality countries in the world. That is mostly because of the enormous difference in the average income of the richest compared to the poorest countries—a 'divergence big time' that has grown from perhaps 9 or 10 to 1 in 1900 to 100 to 1 today. However in the last several decades, the decades of increasing integration of markets, inequality across individuals has probably begun to level off—mostly because rapid economic growth in China, India, and other large and poor countries of South Asia has moved millions of people out of poverty, shifting a large enough portion of the world's individuals from the poorest to less poor parts of the overall world income distribution. In other words, the beneficent effects of growth in some large and poor countries on poverty reduction have also meant a reduction across individuals in inequality. The success of these countries is justifiably invoked by proponents of globalization. It is countries that have successfully entered the global market which have grown most.

At the same time the picture is different across countries and within countries. Across countries, and particularly between the richest and the poorest countries, inequality continues to grow simply because of a continuing difference in the rates of growth of the most successful advanced economies compared to the least successful and thus now poorest economies. Today's rich countries—of Europe, North America, and Australia, which were already richer 100 years ago primarily because of the Industrial Revolution—are continuing to grow in per capita terms, and continuing therefore to get richer. Today's poorest countries, many in Africa, are poor in part because they have grown little at all in per capita terms. Some developing countries—China, India, Botswana, Chile—are now growing faster in per capita terms than some advanced economies. Some in the past—Brazil, Korea—grew faster. So convergence is possible. But by definition some of the currently poorest countries are very poor because they have failed to grow; so divergence between them and the richer and richest countries has increased. The problem of divergence can be thought of in terms of the conventional challenge of triggering sustainable growth and development transformation in today's poorest countries—but today in a world where a more integrated global economy is raising the bar of competitiveness.

Within many developing countries, moreover, the evidence is that where inequality is not already high—posing the kind of problems outlined in Part I—it is rising. In the last two decades, income inequality increased in China, where phenomenal income growth has been heavily concentrated in urban areas; in most countries of Eastern Europe and the former Soviet Union, where growth has been minimal and the current poor are worse off than they were before the fall of communism; and in Mexico, Panama, and Peru in Latin America, where it rose during the low-growth years of the 1980s and failed to decline with the return to modest growth in the 1990s. [There has been a] large rise in manufacturing pay inequality for some Eastern European and Latin American countries since 1980. Inequality is probably rising in India, though that is still controversial and to the extent it is the case, as in China, it is the result of a good thing—the new prosperity liberalization has brought to some.

It would be an exaggeration to say that rising inequality within countries has been the norm. In some developing countries, income inequality has simply not changed, and in a few, including Japan, Canada, and Italy among the industrialized countries, and Bangladesh, Ghana, and the Philippines, it appears to have declined. Nor does it make sense to 'blame' globalization and see some inevitable tradeoff between growth and inequality in countries like China and India. The issue is different: To the extent global integration creates pressures that tend to increase inequality, it is worth understanding what those pressures are, how they operate, and how they might best be managed, within countries and at the global level.

Similarly, in the case of the poorest countries that seem unable to exploit the potential of globalization, it is worth understanding whether they are worse off because of the competitive pressures that they face in the more integrated global economy, rather than better off as has generally been assumed because they can exploit the technologies others have developed to catch up.

2.2 Disequalizing Globalization: Three Reasons

Consider three reasons why the global economy tends to sustain or worsen current money inequality—across countries and in particular within developing countries.

- Global markets reward more fully those countries and individuals with more of the most productive assets. (Call this, for simplicity, the market works.)
- In the global economy, negative externalities raise new costs for the vulnerable and compound the risks faced by the already weak and disadvantaged. (Call this, for simplicity, the market fails.)
- In the global economy, existing rules tend to benefit most those countries and individuals who already have economic power; it is natural that the richer and more powerful manage to influence the design and implementation of global rules—even those rules meant to constrain them—to their own advantage.

The Market Works: Global Markets Reward Productive Assets
Globalization is shorthand for global capitalism and the extension of global markets. Markets that are bigger and deeper reward more efficiently those who already have productive assets: financial assets, land, physical assets, and

perhaps most crucial in the technologically-driven global economy, human capital.

For countries, the key productive asset seems to be stable and sound institutions. Countries that are already ahead—with stable political systems, secure property rights, adequate banking supervision, reasonable public services, and so on—are better able to cope with market-driven changes in world prices. Consider the plight of a large group of the poorest countries, including Bolivia and many in Africa. Highly dependent on primary commodity and natural resource exports in the early 1980s, their markets have been 'open' for at least two decades, if openness is measured by their ratio of imports and exports to GDP. But unable to diversify into manufacturing (despite reducing their own import tariffs) they have been victims of the decline in the relative world prices of their commodity exports, and have, literally, been left behind. These countries have not been xenophobic or in any way closed to the global economy. But despite rising exports, tariff reductions, and, in most of them, economic and structural reforms including greater fiscal and monetary discipline and the divestiture of unproductive state enterprises, they have been unable to increase their export income, have failed to attract foreign investment, and have grown little, if at all.

Many of these countries in Sub-Saharan Africa, as well as Haiti, Nepal, and Nicaragua, seem trapped in a vicious circle of low or unstable export revenue, weak and sometimes predatory government, inability to cope with terrible disease burdens (the HIV/AIDS pandemic being only one recent and highly visible example), and failure to deliver the basic education and other services to their children that are critical to sustainable growth. Their governments have made, from time to time, fragile efforts to end corruption, to undertake economic reforms, and, more to the point, to enter global markets. But, caught in one variety or another of a poverty trap, 'globalization' has not worked for them. For these countries, success in global markets might be a future outcome of success with growth and development itself, but does not seem to be a key input.

In contrast, countries that discovered their natural resources already having the 'asset' of strong political and social institutions (e.g., Australia, Norway, and among developing countries Chile and Botswana) have not suffered the same problems. In a similar vein, [one scholar] argues persuasively that in the new global economy, we should not expect the convergence between rich and poor countries . . . [on the basis of the idea] that trade will reduce inequality within the developing countries by raising the wages of plentiful unskilled labour. [Indeed,] in today's globalization era, the evidence contradicts the theory, and suggests instead that existing productivity differences across countries make 'capital' and 'skilled labour' economically scarcer in high-productivity settings, explaining why skilled people move to those settings where their counterparts are plentiful. This also explains why 80 per cent of all foreign investment occurs among the industrialized countries (and just 0.1 per cent of all US foreign investment went to Sub-Saharan Africa last year). The productivity differences arise, presumably, because of longstanding differences in physical infrastructure and human capital, themselves the product of the incentives inherent in environments created by differences in the nature of social and political institutions.

The global market for skilled and talented people is a good example of the general tendency for markets to benefit most the already strong—individuals as well as countries. In today's global economy the advanced economies are now competing with each other in encouraging immigration of the highly skilled. As a result, it is those with the most education and skills that are more likely to emigrate from developing countries. Indian engineers can quadruple their earnings by moving from Kerala to Silicon Valley and Indian Ph.D. bio-chemists from Delhi to Atlanta or Cambridge. More integrated markets thus increase inequality across countries, via emigration from smaller and poorer countries of highly skilled citizens, who naturally are most likely to leave the countries where they are least able to deploy their skills productively.

For the individuals who emigrate, their mobility is a good thing, and this braindrain can generate offsetting remittances that raise welfare in the sending countries. It can also generate substantial return investments if the institutional and policy setting in their home countries improves, as has been the case in India recently. At the same time, however, it makes the task of poorer countries, trying to build those institutions and improve those policies, tougher. The annual loss to India of its braindrain to the US is estimated at US$2 billion, about equal to all the foreign aid it receives. The farmers and workers whose taxes finance education in poor countries are subsidizing the citizens of the rich countries—whose tax revenues are boosted by the immigrants' contributions (and whose cultures, by the way, are also greatly enriched).

Indeed, the braindrain issue illustrates well the fundamental reality that today's globalization can involve at least a short-term tradeoff for poorer countries—even those like India that are growing rapidly. Emigration of its skilled people can bring benefits, but only under certain circumstances. At the same time, it is likely to increase inequality within countries—because the relative wages of those with increasingly scarce skills rise as their skilled counterparts emigrate. That creates political pressures (as in India today) and can even backfire economically, if the rapid rise in wages undermines competitiveness.

That brings us to the implications of global markets for inequality among individuals within countries. At the individual level, the best example of how healthy markets can generate unequal opportunities is the rising gap in earnings between those with and those without higher education. The effect of having a university education compared to secondary education or less has been increasing for years everywhere. [There is an] increase in returns to some higher education compared to some secondary and some primary education estimated on the basis of wage changes by schooling for 18 countries of Latin America.

The relative return to higher education has been rising despite the fact that more and more people are going to university, including across the developing world. More integrated trade markets, capital flows, and global technology, including the internet, are increasing the worldwide demand for skills more rapidly than the supply, despite increasing enrolments. In the US the highly educated have enjoyed healthy earnings gains for three decades, while those with high school education or less have suffered absolute wage losses. In Eastern Europe, with the fall of communism, the wage difference between those with and without post-secondary education has widened considerably.

Just about everywhere in the world (Cuba, China, Kerala state in India, all socialist entities, being exceptions), education is reinforcing initial advantages instead of compensating for initial handicaps.

Rising wage gaps in open and competitive markets may be a short-term price worth paying for higher long-run sustainable growth. They create the right incentives for more people to acquire more education, in principle eventually reducing inequality. The same can be said for the development of institutions at the country level. Many poor countries have responded to global opportunities by strengthening the rule of law, building and strengthening democratic processes, and investing in public health and education. But just as to educate their children poor families need resources to compensate for initially unequal endowments and the incentive that equal opportunity provides, so to build better institutions poor countries need resources and the incentive that at least a level global playing field provides.

The efficiency gains and increased potential for growth of a global market economy are not to be disdained. But even when participation in the global market brings growth, as in China and India, it is a mixed blessing, bringing political pressures for populist measures and, especially if growth falters, for protectionism. Even Europe and the US are subject to those pressures—but with more resilient institutions and well-developed social insurance programmes they can better afford temporary policy errors. The political risks are greater still when engagement in global markets fails to bring growth, as in Latin America and much of Sub-Saharan Africa. The domestic reforms that are key to growth in a global economy are (ironically) resisted. Part of the resistance is due to the fear of job loss, in turn a product of less flexible labour and financial markets in most developing countries (and the comparison of Europe to the US is also apt here with respect to labour markets), and part due to the inadequacy of social safety nets to minimize the welfare effects of job loss and other shocks to household income.

In short, because global markets work well, they tend to increase inequality between rich and poor countries and individuals. Countries caught in an 'institutional poverty trap' will not necessarily benefit from a healthy global market. Within and across countries, individuals who begin life with lesser endowments—by reason of poverty, discrimination, lack of educational and other opportunities—tend to lose out relative to the better-endowed.

The Market Fails: In the Global Economy, Negative Externalities Hurt Most the Already Weak

A second reason why globalization is disequalizing is that global markets are far from perfect. They fail in many domains. The classic example of a market failure is that of pollution, where the polluter captures the benefits of polluting without paying the full costs. At the global level, the rich countries that have emitted the highest per capita greenhouse gas emissions have imposed future costs on poor countries—who have fewer resources to manage or mitigate the effects. As the biggest polluter in per capita terms, the US is imposing costs not only on its own future citizens, but also on the children and grandchildren of the world's poor, who will be particularly vulnerable.

Similarly with global financial crises. The financial crises of the late 1990s that affected Mexico, Thailand, Korea, Russia, Brazil, and Argentina were in part due to policy errors in those countries. But a healthy portion can be blamed on the panic that periodically plagues all financial markets. In East Asia, accumulation of high reserves for self-insurance against future crises has been one reaction; the costs of maintaining high dollar reserves (given the low interest rates received compared to potential returns domestically) represent a perverse transfer from the developing world to the US. In Brazil public sector debt, already high, grew again (due to borrowing) when its markets were attacked in 2002, keeping interest rates high and job and investment growth lower than otherwise.

The problem the emerging market economies of Latin America and East Asia face in global financial markets has not only brought instability and reduced growth; it has affected their capacity to develop and sustain the institutions and programmes they need to protect their own poor. In Korea, Mexico, and Thailand, financial crises reduced the income shares of the bottom 80 per cent of households compared to the top 20 per cent. During the accompanying recession in Mexico in 1995, many children of the poor dropped out of school—and subsequent studies show that many never returned.

The volatility and financial risks that come with participation in global markets tend to be disequalizing over the long run within countries. Analysis by Lundberg and Squire indicates that negative terms of trade shocks hurt lower quintiles of the income distribution disproportionately. That should not be a surprise. [Several recent studies] find evidence that volatility, whatever its source, is particularly bad for the poor. The biggest culprit, however, seems to be the premature opening of capital markets, which are particularly implicated in volatility in developing countries, with limited if any benefits in terms of higher growth.

Premature opening of the capital market—before adequate banking supervision and financial regulation are in place—brings pressures for increased inequality along with volatility, for at least two reasons. One is a function of being a 'developing' or 'emerging' market. With global market players doubting the commitment of nonindustrialized countries to fiscal rectitude at the time of any shock, countries are forced to resort to tight fiscal and monetary policy to reestablish market confidence, just when in the face of recession they would ideally implement macroeconomic measures to stimulate their economies. The (procyclical) austerity policies that the global capital market demands of emerging markets are the opposite of what the industrial economies implement, such as reduced interest rates, unemployment insurance, increased availability of food stamps, and public works employment: fundamental ingredients of a modern social contract. The effects of unemployment and bankruptcy can be permanent for the poor, so that repeated shocks constitute a structural factor in increasing inequality.

Second, the bank bailouts that follow crises generate high public debt (amounting to 10 to 40 per cent of annual GDP compared to 2–3 per cent on average in advanced economics). High public debt keeps domestic interest rates high, stifling investment, growth, and job creation—all bad for the poor—and increases the pressure on emerging market economies to generate primary fiscal surpluses, in the long run reducing their ability to finance sound broad-based investment in health and education—and their ability to spend more on the unemployment and safety net programmes that would protect the poor in bad times.

The risks of global warming and the problems of global financial contagion are only two examples of market failures that entail asymmetric costs and risks for poor countries and, within developing countries, for their poor people. The same can be said of contagious disease that crosses borders, and of a host of 'policy' and 'regulatory' failures associated with more open borders and more integrated markets such as increased transnational crime and sex trafficking. In general, the ability to adjust to change, or to finance mitigation costs, is smaller for poorer countries, and within countries, for poorer people. In that sense these market failures have a tendency to contribute to increased inequality—between countries and within developing countries, where safety nets and the capacity for social, political, and economic adjustments to changing conditions is more limited.

Global Rules and Regimes Tend to Favour the Already Rich—Countries and People

Finally, global markets tend to be disequalizing because trade, intellectual property, and migration regimes at the global level naturally reflect the greater market power of the rich.

Today's battle to reduce rich country agricultural subsidies and tariffs that discriminate against poor countries is a good example. The problem arises not because of any conspiracy but because domestic politics in Europe, the US, and Japan, as perverse as they are even for those countries themselves, matter more at the negotiating table than unequal opportunities for cotton farmers in West Africa.

What is true of the design of multilateral rules is also true of implementation. In 2003 developing countries finally got clarity on their right to issue compulsory licenses to import as well as produce generic (rather than expensive patented) medicines during public health emergencies. But the rules for exercising that right to import are complicated, and many countries eager to maintain or improve their access to the huge US market for their own exports are acceding to WTO 'plus' patent protection, in effect giving up those rights, in bilateral trade with the US.

In the WTO and other multilateral settings, the cost and complexity of negotiation and dispute resolution processes put poor and small countries with limited resources at a disadvantage. An example is antidumping actions brought by US producers, even when they are unlikely to win a dispute on its merits. These create legal and other costs to current producers in developing countries, and are likely to chill new job-creating investment in sensitive sectors. About one-half of antidumping actions are initiated against developing country producers, who account for 8 per cent of all exports.

International migration is governed by rules that clearly exacerbate inequality between the richest and poorest—countries and individuals. Permanent migration is small relative to the past because today higher-income countries restrict immigration. In the last 25 years, only 2 per cent of the world's people have changed their permanent country residence, compared to 10 per cent in the 25 years before the First World War. Yet more movement, especially of less-skilled workers, would reduce world inequality considerably, as did the tremendous movements of Europeans to the Americas in the nineteenth century. An auto mechanic from Ghana can at least quintuple his income, just by moving from Ghana to Italy; as can a Nicaraguan agricultural worker, by moving to Arizona.

As discussed above, the rich countries actively encourage immigration of the highly skilled. During the recent boom in the information technology sector, the US established a special programme to allow highly skilled workers to enter with temporary visas—a good thing, of course, for the individual beneficiaries. The irony is that movement of the highly skilled into the more advanced economies probably reduces inequality within those economies, all other things the same, but increases inequality in the sending countries. In the sending countries, it increases the wages of the highly skilled that stay, and implies a tax on the working taxpayers in poorer countries who helped finance the education of the emigrants.

Economic power also affects the rules and the conduct of those rules by the international institutions. The International Monetary Fund is the world's institution meant to help countries manage macroeconomic imbalances and minimize the risks of financial shocks. But in the 1990s, the IMF was more enthusiastic about developing countries' opening their capital accounts than subsequent evidence about the costs warranted. This is one example where the IMF and the World Bank have been insufficiently humble in their recipes, perhaps too heavily influenced by their more powerful members. Another is their indiscriminate support for adjustment programmes that in some countries, though technically sound on paper, worsened the situation of the poor (for example maize farmers in southern Mexico) and exacerbated existing inequalities (as did financial sector liberalization and the opening of capital markets in Latin America) because transition costs were inadequately considered and safety net programmes underfunded. Even if most of the policies supported make sense—and for the most part they do—the ability of enlightened leaders to implement them has been reduced because their international sponsors lack legitimacy. . . . The risks to their effectiveness as well as legitimacy are contributing to growing pressure for greater representation of the developing countries in the governance of these international institutions.

Conclusion: Managing Globalization

Inequality within developing countries interacts with their weaker capital markets and institutions to stall growth, encourage perverse economic and social policies, and, in a potential vicious circle, inhibit the creation and strengthening of effective social and political institutions. The global market economy adds to the challenge. Though not the root cause of global inequality it does tend to exacerbate inequality all other things being the same—within developing countries and between rich and poor countries as well. The resulting inequality within and across countries is a development issue. What can be done about the resulting challenge to global security, stability, shared prosperity, and most fundamentally to global social justice?

3.1   A Global Social Contract

In the advanced market economies there is a well-defined social contract that tempers the excess inequalities of income and opportunity that efficient markets naturally generate. Progressive tax systems provide for some redistribution, with the state financing at least minimal educational opportunities for all and some social and old age insurance. The social contract is less well developed in developing countries, almost by definition since they are 'developing'. Yet the economic reforms that competitiveness in global markets requires, and the risks to economic stability it brings, tend to exacerbate existing market-based inequality, generating political pressure for populist redistribution. There is a sense in which the political leadership in many developing countries must manage a delicate balance between undertaking the structural reforms that will generate growth, and minimizing the short-term political risks that it often entails.

Politics is local, and the politics of inequality is doubly so. One lesson for the international community is to do no harm. Volumes have and will be written about the effects of donors' efforts to use conditionality (the 'policy' conditionality of the 1980s and 1990s, and now today's 'process' conditionality). Scepticism and humility about changing politics and policy from the outside seem warranted now. At the same time, in terms of actual resource transfers, the international community has yet to go beyond the shadow of any 'global social contract'. Because global markets work better for the already rich (for individuals with higher education and for countries with stable and sound institutions), the international community needs something closer to a global social contract to address unequal endowments—to rapidly ramp up educational opportunities for the poor in developing countries, and to find ways to help societies build their own sound institutions. Spending by the rich world on the 'global social contract', now reflected in the idea of the Millennium Development Goals, is less than 1 per cent of rich country GDP. That is surprisingly low compared to the typical 20 per cent spent on public transfers for education and social insurance within rich countries. It is a relevant comparison to the extent we now have a more and more integrated global economy—creating legitimate new demands for more shared prosperity.

The business of foreign aid is more effective and sensible than in the Cold War era, but that business itself needs to be reinvented if it is to become reasonably effective—with a premium on the financing of global public goods such as agricultural research and development, on results or output-based transfers, and on systematic evaluation. At the same time, the need to do better should not be an excuse for the rich countries' minimal spending on foreign aid.

Most important, the global and regional institutions we have that are the world's most obvious mechanisms for managing a global social contract need to be reformed. It is ironic that the World Bank and the IMF have been the lightning rod for anti-globalization protests. It may be not that they are too powerful but too ineffective and limited in their resources. To play their role in managing a global social contract they need to become more representative and accountable to those most affected by their programmes, and thus more effective.

3.2 Addressing Global Market Failures

Within countries, governments are meant to temper market failures through regulations, taxes and subsidies, and fines, and to share the benefits of such public goods as public security, military defence, management of natural disasters, and public health through their tax and expenditure decisions. Ideally the latter are made in a democratic system with fair and legitimate representation of all people, independent of their wealth. At the global level, for the global community, an equivalent system to manage global market failures only barely exists.

Because global markets are imperfect, we need global regulatory arrangements and rules to manage the global environment (Kyoto and beyond), help emerging markets cope with global financial risks (the IMF and beyond), and ways to discourage corruption and other anti-competitive processes (a global anti-trust agency for example . . .). Global agreements on bankruptcy procedures, on reducing greenhouse gas emissions, on protecting biodiversity and marine resources, on funding food safety and monitoring public health are all development programmes in one form or another—because they reduce the risks and costs of global spillovers and enhance their potential benefits for the poor.

Similarly with the provision of global public goods—the returns to spending on global public goods that benefit the poor have been extraordinarily high. This is the case of tropical agricultural research, public health research and disease control, and the limited global efforts to protect regional and global environmental resources. These global programmes need to be financed by something that mimics taxes within national economies. Proposals for a tax on international aviation or on carbon emissions fall squarely into this category, and might be more attractive (even in the anti-tax US) were they to be used to increase provision of such global public goods.

3.3 Just Global Rules and Full and Fair Implementation

Within the advanced market economies, democratic politics help temper the inevitable tendency for the rich and powerful to set the rules to their own short-term advantage. At the global level there is no equivalent global polity—only the hope that the rich world will resist short-term advantages in favour of its long-term enlightened self-interest (provided at various times in the past by a benign hegemon—the Roman Empire, the British Empire, and the post-war American empire).

Reducing protection in rich country markets belongs on the agenda of all those fighting for global justice and the elimination of world poverty. Many developing countries are at an unfair disadvantage in global trade and other negotiations, and they need transfers from rich countries simply to effectively participate. This is especially the case for smaller and poorer countries.

Rich countries would do well to open their doors further to unskilled and not just skilled immigrants, allocating resources at home to ease the adjustment of native workers through job training. Even within political constraints, much more could be done by the rich countries in their own interests to make immigration regimes more sensible and more consistent with their overall policies in support of developing countries a part of their overall development policy. Sharing of tax receipts of skilled immigrants across sending and receiving countries is one example. Another is the effort to reduce the transaction costs of remittances. These could help offset the perverse effects of the brain drain on poor countries.

The global approach to intellectual property rights embedded in current WTO rules has struck the wrong balance between incentives for new research and public health needs.

In general the developing countries should be more fully and fairly represented in international institutions; this is especially the case in the international financial institutions, whose policies and programmes are so central to their development prospects. The same can be said for other international fora: the UN Security Council, the Basle Committee for Banking Regulation and Supervision, the G-8, and so on.

We have a potentially powerful instrument to increase wealth and welfare: the global economy. But to complement and support that economy we have an inadequate and fragile global polity. A major challenge of the twenty-first century will be to strengthen and reform the institutions, rules, and customs by which nations and peoples complement the global market with collective management of the problems, including persistent and unjust inequality, which global markets alone will not resolve.

POSTSCRIPT

Is Economic Globalization a Positive Trend?

Globalization is both old and new. It is old in that the efforts of humans to overcome distance and other barriers to increased interchange have long existed. The first canoes and signal fires are part of the history of globalization. The first event in true globalization occurred between 1519 and 1522, when Ferdinand Magellan circumnavigated the globe. MNCs have existed at least since 1600 when a group of British merchants formed the East India Company. In the main, though, globalization is mostly a modern phenomenon. The progress of globalization until the latter half of the 1800s might be termed "creeping globalization." There were changes, but they occurred very slowly. Since then, the pace of globalization has increased exponentially. A brief introduction to globalization is available in Jurgen Osterhammel, Niels P. Petersson, and Dona Geyer, *Globalization: A Short History* (Princeton University Press, 2005). A contemporary look at globalization mentioned in Birdsall's article is Thomas L. Friedman's updated and expanded *The World Is Flat: A Brief History of the Twenty-first Century* (Picador, 2007).

The recent rapid pace of globalization has sparked an increasing chorus of criticism against many of its aspects including economic interdependence. Now it is not uncommon for massive protests to occur when the leaders of the world countries meet to discuss global or regional economics or when the WTO, IMF, or World Bank hold important conferences.

One of the oddities about globalization, economic or otherwise, is that it often creates a common cause between those of marked conservative and marked liberal views. More than anything, conservatives worry that their respective countries are losing control of their economies and, thus, a degree of their independence. Echoing this view, archconservative political commentator Patrick Buchanan has warned that unchecked globalization threatens to turn the United States into a "North American province of what some call The New World Order."

Some liberals share the conservatives' negative views of globalization but for different reasons. This perspective is less concerned with sovereignty and security; it is more concerned with workers and countries being exploited and the environment being damaged by MNCs that shift their operations to other countries to find cheap labor and to escape environmental regulations. During the 2008 campaign for the Democratic presidential nomination, both Barack Obama and Hillary Clinton expressed concern about the impact that U.S. free trade agreements were having both on American and foreign workers and on their environments. One widely read critique of economic globalization is Joseph E. Stiglitz, *Making Globalization Work* (W. W. Norton, 2006).

Despite the upsurge of criticism, globalization continues to have many supporters. Most national leaders, especially among the industrialized countries, continue to support free economic interchange. In the United States, both President Bill Clinton and President George W. Bush took that stand, although they sometimes also applied protectionist practices to shield U.S. business and workers. The support for globalization is also strong among economists, including Jagdish Bhagwati, *In Defense of Globalization* (Oxford University Press, 2004).

What many analysts argue is that globalization is not good or bad, as such. Rather, it is how it is applied that makes the difference. A study that takes a balanced view is Daniel Cohen, *Globalization and Its Enemies* (MIT Press, 2006). Books that look toward reform and discuss new ways of thinking are Frederic Mishkin, *The Next Great Globalization* (Princeton University Press, 2006) and Kemal Dervis, *A Better Globalization* (Center for Global Development, 2005). The Internet provides further resources that examine globalization. A good site is The Globalization Web site, http://www.sociology.emory.edu/globalization, hosted by Emory University. It is even-handed and is particularly meant to support undergraduates.

ISSUE 2

Does Globalization Threaten Cultural Diversity?

YES: Julia Galeota, from "Cultural Imperialism: An American Tradition," *The Humanist* (May/June 2004)

NO: Philippe Legrain, from "In Defense of Globalization," *The International Economy* (Summer 2003)

ISSUE SUMMARY

YES: Julia Galeota of McLean, Virginia, who was seventeen years old when she wrote her essay that won first place for her age category in the 2004 *Humanist* Essay Contest for Young Women and Men of North America, contends that many cultures around the world are gradually disappearing due to the overwhelming influence of corporate and cultural America.

NO: Philippe Legrain, chief economist of Britain in Europe, an organization supporting the adoption by Great Britain of the euro as its currency, counters that it is a myth that globalization involves the imposition of Americanized uniformity, rather than an explosion of cultural exchange.

Globalization is often thought of in terms of economic integration, but it is a much broader phenomenon. Another important aspect of globalization is the spread of national cultures to other countries, regions, and, indeed, the world. One impetus for cultural globalization is economic globalization, as products spread around the world and as huge multinational corporations establish global operations. Additionally, cultural globalization is a product of advances in transportation that allow an increasing number of people to travel to other countries and of radio, television, the Internet, and other advances in communications that permit people to interact passively or actively with others around the world.

To a degree, the culture of many nations is spreading, with Japanese shushi bars now a common site in the United States, Europe, and elsewhere. Cultural globalization also involves a certain amount of cultural amalgamation, with influences merging to create new cultural realities. A third possibility, and the one that is at the heart of this debate, is when the spread of one culture is far greater than the spread of others. Arguably, that is what is currently occurring, with American "cultural exports" much greater than those of any other country.

There is significant evidence of the spread of Western, particularly American, cultural. Casual dress around the world is more apt to include jeans, T-shirts, and sneakers than traditional dress. Young people everywhere listen to music by Beyonce, Jay-Z, and other artists, and fast-food hamburgers, fries, and milk shakes are consumed around the world. Adding to the spread of American culture, U.S. movies are everywhere, earning the majority of all film revenues in Japan, Europe, and Latin America, and U.S. television programming is increasingly omnipresent, with, for instance, about two-thirds of the market in Latin America.

Another indication of the spread of American culture is that English is increasingly the common language of business, diplomacy, communications, and even culture. Among Europeans, for instance, nearly all school children receive English instruction, and two-thirds of younger Europeans speak at least some English compared to less than 20 percent of retirement-age Europeans.

It is important to not trivialize cultural globalization even though it involves, in part, fast food, sneakers, rock music, and other elements of pop culture. Some scholars argue the elimination of culture differences will help reduce conflicts as people become more familiar with one another and, indeed, more similar to each other.

Others, however, believe the cultural globalization has negative aspects. One argument is that it is causing a backlash as people face the loss of their own cultures. Some analysts contend that the growth of religious fundamentalism and even terrorism is a reaction to cultural threats. Other analysts believe that defense of cultural traditionalism could even lead to culture wars in the future, with the world dividing itself into antagonist cultural groups. A third worry is represented by Julia Galeota in the first reading, who worries that the spread of American culture amounts for cultural imperialism that is destroying the rich cultural variety that has heretofore marked human society. Galeota suggests that the spread of American culture is a product of American economic and other forms of power, rather than the result of the superiority of American culture and its attractiveness to others. As such, she depicts the Americanization of global culture as cultural imperialism. Philippe Legrain is much more at ease with cultural globalization. He contends that it reflects new realities and is making many contributions, such as giving people the freedom to adopt whatever language, style of dress, or other cultural aspect that they find most compatible with their tastes and needs.

YES

Julia Galeota

Cultural Imperialism: An American Tradition

Travel almost anywhere in the world today and, whether you suffer from habitual Big Mac cravings or cringe at the thought of missing the newest episode of MTV's *The Real World,* your American tastes can be satisfied practically everywhere. This proliferation of American products across the globe is more than mere accident. As a byproduct of globalization, it is part of a larger trend in the conscious dissemination of American attitudes and values that is often referred to as *cultural imperialism.* In his 1976 work *Communication and Cultural Domination,* Herbert Schiller defines cultural imperialism as:

> The sum of the processes by which a society is brought into the modern world system, and how its dominating stratum is attracted, pressured, forced, and sometimes bribed into shaping social institutions to correspond to, or even to promote, the values and structures of the dominant center of the system.

Thus, cultural imperialism involves much more than simple consumer goods; it involves the dissemination of ostensibly American principles, such as freedom and democracy. Though this process might sound appealing on the surface, it masks a frightening truth: many cultures around the world are gradually disappearing due to the overwhelming influence of corporate and cultural America.

The motivations behind American cultural imperialism parallel the justifications for U.S. imperialism throughout history: the desire for access to foreign markets and the belief in the superiority of American culture. Though the United States does boast the world's largest, most powerful economy, no business is completely satisfied with controlling only the American market; American corporations want to control the other 95 percent of the world's consumers as well. Many industries are incredibly successful in that venture. According to the *Guardian,* American films accounted for approximately 80 percent of global box office revenue in January 2003. And who can forget good old Micky D's? With over 30,000 restaurants in over one hundred countries, the ubiquitous golden arches of McDonald's are now, according to Eric Schlosser's *Fast Food* Nation, "more widely recognized than the Christian cross." Such American domination inevitably hurts local markets, as the majority of foreign industries are unable to compete with the economic strength of U.S. industry.

From *The Humanist,* vol. 64, no. 3, May/June 2004, pp. 22–24, 46. Copyright © 2004 by Julia Galeota. Reprinted by permission from American Humanist Association and Julia Galeota.

Because it serves American economic interests, corporations conveniently ignore the detrimental impact of American control of foreign markets.

Corporations don't harbor qualms about the detrimental effects of "Americanization" of foreign cultures, as most corporations have ostensibly convinced themselves that American culture is superior and therefore its influence is beneficial to other, "lesser" cultures. Unfortunately, this American belief in the superiority of U.S. culture is anything but new; it is as old as the culture itself. This attitude was manifest in the actions of settlers when they first arrived on this continent and massacred or assimilated essentially the entire "savage" Native American population. This attitude also reflects that of the late nineteenth-century age of imperialism, during which the jingoists attempted to fulfill what they believed to be the divinely ordained "manifest destiny" of American expansion. Jingoists strongly believe in the concept of social Darwinism: the stronger, "superior" cultures will overtake the weaker, "inferior" cultures in a "survival of the fittest." It is this arrogant belief in the incomparability of American culture that characterizes many of our economic and political strategies today.

It is easy enough to convince Americans of the superiority of their culture, but how does one convince the rest of the world of the superiority of American culture? The answer is simple: marketing. Whether attempting to sell an item, a brand, or an entire culture, marketers have always been able to successfully associate American products with modernity in the minds of consumers worldwide. While corporations seem to simply sell Nike shoes or Gap jeans (both, ironically, manufactured *outside* of the United States), they are also selling the image of America as the land of "cool." This indissoluble association causes consumers all over the globe to clamor ceaselessly for the same American products.

Twenty years ago, in his essay "The Globalization of Markets," Harvard business professor Theodore Levitt declared, "The world's needs and desires have been irrevocably homogenized." Levitt held that corporations that were willing to bend to local tastes and habits were inevitably doomed to failure. He drew a distinction between weak multinational corporations that operate differently in each country and strong global corporations that handle an entire world of business with the same agenda.

In recent years, American corporations have developed an even more successful global strategy: instead of advertising American conformity with blonde-haired, blue-eyed, stereotypical Americans, they pitch diversity. These campaigns—such as McDonald's new international "I'm lovin' it" campaign—work by drawing on the United State's history as an ethnically integrated nation composed of essentially every culture in the world. An early example of this global marketing tactic was found in a Coca Cola commercial from 1971 featuring children from many different countries innocently singing, "I'd like to teach the world to sing in perfect harmony/I'd like to buy the world a Coke to keep it company." This commercial illustrates an attempt to portray a U.S. goods as a product capable of transcending political, ethnic, religious, social, and economic differences to unite the world (according to the Coca-Cola Company, we can achieve world peace through consumerism).

More recently, Viacom's MTV has successfully adapted this strategy by integrating many different Americanized cultures into one unbelievably influential American network (with over 280 million subscribers worldwide). According to a 1996 "New World Teen Study" conducted by DMB&B's BrainWaves division, of the 26,700 middle-class teens in forty-five countries surveyed, 85 percent watch MTV every day. These teens absorb what MTV intends to show as a diverse mix of cultural influences but is really nothing more than manufactured stars singing in English to appeal to American popular taste.

If the strength of these diverse "American" images is not powerful enough to move products, American corporations also appropriate local cultures into their advertising abroad. Unlike Levitt's weak multinationals, these corporations don't bend to local tastes; they merely insert indigenous celebrities or trends to present the facade of a customized advertisement. MTV has spawned over twenty networks specific to certain geographical areas such as Brazil and Japan. These specialized networks further spread the association between American and modernity under the pretense of catering to local taste. Similarly, commercials in India in 2000 featured Bollywood stars Hrithik Roshan promoting Coke and Shahrukh Khan promoting Pepsi (Sanjeev Srivastava, "Cola Row in India," BBC News Online). By using popular local icons in their advertisements, U.S. corporations successfully associate what is fashionable in local cultures with what is fashionable in America. America essentially samples the world's cultures, repackages them with the American trademark of materialism, and resells them to the world.

Critics of the theory of American cultural imperialism argue that foreign consumers don't passively absorb the images America bombards upon them. In fact, foreign consumers do play an active role in the reciprocal relationship between buyer and seller. For example, according to Naomi Klein's *No Logo*, American cultural imperialism has inspired a "slow food movement" in Italy and a demonstration involving the burning of chickens outside of the first Kentucky Fried Chicken outlet in India. Though there have been countless other conspicuous and inconspicuous acts of resistance, the intense, unrelenting barrage of American cultural influence continues ceaselessly.

Compounding the influence of commercial images are the media and information industries, which present both explicit and implicit messages about the very real military and economic hegemony of the United States. Ironically, the industry that claims to be the source for "fair and balanced" information plays a large role in the propagation of American influence around the world. The concentration of media ownership during the 1990s enabled both American and British media organizations to gain control of the majority of the world's news services. Satellites allow over 150 million households in approximately 212 countries and territories worldwide to subscribe to CNN, a member of Time Warner, the world's largest media conglomerate. In the words of British sociologist Jeremy Tunstall, "When a government allows news importation, it is in effect importing a piece of another country's politics—which is true of no other import." In addition to politics and commercials, networks like CNN also present foreign countries with unabashed accounts of the military and economic superiority of the United States.

The Internet acts as another vehicle for the worldwide propagation of American influence. Interestingly, some commentators cite the new "information economy" as proof that American cultural imperialism is in decline. They argue that the global accessibility of this decentralized medium has decreased the relevance of the "core and periphery" theory of global influence. This theory describes an inherent imbalance in the primarily outward flow of information and influence from the stronger, more powerful "core" nations such as the United States. Additionally, such critics argue, unlike consumers of other types of media, Internet users must actively seek out information; users can consciously choose to avoid all messages of American culture. While these arguments are valid, they ignore their converse: if one so desires, anyone can access a wealth of information about American culture possibly unavailable through previous channels. Thus, the Internet can dramatically increase exposure to American culture for those who desire it.

Fear of the cultural upheaval that could result from this exposure to new information has driven governments in communist China and Cuba to strictly monitor and regulate their citizens' access to websites (these protectionist policies aren't totally effective, however, because they are difficult to implement and maintain). Paradoxically, limiting access to the Internet nearly ensures that countries will remain largely the recipients, rather than the contributors, of information on the Internet.

Not all social critics see the Americanization of the world as a negative phenomenon. Proponents of cultural imperialism, such as David Rothkopf, a former senior official in Clinton's Department of Commerce, argue that American cultural imperialism is in the interest not only of the United States but also of the world at large. Rothkopf cites Samuel Huntington's theory from *The Clash of Civilizations and the Remaking of the World Order* that, the greater the cultural disparities in the world, the more likely it is that conflict will occur. Rothkopf argues that the removal of cultural barriers through U.S. cultural imperialism will promote a more stable world, one in which American culture reigns supreme as "the most just, the most tolerant, the most willing to constantly reassess and improve itself, and the best model for the future." Rothkopf is correct in one sense: Americans are on the way to establishing a global society with minimal cultural barriers. However, one must question whether this projected society is truly beneficial for all involved. Is it worth sacrificing countless indigenous cultures for the unlikely promise of a world without conflict?

Around the world, the answer is an overwhelming "No!" Disregarding the fact that a world of homogenized culture would not necessarily guarantee a world without conflict, the complex fabric of diverse cultures around the world is a fundamental and indispensable basis of humanity. Throughout the course of human existence, millions have died to preserve their indigenous culture. It is a fundamental right of humanity to be allowed to preserve the mental, physical, intellectual, and creative aspects of one's society. A single "global culture" would be nothing more than a shallow, artificial "culture" of materialism reliant on technology. Thankfully, it would be nearly impossible to create one bland culture in a world of over six billion people. And nor should we want to. Contrary to Rothkopf's (and George W. Bush's) belief that, "Good and evil, better and worse coexist in this world," there are no such absolutes in this world. The United States should not be able to relentlessly force other nations to accept its definition of what is "good" and "just" or even "modern."

Fortunately, many victims of American cultural imperialism aren't blind to the subversion of their cultures. Unfortunately, these nations are often too weak to fight the strength of the United States and subsequently to preserve their native cultures. Some countries—such as France, China, Cuba, Canada, and Iran—have attempted to quell America's cultural influence by limiting or prohibiting access to American cultural programming through satellites and the Internet. However, according to the UN Universal Declaration of Human Rights, it is a basic right of all people to "seek, receive, and impart information and ideas through any media and regardless of frontiers," Governments shouldn't have to restrict their citizens' access to information in order to preserve their native cultures. We as a world must find ways to defend local cultures in a manner that does not compromise the rights of indigenous people.

The prevalent proposed solutions to the problem of American cultural imperialism are a mix of defense and compromise measures on behalf of the endangered cultures. In *The Lexus and the Olive Tree,* Thomas Friedman advocates the use of protective legislation such as zoning laws and protected area laws, as well as the appointment of politicians with cultural integrity, such as those in agricultural, culturally pure Southern France. However, many other nations have no voice in the nomination of their leadership, so those countries need a middle-class and elite committed to social activism. If it is utterly impossible to maintain the cultural purity of a country through legislation, Friedman suggests the country attempt to "glocalize," that is:

> To absorb influences that naturally fit into and can enrich [a] culture, to resist those things that are truly alien and to compartmentalize those things that, while different, can nevertheless be enjoyed and celebrated as different.

These types of protective filters should help to maintain the integrity of a culture in the face of cultural imperialism. In *Jihad vs. McWorld,* Benjamin Barber calls for the resuscitation of nongovernmental, noncapitalist spaces—to the "civic spaces"—such as village greens, places of religious worship, or community schools. It is also equally important to focus on the education of youth in their native values and traditions. Teens especially need a counterbalance images of American consumerism they absorb from the media. Even if individuals or countries consciously choose to become "Americanized" or "modernized," their choice should be made freely and independently of the coercion and influence of American cultural imperialism.

The responsibility for preserving cultures shouldn't fall entirely on those at risk. The United States must also recognize that what is good for its economy isn't necessarily good for the world at large. We must learn to put people before profits. The corporate and political leaders of the United States would be well advised to heed these words of Gandhi:

> I do not want my house to be walled in on all sides and my windows to be stuffed. I want the culture of all lands to be blown about my house as freely as possible. But I refuse to be blown off my feet by any.

The United States must acknowledge that no one culture can or should reign supreme, for the death of diverse cultures can only further harm future generations.

Philippe Legrain

In Defense of Globalization

Fears that globalization is imposing a deadening cultural uniformity are as ubiquitous as Coca-Cola, McDonald's, and Mickey Mouse. Many people dread that local cultures and national identities are dissolving into a crass all-American consumerism. That cultural imperialism is said to impose American values as well as products, promote the commercial at the expense of the authentic, and substitute shallow gratification for deeper satisfaction.

Thomas Friedman, columnist for the *New York Times* and author of *The Lexus and the Olive Tree,* believes that globalization is "globalizing American culture and American cultural icons." Naomi Klein, a Canadian journalist and author of *No Logo,* argues that "Despite the embrace of polyethnic imagery, market-driven globalization doesn't want diversity; quite the opposite. Its enemies are national habits, local brands, and distinctive regional tastes."

But it is a myth that globalization involves the imposition of Americanized uniformity, rather than an explosion of cultural exchange. And although—as with any change—it can have downsides, this cross-fertilization is overwhelmingly a force for good.

The beauty of globalization is that it can free people from the tyranny of geography. Just because someone was born in France does not mean they can only aspire to speak French, eat French food, read French books, and so on. That we are increasingly free to choose our cultural experiences enriches our lives immeasurably. We could not always enjoy the best the world has to offer.

Globalization not only increases individual freedom, but also revitalizes cultures and cultural artifacts through foreign influences, technologies, and markets. Many of the best things come from cultures mixing: Paul Gauguin painting in Polynesia, the African rhythms in rock 'n' roll, the great British curry. Admire the many-colored faces of France's World Cup-winning soccer team, the ferment of ideas that came from Eastern Europe's Jewish diaspora, and the cosmopolitan cities of London and New York.

Fears about an Americanized uniformity are overblown. For a start, many "American" products are not as all-American as they seem; MTV in Asia promotes Thai pop stars and plays rock music sung in Mandarin. Nor are American products all-conquering. Coke accounts for less than two of the 64 fluid ounces that the typical person drinks a day. France imported a mere $620 million in food from the United States in 2000, while exporting to America three times

From *The International Economy* by Philippe Legrain, vol. 17, no. 3, Summer 2003, pp. 62–65.

that. Worldwide, pizzas are more popular than burgers and Chinese restaurants sprout up everywhere.

In fashion, the ne plus ultra is Italian or French. Nike shoes are given a run for their money by Germany's Adidas, Britain's Reebok, and Italy's Fila. American pop stars do not have the stage to themselves. According to the IFPI, the record-industry bible, local acts accounted for 68 percent of music sales in 2000, up from 58 percent in 1991. And although nearly three-quarters of television drama exported worldwide comes from the United States, most countries' favorite shows are homegrown.

Nor are Americans the only players in the global media industry. Of the seven market leaders, one is German, one French, and one Japanese. What they distribute comes from all quarters: Germany's Bertelsmann publishes books by American writers; America's News Corporation broadcasts Asian news; Japan's Sony sells Brazilian music.

In some ways, America is an outlier, not a global leader. Baseball and American football have not traveled well; most prefer soccer. Most of the world has adopted the (French) metric system; America persists with antiquated British Imperial measurements. Most developed countries have become intensely secular, but many Americans burn with fundamentalist fervor—like Muslims in the Middle East.

Admittedly, Hollywood dominates the global movie market and swamps local products in most countries. American fare accounts for more than half the market in Japan and nearly two-thirds in Europe. Yet Hollywood is less American than it seems. Top actors and directors are often from outside America. Some studios are foreign-owned. To some extent, Hollywood is a global industry that just happens to be in America. Rather than exporting Americana, it serves up pap to appeal to a global audience.

Hollywood's dominance is in part due to economics: Movies cost a lot to make and so need a big audience to be profitable; Hollywood has used America's huge and relatively uniform domestic market as a platform to expand overseas. So there could be a case for stuffing subsidies into a rival European film industry, just as Airbus was created to challenge Boeing's near-monopoly. But France's subsidies have created a vicious circle whereby European film producers fail in global markets because they serve domestic demand and the wishes of politicians and cinematic bureaucrats.

Another American export is also conquering the globe: English. By 2050, it is reckoned, half the world will be more or less proficient in it. A common global language would certainly be a big plus—for businessmen, scientists, and tourists—but a single one seems far less desirable. Language is often at the heart of national culture, yet English may usurp other languages not because it is what people prefer to speak, but because, like Microsoft software, there are compelling advantages to using it if everyone else does.

But although many languages are becoming extinct, English is rarely to blame. People are learning English as well as—not instead of—their native tongue, and often many more languages besides. Where local languages are dying, it is typically national rivals that are stamping them out. So although, within the United States, English is displacing American Indian tongues, it is not doing away with Swahili or Norwegian.

Even though American consumer culture is widespread, its significance is often exaggerated. You can choose to drink Coke and eat at McDonald's without becoming American in any meaningful sense. One newspaper photo of Taliban fighters in Afghanistan showed them toting Kalashnikovs—as well as a sports bag with Nike's trademark swoosh. People's culture—in the sense of their shared ideas, beliefs, knowledge, inherited traditions, and art—may scarcely be eroded by mere commercial artifacts that, despite all the furious branding, embody at best flimsy values.

The really profound cultural changes have little to do with Coca-Cola. Western ideas about liberalism and science are taking root almost every-where, while Europe and North America are becoming multicultural socie-ties through immigration, mainly from developing countries. Technology is reshaping culture: Just think of the Internet. Individual choice is fragmenting the imposed uniformity of national cultures. New hybrid cultures are emerg-ing, and regional ones re-emerging. National identity is not disappearing, but the bonds of nationality are loosening.

Cross-border cultural exchange increases diversity within societies—but at the expense of making them more alike. People everywhere have more choice, but they often choose similar things. That worries cultural pessimists, even though the right to choose to be the same is an essential part of freedom.

Cross-cultural exchange can spread greater diversity as well as greater similarity: more gourmet restaurants as well as more McDonald's outlets. And just as a big city can support a wider spread of restaurants than a small town, so a global market for cultural products allows a wider range of artists to thrive. If all the new customers are ignorant, a wider market may drive down the qual-ity of cultural products: Think of tourist souvenirs. But as long as some cus-tomers are well informed (or have "good taste"), a general "dumbing down" is unlikely. Hobbyists, fans, artistic pride, and professional critics also help maintain (and raise) standards.

A bigger worry is that greater individual freedom may undermine national identity. The French fret that by individually choosing to watch Hollywood films they might unwittingly lose their collective Frenchness. Yet such fears are overdone. Natural cultures are much stronger than people seem to think. They can embrace some foreign influences and resist others. Foreign influ-ences can rapidly become domesticated, changing national culture, but not destroying it. Clearly, though, there is a limit to how many foreign influences a culture can absorb before being swamped. Traditional cultures in the devel-oping world that have until now evolved (or failed to evolve) in isolation may be particularly vulnerable.

In *The Silent Takeover,* Noreena Hertz describes the supposed spiritual Eden that was the isolated kingdom of Bhutan in the Himalayas as being defiled by such awful imports as basketball and Spice Girls T-shirts. But is that such a bad thing? It is odd, to put it mildly, that many on the left support multiculturalism in the West but advocate cultural purity in the developing world—an attitude they would tar as fascist if proposed for the United States. Hertz appears to want people outside the industrialized West preserved in unchanging but supposedly pure poverty. Yet the Westerners who want this supposed paradise preserved in aspic rarely feel like settling there. Nor do most people in developing countries want to lead an "authentic" unspoiled life of isolated poverty.

In truth, cultural pessimists are typically not attached to diversity per se but to designated manifestations of diversity, determined by their preferences. Cultural pessimists want to freeze things as they were. But if diversity at any point in time is desirable, why isn't diversity across time? Certainly, it is often a shame if ancient cultural traditions are lost. We should do our best to preserve them and keep them alive where possible. Foreigners can often help, by providing the new customers and technologies that have enabled reggae music, Haitian art, and Persian carpet making, for instance, to thrive and reach new markets. But people cannot be made to live in a museum. We in the West are forever casting off old customs when we feel they are no longer relevant. Nobody argues that Americans should ban nightclubs to force people back to line dancing. People in poor countries have a right to change, too.

Moreover, some losses of diversity are a good thing. Who laments that the world is now almost universally rid of slavery? More generally, Western ideas are reshaping the way people everywhere view themselves and the world. Like nationalism and socialism before it, liberalism is a European philosophy that has swept the world. Even people who resist liberal ideas, in the name of religion (Islamic and Christian fundamentalists), group identity (communitarians), authoritarianism (advocates of "Asian values") or tradition (cultural conservatives), now define themselves partly by their opposition to them.

Faith in science and technology is even more widespread. Even those who hate the West make use of its technologies. Osama bin Laden plots terrorism on a cellphone and crashes planes into skyscrapers. Antiglobalization protesters organize by e-mail and over the Internet. China no longer turns its nose up at Western technology: It tries to beat the West at its own game.

Yet globalization is not a one-way street. Although Europe's former colonial powers have left their stamp on much of the world, the recent flow of migration has been in the opposite direction. There are Algerian suburbs in Paris, but not French ones in Algiers. Whereas Muslims are a growing minority in Europe, Christians are a disappearing one in the Middle East.

Foreigners are changing America even as they adopt its ways. A million or so immigrants arrive each year, most of them Latino or Asian. Since 1990, the number of foreign-born American residents has risen by 6 million to just over 25 million, the biggest immigration wave since the turn of the 20th century. English may be all-conquering outside America, but in some parts of the United States, it is now second to Spanish.

The upshot is that national cultures are fragmenting into a kaleidoscope of different ones. New hybrid cultures are emerging. In "Amexica" people speak Spanglish. Regional cultures are reviving. The Scots and Welsh break with British monoculture. Estonia is reborn from the Soviet Union. Voices that were silent dare to speak again.

Individuals are forming new communities, linked by shared interests and passions, that which cut across national borders. Friendships with foreigners met on holiday. Scientists sharing ideas over the Internet. Environmentalists campaigning together using e-mail. Greater individualism does not spell the end of community. The new communities are simply chosen rather than coerced, unlike the older ones that communitarians hark back to.

So is national identity dead? Hardly. People who speak the same language, were born and live near each other, face similar problems, have a common experience, and vote in the same elections still have plenty in common. For all our awareness of the world as a single place, we are not citizens of the world but citizens of a state. But if people now wear the bonds of nationality more loosely, is that such a bad thing? People may lament the passing of old ways. Indeed, many of the worries about globalization echo age-old fears about decline, a lost golden age, and so on. But by and large, people choose the new ways because they are more relevant to their current needs and offer new opportunities.

The truth is that we increasingly define ourselves rather than let others define us. Being British or American does not define who you are: It is part of who you are. You can like foreign things and still have strong bonds to your fellow citizens. As Mario Vargas Llosa, the Peruvian author, has written: "Seeking to impose a cultural identity on a people is equivalent to locking them in a prison and denying them the most precious of liberties—that of choosing what, how, and who they want to be."

POSTSCRIPT

Does Globalization Threaten Cultural Diversity?

Cultural globalization, dominated by the spread of Western, primarily American, culture is likely to continue into the foreseeable future. For example, English may not be a common global language, but the possibility of that occurring is given some credence by a survey of people in 42 countries that recorded the vast majority in every region agreed with the statement, "Children need to learn English to succeed in the world today."

Attitudes toward cultural globalization are less clear-cut and are even contradictory. A global survey found that, on average, three-quarters of all people thought culture imports were good. Regionally, that favorable response ranged from 61 percent in the Middle East to 86 percent in western Europe. At the same time, though, an approximately equal percentage of people thought cultural imports were eroding their traditional way of life, with Africans, at 86 percent, the most likely to think so. Not surprisingly, this sense of cultural threat also leads to a desire to protect traditional cultures. The survey found that about 70 percent of its respondents felt that their way of life needed protection from foreign influence. At 79 percent each, people in Africa and the Middle East were most likely to feel their traditional cultures needed protection; western Europeans (56 percent) were the least insecure. Whether this sense of cultural loss is all due to globalization is unclear. It may well be that the changes that are unsettling most people worldwide are also part of the even broader phenomenon of rapid technological modernization that is spurring globalization.

An oddity of the cultural globalization phenomenon is that American attitudes are not much different from those of other people, despite the worry that American culture is becoming dominant. The poll showed that the overwhelming majority of Americans were favorable to the increased availability of goods, music, films, and other cultural imports. Yet two-thirds of all Americans replied to the survey that their traditional way of life was being lost, and a similar percentage responded that they believed that their way of life needed to be protected against foreign influences.

For more on the progress of globalization, visit the British Broadcasting Corporation's Web site at http://www.bbc.co.uk/worldservice/programmes/globalisation/ and Randolph Kluver and Wayne Fu, "The Cultural Globalization Index," posted on the Web site of *Foreign Policy* at http://www.foreignpolicy.com. An overview of cultural globalization is Paul Hopper, *Understanding Cultural Globalization* (Wiley, 2007). For a mostly negative view of F. Jan Nederveen Pieterse, *Globalization and Culture* (Rowman & Littlefield, 2003) views the process as a cultural hybridization rather than Americanization. Of all countries, the less-developed ones are the most strongly impacted by cultural globalization, as discussed by Jeff Haynesin, *Religion, Globalization, and Political Culture in the Third World* (St. Martin's Press, 1999). A discussion of maintaining cultural distinctiveness can be found in Harry Redner, *Conserving Cultures: Technology, Globalization, and the Future of Local Cultures* (Rowman & Littlefield, 2003).

ISSUE 3

Does Capitalism Undermine Democracy?

YES: Robert B. Reich, from "How Capitalism Is Killing Democracy," *Foreign Policy* (September/October 2007)

NO: Anthony B. Kim, from "The Link between Economic Freedom and Human Rights," *Heritage Foundation Web Memo,* #1650 (September 28, 2007)

ISSUE SUMMARY

YES: Robert B. Reich, professor of public policy at the University of California, Berkeley, and former U.S. secretary of labor, writes that capitalism leaves democratic societies unable to address the trade-offs between economic growth and social problems.

NO: Anthony B. Kim, a policy analyst at the Heritage Foundation's Center for International Trade and Economics, contends that economic progress through advancing economic freedom has allowed more people to discuss and adopt different views more candidly, ultimately leading societies to be more open and inclusive.

T he intersection of politics and economics is called the study of political economy or, at the global level, international political economy (IPE). Through most of history, monarchs and other types of authoritarian rulers almost always wielded political power, and they saw the economy in their realms as a way to increase their personal wealth and power by enhancing the might of the empire, country, or other political units they ruled.

The assumption of monarchial rights began to wane noticeably about three centuries ago, and the countervailing concept of democracy, rule by the people, began to slowly gather strength. The most obvious symbols of this shift were the American Revolution of 1776 and the French Revolution of 1789.

Accompanying the idea that a government should be of, for, and by the people was the notion that the economic activity of people should be aimed at benefiting themselves, not the state or its rulers. This "liberal" idea became known as capitalism. One early proponent of capitalist theory was the English philosopher, Adam Smith, who published his famous *The Wealth of Nations* in 1776, the same year that Americans were rejecting the British monarchy and establishing their independent democracy. Smith saw humans as inherently self-interested; argued that prosperity was best gained by people investing their labor and assets in improving production; and further asserted that people would be most likely to do so if they personally profited from their efforts. He believed all would benefit because competition would keep prices down and increased production would keep the need for labor high. Smith, therefore, opposed any political interference in the economy.

Within a century, it has become clear that the pure capitalism advocated by Smith did not work as he had envisioned. The economy and people were perhaps more free from political control, but capitalism had also created vast differences in wealth, with most capitalist countries, including the United States, having a gulf between wealthy manufacturing, banking, and other moguls and a limited middle class and large poor class working in the fields and factories. Business practices such as monopolies, which stifled Adam Smith's vision of competition, were a major factor.

Beginning in the late 1800s, the countries of Western Europe, the United States, and other capitalist, industrialized countries began to reassert political control over their economies, in part, to restrain monopolies and other ill practices of capitalism and to limit its impact by providing more social services to the needy. The U.S. Progressive Era at the turn of the twentieth century and, later, Franklin Roosevelt's New Deal beginning in 1933 are examples of this change.

How far the "leveling" effect should go has been in great dispute. Some believe that government control of the economy should be kept to a minimum. Favoring greater control and spread of wealth are liberals. Favoring yet greater government controls and even greater wealth redistribution are Socialists, and the furthest extreme are Communists, who, in pure Marxist theory, believe in total public control of the economy and elimination of all economic class distinctions.

All these tie into the issue about whether capitalism undermines democracy because of the dispute over what economic model countries, especially developing ones, should follow to achieve and maintain prosperity. Because of the global power of the decidedly capitalist United States during the years since World War II, when many countries gained independence and began to develop and also when economic globalization gained momentum, countries have been under a great deal of pressure to follow the capitalist model of the United States.

Some, such as Robert B. Reich in the first reading, believe that the relatively unfettered capitalist approach to development and globalization has not only created numerous economic harms (see Issue 1) but also undermined democracy. Reich believes that capitalism in the age of globalization is weakening democracy because global corporations have become ever more powerful and their political influence is increasingly drowning out the voices of average citizens. Anthony B. Kim heartily disagrees and, as you will see in the second reading, maintains that capitalism's economic freedom empowers people and, thereby, unleashes powerful forces of choice and opportunity that promote and strengthen democracy.

YES

Robert B. Reich

How Capitalism Is Killing Democracy

It was supposed to be a match made in heaven. Capitalism and democracy, we've long been told, are the twin ideological pillars capable of bringing unprecedented prosperity and freedom to the world. In recent decades, the duo has shared a common ascent. By almost any measure, global capitalism is triumphant. Most nations around the world are today part of a single, integrated, and turbocharged global market. Democracy has enjoyed a similar renaissance. Three decades ago, a third of the world's nations held free elections; today, nearly two thirds do.

Conventional wisdom holds that where either capitalism or democracy flourishes, the other must soon follow. Yet today, their fortunes are beginning to diverge. Capitalism, long sold as the yin to democracy's yang, is thriving, while democracy is struggling to keep up. China, poised to become the world's third largest capitalist nation this year after the United States and Japan, has embraced market freedom, but not political freedom. Many economically successful nations—from Russia to Mexico—are democracies in name only. They are encumbered by the same problems that have hobbled American democracy in recent years, allowing corporations and elites buoyed by runaway economic success to undermine the government's capacity to respond to citizens' concerns.

Of course, democracy means much more than the process of free and fair elections. It is a system for accomplishing what can only be achieved by citizens joining together to further the common good. But though free markets have brought unprecedented prosperity to many, they have been accompanied by widening inequalities of income and wealth, heightened job insecurity, and environmental hazards such as global warming. Democracy is designed to allow citizens to address these very issues in constructive ways. And yet a sense of political powerlessness is on the rise among citizens in Europe, Japan, and the United States, even as consumers and investors feel more empowered. In short, no democratic nation is effectively coping with capitalism's negative side effects.

This fact is not, however, a failing of capitalism. As these two forces have spread around the world, we have blurred their responsibilities, to the detriment of our democratic duties. Capitalism's role is to increase the economic pie, nothing more. And while capitalism has become remarkably responsive to what people want as individual consumers, democracies have struggled to

From *Foreign Policy,* September/October 2007. Copyright © 2007 by the Carnegie Endowment for International Peace. Reprinted with permission. www.foreignpolicy.com

perform their own basic functions: to articulate and act upon the common good, and to help societies achieve both growth and equity. Democracy, at its best, enables citizens to debate collectively how the slices of the pie should be divided and to determine which rules apply to private goods and which to public goods. Today, those tasks are increasingly being left to the market. What is desperately needed is a clear delineation of the boundary between global capitalism and democracy—between the economic game, on the one hand, and how its rules are set, on the other. If the purpose of capitalism is to allow corporations to play the market as aggressively as possible, the challenge for citizens is to stop these economic entities from being the authors of the rules by which we live.

The Cost of Doing Business

Most people are of two minds: As consumers and investors, we want the bargains and high returns that the global economy provides. As citizens, we don't like many of the social consequences that flow from these transactions. We like to blame corporations for the ills that follow, but in truth we've made this compact with ourselves. After all, we know the roots of the great economic deals we're getting. They come from workers forced to settle for lower wages and benefits. They come from companies that shed their loyalties to communities and morph into global supply chains. They come from CEOs who take home exorbitant paychecks. And they come from industries that often wreak havoc on the environment.

Unfortunately, in the United States, the debate about economic change tends to occur between two extremist camps: those who want the market to rule unimpeded, and those who want to protect jobs and preserve communities as they are. Instead of finding ways to soften the blows of globalization, compensate the losers, or slow the pace of change, we go to battle. Consumers and investors nearly always win the day, but citizens lash out occasionally in symbolic fashion, by attempting to block a new trade agreement or protesting the sale of U.S. companies to foreign firms. It is a sign of the inner conflict Americans feel between the consumer in us and the citizen in us—that the reactions are often so schizophrenic.

Such conflicting sentiments are hardly limited to the United States. The recent wave of corporate restructurings in Europe has shaken the continent's typical commitment to job security and social welfare. It's leaving Europeans at odds as to whether they prefer the private benefits of global capitalism in the face of increasing social costs at home and abroad. Take, for instance, the auto industry. In 2001, DaimlerChrysler faced mounting financial losses as European car buyers abandoned the company in favor of cheaper competitors. So, CEO Dieter Zetsche cut 26,000 jobs from his global workforce and closed six factories. Even profitable companies are feeling the pressure to become ever more efficient. In 2005, Deutsche Bank simultaneously announced an 87 percent increase in net profits and a plan to cut 6,400 jobs, nearly half of them in Germany and Britain. Twelve hundred of the jobs were then moved to low-wage nations. Today, European consumers and investors are doing better than ever, but job insecurity and inequality are rising, even in social democracies that were established to counter the injustices of the market. In the face of such change, Europe's democracies have shown themselves to be so paralyzed that the only way citizens routinely express opposition is through massive boycotts and strikes.

In Japan, many companies have abandoned lifetime employment, cut workforces, and closed down unprofitable lines. Just months after Howard Stringer was named Sony's first non-Japanese CEO, he announced the company would trim 10,000 employees, about 7 percent of its workforce. Surely some Japanese consumers and investors benefit from such corporate downsizing: By 2006, the Japanese stock market had reached a 14-year high. But many Japanese workers have been left behind. A nation that once prided itself on being an "all middle-class society" is beginning to show sharp disparities in income and wealth. Between 1999 and 2005, the share of Japanese households without savings doubled, from 12 percent to 24 percent. And citizens there routinely express a sense of powerlessness. Like many free countries around the world, Japan is embracing global capitalism with a democracy too enfeebled to face the free market's many social penalties.

On the other end of the political spectrum sits China, which is surging toward capitalism without democracy at all. That's good news for people who invest in China, but the social consequences for the country's citizens are mounting. Income inequality has widened enormously. China's new business elites live in McMansions inside gated suburban communities and send their children to study overseas. At the same time, China's cities are bursting with peasants from the countryside who have sunk into urban poverty and unemployment. And those who are affected most have little political recourse to change the situation, beyond riots that are routinely put down by force.

But citizens living in democratic nations aren't similarly constrained. They have the ability to alter the rules of the game so that the cost to society need not be so great. And yet, we've increasingly left those responsibilities to the private sector—to the companies themselves and their squadrons of lobbyists and public-relations experts—pretending as if some inherent morality or corporate good citizenship will compel them to look out for the greater good. But they have no responsibility to address inequality or protect the environment on their own. We forget that they are simply duty bound to protect the bottom line.

The Rules of the Game

Why has capitalism succeeded while democracy has steadily weakened? Democracy has become enfeebled largely because companies, in intensifying competition for global consumers and investors, have invested ever greater sums in lobbying, public relations, and even bribes and kickbacks, seeking laws that give them a competitive advantage over their rivals. The result is an arms race for political influence that is drowning out the voices of average citizens. In the United States, for example, the fights that preoccupy Congress, those that consume weeks or months of congressional staff time, are typically contests between competing companies or industries.

While corporations are increasingly writing their own rules, they are also being entrusted with a kind of social responsibility or morality. Politicians praise companies for acting "responsibly" or condemn them for not doing so. Yet the purpose of capitalism is to get great deals for consumers and investors. Corporate executives are not authorized by anyone—least of all by their investors—to balance profits against the public good. Nor do they have any expertise in making such moral calculations. Democracy is supposed to represent the public in drawing such lines. And the message that companies are moral beings with social responsibilities diverts public attention from the task of establishing such laws and rules in the first place.

It is much the same with what passes for corporate charity. Under today's intensely competitive form of global capitalism, companies donate money to good causes only to the extent the donation has public-relations value, thereby boosting the bottom line. But shareholders do not invest in firms expecting the money to be used for charitable purposes. They invest to earn high returns. Shareholders who wish to be charitable would, presumably, make donations to charities of their own choosing in amounts they decide for themselves. The larger danger is that these conspicuous displays of corporate beneficence hoodwink the public into believing corporations have charitable impulses that can be relied on in a pinch.

By pretending that the economic success corporations enjoy saddles them with particular social duties only serves to distract the public from democracy's responsibility to set the rules of the game and thereby protect the common good. The only way for the citizens in us to trump the consumers in us is through laws and rules that make our purchases and investments social choices as well as personal ones. A change in labor laws making it easier for employees to organize and negotiate better terms, for example, might increase the price of products and services. My inner consumer won't like that very much, but the citizen in me might think it a fair price to pay. A small transfer tax on sales of stock, to slow the movement of capital ever so slightly, might give communities a bit more time to adapt to changing circumstances. The return on my retirement fund might go down by a small fraction, but the citizen in me thinks it worth the price. Extended unemployment insurance combined with wage insurance and job training could ease the pain for workers caught in the downdrafts of globalization.

Let us be clear: The purpose of democracy is to accomplish ends we cannot achieve as individuals. But democracy cannot fulfill this role when companies use politics to advance or maintain their competitive standing, or when they appear to take on social responsibilities that they have no real capacity or authority to fulfill. That leaves societies unable to address the tradeoffs between economic growth and social problems such as job insecurity, widening inequality, and climate change. As a result, consumer and investor interests almost invariably trump common concerns.

The vast majority of us are global consumers and, at least indirectly, global investors. In these roles we should strive for the best deals possible. That is how we participate in the global market economy. But those private benefits usually have social costs. And for those of us living in democracies, it is imperative to remember that we are also citizens who have it in our power to reduce these social costs, making the true price of the goods and services we purchase as low as possible. We can accomplish this larger feat only if we take our roles as citizens seriously. The first step, which is often the hardest, is to get our thinking straight.

Anthony B. Kim  **NO**

The Link between Economic Freedom and Human Rights

In his address to the United Nations General Assembly on September 25, [2007,] President [George W.] Bush urged the nations of the world to work together "to free people from tyranny and violence, hunger and disease, illiteracy and ignorance, and poverty and despair." That message echoes the enduring confidence that Americans have in freedom as a moral and liberating force for all peoples. It is the foundation of true democracy and human rights. Freedom is the engine that drives sustainable economic growth and provides increased access to prosperity for all people everywhere.

Economic Freedom Empowers People

Economic freedom is essentially about ensuring human rights. Strengthening and expanding it guarantees an individual's natural right to achieve his or her goals and then own the value of what they create. Amartya Sen, a Nobel laureate economist who has made considerable contributions to development economics, once noted that "Development consists of the removal of various types of unfreedoms that leave people with little choice and little opportunity for exercising their reasoned legacy." People crave liberation from poverty, and they hunger for the dignity of free will. By reducing barriers to these fundamental human rights, forces of economic freedom create a framework in which people fulfill their dreams of success. In other words, the greater the economic freedom in a nation, the easier for its people to work, save, consume, and ultimately live their lives in dignity and peace.

This relationship is well documented in the Index of Economic Freedom, published annually by The Heritage Foundation and *The Wall Street Journal*, which measures economic freedom around the globe. The Index identifies strong synergies among the 10 key ingredients of economic freedom, which include, among others, openness to the world, limited government intervention, and strong rule of law. The empirical findings of the Index confirm that greater economic freedom empowers people and improves quality of life by spreading opportunities within a country and around the world. [The Index] . . . clearly demonstrates, there is a robust relationship between economic freedom and prosperity. People in countries with either "free" or "mostly free" economies enjoy a much higher

From *The Heritage Foundation Web Memo*, #1650, September 28, 2007 (excerpts). Copyright © 2007 by Heritage Foundation. Reprinted by permission.

standard of living than people in countries with "mostly unfree" or "repressed" economies.

Citizens in nations that are built on greater economic freedom enjoy greater access to ideas and resources, which are the forces that let "all of us exchange, interact and participate" in an increasingly interconnected world. Access, another form of freedom that has practical promise, is an important transmitting mechanism that allows improvements in human development and fosters better democratic participation. A new cross-country study, recently commissioned and published by the FedEx Corporation, measures the level of access that a nation's people, organizations, and government enjoy in comparison to the world and to other countries. The study looks into trade, transport, telecommunication, news, media, and information services in 75 countries.

There is strong positive linkage between degrees of economic freedom and levels of access. [Research shows that] . . . greater economic freedom allows people to have more access to necessary means to success such as new ideas and resources. Reinforcing each other, greater economic freedom and better access to ideas and information combine to empower people, improve their quality of life, and expand opportunities for nations to benefit from global commerce.

Higher economic freedom also has a strong positive correlation with the United Nation's Human Development Index, which measures life expectancy, literacy, education, and standard of living for countries worldwide. By creating virtuous cycles and reinforcing mechanisms, the prosperity created by economic freedom results in reduced illiteracy (through greater access to education) and increased life expectancy (through access to higher quality health care and food supplies).

Economic Freedom Paves a Path to Political Liberty

Debate over the relationship between economic freedom and political freedom and the question of causation has been somewhat controversial due to the complex interplay between the two freedoms. Yet it is well recognized that economic freedom leading to economic prosperity can enhance political liberty. As the late Milton Friedman, the father of economic freedom, once noted in his book *Capitalism and Freedom*:

> Economic freedom plays a dual role in the promotion of a free society. On the one hand, freedom in economic arrangements is itself a component of freedom broadly understood, so economic freedom is an end in itself. In the second place, economic freedom is also an indispensable means toward the achievement of political freedom.

As we have witnessed over the past decades, economic progress through advancing economic freedom has allowed more people to discuss and adopt different views more candidly, ultimately leading societies to be more open and inclusive. Although transformation has been somewhat slower than one might hope, the process has been facilitated by the battle of ideas and greater access to information, guided by forces of economic freedom and innovation. Economic freedom makes it possible for independent sources of wealth to counterbalance political power and to cultivate a pluralistic society. In other words, economic freedom has underpinned and reinforced political liberty and market-based democracy.

Conclusion

The cause of freedom has swept around the world over the last century. It is the compelling force of economic freedom that empowers people, unleashes powerful forces of choice and opportunity, and gives nourishment to other liberties. As the 21st century progresses, freedom's champions must confront both the dark ideology of extremists and those who would restore the failed socialist models of the past. Confidence in, and commitment to, economic freedom as a liberating force must continue to serve as the foundation of open societies and human rights.

POSTSCRIPT

Does Capitalism Undermine Democracy?

Neither Adam Smith–style pure capitalism nor Karl Marx–style pure communism has ever been tried successfully or for very long at either the national or the international levels. For example, the United States is among the most capitalist of countries, but it still has many "uncapitalist" policies, such as outlawing monopolies and requiring a minimum wage, which manipulate the economy. Even as conservative a think tank (a policy research and advocacy institute) as Kim's Heritage Institute would hardly advocate a totally unrestrained economic process. At the other economic end of the spectrum, Marxism has been largely discredited, and socialism is not in very good shape globally either. Thus, advocates such as Reich are not seeking the demise of capitalism. Instead, they call for greater government regulation of the economy to restrain the power of corporations and banks and spread wealth more equitably. Doing so, they contend, will provide the average person greater democratic influence.

It is important to note that this debate is not just a matter of academic theory. A widely accepted theory, for example, suggests that democratic countries do not or, at least, are much less likely to go to war with one another than authoritarian countries could with each other or with democracies. From the perspective of the links between capitalism and democracy and between democracy and peace, many believe, for example, that the best way to ensure that increasingly powerful China is a peaceful member of the international community is by promoting its continuing capitalist path in the belief that this will eventually lead to a more democratic China. Conversely, if the current level of capitalism in the globalizing world is actually undermining democracy, that could augur ill for world peace.

There are numerous paths to continue your further exploration of this issue. One place to begin by reading the author of the first article, Robert B. Reich *Supercapitalism: The Transformation of Business, Democracy, and Everyday Life* (Alfred A. Knopf, 2007). For a view closer to that of Kim's, read Martin Wolf, "The Morality of the Market," *Foreign Policy* (September 2003). What the future of capitalism is, domestically and internationally, remains to be seen of course. From the long historical perspective, political economy has moved away from unrestrained capitalism and toward increasing limits and even the alternatives: socialism and communism. However, the trend has somewhat been reversed in the more recent past as a result of the near total eclipse of communism, the retreat of socialism in Europe and elsewhere, and the seeming triumph of American-style capitalism. That may prove only a short-term shift, though. Joseph A. Schumpeter was possibly right in his *Capitalism, Socialism, and Democracy* (Harper & Brothers, 1942) when he predicted that capitalism would eventually give way to socialism, in part, because capitalism is not really about freedom but has only replaced one type of despot, a king, with another, the corporation.

Internet References . . .

Country Indicators for Foreign Policy (CIFP)

Hosted by Carlton University in Canada, the Country Indicators for Foreign Policy project represents an ongoing effort to identify and assemble statistical information conveying the key features of the economic, political, social, and cultural environments of countries around the world.

http://www.carleton.ca/cifp/

U.S. Department of State

The information on this site is organized into categories based on countries, topics, and other criteria. "Background Notes," which provide information on regions and specific countries, can be accessed through this site.

http://www.state.gov/index.cfm

http://www.state.gov/countries/

WorldAtlas.com

The world may be "getting smaller," but geography is still important. This organization's site contains a wide variety of maps and a range of other useful information.

http://www.worldatlas.com/aatlas/world.htm

Regional and Country Issues

*T**he issues in this section deal with countries that are major regional powers. In this era of interdependence among nations, it is important to understand the concerns that these issues address and the actors involved because they will shape the world and will affect the lives of all people.*

- Should the United States Substantially Limit Its Global Involvement?
- Has Russia Become Undemocratic and Antagonistic?
- Will China Soon Become a Threatening Superpower?
- Would It Be an Error to Establish a Palestinian State?
- Should All Foreign Troops Soon Leave Iraq?
- Does Hugo Chávez Threaten Hemispheric Stability and Democracy?
- Is Military Intervention in Darfur Justified?

ISSUE 4

Should the United States Substantially Limit Its Global Involvement?

YES: Ivan Eland, from "Homeward Bound?" *The National Interest* (July/August 2008)

NO: Barack Obama, from "The American Moment," Remarks to the Chicago Council on Global Affairs (April 23, 2007)

ISSUE SUMMARY

YES: Ivan Eland, senior fellow at the Independent Institute, a libertarian think tank in Oakland, California, and Washington, DC, contends that neither the Republican nor the Democratic Party in the United States has shown any inclination to follow the wise counsel of the country's founders such as George Washington and practice restraint in the country's overseas involvement.

NO: Barack Obama, then a Democratic U.S. senator from Illinois and the 2008 nominee of the Democratic Party for president, sharply criticizes the foreign policy of President George W. Bush for undercutting American leadership of the world and argues that it is time to reclaim that leadership through a new approach.

$\mathbf{A}$t its beginning in the late 1700s, the United States was a relatively weak and isolated country, and leaders such as Presidents George Washington and Thomas Jefferson warned that the country should avoid getting overly involved in world affairs to avoid conflict with powerful countries in Europe. That did not mean economic isolationism, and foreign trade was and has remained an important part of U.S. global activity. Nor did avoiding foreign entanglements dissuade the country from clashing with other powers, as it grew. Indeed American expansionism from its original territory involved land acquisitions, disputes, and even wars with Great Britain, France, Russia, Spain, and Mexico.

Moreover, as the country grew stronger, U.S. foreign political involvement increased. By the late 1800s and early 1900s, the country was acquiring foreign territories such as Hawaii, Samoa, Puerto Rico, and the Philippines, mediating

the Russo-Japanese War, sending troops to China to subdue the Boxer uprising, and building a fleet capable of global operations. The new century brought
even greater strength and greater involvement, with the U.S. participation and
victory in World War I and later World War II as leading examples.

The second of these two world wars shattered Great Britain, Germany,
and most of the other major powers, and left the United States as a global
superpower, rivaled only by the Soviet Union. In part because of its exuberant
assertion of its new superpower status and in part because of its fear of the
ideology and military might of the Soviets, the United States became active
in every corner of the world. Often, this led to military action, with American troops fighting in Korea, Vietnam, Grenada, Panama, Lebanon, Somalia,
Kuwait, Iraq, and elsewhere.

Then in 1991, the Soviet Union imploded, leaving the United States as the
world's sole superpower. No other country could or can rival it militarily, and
the United States was and is also in an unparalleled economic position, now
accounting for over 27 percent of the world's measured economic production.

None of this has meant that the country can always prevail internationally.
Americans are subject to terrorist attacks, and the possibility of a nuclear attack
remains. American troops have fought in Somalia, Haiti, the Balkans, Afghanistan,
and Iraq. Yet the United States has often not been able to control events because
its assets are limited and because Americans' willingness to support many aspects
of U.S. activity, such as the occupation of Iraq, is also limited.

Certainly, there are many advantages to U.S. global activity and leadership. While the United States does not always prevail, it does so far more
than any other country. But there is also a price to pay for global leadership.
Almost 100,000 U.S. troops have died in conflicts since the end of World War
II, including over 3,000 in Iraq since 2003. The current military budget is
over a half trillion dollars, and controlled for inflation, U.S. defense spending
between 1945 and 2008 cost about $20 trillion. Furthermore, U.S. leadership
has often sparked opposition and sometimes even attacks. The terror attacks
on 9/11 were one consequence, and foreign opinion of the United States has
often sagged dramatically, most recently in response to U.S. activity in Iraq.
Global economics have also not been uniformly good for the United States.
Led by a massive trade deficit, the total flow of money into and out of the
United States (the balance of payments) for 2007 was a deficit of $731 billion.

The issue here is what the future of U.S. global activity should be. In the
first reading, Ivan Eland points out that since at least World War II, the United
States has followed an activist foreign policy whether the U.S. president has
been Republican or Democrat and that current party leaders remain committed to extensive U.S. international involvement. The remarks by Barack
Obama, then the 2008 Democratic nominee for president shows that is true
for his party, and it is also the case for John McCain and the Republicans. The
two candidates differed on details of U.S. foreign policy, but each favored
continued leadership in his vision. Eland thinks that they are both wrong, that
a meaningful debate on the U.S. role in the world is long overdue, and that a
much more restrained U.S. presence abroad would have numerous benefits.

YES

Ivan Eland

Homeward Bound?

Both U.S. political parties—the Democrats and the Republicans—compete to see who can be more interventionist in world affairs. Although many liberal Democrats emphasize working through international institutions and organizations, such as the United Nations, and many conservative Republicans focus more on unilaterally employing U.S. power, they all end up trying to meddle in the policies of other nations and peoples, often using military force. Both parties want to fix the Middle East and Afghanistan, aggressively advance democracy and human rights around the world, attempt to stop the drug trade and international crime, and so on. For example, the candidates of both parties would have the United States become more involved in the affairs of Myanmar, Pakistan, Iran, Georgia and Zimbabwe.

Neither party has shown much interest in returning to the original inclination of the nation's founders toward military restraint overseas, as epitomized in Washington's Farewell Address—and practiced, with a few exceptions, from the founding all the way up to the Korean War. The foreign-policy disaster in Iraq should have spurred a long-needed national debate that could lead to such an urgently needed policy switch—[but that was not reflected in the 2008 presidential race.]

Perhaps this is because elections are usually decided on the basis of domestic issues; foreign policy seems more remote to the daily concerns of the general public than do bread-and-butter issues at home. This maxim has been recently demonstrated even during wartime, when bad economic news pushed out the Iraq War as the dominant issue in the 2008 presidential-election campaign.

In addition, there have been far-fewer mass protests in the United States against the drawn-out Iraq War than its Vietnam counterpart because the domestic consequences are much lower. Although the monetary costs of the Iraq War have exceeded the Vietnam War, the cost in lives is much lower (forty-one hundred at this writing versus fifty-eight thousand in Vietnam) and those fatalities are volunteers, not people yanked off the street involuntarily and into a conflict by conscription. People do act in their self-interest, and young people and their parents are more apt to become active, rather than passive, opponents of a war in which they or their loved ones have a higher probability of fighting and dying. But if the public—almost two-thirds of which believe that the Iraq War was not worth fighting—cannot stop the most-celebrated foreign-policy fiasco of our time, they are much less likely to stop, or even be inclined to stop, lesser-known interventions in foreign countries (for example, U.S. assistance to the Ethiopian invasion and continued occupation of Somalia) that don't seem to have much immediate impact on their daily lives.

Perhaps this could be explained because the average American believes that increased U.S. activism—especially maintaining a large military footprint in the greater Islamic world—is necessary to make the country safe by "promoting freedom" and waging the "war against terror." President Bush has echoed both of these sentiments. But let's disassociate slogans from empirical results.

First, Christopher Coyne, a professor of economics at West Virginia University, has studied U.S. efforts to bring liberal democracy to various countries around the world at gunpoint. He concluded that since the late 1800s, countries in which the United States has intervened militarily have achieved some semblance of an institutionalized democracy only 28 percent of the time ten years after the intervention, only 39 percent of the time after fifteen years and 36 percent of the time after twenty years. Moreover, Coyne uses a fairly low standard for achieving institutional democracy—a level slightly better than today's Iran. And even these percentages may overstate the success rate because in some cases the U.S. intervention may have had little to do with the change for the better. Coyne noted that as the length of time passes between the U.S. intervention and progress toward the creation of a liberal democracy, the effect of the former on the latter becomes more cloudy. He uses the examples of Lebanon and the Dominican Republic achieving his modest threshold fifteen years after U.S. interventions in 1958 and 1965, respectively. In the case of Lebanon, the progress unraveled in a civil war, which began two years after the fifteen-year mark in the mid-1970s.

Second, the "offense is the best defense" strategy has been counterproductive for countering terrorism—international terrorism is up markedly since the United States invaded Iraq, and the number of suicide-bombing attacks has skyrocketed from 75 incidents in 2002 to 658 in 2007. In fact, invading, occupying and conducting nation-building operations in "failed states" (as the United States has done in Iraq or Afghanistan) or visibly supporting proxies to do the same (Ethiopia in Somalia) exacerbates the problem twofold; it not only creates new pools of recruits but also allows terrorist groups to hone their skills in direct combat with U.S. and allied forces. Moreover, continued U.S. interventions, particularly in the Arab and Islamic world, dissipate whatever favorable rating the United States receives for its political and economic freedoms in favor of highly negative reactions to the actual consequences of U.S. foreign policy.

So, if the most-important purpose of the U.S. government is to make its citizens and territory secure and U.S. interventionism overseas is making them less so, then the rational response, especially after 9/11, would have been to go after al-Qaeda in the shadows (as opposed to a wider and more-public general "war on terror") while reducing the U.S. footprint overseas and withdrawing from commitments that make little strategic sense in a post-cold-war environment.

But this runs up against the logic of what has been termed the military-industrial-congressional complex. After a crisis such as 9/11, politicians—both in Congress and in the executive branch—have to be seen as "doing something" to make America safer, even though their actions may have little effect, be too costly or cumbersome, or even be counterproductive. Meanwhile, a whole host of special interests found ways to hook their chariots to the desire of Americans to feel safe and protected.

Take this example. The government has overinvested in visible airport-security measures because many voters travel by air and want to see that the government is doing something to protect them. In contrast, much less has been spent on port security—even though this is where we remain vulnerable, maybe even to a nuclear terrorist attack—because few people go down to the docks to see their new Toyota unloaded.

The departments of Defense, State, Treasury and Homeland Security have an incentive to promote an interventionist foreign policy because their departments become more useful and they get more authority and money for their programs. For example, even though a fight against al-Qaeda in the shadows using law enforcement, intelligence, special forces and drones would have been relatively cheap, the Pentagon used 9/11 to justify buying more gold-plated weapons—such as expensive submarines, ships and fighter aircraft—that have little role in such a clandestine war. A wider war on terror against countries that sponsor terrorism was needed to justify purchasing such armaments.

And of course defense, homeland-security and university contractors, which research and build such big-ticket weapons technology and security systems, make huge amounts of money when military interventions burn equipment, justify increased spending on new high-tech weapons and cause the threat of blowback terrorism to increase. But the military-industrial-congressional complex is not the only special interest to benefit from the interventionist U.S. foreign policy. U.S. private nondefense companies operating overseas—for example, U.S. oil companies in the Middle East—get a hidden government subsidy by the U.S. military's efforts to "stabilize" the regions in which they operate. Even private U.S. citizens—such as academic scholars, former politicians and bureaucrats, representatives from nonprofit organizations and think tanks, and U.S. lobbyists for foreign countries—get invited to conferences, appear on television and are consulted with reverence about happenings in the superpower. Thus, even they have an interest in an activist foreign policy.

Seemingly, the only group that doesn't really have an interest in a post-cold-war interventionist foreign policy is the general citizenry, who have to then pay the costs of the policy.

Costs of an Activist Foreign Policy

To support the informal worldwide network of alliances, overseas bases and deployed personnel, which are used to justify and conduct profligate military interventions, the United States spends vast sums on security compared to other countries. The United States spends more on defense than the combined security expenditures of the next sixteen highest-spending countries and accounts for 48 percent of the world's defense spending.

This comparison, along with the strain that the two small wars in Iraq and Afghanistan have imposed on U.S. forces, indicates that the U.S. superpower might be overextended. Many prior empires have declined because their security spending and overseas military commitments, bases, and interventions exceeded their ability to pay for them. Even the British and French Empires, on the winning side of both world wars, became financially exhausted—because of fighting those wars and maintaining their vast empires—and went into decline. More recently, the Soviet Union's empire, and even the country itself, collapsed because its giant military, Eastern European alliances and military interventions in the developing world became too much for its dysfunctional socialist economy to bear.

Many in the United States say that the U.S. economy is much larger than those of such failed empires and that decline cannot happen here. But other formerly dominant, but fallen, empires believed they were invincible too. Economic power is relative to that of other countries—with only about a quarter of the world's GDP, the United States may be a military superpower but is only an economic "first among equals." Furthermore, over time, small differences in economic growth rates between competing countries can lead to a reordering of great powers on the world scene. Some of the Washington's primary current and future economic competitors have far-less defense spending to drag their economies down.

And those who consider themselves conservatives, even those who label themselves "national greatness" conservatives, should be leery of too much defense spending, excessive military commitments and bases overseas, and unnecessary wars, such as Iraq, that sap national resources. Conservatives should also be worried that government activism and spending abroad (which many seem to support) leads to government activism and spending at home in nondefense matters (which many seem to oppose). Domestic government spending balloons as the price a president has to pay to generate continuing support for his overseas war or wars increases. For example, President George W. Bush has increased domestic spending drastically—the greatest increase by a president since Lyndon Johnson—at the same time he has fought wars in Iraq and Afghanistan. During wartime, the government usually intrudes more into the private sector to direct greater resources and productive capacity to the war effort. After the war is over, wartime precedents for government activism in private economic decisions often linger. Over history, war has been the biggest cause of government expansion.

Both liberals and conservatives should be concerned about the effects of repeated wars on domestic civil liberties, which make this country unique. The seemingly perpetual war on terror, like the long cold war, might be more injurious to such liberties than past conventional wars—usually of limited duration—because no end to hostilities terminates the government clampdown. Also, some of the adversaries' attacks may be on the homeland, thus generating more fear—and pressure for a tightening of the domestic-security vise—than would a strictly foreign war.

All Americans should be concerned about an interventionist foreign policy because it endangers U.S. citizens, their property, and the system of checks and balances enshrined in the Constitution, which is supposed to prevent an excessive accumulation of power by any one branch of government. Taking advantage of the war on terror, President Bush has claimed breathtaking executive authority during wartime—including the right as commander in chief, and in signing statements, to ignore laws passed by Congress; by flagrantly violating the law and Constitution in authorizing domestic surveillance without a warrant; and by unilaterally suspending the writ of habeas corpus by which prisoners can challenge their incarceration. If a more-modest foreign policy is not adopted to reduce the likelihood of anti-U.S. terrorism, future presidents will also take advantage of the "war" against terrorists to expand their powers, much to the peril of the Republic.

Foreign military excursions led the Roman Republic to slowly transform into the autocratic Roman Empire; similarly, foreign intervention turned the French revolution into the "terror" at home. It is not out of the realm of possibility that the same could happen in the United States. We have already started down that path. Erosion of republican institutions is the most-important ill effect of war, but the one least mentioned.

Parameters of a New Policy of Global Restraint

The collapse of the United States' principal superpower rival, the Soviet Union, should have rendered many places in the world less strategic to vital U.S. interests (if they ever were). Potentially ascending powers—such as China, India or a resurgent Russia—will probably take decades to challenge the United States militarily, if they ever do.

Even if another potential hegemonic power arises, the United States might adopt a less-expensive and less-dangerous strategy than it did during the cold war vis-a-vis the Soviet Union. Even assuming that Russia and China become more hostile in the future—the so-called Eurasian entente—the United States should be prepared to let its wealthy allies in Europe and East Asia be the first line of defense. The European Union now has a GDP [gross domestic product] that exceeds that of the United States and could do much more for its own defense. In East Asia, the now-wealthy nations of Japan, South Korea, Taiwan and Australia could band together to be the first line of defense against any turn by China toward militarism. In each of these two regions, the United States should act as a second line of defense—that is, as a balancer of last resort—intervening only if the balance of power was disrupted and an aggressive hegemonic power threatened to overrun either of them.

Other regions of the world are much less developed and therefore nonstrategic. If any other hegemonic power wants to conquer them, they will have to pay the exorbitant cost of securing, administering and aiding them—thus increasing the likelihood of imperial overstretch and decline. Learning from the overextension and demise of the Soviet Union, China—at least presently— does not seem willing to spend trillions of its own on such foreign adventures. Unfortunately, now it is the United States that is in danger of experiencing such overstretch as it tries futilely to police the world and convert countries to democracy.

But don't we need U.S. military power in the Persian Gulf to protect vital supplies of oil for the United States? Oil is a valuable commodity, and Persian Gulf countries are heavily dependent on it to earn foreign exchange because they export little else. Oil-producing countries often need to pump and sell the oil as much or more than Western nations need to buy it. Thus, the market will ensure that oil reaches the United States and its Western allies. The triumph of the market over ideology or political turmoil is illustrated by the fact that even the radical Islamic government in Iran sells its oil to the hated West, and oil and other resources make it to market from parts of Africa—for example, from Nigeria—wracked by internal strife.

Even if instability in the Gulf or in other oil-producing countries makes the price go up, recent experience has shown that industrialized economies are very resilient to even high oil-price increases. For example, the oil price is high now by historical standards, but the U.S. economy hasn't collapsed and will likely adjust—just as the German economy did with continued economic growth and low unemployment and inflation while weathering a 211 percent oil-price increase during the 1998–2000 period. Contrary to popular belief, it is unlikely that inflation, a general rise in prices, will be triggered by even significant oil-price increases because economic actors will have less money to spend on other items, thus driving their prices down.

Furthermore, it is cheaper to just pay the occasionally higher prices for oil induced by instability or market factors—contingent expenses—than it is to annually pay to operate expensive military forces in the Gulf to defend oil that will flow anyway.

Nevertheless, if U.S. leaders insist on accepting the myth that the United States must have military power in the Persian Gulf to guard oil, they should at least withdraw U.S. land-based forces (the army, marines and air force) stationed in the Gulf and bring in such forces from offshore only if a major danger to the oil arises. This change in policy would eliminate the lightning rod of non-Muslim forces on Muslim lands, which drives radical Islamists into the ranks of anti-U.S. terrorists. The oil fields were successfully defended using over-the-horizon forces brought in as needed during Desert Shield and Desert Storm in 1991, with only a U.S. naval presence there prior to Saddam's invasion of Kuwait. At minimum, the United States should go back to this posture, minimize or eliminate much of its land-based military presence in the Persian Gulf and abroad, and rely on the American Navy overseas to deter anti-U.S. aggression and protect U.S. trade.

With this much-lighter footprint abroad, the United States also needs to change its mindset. The country's exhausted armed forces cannot withstand many more Iraqi quagmires. The good news is that, to ensure U.S. security, they don't have to do so. In the post-cold-war and post-9/11 era, only a few regions in the world are strategic to the United States. Thus, the United States is only endangering its homeland by meddling in other nonstrategic areas, thus generating the potential for blowback anti-U.S. terrorism. To reduce this risk, the United States should resist the unnecessary urge to control events in remote regions of the world. Instead, America can act as a balancer of last resort in Europe and East Asia and, if the United States needs limited strikes to destroy terrorist bases or camps, it can rely on the navy or air-force bombers flying from the United States. A smaller footprint abroad, especially in the Persian Gulf, and a policy of U.S. global military restraint would cost less in blood and treasure, allow wealthy U.S. allies to take more responsibility for their own defense, be less dangerous to the American public, and allow the U.S. government to better carry out its constitutional duty to defend U.S. citizens and property without destroying its republican system of government.

A meaningful debate on the U.S. role in the world is long overdue. If politicians don't want to engage the issue in the 2008 election campaign, the expensive and continuing quagmires in Iraq and Afghanistan will likely force them to confront the hard reality of imperial overextension. If nothing else, the U.S. military's inclination to purchase evermore-expensive weapons for fighting large conventional wars—thus enabling it to afford fewer and fewer numbers of aircraft, ships, artillery, armored vehicles, etc.—will continue to shrink the quantifies of military hardware available to police the entire world. This Herculean task is what the current interventionist foreign policy essentially requires. Therefore, difficult decisions need to be made about where on the globe America has truly vital interests and what the U.S. role in those regions should be. If reasoned debate does not lead to a more-sustainable strategic vision, the United States is more likely to again be pulled off course into future Iraqs at the expense of the nation's real security interests. The election campaign is a good place for this vital national debate to begin.

Barack Obama

The American Moment

We all know that these are not the best of times for America's reputation in the world. We know what the war in Iraq has cost us in lives and treasure, in influence and respect. We have seen the consequences of a foreign policy based on a flawed ideology, and a belief that tough talk can replace real strength and vision.

Many around the world are disappointed with our actions. And many in our own country have come to doubt either our wisdom or our capacity to shape events beyond our borders. Some have even suggested that America's time has passed.

But while we know what we have lost as a consequence of this tragic war, I also know what I have found in my travels over the past two years.

In an old building in Ukraine, I saw test tubes filled with anthrax and the plague lying virtually unlocked and unguarded—dangers we were told could only be secured with America's help.

On a trip to the Middle East, I met Israelis and Palestinians who told me that peace remains a distant hope without the promise of American leadership.

At a camp along the border of Chad and Darfur, refugees begged for America to step in and help stop the genocide that has taken their mothers and fathers, sons and daughters.

And along the crowded streets of Kenya, I met throngs of children who asked if they'd ever get the chance to visit that magical place called America.

So I reject the notion that the American moment has passed. I dismiss the cynics who say that this new century cannot be another when, in the words of President Franklin Roosevelt, we lead the world in battling immediate evils and promoting the ultimate good.

I still believe that America is the last, best hope of Earth. We just have to show the world why this is so. This President may occupy the White House, but for the last six years the position of leader of the free world has remained open. And it's time to fill that role once more.

I believe that the single most important job of any president is to protect the American people. And I am equally convinced that doing that job effectively in the 21st century will require a new vision of American leadership and a new conception of our national security—a vision that draws from the lessons of the past, but is not bound by outdated thinking.

From Remarks to Chicago Council on Global Affairs by Barack Obama, April 23, 2007.

In today's globalized world, the security of the American people is inextricably linked to the security of all people. When narco-trafficking and corruption threaten democracy in Latin America, it's America's problem too. When poor villagers in Indonesia have no choice but to send chickens to market infected with avian flu, it cannot be seen as a distant concern. When religious schools in Pakistan teach hatred to young children, our children are threatened as well.

Whether it's global terrorism or pandemic disease, dramatic climate change or the proliferation of weapons of mass annihilation, the threats we face at the dawn of the 21st century can no longer be contained by borders and boundaries.

The horrific attacks on that clear September day awakened us to this new reality. And after 9/11, millions around the world were ready to stand with us. They were willing to rally to our cause because it was their cause too—because they knew that if America led the world toward a new era of global cooperation, it would advance the security of people in our nation and all nations.

We now know how badly this Administration squandered that opportunity. In 2002, I stated my opposition to the war in Iraq, not only because it was an unnecessary diversion from the struggle against the terrorists who attacked us on September 11th, but also because it was based on a fundamental misunderstanding of the threats that 9/11 brought to light. I believed then, and believe now, that it was based on old ideologies and outdated strategies—a determination to fight a 21st century struggle with a 20th century mindset.

There is no doubt that the mistakes of the past six years have made our current task more difficult. World opinion has turned against us. And after all the lives lost and the billions of dollars spent, many Americans may find it tempting to turn inward, and cede our claim of leadership in world affairs.

I insist, however, that such an abandonment of our leadership is a mistake we must not make. America cannot meet the threats of this century alone, but the world cannot meet them without America. We must neither retreat from the world nor try to bully it into submission—we must lead the world, by deed and example.

We must lead by building a 21st century military to ensure the security of our people and advance the security of all people. We must lead by marshalling a global effort to stop the spread of the world's most dangerous weapons. We must lead by building and strengthening the partnerships and alliances necessary to meet our common challenges and defeat our common threats.

And America must lead by reaching out to all those living disconnected lives of despair in the world's forgotten corners—because while there will always be those who succumb to hate and strap bombs to their bodies, there are millions more who want to take another path—who want our beacon of hope to shine its light their way.

This election offers us the chance to turn the page and open a new chapter in American leadership. The disappointment that so many around the world feel toward America right now is only a testament to the high expectations they hold for us. We must meet those expectations again, not because being respected is an end in itself, but because the security of America and the wider world demands it.

This will require a new spirit—not of bluster and bombast, but of quiet confidence and sober intelligence, a spirit of care and renewed competence. It will also require a new leader. And as a candidate for President of the United States, I am asking you to entrust me with that responsibility.

There are five ways America will begin to lead again when I'm President. Five ways to let the world know that we are committed to our common security, invested in our common humanity, and still a beacon of freedom and justice for the world.

The first way America will lead is by bringing a responsible end to this war in Iraq and refocusing on the critical challenges in the broader region.

In a speech five months ago, I argued that there can be no military solution to what has become a political conflict between Sunni and Shi'a factions. And I laid out a plan that I still believe offers the best chance of pressuring these warring factions toward a political settlement—a phased withdrawal of American forces with the goal of removing all combat brigades from Iraq by March 31st, 2008.

I acknowledged at the time that there are risks involved in such an approach. That is why my plan provides for an over-the-horizon force that could prevent chaos in the wider region, and allows for a limited number of troops to remain in Iraq to fight al Qaeda and other terrorists.

But my plan also makes clear that continued U.S. commitment to Iraq depends on the Iraqi government meeting a series of well-defined benchmarks necessary to reach a political settlement. Thus far, the Iraqi government has made very little progress in meeting any of the benchmarks, in part because the President has refused time and again to tell the Iraqi government that we will not be there forever. The President's escalation of U.S. forces may bring a temporary reduction in the violence in Baghdad, at the price of increased U.S. casualties—though the experience so far is not encouraging. But it cannot change the political dynamic in Iraq. A phased withdrawal can.

Moreover, until we change our approach in Iraq, it will be increasingly difficult to refocus our efforts on the challenges in the wider region—on the conflict in the Middle East, where Hamas and Hezbollah feel emboldened and Israel's prospects for a secure peace seem uncertain; on Iran, which has been strengthened by the war in Iraq; and on Afghanistan, where more American forces are needed to battle al Qaeda, track down Osama bin Laden, and stop that country from backsliding toward instability.

Burdened by Iraq, our lackluster diplomatic efforts leave a huge void. Our interests are best served when people and governments from Jerusalem and Amman to Damascus and Tehran understand that America will stand with our friends, work hard to build a peaceful Middle East, and refuse to cede the future of the region to those who seek perpetual conflict and instability. Such effective diplomacy cannot be done on the cheap, nor can it be warped by an ongoing occupation of Iraq. Instead, it will require patient, sustained effort, and the personal commitment of the President of the United States. That is a commitment I intend to make.

The second way America will lead again is by building the first truly 21st century military and showing wisdom in how we deploy it.

We must maintain the strongest, best-equipped military in the world in order to defeat and deter conventional threats. But while sustaining our technological edge will always be central to our national security, the ability to put boots on the ground will be critical in eliminating the shadowy terrorist networks we now face. This is why our country's greatest military asset is the men and women who wear the uniform of the United States.

This administration's first Secretary of Defense proudly acknowledged that he had inherited the greatest fighting force in the nation's history. Six years later, he handed over a force that has been stretched to the breaking point, understaffed, and struggling to repair its equipment.

Two-thirds of the Army is now rated "not ready" for combat. Fully 88% of the National Guard is not ready to deploy overseas, and many units cannot respond to a domestic emergency.

Our men and women in uniform are performing heroically around the world in some of the most difficult conditions imaginable. But the war in Afghanistan and the ill-advised invasion of Iraq have clearly demonstrated the consequences of underestimating the number of troops required to fight two wars and defend our homeland. That's why I strongly support the expansion of our ground forces by adding 65,000 soldiers to the Army and 27,000 Marines.

But adding troops isn't just about meeting a quota. It's about recruiting the best and brightest to service, and it's about keeping them in service by providing them with the first-rate equipment, armor, training, and incentives they deserve. It's about providing funding to enable the National Guard to achieve an adequate state of readiness again. And it's about honoring our veterans by giving them the respect and dignity they deserve and the care and benefits they have earned.

A 21st century military will also require us to invest in our men and women's ability to succeed in today's complicated conflicts. We know that on the streets of Baghdad, a little bit of Arabic can actually provide security to our soldiers. Yet, just a year ago, less than 1% of the American military could speak a language such as Arabic, Mandarin, Hindi, Urdu, or Korean. It's time we recognize these as critical skills for our military, and it's time we recruit and train for them.

Former Secretary Rumsfeld said, "You go to war with the Army you have, not the one you want." I say that if the need arises when I'm President, the Army we have will be the Army we need. Of course, how we use our armed forces matters just as much as how they are prepared.

No President should ever hesitate to use force—unilaterally if necessary—to protect ourselves and our vital interests when we are attacked or imminently threatened. But when we use force in situations other than self-defense, we should make every effort to garner the clear support and participation of others—the kind of burden-sharing and support President George H. W. Bush mustered before he launched Operation Desert Storm.

And when we do send our men and women into harm's way, we must also clearly define the mission, prescribe concrete political and military objectives, seek out advice of our military commanders, evaluate the intelligence, plan accordingly, and ensure that our troops have the resources, support, and equipment they need to protect themselves and fulfill their mission.

We must take these steps with the knowledge that while sometimes necessary, force is the costliest weapon in the arsenal of American power in terms of lives and treasure. And it's far from the only measure of our strength.

In order to advance our national security and our common security, we must call on the full arsenal of American power and ingenuity. To constrain rogue nations, we must use effective diplomacy and muscular alliances. To penetrate terrorist networks, we need a nimble intelligence community—with strong leadership that forces agencies to share information, and invests in the tools, technologies and human intelligence that can get the job done. To maintain our influence in the world economy, we need to get our fiscal house in order. And to weaken the hand of hostile dictators, we must free ourselves from our oil addiction. None of these expressions of power can supplant the need for a strong military. Instead, they complement our military, and help ensure that the use of force is not our sole available option.

The third way America must lead again is by marshalling a global effort to meet a threat that rises above all others in urgency—securing, destroying, and stopping the spread of weapons of mass destruction.

As leaders from Henry Kissinger to George Shultz to Bill Perry to Sam Nunn have all warned, the actions we are taking today on this issue are simply not adequate to the danger.

There are still about 50 tons of highly enriched uranium—some of it poorly secured—at civilian nuclear facilities in over forty countries around the world. In the former Soviet Union, there are still about 15,000 to 16,000 nuclear weapons and stockpiles of uranium and plutonium capable of making another 40,000 weapons scattered across 11 time zones. And people have already been caught trying to smuggle nuclear materials to sell them on the black market.

We can do something about this. As President, I will lead a global effort to secure all nuclear weapons and material at vulnerable sites within four years—the most effective way to prevent terrorists from acquiring a bomb.

We know that Russia is neither our enemy nor close ally right now, and we shouldn't shy away from pushing for more democracy, transparency, and accountability in that country. But we also know that we can and must work with Russia to make sure every one of its nuclear weapons and every cache of nuclear material is secured. And we should fully implement the law I passed with Senator Dick Lugar that would help the United States and our allies detect and stop the smuggling of weapons of mass destruction throughout the world.

While we work to secure existing stockpiles of nuclear material, we should also negotiate a verifiable global ban on the production of new nuclear weapons material.

As starting points, the world must prevent Iran from acquiring nuclear weapons and work to eliminate North Korea's nuclear weapons program. If America does not lead, these two nations could trigger regional arms races that could accelerate nuclear proliferation on a global scale and create dangerous nuclear flashpoints. In pursuit of this goal, we must never take the military option off the table. But our first line of offense here must be sustained, direct and aggressive diplomacy. For North Korea, that means ensuring the full implementation of the recent agreement. For Iran, it means getting the UN Security Council, Europe, and the Gulf States to join with us in ratcheting up the economic pressure.

We must also dissuade other countries from joining the nuclear club. Just the other day, it was reported that nearly a dozen countries in and around the Middle East—including Syria and Saudi Arabia—are interested in pursuing nuclear power.

Countries should not be able to build a weapons program under the auspices of developing peaceful nuclear power. That's why we should create an international fuel bank to back up commercial fuel supplies so there's an assured supply and no more excuses for nations like Iran to build their own enrichment plants. It's encouraging that the Nuclear Threat Initiative, backed by Warren Buffett, has already offered funding for this fuel bank, if matched two to one. But on an issue of this importance, the United States should not leave the solution to private philanthropies. It should be a central component of our national security, and that's why we should provide $50 million to get this fuel bank started and urge other nations, starting with Russia, to join us.

Finally, if we want the world to deemphasize the role of nuclear weapons, the United States and Russia must lead by example. President Bush once said, "The United States should remove as many weapons as possible from high-alert, hair-trigger status—another unnecessary vestige of Cold War confrontation." Six years later, President Bush has not acted on this promise. I will. We cannot and should not accept the threat of accidental or unauthorized nuclear launch. We can maintain a strong nuclear deterrent to protect our security without rushing to produce a new generation of warheads.

The danger of nuclear proliferation reminds us of how critical global cooperation will be in the 21st century. That's why the fourth way America must lead is to rebuild and construct the alliances and partnerships necessary to meet common challenges and confront common threats.

In the wake of the Second World War, it was America that largely built a system of international institutions that carried us through the Cold War. Leaders like Harry Truman and George Marshall knew that instead of constraining our power, these institutions magnified it.

Today it's become fashionable to disparage the United Nations, the World Bank, and other international organizations. In fact, reform of these bodies is urgently needed if they are to keep pace with the fast-moving threats we face. Such real reform will not come, however, by dismissing the value of these institutions, or by bullying other countries to ratify changes we have drafted in isolation. Real reform will come because we convince others that they too have a stake in change—that such reforms will make their world, and not just ours, more secure.

Our alliances also require constant management and revision if they are to remain effective and relevant. For example, over the last 15 years, NATO has made tremendous strides in transforming from a Cold War security structure to a dynamic partnership for peace.

Today, NATO's challenge in Afghanistan has become a test case, in the words of Dick Lugar, of whether the alliance can "overcome the growing discrepancy between NATO's expanding missions and its lagging capabilities."

We must close this gap, rallying members to contribute troops to collective security operations, urging them to invest more in reconstruction and stabilization, streamlining decision-making processes, and giving commanders in the field more flexibility.

And as we strengthen NATO, we should also seek to build new alliances and relationships in other regions important to our interests in the 21st century. In Asia, the emergence of an economically vibrant, more politically active China offers new opportunities for prosperity and cooperation, but also poses new challenges for the United States and our partners in the region. It is time for the United States to take a more active role here—to build on our strong bilateral relations and informal arrangements like the Six Party talks. As President, I intend to forge a more effective regional framework in Asia that will promote stability, prosperity and help us confront common transnational threats such as tracking down terrorists and responding to global health problems like avian flu.

In this way, the security alliances and relationships we build in the 21st century will serve a broader purpose than preventing the invasion of one country by another. They can help us meet challenges that the world can only confront together, like the unprecedented threat of global climate change.

This is a crisis that cannot be contained to one corner of the globe. Studies show that with each degree of warming, rice yields—the world's most significant crop—fall by 10%. By 2050 famine could displace more than 250 million people worldwide. That means people competing for food and water in the next fifty years in the very places that have known horrific violence in the last fifty: Africa, the Middle East, South Asia.

As the world's largest producers of greenhouse gases, America has the greatest responsibility to lead here. We must enact a cap and trade system that will dramatically reduce our carbon emissions. And we must finally free ourselves from our dependence on foreign oil by raising our fuel standards and harnessing the power of biofuels.

Such steps are not just environmental priorities, they are critical to our security. America must take decisive action in order to more plausibly demand the same effort from others. We should push for binding and enforceable commitments to reduce emissions by the nations which pollute the most—the United States, the European Union, Russia, China, and India together account for nearly two-thirds of current emissions. And we should help ensure that growth in developing countries is fueled by low-carbon energy—the market for which could grow to $500 billion by 2050 and spur the next wave of American entrepreneurship.

The fifth way America will lead again is to invest in our common humanity—to ensure that those who live in fear and want today can live with dignity and opportunity tomorrow.

A recent report detailed Al Qaeda's progress in recruiting a new generation of leaders to replace the ones we have captured or killed. The new recruits come from a broader range of countries than the old leadership—from Afghanistan to Chechnya, from Britain to Germany, from Algeria to Pakistan. Most of these recruits are in their early thirties.

They operate freely in the disaffected communities and disconnected corners of our interconnected world—the impoverished, weak and ungoverned states that have become the most fertile breeding grounds for transnational threats like terror and pandemic disease and the smuggling of deadly weapons.

Some of these terrorist recruits may have always been destined to take the path they did—accepting a tragically warped view of their religion in which God rewards the killing of innocents. But millions of young men and women have not.

Last summer I visited the Horn of Africa's Combined Joint Task Force, which was headquartered at Camp Lemonier in Djibouti. It's a U.S. base that was set up four years ago, originally as a place to launch counter-terrorism operations. But recently, a major focus of the Task Force has been working with our diplomats and aid workers on operations to win hearts and minds. While I was there, I also took a helicopter ride with Admiral Hunt, the commander of the Task Force, to Dire Dawa, where the U.S. was helping provide food and water to Ethiopians who had been devastated by flooding.

One of the Navy captains who helps run the base recently told a reporter, "Our mission is at least 95 percent civil affairs. It's trying to get at the root causes of why people want to take on the U.S." The Admiral now in charge of the Task Force suggested that if they can provide dignity and opportunity to the people in that region, then, "the chance of extremism being welcomed greatly, if not completely, diminishes."

We have heard much over the last six years about how America's larger purpose in the world is to promote the spread of freedom—that it is the yearning of all who live in the shadow of tyranny and despair.

I agree. But this yearning is not satisfied by simply deposing a dictator and setting up a ballot box. The true desire of all mankind is not only to live free lives, but lives marked by dignity and opportunity; by security and simple justice.

Delivering on these universal aspirations requires basic sustenance like food and clean water; medicine and shelter. It also requires a society that is supported by the pillars of a sustainable democracy—a strong legislature, an independent judiciary, the rule of law, a vibrant civil society, a free press, and an honest police force. It requires building the capacity of the world's weakest states and providing them what they need to reduce poverty, build healthy and educated communities, develop markets, and generate wealth. And it requires states that have the capacity to fight terrorism, halt the proliferation of deadly weapons, and build the health care infrastructure needed to prevent and treat such deadly diseases as HIV/AIDS and malaria.

As President, I will double our annual investments in meeting these challenges to $50 billion by 2012 and ensure that those new resources are directed towards these strategic goals.

For the last twenty years, U.S. foreign aid funding has done little more than keep pace with inflation. Doubling our foreign assistance spending by

2012 will help meet the challenge laid out by Tony Blair at the 2005 G-8 conference at Gleneagles, and it will help push the rest of the developed world to invest in security and opportunity. As we have seen recently with large increases in funding for our AIDS programs, we have the capacity to make sure this funding makes a real difference.

Part of this new funding will also establish a two billion dollar Global Education Fund that calls on the world to join together in eliminating the global education deficit, similar to what the 9/11 commission proposed. Because we cannot hope to shape a world where opportunity outweighs danger unless we ensure that every child, everywhere, is taught to build and not to destroy.

I know that many Americans are skeptical about the value of foreign aid today. But as the U.S. military made clear in Camp Lemonier, a relatively small investment in these fragile states up front can be one of the most effective ways to prevent the terror and strife that is far more costly—both in lives and treasure—down the road. In this way, $50 billion a year in foreign aid—which is less than one-half of one percent of our GDP—doesn't sound as costly when you consider that last year, the Pentagon spent nearly double that amount in Iraq alone.

Finally, while America can help others build more secure societies, we must never forget that only the citizens of these nations can sustain them. The corruption I heard about while visiting parts of Africa has been around for decades, but the hunger to eliminate such corruption is a growing and powerful force among people there. And so in these places where fear and want still thrive, we must couple our aid with an insistent call for reform.

We must do so not in the spirit of a patron, but the spirit of a partner—a partner that is mindful of its own imperfections. Extending an outstretched hand to these states must ultimately be more than just a matter of expedience or even charity. It must be about recognizing the inherent equality and worth of all people. And it's about showing the world that America stands for something—that we can still lead.

These are the ways we will answer the challenge that arrived on our shores that September morning more than five years ago. A 21st century military to stay on the offense, from Djibouti to Kandahar. Global efforts to keep the world's deadliest weapons out of the world's most dangerous hands. Stronger alliances to share information, pool resources, and break up terrorist networks that operate in more than eighty countries. And a stronger push to defeat the terrorists' message of hate with an agenda for hope around the world.

It's time we had a President who can do this again—who can speak directly to the world, and send a message to all those men and women beyond our shores who long for lives of dignity and security that says "You matter to us. Your future is our future. And our moment is now."

It's time, as well, for a President who can build a consensus at home for this ambitious but necessary course. For in the end, no foreign policy can succeed unless the American people understand it and feel a stake in its success—and unless they trust that their government hears their more immediate concerns as well. After all, we will not be able to increase foreign aid if we fail to invest in security and opportunity for our own people. We cannot negotiate trade agreements to help spur development in poor countries so long as we provide no meaningful help to working Americans burdened by the dislocations of a global economy. We cannot expect Americans to support placing our men and women in harm's way if we cannot prove that we will use force wisely and judiciously.

But if the next President can restore the American people's trust—if they know that he or she is acting with their best interests at heart, with prudence and wisdom and some measure of humility—then I believe the American people will be ready to see America lead again.

They will be ready to show the world that we are not a country that ships prisoners in the dead of night to be tortured in far off countries. That we are not a country that runs prisons which lock people away without ever telling them why they are there or what they are charged with. That we are not a country which preaches compassion and justice to others while we allow bodies to float down the streets of a major American city.

That is not who we are.

America is the country that helped liberate a continent from the march of a madman. We are the country that told the brave people of a divided city that we were Berliners too. We sent generations of young people to serve as ambassadors for peace in countries all over the world. And we're the country that rushed aid throughout Asia for the victims of a devastating tsunami.

Now it's our moment to lead—our generation's time to tell another great American story. So someday we can tell our children that this was the time when we helped forge peace in the Middle East. That this was the time when we confronted climate change and secured the weapons that could destroy the human race. This was the time when we brought opportunity to those forgotten corners of the world. And this was the time when we renewed the America that has led generations of weary travelers from all over the world to find opportunity, and liberty, and hope on our doorstep.

One of these travelers was my father. I barely knew him, but when, after his death, I finally took my first trip to his tiny village in Kenya and asked my grandmother if there was anything left from him, she opened a trunk and took out a stack of letters, which she handed to me.

There were more than thirty of them, all handwritten by my father, all addressed to colleges and universities across America, all filled with the hope of a young man who dreamed of more for his life.

It is because someone in this country answered that prayer that I stand before you today with faith in our future, confidence in our story, and a determination to do my part in writing our country's next great chapter.

The American moment has not passed. The American moment is here. And like generations before us, we will seize that moment, and begin the world anew. Thank you.

POSTSCRIPT

Should the United States Substantially Limit Its Global Involvement?

The question in this debate is whether and to what degree the United States should continue to be in its present role of global leadership. President-elect Barack Obama favors a less unilateralist foreign policy than had President Bush, but hardly advocates a retreat from power. Candidate McCain's position is somewhere between Obama's and Bush's. Eland does not advocate isolationism, but he does want a major downshift of U.S. activism. As for Americans, an overwhelming majority supports continuing to take an active role in world politics. However, only 12% want their country to try to be the "single leader," while 74% favor a "shared leadership role." Only 16% want the United States to have "no leadership role," and 4% are uncertain. Yet Americans are also reluctant to give up their premier position, with another poll finding that 52% of Americans wanted their country to ensure that no other country becomes a superpower.

Substantial debate continues over what would occur globally if the United States took a more isolationist turn. One argument is that a power vacuum would occur that might destabilize the world. This view is expressed by Deepak Lal, *In Praise of Globalization and Order* (Palgrave Macmillan, 2004) and Nial Ferguson, "A World Without Power," *Foreign Policy* (2003). Other scholars dismiss these worries.

Considerable debate also lingers on whether the United States can and will remain the dominant world power. For the view that U.S. primacy will decline in the foreseeable future, read Christopher Layne, "The Unipolar Illusion Revisited: The Coming End of the United States' Unipolar Moment," *International Security* (2006). Thoroughly disagreeing with Layne's view is Robert Singh, "The Exceptional Empire: Why the United States Will Not Decline—Again," *International Politics* (Spring, 2008).

A third important issue is what U.S. hegemony has meant for the world. A negative view is presented by Louis Janowski, "Neo-Imperialism and U.S. Foreign Policy," *Foreign Service Journal* (May 2004). Michael Mandelbaum's "David's Friend Goliath," *Foreign Policy* (January/February 2006) gives a positive view.

ISSUE 5

Has Russia Become Undemocratic and Antagonistic?

YES: Tucker Herbert and Diane Raub, from "Russian Geopolitik," *The Stanford Review* (June 2, 2006)

NO: Eugene B. Rumer, from Testimony during Hearings on "Developments in U.S.–Russia Relations" before the Subcommittee on Europe and Emerging Threats, Committee on International Relations, U.S. House of Representatives (March 9, 2005)

ISSUE SUMMARY

YES: Tucker Herbert and Diane Raub, both of whom are on the staff of the *Stanford Review,* an independent, student-run newspaper at Stanford University, argue that under President Vladimir Putin, Russia has fallen from the ranks of democracies and is engaged in a foreign policy that pits U.S. interests against those of Russia.

NO: Eugene B. Rumer, a senior research fellow at the National Defense University's Institute for National Strategic Studies in Washington, D.C., recognizes that Russian democracy falls short of full scale and that Russian policy sometimes clashes with that of the United States, but argues that compared with the history of Russian democracy, which was zero before the 1990s, the country is not doing poorly and that Russia's pursuit of its own interests should not be construed as necessarily antagonistic.

Russia has experienced two momentous revolutions during the twentieth century. The first began in March 1917. After a brief moment of attempted democracy, that revolution descended into totalitarian government, with the takeover of the Bolshevik Communists in November and the establishment of the Union of the Soviet Socialist Republics.

The second great revolution arguably began in 1985 when reform-minded Mikhail S. Gorbachev assumed leadership in the USSR. The country's economy was faltering because of its overcentralization and because of the extraordinary amount of resources being allocated to Soviet military forces. Gorbachev's reforms unleashed strong forces within the USSR. The events of the next six years were complex, but suffice it to say that the result was the collapse of the Soviet Union. Of the former Soviet republics (FSRs), Russia is by far the largest, has the largest population, and is in reality and potentially the most powerful. Russia retained the bulk of Soviet Union's nuclear weapons and their delivery systems.

When Russia reemerged in the aftermath of the collapse of the USSR, its president, Boris Yeltsin, seemed to offer the hope of strong, democratic leadership that would economically rejuvenate and democratize Russia internally and that, externally, would work to make Russia a peaceful and cooperative neighbor. However, these prospects soon faded amid Russia's vast problems. The country's economy fell more deeply into shambles, leaving 22 percent of all Russians below the poverty level. Russia's economic turmoil also caused a steep decline in Russia's military capabilities. To make matters even worse, the rekindling of an independence movement by the Chechens, a Muslim nation in the Caucasus Mountains region, led to savage fighting.

Yeltsin's ill-fated presidency ended when he resigned on December 31, 1999. His elected successor, Vladimir Putin, had spent most of his professional career in the KGB (*Komitet Gosudarstvennoi Bezopasnosti*/Committee for State Security), the Soviet secret police, and headed its successor, Russia's FSB (*Federal'naya Sluzhba Bezopasnosti*/Federal Security Service).

For good or ill, Putin brought a level of stability to Russia. Slowly, Russia's economy steadied itself. Moreover, with a well-educated populace, vast mineral and energy resources, and a large (if antiquated) industrial base, Russia has great economic potential. Similarly, while Russian military forces fell into disarray in the 1990s, the country retains a potent nuclear arsenal. Furthermore, its large population, weapons manufacturing capacity, and huge land mass make it likely that the breakdown of Russia's conventional military capabilities and geostrategic importance will only be temporary.

Putin was reelected by an overwhelming margin to a second term in March 2004, but Russia is less democratic than it once was. Putin used the various challenges facing his country as a reason to consolidate Moscow's power. Much of the independent new media is gone, local authorities have lost much of their power, and the country's largest company has been seized and its leader jailed on charges of corruption. Russia's constitution barred Putin from a third-term, but in 2008, after the following articles were written, he engineered the election of a protégé, Dmitry Medvedev, as president. Medvedev then promptly appointed Putin to be prime minister, leaving Putin by most estimates in de facto power.

There are also numerous issues that divide Russia from the United States. For example, Moscow believes that it is threatened by U.S. drive to deploy a ballistic missile defense system and by the expansion of the North Atlantic Treaty Organization (NATO) to even include some FSRs. One of these, Georgia, became a particular flashpoint when in 2008 Russian troops intervened there to protect separatists in South Ossetia.

The question, then, is: What are the chances Russia will once again become antagonistic toward the United States and its allies? In the first of the following readings, Tucker Herbert and Diane Raub are somewhat pessimistic about the future. They fret that old thinking among Russia's foreign and security policy elites has caused the country to return to a strategic posture that is both prickly and at times anti-United States. Eugene Rumer is more optimistic in the second reading. He contends that Russia is neither as undemocratic nor hostile as its critics charge.

YES

**Tucker Herbert
and Diane Raub**

Russian Geopolitik

Today's Russia is a strange political animal. It emerged from decades-long Soviet isolation in 1991 with the prospect of beginning a new era. Many hoped that Russia would finally join the ranks of the G8 [seven wealthy industrialized countries plus Russia] as a Western-style democracy. The yoke of authoritarianism, however, is not easily broken. Democracies are not created overnight, and the Russian Federation is no exception. Over the past fifteen years, both [President] Boris Yeltsin and his successor Vladimir Putin have made a great show of some democratic reforms, and the world has seen Russia undergo considerable changes. But the Russia that is emerging is not a Western-style liberal democracy.

Russia under President Putin holds fundamentally different values from the U.S., and operates under different assumptions. Justice, liberty, and equality have entirely different meanings in Putin's democracy. Regardless of arguments that Putin uses to claim that he governs a free society, Russia receives a Freedom House ranking of 168th of 192 countries in terms of political rights. The World Economic Forum places it 84th out of 102 countries in independence of the judicial system, and Transparency International places it 126th out of 169 countries in terms of corruption.

Just how serious is this divide between Russian and American political values? The short answer is very serious. The long answer can be found in a two-pronged analysis: first, an analysis of the handling of some salient international issues facing both the U.S. and Russia; and second, a glimpse into recent Russian domestic trends which offer insight into Russian motivations and values. The Russians may pose no immediate threat to U.S. interests—but they are still sitting on the opposite side of the chess board. Some day, an issue will arise which could induce Russia to start the game: and Russia has few qualms about exerting her power against U.S. democratic interests.

Foreign Policy

Russia's foreign policy towards its neighbors is often characterized as domineering and brusque. There is little respect for democratically elected leaders. The Kremlin keeps no secret of their preferred victor in the elections of states which they consider within their sphere. When a former-Soviet ally elects pro-Western democratic leadership, the Kremlin claims the CIA must be involved. Russia tacitly supports break-away republics in both Georgia and Moldova. Most recently, Russia has barred exports of Georgian wines and bottled water because of "health concerns" which Russian officials have failed to validate—

again, Russia does not approve of Georgia's democratically elected leader. They affirmed their endorsement of President Islam Karimov of Uzbekistan following the massacre he ordered of hundreds of political demonstrators, despite swift condemnation from the U.S. and European Union. Putin is one of the only allies of the Belarusian dictator Alexander Lukashenko.

With regard to the Middle East, Russia is at times pragmatic while at other times blatantly opportunistic. Their reception of the newly-elected Hamas leadership of the Palestinian Territories was a calculated and measured response that sought to contrast the reactions of the United States and the European Union, while gaining favor in the eyes of other Arab states. Although Russia is making efforts to prevent a nuclear-armed Iran, Russia does not fear for the security of Israel in the same way that the West does. Russia's proposed sale of truck-loaded missiles to Syria is just absurd. Russia will support America's war on terrorism, so long as it fulfills its own ends. By labeling certain groups as terrorists, Putin has justified the use of intensive force against the Chechnyans [a separatist ethnonational group in southern Russia]. Russia's participation in the War on Terror has served as validation of its military buildup.

Military Might

Russian defense officials are making a concerted effort to revamp the Russian military. Most recently, Defense Minister Sergei Ivanov announced widespread cuts in the number of conscripts and officers as part of an effort to make the army more efficient and professional. Moscow is also pouring resources into making the remainder of the army more powerful. So far these resources have helped to deploy a strategic missile regiment of a quality "unmatched by world rivals"; to develop a new nuclear-powered submarine armed with sea-launched ballistic missiles; and to significantly increase the number and level of large-scale military exercises. In a January letter to the Wall Street Journal, Ivanov outlines the motivations behind Russia's "profound and comprehensive modernization" of their armed forces. He emphasizes that Russia intends to use these new forces to thwart any political processes that carry the potential to "change the geopolitical reality in a region of Russia's strategic interest." He condemns "interference in Russia's internal affairs by foreign states—either directly or through structures that they support" and specifies that "our top concern is the internal situation in some members of the Commonwealth of Independent States, the club of former Soviet republics, and the regions around them." Although Ivanov insists that he is not "saber-rattling," his words are chillingly reminiscent of Cold War rhetoric. Russia has also contributed to military buildup in other regimes. Most notable is Hugo Chavez's Venezuela, which has purchased $54 million worth of Russian assault rifles, ammunition, and other light weapons in the past year alone.

China and Russia

A strong Sino-Russo alliance has gradually emerged over the past ten years. Russia and China have made clear their joint desire to achieve a world order that does not orbit around the American superpower. Joint military exercises have demonstrated the possibility that such an order may be reached through means other than peace. Indeed, Russia and China seem to get along better now than they did during the Cold War when they were purportedly comrades allied against the capitalist bastards of the West. In 2005, Russia and China signed a pact ending 40 years of negotiations over centuries-old border disputes. Both nations are pursuing a military buildup in the name of defense of sovereignty; desire to limit U.S. intervention in their spheres of influence; and have established their willingness to support sketchy regimes.

Nevertheless, the two powers remain in competition economically, politically, and militarily. Much of Russia's industrial sector has been replaced by more efficient Chinese manufacturers. China has gained entrance to the World Trade Organization, while Russia has been left in the cold. China may be moving closer to the West on UN security initiatives. The world seems more patient with China's human rights abuses than with those of Russia. Relative to Russia, China places more emphasis on its economic dominance than its military might. China has devoted vast amounts of resources to investment in infrastructure and human capital, while remaining tight-lipped about their military developments and insisting upon the peaceful nature of their rise. The future of this Sino-Russian alliance remains to be seen. Judging from recent developments, however, the two neighbors are more than willing to put aside resource squabbles in favor of good old-fashioned anti-American ideology.

Oil Politics

Russia is the world's largest exporter of natural gas and the second-largest international oil exporter. In the past year, Putin has demonstrated that he is not skittish of using Russia's abundant resource exports as a tool of political manipulation. For a few days in early January, Russia cut off natural-gas deliveries to the Ukraine after a dispute over an extreme price hike. Many believe this was a form of punishment directed at Ukrainian president Viktor Yushchenko for his Westward orientation. Border explosions in gas pipelines running to similarly democratic Georgia have also raised suspicions. The E.U. draws 25% of its natural gas from Russia. E.U. member states are watching Russian oil politics with apprehension while scrambling to diversify their foreign suppliers.

The domestic structure of the Russian oil industry is another cause for concern. In recent years, Putin has cozied up to state-run energy giants, while building an environment increasingly less friendly to the private energy industry. Russia's oil has played a significant role in fueling 6% growth rates since 1998. Oil wealth is a double-edged sword; if international oil prices fall once again they can drag Russia's economy with them. But for now prices are high and Russia is reaping the benefits.

"Managed Democracy"

Though Putin has continued to lower taxes and increase pro-market incentives that encourage consumer spending, some of his policies look dangerously similar to state centralization. In December 2005, one of President Putin's economic advisors resigned in protest over declining political and economic freedom; and the heads of pro-democracy Russian NGOs [transnational nongovernmental organizations] complain routinely of government harassment and efforts to silence them. The government has passed legislation that declares certain international NGOs illegal in Russia. The Duma [Russia's national parliament] has given Putin the authority to appoint regional governors. Corruption is such that bribes regularly determine the outcomes of court cases. The lack of freedom in the press stifles accountability and calls into question the legitimacy of this democracy.

Russia is no longer the rival superpower it used to be. In the past two decades, Russia has suffered considerable losses to its military clout and political influence. From a Russian perspective, Putin can be seen as a great leader who has restored Russian pride. The economy has rebounded and boomed since he took office in 1999. His economic reforms have coincided with increased investment and consumer confidence. Russia justifies its own interference in the surrounding region by citing cases of U.S. "intervention," despite the more democratically-inclined nature of the approach used by the United States. This belies the fact that the two states have fundamentally different political systems and values. The emerging Russia, in some ways, is as diametrically opposed to U.S. values as the Soviet Union was during the Cold War. Putin is playing a different game than his Soviet predecessors, but it is still a game which pits U.S. interests against Russian. Putin has made clear that he does not attach the same value to liberty, democracy, and peaceful rule that the U.S. does. The U.S. must beware of these differences and understand the Russian psyche when forming U.S. foreign policy.

Eugene B. Rumer  **NO**

Developments
in U.S.–Russia Relations

In 2005, two decades after a little-known Communist Party functionary named Mikhail Gorbachev was selected to the leadership of the Soviet Union, Russia presents an elusive target for students of its foreign policy and domestic affairs, both critics, of whom there are growing numbers, and admirers, whose ranks have been dwindling lately. True to the old adage, Russia is neither as strong as its sheer size and geopolitical heft suggest, nor as weak as it appears relative to other continental giants—China and Europe. No longer capable of projecting its power far beyond its borders as it aspired to do a generation ago, Russia remains the critical variable on the map of Eurasia position on the balance sheet of partners vs. adversaries can make or break most, if not all U.S. design on the continent.

Is Russian Democracy Dying?

Any discussion of modern day Russia inevitably turns to the country's uncertain domestic political situation and what many observers, both Russian and foreign, have lamented as retreat from democracy. Critics point to greater consolidation of government control over major media outlets, marginalization of democratically-oriented political parties, use of law enforcements against Kremlin political opponents and abolition of gubernatorial elections as signs of Russia's abandonment of democracy and possible return to its undemocratic past. Major human rights organizations have been critical of Russia's internal developments; Freedom House, a highly regarded human rights advocacy and monitor of freedom worldwide considers Russia as "not free" with the overall rating of 6, with 7 being the least free.

The facts cited by these human rights organizations are not in dispute. The Russian government directly or indirectly controls major media outlets. The most biting programs mocking leading Russian politicians, including presidents Boris Yeltsin and Vladimir Putin can no longer be seen on Russian TV.

However, contemporary Russian media, although more restrained than during the 1990's, is a far cry from what it was during the Soviet era or from what is implied in the short phrase "retreat from democracy." Russian newspapers, sold freely and available on the Internet, are full of diverse opinions; public opinion polls are freely disseminated; news reports ranging from

U.S. House of Representatives, March 9, 2005.

Kremlin infighting to developments in Iraq are published in print and electronic media.

Russian media are certainly not as free-wheeling as they were during the 1990's. But any claim of Russian retreat from democracy ignores the fact that Russia in the 1990's was not a democracy either. Does increased control of the media by the Russian government represent a bigger blow to democracy in Russia than ownership or control of major TV and print outlets by powerful businessmen who did not shy away from editorial interference when their business or political interests so required? Who bears greater responsibility for many Russians' cynical attitudes toward freedom of the press-President Vladimir Putin who has sought to consolidate his control over major media, or those oligarchs who used their media holdings as a tool of their business and political pursuits?

The issue of freedom in Russia too deserves a more nuanced consideration. There is little doubt that a number of steps by the Kremlin toward greater centralization of power and authority in the hands of the federal government is at odds with its stated commitment to greater democracy and open society. But does Russia deserve its "Not Free" rating in 2005 more than it did in 1996, when it held a rather unfair and unbalanced presidential election? Or 1994 and 1995, when it waged a brutal war in Chechnya? Or in 1993, when the Yeltsin government shelled the parliament building in an effort to resolve a constitutional crisis? During all those years, Russia was rated as "Partially Free."

The notion that Russian democracy is dead or dying ignores widespread grass-roots unrest triggered in recent months by the Russian government's unpopular social welfare reforms. People have been organizing and marching in the streets to protest government policies. After months of protests that have confronted the Russian government with a crisis like no other in recent years, Russian democracy is no less alive than it was when Boris Yeltsin was reelected to his second term in an election that was anything but fair.

Rumors of Russian democracy's demise are not only premature, but ignore the impact of such factors as the ever-expanding access to the Internet in many Russian cities in towns; cell phone use; ability to travel abroad; ability by foreigners to travel deep into the Russian heartland. Russia is no longer cut off from the outside world by the Iron Curtain. All this is having impact in many, often immeasurable ways—from the emergence of hundreds of civic organizations at the grass-roots level to academic debates about globalization and its impact on Russia, to the emergence of new independent candidates in the 2008 election to succeed—or challenge, whatever the case may be—President Vladimir Putin. None of these phenomena promise quick change, but they are signs that changes are taking place.

When the Soviet Union dissolved in 1991, it was universally recognized that Russian democracy-building would be a difficult and ambitious generational project. 15 years into that project one thing is clear: the future of Russian democracy will remain uncertain for a long time to come. Any judgment about its quality or condition at this point is premature and inaccurate at best.

Is Russia Moving toward Authoritarianism?

As a corollary to debates about Russian democracy, students of Russian domestic politics have raised the question of whether Russia is moving toward a more authoritarian system of government.

Surface signs have definitely pointed in the direction of a system that places greater power and authority, as well as greater control over resources, into the hands of the federal executive at the expense of regional governors, legislature and even courts. This has manifested itself in the reform of the Federation Council, which diminished the power and authority of popularly elected governors, reform, which was followed by subsequent elimination of gubernatorial elections altogether.

This was further manifested in the emergence of the pro-Kremlin "party of power" and the federal government's domination of the Duma [the dominant house in Russia's parliament] with its help, marginalization of other political parties and proliferation of electoral techniques that while certainly not invented in Russia and imported into Russian political life well before Vladimir Putin's tenure, were put to frequent and widespread use in multiple election campaigns on his watch. Other manifestations of authoritarian tendencies in Russian domestic affairs have taken the form of attempts by the Kremlin to establish greater control over the business community and its role in the nation's political life.

However, this trend, which began soon after President Putin's rise to the presidency of Russia, has progressed against the background of disasters and setbacks that have highlighted the shortcomings and failures of the Russian government and its inability to act in a crisis, respond to new challenges and cope with their aftermath. The Kursk submarine disaster [after it sank with all hands in 2000], the failure to put an end to the war in Chechnya [a rebellious province], the growing threat of domestic terrorism, the hostage dramas in Moscow [where in 2002 Chechen terrorists seized a crowded theater, with 129 hostages and all 42 Chechens eventually killed] and Beslan [where in 2004, 186 children and almost 200 civilians were killed by Chechen terrorists], and most recently the political and social crisis triggered by the welfare reform, have brought to light the fact that far from being authoritarian, the Russian state is dangerously close to being chaotic.

To the people of Russia this comes as no surprise. Public opinion polls consistently demonstrate low confidence on the part of the Russian people in their government's ability to perform the most basic functions—protect the nation's wealth, sovereignty and territorial integrity; provide for the poor and the weak; and protect citizens against crime and violence.

An authoritarian system may be the goal pursued by President Vladimir Putin and his political advisors. Having concentrated a great deal of decision-making authority and resources under its control, the Kremlin should be omnipotent. Yet, real power, the ability to formulate and execute policies, to produce results, to deal with crises and their aftermath, to effect change-all that so far has proven elusive to the degree that various branches of the Russian government and the country's far-flung provinces appear out of control, driven not by a vision of national interest and will imposed from the center, but narrow, parochial concerns or corporate interests of local elites. In December 2004, two percent of participants in a public opinion survey feared introduction of a "dictatorship based on force"; 15 percent feared anarchy and government incompetence; and 16 percent feared the breakup of Russia.

What Is to Be Done about Russian Democracy?

How should the United States react to developments in Russia? As policy experts and leaders on both sides of the Atlantic debate policy toward Russia, calls to expel Russia from G–8 [Group of 8: the 7 leading developed countries plus Russia] have been heard with increased frequency. The most frequently cited reason for it is that Russia does not deserve a seat at the table of the world's most advanced industrialized democracies, especially in the light of its retreat from democracy in recent years.

Indeed, on the one hand, the state and direction of Russia's democratic transformation is uncertain. Russian democracy is not of the same variety as that of the United States, Great Britain or Germany. That is not subject to serious debate.

But on the other hand, to many observers of Russian democracy inside and outside of Russia, the notion that Russia should be kicked out of G–8 now is just as counterintuitive as the notion that Russia belonged among the crème de la crème of industrialized democracies in the 1990's, when it gradually became accepted there as a full member of that select group.

Russian acceptance into G–8 was based on the principle, embraced by several U.S. Administrations of both political parties, that Russia's integration into major international institutions would secure Russia's constructive posture abroad and promote positive change at home. In shaping relations between Russia and the G–7, the leaders on both sides of the Atlantic and Japan took the long view of Russia's transformation. Excluding Russia from that group now would mark a departure from that view, ignore important developments in Russia and abandon the vision the West put in place as the foundation of its relations with Russia at the end of the Cold War—a vision of Russia integrated into the Atlantic and Pacific economic, political and security structures—and abandon it prematurely with the most adverse consequences for both Russia and its G–8 partners themselves.

How should the United States then respond to developments in Russia? As a constructive observer and partner who is fully aware of the complexity of the task ahead, of the national sensitivities and peculiarities due to Russia's historical and cultural preferences and traditions; as an interlocutor who understands that his own record of engagement on this issue has at times lacked consistency and impartiality; and, of course, as a candid critic in those instances where he feels his core interests and principles are at stake.

Russia and Her Neighbors

Russia's pattern of behavior toward her neighbors has been the other major area of recent criticism of Russian international behavior. Russian meddling in Ukraine, Georgia and Moldova has generated further calls for expelling Russia from G–8 and a more confrontational stance toward Russia on the part of its G–8 partners in the international arena.

Once again, the facts are not in dispute. Russian heavy-handed interference in its neighbors' affairs is well documented. However, this is an area where once again Russian behavior is more apt to be interpreted as a sign of weakness, rather than strength.

The public record of Russian involvement in Ukraine's "Orange Revolution," Georgia's "Rose Revolution," recent elections in Moldova and breakaway Georgian province of Abkhazia suggests that Russian influence in the former provinces of the Soviet Union is on the wane. Russia appears to be so unpopular and its interference so heavy-handed that it often produces the opposite effect from what is presumably intended. The results of recent elections in Moldova suggest that a candidate could be well served by Russian interference *against* him, for such interference is likely to help one's credentials as an independent-minded leader.

However, in areas other than politics, Russia plays an important and at times positive role. This may not be the result of its deliberate policies, but Russia, especially as its coffers swell from the flood of petrodollars, remains an important market for excess labor and goods from some of the neighboring countries, where access to Russian market is a matter of critically important remittances, export revenues and as a result social stability and even survival in some of the poorest areas. It is these flows of goods, people, services and money, often undetected or overlooked by the policy community, that comprise many ties that continue to bind Russia to its neighbors.

Perhaps, the biggest problem that Russia poses in relation to its neighbors is in the area of the so-called "frozen conflicts"—in Abkhazia, Moldova, South Ossetia and Nagorno-Karabakh. Russian involvement with a number of these breakaway regimes is a long-standing irritant in Moscow's relations with some of its neighbors, the United States and other countries.

The dilemma facing U.S. policymakers in this area is whether to confront Russia more forcefully or stay the course of patient, albeit unproductive dialogue. The balance of arguments appears to favor dialogue, though one that needs to be intensified if we are to achieve our stated objective of "unfreezing" these conflicts.

Additional arguments favoring dialogue include changes in Russian attitudes toward these conflicts. Increasingly, Russian interlocutors have acknowledged that developments in the South Caucasus have an impact on the situation in the North Caucasus, where Russian authorities face a growing prospect of destabilization. Some Russian analysts have begun to come to terms with the realization that they lack the capabilities to address the problem of security and stability in the Caucasus alone and that they will need to deal with other parties involved in the region, especially as the United States and Europe carry on with greater involvement there.

The discussion of "frozen conflicts" is bound to come to the fore of the trans-Atlantic agenda for one more reason: the final status of Kosovo. As Europe and the United States approach that thorny issue, as the option of independence for Kosovo looms large in discussions on both sides of the Atlantic, the

Abkhaz, the Ossetians and others will ask: if independence is OK for Kosovo, why not for us? It is equally likely to be an issue of considerable importance for Russia, which will be torn between its preference for client-regimes in Abkhazia and Ossetia and its fear that Kosovo's independence may be the harbinger of the international community's attitudes toward Chechnya. A preventive dialogue with Russia on this subject is essential to avoid a crisis in relations over this issue.

Chechnya   One of the thorniest problems on the U.S.-Russian agenda will have to be discussed as well. Long treated as a major human rights concern for the United States, this issue has acquired new dimensions—sovereignty vs. self-determination in the context of Kosovo, as discussed in preceding paragraphs; regional stability and security because of spillover into the South Caucasus; and counterterrorism in the aftermath of hostage-takings in Moscow and Beslan, as well as other terrorist incidents. Recognizing the complex and multi-faceted nature of the problem is the first step toward addressing our respective concerns.

Demands and ultimatums, as well as criticism of Russian crisis response, as was the case in the aftermath of Beslan, can only lead to Russian intransigence on this issue. There are no certain answers or solutions to this problem in advance. However, recognizing Russian sensitivities in times of national tragedies such as Beslan, being honest and realistic about our own ability to advise and to help in very difficult circumstances is the first step toward honest dialogue, possibly shared interests and even solutions.

Iran   In looking at Russia in the context of Iran's WMD ambitions, there is both good news and bad: Russia is neither *the* problem nor is it the solution. On the one hand, Presidents Putin and Bush have jointly stated that Iran should not be allowed to obtain a nuclear weapon. On the other hand, Russia continues to provide equipment for Iranians' nuclear energy program.

From Moscow's perspective, Iran's program represents a major export opportunity for its nuclear industry that has few domestic or international markets. It perceives Iran as a major political player in the region; an Islamic country that has been largely deferential to Russian interests in the past; and a key partner in the Gulf region.

For the Russians, the Iranian issue is not high enough on their list of the most pressing security concerns. While Moscow would prefer the status quo and considers the prospect of a nuclear-armed Iran to be an unwelcome one, the threat it would pose is not so great as to move the Russian Government to jeopardize other Russian interests in Iran in order to resolve this issue. At the same time, Moscow would not want to be cut out of any scheme to solve the issue put together by Europe and the United States.

Russian officials and analysts understand that it is an important issue for the international community, one that is high on the agenda of its (Russia's) principal interlocutors—the United States, United Kingdom, Germany and France. Russian policymakers would most likely view their involvement in solving the Iranian nuclear crisis as a great power prerogative, as well as a function of their interests in that country.

When discussing Iran's nuclear ambitions, Russian analysts appear to be more concerned about a US intervention than about Iran's ambitions as such. US intervention, they fear, would jeopardize Russian commercial interests; complicate relations with the United States, Israel, and others; cause further regional destabilization; and set off other ripple effects that Russia may be ill-equipped to handle. Some in Russia view the Iranian nuclear program as chiefly aimed at the U.S. and therefore a positive in countering growing U.S. "adventurism."

That is not to say that Russia is cavalier about Iranian intentions; they continue to monitor Tehran's behavior for signs of greater ambition and possible mischief. Generally though, while Russia might object to solutions that rely on use of force, it is unlikely to become a true obstacle to U.S. policy in the region. It is unlikely that Russia will ever become a major player in dealing with an Iranian nuclear program and would probably be more reactive than proactive.

At the same time, Russia could play a useful role in the general framework of the international community's response to the crisis. In doing so, Russia is more likely to use the international legal framework than adopt position that could leave senior policymakers vulnerable to domestic charges of caving in to U.S. pressure. For example, Russia's agreement with Iran on spent nuclear fuel ran against U.S. policy preferences, but instead emphasized compliance with Russian obligations under the NPT Treaty. Perhaps, one collateral benefit of the agreement is that it underscores the point that Iran does not need to develop its own full nuclear fuel cycle.

Russian behavior in the run up to OIF [Operation Iraqi Freedom, the U.S.-led intervention in Iraq beginning in 2003] could be indicative of Russian behavior in a future crisis involving Iran. Unwilling to jeopardize its bilateral relations with the United States or Europe, Russia would likely adopt a "wait-and-see" attitude and watch the debate unfold among allies on both sides of the Atlantic. Russia would likely shy away from a leadership position in that debate, leaving that role to others, while insisting on keeping the tensions confined to the UN–NPT framework, which would give it a major decision-making role, shield its equities vis-à-vis the United States and Europe, as well as maximize its leverage vis-à-vis Iran and neutralize domestic anti-U.S. sentiments.

Summing up   U.S.–Russian relations are neither as bad as critics charge, nor as good as optimists hope they can be. It is indeed a relationship that has fallen far short of its potential. At the same time, it is a relationship that has avoided many very real downturns and certainly avoided the worst. For the United States, it remains a relationship that could facilitate enormously U.S. pursuit of its geopolitical and strategic objectives—stability and peace in Europe, balanced relations with China, global war on terror, counterproliferation and energy security. It is a relationship that if it turns sour and adversarial, could seriously complicate U.S. pursuit of these objectives and the prosecution of the war on terror in Eurasia, as well as elsewhere in the world. It is a relationship that was founded at the end of the Cold War on the realization that the road ahead would be long, difficult and involve change that would be nothing short of generational. It is also a relationship that has paid off in a number of key areas—NATO [North Atlantic Treaty Organization] and EU [European Union] enlargement, Cooperative Threat Reduction, cooperation in the war on terror, etc. It has paid off for the United States through perseverance and adherence to the long view. There is little in the balance of Russia's domestic trends or international behavior to warrant a fundamental reassessment of U.S. commitment to that relationship, let alone a radical departure from it.

And while on the subject of radical departures, anyone considering a fundamental change in this relationship ought to consider the implications and costs of the alternative—a policy of neo-containment of Russia. They would be enormous, ranging from the added burden of military encirclement of Russia to political, involving a new rift in trans-Atlantic relations, for such a radical turnaround is unlikely to be endorsed by Europe. To paraphrase an old-fashioned Soviet phrase, the correlation of factors favors staying the course.

POSTSCRIPT

Has Russia Become Undemocratic and Antagonistic?

The debate over the future of Russia is not a matter of idle speculation. There are two very real policy considerations. The first involves the fact that the direction Russia takes in the future is likely to have important consequences for the world. During the decade after the collapse of the Soviet Union in 1991, Russia was in great economic and military disarray. President Yeltsin and President Putin sometimes strongly criticized such U.S.-favored actions as the expansion of NATO's expansion, but Moscow's weakness constrained it from trying to block U.S. preferences.

More recently, Russia's economic fortunes have improved. The global demand for energy and the increasing revenue that Russia gets from its oil and natural gas exports have given a particular boost to Russia's economy. It is yet unclear how much Russia's military has recovered, but there are some signs that its morale, training, and operational capability are on the upswing.

All this has given Russia greater confidence to oppose U.S. policy preferences where the two countries disagree. Moscow opposed the U.S. invasion of Iraq in 2003 and has helped block Washington's effort to get sanctions on Iran for its Nuclear Development Program passed by the UN Security Council, on which Russia has a permanent seat and a veto. Russia has also grown increasingly vocal about the U.S. effort to build and deploy a ballistic missile defense (BMD) system in part in Eastern Europe, with Putin, and now Medvedev warning that countries that accept the U.S. anti-missile missiles put themselves at nuclear risk. New issues continue to emerge, including the friction between Washington and Moscow over Russia's dismay over the U.S. push for an independent Kosovo in the Balkans and Russia's military move into Georgia. To explore both relatively optimistic and pessimistic views of the future of Russia's foreign policy, go to the spring 2007 issue of *Washington Quarterly*, which as several good articles, including Dmitri Trenin, "Russia Redefines Itself and Its Relations with the West"; Celeste A. Wallander, "Russian Transimperialism and Its Implications"; and Jeffrey Mankoff, "Russia and the West: Taking the Longer View."

There are also increasing doubts about the future of democracy in a country that has no democratic tradition. Even since the two readings, there have been new curbs on a free press and other essential democratic elements, including the barely disguised retention by Putin of at least most of his power. This concern with Russian democracy arguably has important implications for foreign policy. Many scholars contend that democracies generally do not go to war with one another, which means that the collapse of democracy in Russia might increase the potential for its clashes with the Western democracies. One look at the state of democracy in Russia is Stephen E. Hanson, "The Uncertain Future of Russia's Weak State Authoritarianism European," *Politics & Societies* (2007). For the attitudes of the Russia's people about democracy, read Ellen Carnaghan, "Do Russians Dislike Democracy?" *PS: Political Science & Politics* (2007).

It is too early to accurately predict what course Russia and its foreign relations will take in the decade ahead. What can be said is that Russia has seemed to be down and out financially and military at more than one juncture in its history, and it has always recovered, as it seems to be doing now. If the trend continues, Russia will regain the economic and military muscle necessary to play an important role in global affairs. A number of outstanding policy disputes still divide Moscow from Washington. How those are managed by both sides will be an important determinant of the general tone of future relations. Contrasting views of what to do are offered by Yuliya Tymoshenko, "Containing Russia," *Foreign Affairs* (2007) and Dimitri K. Simes, "Losing Russia: The Costs of Renewed Confrontation," *Foreign Affairs* (2007).

ISSUE 6

Will China Soon Become a Threatening Superpower?

YES: John J. Tkacik, Jr., from "A Chinese Military Superpower?" *Heritage Foundation Web Memo* #1389 (March 8, 2007)

NO: Samuel A. Bleicher, from "China: Superpower or Basket Case?" FPIF Discussion Paper, *Foreign Policy In Focus,* a project of the Institute for Policy Studies (May 8, 2008)

ISSUE SUMMARY

YES: John J. Tkacik, Jr., a senior research fellow in China policy at the Asian Studies Center of the Heritage Foundation in Washington, DC, contends that the evidence suggests instead that China's intent is to challenge the United States as a military superpower.

NO: Samuel A. Bleicher, principal in his international consulting firm, The Strategic Path LLC, argues that while China has made some remarkable economic progress, the reality is that the Chinese "Communist" central government and Chinese economic, social, political, and legal institutions are quite weak.

$\mathbf{C}$hina has a history as one of the oldest and at times most powerful countries (and empires) in the world. During the Yuan dynasty (1271–1368) and most of the Ming dynasty (1368–1644), China was also arguably the world's most powerful empire, dominating most of Asia.

However, China's power compared with Europe's began to ebb with the Industrial Revolution beginning in Europe in the mid-1700s playing a major role. By the 1800s, the European powers, joined by the United States in the last years of the century, came to increasingly dominate China. The Chinese consider these years a period of humiliation, emblemized by a park in a European enclave in Shanghai that bore the sign, "Dogs and Chinese Not Allowed."

China's road back began in 1911 when Nationalist forces under Sun Yatsen overthrew the last emperor. Internal struggles and the invasion by Japan (1931–1945) blocked much advance in China's economic and political power until the Communists under Mao Zedong defeated the Nationalists under Chiang Kai-shek who fled and set up the remnants of the Nationalist government on Formosa (Taiwan) as the Republic of China.

Gradually, Communist China (the People's Republic of China, PRC) built up its strength. Military power came first. China's military was saddled by obsolete weapons, but it was the world's largest military force, numbering as many as 4.2 million troops in the 1980s. China also sought to acquire nuclear weapons and delivery capability, and succeeded in that quest by the mid-1960s.

Fundamental changes in China's status began in the 1970s. In 1971, the United Nations changed the rightful owner of China's seat, including its position as a permanent member of the Security Council, from the Nationalist government on Taiwan to the PRC. The following year, the United States relaxed its hostility, and President Richard Nixon visited China. In 1979, President Jimmy Carter shifted U.S. diplomatic recognition of the "legitimate" government of China from the Taiwan government to the PRC government. Domestically, the two great leaders of the Communist Revolution and government, Premier Zhao Enlai and Communist Party Chairman Mao Zedong both died in 1976. This opened the way for a less ideological approach to improving China's economy.

Since then, China has changed rapidly. It retains a communist government, but it has adopted many of the trappings of a capitalist economy. Where once China rejected global trade and other international economic organizations, it has now embraced them.

Economically, it is possible to argue that China is still a poor country, one whose 2006 per capita gross domestic product (GDP) of about $2,000 was less than one-twentieth the U.S. per capita GDP. But China has also become one of the largest economies in the world. China's 2006 GDP was $2.6 trillion. That makes it the fourth largest economy in the world, still far behind the United States ($13.4 trillion), but about equal to Great Britain. China has also become a major global trader, with its $1.9 trillion in exports and imports placing it third among countries after only the United States and Germany. China is also the fastest growing large economy, expanding by an annual average of over 8 percent since 1975. Much of this is industrial growth, and China is the world's fourth largest producer of automobiles and commercial vehicles and third greatest steel manufacturer.

China's growing economy and industrialization has allowed it to upgrade its military technology. The country's 2008 official defense budget was only $59 billion dollars, but there is little doubt that actual spending is higher than that. Still the amount, whatever it is, falls far short of the 2008 U.S. defense budget ($711 billion).

What all this portends is the issue here. In the first reading, John J. Tkacik, Jr., warns that it is time to take China's military expansion seriously. Samuel A. Bleicher takes a much more restrained view of China's power and intentions in the second reading, believing that China could easily suffer major economic and political reversals.

YES

John J. Tkacik, Jr.

A Chinese Military Superpower?

On March 4, [2007,] China's National People's Congress announced that it would increase the country's military budget 17.8 percent in 2007 to a total of $45 billion. Despite the fact that this was the biggest single annual increase in China's military spending, the Chinese government reassured the world that this spending hike was normal and need not worry anyone. "China is committed to taking a path of peaceful development and it pursues a defensive military posture," a spokesman said. But the evidence suggests instead that China's intent is to challenge the United States as a military superpower.

A closer look at China's military spending raises profound questions about China's geopolitical direction. In terms of purchasing power parity (PPP), China's effective military spending is far greater than $45 billion, or even the U.S. Department of Defense's $105 billion estimate. In fact, it is in the $450 billion range, putting it in the same league as the United States and far ahead of any other country, including Russia. This figure reflects the reality that a billion dollars can buy a lot more "bang" in China than in the United States.

Within a decade, perhaps much sooner, China will be America's only global competitor for military and strategic influence. [U.S.] Director of National Intelligence Michael McConnell told the [U.S.] Senate on February 27[, 2007,] that the Chinese are "building their military, in my view, to reach some state of parity with the United States," adding that "they're a threat today, they would become an increasing threat over time." Nor is this a revelation to Washington policy-makers. McConnell's predecessor John Negroponte testified to the Senate Intelligence Committee in February 2006 that "China is a rapidly rising power with steadily expanding global reach that may become a peer competitor to the United States at some point." In June 2005, Secretary of State Condoleezza Rice observed that the U.S. must help integrate China into the international, rules-based economy before it becomes a "military superpower." Rice, with a doctorate in Soviet studies and years of experience in the White House during the last days of the Cold War, would not use the term "superpower" lightly.

It remains to be seen whether China's now massive stake in the global economy will result in Beijing becoming a responsible stakeholder in global affairs, but Beijing seems poised for true global status as a "military superpower."

From *The Heritage Foundation Web Memo*, #1389, March 8, 2007. Copyright © 2007 by Heritage Foundation. Reprinted by permission.

The latest figures from the econometricians at the Central Intelligence Agency—whose data come from the World Bank—peg China's 2006 GDP, adjusted for purchasing power parity, at $10 trillion, with a nominal exchange-rate value of $2.5 trillion.

Despite the Chinese Communist Party leadership's espousal of China's "peaceful rise," the unprecedented peacetime expansion of China's military capabilities betrays a clear intent to challenge the United States in the Western Pacific and establish itself as the region's predominant military power. With China's massive GDP [gross domestic product] and military spending at an estimated 4.5 percent of GDP, the resources that Beijing now devotes to its armed forces surely make it a top global power. The exact methodology that U.S. intelligence agencies use to arrive at this estimate is classified, but it reportedly takes into account the fact that China's budget figures do not include foreign arms purchases, subsidies to military industries, any of China's space program (which is under the command of the Central Military Commission), or the costs of the 660,000 strong "People's Armed Police." It appears that some defense spending sectors that are not counted in the defense budget have increased much faster than the budget itself.

At a time when The Heritage Foundation is encouraging sustained U.S. defense spending of 4 percent of GDP in an initiative called "Four Percent for Freedom," China's military budget could be called "Four-and-a-Half Percent Against Freedom" due to its involvement in countries like Burma, Sudan, Zimbabwe, North Korea, Uzbekistan, and Iran, not to mention its actions against freedom in Taiwan and, of course, in China itself.

U.S. intelligence agencies can plainly see where the money is going. China is assembling a blue-water navy, with a submarine fleet of 29 modern boats, including 13 super-quiet Russian-made Kilo class subs and 14 Chinese-made Song and Yuan class diesel electric submarines that are reportedly improved versions of the Kilos. At least 10 more of these submarines are in China's shipyards, together with five new nuclear ballistic missile and attack boats. China's surface fleet is also undergoing a similar modernization.

China's power in the air and in space is also on the rise. The People's Liberation Army (PLA) Air Force has about 300 Russian-designed fourth-generation Sukhoi-27 Flankers and a number of Chinese-built Jian-11 planes and 76 Sukhoi-30 multi-role jets. With Russian and Israeli assistance, the PLA Air Force has acquired an additional 50 or so Jian-10 fighters based on U.S. F-16 technology and reportedly plans to build 250 more. China's rocket forces are also expanding at an unprecedented pace, with production and deployment of short-range ballistic missiles targeted at Taiwan increasing from 50 per year during the 1990s to between 100 and 150 per year today. Presumably, output from Chinese ICBM factories is expanding at a similar pace. Most recently, China's January 12 test of highly sophisticated direct-ascent "kinetic kill vehicle" (KKV) technology, coupled with attempts to blind or laser-illuminate a U.S. reconnaissance satellite in 2006, are convincing evidence of the PLA's intention to neutralize the United States' military assets in space in any conflict.

Indeed, China's 2006 "White Paper" on national defense describes a China that is moving onto the offensive:

> The Army aims at moving from regional defense to trans-regional mobility, and improving its capabilities in air-ground integrated operations, long-distance maneuvers, rapid assaults and special operations. The Navy aims at gradual extension of the strategic depth for offshore defensive operations and enhancing its capabilities in integrated maritime operations and nuclear counterattacks. The Air Force aims at speeding up its transition from territorial air defense to both offensive and defensive operations, and increasing its capabilities in the areas of air strike, air and missile defense, early warning and reconnaissance, and strategic projection. The Second Artillery Force aims at progressively improving its force structure of having both nuclear and conventional missiles, and raising its capabilities in strategic deterrence and conventional strike under conditions of informationization.

The ultimate question must be whether Beijing's leaders have any purpose in assembling a military machine worthy of a superpower other than to have the strength to challenge the United States' strategic position in Asia. It is time to take China's military expansion seriously.

Samuel A. Bleicher **NO**

China: Superpower or Basket Case?

China as an "emerging superpower" makes for a compelling story line in the media. It is reinforced by the propaganda image that the current Chinese leadership would like us to accept. But the reality is quite different. Although recent events in Tibet and western China—and the central government's response—appear to be generating pro-government patriotic feelings, they dramatically display the practical limits of the government's power. Other sources of unhappiness with the regime, including income disparities and the inevitable collapse of unsustainable price controls on fuel and food, could breed both urban and rural discontent that has no ready outlet besides unlawful opposition to the government.

Meanwhile, the West, in its fixation on its own economic difficulties in comparison to the Chinese "juggernaut," is neglecting to prepare for equally likely "weak China" contingencies. Just as we failed to predict and prepare for the implosion of the Japanese economy and the collapse of the Soviet Union, we appear unready for a dramatic economic and political reversal in China that would be a defining event of the 21st Century.

China is in every sense a world under construction, with the physical, social, economic, legal, and institutional blueprints being drawn and revised daily as the construction proceeds. The depth and scale of the transformation taking place in every dimension of Chinese social, economic, and political life is difficult even for the most knowledgeable observers to comprehend. With luck, this great experiment can be one of the most successful developments in human history. If it fails, the consequences for China and for the rest of us could be tragic, and possibly catastrophic.

Wow/Not Wow

As the U.S. economy slips into recession, the American media are filled with impressive-sounding statistics about Chinese economic, social, and military progress. The implicit or explicit tag line is: "Wow!" For example:

Beijing has three million vehicles and is adding 1,000 cars a day to its already gridlocked streets—Wow! In fact, the Beijing metro area of 16,000 square kilometers, with a permanent population of almost 13 million (plus another 4 million "transient" residents), has about three million vehicles. The Los Angeles

From *Foreign Policy In Focus*, May 8, 2008. Copyright © 2008 by The Institute for Policy Studies. Reprinted by permission. www.fpif.org

metro area, with a similar population but one-quarter the area, has over seven million vehicles. Nationally, China has 22 vehicles per 1,000 people, while the United States has 764 vehicles per 1,000. The Beijing gridlock reflects the serious lack of transportation infrastructure, not a large number of vehicles, and the three new subway lines opening this summer will hardly make a dent in this deficiency.

China is the world's third-largest economy and has been growing consistently at 10% per year for more than a decade—Wow! In fact, China's Gross Domestic Product (GDP) of $3.8 trillion, for 1.5 billion people, is less than one-fourth the $13.2 trillion U.S. economy, for 300 million people. (The European Union has a GDP almost five times that of China's with one third the population.) Based on energy consumption and other indicators, China's longer-term growth rate is probably more like 6% per year, according to MIT economist Lester Thurow. Or, if environmental degradation is included in the calculations, China has essentially no net growth, according to World Bank Reports and statements [of] the senior officials in the Chinese Ministry of Environment. Even assuming that the claimed 10% rate could continue uninterrupted indefinitely from China's small economic base, China would just catch up with the United States in GDP in about 20 years—but not nearly approach the United States in GDP per capita. The gap between the average Western citizen and the average Chinese citizen will not close for the indefinite future.

China's consumption of oil is responsible for about one-third of the increase in demand in recent years (and it is also consuming enormous amounts of iron, aluminum, cement, etc.)—Wow! In fact, China consumes about 9% of total global oil consumption, which compares to U.S. consumption of about 25% of the global total and over 10 times the Chinese per-capita consumption. Unquestionably the increase in consumption of oil and other natural resources by China, India, and other developing countries is raising demand more rapidly than supply, and probably more than the planet can deliver for long (even with more dramatic price increases). But the world's growing resource consumption would hardly be sustainable even without China's growing demand.

Of course the American media coverage is not all pure "wow!" Longer articles often embed the dramatic statistics in discussions of China's fundamental problems, which are legion. The disparity in income distribution exceeds even that of the United States, the government provides virtually nothing in the way of a social safety net, and most people have minimal access to health care. Its cities are choking on air pollution, and water is in short supply and unsafe to drink. But even the "balanced" articles often leave the impression that these problems are merely social welfare matters that do not fundamentally impinge on China's "superpower" status.

More scholarly works have also endorsed the "emerging superpower" image—perhaps in the hope that a catchy title will attract the necessary public attention to sell books and ideas. A valuable book of mostly economic analysis and statistics produced jointly by the Center for Strategic and International Studies and the Institute for International Economics, China: The Balance Sheet, carries a cover line, "What the WORLD needs to know now about the emerging SUPERPOWER." An article by G. John Ikenberry in the January/February 2008 issue of *Foreign Affairs* describes China as "on the way to becoming a formidable global power." Even Sinologist Susan Shirk's generally very thoughtful book on China and American foreign policy, *China—Fragile Superpower,* assumes that the country is a superpower and must be dealt with accordingly.

Inherent Weakness

It may not make such interesting reading to say that China is slowly emerging out of feudalism and desperately hopes to use the fruits of Western technology to pull its people away from the edge of starvation, at least for a few decades. And it is extraordinarily difficult to quantify the real economic limitations imposed by China's environmental and natural resource deficiencies. But these concerns are rarely given serious consideration as real constraints on China's future development. Equally important, the international policy consequences of a faltering China are not being seriously discussed or explored.

The reality is that the Chinese "Communist" central government and Chinese economic, social, political, and legal institutions are quite weak. China is ineffectually governed. It will be struggling for decades to get and stay beyond subsistence. It has built an export-dependent economy ill-suited to meeting its domestic needs, and it will shortly face insurmountable environmental and natural resource obstacles to its rapid growth. The central government has succeeded in unleashing the entrepreneurial, profit-driven economic engine, but it is unable to apply any brakes—that is, to address effectively any of the adverse effects of the single-minded focus on profit. The leadership claims that it recognizes the corrosive economic and social consequences of the current situation and is taking remedial actions. Even if it were seriously committed to these policies as a high priority, the government lacks the mechanisms to rein in the runaway horse.

China has satisfactory national laws about minimum wages and hours, child labor, food and other product safety, worker safety, intellectual property, and air and water pollution. But the central government has not effectively empowered judges and prosecutors to enforce these laws, because they are controlled by provincial and local party leaders. These officials, who often benefit personally or professionally from the success of local profit-making enterprises, are rarely inclined toward enforcement.

China's urban transformation is creating a need for a new government-managed social welfare system that disburses retirement, disability, unemployment, and child welfare benefits—functions formerly handled by the now-diluted extended family. This traditional culture is rapidly collapsing in the newly mobile, urban society.

The supposedly all-powerful central government is unable even to end its substantial subsidies of gasoline, electricity, and water consumption—for the same reasons the U.S. government is unable to raise gasoline taxes or end the mortgage interest deduction. Both fear strong popular opposition. Meanwhile, the dramatic increase in wealth has created more opportunities and incentives for corruption. The high visibility of some of this corruption—poorly-compensated expropriations of private property to help developers, for example—is creating an increasing public backlash.

The current Tibet conflict does not threaten the government domestically. But it shows how quickly events can get out of control in a globally linked media world and when there are no opportunities in China for democratic participation to absorb the energy of the dissatisfied. More threatening to the regime in this situation is public unhappiness with internal economic decisions. Though less publicized internationally, recent events like the unauthorized rallies in Shanghai in opposition to a new rail line in a middle class residential neighborhood, organized through Internet and cell phone messaging, and the demand for public hearings about the PX chemical plant in Xiamen, show the risks of decision-making without mechanisms for public participation.

The popular "emerging superpower" picture in our media mostly takes at face value the central government's assertions about the success of its governance. The government claims primary credit for the "economic miracle" and the dramatic transformation of Beijing, Shanghai, and other major cities. It asserts that all of the country's environmental, social, and economic problems are manageable, and that it controls everything that happens in China. The government may indeed be able to lock up or kill off several thousand dissidents (a comparatively easy task logistically, though recent events in Tibet have shown that there is still a significant domestic and international cost). But that is a much easier task than designing and implementing necessary modern economic, regulatory, and social welfare institutions and programs in a society that has almost none. So far it has not demonstrated real success in those arenas.

China is big in almost every dimension, and its international influence has been increasing, as one would expect of a society comprising one-quarter of the world's people. But does that make it a "superpower"? Or even a "power"? What exactly is the "power" of 500 million near-subsistence farmers who mostly lack substantial electricity, safe drinking water, and indoor plumbing, and whose education consists largely of the ability to write and read a few prescribed texts? How much "power" is gained by adding in another 500 million educated city-dwellers with Western consumer aspirations who may well be living in economically and ecologically unsustainable Potemkin Villages? Balanced against its very real difficulties, China's capabilities are certainly not as great as they are often portrayed.

Military Ambitions?

China is expanding its military spending and technical capabilities, but it is hardly a global threat in any rational context. The Pentagon estimates 2006 Chinese military spending at less than $90 billion; most other estimates are lower. Compare that amount to the $440 billion FY 2007 appropriation for U.S. military spending, not counting $50 billion for Iraq and Afghanistan. The growth in the Chinese military budget more likely reflects the Communist

Party's need to buy the army's loyalty, rather than any imperialist military ambitions. Chinese civilian worker productivity is about 4% of American worker productivity, and a roughly similar productivity ratio probably applies to its military machine as well. Against the combined U.S., Japanese, and Taiwanese military forces, any military venture would be nothing less than a catastrophe for China.

This military balance against China severely limits any rational military ambitions. China's only active military focus grows out of its adamant opposition to Taiwan's independence, an issue that appears likely to recede as a result of this year's elections in Taiwan. China certainly wants enough military capability to make its threat of military action credible to Taiwan, the United States, and Japan. The Chinese tradition of military strategy is built around outwitting and outmaneuvering the enemy, not applying overwhelming brute force.

For that purpose the appearance of strength is important, but the actual use of force would reflect a strategic failure. Worse, any serious, long-term military engagement could easily create just the kind of domestic economic dislocations and shortages that, after the initial burst of patriotic enthusiasm, would feed social and political dissatisfaction, which the regime rightly fears most. The months-long adverse consequences of last winter's blizzard show the true vulnerability of China's economic structure.

Economic Power?

China's economic "power" is significantly less than the often-quoted statistics suggest. U.S. industrial imports from China amounted to less than 3% of the U.S. GDP in 2006 (up from less than 0.5% of GDP in 1993). The standard statistics on U.S.–China trade volume vastly overstate China's economic benefit. Only about one-third of the nominal value of China's exports reflects goods actually manufactured in China. China is still largely an assembler, and most of the components come from abroad. China's manufacturing is heavily dependent on imports of components, raw materials, energy supplies, intellectual property, and financial and other management skills, which all result in economic outflows.

Moreover, a significant part of China's current price competitiveness has grown out of its postponement of the costs of safe and sustainable management of its natural and human resources. Recent indications are that some of these postponed costs are coming due. The government is already spending billions of yuan (directly and by ordered closures) to dismantle environmentally unredeemable manufacturing facilities in time for the Olympics. More billions are being invested to divert water from agricultural uses to supply the growing cities of dry northern China.

Thus the much-discussed financial reserves China has accumulated are mostly offset by real-world social welfare and environmental debits to repair and maintain their human and natural resources. And the value of China's international reserves, mostly invested in declining U.S. dollar paper assets, depends almost entirely on the economic viability of the United States, the

EU, and Japan. China was apparently a significant loser in the U.S. subprime mortgage collapse, though the actual amounts have not been revealed. This dependency deprives China of the kind of independent economic power of Saudi Arabia or Russia, which control substantial physical resources.

International political power is largely derived from the world's perception of a nation's independent military and economic resources, and its willingness to invest them—and risk them—in order to change the behavior of other nations. Thus China's international political influence depends in significant part on what the Chinese government says, and what we believe, about its capabilities and intentions. Though it would like the West to believe otherwise, China cannot afford to risk significant military or economic resources in international political competition.

The Real Threat

In light of these realities, the West is overly focused on the Chinese "emerging superpower" threat and giving far too little attention to the real risks and foreign policy challenges that would flow from a serious breakdown in Chinese economic, political, or social structures. A crisis might be triggered by any number of factors. A dramatic slowdown in the Chinese or world economy could disrupt the lives of millions of factory workers. Serious rationing of water, food, or energy, whether by dramatic price increases or some other mechanism, could be unacceptably painful for a large part of the population. The loss of individual savings from a stock market or banking collapse could fuel popular discontent among the new urban elite. Even with continuing economic progress, widening income disparities could generate increasingly serious opposition in rural areas. A widespread farmers' strike might cut off food to the urban centers, leaving them in a state of chaos.

Systemic crisis could then lead to an open challenge to the regime. Here are two scenarios to consider. In one, students, factory workers, and peasants gather again in Tiananmen Square to protest economic conditions and perceived political non-responsiveness. When urban professionals start to join them, the central government calls in the army. It begins a brutal campaign of violently repressing demonstrators, arresting domestic and foreign media representatives, and purging uncooperative members of the Party and civilian government, entirely disregarding the legal system. The demonstrations do not stop, and various groups ask for outside help to protect foreign residents and foreign investment and to end the wholesale disregard of human rights. Overseas Chinese and major U.S. banks and corporations with investments and supply lines at stake argue that the situation is too dangerous to ignore.

In the second scenario, the central government's inability to control the economy or cure the country's problems becomes increasingly obvious. The educated, urbanized residents of Shanghai and the urbanized areas around Hong Kong increase control over their regional governing systems, perhaps through more democratized Party elections, and disregard Beijing's directives. Taiwan offers economic and technical assistance to these areas, with the aim of creating more of a "one China, many systems" environment. In response, the Chinese military threatens to impose military rule on Shanghai and Hong Kong, and to recapture Taiwan. The new local leaders ask for help from Taiwan and other nations to avoid the bloodbath, economic disruption, danger to U.S. and other foreign citizens, and destruction of foreign investment property that will inevitably result if no one comes to their aid.

Responding to Chinese Instability

Some American hardliners may believe that the United States should encourage crisis and regime collapse in China. However, nothing in Chinese history, or in the history of revolutions and coups almost anywhere, gives any reason to believe that a collapse or violent change in Chinese leadership would be followed by a more stable, more reliable, more democratic, or more cooperative international actor than the current central government. The tragedies of the French revolution, the Russian revolution, the post-World War II coups in Eastern Europe, and the Chinese cultural revolution are far better indicators of what might come next if faltering economic progress or other stresses of transformation become unmanageable.

In our globalized economic world, the West could not simply sit back and smile as China disintegrates. Chaos in China is far more threatening, economically, politically, and militarily, to the United States and the world than China's current "peaceful rise." Both for China's sake and our own, we must help the Chinese succeed in their transition to a 21st-century economy and society. Being better prepared for possible failures along the way is an essential component of planning for and realizing that goal. Western leadership needs to think now about how it would rank and balance various potentially conflicting objectives, including protecting diplomats and foreign citizens, salvaging Western investments, ensuring the stability of the global economy, protecting human rights, avoiding unpredictable military action and reaction, and maintaining civil relations with those who claim to be in power in Beijing.

The West needs to act immediately and more vigorously to help strengthen Chinese civil institutions, recognizing the continuing imperative of the Chinese government to show improvements in its domestic economic and social structures. The 2007 Party Congress was filled with rhetoric about "democracy." But real democracy—the broad diffusion of power beyond the Party and its attendant government bureaucracies, to independent legal institutions, media, and non-government organizations—will only be implemented if it is seen as a means of promoting social harmony and strengthening the authority of national laws over local corruption and opportunism. Arguments that China should expand individual human rights as an independent moral objective are unlikely to motivate the central government. Rather, the central government should be persuaded to decentralize power and create a diverse civil society to create the social resilience, adaptability, and sense of participation that will enable it to survive through the coming storms. The current Tibet controversy, because it is perceived by most Chinese as an ungrateful challenge to territorial integrity, is only a shadow of what may lie ahead.

Finally, we must also prepare for the worst. First, our foreign policy and military planners must develop and publicly discuss contingency plans for the consequences of a dramatic setback in Chinese economic growth and resulting breakdowns in domestic order. Second, we need stronger mechanisms to avoid miscommunication of military movements, lest we lurch into a World War I-like disaster as hardline propaganda and sensationalist media lock both China and other governments into inflexible postures. Third, if the physical entry of national or multilateral military forces into any part of China is unthinkable under all circumstances, we must identify other steps that might be taken to minimize and mitigate the destruction of life, property, social order, and global economic activity. What leverage, if any, can the outside world bring to bear on the central government or the military, without military intervention? Can the threat, or imposition, of economic sanctions, embargoes, blockades, or other tools have a significant impact in time to avoid disaster? Can the UN make any difference at all in this context? Timely, coordinated response by the outside world might make a difference; slow reactions and uncoordinated U.S., EU, and Japanese positions will almost certainly accomplish nothing.

The Chinese propaganda machine is doing its best to make us (and the Chinese people) believe the government has everything under control and on track. We must not take its claims of economic and military strength at face value. We need a more realistic understanding and perspective on the nature and scope of China's growing capacity and hidden weaknesses, learning more about its limits as well as its strengths. And we must think seriously about how the West might proceed to address the global interest in conditions in China if a real breakdown occurs.

POSTSCRIPT

Will China Soon Become a Threatening Superpower?

One of the reasons that Richard Nixon sought to begin the process of normalizing relations with China more than three decades ago was that he believed China was not only on the road to becoming a superpower but also that it might become the predominant country in the twenty-first century. While it remains unclear if Nixon was correct or not, there can be no doubt that China's power continues to develop. It still has the world's largest military (about 2.3 million troops), and its array of nuclear weapons and delivery systems, while still smaller than those of the United States and Russia, is substantial. Preliminary data for 2008 indicate that China's economy and its defense spending continue to grow rapidly.

How to react to the growth of China is one of the hottest topics in national security circles. To a degree, it is only natural for China to seek a military capability to protect itself and to promote its interests in Asia and perhaps globally. That is what the United States does and, to a lesser degree, other countries do as well. Certainly China has come a long way toward that goal, but the Chinese began from a very low military technology point and their weaponry remains far behind U.S. standards. Still, China's military technology has improved substantially, and it is most likely to use its military muscle in Asia, where it has a geographical advantage over the far distant United States. Moreover, China's forces are concentrated in Asia; those of the United States are dispersed globally.

For a view that the status of Taiwan is the point of greatest peril for relations between China and the United States, see Richard C. Bush, Michael E. O'Hanlon, *A War Like No Other: The Truth about China's Challenge to America* (Wiley, 2007).

One key to China's intentions will be not only how much weaponry it acquires, but the configuration of those weapons. Those "power projection" weapons systems, such as aircraft carriers or amphibious landing capabilities, which would allow China to apply military power far from its own territory, are the most likely to signal expansive Chinese diplomatic ambitions. There are numerous sources to keep track of China's weapons and military policy. Since many have a point of view, it is better to consult more than one. Three such sites are the Project on Defense Alternatives' "Chinese Military Power" Web page at http://www.comw.org/cmp/, that of GlobalSecurity.org at http://www.globalsecurity.org/military/world/china/index.html, and that of China Defense Today at http://www.sinodefence.com/.

Whatever China's long-term intentions and prospects to be a global superpower may be, there is no doubt that the country is becoming increasingly important in the regional balance of power in Asia, a status explored by David Shambaugh in *Power Shift: China and Asia's New Dynamics* (University of California Press, 2006).

There are numerous articles and books with policy prescriptions for the United States related to the future role of China. Among the recent additions to this genre are David M. Lampton, "The Faces of Chinese Power," *Foreign Affairs* (2007); Susan L. Shirk, *China: Fragile Superpower* (Oxford University Press, 2007); and Jeffrey W. Legro, "What China Will Want: The Future Intentions of a Rising Power," *Perspectives on Politics* (2007). For China's view of itself and its relations with the United States, visit the embassy Web site of China's embassy in Washington, D.C., at http://www.china-embassy.org/eng/.

ISSUE 7

Would It Be an Error to Establish a Palestinian State?

YES: Patricia Berlyn, from "Twelve Bad Arguments for a State of Palestine," An Original Essay Written for This Volume (2006)

NO: Rosemary E. Shinko, from "Why a Palestinian State," An Original Essay Written for This Volume (October 2006)

ISSUE SUMMARY

YES: Patricia Berlyn, an author of studies on Israel, primarily its ancient history and culture, refutes 12 arguments supporting the creation of an independent state of Palestine, maintaining that such a state would not be wise, just, or desirable.

NO: Rosemary E. Shinko, who teaches in the department of political science at the University of Connecticut, contends that a lasting peace between Israelis and Palestinians must be founded on a secure and sovereign homeland for both nations.

The history of Israel/Palestine dates back to biblical times when there were both Hebrew and Arab kingdoms in the area. In later centuries, the area was conquered by many others; from 640 to 1917 it was almost continually controlled by Muslim rulers. In 1917 the British captured the area, Palestine, from Turkey.

Concurrently, a Zionist movement for a Jewish homeland arose. In 1917 the Balfour Declaration promised increased Jewish immigration to Palestine. The Jewish population in the region began to increase slowly, then it expanded dramatically because of refugees from the Holocaust. Soon after World War II, the Jewish population in Palestine stood at 650,000; the Arab population was 1,350,000. Zionists increasingly agitated for an independent Jewish state. When the British withdrew in 1947, war immediately broke out between Jewish forces and the region's Arabs. The Jews won, establishing Israel in 1948 and doubling their territory. Most Palestinian Arabs fled (or were driven) from Israel to refugee camps in Gaza and the West Bank (of the Jordan River), two areas that had been part of Palestine but were captured in the war by Egypt and Jordan, respectively. As a result of the 1967 Six Day War between Israel and Egypt, Jordan, and Syria, the Israelis again expanded their territory by capturing several areas, including the Sinai Peninsula, Gaza, the Golan Heights, and the West Bank. Also in this period the Palestine Liberation Organization (PLO) became the major representative of Palestinian Arabs. True peace was not possible because the PLO and the Arab states would not recognize Israel's legitimacy and because Israel refused to give up some of the captured territory.

Since then, however, continuing violence, including another war in 1973, has persuaded many war-exhausted Arabs and Israelis that there has to be mutual compromise to achieve peace. Perhaps the most serious remaining sore point between the Arabs and Israelis is the fate of the Palestinians, who live primarily in the West Bank and Gaza.

In 1991 Israelis and Palestinians met in Spain and held public talks for the first time. Israeli elections brought Prime Minister Yitzhak Rabin's liberal coalition to power in 1992. This coalition was more willing to compromise with the Arabs than had been its more conservative predecessor. Secret peace talks occurred between the Israelis and Palestinians in Norway and led to the Oslo Agreement in 1993. Palestinians gained limited control over Gaza and parts of the West Bank and established a quasi-government, the Palestinian authority led by Yasser Arafat.

The peace process was halted in 1995 when Prime Minister Rabin was assassinated by a Jewish fanatic opposed to Rabin's policy of trying to compromise with the Palestinians. Soon thereafter, conservative Prime Minister Benjamin Netanyahu came to power. He dismissed any possibility of an independent Palestine, made tougher demands on the PLO, and moved to expand Jewish settlements in the West Bank. With some 200,000 Jews already in the West Bank and East Jerusalem, these actions compounded the difficult issue of the fate of those people in a potentially Palestinian–controlled area.

Pressure from a number of quarters, including the United States, have kept the government of Israel and the Palestinians talking, at least at times. President George W. Bush announced his support of a Palestinian state, declaring in 2003, "A two-state solution to the Israeli-Palestinian conflict will only be achieved through an end to violence and terrorism." At times there has been optimism in the region. Arafat died in late 2004 and was succeeded by a seeming moderate, Mahmoud Abbas. Then Israel withdrew the last of its troops from Gaza in 2005, leaving it under full Palestinian control. Just a few months later, though, much of the world was appalled when the Palestinians gave representatives of Hamas, a terrorist organization, control of the Palestinian parliament. Matters worsened in June 2006 when Palestinian gunmen entered Israel and seized an Israeli soldier. The Israelis responded with a sharp military attack on Gaza. The next month, members of the militant Muslim group Hezbolla based in south Lebanon captured two other Israeli soldiers in a cross-border raid. The incident set off a major Israeli military response, which pummeled Lebanon for weeks, destroying a good part of the country infrastructure. It is at this juncture that Patricia Berlyn wrote her essay arguing that creating an independent Palestinian state would be a grave error and Rosemary E. Shinko wrote her reply contending that there is no hope for peace without a Palestinian state.

YES

Patricia Berlyn

Twelve Bad Arguments for a State of Palestine

In 1991, during the administration of President George H. W. Bush, the government of the United States officially pledged to the government of Israel:

> In accordance with the United States' traditional policy, we do not support the creation of an independent Palestinian state. . . . Moreover, it is not the United States' aim to bring the PLO into the [peacemaking] process or to make Israel enter a dialogue or negotiations with the PLO.

A decade later, President George W. Bush announced his administration's "vision" of establishing an Arab State of Palestine west of the Jordan River. The vision was quickly ensconced in a U.N. Security Council Resolution.

This reversal of policy is based on the supposition that the pesky Israel-Palestine-Arab problem can be solved via a Two-State Solution (Israel and Palestine). Actually, it would be a Three-State Solution, because both Israel and Jordan are states within the bounds of Mandate Palestine (see Argument 3).

The necessity of an additional division of that very small area is promoted with twelve arguments that have become a kind of mantra.

1. Israel's Occupation of Palestinian Territory is the Cause of an Islamic Jihad That Spreads Much Discomfiture Across Several Continents. Only the End of Occupation and the Proclamation of a State of Palestine Can Relieve the World of this Discomfiture

On the contrary There is no Israeli occupation and no Palestinian Territory. Rather, there is Israeli administration of a section of Mandate Palestine that still has no assigned sovereignty. The right to this land may be debated, but it should not be dictated with a foregone conclusion based on casual assumptions.

This sliver of land, viewed as an issue of prime and urgent global importance, is hard to find on a map of the world without a magnifying glass. Israel knows it by its biblical name of Judea-Samaria. Jordan dubbed it the West Bank. It is not the crux of the Palestine problem and its growing international repercussions, and transforming it into a State of Palestine will exacerbate not solve that problem.

A realistic view depends on understanding the Muslim belief that the world is divided into two sections: *Dar al-Islam* [House of Islam] and *Dar al-Harb* [House of War]. Any land once acquired by Dar al-Islam must remain within it forever and ever. If it is lost—as in Spain—it must one day be regained. Dar al-Harb will eventually be conquered by *jihad* [struggle for the faith], military or otherwise.

"Palestine" was once part of the Ottoman Turkish Caliphate, and thus Dar al-Islam. It must never be yielded to any infidel, least of all to Jews, those despised and downtrodden *dhimmis*, the "sons of apes and pigs." Thus, Israel's existence as a sovereign nation is permanently intolerable, and will be so wherever its borders are set. The goal, whether declared or disguised, is the total obliteration of Israel. [Note: *Dhimmis*, an Arabic word, are non-Muslims living in a country government by the sharia, Muslim religious law.]

The current half-and-half approach to the Palestine problem is futile. It will not satisfy Israel's foes nor lead them toward genuine peace. Rather, it will dilute Israel's ability to defend itself against those foes and thereby encourage them to go to war. Policymakers who grasp the real issue have two options: (1) Facilitate the destruction of Israel, in hopes that it will mollify Dar al-Islam and postpone jihad against Dar al-Harb. (2) Strengthen, not weaken, Israel because it is the frontline of defense against jihad, and if the jihadis can overcome so staunch a nation they will be emboldened to move on to other prey.

2. The United States Will Benefit from Establishing a State of Palestine, and Win Arab Support for Its War on Terror

On the contrary   A Palestine-Arab State will be an enemy of the United States, not a friend or ally. The "vision" of a State of Palestine that is a democracy, has leaders untainted by terror, and wants to live peacefully side-by-side with Israel is not a vision but a mirage.

Under the Oslo Accords of 1993, Israel put much of Judea-Samaria under the control of the PA [Palestine Authority], and it quickly became a terrorist entity. In advance of Israel's withdrawal from Gaza in 2005, President Bush stated: "I can understand why people think this decision is one that will create a vacuum into which terrorism will flow. [. . . .] I think this will create an opportunity for democracy to emerge. And democracies are peaceful." The Hamas/Fatah regime that was soon elected in Gaza quickly demonstrated that terrorism flows and democracy does not emerge.

The Palestine-Arabs for whom the U.S. administration evinces much sympathy are fiercely anti-American. They admire and side with every enemy of the United States: Nazi Germany, the Soviet Union, Saddam Hussein, Al-Qaeda. They rejoice at events that bring pain and loss to the American people, and celebrate them with cheering, singing, dancing, and distributing sweets. The official religious leaders of the Palestine Authority curse America and pray for its destruction.

Israel, in contrast, is strongly and sincerely pro-American, and shares its values, many of them rooted in a shared biblical heritage. The American people sense this affinity, and strongly oppose the notion of a State of Palestine imposed on the Land of Israel.

If the Administration compulsively pursues its vision, it will create a dysfunctional terrorist entity that is both hostile to the United States and a perpetual dependent of the American taxpayers who have already been made to waste billions of ill-spent dollars on the Palestinian experiment.

3. It Will Rectify an Historic Injustice to the Palestine-Arabs

On the contrary Of all that Arabs have demanded for themselves since the end of World War I, they have been given 99.5 percent. They were given 22 states, with a combined area of 6,145,389 square miles. Israel has 8,000 square miles of sovereign territory and 2,000 square miles of disputed territory.

Judea was conquered by Rome 2000 years ago, and renamed "Palastina." It was not again a nation or sovereign state until 1948. In the interval, it was a province of one foreign empire or another; usually a backward, neglected, and misgoverned province. In recent centuries Western travelers to the Holy Land found the Land of Milk and Honey now desolate, barren, decayed, uncultivated, and almost empty of population.

From the late nineteenth century onward, Jewish pioneers came to restore the land of their fathers, bringing it back to life by clearing rocks, draining swamps, carrying water, planting crops, and building villages and towns.

After World War I and the collapse of the Ottoman Turkish Empire, Great Britain governed Palestine under a League of Nations Mandate that covered the area that is now Israel, Jordan, the West Bank, and Gaza. The terms of the Mandate repeated those proclaimed by Great Britain itself in the Balfour Declaration, issued by Foreign Secretary Arthur Balfour in 1917: Palestine was to be developed as a "Jewish National Home," open to "close Jewish settlement."

If Britain had honored these terms, there might never have been a Palestine problem. Instead, the British government violated them.

First, it detached all the land east of the Jordan River, more than three-quarters of Mandate Palestine, to provide a kingdom for a protégé Arab emir who had been expelled from Saudi Arabia. There was no historic name suitable for this kingdom so it was called after a river: Trans-Jordan and later Jordan.

In the remaining sector west of the Jordan River, Jewish immigration and settlement were progressively restricted and then banned. There was a rigid blockade against Jews trying to escape the hell-fires of Nazi Europe that consigned an incalculable number of them to death. At the same time, Britain allowed massive immigration of Arabs into Mandate Palestine, filling up the empty places meant for but denied to the Jews.

The offspring of these recent Arabs migrants and those who had preceded them by a few decades are today's "Palestinians" who claim the Land of Israel as their ancient ancestral heritage. Neither the name nor the claim predates the year 1967. Until then, Arab spokesmen and scholars insisted that there was not and never had been any such place as Palestine—only Southern Syria.

In 1948, the United Nations undertook a second partition of the Jewish National Home to create a second Arab state therein. Had the Arabs accepted the offer, they would have had 83 percent of Mandate Palestine. Instead, they went to war to get 100 percent of it. The series of wars that the Arab states launched were for the destruction of Israel and for their own aggrandizement. There was no interest in a state for the Palestine-Arabs.

The failure of the concerted Arab attack on Israel in the Six-Day-War of 1967, led to a revision in Arab rhetoric. The fight against Israel would continue, but it would win more sympathy if it were fought in the cause of "Falastin." This name is an Arabic mispronunciation of the Greco-Roman Palastina. The would-be-nation that claims to have held this land since the dawn of history has no name of its own. The ploy was so successful, that soon most of the world's governments, media, and academics adopted and disseminated with precipitate enthusiasm the fabrication of a Palestine unjustly stolen and unlawfully occupied by the Jews.

It is not unjust that the Arab world should have to make do with 22 states instead of 23. It is not unjust that there should be only one Arab state in Mandate Palestine instead of two. The injustice would be to deprive Israel of the heartland of its historic homeland, an erstwhile wilderness that it toiled to rebuild and restore.

4. It Will Satisfy the Demands of the Palestine-Arabs, Who Will Give Up Terrorism and War and Settle Down to Building a Society

On the contrary   The charters of Fatah, Hamas and Hezbollah define their goal as the destruction of Israel and they cling to that goal even when they fight each other for control of the areas that Israel gives up.

Hamas does not disguise its bloody intentions. Fatah's Mahmoud Abbas/ Abu Mazen, chairman of the PA, speaks literally in two tongues: In English he professes a willingness to recognize Israel and co-exist with it; in Arabic he says the opposite. He is a lifelong terrorist, former second-in-command to Yasser Arafat, but if he says the right word in at least one language, Western policymakers can embrace him without violating their own rule of not dealing with terrorists, and demand that Israel jeopardize its own most vital interests to strengthen him in the interests of the Peace Process.

A plurality of the Palestine-Arab population has demonstrated through both election polls and opinion polls that it prefers the Hamas line, approves of suicide bombings and murder of Israelis, and believes that a prospective State of Palestine should keep up such attacks until Israel disappears.

Where the Palestine Authority is in power, maps show Palestine as an all-Arab entity with Israel obliterated. In the year 2006 it is declared that the Israeli Occupation has been going on for 58 years—dating it back to Israel's Declaration of Independence in 1948, not the loss of territory in 1967. In schools and summer camps, children are taught to aspire to martyrdom by killing Jews. None of this suggests that Palestine-Arabs plan ever to co-exist with Israel on any terms.

The PLO (Palestine Liberation Organization) in 1974 formally adopted a plan to be carried out in two stages: (1) Take whatever territory Israel can be persuaded or forced to yield. (2) Use that territory as a base for the future war to take all of Israel. Stage 1 was achieved with the Oslo Accords and the empowerment of the PA. Yet one of its top ministers and spokesmen, Faisal al-Husseini, defined the forthcoming Stage 2 as: "Whatever we get now, cannot make us forget this supreme truth. If we agree to declare our state over . . . the West Bank and Gaza, our ultimate goal is the liberation of all historic Palestine from the River [Jordan] to the Sea [Mediterranean]."

This purpose and intent has never been changed.

5. It Will Bring Peace and Stability to the Middle East

On the contrary   It will establish a sovereign national base for violent jihad. This can be deduced from the evidence of experience.

Every area from which Israel withdrew its administration and security patrols is now a base for terrorism and/or preparation for military attack: In Ramallah and other PA enclaves, bombings are planned and perpetrators dispatched to their targets. In the border zone of Lebanon, the Iranian-sponsored Hezbollah installed missile bases and launchers, whence they have so far fired some 4,000 deadly Katyusha missiles into Israel and brought devastation to Lebanon. In Gaza, Fatah and Hamas steadily shoot Kassam rockets into Israeli towns. When Israel relinquishes control, it opens the way for massive imports of weapons and explosives, and infiltration by Al-Qaeda. These are consequences of withdrawal, and no measures to prevent or counter them have any effect.

There is no reason to suppose that a State of Palestine will deviate from this pattern. It will be a base for terror and jihad, in a location where it can imperil both Israel and Jordan. Secretary of State Condoleeza Rice has said, "There can be no peace without a Palestinian state." That forecast can be amended by cutting a mere three letters: "There can be no peace with(~~out~~) a Palestinian state."

6. A State of Palestine Will Be Demilitarized and Not a Danger to Israel

On the contrary   A State of Palestine cannot be kept demilitarized. If it signs an agreement or treaty to that effect it will be worthless because promises to infidels are not binding. Arafat compared the Oslo Accords to a treaty Muhammad made with an Arabian tribe that he then attacked and annihilated.

The PA was bound by signed agreement to have only a police force of no more than 8,000 with no heavy weapons. It acquired a military force of at least 50,000 with heavy weapons. Nothing was done about this violation because neither Israel nor any other nation demands that Arabs adhere to agreements. It is prudent to anticipate that a State of Palestine will not be subject to any effective restrictions on its doings. As in Gaza and the Lebanese border zone there will be a massive influx of heavy weapons and trained fighters.

The strategic danger to Israel of a Palestine-Arab state was analyzed by the U.S. Joint Chiefs of Staff, who reported that Israel must at the very least keep control of the highlands of Judean Hills and the Jordan valley. Without them, Israel at its narrowest point is only nine miles wide. "Palestine" holding the adjacent highlands can bombard much of Israel with missiles and rockets and shoot down civilian aircraft. Foreign troops can sweep in across the Jordan Valley without hindrance.

An administration that forces Israel out of these vitally strategic points rejects the counsel of its own highest-ranking military men. As though this were not ill-advised enough, it also demands that a State of Palestine must have "contiguity." That is: Judea-Samaria and Gaza must be linked together. It is geographically impossible to satisfy this demand without splitting Israel in half.

To render Israel so vulnerable is an invitation to massive military attack upon it.

7. If a State of Palestine Commits Aggression Against Israel, Then Israel Can Take Back the Land it Gave Away

On the contrary   The supporters of the Oslo Accords said. "If they [the PLO] do not keep their commitment to peace, we will just take the land back." No commitment was kept, and nothing was taken back.

Regaining the forfeited land would require a military campaign, difficult, perhaps long, and costly in casualties. It would be carried out against a background chorus of denunciations and demands to cease and desist. In the past, when the Israel Defense Force has gone into PA-held areas even briefly, to close down terrorist bases and weapons factories and depots, there were international howls for Israel to "get out of Palestinian territory immediately." Any such defensive move against a State of Palestine would be branded as aggression against a sovereign state, perhaps even with a threat of sanctions against Israel and/or intervention by foreign troops.

In the event of a full-scale military attack on Israel, it might be granted some right of self-defense, but even that would be limited. If Palestine were on the verge of crumbling, the United Nations would likely save it with an imposed ceasefire. If Israel were to regain any or all of its forfeited land, there would be international pressure for it to yield the land to the defeated aggressor, just as there has been with territories won in the Six-Day War.

8. If Israel Does Not Cut Away from Regions With Large Arab Populations, the Arabs Will Soon Become a Majority and Rule Over the Jews

On the contrary   This argument, sometimes dubbed "The Demographic Time-Bomb," rests on erroneous statistics and unsound projections.

The calculations are based on a census by the Palestine Authority. An examination of the statistics and the methods of compiling them found that the number of Arabs was over-estimated by one million or more. Estimates of population growth depend on an inflated anticipated Arab birthrate.

More precise calculations yield both a smaller Arab population and an ongoing drop in the Arab birthrate. Furthermore, there is little if any immigration to PA areas, and indeed a high percentage of the residents say they would like to emigrate if they had the means. In Israel, in contrast, the birthrate is steady or rising, and there is ongoing immigration.

9. It Will Secure the Human Rights of the Palestinian Arabs and Solve the Arab Refugee Problem

On the contrary   The PA regime in areas of Judea-Samaria and with full sway in Gaza has nothing to its credit in human rights.

Wherever Fatah and/or Hamas rules, there are no human or civil rights or rule of law. Those under their rule are subject to oppression, extortion, and brutality. Those accused of offenses have no right of fair trial, and at times are lynched without trial. Christians are especially vulnerable to harassment and abuse, and desecration of their churches. Their communities, which long predate the Muslim incursion into the region, are shrinking and dwindling away. There would not be a live Jew anywhere in a State of Palestine.

To the Arab refugees, whose plight the United Nations has deliberately perpetuated for almost 60 years, a State of Palestine would bring no relief. The chieftains of Fatah and Hamas, along with the rulers of Saudi Arabia and other Arab states, insist on a Right of Return. That is: Israel itself must take in the massive population of the United Nations camps for Palestine refugees and their descendants, who are taught and trained to loathe it and dedicate themselves to destroying it. This impossible demand is designed to evade solving a problem deliberately perpetuated for propaganda.

10. It Will Encourage Civic and Economic Development, Raise the Standard of Living and Bring Contentment to the People

On the contrary   In areas under PA control, the standard of living drops and hardship increases.

When the disputed territories were entirely under Israeli administration, there was economic growth, a rise in the standard of living, improved health care, and the establishment of the first universities. Since administration was turned over the PA, there has been a slide backwards. Economic development is strangled by graft and corruption, and revenues are squandered. The development of an economy and a civic infrastructure are not a priority.

The United States and the European Union have subsidized the PA so lavishly that the Palestine-Arabs have received per capita more donations than any other group in the world. The bulk of the money melted away, ended up in private foreign bank accounts, or was spent on buying weapons and training terrorists. Some individuals have gotten very rich, but little benefit has seeped down to the working-class or the unemployed-class.

In civil society, schools are for the indoctrination of martyrs-to-be; radio and television stations are for propaganda, recruitment of terrorists, and curses upon Israel and America; streets are for gang-warfare. There is water and electricity only because Israel still provides it.

As the standard of living sinks, international agencies cry "Humanitarian Crisis!" and blame it on Israel—especially in Gaza, where there has been no Israeli presence or control since August 2005.

11. Israel Must Comply With United Nations Resolutions

On the contrary   The United Nations is a world epicenter of corruption engaged in active hostility against Israel. It has made itself a foe and should be treated as such.

Israel has never been granted the rights and protections due to a member state. Since 1948, Arab states that are U.N. members have perpetrated every form of aggression against Israel, without interference or even rebuke. There is a built-in anti-Israel majority that churns out anti-Israel resolutions, while no resolution with even a shade of balance can pass.

The Secretariat that is the administrative branch of the United Nations celebrates an annual Day of Solidarity with the Palestinian People, and the Secretary-General poses in front of a map of Palestine from which Israel has been obliterated. Peacekeeping troops aid and abet Arab terrorists in the kidnapping and murder of Israelis. Demands for Israeli compliance focus on the obsolete Security Council Resolution 242, passed in the wake of the Six Day War of 1967. The Council did nothing to hinder the Arab states in their openly announced intent of launching a war to exterminate Israel. When they had lost the war and along with it control of Judea-Samaria [West Bank], East Jerusalem, Gaza, the Sinai Peninsula, and the Golan Heights, the Council presumed to dictate the terms of a future peace settlement: Israel should withdraw from unspecified "territories" to "agreed and secure borders." The United States and Great Britain, who wrote the resolution, gave official and unequivocal assurances that it did not mean Israel's return to the pre-war frontiers, which were merely the ceasefire lines of the War of Independence of 1948–1949. This Resolution is widely misquoted in a falsified version that requires Israel's full and unconditional withdrawal from all of the land the Arabs lost in 1967, and the establishment of a Palestinian state. This is not true.

The United States and Great Britain, the authors of Resolution 242, have since reneged on the words of their own past governments and call for Israel's full or near-full surrender of the disputed territories to a Palestine-Arab state-to-be. This flip-flop demonstrates that if Israel makes any sacrifice in deference to the United Nations there will be more demands for more severe sacrifices.

12. It Will Win the Respect of World Opinion for Israel

On the contrary   Honest and informed opinion does not need to be bought. Dishonest and ignorant opinion is not worth buying.

Some holders and makers of opinion are fair-minded or even friendly toward Israel. Their views can include reasonable disagreements and criticisms made without malice.

Some are automatically hostile to Israel because of Judeophobia, or ideology, or financial interests in the Arab world, or a desire to curry favor with Israel's foes, or simply because it is a fad. They do not make their judgments according to anything Israel does or does not do, and Israel cannot affect them.

Some judge only by what they hear from teachers—many of whom fit into the "automatically hostile" category—and the popular news media, whose practitioners have slipped from slanting news against Israel to complicity in lies and hoaxes.

Israel can and should do more to bring accurate facts and explanations to public attention. It should never compromise its own best interests and jeopardize its own security to oblige distant opinion-makers.

Conclusion

Giving up Judea-Samaria would cut the Jewish People off from the heart of the land to which they have been bound for almost 4,000 years. Arabs would destroy ancient Jewish sites and relics, as they have already done in Jerusalem. There would be no chance for scholars and archeologists to make new discoveries, and much knowledge of the past would be lost. And all this loss would be on behalf of an ill-advised political experiment.

Even so, it may be said "It is useless to oppose a State of Palestine—it is inevitable." Such passive submission is moral indolence, a limp acceptance of a plan regardless of the harm it is bound to do.

For 2000 years, the Jewish people did not despair of restoration to their land. When the restoration has at last come, those who toss it away betray both their ancestors and their descendants.

Why a Palestinian State

A Two State Solution

On July 8, 1937, the Palestine Royal Commission (Peel Commission) offered its recommendations to the British government regarding the disposition of the Palestinian question. The commission expressed serious reservations about the possibility of reconciliation between Arabs and Jews and thus concluded; "only the 'surgical operation of partition' offers a chance of ultimate peace. The commission proposed the establishment of two separate states—a sovereign Arab State and a sovereign Jewish State.

President, Bill Clinton reiterated these same sentiments in a speech he delivered on January 7, 2001. "I think there can be no genuine resolution to the conflict without a sovereign, viable, Palestinian state that accommodates Israel's security requirements and the demographic realities." Any settlement, he continued, must ultimately be "based on sovereign homelands, security, peace and dignity for both Israelis and Palestinians." In 2002 the UN Security Council adopted a US supported resolution supporting the establishment of an independent Palestinian state. The current Bush administration has also expressed support for statehood as part of its roadmap for peace in the Middle East.

Why is it then that Patricia Berlyn argues that the creation of a 23rd Arab state would be unwise, unjust and undesirable? Her arguments revolve around the following five main assertions: (1) there is no such thing as a 'Palestinian territory' (2) nor do the Arabs constitute a 'Palestinian people,' (3) if such a state were established the Arabs would be unable to fulfill the rights and duties associated with statehood, (4) it would not be in the self-interest of the State of Israel because its [the Palestinian state's] aim would be Israel's demise, and finally it would betray the sacrifices of the past and the promises of the future of the Jewish people.

Berlyn's arguments follow an all too familiar pattern, one which seeks to denigrate the 'other,' in this case the Palestinian other, at the expense of constituting an Israeli identity that encircles itself with all of the admirable qualities, distances itself from any responsibility for the plight of the Palestinians, and claims the moral high ground of victimization at the hands of an illegitimate, infidel other. For instance she equates all Palestinians with former and current enemies of the United States; the Nazis Communists, Saddam Hussein and al-Qaeda. Jewish settlements in the late 19th century are characterized as making profitable and industrious use of land that was otherwise wasted, uncultivated, and barren. These characterizations bear a striking resemblance to [English philosopher John] Locke's arguments in his fifth chapter on property in the *Second Treatise of Government* [1689], which were a carefully crafted argument intended to justify European colonization and deny the consent of the wasteful, non-industrious indigenous inhabitants whose land was taken from them.

What is a 'state' and why does the possibility of the creation of a Palestinian state; in particular, provoke such a strong, emotional response from Berlyn? What does the term 'state' signify? According to [German philosopher Georg Wilhelm Friedrich Hegel (1770–1831)], "only those peoples that form states can come to our notice" because it is the state that provides the foundation for "national life, art, law, morality, religion, [and] science." The political identity of most peoples is inextricably bound up with the notion of statehood. According to an international relations text, *International Politics on the World Stage*, written by John Rourke and Mark Boyer, "States are territorially defined political units that exercise ultimate internal authority and that recognize no legitimate external authority over them." The political implications of legitimacy that would flow from the establishment and recognition of a Palestinian state are extremely significant in this particular instance.

As scholar Malcom Shaw notes in his 1999 Cambridge University Press book *International Law*, a state is recognized as having a 'legal personality,' which includes the capacity to possess and exercise certain rights and to perform specific duties. These rights and duties encompass the attributes of independence, legal equality, and peaceful coexistence. Thus a Palestinian State would claim the right to exercise jurisdiction over its population and territory, as well as, the right to self-defense. Such a state would also have a concomitant duty not to intervene in the internal affairs of another state and a duty to respect the territorial integrity and sovereignty of other states.

The Palestinians have been denied anything that has even remotely resembles an independent sovereign existence that is not determined by and ultimately reliant upon Israeli dictates. Israeli settlements have served to cut the West Bank in half, isolating East Jerusalem, and carving the economic heart out of the Palestinian territories, according to Jeff Halper in the *Catholic New Times* on April 24, 2005. The patchwork of Palestinian designated areas currently resembles apartheid inspired Bantustans, which serve to further isolate and impoverish their residents. [Note: Bantustan was one of the segregated, theoretically autonomous enclaves in South Africa in which white South Africans once forced many of the country's blacks (who speak Bantu and other languages) to live.]

Legitimacy and Equality

The establishment and recognition of a Palestinian state would confirm the political legitimacy and legal equality of the Palestinian people. Historically they have been denied recognition as a people, and the legitimacy of their claims to the territory of Palestine has been dismissed. Berlyn's arguments are designed to foster the sense of Palestinian illegitimacy with her intimations that the Arabs have 'no roots and no history' in Palestine and that there is 'no such thing as a Palestinian territory'. To round out her argument, she employs the [traditional Hebrew] term 'Judea-Samaria' when referring to the territory that would constitute a Palestinian State in order to historically delegitmate and rupture Palestinian connections to their homeland, while attempting to privilege the historical primacy and unbroken continuity of Israeli claims. Only a state troubled by its own legitimacy would find it necessary to work so hard to represent their historical lineage in the form of an unbroken line from the dim mists of the past to the clarity of the present.

All states are man-made creations; all states are reflective of the political, legal, social, and economic conditions which led to their rise. All states, even the State of Israel, are current and ongoing political creations of contemporary men and women. But more importantly, she attempts to cover over the fact that states are not divinely sanctioned nor guaranteed by claims to lineage alone, but instead created out of hard fought political struggles, compromises, and bargains. Berlyn's arguments, which are framed to effect the dismissal of a Palestinian presence and history, are an extension of earlier Zionist attempts to portray Palestine as a 'land without people for a people without land'. Such a perception promotes the view that the territory of Palestine was 'empty' and that its only inhabitants were uncivilized, backward nomads.

Demographic realities, however, prove otherwise. "There were always real, live Palestinians there; there were census figures, land-holding records, newspaper and radio accounts, eyewitness reports and the sheer physical traces of Arab life in Palestine before and after 1948," according to Edward W. Said, and Christopher Hitchens in their 1988 study, *Blaming the Victims, Spurious Scholarship and the Palestinian Question*. In 1947 when the United Nations Committee on Palestine (UNSCOP) made its recommendation that Palestine be portioned into two separate states, there were 1.2 million Arabs as compared to 570,000 Jews living in the territory. Clearly the Arabs formed the majority of the population in Palestine. On what basis then can it be maintained that the Palestinians had no history, had no roots, and had no presence in Palestine? "The fact is that [when] the people of Israel . . . came home, the land was not all vacant," President Clinton commented in 2001. Statehood confirms presence, establishes legitimacy, confers recognition, and provides a focal point for a peoples' identity.

Recognition and Self-Determination

David Shipler in an October 15, 2000 article in the *New York Times* commented astutely that "Recognizing the authenticity of the other in that land comes hard in the midst of the conflict. Yet the conflict cannot end without that recognition." Ultimately legitimacy and recognition are the keys to the end of conflict and to the establishment of peace in the Middle East. Peace cannot occur without the recognition of the Palestinian people's right to self-determination and without their consent to a government that exercises authority within a territorial sovereign entity of their own. "The six wars with the Arabs created a situation in which 3 million Jews came to control territories that contained nearly 2 million Arabs," scholar John G. Stoessinger observed in his 2001 book, *Why Nations Go to War.* The United Nations General Assembly also concluded that without "full respect for and the realization of these inalienable rights of the Palestinian people," namely the right to self-determination and the right to national independence and sovereignty, there would be no resolution of the question of Palestine.

Statehood implies the capacity to maintain certain rights and the performance of specific duties. Berlyn maintains that even if the Palestinians were granted their own state they would not live up to the duties of a state because a Palestinian State would be committed to the destruction of Israel and would merely serve as a base for further acts of terror. In her estimation a Palestinian State would not respect the territorial integrity and sovereignty of the State of Israel. Furthermore, she even questions the ability of such a state to be able to fulfill the requirements of statehood, including civic and economic development and the promotion of human rights. Fundamentally such a negative assessment rests on conjecture and an underlying sense of distrust born of conflicting claims of legitimacy to the same parcel of land.

No one can claim to profess the future, and not even Berlyn can with any certainty predict the actions of a State of Palestine, much less characterize an entire people as terrorists. One thing does however appear to be foreseeable, and that is the continued agitation of the Palestinians for recognition, self-determination and legitimacy. As Professor Stoessinger concluded in *Why Nations Go to War,* "The shock inflicted on the Arab consciousness by the establishment of Israel and the resulting homelessness of a million native Palestinians grew more, rather than less, acute as Arab nationalism gathered momentum." The Arabs perceive Israel as the ever-expanding and ever-growing threat to their survival, thus a state is the only way to insure their continued existence as a people. Declaring that a Palestinian State would be unable to fulfill the requirements of statehood is merely a thinly veiled ethnocentric critique, which smacks of patronization and cultural superiority. What precisely do the Palestinians lack that would deem them ill suited to exercise self-rule and incapable of founding a government that rests on consent which would secure their rights to life, liberty and property? The Lockean assertion that the only legitimate form of government is that which rests on consent is as true for the Jews as the Arabs of Palestine.

Equivalence and Justice

Israel feels exposed and vulnerable as a direct result of the Palestinians unrelenting quest for legitimacy and recognition. Israel's economic strength and military power dwarfs that of the Palestinians, yet despite all of the material aspects of power, the Israeli quest for security remains more elusive than ever. Berlyn's arguments reiterate the mantra that Israel will never be secure unless the Palestinians are erased via absorption into neighboring Arab states. The very existence of the Palestinians serves as a constant reminder of the ongoing exclusionary colonization practices carried out in furtherance of Israel's quest for ethnic and religious homogeneity. Thus a case can be made that Israel ultimately wishes to expunge the Palestinians and obliterate any traces of their existence.

However, Israel's self-interest may ultimately rest with the establishment of a separate Palestinian state in order to diffuse the longstanding animosities and hatreds that have arisen between the two peoples. Walid Khalidi, in a 1978 article in *Foreign Affairs*, forcefully argued that a sovereign Palestinian state would end their "anonymous ghost-like existence as a non-people" because their own state could serve as "a point of reference, a national anchorage, a center of hope and achievement." We have seen where the denial of legitimacy has taken us, and it has not nurtured the seeds of peace. In a spasm of frustration in January 2006 the Palestinians elected a Hamas-dominated leadership to the Palestinian Legislative Council. In a setting in which all of the really significant political decisions are made by Israel, moderation has no chance to prevail when desperation is the defining attribute of life itself within the occupied territories. Peace can only be established in the wake of the recognition of legitimacy and equality between the two peoples.

Berlyn offers us 12 justifications why a Palestinian state is a bad idea; however, the Palestinian case rests on only one singular point; that justice demands equivalence. In order to secure the national character and the cultural identity of the Israelis, the national character and the cultural identity of the Palestinian Arabs must likewise be secured. This can only occur with the establishment of a separate, sovereign Palestinian State.

POSTSCRIPT

Would It Be an Error to Establish a Palestinian State?

To learn more about the history of the current conflict between Jews and Palestinian Arabs, consult Bernard Wasserstein, *Israelis and Palestinians: Why Do They Fight? Can They Stop?* 3rd ed. (Yale University Press, 2008). A somewhat critical view of Israel's position is former President Jimmy Carter's *Palestine: Peace Not Apartheid* (Simon & Schuster, 2006), a book that evoked a spirited response by Alan Dershowitz in *The Case Against Israel's Enemies: Exposing Jimmy Carter and Others Who Stand in the Way of Peace* (Wiley, 2008).

Complicating matters for Israel is the fact that the country is divided between relatively secular Jews, who tend to be moderate in their attitudes toward the Palestinians, and Orthodox Jews, who regard the areas in dispute as land given by God to the Jewish nation and who regard giving up the West Bank and, especially, any part of Jerusalem as sacrilege. Furthermore, some 200,000 Israelis live in the West Bank, and removing them would be traumatic for Israel. The issue is also a matter of grave security concern. The Jews have suffered mightily throughout history; repeated Arab terrorism represents the latest of their travails. It is arguable that the Jews can be secure only in their own country and that the West Bank (which cuts Israel almost in two) is crucial to Israeli security. If an independent Palestine centered in the West Bank is created, Israel will face a defense nightmare, especially if new hostilities with the Palestinians occur. Additional material on a prospective Palestinian state is available in Robert E. Hunter, *Building a Successful Palestinian State* (Rand, 2006).

Thus, for the Israelis the "land for peace" choice is a difficult one. Some Israelis are unwilling to cede any of what they consider the land of ancient Israel. Other Israelis would be willing to swap land for peace, but they doubt that the Palestinians would be assuaged. Still other Israelis think that the risk is worth the potential prize: peace.

Palestinians do not march in political lockstep any more than do Israelis. Indeed, there has been serious tension and even fighting between Fatah, the more moderate Palestinian faction led by Palestinian National Authority Mahmoud Abbas, and the more militant group Hamas, which the United States considers a terrorist organization. Further complicating matters, Israel's government has been somewhat unstable in recent years. The failure of the intervention in Lebanon left him very unpopular in Israel. Charges of corruption have also dogged Olmert, and although an official investigation found insufficient evidence to prosecute him, he was weakened. In 2008, he announced he would step down. In Palestinian-Israeli relations do not exist in a vacuum, and actions like the Hamas kidnapping of two Israeli Symbolic of the turmoil in the region, the Palestinian National Authority used to have a Web site, but it no longer operates. However, one source of the viewpoint of Palestinians is the Palestine Media Center at http://www.palestine-pmc.com/. The government of Israel's home page is at http://www.gov.il/firstgov/english. The United States has tried to encourage peace in the area, but U.S. leverage is constrained, as related in Douglas Sturkey, *The Limits of American Power: Prosecuting a Middle East Peace* (Edward Elgar, 2007).

ISSUE 8

Should All Foreign Troops Soon Leave Iraq?

YES: Lawrence B. Wilkerson, from Testimony during Hearings on "Iraq: Alternative Strategies in a Post-Surge Environment," before the Subcommittee on Oversight and Investigations, Committee on Armed Services, U.S. House of Representatives (January 23, 2008)

NO: Michael Eisenstadt, from Testimony during Hearings on "Iraq: Alternative Strategies in a Post-Surge Environment," before the Subcommittee on Oversight and Investigations, Committee on Armed Services, U.S. House of Representatives (January 23, 2008)

ISSUE SUMMARY

YES: Lawrence B. Wilkerson, the Pamela C. Harriman Visiting Professor of Government and Public Policy at the College of William and Mary and formerly chief of staff to Secretary of State Colin Powell, tells Congress that most U.S. forces in Iraq should be quickly withdrawn because they are poorly positioned to protect U.S. interests and are exacerbating the antagonisms that make it difficult to defeat terrorism.

NO: Michael Eisenstadt, a senior fellow and director of The Washington Institute's Military and Security Studies Program, contends that there is no doubt that the surge of U.S. forces into Iraq in 2007 has dramatically improved the security environment in Iraq, and that too rapid a withdrawal would reverse the gains that have been made.

In August 1990 after Iraq overran Kuwait, President George H. W. Bush sent U.S. troops to protect Saudi Arabia. A UN resolution demanding that Iraq withdraw and authorizing UN members to use force if necessary to free Iraq soon followed. When Iraq refused to withdraw, a U.S.-led attack in January 1991 quickly defeated Iraqi forces. In the aftermath, huge stocks of Iraqi chemical weapons were uncovered, and as part of the peace terms, the Security Council barred Iraq from possessing, producing, or seeking to acquire any weapons of mass destruction (WMDs) and required that Iraq give UN arms inspectors unhindered access to ensure that Iraq was complying. During the following dozen years, a cat-and-mouse game ensued. Iraq claimed to be complying but often blocked or delayed UN inspections, and in 1998, it even expelled the inspectors. In response, economic sanctions continued, and there were periodic attacks by U.S. warplanes and cruise missiles under President Bill Clinton. The U.S. attitude hardened even more once George W. Bush became president, especially after the terrorist attacks of September 11, 2001. In Iraq, UN inspectors found no hard evidence of Iraqi WMDs, but they also reported repeated barriers to their inspections. In this tense atmosphere, the U.S. Congress authorized (October 2002) the use of U.S. force against Iraq if necessary, but the UN Security Council would not do so. Frustrated and claiming that intelligence reports indicated that Iraq was seeking to acquire nuclear weapons and supporting terrorism, President Bush in March 2003 demanded that Saddam Hussein and his sons leave the country and that Iraqi forces surrender their arms. Iraq refused, and another U.S.-led invasion ensued.

Iraq's forces were soon vanquished, but securing the peace proved much more difficult. No WMDs were ever found. Terrorist-style operations began against occupying U.S. and other coalition troops, civilians, and anyone, including Iraqis, who cooperated with them. American troop casualties mounted, and by the end of 2006, more than 3,000 had died. Americans were also frustrated by the cost of the war, which by that time was nearing $300 billion. Also disheartening to many Americans was the fact that trying to bring Iraqis together proved maddening. The country was divided between warring groups, including two Arab Muslim denominations, the Shiites and the Sunnis, and the Kurds, who are of non-Arab Muslims denomination. Amid all this, public opinion had turned decidedly against the war, and anti-war feeling was a key factor in the Republicans' electoral disaster in 2006 and their loss of control in Congress.

Amid tremendous political pressure to begin a U.S. withdrawal, President Bush did the opposite. He announced in January 2007 that he would send a "surge" of more than 20,000 additional U.S. troops into Iraq to bolster U.S. chances there. In a televised speech from the Oval Office, the president told Americans that their country was now "engaged in a new struggle that will set the course for a new century," and he assured them, "We can, and we will, prevail." The congressional hearings from which the following two readings are drawn took place a year after President Bush ordered the surge. In the first reading, Lawrence B. Wilkerson says that it was absurd to think that only an additional few brigades of troops could make a major difference, that the situation in Iraq is still a quagmire, and that a quick U.S. withdrawal would be the wisest course. Taking the opposite side, Michael Eisenstadt points to a number of positive signs, including a significant drop in the U.S. casualty rate, and argues that the surge has made a difference, and that the United States can achieve its goals in Iraq if holds steady.

YES

Lawrence B. Wilkerson

Iraq: Alternative Strategies in a Post-Surge Environment

I've been watching Iraq closely since 1990 when I served as Special Assistant to the Chairman of the Joint Chiefs of Staff and we were all, I will have to admit, bowled over by Saddam Hussein's invasion of Kuwait in August of that year.

I recall vividly sitting up very late one night in the Pentagon, smoking a cigar with Colonel Tom White—later Secretary of the Army but then Executive Assistant to the Chairman—and pouring over the map of the "left-hook" that General [Norman] Schwarzkopf was getting ready to execute in the western desert and, together, Tom and I trying to predict the number of U.S. casualties that would result. Thankfully, we were off by a considerable amount. Neither of us at the time realized how significantly the eight long, bloody and bitter years of war with Iran had decimated the Iraqi Army and the country's infrastructure.

I recount this short history simply to inform you that when, as chief of staff of the State Department in 2002–2003 when the U.S. once again contemplated war with Iraq, I was not exactly a newcomer to this business. In fact, in the intervening years, I had made a study of Iraq for educational purposes as I helped to lead the U.S. Marine Corps War College in its efforts to educate a new generation of joint leaders in our armed forces, and, later, as I continued to work for Colin Powell as an advisor and consultant. It is enough to say that Saddam Hussein was a much-studied man. Perhaps too studied, as later some of us in this country came to believe that we knew him better than we did, particularly with regard to his possession of weapons of mass destruction.

Now he's gone from the scene in Iraq and many of us, including I expect you and the members of this committee, are trying to estimate what may follow him, for surely something or someone will and just as surely it will not be a continued American or coalition occupation. Note I said "estimate" and not "determine". One thing I've learned conclusively about Iraq is that the best we can do is estimate. In the vernacular, of course, that means "guess".

But before I add my guess to the pile, let me make a few brief comments about why we are in a slightly better position today in Iraq than prevailed in 2004, 2005 and 2006, or even early 2007. That better situation has come about largely in conjunction with the so-called surge and not because of it. To believe that the equivalent of two small divisions of troops—or five or six combat

U.S. House of Representatives, January 23, 2008.

brigades in the new military lexicon—could make a significant difference in a country of some twenty-seven and a half million people, or even in the city of Baghdad or the province of al-Anbar, is to believe in pipe dreams.

Moreover, to recognize this reality and to acknowledge what actual confluence of circumstances has in fact caused the situation to improve, is essential to making a good guess about what may be coming in Iraq in the future.

One of the most significant reasons violence in Iraq has abated somewhat is that [militant Shiite religious leader] Moqtada al-Sadr has gone to ground. The strongman most likely to have replaced Saddam Hussein had we left the country very soon after our invasion in 2003—what the Secretary of Defense at the time, Donald Rumsfeld and his cohorts wanted to do—was not Ahmad Chalabi as they wished and planned for. Chalabi may have lasted a few weeks or even months but eventually Moqtada al-Sadr, or someone who looked very much like him, would have risen to power. My pick would be the man himself, al-Sadr.

And today, his decision to more or less go to ground and to take his militia with him, the most powerful militia in Iraq, has been one of the significant factors leading to the reduction in violence and the modicum of stability that currently exists in Iraq. (Moqtada al-Sadr's recent statement that he may revisit this decision soon and re-enter the fray in Iraq is, therefore, very disquieting.)

Likewise, the decision of many Sunni leaders in key areas to place their operations and their support in line with coalition tactical objectives and to take arms and undergo training in order to do this, has contributed majorly to this improved situation. In addition, the combat operations that started well before the surge, particularly in the most terrorist- and insurgent-infested areas, were remarkably successful in rooting out al-Qa'ida remnants and putting a high premium on continued insurgent operations, this latter particularly the case when Sunni tribal leaders began to realize that money, arms, and training could be had if they "changed their ways". As Andrew Bacevich suggested in the *Outlook Section* of Sunday's *Washington Post*, these Sunni leaders decided for the time being that money and arms and awaiting more propitious times was a better plan than continuing the current fight.

And we must not fail to mention the war-weariness of the general Iraqi population, as testified to most dramatically by the exodus of some two-plus million Iraqis into Jordan and Syria primarily and the displacement within Iraq of an almost similar number of citizens without the wherewithal or means to escape.

And we must not forget that by the time of the surge, most of the significant ethnic cleansing that had been going on in Iraq had been completed and had accomplished the purposes of the largely Shiite groups that were perpetrating it. So, we might say that Iraq had reached a sort of weird equilibrium when the surge occurred and that General [David H.] Petraeus [commander of coalition forces in Iraq] was astute enough to recognize this, as was Ambassador Ryan Crocker, and between the two of them, with a new and much more effective set of military tactics and a far better approach to letting the Iraqis do much of the heavy-lifting, they began to widen and expand the stability and reduction in violence that was already occurring. This is a good development, of course, but it has hardly proven its sustainability. Nor has it eliminated major violence or large numbers of deaths in Iraq, as the last few days have amply demonstrated.

What it has done is helped the current administration to implement what was its fundamental decision with regard to Iraq earlier in 2007, and that was to pass the problem of Iraq to the new administration. Admittedly, the Bush Administration wants to pass Iraq on with as many encumbrances as possible so that the new administration will be bound by certain restraints and will have to continue some of the old administration's policies; but the success or failure of that attempt will in large measure be decided here in the corridors of this Congress as much as on the battlefields of Iraq.

I have had people in Iraq since the invasion—some of whom I put there, others who Secretary of Defense [Donald] Rumsfeld put there but who communicated with me nonetheless, still others who Secretary of State Powell put there. These people have worked in the Iraqi ministries, in the Multi-National Security Transition Command (MINSTICI), in the U.S. embassy group, the U.S. Marine Corps, the U.S. Air Force, the U.S. Army, and elsewhere. My son, a USAF captain, was just in Iraq, in Kirkuk, working with the Third Iraqi Air Force for six months. Such people have kept me fully apprised of what is happening there and I am infinitely grateful to them because in many cases they have been in grave danger on a number of occasions and my hat is off to their bravery, courage, and daring in trying to make some sense out of a situation and bring some coherence to U.S. operations when leadership from Washington was so utterly lacking. At the end of the day, it is somewhat unbelievable to me, a veteran of Vietnam and of three decades under the Pentagon's aegis, that Washington first so badly micro-managed the war in Iraq that we were doomed to fail and, then, as if in horrible recognition of this fact, completely relinquished control and allowed a vacuum of leadership to develop that was just as bad. General Petraeus and Ambassador Crocker represent the first real leadership that America has exercised in its use of the military and diplomatic instruments to achieve political objectives in Iraq. That alone is reason to damn this administration a thousand times over.

In fact, it becomes clear that Ambassador Barbara Bodine—the "mayor of Baghdad", as she became known at the time—was correct when she intimated that, in the beginning, just after the toppling of the statue in Baghdad, experts such as she knew that there were 500 ways to get things wrong in post-invasion Iraq and perhaps two or three ways to get things right. What was not known was that the U.S. would try all 500 of the wrong ways before it would stumble onto one of the right ways.

I've also remained in contact with Iraq's very capable ambassador to the U.S., Samir Sumayda'ie, who as you know was Minister of the Interior for Iraq early-on, and I have valued his counsel as well with regard to what is happening in his much-troubled country. Our most recent conversation took place as he visited the campus at William and Mary, where I teach.

Again, I relate these matters to you and to your committee members so that you are aware that what I am saying is not my punditry or surmise but what I have gleaned from some very talented people doing very difficult jobs.

What follows, however, is indeed my surmise for I'm not certain any of my contacts in Iraq—or perhaps even Ambassador Sumayda'ie—would be able to or want to make such characterizations and predictions as I am about to indulge in.

First, I want to talk geostrategically for a moment or two. We—the United States—have major and abiding interests in the Middle East. These include, but are not limited to, the flow of oil through the region's pipelines and through the Strait of Hormuz [between Oman and Iran, the exit/entry to the Persian Gulf] and the security of the state of Israel. The latter is no longer a vital strategic interest in the sense that Israel is an unsinkable aircraft carrier in a region endangered by a superpower with an expansive strategy, but it is an important interest because America and Israel are joined at the hip—if for no other reason than Jewish Americans form a very powerful political lobby in this country. In my view there are other reasons than that one, not the least of which is that Israel is a democracy and that we and Israel have ideological connections as well.

In addition to oil and Israel, there are other very important U.S. interests. For example, there is Turkey and our strategic relationship with that potentially very powerful Muslim country—a relationship that was on the rocks until very recently because of the ineptitude of the Bush administration but lately has been recovering due to some hard work on the part of Secretaries [of Defense Robert] Gates and [State Condoleezza] Rice; there is Lebanon and what that country means to the stability of the eastern Mediterranean; and there are the relationships with Saudi Arabia, Egypt and others.

Currently with about 160,000 U.S. troops on Iraqi soil, we are poorly-positioned to protect these very important interests. Moreover, we are exacerbating the antagonisms that make our challenge to defeat the terrorists who wish us harm so difficult. For example, by having so many U.S. boots on Arab soil, we make it extremely difficult to energize the moderate Muslim world—a world we seriously need if we are to defeat these terrorists.

We need to re-position our forces. We need them to be over-the-horizon in carrier battle groups and amphibious ready groups, in pre-positioned stocks in key areas, and participating in critical exercises with Gulf Cooperation Council (GCC) countries and others in the region—not permanently deployed to and tied down in Iraq. This situation must cause Admiral William J. Fallon [commander, U.S. Central Command] to pull out his hair nightly as he contemplates how badly deployed his forces are to protect America's real interests in the region. I served from 1984 to 1987 as Executive Assistant to Rear Admiral Stewart Ring who was then the J5 [political-military affairs officer] for, first, Admiral William Crowe and, later, Admiral Ron Hays as USCINCPACs [U.S. commander-in-chief Pacific]—back when it was permissible to call these good men "commanders in chief." I know of what I speak.

Now, let me relate this very brief geostrategic analysis to the purpose of this hearing—alternative strategies for Iraq in the post-surge environment. I think you can see where I'm headed.

We need to reposition our forces to protect our real interests in the Middle East and to better our position in the war against those terrorists such as al-Qa'ida who wish us harm.

And incidentally, when we are long gone from Iraq there will be no al-Qa'ida presence there, just as there was no al-Qa'ida presence there when we invaded. This is because the Iraqi people—Sunni, Shia, Kurd of either religious persuasion, Turcoman, Christian, or other ethnic or religious grouping—will not tolerate an al-Qa'ida presence in their country.

Because of this need to reposition our forces, it is imperative that we not remain embroiled in Iraq. It is also imperative that we remove substantial numbers of our ground forces from Iraq because our ground forces are on the verge of self-destructing. It is both a source of amusement and chagrin to me that, for example, while General George Casey was in Iraq he could not admit to this fact but now that he is Chief of Staff of my beloved Army he has discovered it. I fear that over the past seven years the uniformed leadership in our Army in many instances has proven itself very nearly as incompetent as the civilian leadership above and around it.

How do we accomplish this down-sizing and departure without jeopardizing the modicum of stability that has come to Iraq of late? In short, how do we leave Iraq in some semblance of order—particularly if what I've said about the Sunnis is true and they are simply waiting until we depart before they use our arms and our training to begin anew their struggle for a return to power against the Shiites?

It ain't gonna be easy—that's the first reality in my view. But, that said and admitted, I believe it can be done; indeed, as I've highlighted it *must* be done.

Over the course of the next two years, starting as soon as possible but no later than this summer, we must start withdrawing our forces from Iraq. We need to do this carefully, slowly, and in accordance with a withdrawal plan that has what we in the military used to call "branches and sequels". In layman's terms you may refer to them as plan B's, offshoots, or on- and off-ramps. In essence, branches and sequels are designed to exploit a sudden and perhaps unexpected success or to hedge against a similarly sudden and unexpected failure or adverse development.

Of these possible developments, the most dire situation would be a planned withdrawal that, once the bulk of the troops were withdrawn, abruptly turned into what the military calls a withdrawal under pressure, i.e., a fighting withdrawal. I don't envision that happening but we should have a plan for it nonetheless. That plan would envision all remaining forces leaving Iraq in 60–90 days, executing non-combatant evacuation (NEO) operations from the over-built complex that is our embassy in Baghdad, as well as from elsewhere in Iraq, and leaving in Iraq—with the Iraqi military and police forces or destroyed in place—what remained of the heavy equipment and facilities that we have in typical American fashion built-up over the last few years in Iraq. An interesting wrinkle here would be how the thousands upon thousands of contractors in Iraq would escape. I don't believe we have given much thought to that, nor have the contractors themselves—just as we neglected giving any thought to a Status of Forces Agreement with the Iraqis that would cover contractor crimes and misadventures in Iraq. But, as I said, this planning for a withdrawal under pressure is just good contingency planning and not something I envision being necessary. Unlike Vietnam in 1975, in Iraq there is no large, capable and battle-hardened conventional army waiting to invade. But we must remember: in Iraq, anything is possible.

The most likely context for our withdrawal will be a relatively peaceful one because those who would most likely interfere with it—the Sunni insurgents—are largely co-opted at this point for whatever reason. And therein lies the rub.

If the Sunnis are indeed converts to the American way, if they are committed to a unified Iraq, however imperfectly conceived, and convinced that workable and acceptable power-sharing arrangements are in place and that their rights as the largest minority in Iraq will be reasonably looked after, then the withdrawal will not lead to an even more vigorous civil war than what we've witnessed so far. In short, a fair amount of security, stability, and in that context, economic progress, will be possible. Iraq will muddle through, U.S. forces will be largely repositioned, regional forces in Iraq will rise to the forefront of the power management structure—centered of course in the north, the center, and the south—and a largely feckless national government will be tolerated until another strong man comes along to challenge the status quo and consolidate power once again in Baghdad, the most likely ultimate result in Iraq. But the U.S. will be gone, our true interests in the region will be once again reasonably secure, and coalition troops and Iraqi citizens will not be dying in the high numbers of recent years.

On the other hand, if key Sunni leaders are just biding their time and undergoing the training, taking the arms, building the formal infrastructure to eventually—once coalition forces are gone—strike at the Shiites and recover what they believe to be their rightful place in Iraq (and with ample financial and even manpower support from the Saudis in the process), then we have the same outcome for the U.S. but a very different situation in Iraq. In fact, we have an even bloodier civil war than the one we've experienced for the past several years.

The salient question then becomes—as sometimes we forget was the same question in Vietnam in 1975—does the U.S., with whatever remnants of the coalition that can be mustered, go back in?

My answer to that question is a resounding "no."

Instead, we let one of the parties in the resulting civil war win.

Through diplomacy and an exquisite mixture of hard and soft power we then try to come to some accommodation with the new power structure in Iraq. At worst, due to the power dynamics in the Persian Gulf, we will have not a warm but a tolerable relationship. At best, we will have a reasonable if not warm relationship. More importantly, the U.S. will have returned to a far better strategic position with respect to its genuine interests in the region and will no longer be exacerbating its struggle with jihadist terrorists by having an enormous American presence on Arab soil.

There are two other very vital components of these potential outcomes that I must mention: the Israeli-Palestinian situation and Iran. Let me close by briefly explaining why.

First, Iran.   Iran is the hegemon of the Persian Gulf. We recognized this when we helped orchestrate the overthrow of the first democratically-elected government in the history of Persia, led by Mohamad Mossadegh, in 1953. We installed the Shah and he was in power for 26 years and was, so to speak, our hegemon. When the oil crisis of 1973 struck and oil prices soared, then National Security Advisor Henry Kissinger and his president, Richard Nixon, sold more than $20B worth of arms to the Shah to keep him "our hegemon" and to try to offset some of the huge transfer of wealth that was occurring in the direction of the oil-producing states of the Middle East.

The "our hegemon" part changed in 1979 when the Shah was overthrown. But the hegemon part stayed the same—as geography, demography, and military power tend to stay the same—though we have tried to deny it for almost 30 years. We tried to build up Iraq to counter Iran, but as the bloody Iraq-Iran war demonstrated, Iraq without our help could not stand up to Iran. The reason is clear: Iran is the regional hegemon because Iran is more powerful than any other country, period.

Israel, were it in a different geographical situation, could compete, particularly because Israel is a nuclear power (another reason why Iran wants a nuclear weapon of course), but we cannot simply slice Israel away from the Mediterranean and plop it down in Oman next to the Gulf.

Iran has more people, more territory, better organization, a more nationalistic people, and frankly far superior armed forces than any other Gulf power. Again, let me repeat the reality: for all the strategic, geographic, demographic, and power reasons one declares such things, Iran is the hegemon in the Persian Gulf.

Ironically, by invading Iraq in 2003 and introducing barely-controlled chaos onto its territory, we destroyed what balance of power there was in the Gulf, largely between Iran and Iraq, and we did so to the overwhelming advantage of the real regional hegemon, Iran. Today, our presence on the ground in Iraq is the only thing keeping the scales from tilting dramatically toward Iran.

So, when we withdraw from Iraq we need to get over our strategic myopia and passionate hatred for the government in Teheran, act more like George Washington than George Bush, and in parallel with our slow, careful withdrawal from Iraq negotiate a very much-improved and increasingly amicable relationship with the Gulf's true hegemon, Iran.

That would be the best of all possible solutions; however, if that proves impossible—and so far we have not even tried—we have even more urgent reason to reposition our forces in the region because they will remain the "balancer" of power in the Gulf and they must be far more flexible and agile to do that. They are anything but flexible and agile while they are largely stuck in Iraq.

In addition to an improved U.S.-Iran relationship, key to any realization of a more stable, more peaceful and ultimately more prosperous Middle East, is a final settlement to the Israeli-Palestinian situation. I had the pleasure of recently dining with a current member of the Israeli legislature, the Knesset. He asked me how it was that the present administration finally, after seven long and painful years, has apparently arrived at this epiphany. You don't want to hear the answer I gave him.

It is well beyond time that the entire leadership in this country, here in the Congress and over there in the White House, not only recognized this reality but put considerable energy, time, and power into bringing about a final solution that addresses borders, settlements, right of return, Jerusalem, and two states—two *politically, economically and security-wise viable states*—living side by side, Israel and Palestine.

All bets are off for any workable, effective, sustainable solution to a post-surge, post-withdrawal Iraq, if strong, parallel and ultimately successful efforts to resolve this issue of Israel and Palestine are not forthcoming. Moreover—and this is very crucial—if in the process of working toward a final solution the majority of the people on both sides, Israelis and Palestinians, do not believe that the U.S., Israel, and the Palestinians are genuinely serious and committed to a solution, all bets are off too. That is why what Dr. Rice and President Bush started at Annapolis in late November of last year is so important and so connected to everything else in the Middle East, including post-surge Iraq. The least important aspect of this Annapolis process is lining up all the Arab states against Iran—which I fear may be the principal objective of the Bush administration. Let me say again: the most important aspect is bringing about a final solution to the Israeli-Palestinian problem as speedily as possible.

Michael Eisenstadt  **NO**

Iraq: Alternative Strategies in a Post-Surge Environment

There is no longer any doubt that the security environment in Iraq has improved dramatically in the past six months. Understanding how this came about is key to assessing U.S. post-surge options in Iraq.

Dramatically Improved Security

After violence in Iraq hit all-time highs in late 2006 and early 2007, attacks on and casualties among Iraqi civilians, Iraqi Security Forces (ISF), and Coalition forces are down more than 60 percent. A combination of factors accounts for this dramatic development:

- *The Sunni Arab Tribal Awakening.* The extreme ideology and brutal tactics of al-Qaida in Iraq (AQI), and the threat it posed to more mainstream Islamo-nationalist insurgent groups, as well as to traditional tribal power structures and economic interests, eventually engendered a backlash in the form of an anti-AQI tribal uprising in the largely Sunni Arab regions of Iraq. The principal manifestation of this backlash was the creation of various tribal "Awakening Councils" in Anbar province and elsewhere. While this development predated the surge, the latter gave additional impetus to this trend, particularly after Coalition forces started working, in about June 2007, with local tribal elements to create armed Concerned Local Citizen (CLC) groups to fight AQI. Because many CLC members had worked previously with AQI as facilitators or co-belligerents, they knew the local AQI members, and were therefore able, with the help of Coalition forces, to root them out and roll up their networks.
- *The Surge.* The commitment of five additional Brigade Combat Teams to Iraq in tandem with a parallel surge by Iraqi Security Forces, enabled Coalition forces to not only "clear," but also to "hold" areas that they had been unable to hold previously due to the paucity of forces on the ground. Coalition forces set up 68 combat outposts and joint security stations throughout Baghdad, permitting them to maintain a 24 hour presence throughout the capital—conveying in the most dramatic way possible the U.S. commitment to protecting the civilian population. One of the benefits of this new approach was a torrent of fresh intelligence from the civilian population concerning AQI. Coalition forces

U.S. House of Representatives, January 23, 2008.

have pursued AQI relentlessly, killing many, and forcing their remnants to go to ground, or to flee to Ninawa and Diyala provinces where they are attempting to regroup.

- *Taking on Shiite Militias.* Coalition forces have also taken on Iranian-supported "special groups" that targeted Coalition forces, and have sought to roll up Mahdi Army/Jaysh al-Mahdi (JAM) cells engaged in sectarian cleansing in various neighborhoods of Baghdad. After clashes between JAM cells [Shiite militia force, Jaish al Mahdi] and ISF units in Karbala in August 2007, Muqtada Sadr stood down the JAM in order to clean house and consolidate control over an organization that was fragmenting, that was increasingly unresponsive to central direction, and that had alienated the movement's popular support base. Coalition forces have tried to exploit this growing alienation between JAM and its popular base by attempting to establish tribal "Awakening Councils" and CLC groups in largely Shiite regions of Iraq.
- *Diminished Flow of Foreign Fighters.* Syria and Iran have contributed greatly to the violence in Iraq: the former by serving as a conduit for foreign fighters, the latter as a training base for Shiite militias and as a supplier of arms and advanced IEDs [improvised explosive devices] for these groups. Though small in number, foreign fighters are a combat multiplier for the insurgents, as a significant proportion of them end up as suicide bombers. As a result, they have had had an impact out of all proportion to their numbers. Recently, however, the number of foreign jihadists [Muslim religious fighters] entering Iraq from Syria has decreased, due at least in part to efforts by Syria and the countries of origin to stanch the flow of foreign fighters. There has also been some speculation that Iran has reduced the flow of EFP [explosively formed projectiles/penetrators: a shaped charge designed to penetrate armor] components and bombs to Iraq recently, though Coalition commanders are emphatic in asserting that Iran continues to train and fund the so-called "special groups" operating in Iraq.

In sum, the improved security situation can be attributed to a sustained effort to neutralize the main drivers of the escalating civil violence in Iraq prior to the surge—AQI suicide bombings on the one hand, and JAM cells engaged in revenge killings and ethnic cleansing on the other. By capturing or killing the members of these organizations, and thereby disrupting their operations, the Coalition was able to break what previously appeared to be a self-sustaining cycle of civil violence. In this, the Coalition was assisted greatly by its new alliance of convenience with Sunni Arab tribal elements that included in their ranks former anti-Coalition insurgents, and the decision of the Sadr organization to temporarily halt military operations.

Several policy-relevant conclusions can be drawn from this experience: 1) while the U.S. presence may have stoked insurgent violence in Iraq between 2003–2006, the U.S. is, for now, a force for stability; 2) while some violence in Iraq is undoubtedly the product of random and revenge killings, it is for the most part, neither spontaneous nor self-sustaining; rather, violence is used in an instrumental fashion by armed groups whose activities can be disrupted and whose decision calculus can be influenced by various military and non-military means.

These conclusions have a direct bearing on the prospects for improving security and achieving local accommodations (if not national reconciliation) in Iraq. At the same time, it must be stressed, Iraq is still a fairly violent place; there are still large numbers of Iraqis committed to pursuing their goals by violent means. And needless to say, should the groups that have halted attacks on Coalition forces and the ISF decide to resume these operations, the security situation in Iraq could very quickly take a turn for the worse.

Preserving Recent Gains

The immediate challenge faced by Coalition forces in Iraq is how to preserve recent security gains in the face of a pending U.S. drawdown, as the surge comes to an end. Has the security environment changed in such a way that it is unlikely to be affected by the drawdown? Or is violence likely to spike as the surge comes to an end?

Ultimately, there is no way to answer this question with any degree of confidence. Iraq continues to confound even experienced observers, so it would be prudent to plan for both pleasant and unpleasant surprises. However, given continuing levels of violence, it is reasonable to assume that groups still engaged in violence will seek, and likely find new opportunities to act, as the surge comes to an end. There are a number of other developments, moreover, that could complicate the security situation; it is vital to nip these developments in the bud (if possible), or to be prepared to deal with them should they come to pass. These include:

- The defeat of AQI leads to the collapse of the tribal coalitions underpinning the various "awakening" movements, leading to infighting among rival tribes, or a resumption of anti-Coalition violence by tribal and insurgent militias;
- Tensions over influence and access to resources between the various tribal awakening movements, and the Sunni Arab parliamentary parties erupts into violence;
- Muqtada Sadr opts not to renew his order to JAM to stand down, resulting in the resumption of attacks on Sunni Arab civilians and militias, Coalition forces, and rival Shiite parties and militias;
- Intermittent violence among various Shiite movements and parties or between various Shiite movements and the ISF expands in scope and intensity;
- Simmering tensions around Kirkuk deriving from Kurdish demands for a referendum over the city's future (as called for in Article 140 of the Iraqi Constitution) explode into open violence involving Kurds, Arabs, Turkmen, and other groups;
- Turkey and/or Iran intensify military operations against expatriate Kurdish separatist groups based in northern Iraq;
- Returning internally displaced persons (IDPs) or refugees resort to violence to evict squatters from their homes, or are met by violence upon their return, reigniting sectarian violence in previously "cleansed" neighborhoods or communities.

Some of these developments would have only local consequences. Others could have far-reaching implications for stability and security in large parts of Iraq. Dealing with these ongoing problems and potential challenges will require the active involvement of the Iraqi government, and the sustained engagement of U.S. military and diplomatic personnel, as well as the President of the United States.

In some cases, the political process already offers the means to deal with these problems (for instance, new provincial elections could reduce tensions between the de facto tribal leadership and established elected politicians in predominantly Sunni Arab regions of Arab). In others, new mechanisms will have to be devised to deal with the problem (such as that of returning IDPs and refugees). Much will depend on the success of the Iraqi Security Forces in taking up the slack as the U.S. draws down, and on the political savvy and negotiating skills of Iraqi politicians and U.S. diplomats.

A Growing Role for Coalition Air Power

The U.S. also has to prepare for the possibility that as it draws down, violence might flare up again. Under such circumstances, it will probably not be feasible, for political and/or military reasons, to recommit large numbers of ground forces. For this reason, the U.S. will likely become increasingly reliant on air power, in conjunction with residual U.S., and Iraqi ground forces, to respond to future contingencies. Increased emphasis, therefore, need be put on improving U.S.-Iraqi air-ground coordination—if this is not being done already, and on employing tactics, techniques, and procedures developed for targeting terrorists from the air, against insurgents, sectarian militias, and warlords. While Coalition airpower can backstop the ISF on a stopgap basis, it is ultimately not a substitute for effective Iraqi ground forces.

Toward a Political Solution

Assuming that security gains of recent months can be preserved, the next challenge is to translate these gains into political achievements. Experience elsewhere shows that the factors that make an inconclusive insurgency or civil war ripe for settlement often include: (1) a military stalemate that leads both sides to conclude that they cannot achieve their objectives by violent means; (2) an emerging consensus among the belligerents over the terms of a settlement; and (3) authoritative leaders capable of speaking and negotiating on behalf of their respective constituencies. These conditions are not currently present in Iraq, though there have been signs of progress toward fulfilling some of these conditions during the past year.

The Utility of Violence. Most Iraqis are weary of violence, though tactical adjustments by Sunni insurgent and Shiite militia leaders in the past year seems to derive more from the imperatives of organizational survival than from an assessment that they cannot achieve their goals by military means. Thus, many Sunni Arabs, fearing an AQI takeover of their communities and Iranian domination of Iraq, apparently concluded that they risked marginalization, or worse, if they did not cut a deal with the U.S. Doing so, however, has enabled them to weather the AQI challenge, and position themselves for possible future phases of conflict. Conversely, Muqtada Sadr, fearing the loss of control over his movement, ordered them to stand down in August while he sought to reassert control over his cadres. Recent news reports indicate that Sadr may be reconsidering his decision. It is not clear, however, how the arrest of hundreds of his followers in recent months have affected the military capabilities of JAM.

Consensus on Terms of Settlement. The political gap at the national level between many Sunnis and Shiites remains broad and deep. Many Sunni Arabs reject negotiations with a government that is the product of a foreign occupation, and composed of Iran-affiliated Shiite parties committed to consolidating their own primacy, though there has recently been signs of growing willingness on both sides to engage (e.g., the willingness of many CLC members to join the ISF, and recent complements by 'Abd al-'Aziz al-Hakim of the Supreme Islamic Iraqi Council [SIIC] concerning the CLCs). Major differences over key policy issues (e.g., oil, federalism, and implementation of the recently approved de-Baathification law) also remain. For instance, the Kurdish parties and SIIC support a loose form of federalism, while the Sadrists and most Sunni Arabs favor a strong unitary state.

Authoritative Leadership. While the Kurds seem to have transcended their internal divisions (at least for now), the Shiite and Sunni Arab communities remain bedeviled by internal divisions and lack authoritative leaders capable of speaking with a single voice or of negotiating on their behalf. If anything, the trend has been toward fragmentation of political and religious authority in both communities. In the Shiite camp, Prime Minister Nouri al-Maliki has been largely ineffective, Ayatollah 'Ali Hussein al-Sistani [Iraq's ranking Shiite cleric] proved unable to stem the slide toward sectarian violence, and Muqtada al-Sadr has not been able to control elements of JAM. Moreover, JAM and SIIC have been engaged in a bitter power struggle in the south (which sometimes has also involved the Fadhila Party); and in recent months, Coalition forces and ISF units (often police units associated with the SIIC) have detained or arrested hundreds of JAM members in Baghdad and the south, perhaps portending a shift in the balance of power in some parts of southern Iraq.

As for the Sunni Arabs, while many revile the current government, there is apparently growing support for joining the political process and for seeking employment by the ISF as a way of protecting the equities of the community. This has led to splits in the ranks of the Sunni Arab insurgency between those who embrace and reject politics (e.g., the reported split in the 1920 Revolution Brigades in March 2007), and splits in the broader community between de facto and elected leaders (e.g., the members of the various Awakening Councils, and the Iraqi Islamic Party). At the same time, there are signs that the possibility of a precipitous U.S. withdrawal has caused some Sunni Arab insurgent groups to come together, in order to preclude a self-destructive power struggle in the aftermath of such a possible eventuality (e.g., the formation of the Political Council of the Iraqi Resistance in October 2007, made up of six Islamist and nationalist insurgent groups).

Finally, events of recent months show that despite the trend toward fragmentation of authority at the national level, local leaders frequently retain sufficient influence to negotiate on behalf of their constituents. Thus, local accommodations may be possible in parts of Iraq, even if national reconciliation remains a distant, unattainable goal at this time. The failure to achieve national reconciliation in such a short timeframe should, however, come as no surprise: national reconciliation remains an elusive goal in other deeply divided societies (e.g., Yugoslavia, Lebanon, Afghanistan), and may take years, if not decades to achieve—if it is achieved at all.

Conclusions

While Iraq remains a dangerous place, the security situation has improved greatly, creating the possibility of political and economic progress in the coming year. Many challenges lay ahead, and there is no guarantee that recent security gains can be sustained. But for the first time in a long time, there is reason to believe that an acceptable outcome (defined as a reasonably stable Iraq that can offer its citizens the opportunity to live in peace and dignity) may be feasible. The key is continued U.S. military and diplomatic engagement.

An acceptable outcome in Iraq could, beyond its inherent benefits for the long-suffering people of Iraq, help rehabilitate America's reputation and reestablish its credentials in the Middle East and elsewhere as a reliable ally and force for stability—at a time when the region faces growing threats. For this reason, as long as there remains a reasonable prospect for success in Iraq, no matter how modestly defined, it is vital that the U.S. work toward such an outcome, and accept the risks and costs that a long-term commitment to the people and government of Iraq is likely to entail.

POSTSCRIPT

Should All Foreign Troops Soon Leave Iraq?

One thing to beware of in this debate is accepting as a given the argument by some people that since the U.S. invasion of Iraq was a mistake in the first place, it follows that the United States should quickly withdraw its troops. The problem with that argument is that the equation changed dramatically once the invasion occurred and that action cannot be undone. For example, Iraq was a brutal dictatorship, but it was a relatively stable country. When the U.S.-led coalition toppled Saddam Hussein, it created a power vacuum in Iraq that has yet to be filled fully by the Iraqi government. In that atmosphere, a rapid withdrawal might well lead to a bloodbath among Kurds, Shiites, and Sunnis and even among factions within those groups. An uncertain, but probably very high, number of innocent Iraqis would be killed in a civil war. Also, the country might fall apart. That could lead to a nearly independent Kurdish area, a Kurdistan, which might set off a war with Turkey trying to prevent its own sizeable Kurdish minority from seceding and joining its territory to Iraqi Kurdistan. Furthermore, an Iraqi collapse would serve to further enhance the relative power of Iran in the region, a state of affairs arguably counter of U.S. interests. Yet there is also no point in pouring money and lives into Iraq if Colonel Wilkerson is correct. Perhaps the damage was done in March 2003, and nothing the United States can do now can undo it. If the United States will inevitably have to deal with civil war in Iraq and perhaps its dissolution, then arguably sooner is better than later. Well symbolizing the "damned if you do, damned if you don't" conundrum was a national intelligence estimate (NIE) that leaked to the press in September 2006. Those wanting a speedy withdrawal seized on the reports finding that "The Iraq conflict [has been] . . . breeding a deep resentment of U.S. involvement in the Muslim world and cultivating supporters for the global jihadist movement." Yet the very next sentence arguably supported staying the course by predicting that if the jihadists fail to force the United States out of Iraq, "fewer fighters will be inspired to carry on the fight" and implying that jihadist success would embolden the terrorist movement.

For an overview of a very complex situation, start with William R. Polk, *Understanding Iraq: The Whole Sweep of Iraqi History, from Genghis Khan's Mongols to the Ottoman Turks to the British Mandate to the American Occupation* (Perennial, 2006). Current information on the situation in Iraq, including casualties, is available from CNN at http://www.cnn.com/SPECIALS/2003/iraq/. The National Priorities Project has a counter for its up-to-the-minute estimate of the monetary cost of the war is at http://nationalpriorities.org/index.php?option=com_wrapper&Itemid=182.

ISSUE 9

Does Hugo Chávez Threaten Hemispheric Stability and Democracy?

YES: Norman A. Bailey, from Testimony during Hearings on "Venezuela: Looking Ahead," before the Western Hemisphere Subcommittee, Committee on Foreign Affairs, U.S. House of Representatives (July 17, 2008)

NO: Jennifer McCoy, from Testimony during Hearings on "Venezuela: Looking Ahead," before the Western Hemisphere Subcommittee, Committee on Foreign Affairs, U.S. House of Representatives (July 17, 2008)

ISSUE SUMMARY

YES: Norman A. Bailey, a senior fellow at the Potomac Foundation, a conservative think tank in Vienna, Virginia, and formerly senior director of international economic affairs for the National Security Council, argues that Venezuela's President Hugo Chávez is ruining the country economically, destroying its democracy, and undertaking foreign policies which threaten hemispheric stability.

NO: Jennifer McCoy, professor of political science, Georgia State University and director of The Americas Program at The Carter Center, argues that the reforms Hugo Chávez has instituted are very popular there, and that the best course for U.S. foreign policy is to start with positive signals and focus on pragmatic concerns of interest to both countries.

During the nearly 50 years while Fidel Castro was in power in Cuba (1959–2008), the country and its leader have been officially Washington's most prominent opponent in the Western Hemisphere. Much of this history is contained in the material associated with previous edition's Issue 8 ("Are Strict Sanctions on Cuba Warranted?"). Castro has been in ill-health, however, and it may well be that President Hugo Chávez of Venezuela will take his place as Washington's official bête noire in the hemisphere.

Chávez was born in 1954 and graduated in 1975 from Venezuela's equivalent of West Point with an engineering degree. Chávez's military career led him into the elite paratroopers and also, along with other young officers, into a secret organization named after and espousing its interpretation of the principles of Símon Bolívar (1783–1830), the leader of the struggle for independence in northern South America. Although Venezuela was at least a limited democracy, Chávez and his colleagues believed that the two main parties were dominated by the wealthy classes and ignored the country's vast impoverished mass.

Venezuela's economy was suffering in the early 1990s. In return for assistance from the International Monetary Fund and its dominant member, the United States, Venezuela agreed to a series of economic steps that by now Colonel Chávez and his followers believed benefitted the country's rich at the expense of its poor. Chávez reacted in 1992 by twice trying to overthrow the government under the banner of the Bolivarian Revolutionary Movement. Both attempts failed, and he was jailed for two years. Out of prison, Chávez reentered the political fray, this time campaigning for the presidency in 1998. He won by a landslide victory and has been reelected twice since then.

Much of Chávez's years as president can be understood in terms of the ideas of Bolívar and their implementation in the Bolivarian Revolution. In modern terms, Bolívar might be termed a social democrat, or perhaps a populist. Domestically, he proclaimed the importance of the masses and condemned the powerful and wealthy oligarchy (elite class). Internationally, he fought against outside control. He ended Spanish rule in his region and was also wary of other outside powers. This included the United States.

Domestically, Chávez, like Bolívar did, portrays himself as the protector of the masses and the opponent of "the establishment." Oil is the country's greatest resource, and Chávez has charged that the oil companies are led by those living in "luxury chalets where they perform orgies, drinking whisky." Critics charge that he has done little to improve the lot of poor Venezuelans, but he has enjoyed strong support among them.

Also like Bolívar domestically, Chávez has responded to opposition by consolidating his power. Bolívar tried to keep an area composed of what is now Colombia, Ecuador, Venezuela, and Panama together as a large single country, Gran Colombia. Faced with opposition, he became increasingly autocratic, making himself the all-powerful president for life under the Organic Decree of Dictatorship of 1828. Similarly, Chávez, as detailed by Norman A. Bailey in the first reading, has moved steadily to consolidate government power in his hands and to silence both the press and political opponents. Bolívar justified such actions as necessary to protect the masses. So does Chávez—who argued at one point, "What my rivals don't understand . . . is that Hugo Chávez is not Chávez but the people of Venezuela."

Internationally, Chávez echoes Bolívar's anti-imperial sentiments. He accuses the United States of meddling in the affairs of Venezuela, its hemispheric neighbors, and countries around the world. He has also worked to block such efforts backed by Washington as the hemispheric trade pact, the Free Trade Area of the Americas. Whether or not these domestic and international plans and moves bode well for Venezuelans and the hemisphere is the subject of the following exchange between Norman A. Bailey and Jennifer McCoy.

YES

Norman A. Bailey

Venezuela: Looking Ahead

Thank you for the opportunity to testify before you on the subject of the current domestic and international situation of Venezuela and its relations with The United States. I wish to emphasize that everything in this testimony is backed by extensive, detailed and cross-checked information, in many cases with original documentation, which demonstrate that under its present leadership Venezuela is a clear and immediate threat to the national security of The United States, especially due to its extensive and growing ties to the Islamic Republic of Iran. With reference to the internal situation in Venezuela at the present time, the following points need to be emphasized:

1. Caracas and the other major cities of Venezuela currently have the highest rates of common crime in the Hemisphere.
2. Venezuela currently has the highest rate of inflation in the Hemisphere.
3. There are shortages of many staple products such as eggs, milk, bread, etc. Venezuela imports the vast bulk of its consumer goods because of the serious deterioration of domestic production in the last few years.

The financial situation of the country is very poor. The free reserves of the central bank are negative and the state oil company, PDVSA [Petróleos de Venezuela S.A.], had to borrow sixteen billion dollars in 2007. The Venezuelan crude mix gets about $20 per barrel less than the international benchmark rate. Production has been falling for years due to lack of investment and maintenance. Domestic demand is huge because gasoline is sold at four to six cents per liter. Much of what is exported is given away (such as to Cuba) or sold at a discount [to Central American and Caribbean countries] for political reasons, through PetroCaribe and elsewhere.

Refinery downtime is extensive because of poor maintenance and security, much gasoline is smuggled into Colombia and PDVSA management is so poor that the company is subject to dozens of lawsuits internationally for non-performance of supply contracts. PDVSA does not receive the proceeds from advanced sales to raise cash, such as the $3.5 billion loan from Japan and the $4bn loan from China collateralized with future oil deliveries. These funds go directly into the so-called development bank, BANDES, which along with the equally so-called development fund, FUNDES, is used as a slush fund for international operations by the government with no controls or supervision or transparency whatsoever. PDVSA in 2007 not only borrowed extensively (including

U.S. House of Representatives, July 17, 2008.

from its U.S. subsidiary, CITGO, which in order to lend its parent one billion dollars had to borrow it itself, thereby affecting its bond rating), but began to sell off international assets, such as an important storage facility in the Bahamas.

The crown jewels of the Venezuelan economy, formerly well-run companies, especially Electricidad de Caracas (EDC) and CANTV, the telephone company, were nationalized and are now run with the same degree of efficiency as PDVSA. Many productive agricultural properties have been confiscated from their owners and given to the workers and are now much less productive.

On the political side, the deterioration of Venezuelan democracy is a well-known story. All of the major institutions of government are now in the hands of administration supporters as well as the vast majority of state governorships and municipal governments. The principal opposition television network, RCTV, was seized without compensation and remaining opposition media are constantly harassed.

The most recent outrage, however, is the disqualification of about 200 opposition candidates for governorships, mayoralties and legislatures. This is directly out of the Iranian playbook and the reasons given for the disqualifications range from the ludicrous to the absurd. Although all the disqualifications have been appealed, without outside pressure it is unlikely the bans will be lifted since all the electoral and judicial authorities are controlled by the administration. In any case, there is no reason to think that the electoral campaign will be conducted with any greater even-handedness than previous electoral contests in past years.

Finally, corruption in this administration in Venezuela is nothing less than monumental, with literally billions of dollars having been stolen by government officials and their allies in the private sector over the past nine years. One of the principal of these collaborators recently had his bank accounts closed by the Hong Kong and Shanghai Banking Corporation (HSBC) in London. They contained one and a half billion dollars. Some of this corruption and much of the money laundering taking place in Venezuela is connected with drug trafficking. At present, Venezuela and West Africa are the principal routes for Colombian cocaine going to Europe, and much of the resulting income stays with Venezuelan entities and individuals and is facilitated by the Venezuelan financial system, including both public and private institutions.

All of the above is aside from the billions that Venezuela has spent on military equipment, including advanced fighter planes and submarines, way beyond any conceivable needs of the country for legitimate self-defense. Much of the money collected by the official funds and banks has been used to try to influence policy and elections in the rest of the Hemisphere and beyond. A recent compilation indicates that at least $33 billion has been used in this way, including buying billions of dollars worth of Argentine bonds at ruinous rates of interest, since Argentina has had no access to the international financial markets since defaulting on its international debt. Election contributions have been made in Nicaragua, Ecuador, Peru, and Argentina. . . . In some cases this activity has been successful and in others, such as Peru, not, although it was a close call. Additionally, financial support has been provided to insurgent groups in certain countries, most notoriously to the FARC in Colombia, as well as to ETA, the Basque separatist organization, and most importantly to Hamas, Hezbollah and Islamic Jihad, through their extensive network in Venezuela and elsewhere in Latin America. This is done directly through the Islamic Center on the island of Margarita and subsidiary centers in Barquisimeto, Anaco, Puerto Ordaz and Puerto Cabello, as well as a result of Iranian penetration in the Hemisphere, which has been assiduously cultivated by the current Venezuelan administration. Regular flights tie the two countries together (although ordinary citizens cannot buy passage on those flights), Iranians are provided with Venezuelan passports and other documents and more recently the Iranians opened a bank in Caracas, called the Banco Internacional de Desarrollo. This bank has an entirely Iranian board and was authorized in 72 hours in a process that usually takes months. It is an obvious and apparently successful attempt to circumvent the financial sanctions that have been imposed on Iran by the United States and other countries and of course has unlimited access to the facilities of the Venezuelan financial system. In short, should hostilities break out between the U.S. and/or Israel and Iran, the Iranians directly or through their proxies now have the ability to seriously damage U.S. interests in our own Hemisphere, including the Panama Canal.

As a final note, the current Venezuelan regime is notoriously anti-semitic, as documented by the American Jewish Committee (AJC) and others. Jewish institutions are frequently harassed and government publications print scurrilous cartoons, reminiscent of Nazi Germany. U.S. policy towards Venezuela has been characterized by an essential passivity in the face of many provocations, including gross insults directed at the president and secretary of state, among others. That the current regime there has been taking multiple measures contrary to our national interest is beyond question. That it represents a threat to the national security of the United States and our allies in the region should also be beyond question, not least due to the tapes captured from the FARC leader Raul Reyes' camp inside Ecuador. This passivity is apparently motivated by the belief that the regime will eventually self-destruct and in any case more active measures would threaten to exacerbate the oil markets leading to even higher prices for crude. This is a policy that I can understand but with which I do not agree.

It is not necessary to declare Venezuela a state sponsor of terrorism although it obviously is, and not only with reference to the FARC but also to Hamas, Hezbollah, etc. Through current legislation on money laundering, drug trafficking and terrorism measures could be taken against Venezuelan banks which would cripple the Iranian attempt to bypass sanctions on their own financial system by using Venezuela's. However, if Venezuela were to be declared a state sponsor of terrorism and as a result oil imports from that country were blocked, it would be impossible for Venezuela to divert any substantial amount of its exports elsewhere because refining of its quality of crude (predominantly heavy, sour crude) is primarily concentrated in the CITGO refineries in the U.S. By simply releasing about two million barrels a day of crude from the Strategic Petroleum Reserve (SPRO), that oil would be effectively and immediately replaced, and with better quality crude. The effect on Venezuela, however, would be devastating.

Venezuela: Looking Ahead

Thank you for the opportunity to address the committee on the current state of Venezuelan politics and relations with the United States. My written testimony will do three things:

- Analyze the background, goals and challenges of the Chávez administration's "Bolivarian Revolution" focusing on democracy and governability.
- Address two issues of current concern as requested by the committee: the disqualification of candidates for the upcoming subnational elections and the implications of the information in the FARC [leftist rebels in Colombia] laptops.
- Suggest some changes for U.S. policy towards Venezuela and Latin America.

I. Background, Goals and Challenges of the Chávez Administration's "Bolivarian Revolution"

Venezuela democracy and governance must be understood in the context of the demand for radical change expressed by the voters in the 1998 election of Hugo Chávez. A near tripling of poverty rates from the 1970s to the 1990s had produced a serious social dislocation, and a profound rejection of the traditional political elites that led to the collapse of what had been one of the strongest political party systems in the region.

Venezuela today remains in a transitory state, as one political system was dismantled and another is still being created. The constitutional "refounding" promised by Hugo Chávez in his campaign initiated a process of sweeping elite displacement, major redistribution of economic and political resources, and experimentation with new forms of participatory democracy. Venezuela is the first of several Latin American countries seeking a fundamental change in the balance of social relations in the 21st century. This process has been very conflictive. Venezuela has not yet achieved a new social contract including all sectors of the society, and the society remains polarized.

The process referred to by its proponents as the Bolivarian Revolution actually retains many of the basic traits of the previous democratic period known as the "Punto Fijo" political system (1958–98): dependence on oil

U.S. House of Representatives, July 17, 2008.

revenues; highly centralized decision-making structures, with a new set of privileged actors displacing the traditional elites; reliance on the distribution of oil rents; and failure to restore the regulative and administrative capacities of the state (though there is increased tax collection capability). The changes lie in the centralization of decision-making in one person (Chávez) rather than two hierarchical political parties; a new emphasis on class divisions rather than cross-class alliances; an emphasis on confrontation and elimination of opponents to achieve change rather than consensus-seeking to achieve stability; and the dismantling of traditional representative institutions and weakening of checks and balances in favor of new forms of participatory democracy and accountability.

In broad terms, the "Bolivarian Revolution" is an attempt to reformulate the political economy to be more inclusive of those who perceived themselves to be excluded in the latter half of the Punto Fijo period (which included urban poor, middle class civil society organizations, intellectuals, and junior ranks of the military). It is full of contradictions: nationalistic and integrationist, top-down and bottom-up change, centralized and participatory. It seeks to move beyond representative, liberal democracy to achieve a new form of participatory, protagonistic democracy which in its utopian form allows for empowered citizens to hold the state accountable without intermediary institutions. It follows a Bolivarian inspiration comprised of both a Latin American integrationist dream and a centralization of domestic power. Foreign policy is fundamental to the project, with its goal of counter-balancing U.S. global and regional hegemony with a more multipolar world. Like its domestic version, Venezuela's foreign policy is confrontational and conflictive.

Chávez' reelection with 63% of the vote in 2006 apparently encouraged him to propose even more radical change in a second constitutional project in 2007, which was ultimately rejected by the voters. Institutionally, the 2007 (failed) constitutional reforms would have deepened the executive control of the political system, concentrating power to an extraordinary degree. Since then he has reached out to dissidents within his own movement; reshuffled his cabinet to attempt to address severe problems in government services, crime, and inflation; and restored relations with neighboring Colombia while calling on the FARC to end kidnapping and unilaterally release hostages. The retreat from "deepening the revolution" is most likely aimed at the November 2008 mayoral and gubernatorial elections, in which the government faces stiff competition if the opposition unifies. It does not mean that the government or the president has abandoned the goals of "21st Century Socialism".

State of Democracy

In formal terms, Venezuela is a constitutional democracy whose citizens have the right to change their government peacefully through regular elections based on universal suffrage. Democratic legitimacy in Venezuela is based on electoral legitimacy and popular participatory mechanisms. The concerns lie in an erosion of separation of powers and mechanisms of horizontal accountability (checks and balances), and the dominance of the governing party in representative institutions.

A dozen elections and referenda have been conducted in the ten years of the Chávez administration. President Chavez has consistently won between 56% and 63% of the popular vote in every election in which he has participated since 1998.

The perceptions of social inclusion, political representation and personal empowerment and hope provided by Hugo Chávez to the majority of impoverished citizens are a powerful factor, often ignored in external evaluations of Venezuelan democracy. The Chávez administration has accepted elections as a mechanism for citizen participation and choice, and they will continue to provide the best opportunity to achieve pluralistic representation at local, regional and national levels.

Electoral Processes

After a period of politicized electoral processes, erosion of public confidence, and abstention by the opposition, Venezuela's electoral processes are regaining widespread confidence and include one of the most advanced electronic systems in the world. Continued focus on improving equitable campaign conditions (finance, control of use of state resources) can provide more options to voters while enhancing the legitimacy of the victorious candidates.

The November 2008 elections for governor and mayor present an opportunity for additional political leaderships to develop, both within chavismo and outside of it, thus providing a route for a healthy dynamism and generational renewal within Venezuela's political class.

Participatory Mechanisms

Direct democracy mechanisms and experimental community-based political organization provide important opportunities for citizen participation, but have mixed reviews to date.

Venezuelans have voted in at least four significant referenda on constitutional reforms and presidential recall. Further, one of the hallmarks of the Bolivarian Revolution has been the experimentation with various forms of citizen organization and community-based political organization, from the early Bolivarian Circles to the Election Battle Units to local Water Committees and the more recent Community Councils (now an estimated 30,000). The effectiveness of these experiments in terms of bringing citizen empowerment, technical expertise, autonomy and sustainability, and their ability to hold the government accountable has been mixed to date.

Political Party System

The recomposition of the political party system is another challenge for Venezuela, after the collapse of the Punto Fijo party system in the 1990s. The ability of the small, new opposition parties to challenge the current hegemonic position of the governing party remains to be seen.

Chávez' own party started as a clandestine movement within the military, then morphed into a political-electoral movement, then a political party within a coalition, and finally (in 2007–08) an attempted single official party (PSUV).

The opposition parties are now led by Primero Justicia (a relatively new young, technocratic party), Un Nuevo Tiempo (based in Zulia and led by Zulia's governor and 2006 presidential candidate Manuel Rosales), and MAS (one of the few remaining parties from the Punto Fijo years), while Podemos has left the governing coalition and occupies a centrist position. The two dominant parties of Punto Fijo – Acción Democrática and Copei – have virtually disappeared.

Party identification of voters with the opposition parties totals only 10%, and the government's party obtains about 20% identification, with the bulk of the population claiming to be independents (Datanalisis, February 2008). The possibilities of re-creating a pluralist political system in Venezuela rest today on creating equitable campaign conditions and on the opposition's ability to do two things: i) convince its supporters to vote after years of alleging fraud and sowing distrust in the electoral system; and ii) craft a convincing message that the opposition provides a credible alternative that will work to achieve social inclusion and redistribution as the Bolivarian Revolution has promised.

State of Rule of Law

Traditional mechanisms of horizontal accountability under liberal democracy – separation of powers and independent organs of control – are largely absent in Venezuela today.

Due to electoral weakness of the opposition and the decision to boycott the 2005 National Assembly elections, the government coalition controls 100% of the legislative seats and the vast majority of the elected gubernatorial and mayoral posts. The National Assembly, in turn, appoints the other independent powers of the Supreme Court, the National Electoral Council, and the "Citizen's Power" made up of the Ombudsman, Attorney General and Comptroller General. All of these institutions are widely perceived today to be partisan in favor of the government. The ability of the democratic institutions to protect individual civil and human rights and provide equality before the law has thus been questioned.

Civil Rights
The government generally respects most civil liberties, with some concerns of infringements on assembly, dissent and speech.

One current concern is the attempt by the government to introduce legislation requiring NGO registration and regulating foreign funding of NGOs. A similar provision was included in the defeated constitutional reforms of 2007. The draft law is currently in the National Assembly.

Additionally, there is strong debate over the degree of freedom of speech and of the media. Venezuelan media have long been politicized, but with the polarization and conflict beginning in 2002, both private and public media, especially television, took on overt political roles. Two virtual realities of the country were presented in the media, and the opposition and the president engaged in public discourse and mutual accusations through the airwaves. After the 2004 recall referendum, several changes occurred: the government opened several new television stations and sponsored hundreds of community radio programs, changing the balance from overwhelmingly oppositionist media to a majority of official broadcast media; the National Assembly passed the Social Media Responsibility law to regulate violence and pornography during primetime television; and some media decided to make peace with the government and take on a less political role.

Vigorous criticism of the government and the president in the private media continues, and there is no formal censorship. Nonetheless, legal, economic and regulatory mechanisms create a climate of self-censorship. The state-owned media is characterized by strong pro-government politicization, while private media continue to be anti-government. Private media complain that they are denied equal and full access to government facilities and official events. Perhaps even more concerning, reforms to the criminal code in March 2005 increased the penalties for libel and defamation of public officials from a maximum of 30 months to 4 years in prison, directly counter to the direction of most of the rest of the region and the rulings of the Inter-American Court of Human Rights. Human Rights Watch reported that in 2007 at least eight reporters were charged with libel, defamation or related offenses (Human Rights Watch 2008). Nevertheless, international watchdog groups report that from 2002–2006, only 2 journalists were reported killed while working, and none were imprisoned or missing, a considerably better record than either of Venezuela's neighbors (Committee to Protect Journalist, Reporters Without Frontiers).

The government also places restrictions on the media through its administration of broadcasting licenses, which is not always transparent and may be motivated by political concerns. On May 28, 2007 the government declined to renew the broadcasting license of the country's oldest commercial network and most vocal critic, Radio Caracas Television (RCTV), for allegedly supporting the 2002 coup and violating broadcast norms. In addition, under the Law of Social Responsibility in Radio and Television, media outlets that fail to comply with regulations can receive large fines and risk suspension of their broadcasts.

State of Governance

Weak state capacity, long deteriorating public services, political instability, and a continual climate of electoralism plague the government's ability to respond to the needs of the populace through effective governance.

Venezuela's public services have been deteriorating since the 1970s, causing much of the dissatisfaction with the prior Punto Fijo regime and increasingly with the current regime. Both regimes have relied on external petroleum rents to finance a distributive policy and failed to develop effective regulatory policies. Venezuela's oil booms have historically fueled a paternalistic state and petrodiplomacy in foreign policy, and the external criticism of Chávez' programs as unsustainable populist give-aways have been directed to past governments as well.

The government gained political control over the petroleum industry in 2003 after the 2-month oil strike, and has since used the rise in oil prices to fund many newly created social programs or misiones. The government has not only maintained the proportion of central government spending spent on pro-poor programs, but has added direct social spending by the petroleum industry. Thus, the percentage of pro-poor spending as a proportion of GDP appears to have increased under Chávez.

In addition to personal insecurity and unemployment, a new problem has emerged in 2007 and 2008 as a pressing problem in public opinion polls: food shortages. A combination of foreign exchange controls, price controls, rising consumer demand and lack of producer confidence have created serious food shortages in milk, oil, sugar, eggs and meat. With worldwide demand and food prices rising, Venezuela's traditional reliance on imported food is becoming a real vulnerability for the government. The rise in social spending has contributed to inflationary pressures making Venezuela the country with the second highest inflation in the world (expected to reach 25–30% in 2008).

Despite all these issues, satisfaction with democracy in Venezuela, perhaps surprisingly, has risen over the last five years and is now the second highest in Latin America with 59%, while the average for the region is 37% (Latino-barometer, *The Economist* 2007). Moreover, Venezuelan citizens' approval of their government is 66%, while the average for Latin America is 39%, and their confidence in the president is 60%, while the regional average is 43% (Venezuela Information Center 2007). These numbers reveal that Venezuelans, compared to the rest of the region, have a generally positive perception of their democratic system.

II. Two Issues of Current Interest

Venezuela's Relationship with the FARC

The laptop computers captured by the government of Colombia in the March 1 raid into Ecuador have spawned a number of news stories about the alleged relationship between Venezuela, Ecuador and the FARC. Interpol was asked to investigate the laptops in order to ascertain whether they had been tampered with after the capture, but it did not investigate the content of the materials. The Government of Ecuador asked the OAS to investigate the content of the materials with reference to Ecuador. Interpol released their report in May, but the OAS has not yet released a report.

The Interpol report concluded three things about the captured laptops, CDs and memory sticks: that the materials were not handled according to international standards during the first two days of Colombian government possession; that they were handled properly during subsequent days, when copies were made and accessed rather than the original files directly accessed; and that no evidence of manipulation of the files after they were captured was found. The report also said that Interpol would make no evaluation of the veracity of the content of the files, the origin of the files, or interpretations of the files that various governments might make.

The report asserts that the Colombian government did not introduce the files, but it does not prove that Raul Reyes actually wrote the files, nor whether the statements in the files are true. The latter will require corroboration from other sources – that is, a full investigation that may not be physically or politically feasible.

There are issues of evidence and perception. The evidence thus far rests in the files of guerrilla leaders intimating offers of material and financial support from the government of Venezuela. Corroborating evidence would require viewing the responses of the Venezuelans, evidence of approval at the highest levels, and evidence of actual support. Some of the interpretations of the information leaked from the laptops has been found to be false (e.g. the alleged photo of an Ecuadoran minister turned out to be an Argentine), and others to be true. In addition, the timing of the emails suggests an increase in contacts during the fall of 2007 when President Chávez was authorized by President Uribe to negotiate a hostage exchange.

Nevertheless, expressions of solidarity with the FARC from Venezuelan officials and the early 2008 request by President Chávez for the international community to recognize the FARC as a belligerent force give the impression of at least ideological solidarity. The recent change in policy expressed by President Chávez in his request to the FARC to unilaterally release the hostages is most likely a result of two things: a) an attempt to distance himself from the perception of close ties with the FARC; and b) the need to reestablish a more cooperative relationship with the government of Colombia for pragmatic reasons of trade, as evidenced in the July 11 meeting between Uribe and Chávez. Bilateral trade between the two countries is extremely important and Venezuela is dependent on Colombian food imports during the current food shortages.

Given the stakes of the United States declaring a country to be a state-sponsor of terrorism (affecting the vital oil trade with Venezuela), it is extremely important to base such a decision on firm evidence rather than perception.

Disqualification of Candidates

A current controversy involves the disqualification (inhabilitación) of 386 individuals from holding appointed public office, or running for elected office. The controversy includes both legal questions and questions of political bias.

The disqualification is an administrative sanction applied by the Controller General according to the Law of the Controller General, approved by the majority of the National Assembly, including many opposition representatives, in 2001 in order to curb corruption. Article 105 of that law gives the Controller General not only the right to apply a fine when an administrative irregularity (corruption) is documented, but also to remove the person from an appointed position and to prohibit the person from running for elected office. The Supreme Court previously ruled that this latter sanction would apply to an elected official only at the end of their current term, prohibiting them from running for reelection or another position for the specified time period. Some of the potential candidates for the municipal and state elections on November 23, 2008 are on the list.

There are currently at least 15 appeals in front of the Supreme Court of Justice requesting nullification of the finding of irregularity in specific cases, nullification of specific disqualifications, and nullification of the Article 105 of the law as unconstitutional. These appeals include both pro-government and opposition persons. It is hoped that the Supreme Court of Justice will rule on these issues before the August 512 period for candidates to register to compete in the November 23, 2008 elections. The National Electoral Council has thus far said that it will abide by the Controller General's list of disqualified candidates unless the Supreme Court rules otherwise.

The problem is that the law appears to contradict the constitution. The constitution specifies that the political right to run and be elected to office can be disqualified only by a judicial sentence, and that those sentenced for crimes while in public office or damaging public patrimony are not eligible to run (Articles 42 and 65). The constitution also gives the Controller General the authority to investigate and apply administrative sanctions for irregularities against the public patrimony (Article 289).

The second issue has to do with the definition of "administrative sanction" and whether that should include only monetary fines, or can include the right to hold office. The appeals before the Supreme Court argue that an administrative sanction impeding the right to hold office in the absence of a criminal sentence by the courts violates both the constitution and the Inter-American Convention on Human Rights.

Clearly, Venezuela needs a resolution of the legal questions from the Supreme Court. In addition to the legal questions, however, is the perception of political bias. Although the list of persons having received administrative sanctions includes many chavistas, perhaps a majority, and several have been removed from their public positions, it is not as evident that there are aspiring chavista candidates for elected office being disqualified. The persons most in the news or traveling to international circles are well-known opposition candidates. There is a perception, then, that these are popular candidates with viability to be elected who are being disqualified in order to prevent true competition with government-sponsored candidates. This perception has the potential to damage the legitimacy of the November 23 elections and those elected in them, particularly if the legal issues are not resolved by the Supreme Court before the candidate registration period.

III. International Engagement with Venezuela – 2009 and Beyond

In general, international leverage over a resource-rich state is strictly limited. Political conditionality of loans and aid is unavailable as a foreign policy or a democracy-promotion tool. Venezuela itself is becoming a donor to neighboring states, and even to the United States, with discounted oil payment terms to Caribbean and Central American countries, cheap heating oil in parts of the U.S., significant bond purchases in Argentina, and barter trade through its Bolivarian Alternative for Latin America (ALBA).

On the other hand, mutual commercial dependence between Venezuela and the U.S., as well as with its neighbors, both encourages moderation and prevents serious threats between Venezuela and its neighbors. For example, 11–14% of the oil imported into the U.S. comes from Venezuela; Venezuela sells about 55% of its oil exports to the U.S. Colombia is Venezuela's other major trading partner, the importance of which was demonstrated during the brief break in diplomatic relations after Colombia's incursion into Ecuador in March 2008. The disruption of Venezuelan-Colombia trade (and especially imported food) contributed to Venezuela's rapid restoration of ties with Colombia, despite deep political disagreements.

A change in U.S. attitude and policy toward Latin America can reduce the impact of Venezuela's anti-Americanism in the region, and may gain receptivity within Venezuela as well.

Chávez' anti-Americanism resonates at home and abroad because of general antipathy toward U.S. unilateralness and perceived bullying. The new nationalism led by Hugo Chávez and joined by other Latin American countries seeks to assert greater independence of U.S.-dominated multilateral organizations such as the IMF and World Bank, and greater control and equity in their own natural resources (reflected in the renegotiation of contracts and rise in royalty and tax payments for extractive industries). A more consultative and responsive American foreign policy that addresses the agenda of Latin America would ameliorate the negative attitudes towards the U.S., opening the door over time to greater receptivity of U.S. ideas and assistance in Venezuela and elsewhere.

Several lessons from U.S. policy toward Latin America and Venezuela over the last eight years are evident:

- U.S. neglect of the region since 2001 left a political vacuum which Venezuela has been able to enter, primarily by providing alternative ideas on organizing the polity, economy and foreign relations.
- The U.S and Venezuela have engaged in a Western Hemisphere "Cold War" in recent years, attempting to divide up countries among them. This is counterproductive. Latin governments do not want to be forced to choose and U.S. attempts to strong-arm Latin governments into isolating Venezuela failed miserably, as shown in the drawn-out affair to elect a new Secretary General of the Organization of American States.
- The U.S. lost much of its moral authority in the realm of democracy promotion in Venezuela with its welcoming of the 2002 coup against Chávez, leading to a deepening suspicion of U.S. intent to carry out "regime change" in Venezuela and a radicalization of Venezuela policy toward the U.S. In Latin America more broadly, the U.S. unilateral policy on Iraq, in which "regime change" aims were promoted as democracy promotion, and the attempt to strong-arm Chile and Mexico in the UN Security Council to vote for the invasion was resented.
- The Bush Administration has learned to ignore rather than respond to much of Chávez' inflammatory rhetoric. This change in attitude will help to mitigate the U.S. role as a "foil" to Venezuela's anti-imperialist stance and should be continued.
- The U.S. refusal to extradite to Venezuelan citizen Luis Posadas Carriles on charges of terrorism (accused of masterminding the 1976 bombing of a Cuban plane) presents a U.S. double-standard on issues of terrorism. Lessons for the future – what can and should the U.S. do?

A new U.S. administration offers the opportunity to begin anew with Venezuela in a more amicable and cooperative relationship. However, Washington should not expect major change given the fundamental foreign policy goals of the Chávez administration and the Bolivarian Revolution: to increase Venezuela's national autonomy, to increase the global South's autonomy vis-à-vis the North, and to lessen U.S. dominance in the region and the world. Venezuela will continue its attempts to diversify its oil export markets and to build coalitions to create a more multipolar world and a more integrated South.

A new U.S. foreign policy toward Venezuela should start with positive signals and focus on pragmatic concerns of interest to both countries – commercial relations, counter-narcotics, and security on the Venezuelan-Colombia border. The U.S. should make clear that it respects the sovereign right of the Venezuelan people to choose their leadership (as they have done consistently in voting for Hugo Chávez) and that the U.S. has no intent to engineer regime change in Venezuela. A more consistent policy across the executive branch would help to reinforce this message, as in the past the Pentagon has continued negative descriptions of the Chávez administration even while the State Department tried to moderate its rhetoric.

In analyzing Venezuelan democracy, U.S. policymakers should recognize the social roots of the political change happening in Venezuela and Latin America, and acknowledge the pressing demand for jobs and personal safety, for poverty reduction and closing the huge income gap. We need to understand the hunger for recognition and inclusion by populations marginalized from economic and political power. Procedural democracy is not a priority for many in this situation. Having greater control and participation in the forces that determine their daily lives is.

Finally, the U.S. should recognize and have confidence in the capacity of Venezuelan citizens to provide their own constraints on their government when it crosses their threshold of acceptable change, as evidenced in the 2007 constitutional referendum vote. Given the limited direct influence that the U.S. can have in Venezuela in terms of its political-economy choices, a focus on providing the space and mechanisms for the Venezuelan people to determine their own direction should be a guiding principle for U.S. policy, working through multilateral forums and broader regional networks.

POSTSCRIPT

Does Hugo Chávez Threaten Hemispheric Stability and Democracy?

Hugo Chávez's power has been greatly augmented in recent years by the high price of oil, which produces about 80 percent of Venezuela's export earnings and 50 percent of the government's revenue. The increased revenue has allowed Chávez to greatly increase the money going to social service programs since 2004. Oil income has also allowed Chávez to spread his influence abroad, in part by giving over $1 billion in foreign aid in recent years to numerous countries in the hemisphere. Venezuela has even provided low-cost heating oil to poor people in many locations in the United States through CITGO, Venezuela's U.S. subsidiary.

Chávez remains popular in Venezuela, winning reelection in 2006 with 63 percent of the votes in what was, again, certified as a fair contest by the OAS. Less positively, he has also continued to consolidate his power. For example, he refused to renew the license of Venezuela's second largest television station and replaced it with a state-owned station. In January 2007, he also had the compliant of the National Assembly give him the power to rule by decree in certain areas for 18 months. Yet he has not always succeeded. He sponsored a referendum that would have allowed him to run reelection without limit and also give him as president broad reaching economic power, but Venezuelans rejected the changes by a narrow margin in December 2007.

Relations between Venezuela and the United States have worsened. When Venezuela launched an effort to win a seat on the UN Security Council beginning in 2007, the United States countered by backing Guatemala. A standoff ensued, and Panama was seated as a compromise candidate. Another sore point has been Venezuela's increased purchases of military weaponry from abroad, including a $3-billion purchase of fighter planes and other arms from Russia, and Washington's warning that Venezuela is a threat to its neighbors. Chávez counters these by claiming that the weapons are necessary to protect his country from a possible U.S. intervention. Most recently, in late 2007, Chávez threatened Colombia with war. The crisis began when Colombia bombed a camp of FARC rebels inside Ecuador. Chávez, who has supported both the FARC and Ecuador's leftist President Rafael Correa, condemned Colombia for U.S.-backed aggression and sent tanks to the Colombia border. Soon however, and for reasons yet unclear, Chávez reversed course. He withdrew the tanks, and in July 2008, he met with Colombia's President Álvaro Uribe to, as Chávez put it, "turn the page on the stormy past" and begin a "new era" of friendship.

What the future holds is unclear, but Chávez may not want to fully follow Simon Bolívar's course. Bolivar failed to create a South American federation or even hold Gran Colombia together. Instead, he was driven from power, and was so unpopular that when he died soon thereafter, authorities in Venezuela would not allow his body to be returned there for burial. Bolívar wrote just before his death that Gran Columbia was "ungovernable," and "will fall inevitably into the hands . . . of petty tyrants." The issue is whether Hugo Chávez is disproving or fulfilling that prophecy.

An interesting look at Chávez is in Cristina Marcano et al., *Hugo Chávez: The Definitive Biography of Venezuela's Controversial President* (Random House, 2007). Because he is so important in the thinking of Chávez, learn more about Bolívar in John Lynch's, *Símon Bolívar: A Life* (Yale University Press, 2006). The view of the government of Venezuela is on the Web site of its embassy in Washington at http://www.embavenez-us.org/.

ISSUE 10

Is Military Intervention in Darfur Justified?

YES: Susan E. Rice, from "Dithering on Darfur: U.S. Inaction in the Face of Genocide," Testimony during Hearings on "Darfur: A 'Plan B' to Stop Genocide?" before the Committee on Foreign Relations, U.S. Senate (April 11, 2007)

NO: Alex de Waal, from "Prospects for Peace in Darfur Today," Testimony during Hearings on "Current Situation in Darfur," before the Committee on Foreign Affairs, U.S. House of Representatives (April 19, 2007)

ISSUE SUMMARY

YES: Susan E. Rice, a senior fellow in foreign policy and global economics and development at the Brooking Institution, formerly U.S. assistant secretary of state for African affairs and nominated to be U.S. Ambassador to the UN in January 2009, says that using military force is long overdue to halt what she portrays as an ongoing genocide in Darfur.

NO: Alex de Waal, program director at the Social Science Research Council, a research organization in New York City, contends that inserting a military force into a very unstable situation would not likely bring success and that using diplomacy to create a situation where all sides want peace is a better strategy for now.

Darfur is a mostly arid region in western Sudan along its border with Chad. The region encompasses about 190,000 square miles, an area 15 percent larger than California, and makes up about 20 percent of Sudan. Darfur's population is (or was before the fighting began) about 6 million, or about 15 percent of Sudan's overall population. The racial/ethnic/religious make up of Sudan and, even more so, Darfur is very complex and is a source of division. Racially, 52 percent of Sudanese are akin to the black sub-Saharan Africans living in countries to the south and southwest of Sudan. Another 40 percent of Sudanese are more closely related to the Arab populations living in countries to Sudan's north and northwest. Bejas and other ethnoracial groups make up the rest of Sudan's population. Some 70 percent of the Sudanese are Muslims, 25 percent have traditional religious beliefs, and 5 percent are Christians.

The word "Darfur" is from Arabic and means the "area of the Fur," a people who are black, Muslim, and mostly grain and cattle farmers. However, the population of Darfur is more complex than that. The more than one million Fur live in central Darfur along with the Masalit and other related groups, while other parts of Darfur are populated by groups such as the Zaghawa and Baqqara, who are traditionally nomadic people herding camels, cattle, and other livestock. An essential point by one analysis is that "no part of Darfur was ever ethnically homogeneous."

Until the late 1800s, Darfur was a quasi-independent area, but it came under Egyptian, then Egyptian-English control, then Sudan's in 1956 when it gained independence. Sudan has been beset by ethnonational violence since the mid-1980s. In 2005, after 20 years of bloody fighting, the largely black and Christian/traditional belief groups of southern Sudan gained a measure of autonomy. Some trace the violence in Darfur to this period when the Sudanese government armed the Baqqara and other Muslim-Arabic-speaking groups in south Darfur to protect themselves against and attack the rebels in southern Sudan. Reportedly, the Baqqara and other nomadic groups also used their arms to try to take lands from the Fur. The militia groups attacking the Fur became known as the Janjaweed, an Arabic colloquialism that means "armed horse-man." Conditions worsened after 1989, when the Arab-oriented National Islamic Front seized power in Sudan, and Omar al-Bashir became president. By 2003, rebel groups from Darfur were in full revolt against Khartoum, accusing it of oppressing black Africans in Darfur and demanding autonomy and a substantial share of any oil revenues that the region might produce.

The Sudanese government responded with direct attacks and by further arming and otherwise supporting the Janjaweed. Their attacks drove many Fur and related groups into refugee camps or across the western border into Chad. The number of dead is uncertain, but 250,000 is a reasonable estimate, and rapes of Darfurian women and other atrocities have also been numerous. At least a million others have been displaced.

Peace efforts have failed so far. An African Union (AU) peacekeeping force beginning in 2006 with the addition of UN peacekeeping forces in 2007 have proven insufficient because there are too few of them, they are inadequately equipped, and their ability to operate is too limited by political agreements with Khartoum. Talks between Khartoum and the rebels have also failed, in part because of the unwillingness of Khartoum to give much ground and in part because the rivalries among the dozen or so rebel groups have made negotiating nearly impossible.

In the mean time, the atrocities have continued. Former U.S. Secretary of State Colin Powell had called them "genocide," the international spotlight on the crisis has been kept focused by the calls for action by celebrities such as George Clooney and Angelina Jolie. That was about the situation when Susan E. Rice and Alex de Waal testified before Congress. In the two readings drawn from that testimony, Rice gives a clarion call for immediate strong action, including military force if necessary. de Waal is more cautious, believing that military force would be unlikely to help and could even hurt.

YES

Susan E. Rice

Dithering on Darfur: U.S. Inaction in the Face of Genocide

Thank you for the opportunity to testify on the vitally important issue of the escalating crisis in Darfur. Let me also take this opportunity to thank you, Mr. Chairman [Senator Joseph Biden, D-DE], and many of your colleagues in both Houses and on both sides of the aisle for your committed leadership in trying to halt the ongoing genocide in Darfur. I commend your efforts to enable all the people of Sudan to live in peace, free from persecution on the basis of their race, religion or ethnicity.

Where's Plan B?

I feel compelled to begin with a simple observation: today is the 11th of April, 2007. The genocide in Darfur has lasted four years and counting. An estimated 450,000 people are dead. More than 2.5 million have been displaced or rendered refugees. Every day, the situation worsens. One-hundred and one days have come and gone since the expiration of the very public deadline the President's Special Envoy Andrew Natsios set at my very own Brookings Institution. Last year, on November 20th, Natsios promised that harsh consequences would befall the government of Sudan, if by January 1, 2007, it failed to meet two very clear conditions. First, Khartoum must accept unequivocally the full deployment of a 17,000 person UN-African Union "hybrid" force. And, second, it must stop killing innocent civilians.

In spite of this threat – the so-called "Plan B" – the government of Sudan continues to kill with impunity. Khartoum still has not accepted UN troops as part of a hybrid force. Bashir sent a letter late last December to Kofi Annan [UN Secretary-General] implying his acquiescence to UN troops – but offering no explicit acceptance. The next day Sudan's ambassador to the UN ruled out any UN forces. Sudan keeps playing this bait and switch game to its advantage, and the U.S. keeps being played. And, still, no Plan B.

In early February, the *Washington Post* reported, and Natsios confirmed, a leaked story that the President had finally approved "Plan B" – a three stage punitive package that could begin with the United States blocking Sudan's oil revenue. This "Plan B" should have been implemented swiftly, not leaked. This kind of leak gives Sudan advance warning, enabling it to try to evade sanctions.

U.S. Senate, April 11, 2007.

Still, it remains unclear what the "three tiers" of the administration's Plan B are. In testimony in February before the House Committee on Foreign Affairs, Special Envoy Natsios revealed nothing of the substance or timing of Plan B. One cannot help but wonder: is there any beef behind the Administration's repeated threats? We have no idea if the promised penalties will ever be implemented and, if so, whether they would be powerful enough to change Khartoum's calculus.

The sad truth is: the United States continues to be taunted, and our conditions continue to be flaunted by the Sudanese government. Plan B is long past its sell-by date and getting staler by the day.

In January, a bipartisan group of 26 U.S. senators wrote to President Bush saying, "We appreciate your Administration's efforts at aggressive diplomacy and negotiation, but it seems clear that the Sudanese are not responding to such tactics." The Senators insisted ". . . the time has come to begin implementing more assertive measures."

In March, a bipartisan group of 31 senators reiterated the call for action in another letter to President Bush urging that the administration ask the UN Security Council to impose sanctions on the Sudanese government. Many members of this committee correctly argued that "a threatened veto should not silence us" and that we should "let a country stand before the community of nations and announce that it is vetoing the best effort we can muster to build the leverage necessary to end ongoing mass murder." Yet, to date, the Bush Administration has failed to press for tough action against the Sudanese government at the UN Security Council.

Worse still are this Administration's diversionary tactics – recently asserting that Sudan had accepted, in principle, so-called Phase III – the full deployment of the hybrid force, including its UN elements. In fact, the Sudanese made no such clear commitment, not even in principle. The State Department's spokesman said some weeks ago that the Administration will defer further consideration of any punitive measures until after the UN is ready to deploy all its forces for the hybrid mission. In other words, the new due date for consideration of Plan B, may, be months away at the earliest, and may occur only if the Sudanese block deployment of UN forces once they are fully ready to go.

In testimony before the Senate in February, Secretary [of State Condoleezza] Rice went even further in ratcheting down the pressure on Khartoum. In response to you, Mr, Chairman, when you said "I think we should use force now and we should impose [a no fly zone]", Secretary Rice took the option of unilateral U.S. military action off the table, noting its "considerable down-sides." She made no mention of the "considerable downsides" of allowing genocide to continue unabated.

Perhaps that is because the Administration appears to have reversed itself and decided that genocide is not happening in Darfur. Quoted in the *Georgetown Voice*, Natsios told a student group that: "The ongoing crisis in Darfur is no longer a genocide situation" but that "genocide had previously occurred in Darfur." President Bush conspicuously failed to use the term "genocide" when speaking of Darfur in his latest State of the Union address.

Such language games shock the conscience, especially given recent escalating attacks on civilians and aid workers.

Reflect on what's at stake. If any progress at all has been made on the subject of Darfur, it is that we in the United States have gotten past the debate about whether this is, or is not, a genocide. To regress, to re-open this issue, is to further slow-roll any action, to reduce any sense of urgency, and to allow more and more people to continue dying. Make no mistake: Darfur has been a genocide. It continues to be a genocide. And unless the United States leads the world in halting the killing, it will remain a genocide.

Why do you suppose the Administration is equivocating and temporizing? Why would it re-open old debates? Why would it, yet again, issue threats to the Sudanese regime and fail to follow through on them? What damage is done to our interests, to our credibility, to our already diminished international standing by the Administration's seemingly empty threats?

One possible explanation is that the administration accepts Khartoum's line that what is occurring in Darfur is a complex civil conflict that requires primarily a political solution. It is obvious that there are rebel groups operating in Darfur, that these groups have attacked civilians and peacekeepers, and that the splintering and disunity amongst these groups hampers political negotiations. It is also obvious that a long-term solution in Darfur will require political accommodation and reconciliation.

However, negotiations cannot end a genocide: genocide is not a mere counter-insurgency tactic. Genocide results from the conscious decision of one party to a conflict to seek to eliminate another distinct group in whole or in part. This is the choice the Sudanese government made in the case of Darfur. There are only two ways to end a genocide: to apply powerful enough pressures or inducements to persuade the perpetrators of genocide to stop; or to protect those who are the potential victims of genocide. A negotiated solution would do neither, though it is necessary, ultimately, to resolve the underlying conflict.

Yet, diplomacy takes time. Political negotiations require patience, coordinated pressure and energetic diplomacy married with the credible threat of powerful sanctions and the use of force. While the Administration negotiates without credibly threatening more powerful action, Khartoum continues the killing at an alarming pace. America's principal priority in Darfur must be to stop the suffering and killing, and to do so quickly.

Another explanation for the Administration's dithering is that they simply do not have a coherent Darfur policy. In fact, the U.S. approach to the genocide in Darfur has been simultaneously anemic and constipated. The coming and going of deadlines and the shifting personnel assignments are indicative of the fact that we have no comprehensive strategy for stopping the killing.

This week, Deputy Secretary [John D.] Negroponte is traveling to Khartoum to take yet another stab at negotiations with the Sudanese junta. Undoubtedly, Ambassador Negroponte will learn for himself what Condi Rice, [former Deputy Secretary of State] Robert Zoellick, [U.S. Assistant Secretary of State for African Affairs] Jendayi Frazer, Andrew Natsios, Kofi Annan and [former U.S. ambassador to the UN] Bill Richardson have discovered all before him: Khartoum's word means nothing. The Sudanese government cannot be trusted to keep its promises nor to take concrete steps to end the killing. Yet, while U.S. officials re-learn old lessons, Khartoum is using diplomacy as a foil to continue the genocide.

How can the Administration explain to the dead, the nearly dead and the soon to be dead people of Darfur that, at the end of the day – even after we declare that genocide is occurring, even after we insist repeatedly that we are committed to stopping it – the United States continues to stand by while killing persists. This genocide has endured now, not for 100 days, not for 1,000 days, but for four long years.

In January, the UN reported that the situation in Darfur was deteriorating rapidly. December 2006 was the worst month in Darfur in over two years. This nadir followed six months of escalating violence – a period which coincided with Khartoum's bid to expel the African Union force, to block the UN deployment and to throw its killing machine into high gear. Rebel activity has also increased, and their violence is harming civilians and humanitarian agents. In those six months: thirty humanitarian compounds suffered attacks; twelve aid workers were killed, and over 400 were forced to relocate. On December 18, four aid organizations were attacked at a massive refugee camp housing 130,000 at Gereida in South Darfur. All humanitarian operations there ceased, and innocent people went weeks without food shipments. Sudanese aircraft have attacked rebel-held areas and killed many innocent civilians.

At the same time, the fighting in Darfur is destabilizing neighboring Chad and Central African Republic. Khartoum has backed rebels that seek to overthrow these governments. Indeed this past week, 65 people were killed and 70 wounded by janjaweed militias in Chad. UN Undersecretary General for Humanitarian Affairs John Holmes reported last week that, since the fall of 2006, the number of displaced persons in eastern Chad has risen from 50,000 to 140,000; the number of displaced people in the northeast of the Central African Republic has grown from 50,000 to 212,000. The UNHCR is now reporting that refugees from Chad are actually spilling into Darfur. The security situation along these borders is so bad that the UN is reluctant to deploy forces there without an effective ceasefire.

The administration has been slow to recognize the impending collapse in Chad and CAR. The Administration's FY 2008 budget request includes a scant $100,000 of assistance for the Central African Republic, this is a decrease from FY 2006's meager $670,000 appropriation. The requests for Chad are somewhat more robust – totaling $5.3 million, most of which is food aid; however neither country is likely to receive the money to avert worsening political, security, and humanitarian conditions. The UN's John Holmes estimates that the UN will require $174 million for humanitarian assistance in Chad and $54 million in the Central African Republic. While this will require a global effort, the United States should be leading efforts to provide this money.

As the humanitarian situation in these countries worsens, I begin to worry that, in the absence of swift action to stop the genocide in Darfur and stabilize the region, we may be forced to change the advocacy campaigns from "Save Darfur" to "Save Central Africa." I commend Senator Feingold and others who introduced Senate Resolution 76, which calls on the administration to press for a UN force on the Chadian side of the border and to "develop, fund, and implement a comprehensive regional strategy in Africa to protect civilians, facilitate humanitarian operations, contain and reduce violence, and contribute to conditions for sustainable peace in eastern Chad, the Central African republic, and Darfur." As you recognize, the disastrous implications of another round of cancerous violence spilling from one country to another are too numerous to catalogue here. At the same time, we cannot allow the search for a comprehensive political solution to a complex regional crisis to slow us from stopping the on-going genocide in Darfur. Both efforts must proceed in tandem, but the stopping of mass murder must be the most urgent task.

Bluster and Retreat

Instead, what we are witnessing is part of a three year pattern: the Administration talks tough and then does little more than provide generous humanitarian assistance. It blusters and, then, in the face of Sudanese intransigence or empty promises, the Administration retreats.

When the rebels started fighting in Darfur in February 2003, the Administration at first chose to ignore it. Despite the rampaging reprisals of janjaweed killers and rapists, the torching of whole villages, the wanton bombing of innocent civilians and massive humanitarian suffering, the Administration was slow to act. It seems to have calculated that pressing the government of Sudan to halt its customary scorched earth tactics in Darfur ran counter to our interests in getting Khartoum's cooperation on counter-terrorism, which began abruptly after September 11, 2001. Confronting the genocide, the Administration calculated, might also jeopardize U.S. efforts to cajole the regime to sign a North-South peace agreement with the SPLM.

But by 2004, the human toll was mounting. On the tenth anniversary of the Rwandan genocide, many noted the contrast between the hollow pledges in many capitals of "never again" and the dying in Darfur. With, a presidential campaign underway, Congress and Democratic candidates went on the record characterizing the atrocities as genocide. This prompted the Administration to decide, belatedly, that its comparative silence was deafening. Secretary Powell and Kofi Annan visited Darfur and obtained hollow promises from Bashir that his government would disarm the janjaweed, allow unfettered humanitarian access and permit an African Union force to deploy.

Yet, predictably, the killing and dying continued. Over the summer of 2004, Secretary Powell ordered a comprehensive investigation of the atrocities, drawing upon hundreds of first hand accounts from victims and witnesses. Faced with the evidence, Secretary [of State Colin] Powell embraced the investigators conclusions: genocide was taking place. To his credit, he testified to that effect, and the President in September powerfully repeated that judgment before the UN General Assembly. But then, again, the Administration did nothing effective to stop the killing.

With Western encouragement, the African Union mounted its first-ever peacekeeping mission – in Darfur. To seasoned analysts, this approach was clearly flawed from the start: the nascent AU [African Union] could not hope to secure millions of people at risk in an area the size of France. Hobbled by a weak mandate, perpetual troop shortages, an uncertain funding stream, and little institutional back-up at a brand-new regional organization, the AU was bound to fall short, despite its best intentions. It was slow to deploy, but deploy it did – with U.S. and NATO logistical and financial support.

The African Union has been the target of a lot of criticism for its short-comings in Darfur. I think unfairly so. While the United States blusters, the African Union forces have been the only ones willing to take bullets to save Darfurians. Just this past month five Senegalese soldiers died guarding a water point in Darfur, this brought the total number of AU soldiers killed in Darfur since 2004 to 15. These courageous soldiers are part of a force that has deployed without adequate international support and under constant restrictions imposed by Khartoum. They have saved thousands of lives and we owe them our honor and gratitude. Their presence also provided the U.S. with a ready, if cynical, foil for declaring the genocide under control. It wasn't.

By 2005, the AU finally fielded almost 7,000 troops. It pledged to add another 6,000 within a year. It couldn't. By then, it was obvious to all: the African Union was in over its head. Many experts, I among them, pled for NATO [North Atlantic Treaty Organization] to step in, with US support, to augment the AU force. Those calls went unheeded. Certain African leaders continued to insist on "African solutions to African problems." It was a convenient conspiracy of absolution, which enabled Washington to claim that further U.S. action was not desired. The Africans were responsible. But genocide is not and never will be an African responsibility. It is a human responsibility, requiring the concerted efforts of all humanity to halt decisively. To date, we have not.

In 2005, Secretary Rice visited Darfur, and Deputy Secretary Zoellick took over the U.S. negotiating effort. In early 2006, the AU itself accepted reality and recommended that the UN subsume its force and take over its mission. In parallel, Mr. Zoellick was trying to nail a peace agreement before he left the State Department. His efforts culminated in May 2006, in the signing of the Darfur Peace Agreement (DPA).

This deal was doomed before the ink on it was dry. It left out two key rebel groups. The one that signed did so under extreme duress – one day after its leader's brother was killed by the regime. Moreover, Khartoum made little in the way of power-sharing concessions to the rebels; there was no firm requirement that the government accept a UN peacekeeping force. There were rewards secretly pledged for Khartoum like the lifting of U.S. sanctions and a White House visit, but no penalties for non-compliance. As many feared, the ceasefire collapsed almost immediately. The rebels fractured. The killing intensified, and the people of Darfur suffered more.

After Zoellick left State, U.S. policy foundered. But, by late August 2006, it seemed back on track. The U.S. obtained UN authorization for a robust Chapter VII force for Darfur – 22,000 peacekeepers with a mandate to protect civilians. In September, President Bush and Secretary Rice visited the UN General Assembly. They appointed Andrew Natsios Special Envoy and promised tough consequences, if Khartoum did not accept the UN force mandated by UN Security Council Resolution 1706.

Mr. Natsios went to work. By November in Addis Ababa, he had joined the UN, African Union and European leaders in preemptively capitulating to Khartoum. In an effort to win Sudan's acquiescence, the U.S. and others jettisoned the robust UN force and embraced a fall-back: a smaller, weaker, AU-UN "hybrid" force. In December, the UN Security Council, with the U.S. leading the way, abandoned Resolution 1706 and endorsed the Addis agreement. This hybrid force is to be 17,000 troops versus the 22,000 called for in United Nations Resolution 1706. It would derive its mandate from the AU, which Khartoum readily manipulates. It is to draw its troops principally from Africa. But overstretched by deployments to hotspots all over the continent, Africa has very little peacekeeping capacity to spare. The hybrid would enjoy UN funding but suffer from the same "dual-key" problems that plagued the UN and NATO in the Balkans in the 1990s.

One of the greatest shortcomings of the hybrid force is that each and every aspect of it must be negotiated by all the parties involved. As negotiations persist, people in Darfur die. On March 29th at the Arab League Summit in Riyadh, [the new] UN Secretary General Ban Ki Moon reportedly won Khartoum's acceptance in principle of phase two of the UN/AU deployment. On Monday, experts from the United Nations met with Sudanese officials and appear to have worked out terms for deploying the UN "heavy support package," but not the hybrid force itself. Secretary Ban plans to meet with AU Chief Executive Alpha Oumar Konare on April 16th to discuss how to move forward. In the interim, innocent civilians remain at grave risk without adequate protection. While Secretary Ban's diplomatic efforts are laudable, they have far fallen short of delivering what is so urgently needed a robust international force, led by the United Nations that is capable of stopping the genocide in Darfur.

In reality, the "hybrid" is an ill-conceived, short-sighted and failed expedient to appease, yet again, the perpetrators of genocide. How perverse is it that the U.S. is expending all of its diplomatic capital politely negotiating the terms of a hybrid force that falls well short of what is needed to halt the genocide?

As the back and forth with Sudan persists, U.S.-imposed deadlines have come and gone. Khartoum continues to lead the international community through a diplomatic dance that defies definition. Darfurians continue to die. Chadians continue to die. The region is coming unglued.

This is, by any measure, a collective shame. The American people know it. And, by all accounts, they don't much like it. A December *Newsweek* poll as well as a PIPA poll released last week found that 65% of Americans support sending U.S. troops, as part of an international force, to Darfur.

The Way Forward

The time for fruitless and feckless negotiations has long since passed. However well-intentioned the mediators, negotiations only serve Khartoum's interests – in diverting international attention and delaying meaningful international action. They buy Khartoum time to continue the killing.

If the Administration were serious about halting this four year-old genocide and protecting civilians in Darfur, it would act now to show Khartoum
that we are done talking and are ready to turn the screws.

We should take the following four steps:

Step One: The President should issue an Executive Order implementing the
financial measures in Plan B immediately. The Order should include safeguards
to ensure that revenue flows to the government of South Sudan remain unaf-
fected. Given the leak of Plan B, the President should act now or risk squander-
ing the potentially significant impact of these measures. The Administration
should couple unilateral sanctions with a sustained push for tough UN sanctions, including those that target the oil sector. The U.S. should then dare
China or another permanent member to accept the blame for vetoing effective
action to halt a genocide.

Step Two: The Bush Administration should state clearly that these financial
penalties will not be lifted unless and until the Sudanese government permanently and verifiably stops all air and ground attacks and allows the full and
unfettered deployment of the UN force authorized under UNSC Resolution
1706. The U.S. should declare the so-called "hybrid" force dead and take it off
the negotiating table. The hybrid was an unfortunate concession to Khartoum,
which Khartoum has been foolish enough not to embrace. It's time to tell
Khartoum that it has a simple choice: accept the UN force as mandated by
Resolution 1706 or face escalating pressure from the U.S.

Step Three: The 110th Congress should swiftly adopt new legislation on Darfur.
It should build upon a bill introduced in the last Congress by Representative
Payne, which garnered the bipartisan support of over 100 co-sponsors. The
new legislation should:

- Authorize the President to stop the genocide in Darfur, including by
  imposing a no-fly zone, bombing aircraft, airfields and the regime's
  military and intelligence assets.
- Authorize funds to upgrade Abeche airfield in Chad, with the agreement of the government of Chad, in order to support potential NATO
  air operations, to facilitate a UN deployment to Chad and Darfur, and
  for humanitarian purposes.
- Urge the Administration to press for the deployment of UN peacekeepers to the borders of Chad and the Central African Republic to protect
  civilians and serve as advance elements for the UN force in Darfur
  authorized under UNSCR 1706.
- Impose capital market sanctions on companies investing in Sudan.
- Freeze the Sudanese government assets and those of key Sudanese military, government and janjaweed leaders and their families. Prohibit
  their travel to the U.S.
- And, require the Administration to report every 30 days (in unclassified and classified form) on the financial, military, and covert steps it is
  prepared to take to compel the GOS to accept unconditionally a robust
  UN force and halt attacks on civilians.

Step Four: If within fifteen days of the issuance of the "Plan B" Executive Order, the government of Sudan has failed to meet these conditions, the Bush Administration should use force to compel Khartoum to admit a robust UN force and stop killing civilians.

What I wrote with Anthony Lake and Donald Payne in the *Washington Post* on October 2, 2006, still applies six months, and thousands of lives later:

> History demonstrates there is one language Khartoum understands: the credible threat or use of force. It's time again to get tough with Sudan. The U.S. should press for a Chapter VII UN resolution that issues Sudan an ultimatum: accept the unconditional deployment of the UN force within one week, or face military consequences. The resolution would authorize enforcement by UN member states, collectively or individually. International military pressure would continue until Sudan relents. The U.S., preferably with NATO involvement and African political support, would strike Sudanese airfields, aircraft and other military assets. They could blockade Port Sudan, through which Sudan's oil exports flow. Then, the UN force would deploy – by force, if necessary, with U.S. and NATO backing.

If the U.S. fails to gain UN support, we should act without it as it did in 1999 in Kosovo – to confront a lesser humanitarian crisis (perhaps 10,000 killed) and a much more formidable adversary. The real question is this: "will we use force to save Africans in Darfur as we did to save Europeans in Kosovo?"

Not surprisingly, our proposal has been controversial.

Some argue that it is unthinkable in the current context. True, the international climate is less forgiving than it was in 1999 when we acted in Kosovo. Iraq and torture scandals have left many abroad doubting our motives and legitimacy. Some will reject any future U.S. military action, especially against an Islamic regime, even if purely to halt genocide against Muslim civilians. Sudan has also threatened that Al Qaeda will attack non-African forces in Darfur – a possibility since Sudan long hosted bin Laden and his businesses. Yet, to allow another state to deter the U.S. by threatening terrorism would set a terrible precedent. It would also be cowardly and, in the face of genocide, immoral. Others argue the U.S. military cannot take on another mission. Indeed, our ground forces are stretched thin. But a bombing campaign or a naval blockade would tax the Air Force and Navy, which have relatively more capacity, and could utilize the 1,500 U.S. military personnel already in nearby Djibouti.

Still others insist that, without the consent of the UN or a relevant regional body, we would be breaking international law. But the Security Council last year codified a new international norm prescribing "the responsibility to protect." It commits UN members to decisive action, including enforcement, when peaceful measures fail to halt genocide or crimes against humanity.

Some advocates prefer the imposition of a no-fly zone over Darfur. They seem to view it as a less aggressive option than bombing Sudanese assets. It is a fine option, but let's be clear what it likely entails. Rather than stand-off air strikes against defined targets, maintaining a no-fly zone would require an asset-intensive, 24 hours per day, 7 day per-week, open-ended military commitment in a logistically difficult context. To protect the no-fly area, the air cap would have to disable or shoot down any aircraft that took off in the zone. It would mean shutting down Sudanese airfields in and near Darfur to all but humanitarian traffic. In short, it would soon require many of the same steps that are necessary to conduct the air strikes we recommend, plus much more.

Finally, humanitarian organizations express concern that air strikes could disrupt humanitarian operations or cause the government of Sudan to intensify ground attacks against civilians in camps. These are legitimate concerns. Yet, there are ways to mitigate these risks. Targets could be selected to avoid airfields used by humanitarian agencies operating in Darfur. To protect civilians at risk, the U.S., France or other NATO countries could position a light quick reaction force in nearby Chad to deter and respond to any increased attacks against camps in Darfur or Chad. While the risks may be mitigated, we must acknowledge they cannot be eliminated.

Yet, we must also acknowledge the daily cost of the status quo – of a feckless policy characterized by bluster and retreat. That cost has been and will continue to be thousands and thousands and thousands more lives each month. That cost is an emboldened Khartoum government that continues to kill with impunity. That cost is a regime that literally has gotten away with murder, while the U.S. merely remonstrates.

I would submit that this cost is too high. Too many have already died. Too many more are soon to die. When, if ever, will the Bush Administration decide that enough is finally enough?

Prospects for Peace in Darfur Today

It is a pleasure to be invited here to testify at this hearing and to present some of my views and analysis on the situation in Darfur, a part of the world that I knew intimately in the 1980s, and whose travails I have followed closely since then.

I will focus my remarks on two major points. One is that Darfur today is different to the Darfur of 2003–04, when, on the tenth anniversary of the Rwanda genocide, the conscience of the world—and notably this House—was awoken to condemn the massacres, dispossession and rape as "genocide." Many realities in Darfur have changed and we need an accurate appraisal and analysis of the situation if we are to take the right decisions. The crisis in Darfur has been characterized as "genocide," as "war" and as "anarchy." None of these descriptions does justice to the complexity of the situation and the changes in the political and military landscape, especially in the last year. I submit that in order for us to respond appropriately, it is important to recognize the realities—notably that Darfur today cannot be described as a conflict between Arabs and Africans.

My second point is that the essential test of any policy for Darfur—or indeed Sudan—is that it should work. "Ought" implies "can": in framing our actions we should be aware of what can succeed.

In that regard, I draw upon my experience as a member of the AU [African Union] mediation team in Abuja, [Nigeria,] when I was tasked with mediating a comprehensive ceasefire for Darfur and convening a task force to draw up an implementation plan for AU or UN forces. We must be aware of the considerable limitations on what international forces, such as are proposed under UN Security Council Resolution 1706, can achieve in Darfur. What they can do is to monitor and selectively enforce a ceasefire including demilitarization of displaced camps and humanitarian access routes. What they cannot do is to police Darfur, disarm the Janjaweed [Muslim militia linked to the Sudanese government] or provide protection to the majority of Darfurian civilians in the event of an eruption of major violence. The proposed UN troop deployment could not fulfill these latter tasks, even with a workable ceasefire, and certainly cannot undertake them in the middle of ongoing hostilities.

The current political alignment is not favorable for a rapid peace settlement for Darfur. Nonetheless, without the warring parties having confidence that there

U.S. House of Representatives, April 19, 2007.

is progress towards such a settlement, the task of any international peacekeeping or protection force in Darfur will be infinitely harder. Our immediate aim should be a robust and monitorable ceasefire. In turn, a credible political peace process for Darfur requires putting Sudan's Comprehensive Peace Agreement back on track, and restoring Sudanese confidence in that peace agreement. I urge the U.S. government to keep this primary aim clearly in focus.

My Personal Involvement in Darfur

I lived and worked in Darfur from 1985–87, when I conducted research for my Ph.D. thesis. Of the villages and nomadic camps where I lived, three are completely destroyed—one of them occupied by Janjaweed—two are partly destroyed, one is a government garrison, and one a stronghold of the SLA [Sudanese Liberation Army, one of the major opposition groups in Darfur to the Sudanese government], which was attacked and bombed by the government. Another where I stayed as a guest of Sheikh Hilal Abdalla, father of Musa Hilal [widely regarded as the top Janjaweed leader in Darfur]—is a camp for the Janjaweed. One day I hope to return to these places and document what has happened to the people I knew who lived in each of them.

During the 1990s, and during the period of the peace talks between the Sudan government and the SPLM [Sudan People's Liberation Movement, the political counterpart of the SLA] during 2001–04, I focused much of my energy on the question of the marginalized peoples of northern Sudan—including the Nuba, the Beja and the peoples of Blue Nile. International attention to the plight of the South tended to overlook these people, who on occasions were suffering from massacre, systematic rape and forced displacement every bit as horrendous as that inflicted on the people of Darfur during the peak of the counter-insurgency campaigns by government army and Janjaweed in 2003–04. I was concerned that the North-South focus of the Naivasha peace talks would leave the marginalized peoples of northern Sudan politically short-changed and vulnerable. I also followed Darfur and brought Darfurians into the various fora I helped organize, though their effective participation was always hampered by their internal divisions.

When Darfur erupted into large-scale violent conflict in 2003 I was saddened and angered, but not entirely surprised. The pattern of the violence in Darfur replicates in most respects the experience of other Sudanese peripheries. In an article I wrote in 2004, entitled "Counterinsurgency on the cheap," I described the atrocities as "genocide by force of habit." We can learn much about the conflict in Darfur by placing it in the context of the previous wars in Sudan and the sadly consistent methods used by the government of Sudan to pursue its war aims.

I spent much of 2005 and 2006 as an advisor to Dr Salim Ahmed Salim, the African Union's chief mediator for the Darfur conflict, dealing with many of the places and some of the people I knew from my years in Darfur. My principal role in the peace talks was facilitating the negotiations on security issues. The main focus of this was working on a text of a comprehensive ceasefire and final status security arrangements—a text that was subsequently enhanced in certain details by the efforts of [U.S.] Deputy Secretary Robert B. Zoellick and his team on May 2–4, 2006. I am happy to say that all the three leaders of the Darfur armed movements judged the security arrangements section of the Darfur Peace Agreement acceptable at that time, with the sole objection coming from Dr. Khalil Ibrahim, President of the Justice and Equality Movement [another Darfurian opposition group], who demanded that his troops be paid salaries from the government budget during the interim period.

My role also included overseeing an implementation task force, consisting of military officers from the UN and AU, who designed the ceasefire implementation modalities, a plan that in turn was the basis for the troop strengths and tasks envisioned in UN Security Council Resolution 1706, which calls for the dispatch of UN forces to Darfur.

My final task in Abuja was to stay on when all the other members of the mediation team had left, in a last-ditch effort to persuade Abdel Wahid al Nur [leader of a faction of the SLA] to join the peace agreement. I came close but did not succeed.

How to Describe Darfur Today?

Darfur's nightmare continues. It is taking new forms. The violence today is different in both scale and nature to that of three years ago. Many fewer people are being killed than during the peak of atrocity in 2003–04, and many fewer are dying from hunger and disease. The humanitarian agencies have done a remarkably good job.

The number of deaths should not be the sole or the overriding measure of the crime and tragedy in Darfur. Millions of people live in displaced camps, unable to return home. They live in fear. The legacy of the immense military campaigns of 2003–04 is that significant areas of Darfur have been ethnically cleansed of their former population. This crime cannot be allowed to stand: one basic measure of peace is that it entitles and empowers displaced people to return to their places of origin, to resume their lives under a local administrative system of their choice that provides them with physical and legal security, including tenure over their land.

Moreover, the capacity for renewed violence on a comparable scale has not diminished. Darfur is awash with weaponry. The army, paramilitaries, rebel groups and local self-defense groups are all heavily armed. Decades of experience in Sudan tells us that war consists of occasional sweeping campaigns in which the army, air-force and paramilitaries destroy everything in their path, followed by longer periods in which the violence subsides somewhat, but the underlying causes of conflict remain unaddressed. Any new explosion of violence rarely follows the same pattern as the previous peak in killing—the location may be different (for example in urban areas or displaced camps, or across an international frontier), and the belligerents may be configured differently (some militia may switch sides to join the rebels, some rebel factions may cut deals with the government). New armed groups may emerge, perhaps among the angry and politicized groups of displaced people, or in neighboring regions of Sudan. These patterns are familiar from Sudan's long-running wars and it would be unwise to assume that Darfur's violence will not surge again and take on new forms.

I submit that we can no longer describe the conflict as "Arab" versus "African." That was always an inadequate description, even during the height of the killing in 2003–04, when racial labels were particularly salient. The ethnic politics of Darfur are much more complicated now. Having armed numerous Arab militia, including the Janjaweed, the government no longer commands the loyalties of its erstwhile proxies. Army generals are fearful of the might of the Janjaweed, who in some locations are more numerous and better armed than the regular army. The generals know it is impossible to dis-arm the militia by force. Their greatest fear is that some of the Arab militia will desert the government for the rebels. This fear is not without foundation: many Darfurian Arabs are talking to the insurgents and making local pacts. In the other direction, one of the most unfortunate consequences of the Darfur Peace Agreement was the way in which some commanders of the SLA-Minawi, most of them ethnic Zaghawa, became government proxies, to the extent that local people called them "Janjaweed-2."

There is no doubt that individual atrocities in Darfur continue to bear the hallmarks of ethnically-targeted genocidal massacre. But these atrocities do not follow any straightforward "Arab"-"African" dichotomy. One of my concerns about the use of the word "genocide" to describe these crimes is that it seems to imply that Darfur's crisis consist of Arabs killing Africans. Such a depiction is inaccurate.

Many Darfurians characterize the situation as "anarchy." That is cor-rect insofar as the institutions and mechanisms that maintained law and order have broken down or been dismantled, and the government is failing in its basic obligation of providing security. It is accurate insofar as much of the violence witnessed in the last year is localized conflict (including clashes between Arab tribes), fighting among rebel groups, and banditry. Describing the situation as "war" does not do justice to the complexity of the conflict and the extent of multiplication of armed groups. But "anar-chy" is also an incomplete description: it fails to capture the way in which the situation is manipulated by the strongest actor, the government of Sudan, which has co-opted many institutions for civil administration into its paramilitary structure.

What is clear is that Darfur's crisis is complicated and has changed. Last year's solutions can no longer work. Last year's labels may no longer fit.

Prospects for Peace and Security

The prospects for peace in Darfur are not encouraging. The political alignment for peace was most favorable in the first half of 2005, when there was enthusi-asm for the Comprehensive Peace Agreement (just signed by Khartoum and the SPLM) and its promise of national democratic transformation. At that time, pro-peace figures in Khartoum [capital of Sudan] such as vice president Ali Osman Taha were in the ascendant, the Darfur rebels had a semblance of political coor-dination, and Chad was still part of the solution, not part of the problem.

That favorable alignment slipped during late 2005 and early 2006, and by the time the Abuja peace talks reached their denouement, the political context was becoming less favorable week-by-week. Peace in Abuja was missed by a hair's breadth, but that slender miss was disastrous. The adverse trend has continued over the subsequent eleven months.

I recall some tribal elders arriving at Abuja to encourage the rebels to sign the agreement, making the argument that if the chance for peace is not taken, Darfur faces the prospect of a war of all against all. That Hobbesian scenario may yet materialize. Local disputes are multiplying and the mechanisms to resolve them are too weak.

Today, the Darfur armed groups are more fractured than at any time in their short history. The prospects for unifying them are remote. Arabs groups have emerged as independent actors and should be represented in any new peace process.

External interference—by Chad, Eritrea and Libya—has intensified. The leaders of these countries see turmoil in Darfur as a means of furthering their own political interests.

Implementation of the Darfur Peace Agreement is farcical. Minni Minawi [leader of the combined SLA/SPLM] possesses no power, the key institutions do not exist or have no resources, and the National Congress Party is choosing the candidates to fill the ministerial and gubernatorial posts provided for the SLM. Contrary to the provisions of the DPA, the Security Arrangements Implementation Commission is headed by an army general, not a nominee of the SLM. The most important institution of all—the Ceasefire Commission—has become completely dysfunctional. The government is practicing "retail politics"—purchasing the allegiance or cooperation of individuals on a case-by-case basis, and describing this as fulfilling the requirements of the DPA.

Credible mediation is needed, but the most important interlocutors face conflicts of interest. The African Union has the mandate to implement the DPA as it stands, and is also tasked with negotiating a new agreement with the non-signatory rebels. It is hard for it to do both. In due course the UN will find itself in a similar position—the UN Mission in Sudan is mandated to implement the Comprehensive Peace Agreement, and Special Representative Jan Eliasson is also tasked to mediate with Darfurian groups which demand that the CPA be revised to accommodate their demands.

This points us to perhaps the most significant single challenge to peace in Darfur: any peace agreement for Darfur must be a buttress to the CPA. But most Darfurians see the CPA, not as a charter for national democratization, but rather as (at best) a ceiling for their aspirations and (at worst) a sinking ship. While such beliefs continue, there is little chance that they will be ready to make peace. Peace in Darfur is possible only if there is widespread confidence in the CPA among ordinary Sudanese, and at present this does not exist.

In these circumstances, many advocate that the priority should be to send a strong international force to Darfur to protect civilians there, so that the Darfurian people who have already suffered enough do not continue to die while the politicians argue interminably about peace over the coming months and years. There is no doubt that a larger, better equipped and better man-dated international force could improve conditions in Darfur. But we must also be frank and realistic about what such a force can achieve, both under the current circumstances of ongoing hostilities, and under any future conditions of a fully signed-up peace agreement.

In facilitating the discussions on the security arrangements for the DPA, the African Union security team took advice from a number of senior and experienced military officers and security advisers from Africa, the UN and the U.S. The team concluded that a force of about 20,000 peacekeepers could police a ceasefire agreement between government and rebels, monitor airfields to ensure that the ban on offensive military flights is respected, ensure the demilitarization of displaced camps and humanitarian supply routes, train a community police force to provide security for displaced people, and monitor government efforts to neutralize and selectively disarm the militia. It could fulfill these tasks in the context of a fully-signed up peace agreement with the active cooperation of the parties.

Even with a Chapter VII [of the UN Charter] mandate and the consent of the Sudan government, what such a force could not do is to provide security for all, or even most, Darfurian civilians in their home villages. It could not disarm the Janjaweed. It could not remove the government army and police from Darfur and take over their functions.

In the context of ongoing hostilities, the capability of a peacekeeping force would be even more limited, as it would need to devote much of its capacity to force protection. As we have learned from many other conflicts, international forces do not, as a general rule, protect civilians at risk during an explosion of violence.

The main security discussion that is needed concerns the strategic plan and concept of operations for an international force in Darfur. This was a discussion that we began but did not conclude in Abuja. But in our truncated discussions, some basic principles became clear.

A first consideration is time. Any international force dispatched to Darfur should expect to be there for a minimum of five years. It is not realistic to expect the region to be stabilized in a shorter period of time.

Second, disarmament can only be undertaken by consent, in a staged and reciprocal manner across all armed groups. Arms control is primarily a political process, not a technical one. The government's cooperation in this is also necessary. While Khartoum is most of Darfur's problem, Darfur's solutions must also come through Khartoum.

Third, for an international force to be effective, it must devote the major-ity of its energy to political work and community liaison, with the threat and use of force comprising only a small part of its activities.

And finally, the force levels envisaged for the implementation of the DPA security arrangements would be woefully insufficient to provide physical protec-tion to all civilians at risk during any possible future eruption of violence. Other measures would be required to prevent such violence or protect civilians at risk.

It is important to be soberly realistic about what the UN—or indeed any international force—can achieve in Darfur. Many Darfurians have exaggerated expectations that the UN will solve all their problems, and these false hopes deter them from engaging realistically with the political challenges they face. It is important for the U.S. and UN to give the right message: peace is the goal; peacekeeping is a tool.

A comprehensive, robust and monitorable ceasefire in Darfur, and a political process leading to a peace agreement for Darfur, and a properly implemented CPA must be the priority. Let us have no illusions that these goals will be easy to achieve. But a credible political process in this direction is essential and can create sufficient confidence that an international force can function effectively.

The lesson of Sudan's wars over the last quarter century is that peace is possible, if it is pursued relentlessly and with an international consensus. The lesson of Sudan's peace deals is that whatever is on paper is never good enough: the challenge lies in the implementation. Sudan and its problems will be with us for some time to come: we must take a long view.

POSTSCRIPT

Is Military Intervention in Darfur Justified?

Fighting in Darfur eased some in late 2007 and into 2008, but escalated anew during the summer of 2008. There was some hope that the UN peace-keeping force authorized in 2007 would bring some relief, but its strength and mission order have been restrained by its inability to raise forces and by the opposition of China in the UN Security to a robust UN force. China has long opposed outside intervention, even by the UN in other countries, and some also accuse China of seeking to curry favor with Khartoum to increase Beijing's oil imports from Sudan. The UN and AU have also sponsored or supported various efforts to renew peace talks, but these efforts have been rejected by some or many of the rebel groups, who make several demands, such as an end to attacks by the Sudanese military and the Janjaweed, prior to negotiations. Another development in 2008 came at the International Criminal Court when its prosecutor accused Sudan's President al-Bashir of war crimes in Darfur and asked the court's judges to issue an arrest warrant against him.

Rice's call on the White House to send U.S. troops to Sudan went unheeded. U.S. commitments in Iraq and Afghanistan were one reason; a reluctance to become involved in a complex situation is another. Clearly atrocities, even genocide, have occurred, and also clearly, Khartoum and the Janjaweed bear the majority of guilt. But it is also true, as de Waal points out, that the political situation is very murky and that not all the barriers to peace are attributable to Sudan's government. Further it is unclear what Americans think about U.S. troops going to Darfur. A recent poll found 61 percent of Americans saying they favored sending U.S. ground troops to Darfur as part of an international force. Yet in another poll, 65 percent say they hardly or do not much follow the situation in Darfur. Perhaps most revealing was a poll that asked about U.S. involvement in Darfur that "may cost more than one hundred U.S. lives." Faced with the possibility of even very limited U.S. casualties, support for intervention dropped to 37 percent, with 58 percent opposed, and 5 percent unsure.

A good and up-to-date overview of the situation in Darfur is available through the Council on Foreign Relations' *Crisis Guide: Darfur* at http://www. cfr.org/publication/13129/. An alliance of 100 or more humanitarian groups calling for immediate and strong international efforts in Darfur is Save Darfur at http://www.savedarfur.org. For the Sudan government's perspective, go to the Web site of its embassy in the United States at http://www.sudanembassy.org/. The view that the conflict in Sudan could threaten that country's survival and the implications of a collapse can be found in Andrew S. Natsios, "Beyond Darfur: Sudan's Slide Toward Civil War," *Foreign Affairs* (May/June 2008).

Internet References . . .

IPE Net

The International Political Economy Network hosted by Indiana University and sponsored by the IPE section of the International Studies Association is a good starting point to study the intersection of politics and economics globally.

http://www.indiana.edu/~ipe/ipesection/

United Nations Development Programme (UNDP)

This United Nations Development Programme (UNDP) site offers publications and current information on world poverty, the UNDP's mission statement, information on the UN Development Fund for Women, and more.

http://www.undp.org

Office of the U.S. Trade Representative

The Office of the U.S. Trade Representative (USTR) is responsible for developing and coordinating U.S. international trade, commodity, and direct investment policy and leading or directing negotiations with other countries on such matters. The U.S. trade representative is a cabinet member who acts as the principal trade adviser, negotiator, and spokesperson for the president on trade and related investment matters.

http://www.ustr.gov

The U.S. Agency for International Development (USAID)

This is the home page of the U.S. Agency for International Development (USAID), which is the independent government agency that provides economic development and humanitarian assistance to advance U.S. economic and political interests overseas.

http://www.usaid.gov/

World Trade Organization (WTO)

The World Trade Organization (WTO) is the only international organization dealing with the global rules of trade between nations. Its main function is to ensure that trade flows as smoothly, predictably, and freely as possible. This site provides extensive information about the organization and international trade today.

http://www.wto.org

Third World Network

The Third World Network (TWN) is an independent, nonprofit international network of organizations and individuals involved in economic, social, and environmental issues relating to development, the developing countries of the world, and the North-South divide. At the network's Web site you will find recent news, TWN position papers, action alerts, and other resources on a variety of topics, including economics, trade, and health.

http://www.twnside.org.sg

Economic Issues

*I*nternational economic and trade issues have an immediate and personal effect on individuals in ways that few other international issues
do. They influence the jobs we hold and the prices of the products we
buy—in short, our lifestyles. In the worldwide competition for resources
and markets, tensions arise between allies and adversaries alike. This
section examines some of the prevailing economic tensions.

- Is World Trade Organization Membership Beneficial?
- Do Sovereign Wealth Funds Threaten Economic Sovereignty?
- Is Immigration an Economic Benefit to the Host Country?

ISSUE 11

Is World Trade Organization Membership Beneficial?

YES: Peter F. Allgeier, from Testimony during Hearings on "The Future of the World Trade Organization," before the Subcommittee on Trade, Committee on Ways and Means, U.S. House of Representatives (May 17, 2005)

NO: Lori Wallach, from Testimony during Hearings on "The Future of the World Trade Organization," before the Subcommittee on Trade, Committee on Ways and Means, U.S. House of Representatives (May 17, 2005)

ISSUE SUMMARY

YES: Peter F. Allgeier, Deputy U.S. Trade Representative, Office of the U.S. Trade Representative, describes the World Trade Organization as beneficial to U.S. strategic and economic interests and argues that there is overwhelming value to be gained through continued U.S. participation in the organization.

NO: Lori Wallach, director of Public Citizen's Global Trade Watch, part of Public Citizen, a Washington, D.C.–based advocacy group, maintains that Congress should demand a transformation of WTO trade rules because they have failed to achieve the promised economic gains and have also undercut an array of nontrade, noneconomic policies and goals advantageous to the public interest in the United States and abroad.

The debate here is an extension of the controversy over economic globalization found in Issue 1. A key component of the growth of interaction and interdependence among the countries of the world has been the expansion of international trade through the lowering of tariffs and nontariff barriers to trade, such as quotas on imports and government subsidies for domestic producers. On the global level, the World Trade Organization (WTO) is at the center of the drive to continue to remove trade barriers and the resolution of disputes among countries over trade policy.

The origins of the WTO extend back to the General Agreement on Tariffs and Trade (GATT), an organization confusingly named after the treaty that established it in 1947 to promote free trade. The confusion was ended in 1995 when the treaty was amended to change the name of the organization to the World Trade Organization. One mark of the WTO's importance is that from an initial 23 countries, almost all countries are now either a member (149 countries) or an observer (32 countries) on the path to membership.

Since the GATT/WTO began, there have been nine "rounds" of trade talks among its members aimed at further reducing trade barriers. The eighth and most recently completed round, the "Uruguay Round" named after the site of the initial meeting, was begun in 1986 and concluded in 1994. This complex agreement is about 26,000 pages long and covers not just exporting and importing raw materials and manufactured goods, but also buying and selling services abroad, protecting copyrights and patents, and virtually everything else that impacts the flow of goods and services among countries.

Hoping to build on the Uruguay Round, the WTO launched its ninth round at a meeting in Doha, Qatar, in 2001. The Doha Round has floundered. One issue is between the economically less developed countries (LDCs) and economically developed countries (EDCs). The LDCs believe that the EDCs have created trade rules that have benefited themselves and disadvantaged the LDCs. There are also disputes between the EDCs, especially pitting the United States versus the European Union. Several meetings to negotiate new revisions to the GATT have failed to make progress, and the success of the Doha Round is doubtful.

Adding to the LDCs' criticism of the rules under the WTO are a wide range of other complaints about the organization and even the very concept of free trade. Critics argue, for example, that WTO rules prevent countries from refusing to import goods that are produced in low-wage "sweatshops" or in a manner that damages the environment. Labor unions, among others, argue that free trade is undermining employment in their country by allowing low-cost imports to undercut domestic production. U.S. trade unions, for example, are very skeptical of free trade. Other groups oppose it because they do not believe that all countries abide by the rules. American software, movie, and music producers, for example, complain that their copyright-protected "intellectual property" is pirated in other countries with at least the passive complicity of the government. Yet another issue concerns national sovereignty. Treaties legally bind countries, and, for example, a country that believes another is not living up to the WTO treaty can file a suit against the offending country in what amounts to a WTO court. The fact that an international organization can, in effect, find a country wrong and direct it to change its policy is an affront to those who defend absolute sovereignty for their country. Without denying that there is a range of important concerns that face the WTO, Peter F. Allgeier argues in the first reading that the WTO has contributed to American and world prosperity and indicates U.S. support for even further reductions in trade barriers. Lori Wallach does not argue for withdrawing precipitously from the WTO, but depicts it and the GATT as deeply flawed and in need of major repair.

YES

Peter F. Allgeier

Supporting the World Trade Organization

Introduction

I am pleased to be here to discuss the World Trade Organization (WTO) and the WTO Agreements, the relationship to the strategic and economic interests of the United States, and the overwhelming value of continued U.S. participation in the WTO. . . .

My testimony today provides an opportunity to look back at the creation of the WTO and our participation over the last 10 years and, equally important, to focus on our agenda for the next several months leading up to the Sixth WTO Ministerial in Hong Kong this December and head toward a successful conclusion of the Doha Development Agenda negotiations in 2006.

Historical Context for the WTO

The creation of the WTO represented the culmination of a decades-long bipartisan U.S. commitment to lead the world away from economic isolationism and toward the imperative of an open, rules-based global trading system. The GATT [General Agreement on Tariffs and Trade] had been created in 1947—drawn up in an unsteady post-war world that collectively was determined to strengthen global security and peace through economic opportunity and growth in living standards.

Today, we continue to exercise our leadership in a world that faces new challenges to maintaining global security and stability, underscoring the continuing important strategic interest of the United States in an open global trading system governed by the rule of law. The United States is fully engaged in the WTO work under the Doha Development Agenda [DDA], and the United States aggressively uses the existing WTO machinery to effectively enforce our rights.

WTO membership now stands at 148. Accession to the WTO carries more stringent requirements than what was used in the GATT. Key entries during the past decades include not only China, but also a wide array of other countries that each carry their own strategic and economic importance, such as Jordan, Cambodia, and several former Soviet Republics. Negotiations toward entry into the WTO are ongoing at various stages for more than 25 countries, ranging from Russia and Vietnam, to Iraq, Ukraine, Saudi Arabia, and

U.S. House of Representatives, May 17, 2005.

Afghanistan. Each effort underscores the importance attached to membership in the WTO, and the importance of moving forward with a member-driven, rules-based approach to the global trading system.

Commercial Significance for the United States of Uruguay Round and the WTO

During the five years since the last review under the Uruguay Round Agreements Act, unprecedented growth in trade and global economic integration has continued—led by continuing advances in technology, communications, manufacturing, and logistics. Five years ago we did not have ubiquitous cell phones that captured and transmitted photos miles away, nor was it yet routine to use the Internet to order overnight delivery of a product from thousands of miles away. Advances such as these demonstrate that the trade environment is always changing, the citizens of the United States—like the rest of the world—are being presented with new products, new services and, most important, new economic opportunities that did not exist in 1995, or 2000. At the same time, globalization also undoubtedly presents new issues, new competitive challenges and new economic pressures.

Simply put, the WTO exists as the most important vehicle to advance U.S. trade interests, and is critical to America's workers, businesses, farmers, and ranchers. Many are dependent and all are affected by a global trading system that must operate with predictability and transparency, without discrimination against American products, and providing for actions to address unfair trade practices. The United States remains the world's largest exporter. During the first 10 years of the WTO—from 1994 to 2004—U.S. exports of goods and services have risen 63 percent, from $703 billion to over $1.1 trillion.

To ensure equal opportunities for U.S. businesses, farmers, ranchers, and other exporters, the United States has brought more WTO dispute settlement cases than any other member. Since establishment of the WTO, the United States has initiated 74 cases. Examples of cases include those focusing on: dairy, apples, biotechnology, telecommunications, automobiles, apparel, unfair customs procedures, and protecting intellectual property rights. Of those, we have won 23 on core issues, lost four, and settled 23 before decision. The remaining 24 are "in process" (in panel, in consultations, or monitored for progress or otherwise inactive). In the last five years, our record to-date in cases—both offensive and defensive—is 16 wins and 14 losses. From 1995 to 2000, the U.S. record was 18 wins and 15 losses. The United States represents roughly 17 percent of world trade, yet has brought nearly 22 percent of the WTO disputes between January 1, 1995 and December 31, 2004.

This year marks the full implementation of many key Uruguay Round agreements, such as completion of the 10 year phased implementation of global tariff cuts on industrial and agricultural goods and reductions in trade-distorting agricultural domestic support and export subsidies; elimination of quotas and full integration of textile trade into the multilateral trading system; and improvements in patent protection in key markets such as India. The Uruguay Round was highlighted by the negotiating results being adopted in a "single undertaking" by all members, who together rejected any notion of a two or three-tier global trading system.

The WTO also provides opportunities on a day-to-day basis for advancing U.S. interests through the more than 20 standing WTO committees—not including numerous additional Working Groups, Working Parties, and Negotiating Bodies—which meet regularly to administer agreements, for members to exchange views, work to resolve questions of members' compliance with commitments, and develop initiatives aimed to improve the agreements and their operation.

The United States has advocated greater transparency and openness in WTO proceedings. The WTO has taken important steps to increase the transparency of its operation across the board, from document availability to public outreach. WTO members continue to set the course for the organization, and the members themselves remain responsible for compliance with rules.

Responding to U.S. leadership, during the past 10 years the WTO has shown itself to be a dynamic organization, one where our interests are advanced toward achievements with concrete positive effect. We have seen to it that the substantive agenda has provided the path for significant market-opening results over the past decade, such as concluding the Information Technology Agreement (ITA) to eliminate tariffs worldwide on IT products, and bringing the Basic Telecommunications Agreement into effect, which opened up 95 percent of the world's telecommunications markets. Both are achievements that continue to contribute to the ability of citizens around the globe to take advantage of the Information Age.

The 1997 Agreement on Trade in Financial Services has achieved fair, open and transparent practices across the global financial services industry, fostering a climate of greater global economic security. The agreement helps ensure that U.S. banking, securities, insurance, and other financial services firms can compete and invest in overseas markets on clear and fair terms.

In a world where over 95 percent of consumers live beyond our borders, the WTO is an essential tool for U.S. interests. Increasingly, small businesses are important players in the global economy and an important stake holder in advancing U.S. interests in the WTO agenda. Between 1992 and 2002, U.S. exports from small and medium-sized enterprises rose 54 percent, from $102.8 billion to $158.5 billion—a faster pace than the rate of growth for total U.S. exports during the same time.

Falling trade barriers—many of which reflect the 10 year implementation of the results of the Uruguay Round—have helped rapidly increase the value of trade relative to the U.S. economy. U.S. goods and service trade (exports plus imports) reached the levels of 18 percent of the value of U.S. GDP in 1984, 21.7 percent in 1994 and 25.2 percent in 2004. Both U.S. manufacturing exports and U.S. agricultural exports have grown strongly during our 10 years in the WTO. Between 1994 and 2004, they were up 65 percent and 38 percent, respectively. U.S. exports of high technology products grew by 67 percent during the past 10 years and accounted for one-quarter of total goods exports.

During this time period, U.S. exports to Mexico more than doubled, while exports to Canada and the EU grew by 66 percent and 56 percent, respectively.

Among major countries and regions, exports to China exhibited the fastest growth, nearly quadrupling over the past 10 years. China's entry into the WTO in December 2001 locked in improved market access opportunities, committing to reduce its tariffs on industrial products, which averaged 24.6 percent, to a level that averages 9.4 percent. The growth in services exports between 1994 and 2004 (69 percent) slightly exceeded that of goods (61 percent). Nearly all of the major services export categories have grown between 1994 and 2004.

Development

The United States has been the engine of economic growth for much of the world economy. Strong growth of the U.S. economy and openness to trade assisted the recovering countries involved in the Asian financial crisis of the late 1990s and further helped pull the global economy back from the brink of severe recession in the early part of the current decade. The completion of the Uruguay Round and creation of the WTO have figured prominently in helping our nation to sustain not only our own domestic economic strength but also our leadership role within the global economy.

The United States continues to be second to none in actively working with developing countries to encourage trade liberalization that will boost economic growth and development. Trading partners with strong economies make good allies and provide important consumers for US goods and services. Study after study shows that the WTO's rules-based system promotes openness and predictability leading to increased trade and improved prospects for economic growth in member countries. By promoting the rule of law, the WTO fosters a better business climate in developing country members, which helps them attract more foreign direct investment and helps to increase economic growth around the globe, while also helping to lift the least developed countries out of poverty. Economic literature confirms that countries that have more open economies engage in increased international trade and have higher growth rates than more closed economies. Several World Bank studies in 2004 found that trade and integration into the world economy lead to faster growth and poverty-reduction in poor countries. The developing countries that were most open to trade over the past two decades also had the fastest growing wages.

Looking Ahead: Advancing the Doha Development Agenda

Two months after the events of September 11th, 2001, U.S. leadership played a critical role in the launch of a new round of multilateral trade negotiations, the first to be conducted under the WTO. The negotiations under the Doha Development Agenda reflect the dynamic complexities of today's economic world, and present new opportunities to make historic advancements on the idea of open markets and a respect for the rule of law.

The main focus of the negotiations is in the following areas: agriculture; industrial market access; services; trade facilitation; WTO rules (i.e., trade remedies, regional agreements and fish subsidies); and development. In addition, the mandate gives further direction on the WTO's existing work program and implementation of the Agreement. The goal of the DDA is to reduce trade barriers so as to expand global economic growth, development and opportunity.

The market access related negotiations of the DDA offer the greatest potential to create high-quality jobs, advance economic reform and development, and reduce poverty worldwide. We recognize that the national economic strategies of our developing country partners include many important issues, but at the same time we believe that the focus of the WTO should be concentrated on reducing trade barriers and providing a stable, predictable, rules-based environment for world trade.

The DDA provides us with historic opportunities to achieve agriculture reform and greatly diminish current market distortions that present barriers to American farmers and ranchers. We are also aiming to achieve significant new market access for our manufactured goods through broad tariff cuts while working to reduce non-tariff barriers. We are also pressing for ambitious global market opening for our services industries. The WTO negotiations on trade facilitation will result in less red tape and more efficiency and predictability for moving goods across borders. And less corruption in customs activities.

The WTO's Doha Development Agenda is part of President Bush's strategy to open markets, reduce poverty, and expand freedom through increased trade among all countries in the global trading system, developed and developing. The U.S. role in the WTO is at the core of this strategy.

Dismantling trade barriers multilaterally holds immense potential. From 1994 to 2003, the world economy expanded at an average rate of about 2.5 percent, but exports have grown at more than double that pace—about 5.5 percent, a harbinger of accelerating globalization.

Obstacles to the free flow of commerce undermine our ability to maximize this potential and its benefits. We need to move toward a system that provides incentives for innovation and growth in the most competitive aspects of our productive sectors. The best way to do this is successfully to complete the WTO Doha Development Agenda negotiations.

Last August, we made a crucial step forward by adopting negotiating frameworks. Much of our work this year has been on fleshing out the technical details to set the negotiating table. Looking ahead, the next major challenge for the WTO will be preparations for the 6th Ministerial Conference in Hong Kong, China, December 13–18, 2006, where Ministers will be providing direction and guidance as to how to bring the Doha negotiations to a successful conclusion. Final negotiations need to be underway, with offers on the table in the first quarter of 2006. Once we agree on modalities, we have tough bargaining ahead.

One important lesson we drew from the meetings in Seattle and Cancun is that such meetings only succeed if they are well prepared. Simply put, most of the work needs to be done before arriving at the Ministerial meeting. This gives all of us the necessary time at home, and with our partners to build the needed consensus among the wider WTO membership on any given issue.

For Hong Kong, we clearly need to have an agreement on the modalities for negotiation in agriculture and non-agricultural market access, prospects in hand for a significant result in services, directions for how to ensure that WTO rules remain effective and in some cases are strengthened (e.g., by adding new disciplines to subsidies to deal with over fishing) and the outlines of an agreement on Trade Facilitation.

If we are to secure such results in Hong Kong, we will need to be very far along in the process before the August recess in Geneva, and have an outline of the agreements to be affirmed at Hong Kong. To meet this timetable, we believe that there is an urgent need to reinvigorate the negotiations Doha provides us an opportunity we cannot afford to waste. We can set a vision for the global economy for the next decades and make a major contribution to development.

We will conclude in 2006 only if we achieve a balanced outcome with results that will benefit all members. That's why agriculture, non-agricultural market access (NAMA), services, rules and development are the major issues for the negotiations. We have learned that while agriculture may be the engine for negotiations, success requires us to secure strong results across the broad range of issues in the Round. We believe we can secure results that provide new opportunities for America's workers, farmers, ranchers, service providers, and consumers. And, at the same time secure a result that strengthens the rules of the global trading system to meet America's trade interests.

On agriculture, we have work to do in all three pillars of agriculture: market access, export competition and domestic support. The 2004 Geneva framework envisions reforms in global agricultural trade: the complete elimination of export subsidies by a date to be negotiated; a framework for negotiating substantial reductions in domestic agricultural supports, including a significant down payment up front in the form of a 20 percent cut in the allowable level of domestic supports; and a commitment to making substantial improvements in agricultural market access.

Until last week, the negotiations were blocked on a technical issue. It is clear that how deeply and broadly tariffs are cut will determine the level of ambition for the agriculture negotiations overall. The World Bank recently reported that the 92% of the welfare gains from liberalization in agriculture will come from improvements in market access, compared to 6% from reduction of domestic subsidies and 2% from the elimination of export subsidies. So, the stakes are high, and highest for our partners in the developing world.

On non-agricultural market access, the key standard of success will be increased market access in manufactured goods, which account for nearly 60 percent of all global trade. The mandate from Doha lays the groundwork for broad cuts in tariffs through a formula that would make deeper cuts in higher tariffs, and it provides the possibility of complete tariff elimination in key sectors.

Negotiations now are focused on the technical details of how we get a big result. We need to find common ground on the centerpiece of the proposal—the Swiss formula—combined with appropriate forms of flexibility for developing countries in order to proceed. Other issues—work on sectoral initiatives and non-tariff barriers—must also be addressed. There are concerns and sensitivities—we all have them—and we need to understand one another. We have a big opportunity to open markets for the future—particularly for developing countries—but we need to find a way to ensure that all contribute fairly to the outcome.

We cannot afford to be anything but ambitious and ensure that we are looking to markets of the future. We did so in the Uruguay Round with great success—we accomplished a number of sectoral initiatives where growth has been substantial (e.g., chemicals, medical equipment, pharmaceuticals). We want to look at the most aggressive ways to create market opportunities. As a result of the market openings in the Uruguay Round on the sectoral initiative on medical equipment, that sector grew nearly 165% in global exports (U.S. exports grew 89.2%).

On services, in July 2004 WTO members agreed to intensify the negotiations on opening markets and made clear that services are definitely on par with agriculture and manufacturing as a "core" market access area. Services are playing an increasing role in both developed and developing economies. Indeed, the World Bank recently reported on the force multiplier effect of open services markets: developing countries with open telecommunication and financial services markets grew 1.5 percent faster than countries where those two markets remained closed. Services, investment and trade go hand-in-hand, and liberalization in services will be a powerful engine for growth and job creation—especially in higher value added and therefore higher paying jobs.

This month, members are expected to table revised market access offers, according to the timetable established for negotiations. The process is slower than we would like, but we are encouraged that governments are beginning to see the important role that services plays in development. For developing countries, for example, over 55% of GDP comes from services trade—and much of this trade is done with other developing countries. Working with industry, we want to build out the negotiations and supplement the current process to ensure that the degree of openness and liberalization now provided by the United States is matched by others.

On rules, negotiations are underway on subsidies and antidumping. We have found convergence with our trading partners on a number of issues, notably the importance of creating greater transparency, certainty and predictability in the ways in which the rules are administered—and we have vigorously questioned any proposal that would undermine the effectiveness of our trade laws. We have also seen that there is enormous interest in building out the subsidy disciplines further to address new and emerging issues, including those that challenge the environment. . . .

WTO members are currently negotiating clarifications and improvements to the WTO Dispute Settlement Understanding. The United States recognizes that an effective dispute settlement system advantages the United States not only through the ability to secure the benefits negotiated under the agreements, but also by encouraging the rule of law among nations. The DSU negotiations offer members the opportunity to assess the strengths and weaknesses of the WTO dispute settlement system and to work together to improve the system.

In those negotiations, the United States has taken an active role. The United States has tabled proposals that would provide greater flexibility and member control in the dispute settlement process, including the ability to more effectively address errant or unhelpful panel reasoning. Moreover, the United States has tabled proposals to open up the dispute settlement process to the public—there is no reason the public should not be able to see the briefs filed or the panel and Appellate Body hearings.

After substantial delay, in July last year we managed to have an agreement to launch negotiations on trade facilitation. These negotiations are aimed at updating and improving border procedures to be more transparent and fair, and to expedite the rapid release of goods. The goal will be to overhaul 50 year-old customs rules that no longer match the needs of today's economy, much less tomorrow's. This work on trade facilitation will round out the market access elements of the overall Doha negotiating agenda and present the opportunity for true win-win results for every WTO member—developed and developing country alike.

This leads me to the question of development. It is clear that the biggest gains to development will be in the core areas of goods, services and agriculture. I am pleased to report that many of our trading partners see the issue in the same way. Liberalizing trade among developing countries is an essential part of this effort. Some 70 percent of the duties collected on developing country trade are due to tariffs imposed by developing countries. This is significant.

In addition to the negotiations, the United States will continue to contribute in various ways to development. On the technical assistance and capacity building side, I am pleased to announce that the United States will contribute an additional $1 million this year to the WTO's DDA Trust Fund. The appropriation by Congress for this purpose is something that we appreciate, as yet another example of our working together to support our overall strategic efforts. In this regard, I would also note that our total trade capacity building activities last year were close to $1 billion ($903 million).

In sum, the Doha negotiations hold the potential to make an important contribution to global growth and development. The Uruguay Round was launched in 1986, finalized in 1994, and we are just now seeing the final implementation of results. With care and attention, we can use the WTO to make a further substantial contribution to global growth and development. The United States is prepared to lead by example, but we need to ensure that we secure real gains and market opportunities in the decades ahead.

Conclusion

The first 10 years of the WTO have demonstrated why the United States must continue its active participation and leadership role. A turn away from the work of the past six decades to bring about a rules-based liberalized global trading system would bring certain closure of markets to those American workers and farmers dependent on continued trade liberalization and would ignite persistent trade conflicts that would distort the global economy beyond anything imaginable today. A world where the United States steps away from a rules-based global trading system would be a world where trade no longer would be a positive contribution toward solving broader international tensions; instead, trade issues would simply act as an additional dimension exacerbating larger strategic conflicts.

We know that the global trading system is not perfect, and remains—and perhaps always will remain—a work in progress. But through American leadership within the WTO, the core U.S. trade agenda of promoting open markets and the rule of law remains the core agenda of the global trading system. The work toward these objectives is complex and often difficult, especially in a dynamic global economy unfolding as never before. But this work is no less vital today than it was in those first decades after a catastrophic world war. The participation and leadership of the United States in the global trading system remains a critical element for ensuring America's continued prosperity, and for meeting the new challenges in seeking a more stable and secure world.

Lori Wallach  **NO**

Problems with World
Trade Organization Membership

On the basis of the ten-year record of the WTO [World Trade Organization] in operation, Public Citizen urges Congress to demand a transformation of the current global 'trade' rules which have not only failed to achieve the economic gains we were promised when Congress debated the establishment of the WTO in 1994, but have resulted in unacceptable reversals in an array of non-trade, non-economic policies and goals which promote the public interest in the United States and abroad. While this hearing is focused on the WTO's record, I urge this committee to hold a future hearing about ideas for transforming the current system to one that is more economically and environmentally sustainable and democratically accountable. Unfortunately the Bush administration's March annual trade report to Congress, which was also to be understood as fulfilling its statutorily required five-year report on the WTO, did not satisfy the statutory language by answering the specific questions set forth there which were designed to measure both the positive and negative results of the WTO on the United States. Rather, the March 1 report only touted the administration's view of the WTO's benefits for the United States.

We have spent the last ten years closely monitoring and documenting the outcomes of numerous trade agreements. Beginning in 2001, we compiled these findings for a book released in 2003, entitled *Whose Trade Organization? A Comprehensive Guide to the WTO*. This book is unique in its examination of the effect of WTO rules on economic well-being and development, agriculture and food safety, the environment, public health, and democratic policy-making. This testimony summarizes and updates the major findings of the book.

During the Uruguay Round negotiations of the General Agreement on Tariffs and Trade (GATT) which established the WTO and over a dozen new substantive agreements it would enforce, Public Citizen raised concerns about the implications of establishing such broad global rules on non-trade matters in the context of an international regime whose goal was expanding trade. While expanded trade has the ability to bring benefits to consumers, workers, and farmers, setting broad non-trade rules in a body whose aim was trade expansion, threatened to undermine an array of consumer, environmental and human rights goals, the implementation of which, sometimes limits trade, such as in food containing banned pesticides. Effectively our concern was

U.S. House of Representatives, May 17, 2005.

that the WTO did not mainly cover 'trade,' but rather served to implement a much more expansive corporate globalization agenda that required countries to change their domestic policies worldwide to meet the needs and goals of the world's largest multinational business interests.

We also raised deep concerns about the WTO's threat to citizen-accountable, democratic policy-making processes—in which the people who would live with the results participate in making decisions and are able to alter policies that do not meet their needs. While some problems require a global approach—such as transboundary environmental problems or weapons proliferation—others, such as setting domestic food or product safety standards or developing policies to ensure a country's inhabitants have access to afford-able medicine or basic services such as healthcare, education, transportation, water or other utilities do not require global redress and moreover, setting global rules on these matters can undermine democratic policy making that reflects the needs and desires of different countries' inhabitants at different times.

We sought to alert Congress as to what a dramatic shift WTO would affect in how and where non-trade policy would be set. Yet even in this hearing, much of the focus remains on the important, but not singular implications of the WTO on trade flows. While the GATT covered only traditional trade mat-ters, such as tariffs and quotas, with respect only to trade in goods, the WTO included agreements setting terms on the service sector; food, environmen-tal and product safety standards; patents and copyrights; investment policy; and even the terms by which countries could make procurement decisions regarding their domestic tax dollars. The operative term of the WTO requires that "all countries shall ensure conformity of their domestic laws, regulations and administrative procedures" to all of these broad WTO requirements. As well, the WTO's Dispute Settlement Understanding (DSU) provided for a strin-gent enforcement mechanism, subjecting countries who fail to conform their domestic policies to the WTO dictates to trade sanctions after a tribunal pro-cess that does not guarantee the basic due process protections afforded by U.S. law, such as open hearings, access to documents, conflict of interest rules for tribunalists, or outside appeals.

In 1990 when Public Citizen began working on the Uruguay Round, we were not particularly focused on the potential implications for poor coun-try development or on U.S. wages, income inequality or jobs. However, over 15 years of working on the GATT and then WTO, our relationships with devel-oping country economists and policy experts, as well as our tracking of eco-nomic trends, has expanded the scope of our focus.

Now, after a decade of tracking the WTO's actual outcomes, Public Citi-zen's concerns about the WTO have grown dramatically. We have worked internationally with civil society and governments to promote a transforma-tion of the existing global "trade" rules contained in the WTO and oppose the expansion of the scope of the WTO. Yet, even as the negative conse-quences of the current rules and the model they represent increase, the cur-rent Doha Round WTO negotiations fail to address the existing problems and instead are designed to expand the WTO's jurisdiction into yet greater non-trade matters.

The WTO's Controversial Dispute Settlement Procedure

Unlike the GATT, which required consensus to bind any country to an obligation, the WTO is unique among international agreements in that its panel rulings are automatically binding and only the unanimous consent of all WTO nations can halt their implementation. These rulings are backed up by trade sanctions which remain in place until a WTO-illegal domestic policy is changed. Among our analysis of WTO decisions between 1995 and 2003 are the following findings:

- **U.S. Domestic policies from gambling regulations to tax policies have been repeatedly ruled against by run-away WTO panels.** The recent WTO gambling case is the most recent demonstration that when expansive 'trade' rules come up against public interest laws before WTO tribunals, nondiscriminatory, democratically-created domestic policies can be undercut. Among the WTO panel's outlandish decisions in that case, where the Caribbean nation of Antigua challenged various U.S. state and federal anti-gambling laws, were the following: The *entire* U.S. gambling sector is covered by provisions within the WTO's General Agreement on Trade in Services (GATS) irrespective of the intention of U.S. trade negotiators. As such, the ability of the U.S. government to regulate not only Internet but ALL forms of gambling at the federal, state and local level is limited by the rules of GATS. The panel also announced that GATS rules forbidding numerical restrictions on covered services means that a *ban* on an activity in a GATS-covered sector, even if applied to domestic and foreign service providers alike, is a "zero quota" and thus a violation of GATS rules—with broad implications for bans on an expansive range of pernicious activity. These two elements of the ruling mean that the U.S. is exposed to future WTO challenges in light of limits on gambling common in many states, as well as assorted exclusive supplier arrangements, such as with Indian tribes, and state monopoly gaming, such as the 43 U.S. states and territories which use lotteries to raise revenues. Thus, the WTO panel, in this case, interpreted that a GATS exception for "laws necessary to protect public morals," could be applied if the U.S. eliminates discrepancies between the way in which it regulates domestic and foreign providers, including through the U.S. Interstate Horseracing Act, which waives the three laws challenged by Antigua for certain domestic firms. A week later, a WTO tribunal issued a ruling on the same necessity text within the GATS exceptions clause in a case having to do with the Dominican Republic's alcohol distribution system which explicitly contradicted the inclusive reading in the gambling case. At a minimum this conflict in rulings shows that the lenient decision in the gambling case with regards to the necessity test is not a settled WTO standard. Some WTO observers wonder if the sudden switch back to the past, narrow ruling on the necessary test points to the political nature of the WTO dispute process and an attempt to avoid an explosive WTO ruling just before the U.S. Congress takes up the WTO ten year review.

- **With only two exceptions, every health, food safety or environmental law challenged at the WTO has been declared a barrier to trade.** The exceptions have been the highly-politicized challenge to France's ban on asbestos and a WTO compliance panel's determination that after losing a WTO case on the Endangered Species Act turtle protection regulations, the U.S. had weakened the law to sufficiently comply with the WTO's orders.
- **In most WTO cases, the country that launches the challenge wins.** As a result, mere threats of WTO action now cause many nations to change their policies. The challenging country at least partially prevailed in an astonishing 102 out of 118 completed WTO cases—a success rate of 86.4 percent.
- **Important U.S laws ruled illegal at the WTO.** In 42 out of 48 cases brought against the United States in which a WTO panel has made a ruling, or 85.7 percent of the time, the WTO has labeled as illegal policies ranging from sea turtle protections and clean air regulations to tax and antidumping policies. The United States also lost two high-profile cases that it brought against EU computer tariff classifications and Japan's film policies.
- **U.S. trade safeguard laws have been successfully challenged numerous times in the WTO.** One of the most politically sensitive aspects of Congress' 1994 consideration of the WTO was the degree to which U.S. trade safeguard law would have to be changed to conform to the related WTO agreements. Congress was promised that our laws would remain effective, yet, a decade later, the United States has not been able to successfully defend any of our safeguard laws in 14 out of 14 completed cases brought by other countries against our safeguards on products ranging from steel to lamb to wool shirts. Furthermore, the United States has lost 11 out of 15 antidumping or countervailing duties cases. Additionally, Doha Round "Rules" negotiations are poised to translate these WTO cases against the U.S. into new, more expansive limits on U.S. domestic trade safeguard laws. Meanwhile despite promises that other U.S. trade laws, such as Section 301, would remain operational under a WTO regime, the U.S. withdrew a case against Japan regarding anticompetitive practices in film trade after it became clear that use of Section 301 sanctions would be prohibited under WTO rules.
- **The process is closed, narrow and unbalanced.** Our concerns about the WTO dispute resolution process have born out. Complaints are typically filed at the request of business interests with no opportunity for input from other interested parties. The WTO Secretariat selects panel members from a roster formed using qualifications that ensure a bias towards the WTO's primacy. Panelists' identities are not disclosed and there is no requirement that they disclose conflicts of interest they might have in deciding cases. Tribunals meet in closed sessions and proceedings are confidential unless a government voluntarily makes its submissions public. Far from being a neutral arbiter, the singular and explicit goal of the dispute settlement process is to expand trade in goods and services. Increasingly, WTO panels have rewritten WTO provisions with their broad interpretations, a situation that can find no remedy as there is no outside appeal.

The WTO Decade and the U.S. Economy: Exploding U.S. Trade Deficits, Increased Income Inequality, Stagnant Real Wages, and the Loss of 1 in 6 U.S. Manufacturing Jobs

In the early 1990s, many economists argued that the opening of foreign markets for U.S. exports under WTO (and NAFTA) would create U.S. jobs and increase income for U.S. workers and farmers. When Congress was preparing to vote on WTO in 1994, the President's Council of Economic Advisers informed Congress that approval of the package would increase annual U.S. GDP by $100–200 billion over the next decade. Others claimed that the WTO's adoption would lead to a decline in the U.S. trade deficit. President [Bill] Clinton even went so far as to promise that the average American family would gain $1,700 in income annually from the WTO's adoption, which would have meant that the U.S. real median family income would have been upwards of $65,000 in 2005, or a nearly 35 percent increase since 1995. These growth projections have been shown to be wildly off the mark.

- **U.S. Median Income Growth Meager:** U.S. median income grew only 8 percent to $52,680 in 2003—the latest numbers available. There is little reason to think that this has improved in 2004–05, since median real wages have not grown since that time. In fact, the U.S. real median wage has scarcely risen above its 1970 level (only 9 percent), while productivity has soared 82 percent over the same period, resulting in declining or stagnant standards of living for the nearly 70 percent of the U.S. population that does not have a college degree.
- **Trade Deficit Soars as Imports Boom:** During the WTO era, the U.S. trade deficit has risen to historic levels, and approaches six percent of national income—a figure widely agreed to be unsustainable, putting the U.S. economy at risk of lowered income growth in the future. Soaring imports during the WTO decade have contributed to the loss of nearly one in six U.S. manufacturing jobs.
- **U.S. Has Suffered a Good-Job Export Crisis:** Another factor contributing to this job loss is the shift in investment trends, with China overtaking the United States in 2003 as the leading target for FDI [foreign direct investment: the purchase of realty property abroad or a controlling interest in a foreign business]. WTO Trade Related Investment Rules, (TRIMs), limit the ability of countries to set conditions on how foreign investors operate in other countries, making it more appealing for manufacturers to seek lower wages by relocating. Meanwhile, WTO terms guaranteed low tariff access for products made in low wage countries back into wealthy markets while forbidding rich countries from setting labor or other standards such products must meet. The type and quality of jobs available for workers in the U.S. economy has dramatically shifted during the WTO decade, with workers losing to imports or offshoring [hiring people abroad to do a job] their higher wage manufacturing jobs (which often also provided health care and other benefits) and finding reemployment in lower wage jobs. Labor Department data shows that such workers lose up to 27 percent of their earnings in such shifts.
- **U.S. Income and Wage Inequality Have Jumped:** During the WTO decade these trends have resulted in U.S. income and wage inequality

increasing markedly. In 1995, the top five percent of U.S. households by income made 6.5 times what the poorest 20 percent of households made, while this gap grew by nearly 10 percent by 2003. In wages, the situation was comparable. In 1995, a male worker that ranked at the 95th percentile in wages earned 2.68 times what a worker at the 20th percentile earned. By 2003, that gap had widened nearly 8 percent. Nearly all economists agree that increased trade has partially driven this widening inequality. One study by the non-partisan Center for Economic and Policy Research found that trade liberalization has cost U.S. workers without college degrees an amount equal to 12.2% of their current wages. For a worker earning $25,000 a year, this loss would be slightly more than $3,000 per year. William Cline, at the pro-WTO Institute for International Economics, estimates that about 39 percent of the actually observed increase in wage inequality is attributable to trade trends.

- **Job Export Crisis Is Expanding from Manufacturing to High Tech and Services:** While some commentators, such as Nike CEO Phil Knight, have famously argued that this decline in assembly-line U.S. manufacturing is a result of "Americans simply not wanting to make shoes for a living," job loss and wage stagnation is increasingly affecting workers in those sectors where the United States is understood to have a comparative advantage, such as professional services and high technology. Studies commissioned by the U.S. government have shown that as many as 48,417 U.S. jobs—including many in high-tech sectors—were offshored to other countries in the first three months of 2004 alone. This trend does not appear to be slowing down, as 3.3 million high-end service sector jobs—including physicians, computer programmers, engineers, accountants and architects—are all forecast to be outsourced overseas in the next decade. Another study by the Progressive Policy Institute, a think-tank associated with the pro-WTO faction of the Democratic Party, found that 12 million information-based U.S. jobs—54 percent paying better than the median wage—are highly susceptible to such offshoring.

This manufacturing and high-tech job loss has had direct impact on workers' ability to bargain for higher real wages. Studies commissioned by the U.S. government show that as many as 62 percent of U.S. union drives face employer threats to relocate abroad, with the factory shut-down rate following successful union certifications tripling in the years after WTO relative to the years before.

In short, few of the claims made about the U.S. economic benefits that would flow from greater trade liberalization can be shown to have been close to accurate. This, however, has not stopped another round of WTO expansion from being launched, accompanied by a new set of promises. The WTO and the Developing World: Do As We Say, Not As We Did.

The WTO's failure to deliver the promised economic gains in the United States has also been mirrored abroad. Despite a paucity of evidence, think tanks, public opinion-makers and newspapers editorials have continued to relentlessly promote the notion that developing countries are the primary beneficiaries of WTO globalization. After a decade of the WTO, few if any of the promised economic benefits have materialized for developing countries. For many, poverty and inequality have worsened, while nearly all countries have experienced a sharp slowdown in their rates of economic growth.

- **Poverty on the Rise.** The number and percentage of people living on less than $1 a day (the World Bank's definition of extreme poverty) in the regions with some of the worst forms of poverty—Sub-Saharan Africa and the Middle East—have increased since the WTO went into effect, while the number and percentage of people living on less than $2 a day has gone up in the same time for these regions, as well as for Latin America and the Caribbean. The number of people living in poverty has gone up for South Asia, while the rate of reduction in poverty has slowed nearly worldwide—especially when one excludes China, where huge reductions in poverty have been accomplished, but not by following WTO-approved policies given China only became a WTO member in 2001.

- **Slowdown in global growth rates under WTO model.** The per-capita income growth rates of developing regions before the period of structural adjustment and WTO liberalization are higher than the growth rates after the countries implemented the WTO—International Monetary Fund (IMF) model, many aspects of which are locked in through the WTO's services, investment, intellectual property and other agreements. For low and middle-income countries, per capita growth between 1980 and 2000 fell to half of that experienced between 1960 and 1980. Latin America's per-capita GDP grew by 75% between 1960–1980; however, between 1980–2000—the period during which these countries adopted the package of economic policies required by the WTO and IMF—it grew by only six percent. Even when one takes into account the longer 1980–2005 period, there is no single 25-year window in the history of the continent that was worse in terms of rate of income gains. Sub-Saharan Africa's per-capita GDP grew by 36% between 1960–1980 but declined by 15% between 1980–2000. Arab states' per-capita GDP declined between 1980–2000, after it grew 175% between 1960–1980. South Asia, South East Asia and the Pacific all had lower per-capita GDP growth, subsequent to 1980 than in the previous 20 years. (Only in East Asia was this trend not sustained, but only because China's per-capita GDP quadrupled during this period prior to China joining the WTO).

- **Developing countries that did not adopt the package fared better:** In sharp contrast, nations like China, India, Malaysia and Vietnam, that chose their own economic mechanisms and policies through which to integrate into the world economy had more economic success. These countries had among the highest growth rates in the developing world over the past two decades—despite ignoring the directives of the WTO, IMF or World Bank.

- **Gap between rich and poor widens.** Instead of generating income convergence between rich and poor countries, as WTO proponents predicted, the corporate globalization era of the 1990s exacerbated the income inequality between industrial and developing countries, as well as between rich and poor within many countries. According to one United Nations study, "in almost all developing countries that have undertaken rapid trade liberalization, wage inequality has increased, most often in the context of declining industrial employment of unskilled workers and large absolute falls in their real wages, on the order of 20–30% in Latin American countries." According to another, the richest 5 percent of the world's people receive 114 times the income of the poorest 5 percent, and the richest one percent receives as much as the poorest 57 percent. This trend is widening over time, not closing, with the 20 richest countries earning per-capita incomes 16 times greater than non-oil producing, less developed countries in 1960, and by 1999 the richest countries earning incomes 35 times higher, signifying a doubling of the income inequality.

The track record of the IMF and WTO—condoned policies—which have failed to reduce poverty and inequality or increase growth—are falling into greater ignominy. A recent study by the Inter-American Development Bank found that, of a total of 66 presidential and 81 legislative elections in 17 Latin American countries during the 1985–2002 period, incumbent parties that pursued trade liberalization and privatizations while in office lost between 25 to 50 percent of their previous votes when pursuing reelection. If anything, voter discontent in Latin America, a region widely seen as having most fully implemented the standard "neo-liberal" policies, has increased since 2002.

Even policy-makers who once pursued such liberalization policies, such as former Venezuelan economic minister Ricardo Hausmann and SAIS [school of Advanced International Studies, Johns Hopkins University] economist Riordan Roett, have now advocated a move away from the Washington Consensus policies, due to their utter failure to generate growth and rising living standards. Such a reversal is not surprising, given that no developed country, including the United States, England, or even Korea developed on the basis of "free trade," without managing foreign investment or without government intervention in providing basic services and infrastructure. Indeed, many commentators have observed that developed country's advocacy of WTO liberalization policies is akin to "kicking away the ladder" to development for the poor countries, once the rich countries have already climbed up.

U.S. Becomes Net Food Importer Under WTO, While Poor Countries Face Increased Food Insecurity

The WTO's approach to agriculture is to treat food as if it were any other commodity, like steel or rubber, not something on which every person's life depends. WTO rules on agriculture, both under the Agreement on Agriculture (AoA) and the Trade Related Aspects of Intellectual Property (TRIPS), have led to devastating outcomes for developing countries, while farm income in the wealthy countries has declined as food trade volumes have risen. These WTO rules have forced the elimination of domestic policies aimed at ensuring food sovereignty and security in developing countries, and of policies aimed at balancing power between producers and grain traders and food processors in rich countries. These changes have greatly benefited multinational commodity trading and food processing companies who, in the absence of government price and supply management programs, have been able to manipulate the markets to keep prices paid to farmers low, while at the same time keeping the prices paid by consumers steady or rising. Farmers in rich and poor countries have only seen their incomes decline, with many losing farms and livelihoods under the decade of the WTO regime. In the developing world, the combination of sharply lower prices and the effects of WTO rules regarding the patenting of seeds and plants under TRIPS have led to increased hunger.

- **United States to become net food importer.** According to a U.S. Department of Agriculture (USDA) write-up of the topic, 2005 may be the first time since 1959 that the United States will be a net food importer, thanks to a flood of imports and declining export growth. That the report blames the increased appetite of U.S. consumers for foreign products for this projected deficit is nonsensical given that much of the flood of imports is in the products in which the United States was once considered the leading exporter, such as beef and poultry, while U.S. exports of cotton, soy, red meat have declined dramatically in recent years.
- **Under the AoA, export prices for key U.S. crops have fallen to levels substantially below the cost of production, while consumer prices increased.** Since 1996, U.S. crop prices have generally declined about 40 percent, while the cost of running a farm has risen by as much. The overall tilt of U.S. government farm policy, in line with the WTO's AoA, has been to remove the last vestiges of production management and price support, while topping off the dips in gross farm income through government payments. According to government data, however, real prices for food eaten at home in the U.S. rose by 30% during the WTO era (1994 and 2004), even as prices paid to farmers plummeted.
- **A similar long-term trend holds in the developing world,** where falling real prices for the agricultural commodity exports on which poor countries depend have fallen 50 percent relative to the 1960s, while wild price swings of up to 25 percent off of price trends make planning and subsistence difficult. At the same time, many of the very poorest countries are increasingly reliant on grain imports to meet their food needs, with the share of food imports in national income tripling since the 1960s. This trend has been particularly felt in Mexico, where the consumer price of the staple food corn tortillas has only risen since NAFTA, despite a flood of cheap corn imports into Mexico that have collapsed much of Mexico's domestic small-scale corn production.
- **A dramatic loss of U.S. family farms accompanies sharp falls in income for the poorest farmers under the WTO.** The United States lost 226,695 small and family farms between 1994 and 2003, while average net cash farm income for the very poorest farmers dropped to an astounding –$5,228.90 in 2003—a colossal 200 percent drop since the WTO went into effect.
- **Displacement and hunger the norm in developing countries.** Following the decade of the WTO and NAFTA, over 1.5 million Mexican *campesino* farmers were thrown from their land. The agricultural sector, traditionally a major source of employment in Mexico, was devastated by the dumping of U.S. and foreign agricultural products into their markets. Likewise, the Chinese government projects that as many as 500 million of China's peasants will be made surplus, as the country continues the rapid acceleration of industrial development of its

agriculture sector under WTO rules. In country after country, displaced farmers have had little choice but to join swelling urban workforces where the oversupply of labor suppresses wages and exacerbates the politically and socially destabilizing crisis of chronic under- and unemployment in the cities of the developing world.

- **By dramatically expanding legal definitions of what can be patented under the TRIPS Agreement, the WTO has endangered food sovereignty and security in poor countries.** In most developing countries, the majority of the population lives on the land and feeds itself by replanting saved seeds. Yet over 150 cases have already been documented of research institutions or businesses applying for patents on naturally-occurring plants, some of which have been farmed for generations. After the WTO TRIPS Agreement becomes fully binding for developing countries in 2006, governments that fail to enforce patents on seeds—by pulling up crops or by forcing subsistence farmers who cannot afford to do so to pay royalties—will face trade sanctions.

    These trends and the policies underpinning them are not expected to be improved upon in the current WTO Doha Round negotiations. Increasingly, even pro-trade academics such as Jagdish Bhagwati are arguing that the proposed agricultural reforms will not benefit most poor countries, characterizing claims to the contrary as "dangerous nonsense" and a "pernicious fallacy." The liberalization-led fall in prices has had a negative effect on producers in rich and poor countries alike, as a recent National Bureau of Economic Research study concluded when it found that middle income corn farmers in Mexico saw their incomes fall by more than 50 percent after NAFTA/WTO implementation. After a decade of failed policies, it is clear that the WTO's "one size fits all" approach to agriculture and food security issues has failed at delivering its promised results.

The WTO's Coming to Dinner and Food Safety is Not on the Menu

The WTO's relentless drive toward the "harmonization" of food, animal and plant regulations based on low, industry-preferred international standards, endangers human health and sharply curtails the ability of elected governments to protect the health of their citizens in this critically important area. WTO-approved standards are generally set in private-sector bodies which do not permit consumer or health interests to participate and which make decisions without complying with domestic regulatory procedures for openness, participation or balance. Even if a country's domestic food safety laws treat domestic and foreign products identically, if the policy provides greater consumer protection than the WTO-named international standard, it is presumed to be a WTO violation and must pass a series of WTO test established in the Sanitary and Phytosanitary Agreement that have proved impossible to meet. Some of our key findings include:

- **As required under WTO "equivalency determination" rules, the U.S. declared that dozens of countries ensure their meat** inspection systems are "equivalent" to that of the U.S. even though the countries' standards and performance violated U.S. law and regulation. Many nations maintain their equivalency status and this right to ship meat to the U.S. despite documented violations of U.S. policy. For instance, Argentina's meat inspection system maintains its U.S. equivalency status despite well-documented problems that include contamination of meat with oil, hair and feces. Similarly, the Brazilian system, which allowed companies to pay meat inspectors in violation of U.S. law requiring independent government inspection, was declared "equivalent." USDA [U.S. Department of Agriculture] labeling of imported products makes them indistinguishable to the consumer.

- **Time and time again, WTO tribunals have refused to permit any regulatory action based on the "Precautionary Principle."** Governments have long relied on this principle to shield their populations from uncertain risks from new or emerging products. Previous "precautionary" actions by the U.S. government to ban the morning sickness drug Thalidomide in the 1960s and to prevent the outbreak of Mad Cow disease in the 1980s and 90s helped avert the substantial human and agricultural devastation that occurred in other countries due to these and other policies. Yet the U.S. has used the WTO to systematically attack other countries' precautionary regulations such as those dealing with beef hormones, genetically modified organisms (GMOs), invasive species and agricultural pests.

- **Any domestic standard that provides more health protection than a WTO-approved standard, is presumed to be a trade barrier,** unless the higher standard is supported by extensive scientific data and analysis that clearly shows a specific and significant risk associated with the lower standard. No nation has yet been able to demonstrate the need for higher standards, much to the WTO's satisfaction, despite several lengthy and costly attempts by developed countries to perform WTO-required risk assessments on the dangers posed by artificial hormones in beef, invasive species, pest contamination of native salmon populations, and more.

The WTO's Environmental Impact: First, Gattzilla Ate Flipper

Public Citizen has documented a systematic pattern of WTO attacks on member nations' vital environmental concerns and policy priorities, as well as a series of biases built into WTO rules that promote unsustainable uses of natural resources. Over its ten years of operation, the WTO's anti-environmental rhetoric has been replaced by more political pronouncements, even as WTO tribunals have systematically ruled against every domestic environmental policy challenge that has come before it, and eviscerated whatever GATT Article XX exceptions that might have been used to safeguard such laws. Instead of seeking to resolve conflicts between commercial and environmental goals, the WTO's largely ineffectual Committee on Trade and the Environment has become a venue mainly for identifying green policies that violate WTO rules. Key findings include:

- **To date, all GATT/WTO dispute panel decisions on environmental laws have required that the challenged domestic laws and measures be weakened**—even when the challenged policy treats domestic and foreign goods the same, or when it implements a country's obligations under a Multilateral Environmental Agreement (e.g. the U.S. Endangered Species Act regulations implementing the Convention on International Trade in Endangered Species (CITES)). When the WTO ruled against U.S. Endangered Species Act rules protecting CITES-listed sea turtles from shrimpers' nets, the U.S. complied with the WTO order by replacing the requirement that all countries seeking to sell shrimp in the United States had to ensure that their shrimpers used turtle exclusion devices. The new U.S. regulations were approved several years later, but Thailand and other shrimp exporting countries continue to put pressure on the United States to weaken the rule's enforceability.
- **WTO rules have consistently been interpreted to mean that products cannot be treated differently according to how they were produced or harvested.** This interpretation, for which there is no legal basis in the actual rules, requires, for example, that clear-cut tropical timber cannot be treated differently from sustainably-harvested timber, that fish caught with damaging drift nets cannot be distinguished from sustainably-caught fish, and that products made using child labor or extreme cruelty toward animals must be given the same trade treatment as products made under more humane and ethical conditions.
- **Because WTO panels have systematically ruled against challenged environmental policies, now mere threats of challenges often suffice.** For example, after years of sustained trade law challenges, the Bush administration decided to quietly implement a change to a "dolphin safe" labeling policy which Mexico had demanded as necessary for implementation of a GATT ruling. (Mexico had threatened a new WTO case if their demands were not met). On New Years Eve 2002, when few U.S. citizens were focused on policy matters, the Bush administration announced that it would change the "Flipper-friendly" tuna policy and allow the "dolphin-safe" label to be used on tuna caught using deadly purse seine nets and dolphin encirclement. While this policy was eventually overturned in a challenge brought by environmentalists to federal court, Mexico and other countries continue to make noises about a possible WTO challenge. Another case involved Hong Kong's WTO complaint about U.S. anti-invasive species laws. In this case, U.S. regulatory efforts to fight the costly infestation of the Asian Longhorned Beetle (which is devastating maple and other trees throughout the United States) are being classified as violating WTO rules. The mere threat of a challenge in this regard has provoked the USDA to considering watering down regulations requiring treatment of raw wood packing material to comply with a weaker, WTO-sanctioned "international" standard.

Warning: The WTO Can be Hazardous to Public Health

The WTO's wide-ranging rules have consistently troubled public health advocates, who have found that many policies which have little to do with trade, are being threatened by WTO mandates. The following are some examples:

- **Access to and safety of medicines.** The creation of a worldwide pharmaceutical patenting system under the WTO's TRIPS agreement has raised pharmaceutical costs in the U.S. and further restricted the availability of lifesaving drugs in developing countries. A 1995 study on the overall impact of the TRIPS agreement on U.S. consumers "conservatively estimated" $6 billion in higher U.S. drug prices due to windfall patent extensions under the WTO. Why a business protection scheme guaranteeing monopoly markets would be inserted into a trade 'liberalization' agreement has outraged consumer groups worldwide. Poor country governments and health officials note with fury that even though the current patent and licensing regime has only recently been accepted in developed countries (Switzerland for example, did not recognize drug patents until the 1960s), under WTO rules developing nations around the world are required to adopt monopoly patents on medicines. Concern about public health has grown around the world, with many Members of Congress taking a lead in opposing trade agreements that restrict access to essential medicines. Unfortunately, the U.S. government has often been on the wrong side of this issue, WTO challenging Brazilian and threatening Thai and South African laws on compulsory licensing of pharmaceutical products and pushing to undermine in its new Free Trade Agreements a 2001 WTO Declaration reiterating countries' ability to issue compulsory licenses for medicines. Yet the U.S. itself used the power it seeks to deny other nations in WTO when it threatened a compulsory license after the 2001 anthrax scare.
- **Downward harmonization for drug testing.** In order to fulfill its harmonization obligations under the WTO, the Food and Drug Administration (FDA) in 1996 proposed changes to its guidelines for testing the potential carcinogenicity of medicines being approved for U.S. use. The FDA had previously required companies to test drugs on two species (typically mice and rats) because tests on rats alone often failed to produce evidence of carcinogenicity where it was subsequently found in mice. The new WTO "harmonized" testing standard approved by the FDA, however, allows drug companies to drop long-term mice tests and substitute them with less reliable short-term second species tests.
- **Threatening developing countries with WTO challenges to pressure them into reducing public health protections.** American Gerber Products Company refused to comply with Guatemalan infant formula labeling laws that implemented the WHO/UNICEF "Nestlé's Code" on the grounds that the laws violated trademark protections provided in the WTO's TRIPS agreement. The Guatemalan law forbid pictorial depictions of healthy babies aimed at inducing illiterate people to replace breast feeding with formula which, when mixed with unsanitary water, was causing an epidemic of avoidable infant deaths.

Gerber refused to remove its trademark "Gerber Baby" from its labels. The law might have withstood the threatened WTO challenge. However, to avoid the prohibitive cost of mounting an uncertain defense, Guatemalan authorities instead exempted imported formula from this important public health law, whose success in saving babies' lives had led to Guatemala previously being held up as an example by UNICEF.

Conclusion: The WTO Must Shrink or Sink in Order for the Public Interest to be Served

The WTO, far from being a win-win proposition, has been a lose-lose affair for most people in the United States and abroad, threatening people's livelihoods, the environment, public health, and the right of people around the world to enjoy democratic policy-making processes that allow them to decide what is best for themselves.

The recent WTO gambling ruling and other controversial rulings are widening the coalition of groups questioning U.S. trade policy. Groups such as the Association of State Supreme Court Justices, U.S. League of Cities, National Conference of State Legislatures, National Association of Counties, and National Association of Towns and Townships all have expressed concerns that current and proposed trade rules may undermine our nation's system of federalism and the integrity of our domestic courts. Groups typically considered bedrocks of the "pro-trade" alliance, such as the National Association of State Departments of Agriculture and other agricultural groups, are expressing concerns about depressed commodity prices, lowered farm income, and the United States' "net food importer" status. Associations of immigrant-descended groups such as the League of United Latin American Citizens are expressing concerns that Hispanics and people of color are not sharing in the gains from trade. And high-tech workers and inventors are arguing that the drive to make ever-more protectionist trade law favoring the largest high-tech corporations like Pfizer and Microsoft is cheating workers whose jobs are being offshored, inventors who are seeing few gains for their innovations, and consumers in rich and poor countries alike, who face lessened access to essential medicine and restrictions on legitimate uses of copyrighted items.

Opposition to the WTO's rules is increasingly coming from governments themselves, as the organization's ever-growing crisis of legitimacy bursts into public view again with the collapse of the WTO's Cancun Ministerial. In particular, these countries—led by Brazil, India, South Africa and other nations—demanded that the WTO should not establish one-size-fits all, anti-democratic rules over investment, government procurement, and competition policy, proposed rules that were subsequently dropped from WTO discussion. It is extremely ironic that while the Bush Administration argues that one of its top priorities is promoting democracy worldwide, the status quo WTO and U.S. positions regarding the WTO's future course push in the opposite direction.

We no longer have to guess what might happen under the WTO: we now know. A decade of WTO policy has led to stagnant real national and family incomes around the world, increased poverty in the poorest regions, and undemocratic WTO attacks on national sovereignty and public policy. Based on this evidence, Public Citizen finds it highly unlikely that continuation or expansion of this model will reverse these failures.

Thus, Public Citizen works with a global movement calling for transformation of the current WTO system. While we believe that a system of global trade rules is vital, the current rules are not serving us well. We propose that certain non-trade aspects be eliminated from the WTO. We also propose that the trade rules that would remain be altered so as to better meet the goals of providing sustainable livelihoods to people in rich and poor countries alike, fighting for the elimination of poverty, ensuring sustainable use of natural resources and providing food sovereignty, the essential tool in fighting hunger. For details on these proposals, we [urge] you to review their summary at "WTO—Shrink or Sink! The Turnaround Agenda International Civil Society Sign-On Letter," or for a more thorough review, *Alternatives to Economic Globalization: A Better World is Possible,* which is an edited anthology with contributions from Public Citizen.

To maintain, much less expand, a global 'trade' regime that to date has worsened the economic situation in rich and poor countries alike, threatened food sovereignty and access to essential medicines, and that undermined democratic governance is a recipe for growing economic, social and political instability. At a minimum, the real life outcomes of a continuation of the expansive status quo corporate globalization agenda as implemented by the WTO pose an enormous risk to the legitimacy of trade itself.

POSTSCRIPT

Is World Trade Organization Membership Beneficial?

There can be no doubt that there are winners and losers in globalization, including free trade, both among countries and within them. Moreover, it is much easier to see the negative consequences of free trade and its central organization, the World Trade Organization, than it is to see the positive aspects. Low or no tariffs on imported fabrics and clothing has, for example, meant that most of these commodities sold in the United States are imported from China and elsewhere. Tens of thousands of American workers in fabric mills and clothing manufacturing plants have lost their jobs, and it is easy to empathize with them. Yet it is also the case that imports mean that Americans pay less for their shirts, pants, and other garments than they would have if they were made in the United States given the differing wages and other production costs with China. It is also easy to be offended when a WTO hearing finds that your country has violated trade rules. Yet the WTO's rules, which all member countries have agreed to follow, also mean that your country can file a case against another country when it violates trade laws. It is axiomatic that if your country is free to ignore the rules and the WTO that other countries are also free to do so, even if that negatively impacts your country. It is also the case that almost every country thinks that it is disadvantaged in one way or another by their WTO membership, yet almost all countries are either members of the organization or aspire to membership. The best way to evaluate the WTO, then, is to decide, on balance, whether it is performing well or not.

As the matter stands, the Doha Round remains stalled. Top-level negotiations in Cancun, Mexico (2003), Hong Kong (2005), and at Switzerland, the WTO headquarters in Geneva, on several occasions since then have all failed to make enough progress among the main opponents to revive the more general negotiation process. The most recent negotiations as of this writing ended in July 2008 when diplomats from the United States, European Union, India, Brazil, Australia, China, and Japan could not resolve whether and how to protect farmers in less developed countries, particularly India, against a flood of imports if tariff barriers were removed. About the only things everyone could agree on is the need to keep trying because of the negative implications of having the Doha Round die. As China's Commerce Minister Chen Deming wrote in *Business Week* in September 2008, "In today's globalized world, all countries are going up and down in the same elevator, not sitting on the two ends of a teeter-totter where one's gain is the other's loss. [Only by successfully concluding the Doha Round] . . . will we be able to confront multiple challenges faced by the world economy and realize the goal of achieving global prosperity, sustainable development, and a harmonious world."

To further explore the WTO, good places to start are the Web site of the WTO at http://www.wto.org, and the overview of the organization, its history, and the current issues related to it are found in Judith L. Goldstein, Douglas Rivers, and Michael Tomz, "Institutions in International Relations: Understanding the Effects of the GATT and the WTO on World Trade," *International Organization* (2007); John H. Barton, Judith L. Goldstein, Timothy E. Josling, and Richard H. Steinberg, A study focusing on the Doha Round is Stefan Griller (ed.) At the Crossroads: The World Trading System and the Doha Round (Springer, 2007). The best location to look into the U.S. government's perspective on the WTO and the Doha Round is at the Web site of the U.S. Trade Representative at http://www.ustr.gov/. A recent study on the impact of the WTO are Arvind Subramanian and Shang-Jin Wei, "The WTO Promotes Trade, Strongly but Unevenly, *Journal of International Economics* (2007).

ISSUE 12

Do Sovereign Wealth Funds Threaten Economic Sovereignty?

YES: Patrick A. Mulloy, from Testimony during Hearings on "Sovereign Wealth Fund Acquisitions and Other Foreign Government Investments in the U.S.: Assessing the Economic and National Security Implications," before the Joint Economic Committee, United States Congress (February 13, 2008)

NO: Stuart E. Eizenstat, from Testimony during Hearings on "Do Sovereign Wealth Funds Make the U.S. Economic Stronger or Pose a National Security Risk?" before the Committee on Banking, Housing, and Urban Affairs, U.S. Senate (November 14, 2007)

ISSUE SUMMARY

YES: Patrick A. Mulloy, Washington representative of the Alfred P. Sloan Foundation and formerly a U.S. assistant secretary of commerce for international trade administration, tells Congress that the upsurge of investments in the United States by sovereign wealth funds presents economic and national security problems for the country.

NO: Stuart E. Eizenstat, a partner in Covington & Burling, a Washington, DC, law firm and formerly chief domestic policy adviser to the U.S. president, under secretary of state, and deputy secretary of the treasury, reassures Congress that sovereign wealth funds bolster the U.S. economy and balance a significant net plus for the U.S. economy.

Economic globalization is more than just expanding trade. Another aspect is the globalization of investment. This is the global flow of money being used to buy real property, bonds and other debt instruments of governments and corporations, and stock in private companies. Buying enough shares in a foreign company to gain de facto control of its operations is called foreign direct investment (FDI). The bulk of FDI is by multinational corporations (MNCs). An example in 2008 occurred when a Belgian-based MNC, InBev, spent $52 billion to acquire a controlling share of the stock in the U.S. corporation Anheuser-Busch, brewer of Budweiser, and other beers.

FDI is not a new phenomenon, but, like other aspects of globalization, it has vastly increased in recent decades. Total global FDI rocketed from $700 billion in 1980 to $10.1 trillion in 2005. Another way to measure FDI is through the annual net flow (money invested minus investments liquidated). This annual flow grew from a positive $328 million in 1995 to a positive $1.3 trillion in 2006.

Americans are at the forefront of both investing in foreign assets and having U.S. assets acquired by foreign investors. During 2007, American net FDI abroad increased $333 billion and overseas FDI in the United States grew $238 billion. These flows brought the total FDI holding of Americans abroad to $1.8 trillion and the foreign FDI holdings of U.S. assets to $1.4 trillion. Figures for 2008 are not yet available, but preliminary indicators are that the weakening dollar worked to increase foreign FDI purchase in the United States and to decrease American acquisitions abroad.

The inflow of FDI has often brought negative commentary, especially when iconic U.S. companies or other assets have been bought by foreigners. This was true when the Belgians bought "Bud," or when some years ago Japanese investors bought (and have since sold back to Americans) Rockefeller Center in New York City. Certainly there are negatives to FDI. In the extreme, a country could lose control of most of its economy, and it would also be arguably unwise to allow foreign ownership of a key national security asset, such as a major arms manufacturer. However, foreign FDI also has benefits. For example, when Germany's Daimler Corporation bought Chrysler Motors for $36 billion in 1998, it saved it from bankruptcy and also saved the jobs of most of its 130,000 workers.

Recently there has been a growing amount of FDI flowing into the United States from sovereign wealth funds (SWFs). These are investment sources controlled directly or indirectly by foreign governments. Some of these investment operations are controlled directly by a foreign government or by individuals or groups so closely related to the government as to be considered an extension of it. Investment syndicates controlled by members of Saudi Arabia's royal family would be an example. Other SWFs are organizations like banks and corporations that are owned by a government, instead of being held privately, as is true in most industrialized countries. One example is the China National Offshore Oil Corporation (CNOOC), which is wholly controlled by the Chinese government, and has sought to buy control of foreign oil companies, including those in the United States.

In the first of the following readings, Patrick A. Mulloy gives a congressional committee an overview of SWFs and warns that their increasing role in the U.S. economy presents several worrisome issues. Stuart E. Eizenstat is not oblivious to these concerns in the second reading, but advises that with proper management, SWF investments are positive for the United States.

YES

Patrick A. Mulloy

Sovereign Wealth Fund Acquisitions and Other Foreign Government Investments in the U.S.: Assessing the Economic and National Security Implications

Prior Oversight Hearings

In October 2005 [the committee leaders] invited me to testify on the background of the foreign investment provisions enacted in 1988 and amended in 1992 and how they were being implemented by the Treasury Department chaired Committee on Foreign Investment in the United States or CFIUS. I am delighted that some of the concerns I expressed at that hearing were taken into account by the Committee in the CFIUS reform legislation entitled the "Foreign Investment and National Security Act of 2007" which you formulated on a bipartisan basis and got enacted into law just a few months ago.

In May of this year [2008], International Finance Subcommittee invited me to testify on the "exchange rate" provisions of the 1988 Omnibus Trade Bill and the performance of the Treasury Department in carrying out the statutory obligations given to it by that law to identify and report to Congress the names of countries that were manipulating their currencies to gain trade advantages with the United States. In my May testimony I told the subcommittee that the Treasury Department had failed to carry out the responsibilities given to it by Congress in that 1988 law. That failure is at least one reason we are here today to discuss the issue of sovereign wealth funds and increased foreign ownership of the United States economy. I will explain in my testimony why I make that direct link.

I am pleased, however, that the committee subsequent to the May hearing did formulate and report out for consideration by the full Senate legislation to address some of the measures that were advocated by me and others to address exchange rate manipulation by other nations including China.

Sovereign Wealth Funds

As I begin my discussion of sovereign wealth funds, and knowing that many officials in the Executive Branch along with some business leaders will not be sympathetic to the concerns I will raise, let me remind the Committee that

United States Congress, February 13, 2008.

under Article I, Section 8 of the Constitution it is the Congress, not the Executive Branch, which is charged with the regulation of foreign trade, foreign investment and the value of our nation's currency. Our Founding Fathers knew such matters directly impacted people's lives and wanted them under the control of the branch of government closest to the people. The rise of "sovereign wealth funds" and the increased foreign ownership of our economy are directly related to our mismanaged trade policies which have failed to take into account the government-directed mercantilist trade policies of many of our trading partners.

In June of this year [2008], then Acting Under Secretary of the Treasury Mr. Clay Lowery made a speech in San Francisco on "sovereign wealth funds". He said he would use the term to mean, "a government investment vehicle which is funded by foreign exchange assets and which manages those assets separately from official reserves."

He said such sovereign wealth funds typically fall into two categories based on the foreign government's source of foreign exchange assets. These are:

1. Commodity Funds – which are established through commodity exports such as oil and gas. The tripling of oil prices since 2002 has created a windfall for oil-exporting nations such as Abu Dhabi, Kuwait, and Norway. McKinsey and Company in an October 2007 report entitled "The New Power Brokers," which examines sovereign wealth funds, has estimated that investors from oil-exporting nations collectively owned between $3.4 trillion and $3.8 trillion in foreign financial assets at the end of 2006. That report also said many oil-exporting nations have now set up state-owned investment funds, often called sovereign wealth funds, to invest some of the assets they have acquired through their oil exports. The October 2007 study done by McKinsey and Company tells us that "sovereign wealth funds", unlike "central bank reserves" (also known as "foreign exchange reserves"), have diversified portfolios that range across equity, fixed income, real estate, bank deposits, and alternative investments such as hedge funds and private equity. According to the McKinsey October 2007 study, the largest sovereign wealth fund among oil exporters is the Abu Dhabi Investment Authority which reportedly has total assets of up to $875 billion.

2. Non-Commodity Funds – which are typically established through transfers of assets from official foreign exchange reserves. Large balance of payment surpluses, according to the McKinsey Study, have enabled non-commodity exporters to transfer "excess" foreign exchange reserves to stand alone investment funds to be managed for higher returns. Most of the non-commodity holdings of foreign exchange reserves are held by the Asian central banks. The October 2007 McKinsey study estimates that at the end of 2006 Asian central banks had $3.1 trillion in foreign reserve assets. The study then stated, "to put this in perspective, it is twice as many assets as global hedge funds manage and twice the size of global private equity".

China's central bank had $1.1 trillion in reserves at the end of 2006 and the Bank of Japan had $875 billion. The central banks of Hong Kong, India, Malaysia, Singapore, South Korea, and Taiwan together have another $1 trillion.

Now how are these Asian central banks able to accumulate these vast and fast-growing amounts of "foreign exchange reserves?" The McKinsey study tells us that:

> Exchange rate management has been key. Since the Asian financial crisis, the region's economies have benefited from rapidly growing exports, and apart from Japan, have switched from running current account deficits to large current account surpluses. The logical long-run corollary of these surpluses, combined with foreign capital inflows would be the appreciation of the currencies of the surplus countries. However to preserve the competitiveness of the region's exports, Asian central banks have intervened in the foreign exchange markets to prevent rapid appreciation, buying foreign currencies (mainly the dollar) while selling domestic currency.

The McKinsey study then explores the pros and cons of having the Asian central banks manage the value of the dollar in a system some economists called Bretton Woods II. The study states:

> "For Asia the system has ensured the success of its export-led growth model and continuous and growing current account surpluses. For the United States the benefit has been twofold. American consumers have the advantage of being able to bring in a huge range of cheap goods manufactured in Asia. But of even more importance is the fact that the United States has been able to maintain a large and growing current account deficit while at the same time maintaining significantly lower interest rates than would normally prevail with a large deficit position – because Asia has provided low cost funds to finance the shortfall".

The McKinsey Report then goes on to note that the Bretton Woods II system has two distinct disadvantages for the United States. A higher dollar (propped up by the Asian central banks) hinders our nation's ability to export (and harms import sensitive domestic industries) and there are hazards from an over-reliance on foreign capital.

Recently Asia's governments have begun to shift some of their foreign exchange assets into "sovereign wealth funds". The Government of Singapore Investment Corporation has around $150 billion under management. China has taken at least $200 billion of its foreign reserve assets and put them into its sovereign wealth fund the China Investment Corporation. It can always transfer more from its foreign exchange reserves into its sovereign wealth fund as it is accumulating foreign exchange at a rate of well over $300 billion annually. Its trade surplus with just the United States this year will be over $250 billion.

Problems for the U.S. with Sovereign Wealth Funds

1. Purchases of Strategic Assets and Technologies

Mr. Gerard Lyons, the Chief Economist of the Standard Chartered Bank, issued a paper on October 15, 2007 entitled "State Capitalism: The Rise of Sovereign Wealth Funds". In that paper he noted that sovereign wealth funds are presently valued at $2.2 trillion, but could reach $13.4 trillion in a decade. One concern he identified on page 9 of his paper is that these funds may make purchases (investments) for strategic, rather than economic purposes. He noted that through these funds foreign governments could acquire, "strategic stakes in key industries around the world such as telecommunications, energy, the financial sector, or even to secure intellectual property rights in other fields."

In 1992, the Treasury Department, as part of its CFIUS responsibilities, was tasked by law to report to Congress within one year and every four years thereafter whether any foreign government had a coordinated strategy to acquire U.S. companies involved in the research and development or production of critical technologies. In its 1993 report the Treasury said it could not find credible evidence of such strategies but said that "should not be viewed as conclusive proof" such strategies did not exist. It did indicate some governments did identify "technologies that are critical to national economic development and thus prime targets for acquisition through M&A's" [mergers and acquisitions]. In its first update to that report submitted to the Congress in September of 2007, the Treasury again reported it "did not find strong enough evidence to conclude that any individual company had a coordinated strategy or was acting on a coordinated strategy on behalf of its respective government." The Treasury report did note, however, that "there is significant evidence that foreign governments are involved in other efforts to acquire such technologies." That was in the Treasury's unclassified report. I understand that there is a classified version and I would urge you to have your staffs peruse that and brief you on it. It just seems reasonable to me to assume that if some foreign governments are using illicit means to acquire U.S. developed critical technologies, that they will probably buy companies producing them if they can utilize that means to access these critical technologies.

2. Increasing Foreign Government Ownership of Our Market Economy

Another concern was expressed by SEC [Security and Exchange Commission] Chairman Christopher Cox in an October 24th speech at the Kennedy School of Government at Harvard University. In that speech entitled "The Role of Government in Markets", Chairman Cox noted that sovereign wealth funds, which are already enormous in his view, could "grow as large as $12 trillion over the next eight years". He then went on to state, "The economic rationale for our legislative and regulatory deference to markets is called into question when the major marketplace participants are not profit-maximizing individuals but governments with national interests".

The SEC Chairman then went on to discuss why in the United States we have traditionally been against large government ownership of our economy, noting our emphasis on private ownership is directly tied to America's dedication to individual freedom. He stated, "The fundamental question presented by state-owned public companies and sovereign wealth funds does not so much concern the advisability of foreign ownership, but rather of government ownership".

He then revisited the issue of foreign ownership later in his speech and noted that if ownership is held by our own government, we can at least influence it to use its ownership to "put our nation's interests first." If the owner on the other hand is a foreign government, he said, "the national interests a foreign government will advance will presumably be its own".

So there are, in Chairman Cox's view, legitimate concerns a nation must take into account when it considers whether to follow policies giving foreign owners and particularly foreign governments increasing amounts of control over its domestic economy.

Foreign Ownership and Trade Deficits

On October 26, 2003, *Fortune* magazine carried an article by Warren Buffett [an investor and reportedly the world's richest person] entitled "Why I'm Not Buying the Dollar: America's Growing Trade Deficit is Selling the Nation Out From Under Us". In that article, Mr. Buffett noted that America's trade deficit exceeded 4 percent of GDP (it is closer to 5.5 percent now), and our nation owed the world $2.5 trillion from the cumulative effect of past trade deficits. He then wrote:

> In effect our country has been behaving like an extraordinarily rich family that possesses an immense farm. In order to consume 4 percent more than we produce – that's the trade deficit – we have day after day been both selling pieces of the farm and increasing the mortgage on what we still owe.

He then said it was imperative that we take "action to halt the outflow of our national wealth" and advocated a plan to do so. I will discuss that plan later in my testimony.

In the winter of 2005 Mr. Buffett in his annual letter to the shareholders of his company Berkshire Hathaway, stated that our country's continuing and massive trade deficits are leading us in the direction of becoming a "sharecropper society", not an ownership society. In July of 2005 a debate raged in Washington about whether the Chinese National Offshore Oil Company (CNOOC), which was 70 percent owned by the Chinese government, should be prohibited from purchasing UNOCAL, a privately owned American company. During an interview on CNBC Mr. Buffett was asked to comment on the matter and stated, "If we are going to consume more than we produce, we have to expect to give away a little part of the country".

Associated with the same debate about the CNOOC/UNOCAL merger, the *Washington Post* published an editorial which appeared on August 7, 2005 entitled "A Sharecropper Society". In it the Post expressed concern that Mr. Buffett's vision of where the United States was headed was "distressingly plausible." The editorial noted that "the country is living beyond its means, spending more than it earns, and relying on foreigners to supply the difference." On October 24th of this year the *Washington Post* published an editorial entitled "Countries Buying Companies" about sovereign wealth funds. The editorial stated:

> Sovereign wealth funds, however, offer governments a way to take over businesses for political as well as economic purposes. That's a benign prospect if the buyer is Norway, a member of NATO. It is more troubling if the government behind the money is that of China, Russia, or Venezuela . . . the accumulation of so many dollars in foreign hands is the result of years in which the United States has imported more than it exports.

The fast-increasing surge of sovereign wealth funds are just another indicator that the country is living beyond its means, spending more than it is earning, and relying on foreigners to purchase our assets to supply the difference. Most of the so-called foreign investment in this country is not "green field" investment whereby new assets are being created, but rather the sale of existing assets to new foreign owners. This is what Warren Buffett means by the "sharecropper economy" reference. In allowing this to happen on our watch we are not doing well for future generations of our citizens.

What Is to Be Done: Immediate Steps

America's political leaders must realize that the United States is part of an increasingly competitive global economy in which many of our trading partners, such as China, Korea, Japan and Taiwan have national goals and strategies to move their economies forward. Under pricing their currencies to achieve trade surpluses and attract investment is just one part of their economic strategies. Our nation must begin to develop our own national goals and a strategy to accomplish them to ensure that the Asian countries do not achieve their economic goals at our expense. Some elements of our own "national strategy" or if you prefer "business plan" might be:

1. The development of an energy policy that promptly begins to reduce our reliance on imported oil and gas. Spending on the technologies to accomplish this, which means investing in America, would create new high tech jobs in our nation and in time reduce the speed by which oil and gas exporters are building their sovereign wealth funds with our own dollars.
2. The development of policies to aggressively address the mercantilist trade practices (being used by China and many of our other Asian trading partners) such as currency manipulation, barriers to imports, illegal export subsidies, forced technology transfers, subsidies to attract investment, and the massive theft of intellectual property. This Committee has already developed and reported to the Senate

legislation to begin to address currency manipulation. I hope that additional measures can be added to that legislation when it is taken upon the floor, such as a provision to make an under-priced currency an illegal export subsidy that can be addressed by our countervailing duty laws.

It would also be good public policy to include measures to stop the influx of contaminated toys, foods and other items that threaten the health and welfare of our citizens.

3. A third element of such a strategy is to have in place a CFIUS process for reviewing foreign acquisitions of U.S. companies that ensures our Government does not permit the selling off of assets that are critical to our national security. The CFIUS legislation enacted this summer goes a long way in doing that. It gives the intelligence agencies a key role in the review process and ensures closer scrutiny of purchases made by foreign government-owned corporations.

Under the new statute, however, the more searching CFIUS review process for a foreign government acquisition only takes place if the foreign government acquires "control" over the American assets and it leaves the word "control" to be defined by agency rulemaking. The Treasury Department, which will pursuant to the Administrative Procedures Act engage in "notice and comment" rulemaking, is likely to receive more comments to be lenient in defining control than strict. It was thus reassuring to see that [several senators] have written to Secretary [of the Treasury Henry] Paulson on that matter. Their September 27th letter urged the Treasury in its rulemaking process to take account of the fact that "[i]n some cases passive foreign ownership interests in assets in the United States, including through sovereign investment funds may have national security implications".

It will be very important for this committee to continue its recent close oversight of the CFIUS process to ensure that the Treasury implements the new statute in the manner intended by its Congressional authors. You can be sure interests representing foreign investors, including foreign government investors; will be active participants in the rulemaking now underway at the Treasury Department.

What Is to Be Done: Further Steps

1. Emergency Trade Summit

During the period of August 2006 through January 2007, I had the opportunity to participate as a senior staff member on the Horizon Project, which was established by the Democratic Policy Committee to develop proposals to address America's economic prosperity and security. At the conclusion of their work the leaders of the Project briefed both the Democratic and Republican Policy Committees about their recommendations.

The Horizon Project group of CEOs and policy experts, which included the President of the Sloan Foundation with whom I work, was very concerned about our nation's massive and ongoing trade deficits and recommended, among other things, that, "An Emergency National Summit on the Trade Deficit be convened to be attended by relevant Cabinet officers, the bipartisan leadership of both Houses of Congress and a small number of top corporate and labor leaders".

The Project report stressed that capping the size of the trade deficit had to be a top national priority. One method the report advocated be considered was the so-called Buffett proposal which was put forth by Warren Buffett in the May 2003 edition of *Fortune* magazine which I referred to earlier in my testimony. Under the Buffett plan our nation's trade account could be balanced through a system whereby the Federal Government would issue import certificates to exporters of goods in the amount equal to the dollar value of their exports. Such a system could be phased in over a period of time.

The Alfred P. Sloan Foundation has recently funded a proposal submitted by a group of trade economists and lawyers to examine how the Buffett proposal could actually be implemented. The Horizon Project noted that [two senators] encapsulated the Buffett proposal in S.3899, a bill they introduced in the last Congress, which would phase in balanced trade for regular commerce over five years and for petroleum trade over ten years.

Another way to reduce the trade deficit considered by the Horizon Project was to use unilateral emergency tariff increases as President [Richard M.] Nixon did in August of 1971. Either the Buffett proposal or the tariff increases could be justified under Article XII of the GATT/WTO agreement [General Agreement on Tariffs and Trade/World Trade Organization] which permits parties to take measures to deal with serious balance of payment difficulties. The fast declines of our currency against the currencies of nations which do not prop it up are evidence of our balance of payments problem. Serious discussion in the Congress of either proposal would give us much needed leverage to deal with China and the other Asian countries which under-price their currencies and utilize other mercantilist practices to achieve massive trade surpluses at our expense.

2. Align Corporate and National Interests

America's political leaders must understand that other countries such as China have instituted policies, including subsidies and an under-priced currency, to give incentives to U.S. and other multinational corporations to help them grow their own economies. Our corporations are operating in a system that compels them to focus on making profits for their shareholders. Top corporate officials get significant financial rewards for achieving these objectives. Public officials, who are accountable to America's citizens, must develop policies to counter foreign practices designed to entice our corporations to serve their interests. We must find the means to align the interests of American based multinational corporations with the national interest which includes keeping and creating well-paying high tech jobs in this country and not transferring huge chunks of our productive capabilities out of the country.

3. Craft an Omnibus Globalization Bill

Over 20 years ago the joint House and Senate leadership, acting in a bipartisan manner, decided to craft an omnibus trade bill to address some of the competitive challenges then facing the nation. Each relevant Committee of the Congress was charged to conduct hearings and to elicit ideas and concepts that could be encapsulated into one Omnibus bill. This process began in 1986 and continued in 1987 and resulted in the Omnibus Trade and Competitiveness Act of 1988.

As one who participated in that process and found it exhilarating, I urge the Congress to again institute such a process and use the year 2008 to lay the groundwork through comprehensive hearings for an Omnibus Globalization bill. Such a Bill would be designed to shape our nation's participation in the globalization process in a manner that reduces our current account deficits and lifts the living standards for our citizens. Any new Administration that comes to power in January 2009, will, I am sure, welcome a cooperative relationship with the Congress in crafting such a bill.

Conclusion

The rapidly-rising status of sovereign wealth funds, which the Committee is examining today, are just one more sign that our nation is not doing well in the global economic competition that will only intensify as we move forward into the 21st century. While it is very useful to examine proposals to make such funds more transparent and to establish behavioral guidelines for them, the real lesson we should take from their rise is that we must take action now to forthrightly address our massive trade deficits that are feeding the growth of these funds.

Stuart E. Eizenstat

Do Sovereign Wealth Funds Make the U.S. Economy Stronger or Pose National Security Risks?

The question posed in the title the committee has given this hearing, whether Sovereign Wealth Funds (SWFs) strengthen or imperil the US economy, is the critical question in the SWF debate. Permit me to say at the outset that the challenges provided by the some $3 trillion in SWFs, from China and Russia to the Gulf States and Saudi Arabia, are as much a reflection of our own economic problems as they are about SWFs themselves. Their remarkable growth and decisions to broaden their portfolio beyond the investments of their central banks in Treasury bills, is a reflection of our growing dependence on expensive foreign oil and our massive current account deficit. This committee and the Congress, and all of us, should be spending as much time and energy on dealing with these structural economic problems as on the consequences of those problems. In effect, SWFs are recycling U.S. petro-dollars and our appetite for products from China and Emerging Markets.

In addition, I am a strong believer in the importance of the free flow of capital around the world, and of the value of foreign direct investment (FDI) in creating jobs in the United States, and adding creativity and innovation to our economy. There is a difference, for sure, between private foreign investment and that of SWFs and their close cousins, State Owned Enterprises (SOEs). But even there, the distinction is not always as clear as it may seem. Many European companies, for example, have some government ownership through "golden shares". Moreover, many European governments are trying to create "national champions" to better compete in the global marketplace. We need to be very careful that in dealing with SWFs, we do nothing to deter the free flow of international capital.

I strongly believe that SWFs do bolster the US economy, and that on balance they are a significant net plus for the U.S. economy. If we take off the "welcome sign", they will invest their growing wealth elsewhere in the world. At the same time, there are legitimate concerns about SWFs that need to be addressed. These heavily revolve around the need for "transparency" and good governance. This, in my opinion, does not mean that they must divulge their holdings and investments, but rather that they should be transparent in their governance, in their relationships to their governments, in their processes, in their goals, and in determining whether they obtain subsidized government

U.S. Senate, November 14, 2007.

financing on individual deals – which would create an unfair advantage over U.S. or foreign corporations who must rely on the private credit markets for competing for the same acquisitions. We have a legitimate interest in assuring that SWFs have a purely commercial, not a political or national security, interest in their investments in the U.S.

Beyond transparency, there certainly are a limited number of matters in which national security risks are implicated by SWFs and SOEs acquisition. But in a globalized world economy, in which the U.S. does not have a monopoly on products, it is important that national security not be defined so broadly that it is used as a broad basis to deter foreign investment.

I urge Congress not to seek legislation or to pressure regulators to impose heavy regulations on SWFs at this stage. The reason for this is that Congress has wisely provided the Executive Branch – in the form of last year's bipartisan Foreign Investment and National Security Act (FINSA) – the means to deal with genuine national security threats from SWFs and SOEs. In my opinion we already have the legislative tools necessary to effectively address any national security concerns raised by SWF investments, and we should give the CFIUS process the time to work through SWF/SOE investments on a case by case basis. [CFIUS is the U.S. Department of the Treasury's Committee on Foreign Investment in the United States.]

Moreover, it is critically important that Congress not take unilateral action. It is vital that we try to develop multilateral principles. Europe, for example, has similar concerns with SWFs/SOEs; for instance, Russia's Gazprom [the country's primary producer of natural gas] has expressed interest in acquiring energy assets in Europe. The Bush Administration has wisely agreed to support this multilateral approach. The IMF is now working directly with all the major SWFs on developing a set of "best practices", which they hope to have completed by April. The OECD [Organization for Economic Cooperation and Development composed of 4 mostly economically developed countries] is doing the same exercise with host countries, and their report will be ready in roughly the same time frame. Moreover, the Government Accountability Office is examining SWFs and their report will be an important touchstone. We should allow these activities to play out, and, for example, see how the SWFs react to the IMF effort to develop a set of principles focused on transparency.

The Benefits and Concerns of the "New" Sovereign Wealth Funds

The benefits of foreign investment into the US are well known. Such investments support economic growth and job creation; they help keep domestic industry competitive; they grease the wheels of the international economy by helping to right financial imbalances; and, as we have seen since last summer as SWFs began investing heavily in the US financial industry, foreign investments can be ready sources of assistance to distressed sectors, in this case bolstering the US economy while providing a needed vote of confidence in the US financial system at a difficult time.

Moreover, we know that SWFs are not recent innovations. The first versions beginning in the 1950s and 60s with states as diverse as Kuwait, Kiribati and Norway establishing national investment vehicles, many of which have long invested in the US. SWFs have a strong record of making long-term investments, with a generally passive involvement in the management of the companies in which they invest.

Most SWF and SOE Investments Raise No National Security Risks

For instance, the acquisition of Barney's, the U.S. retailer, by Dubai, hardly impacts on national security. CFIUS approved the sale of IBM's PC division to Lenovo (which our firm handled), which is partly owned by the Chinese government. Further, SWFs' recent investments in U.S. and European financial institutions have been for small stakes, well under 10%, with no board seats or management voice. It is important to recognize that the control test – which can trigger CFIUS review – is not a mechanical test of 10% voting shares. There are a variety of factors to consider, such as whether the SWF/SOE has the right to appoint members of the board of directors; the right to appoint or veto members of management; the right to approve the corporate budget; the right to approve of new investments and divestitures. Generally, SWFs/SOEs have not insisted on this level of control.

Even if a SWF or SOE transaction presents some risk to national security, CFIUS has proven well-equipped to analyze the risk and negotiate appropriate measures to mitigate that risk. If, for some reason, CFIUS determines that the risk cannot be satisfactorily mitigated, the President has the power to block the transaction.

There are some different factors at work in the recent emergence of SWFs. The amount of money under SWF management is greater than it has ever been. Fueled in some cases by high commodity prices (as is the case for the Persian Gulf, Russian and Norwegian funds) and in others by trade surpluses "unequalled as a percentage of the global economy since the beginning of the 20th century" (as for East Asian SWFs) SWFs are thought to control as much as $3 trillion in assets – greater than the global stock of assets invested in either hedge funds or private equity. Even so, SWFs account for no more than 1.3 percent of the world's financial assets.

And, the number of SWFs are increasing, with some new entries representing perhaps the biggest challenges for US regulatory review. There are now more than 40 major SWFs, with as many as a dozen established since 2005. Given the size and number of the new players in the SWF world, some measure of anxiety was expected and prudent.

The timing of the emergence of SWFs also sharpened fears. The 2008 presidential campaign has begun, memories of two highly-politicized bids by foreign government owned companies for key US assets were still raw (CNOOC's bid for Unocal was in 2005, the Dubai Ports World controversy erupted in 2006), and news of SWFs came just as Congress was completing its legislative overhaul of the US investment screening mechanism – the Committee on Foreign Investment in the United States (CFIUS) codified in FINSA – a task that was precipitated by the CNOOC/Dubai Ports World events but took on new urgency once SWFs appeared. [CNOOC is the China National Offshore Oil Corporation; Unocal was the Union Oil Company of California. Congress blocked China's acquisition of Unocal; it soon thereafter was acquired by Chevron. The Dubai Ports World (DPW) involved the bid of DPW, a port-management company based in the United Arab Emirates, to take over the administration of six major U.S. ports. The Bush administration supported the possibility, but DPW withdrew its bid in the face of strong congressional opposition.]

Governance and Transparency – The Critical SWF Reforms

If there has been an underlying theme for most of the concerns verbalized about SWFs in the assertion that these funds, as a whole, are nontransparent, and consequently policymakers cannot be sure what drives the funds' investments, divestments, and other behaviors. It is asserted that SWFs may be political or intelligence-gathering tools out to harm the United States, rather than profit maximizers. And, it is disquiet emanating from this alleged feature of SWFs that has led many of those otherwise positively disposed towards free capital movements – including Treasury Department officials, capital markets regulators, and some in the think tank community – to question whether some regulation is needed. Senior government officials from Robert Kimmitt and Clay Lowery at Treasury to Chris Cox, the Chairman of the SEC [Security and Exchange Commission], to experts like Ted Truman at the Peterson Institute, have raised a number of legitimate concerns:

- whether the governments subsidize individual transactions;
- the potential for imprudent investments to increase risks for market stability;
- whether they have a political agenda, such as Gazprom has exhibited in Ukraine, Georgia and elsewhere;
- whether there is a risk of insider trading;
- whether there is a risk for corruption, if government officials are directly involved from countries with a record of corrupt activities;
- whether there is a risk of leakage of sensitive technology to countries which are not allies of the U.S.

Tellingly, SWFs have followed these debates and concerns and appear to have made recent investments with political sensitivities in mind. As I mentioned, the recent SWF investments in the financial sector have explicitly and invariably been non-controlling minority investments, have not included any board seats for the SWFs or powers to control management, budgets, or new acquisitions or divestitures, and have generally been below 10% voting shares.

Further, some SWFs have already responded to calls for greater openness. I hope that SWFs will take steps to be more transparent. Even in the short run, increasing transparency produces benefits not just for the host states,

but for the SWFs themselves. Real transparency promises to ease the acceptance of SWF investments as host states come to understand SWFs' investment
strategies and management structures, and can be assured that commercial
rather than political interests control investments, and that SWFs do not
receive unfair subsidies that may make competitive bidding with private entities difficult. Finally, SWFs will very likely come to understand that adopting
some measures of transparency and other robust regulation for themselves is
the best way to avoid more heavy-handed regulation from both the US and
other investment recipients.

Across the Atlantic, Joaquin Almunia, the EU [European Union] Commissioner for Economic and Monetary Affairs, has explicitly suggested such a
quid pro quo, stating that there were "good reasons" to ask funds about their
investment strategies and holdings, and if they do not provide such information "we can find good reasons to 'react' in some cases, where these funds try
to invest . . . in strategic sector[s] or . . . specific industries."

Unilateral Rules May Harm the U.S.

My contention that SWF-specific legislation is not needed at this juncture
comes not just from my hope that over time many SWFs will become more
transparent of their own accord. Rather the imposition of unilateral rules on
US investment for SWFs may harm the competitive position of our economy.
After all the United States is only one of many markets in which SWFs can
choose to invest. As former Secretary of State Colin Powell noted, "capital
is a coward," and unilateral rules in the US that are not matched by similar
regulations in other potential host states may adversely impact our ability to
attract FDI and consequently may diminish our competitiveness. It is worth
remembering that the majority of SWF money that has been invested into
the US is actually recycled US dollars resulting from our oil dependence (for
the Middle Eastern funds) and mass current account deficit (for the East Asian
funds). It seems far better to have this money recycled here, than to be moved
elsewhere.

The Way Ahead – Multilateral Discussions and the "New" CFIUS

The necessity for a global solution that evens the playing field between potential recipients of investments provides one of the guideposts to the most
effective future direction for US policy on the SWF issue. Fortunately such a
multilateral approach is underway. Last fall, the Treasury Department, along
with finance ministries from the rest of G8 and those of several states owning
leading SWFs asked the International Monetary Fund [IMF] and the Organization for Economic Cooperation and Development [OECD] to begin working
on best practices.

The IMF process, which is focused on best practices for the SWFs themselves, is due to issue its recommendations in April. Though the IMF will likely

touch on several aspects of reform, it seems evident that a central focus of the guidelines will be on enhancing SWF transparency in order to increase the number of SWFs that publish annual accounts and provide outsiders some insight into governance and investment strategies. In a hopeful sign, some SWFs are closely assisting the IMF efforts.

Working alongside the IMF, the OECD's Investment Committee has begun working on best practices for host countries, and in particular the processes of host country review of SWF investments. The OECD report is due in March. The OECD's primary concern is that some recipient states may overreact to SWFs and erect needless procedural barriers to SWF investments which may chill wider FDI flows. Though still being drafted, the OECD rules will likely borrow from best practices in some of its members, including the US CFIUS process.

The CFIUS process, newly vested with enhanced transparency and predictability, provides the other guidepost for effective domestic response to SWFs. Though as this committee knows the CFIUS regulations are due to be released in April, even before the rules are finalized it is clear that FINSA's improvements on CFIUS are significant and important. Its enhancements include a greater clarity for foreign investors, a result of new transparency regarding the factors CFIUS considers in moving a transaction from a 30-day review to a 45-day investigations, alongside the requirements that CFIUS issue public guidance on the types of transactions that have been reviewed and that have raised national security concerns. Moreover, the law's provision for a "lead agency or agencies" for the government entity with greatest equities in a transaction promises to instill discipline in CFIUS and lead to more routinized review processes. Finally, the law requires the involvement of senior-level officials in major CFIUS actions including with respect to certifications provided to Congress and decisions not to investigate transactions involving foreign government ownership.

We should rely on the wisdom of FINSA and take solace from the CFIUS process and its recent ability to quickly clear transactions – such as the sale of IBM's personal computer business to Lenovo. That the review processes were transparent and efficient, simultaneously promoting both open investment and national security, suggests that the current tools – set to be improved further after the release of the CFIUS regulations – can effectively address SWF investments.

I counsel Congress to withhold judgment on the necessity for further legislation until both the CFIUS regulations are published and can be assessed in practice, and the IMF and OECD have delivered their reports.

History, Transparency and Nuance – The Key to Effective Regulation of SWFs

If the past is prologue, history does not suggest that most SWFs will engage in politically-motivated investments. SWFs have been long-term, stable and passive investors. Though they may be less risk averse than central banks solely investing in T-Bills, most SWFs are run with profit in mind. Quickly unwinding positions, or investing for political as opposed to financial gain, could be as damaging to SWFs (if not more so) as to host countries. Most SWFs have been mandated to secure healthy returns and many have received political and public rebuke at home for unsuccessful investments. Further, SWFs are aware of the growing political sensitivities regarding their investments and most would be loathe to upset host governments for fear of wearing out their welcome.

Even if history and the structure of SWFs suggest that we have little to fear, the current approach adopted by the Bush Administration should be lauded. Unilateral, protectionist regulations have not been contemplated, neither has the Administration raised the potential for imposing reciprocity as a test for SWF investments. In some quarters this has been a commonly suggested response to the SWF influx and asks the reasonable question why the United States should allow unfettered access to its assets to state-backed SWFs when those states to not allow commensurate access to their assets. A successor of mine as Deputy Treasury Secretary, Robert Kimmitt, made the Administration's rejection of reciprocity clear in his recent Foreign Affairs piece: raising reciprocity as a barrier to SWFs "is not on the list" of policy proposals. He argues correctly that the benefits the United States receives from foreign investment are irrespective of whether or not other countries provide US investors similar rights.

Indeed, instead of unilateral restrictions, constructive deliberation on a multilateral basis is critical so as to ease bona fide concerns regarding investors' intentions and fund transparency, while ensuring that host states remain open to receiving the benefits SWF investments can bring – benefits that include both domestic financial stability in distressed sectors and wider global stability as the world's major economies become ever more interdependent.

To that end, transparency coupled with nuance are key. Clearly there should be some limits to SWF acquisitions. However, these prohibitions should be clear, narrowly focused and few and far between. Broad prohibitions are not needed, and with nuanced review that takes into account the transparency of a particular investor and the magnitude of specific investments (differentiating between controlling and passive stakes), there is little reason that our aim of protecting national security cannot be consistent with opening up the vast majority of the American economy to SWF funds. Relying on the CFIUS process makes per se rules even less needed, given that appropriate protections can be negotiated on a case-by-case basis, ranging from insisting that investors establish an arm's length proxy relationship to handle sensitive investments, to striking nuanced mitigation agreements of the kind the Government has forged with scores of foreign investors.

It is my view that a chorus of support for moderated, thoughtful reaction to SWFs must be developed now, before SWFs become a political third-rail and the United States loses out in attracting both needed funds and in retaining the mantle of the world's most dynamic economy.

POSTSCRIPT

Do Sovereign Wealth Funds Threaten Economic Sovereignty?

Sovereign wealth funds are a relatively new financial actor on the global stage. The first of what are now SWFs was not created until 1953, when Kuwait set up an agency to invest its oil revenues. The term sovereign wealth fund itself was not coined until 2005, when Andrew Rozanov did so in "Who Holds the Wealth of Nations," *Central Banking Journal* (August 2005).

There is nothing inherently nefarious about SWFs. Most U.S. state governments and many U.S. public universities, for example, have what amount to SWFs to invest retirement funds or contributions. Some national governments do the same, with the Government Pension Fund of Norway an example. However, concern has mounted as the number of SWFs and their wealth has grown because of their ties to governments and the possibility of manipulating investments for political ends. Currently, just the top 20 directly controlled SWFs have assets over $2.8 trillion, and the assets of smaller directly and indirectly owned SWFs, like CNOOC, would add substantially to that figure.

SWFs first gained wide attention among Americans after CNOOC tried to by the U.S. oil firm UNOCAL. The 2007–2008 mortgage/banking crisis in the United States brought SWF into the news again. When Citigroup, the largest U.S. bank, fell into trouble in 2007, it regained stability because of an infusion of $7.5 billion for stock by the Abu Dhabi Investment Authority (ADIA). The investment made the ADIA Citigroup's largest investor. The bank's second largest shareholder is Kingdom Holding Company of Saudi Arabia. It is technically a public company, but in reality is controlled by Prince Alwaleed bin Talal al Saud, who owns 95 percent of its shares. ADIA releases little about its investments, but in 2008 it is known to have acquired a major stake in Toll Brothers, a major U.S. homebuilders and to have acquired New York City's iconic Chrysler Building for $800 million.

The notice SWFs have drawn and the growing calls to regulate them more and to make their activities more transparent brought 25 SWFs together at the headquarters of the International Monetary Fund in Washington, D.C. in 2008 to create an International Working Group to formulate voluntary SWF principles regarding proper investment practices and objectives.

More on SWFs is available online at SWF Insitute at http://www.swfinstitute.org/. The Peterson Institute for International Economics at http://www.petersoninstitute .org/ is also a good source. Keyboard "sovereign wealth funds" into the site's search window. Also see, Shams Butt, Anil Shivdasani, Carsten Stendevad, and Ann Wyman, "Sovereign Wealth Funds: A Growing Global Force in Corporate Finance," *Journal of Applied Corporate Finance* (March 2008).

ISSUE 13

Is Immigration an Economic Benefit to the Host Country?

YES: Dan Siciliano, from Testimony during Hearings on "Immigration: Economic Impact," before the Committee on the Judiciary, U.S. Senate (April 24, 2006)

NO: Barry R. Chiswick, from Testimony during Hearings on "Immigration: Economic Impact," before the Committee on the Judiciary, U.S. Senate (April 24, 2006)

ISSUE SUMMARY

YES: Dan Siciliano, executive director, Program in Law, Business, and Economics, and research fellow with the Immigration Policy Center at the American Immigration Law Foundation, Stanford Law School, contends that immigration provides many economic benefits for the United States.

NO: Barry R. Chiswick, UIC Distinguished Professor, and program director, Migration Studies IZA—Institute for the Study of Labor, Bonn, Germany, takes the position that legal immigration has a negative impact on the U.S. economy and that illegal immigration increases the problems.

Part of the saga of human history is the migration of people ranging from individuals to entire populations from their homes to new ones in search of a better life. Indeed, the development of some countries, such as the United States, is substantially based on the inflow of immigrants. Sometimes such influxes have gone fairly smoothly. At other times they have met significant opposition within the country of destination. Such is the case currently, with the global tide of refugees and immigrants, both legal and illegal, facing increasing resistance. A poll that asked people in 44 countries whether immigrants were having a good or bad impact found that a plurality in 28 countries said bad, with a plurality answering good in just 13 countries, and 3 countries evenly divided. Moreover, a lopsided 72 percent of the respondents favored stricter controls on immigration. Support for this position averaged 76 percent in the wealthiest countries such as the United States, Canada, and Western Europe. But opposition was even slightly higher in Latin America (77 percent) and sub-Saharan Africa (79 percent) and also strong among East Europeans (67 percent), Asians (61 percent), and Middle Easterners (66 percent).

Opposition to immigration comes from several sources. One is prejudice based on race, ethnicity, religion, or some other characteristic. More legitimate in the view of many is worry that immigrants are diluting the host country's language and other aspects of its national culture. Security concerns are a third source of opposition to immigration. Some critics of immigration argue that crime is higher among immigrant populations, and in recent years the possibility of immigrants being terrorists has increased this worry for some. Economic concerns are a fourth source of opposition to immigrants. One economic argument is that immigrants work for low wages, thereby undercutting the wage of native-born workers. Another charge is that immigrants are an economic burden, requiring far more in terms of welfare, medical care, education, and other services than the migrants return to the economy in terms of productivity and taxes. These charges are met by counterarguments that depict immigrants as providing needed workers and otherwise giving a boost to their new country's economy.

Immigration into the United States has changed markedly in recent decades. One difference is that it has increased significantly, with legal immigration growing almost 300 percent from a yearly average of 330,000 in the 1960s to an annual average of 978,000 in the 1990s and just over 1 million during 2000–2007. A second difference is that immigrants are more likely to be people of color from Africa, Asia, and Latin America. European-heritage whites made up more than 70 percent of all immigrants as late as the 1950s. Now, because of changes in U.S. immigration law, only 14 percent are from such countries, while 48 percent of legal immigrants are from Latin America and the Caribbean, 34 percent are from Asia, and 4 percent are from Africa. Adding to both the overall number of immigrants and the percentage who are not from Europe, Canada, and other European-heritage countries is an estimated 400,000 to 500,000 illegal (undocumented, unauthorized) immigrants who arrive in the United States yearly. Perhaps 11 million such immigrants are currently in the United States, with approximately 80 percent of them from Central America, especially Mexico.

The presence of so many undocumented immigrants has become a major political issue in the United States. At one level, it is a question unto itself. It also relates to the general concerns about immigration that many Americans have regarding culture and security. Certainly, American attitudes are different for legal and illegal immigrants, but there is also an overlap, illustrated by the fact that polls find that most Americans favor decreasing immigration overall. When Americans are asked what bothers them about illegal immigration, about the impact of unauthorized immigrants on wages, job availability, and the cost of social and educational services. Taking up this concern, Dan Siciliano examines the economic impact of both documented and undocumented immigrants on the United States in the first reading and finds that the country benefits. Barry Chiswick disagrees in the second reading, finding economic damage from legal and illegal immigration alike.

YES

Dan Siciliano

Immigration: The Positive Impact

Today's hearing on U.S. immigration policy and its impact on the American economy comes at a critical time. Efforts are underway in the House and in the Senate to repair a system that is generally acknowledged to be broken. I suggest that any reform to immigration policy should be evaluated by considering how immigrants directly, and as the evidence now seems to indicate, positively impact our nation's economic prosperity.

Much of the public debate over immigration in the United States has focused on the rapid growth of the undocumented population over the past decade and a half. However, undocumented immigration is just one symptom of the larger disconnect between U.S. immigration policy and the reality of our economy's fundamental reliance on a diverse and, hopefully, growing pool of available labor. The U.S. economy has become increasingly reliant on immigrant workers to fill the growing number of less-skilled jobs for which a shrinking number of native-born workers are available. Yet current immigration policies offer very few legal avenues for workers in less-skilled occupations to enter the country. Undocumented immigration has been the predictable result of the U.S. immigration system's failure to respond effectively to actual labor demand.

Many critics of immigration point to economic arguments that the presence of immigrants, particularly undocumented immigrants, has broad negative consequences for the native-born workforce. Some claim that immigration reduces employment levels and wages among native-born workers. This is generally not true. These arguments are largely the result of an over-simplified economic model used to measure the impact of immigration on the workforce, while ignoring the role that immigrants play in expanding the economy and stimulating labor demand through their consumer purchases and investments. Moreover, the empirical evidence indicates that businesses expand through the investment of more capital when the labor supply is not artificially constrained. Careful analysis and more recent studies add a dynamic component to the economic analysis of immigration by treating immigrants (both documented and undocumented) as real economic agents: earning, spending, and investing in the economy. Businesses, in turn, are considered dynamic as well: adjusting to the available resources and expanding accordingly. Or, if this issue should be mishandled, rediverting resources and shrinking accordingly.

Few argue with the notion that immigration provides many benefits to the United States. As a nation of immigrants, our culture, customs, and

U.S. Senate, April 24, 2006.

traditions reflect the diverse backgrounds of the millions of individuals who have made their way to America over time. But more than cultural benefits, recent economic analysis, including work by Giovanni Peri of the University of California, shows that the United States sees real economic benefits from immigration. Native-born wages increased between 2.0 and 2.5 percent during the 1990s in response to the inflow of immigrant workers. Overall annual growth in the Gross Domestic Product is 0.1 percentage point higher as a result of immigration—a misleadingly small number that represents billions of dollars in economic output and, when compounded across a generation, represents a significant improvement in the standard of living of our children and grandchildren.

The positive impact of immigration results in part from the fact that immigrants help to fill growing gaps in our labor force. These gaps develop as aging native-born workers, in larger numbers than ever before, succeed in attaining higher levels of education and subsequently pursue higher-skill, higher-wage jobs. If the United States were to reform the immigration system to better address the demand for foreign-born labor, largely through ensuring that such workers were a part of the transparent and competitive "above ground" economy, the economic benefits of immigration could be even greater than what we have already experienced. Immigrants and their employers would likely benefit from a more predictable workforce environment and less time and resources would be spent addressing the dysfunction that is a result of a strong demand for a labor force that our laws do not accommodate.

Undocumented immigration is largely the result of two opposing forces: an immigration policy that significantly restricts the flow of labor and the economic reality of a changing native-born U.S. population. The extent to which the U.S. economy has become dependent on immigrant workers is evident in the labor force projections of the Bureau of Labor Statistics (BLS). According to BLS estimates, immigrants will account for about a quarter of labor force growth between 2002 and 2012. Given that roughly half of immigrants now arriving in the United States are undocumented, this means that 1 in 8 workers joining the U.S. labor force over the coming decade will be undocumented immigrants. Many of the jobs that would be harder to fill without this labor supply are already associated with immigrant labor: construction, agriculture, meatpacking, and hospitality. A growing number of immigrants, however, are also filling jobs in fields that are vitally important to serving America's aging population, such as home healthcare. This indicates that while policymakers debate the relative merits of various immigration reform proposals, immigration beyond current legal limits has already become an integral component of U.S. economic growth and will likely remain so for the foreseeable future.

The Impact of Immigrants on Native-Born Wages

Despite the critical role that immigration plays in preventing labor shortages that might impede economic growth, many critics of immigration argue that foreign-born workers reduce the wages of native-born workers with whom they compete for jobs. However, this argument relies on an overly simplistic understanding of labor supply and demand that fails to capture the true value that immigrants bring to the economy. If you are to gauge accurately the economic impact of immigration, the role that immigrants play in creating jobs is just as important as the role they play in filling jobs.

To analyze the impact of immigration on the U.S. economy as a whole, particularly in the studies relied upon in this debate, economists typically use one of two models: "static" or "dynamic." The static model is the simplest and most frequently used by critics of immigration, yet it is the least realistic because it fails to account for the multi-dimensional role that immigrants play as workers, consumers, and entrepreneurs. The dynamic model, on the other hand, offers a more nuanced portrait of immigrants as economic actors. The net economic benefits of immigration are apparent in both models, but are larger in the dynamic model.

Under the static model, economists assume that immigrant workers serve only to increase the labor supply, which results in slightly lower wages and thus higher profits for the owners of capital. In other words, if there are more workers competing for a job, an employer might pay a lower wage for that job and pocket the difference. For instance, under a popular version of the analysis that utilizes the static model, the 125 million native-born workers in the United States in 1997 would have earned an average of $13 per hour if not for the presence of immigrants. However, the 15 million immigrant workers who were actually in the country increased the labor force to 140 million and, under the static scenario, thereby lowered average wages by 3 percent to $12.60 per hour. Nonetheless, the net benefit to the U.S. economy of this decline in wages would have amounted to about $8 billion in added national income in 1997.

Despite the seeming simplicity of this logic (more workers competing for jobs results in lower wages for workers and higher profits for businesses), the assumptions underlying the static model bear little resemblance to economic reality. Recent evidence supports the contention that the impact of immigration on wages is not as simple, or negative, as the static model would suggest. A 2004 study found that, despite the large influx of immigrants without a high-school diploma from 1980 to 2000, the wages of U.S.-born workers without a diploma relative to the wages of U.S.-born workers with a diploma "remained nearly constant." More importantly, [research shows] . . . that the dynamic response of small and medium sized businesses to this phenomena means that nearly all U.S.-born workers, especially those with a high school education or better, have benefited from higher wages due to the presence of this low skilled, often undocumented, immigrant labor.

The inability of the static model to explain this finding rests in part on the fact that the model incorrectly assumes immigrant and U.S.-born workers are perfectly interchangeable; that is, that they substitute for each other rather than complement each other in the labor force. Common sense alone suggests that this is not always the case. For example, less-skilled foreign-born construction laborers enhance the productivity of U.S.-born carpenters, plumbers, and electricians, but do not necessarily substitute for them. More broadly, the different educational and age profiles of foreign-born and native-born workers indicate that they often fill different niches in the labor market.

More importantly, the static model fails to account for the fact that immigrants spend money or invest capital, both of which create jobs and thus exert upward pressure on wages by increasing the demand for labor. This amounts to more than a minor omission given the scale of immigrant purchasing power and entrepreneurship. For instance, in 2004, consumer purchasing power totaled $686 billion among Latinos and $363 billion among Asians. Given that roughly 44 percent of Latinos and 69 percent of Asians were foreign-born in that year, the buying power of immigrants reached into the hundreds of billions of dollars.

The dynamic model accounts for many of these additional economic contributions by immigrants. In the dynamic scenario, immigrant workers spend some of their wages on housing and consumer goods, which in turn increases the demand for labor by creating new jobs. Rising labor demand then increases wages relative to what would have existed if immigrant workers had not been present in the labor market. Businesses in turn invest more capital, expand, and hire more workers across the spectrum of skill levels. The result is a larger economy with higher employment.

The Impact of Immigrants on Native-Born Employment Levels

An IPC research report released in November of 2005 provides strong demographic evidence that the impact of immigrants on native-born employment levels is extremely limited or, in some cases, positive. The report examines the significant differences between the native-born workforce and the immigrant workforce and finds that immigrants are largely complementary to the native-born in education, age and skill profile. The complementary nature of immigrant labor makes it unlikely that immigrants are replacing a significant number of native-born workers, but are instead moving into positions that allow native-born workers to be more productive.

As the number of less-skilled jobs continues to grow, it will become increasingly difficult for employers to find native-born workers, especially younger workers, with the education levels that best correspond to those jobs. In this sense, immigrant workers are a vital complement to a native-born labor force that is growing older and better educated. On average, foreign-born workers tend to be younger than their native-born counterparts and a larger proportion have less formal education. In addition, immigrants participate in the labor force at a higher rate. As a result, immigrants provide a needed source of labor for the large and growing number of jobs that do not require as much formal education.

Immigrant Workers are More Likely to Have Less Formal Education

Immigrants comprise a disproportionate share of those workers who are willing to take less-skilled jobs with few or no educational requirements. In 2004, 53.3 percent of the foreign-born labor force age 25 and older had a high-school diploma or less education, compared to 37.8 percent of the native-born labor force. Immigrant workers were more than four times as likely as native workers to lack a high-school diploma. In contrast, immigrant workers were nearly as likely to have a four-year college degree or more education, amounting to more than 30 percent of both the native-born and foreign-born labor force.

In general, foreign-born workers are more likely to be found at either end of the educational spectrum, while most native-born workers fall somewhere in the middle. Roughly three-fifths of the native-born labor force in 2004 had either a high-school diploma or some college education short of a four-year degree, whereas three-fifths of the foreign-born labor force either did not have a high-school diploma or had at least a four-year college degree. Given their different educational backgrounds, most native-born workers are therefore not competing directly with foreign-born workers for the same types of jobs.

Immigrant Workers Tend to be Younger

Immigrants also include a large number of younger workers, particularly in the less-skilled workforce. In 2004, 67 percent of the foreign-born labor force with a high-school diploma or less education was between 25 and 45 years old, as opposed to 52 percent of the native-born labor force with no more than a high-school diploma. While relative youth is not a requirement for many jobs, it is an asset in those less-skilled jobs that are physically demanding or dangerous.

Given the different age and educational profiles of foreign-born and native-born workers, it is not surprising that immigrants comprise a disproportionately large share of younger workers with little education. In 2004, immigrants made up more than a quarter of all workers 25–34 years old with a high-school diploma or less, and more than half of workers 25–34 years old without a high-school diploma. Employers searching for younger workers in less-skilled positions therefore often find that a large portion of prospective hires is foreign-born.

The Fiscal Costs of Immigration

Critics of immigration often focus on the fiscal costs of immigration instead of the economic benefits. These costs are often exacerbated by the undocumented status of many immigrants. An immigration policy that acknowledged the economic need for and benefits of immigration would significantly reduce these costs. To support the contention that immigrants are a net fiscal drain, critics cite studies indicating that immigrants contribute less per capita in tax revenue than they receive in benefits. However, these studies fail to acknowledge that this has more to do with low-wage employment than with native-born status. Native-born workers in low-wage jobs similarly receive benefits in excess of the level of taxes paid. However, net tax revenue is not the same as net economic benefit. Generally accepted analysis reveals that the net economic benefit compensates for and exceeds any negative fiscal impact. The "fiscal only" analysis ignores the fact that in the absence of sufficient immigrant labor, unfilled low-wage jobs, regardless of the relative tax implications, hurt the economy.

Conclusion

Immigration is a net positive for the U.S. economy and the presence of immigrants does not generally harm the native-born workforce. Studies that purport to demonstrate a negative impact on native-born wages and employment levels rely on an overly simplistic economic model of immigration and the economy. The most recent demographic analysis in conjunction with more sophisticated economic analysis reveals that most immigrants, including undocumented immigrants, do not compete directly with native-born workers for jobs. Instead, these immigrants provide a critical element of our nation's economic success and continued resiliency: a relatively young, willing, and dynamic supply of essential workers in areas such as healthcare, construction, retail, and agriculture. These are jobs that, once filled, enable our economy to continue the cycle of growth and job creation.

Indeed, this makes clear that the implication of the government's own BLS data cannot be ignored. To prosper, our economy desperately needs workers at both ends of the spectrum: young and less skilled as well as more educated and highly skilled. As a nation, we are in the midst of a slow-motion demographic cataclysm unlike any we have previously experienced. Immigration is not the only tool for seeing our way clear of the coming storm—but it is one without which we will not prosper. Without a continued and normalized flow of immigrant labor our workforce will fall well short of the numbers needed to meet the emerging demand for labor. The result will be an erosion of both the growth and increased standard of living that our citizenry has come to expect and to which future generations are entitled. Until the United States adopts a more articulated and thoughtful immigration policy that accommodates these economic realities, the insufficiency of current immigration and the problematic nature of undocumented immigration, in particular, will continue to hobble the economy.

Barry R. Chiswick  **NO**

Immigration:
The Negative Economic Impact

When I am asked the question "What is THE economic impact of immigration?" where the tone indicates the emphasis on the word "the," I respond that this is not the best way to couch the question. There are two fundamental questions. One is: "What is the optimal size of the immigrant population?" The other is: "What are the different impacts of immigrants that differ in their productivity-related characteristics?"

Impacts on Relative Wages

Let us begin with a discussion of the second question. Conceptually, it is best to think in terms of two types of immigrants, which for simplicity we will call high-skilled and low-skilled, with the same two skill groups represented in the native-born population. High-skilled immigrants will have some characteristics in common, without regard for their country of origin. They tend to have high levels of schooling, which means they tend to have a high degree of literacy, perhaps also numeracy, critical thinking or decision-making skills. Many, but not all, will have a high degree of scientific or technical knowledge, and in the modern era a high comfort level with computer technology. Many, but certainly not all, will either have a degree of proficiency in the destination language (in this case, English) or the ability to acquire proficiency in that language shortly after arrival. These are all characteristics that have been shown to improve the earnings of immigrants and to facilitate their economic adjustment in the host country.

Although particular individuals may differ, low-skilled immigrants generally have little formal schooling, limited literacy proficiency in their mother tongue (the language of their origin country), and limited scientific and technical knowledge. These are characteristics associated with low earnings in the destination.

High-skilled and low-skilled immigrants will, in general, have different impacts on the host economy and labor market. Labor markets behave in a manner similar to other markets, in that a greater supply of a given type of labor tends to depress the market wage of workers with similar characteristics. An increase in the supply of a given type of worker also increases the productivity of the complementary factors of production with which it works, including

U.S. Senate, April 24, 2006.

other types of labor and capital. To give a simple example, an increase in the supply of low-skilled restaurant kitchen help will result in more competition for this type of job and lower wages for ordinary kitchen workers. Yet this will increase the productivity (and hence wages) of the master chefs because with more help for the menial kitchen chores they can spend their time on the highly specialized tasks for which they have trained. By the same token, an increase in the supply of high-skilled chefs would raise the productivity of low-skilled restaurant kitchen workers since they would have more master chefs for whom to work.

The result of high-skilled immigration tends to be an increase in the wages of all low-skilled workers (and reduce their use of public income transfers) and a decrease in the wages of high-skilled natives. This reduces income inequality, which we generally view as a good development. Like high-skilled natives, the taxes paid by high-skilled immigrants tend to be greater than the costs they impose on the public treasury through the income transfers they receive, the schooling received by their children, and the publicly subsidized medical care that they receive. High-skilled immigrants are also more likely to bring with them the scientific, technical and innovative skills that expand the production capabilities of the economy. As a result, the population as a whole tends to benefit from high-skilled immigration, although with some benefiting more than others.

Now consider the impacts of low-skilled immigration. While these immigrants tend to raise the earnings of high-skilled workers, their presence in the labor market increases competition for low-skilled jobs, reducing the earnings of low-skilled native-born workers. This not only increases income inequality, which is rightly considered to be undesirable, it also increases the need among low-skilled natives for public assistance and transfer benefits. Because of their low earnings, low-skilled immigrants also tend to pay less in taxes than they receive in public benefits, such as income transfers (e.g., the earned income tax credit, food stamps), public schooling for their children, and publicly provided medical services. Thus while the presence of low-skilled immigrant workers may raise the profits of their employers, they tend to have a negative effect on the well-being of the low-skilled native-born population, and on the native economy as a whole. These points are not purely theoretical arguments. In the past two decades the real wages of low-skilled workers have remained stagnant even as the real earnings of high-skilled workers have risen. As a result, income inequality has increased. Several factors have been responsible for this development, but one of them has been the very large increase in low-skilled immigration.

The "Need" for Low-Skilled Immigrants

"But," I am often asked, "don't we need low-skilled immigrant workers to do the jobs that native workers are unwilling to do?" I respond: "At what wage will native workers decline to take these jobs?" Consider the following thought experiment: What would happen to lettuce picking or the mowing of suburban lawns if there were fewer low-skilled workers? Earlier this month on ABC's Nightline program a winter lettuce grower in Arizona provided the answer. He acknowledged that he would pay higher wages to attract native-born workers and he would speed up the mechanization of lettuce harvesting. The technology is there, but with low wages for lettuce pickers there is no economic incentive for the growers to mechanize or invest in other types of new technology. If the supply of low-skilled immigrant workers decreased substantially, mechanical harvesting would replace many of them with capital (machines) and more highly paid native workers. How would suburban lawns get mowed if there were fewer low-skilled immigrant workers? Wages for lawn care workers would surely rise. The result would be that more teenagers and other low-skilled native workers would find it worth their while to make themselves available for this work.

In addition to this substitution of one type of labor (youthful and low-skilled natives) for another (low-skilled immigrants), there would be other adjustments to the higher cost of lawn mowing. One would be letting the grass grow longer between mows—say, every ten days instead of weekly. Another would be the substitution of grass that grows more slowly, or the substitution of ground cover or paving stones for grass, etc. The point is that there would be many ways for consumers and employers/producers to respond to the higher wages of low-skilled workers to mitigate the adverse effects of having fewer low-skilled immigrants.

A Century Ago

At this point in the conversation, someone usually points to the period of mass immigration of unskilled workers from the 1880s to the 1920s: If these arguments are valid now, wouldn't they have applied at that time as well?—and we know that immigration was a tremendous net benefit to the United States at that time. The answer is both yes and no. The economy and economic institutions of 100 years ago were quite different from those of today in ways that are both important and relevant to our discussion. Then, rapid industrialization of the American economy generated a very large demand for unskilled workers in mines and in factories producing everything from steel to shirts. This is no longer the case. Technological change, the increased cost of even low-skilled labor (wages plus fringe benefits and employment taxes), the falling cost of capital equipment, and globalization/international trade have sharply reduced the demand for low-skilled workers in U.S. manufacturing, mining, agriculture, and even service occupations and industries. Moreover, 100 years ago income inequality and income distribution issues were not a matter of public policy concern. If there were poor people in the United States—so be it. If private individuals and charities helped the poor—fine, but there was nothing like the tax-funded income transfer system in place today.

Yet in some ways the mass immigration from Europe 100 years ago had a similar impact as the one we are facing today. By holding down the wages of low-skilled workers in the industrializing centers of the economy, especially in the Northern states, rural-urban and South-North migration was slowed. Rural and Southern poverty persisted longer than they might have otherwise, and it was only after war (WWI) and immigration restrictions (in the 1920s) had effectively stopped the European migration that these poverty-reducing internal migrations resumed. While there is no question that there were long-term benefits from the massive wave of immigrants for the country as a whole, it is also true that the low-skilled native-born workers of that time paid a price.

Fallacies in Estimating Immigrant Impacts

In the course of these hearings on the economic impact of immigration, you may receive testimony regarding a body of literature that attempts to estimate this impact. In this literature a statistical technique, regression analysis, is used to show how the wages of native workers (or low-skilled natives in particular) in a state or metropolitan area are affected by the extent to which there are immigrants (or low-skilled immigrants) in the same area. These studies tend to find no relation, or sometimes a very small relation, between the presence of immigrants and wage levels.

There is nothing wrong with regression analysis per se as a statistical technique, but its application in this case is flawed. This application of regression analysis requires us to assume that each state or metropolitan area is a self-contained economy, with little or no in-and-out movement of workers, of capital, or even of goods and services. We know, however, that this is not the case. Labor, capital and goods are highly mobile across state boundaries and metropolitan areas. What we learn from these studies is not that immigrants have no effect on wages, but that these wage effects—whatever they may be—have spread throughout the country. Although it does provide evidence that markets in the United States function quite efficiently, the impacts of immigration cannot be detected by this statistical technique.

At the aggregate level, many analyses consider immigrants as an undifferentiated whole without distinguishing between high-skilled and low-skilled workers. These also provide misleading implications, often to the effect that immigrant impacts on wages and income distribution are small. When the positive economic benefits of high-skilled immigration are lumped together with the more negative consequences of low-skilled immigration, they appear to cancel each other out because there are both gains and losses. In the real world, however, the penalty paid by low-skilled natives because of high levels of low-skilled immigration is not so easily cancelled out by the positive impacts of high-skilled immigration.

Does Country of Origin Matter?

To this point I have not said anything about country of origin. That is because country of origin per se is not really relevant for an analysis of economic impacts. What is most relevant is the skills that immigrants bring with them.

Immigration Law and Low-Skilled Immigrants

I have also not said anything yet about legal status. For various reasons, most individuals working in the United States in violation of immigration law are low-skilled workers. But most low-skilled workers are not "undocumented" aliens. Most low-skilled workers were born in the United States and hence are citizens by birth.

Current U.S. immigration law, however, encourages the legal immigration of low-skilled workers. This encouragement comes through the kinship preferences for various relatives built into our legal immigration system and to the smaller diversity visa program. Our immigration law permits a "snowball effect" where even immigrants granted a visa for the skills they bring to the U.S. labor market can sponsor low-skilled relatives who will then legally work in the U.S.

Of the 946,014 people who received Permanent Resident Alien visas in 2004, 65.6 percent entered under one of the several kinship categories, 8.8 percent entered as refugees or asylees, 5.3 percent entered under "diversity" visas, and 3.5 percent had a cancellation of deportation order. The 155,330 employment-based visas represented only 16.4 percent of the total. However, only about half of those who received an employment-based visa were themselves skill-tested (less than 73,000), while the remainder of these visas were received by their spouses and children. Thus, only about 7.6 percent of the nearly one million visa recipients were asked a question about their skills. . . .

The 1986 Immigration Reform and Control Act (IRCA) was sold to the American public as having two major features—amnesty which was to "wipe the slate clean" of undocumented workers, and employer sanctions which was to "keep the slate clean"—along with some increased border enforcement of the immigration law. Employer sanctions were intended to cut off the "jobs magnet" that attracted undocumented workers to the United States. Half of the political bargain was fulfilled. Under its two major amnesty provisions legal status was granted to nearly 3 million undocumented individuals, nearly all of whom were low-skilled workers, and millions more have subsequently been able to immigrate as their relatives. It is noteworthy that while in 1986 the word "amnesty" was used outright, in the current political debate the "A" word is anathema to the proponents of what is euphemistically called "earned legalization." This by itself is testimony to public perception of the failures of the 1986 Act.

Border and Interior Enforcement

Border enforcement, both at land borders and at airports, is a necessary element in the enforcement of immigration law. Border enforcement by itself has not, cannot, and will not work in controlling illegal entry of undocumented immigrants. If a potential immigrant is unsuccessful in penetrating the border on the first try, success may be had on the second or third try. This may be done by "entry without inspection" (i.e., sneaking across the border) or by using "fraudulent documents" at a border crossing point. Alternatively, a "visa abuser" enters into illegal status by violating a condition of a legally obtained visa—by working while on a tourist visa, for example, or by overstaying the time limit permitted on a temporary visa.

Thus, border enforcement must be complemented with "interior enforcement." The 1986 Act focused on "employer sanctions," penalties for employers who knowingly hire people who do not have the legal right to work in this country. There has, however, been no serious effort over the past two decades to enforce employer sanctions. Modern technology makes it easier to create fraudulent documents, but it also makes it easier to develop more stringent identity checks. There are two major failings in the current system. Employers are not given a "foolproof" mechanism to readily identify those with a legal right to work, and the Federal authorities show no interest in enforcing the law, except for an occasional "show raid."

It is not obvious that new enforcement legislation (e.g., to criminalize an illegal status) is called for. What is obvious is that illegal immigration cannot be controlled without a political will to enforce current immigration law. This includes providing employers with a simple and "foolproof" mechanism for identifying workers with a legal right to work in the U.S. along with more stringent enforcement of employer sanctions.

The Current Immigration System

The current legal immigration system is not serving the best economic interests of the United States. Only a small percentage of the immigrants who enter the U.S. legally in any year (less than 8 percent) are screened for their likely economic contribution to this economy. The vast majority enter under a nepotism system (the kinship preferences), with a smaller group entering under a lottery (diversity visas). To enhance the competitiveness of the U.S. economy in this increasingly globalized world, where efficient competitors are emerging across the world, the U.S. needs to change the basic question from "To whom are you related?" to "What can you contribute to the U.S. economy?"

Other highly-developed democratic countries—Canada, Australia, New Zealand—introduced "skills-based" immigration policies several decades ago. More recently, some countries in Western Europe have done the same. Some, like Canada and Australia, use a "points system" in which points are awarded based on characteristics that research has shown to enhance the earnings of immigrants such as age, schooling, technical training, and proficiency in the host country's language. Those with more than the threshold number of points receive a visa for themselves, their spouse and their minor accompanying children. This shift in emphasis in the rationing of visas would increase the skill level of immigrants and provide greater economic benefits to the U.S. economy than the current system.

A points system has many advantages over the current targeted employment-based visas. Under the current system a complex and very expensive bureaucratic process is required for employers to demonstrate to the U.S. Department of Labor not only that the visa applicant is qualified for a specific job but also that there is no qualified person with a legal right to work in the U.S. who will take the job at "prevailing wages." Even then, the worker who obtains a visa through this process is not obliged to remain on that job or with that employer.

Other proposals would use market mechanisms to "close the gap" between the large demand for visas and the much smaller supply that the U.S. is willing to make available. One possibility would involve auctioning visas; another involves charging a large market-clearing "visa fee." Among other advantages of these market mechanisms is that people in the U.S. can express their preferences for bringing relatives and friends by contributing to the price of their visa. Nor does there need to be only one mechanism—a skill-based system and a market-based system could both be used.

How Many Immigrants?

This returns us to a question posed early in this testimony: "What is the optimal size of the immigration flow?" The optimal immigration policy is neither a completely open door nor a completely closed one. There is no magic number or proportion of the population. Currently, legal immigration is running at approximately one million immigrants per year. This is on a par with the peak period of immigration from 1905 to 1914, when immigration also averaged one million per year. Yet, relative to the size of the U.S. population, current legal immigration is about one-fourth of the ratio in this earlier period. There is no clear evidence that the U.S. has exceeded—or even reached—its absorptive capacity for immigration. The U.S. economy and society exhibits a remarkable adaptability to immigrants, and thus far immigrants continue to show considerable adaptability to the U.S. economy and society. This adaptability means that the U.S. economy can absorb a continuous stream of immigrants without fracturing the system.

The demand for visas to enter the U.S. is very strong and, if anything, it seems to be increasing. This is a credit to the U.S. economy, society, and political system. The number of visas the U.S. political process is willing to supply is not immutable. The greater the economic benefits of immigration, the larger the optimal number of visas and the greater the willingness of the American public to provide them.

A comprehensive immigration policy reform would reduce undocumented migration by more stringent enforcement of existing law. It should also include the adoption of a skill-based points system and/or market mechanisms to ration visas, while limiting kinship migration to the immediate relatives of U.S. citizens (spouse, minor children, aged parents). These policies would increase the benefits of immigration for the American public, providing economic incentives to increase the supply of visas and hence the annual total number of immigrants entering the country legally.

POSTSCRIPT

Is Immigration an Economic Benefit to the Host Country?

Debate over what to do about immigration, especially illegal immigration, has become a staple of American politics. Some want stronger measures to keep illegal immigrants out and to deport those in the United States. Others favored a guest-worker program that permits undocumented immigrants currently in the country to remain for several years as temporary workers but that also requires them to leave the country. Yet others support allowing unauthorized immigrants already in the country to get a work permit and eventually to apply for citizenship. A 2007 poll found 30 percent of Americans favoring the first option, 28 percent supporting the second, and 37 percent preferring the third option, with 5 percent unsure. Opinions were similarly split in the halls of Congress, and as a result it has enacted some piecemeal legislation in recent years dealing with immigration, but has failed to enact a comprehensive plan.

The debate in the United States is very similar to that going on in many countries. Whatever public opinion may be, one certainty is people will abandon their homelands and seek new ones as long as widespread poverty and violence exist in many countries. Border barriers can impede, but not stop, the flow of those desperately seeking physical and economic security. Therefore, it might be wise to address the cause of immigration and also to avoid annual spending of huge amounts on immigration control to help Mexico, Central America, and other developing countries achieve greater prosperity so that the people in those countries would no longer be willing to experience the dislocation and danger that leaving home and slipping into the United States or some other developed country entails.

An overview of the history of U.S. immigration and policy is found in Aristide R. Zolberg, *A Nation by Design: Immigration Policy in the Fashioning of America* (Harvard University Press, 2008). A group that favors fewer immigrant is the Center for Immigration Studies at http://www.cis.org/. Taking a positive view of immigration and immigrants is the National Immigration Forum at http://www.immigrationforum.org/. To read opposing points of view, go to Mark Krikorian, *The New Case Against Immigration: Both Legal and Illegal* (Sentinel, 2008) and Jason L. Riley, *Let Them In: The Case for Open Borders* (Gotham, 2008). For the impact of immigration beyond the United States, read Craig A. Parsons and Timothy M. Smeeding (eds.), *Immigration and the Transformation of Europe* (Cambridge University Press, 2006).

Internet References . . .

Disarmament Diplomacy

This site, maintained by the Acronym Institute for Disarmament Diplomacy, provides up-to-date news and analysis of disarmament activity, with a particular focus on weapons of mass destruction.

http://www.acronym.org.uk

The Center for Security Policy

The Web site of this Washington, DC–centered "think tank" provides a wide range of links to sites dealing with national and international security issues.

http://www.centerforsecuritypolicy.org

National Defense University

This leading center for joint professional military education is under the direction of the Chairman of the U.S. Joint Chiefs of Staff. Its Web site is valuable for general military thinking and for material on terrorism.

http://www.ndu.edu/

Office of the Coordinator for Counterterrorism

This worthwhile site explores the range of terrorist threats and activities, albeit from the U.S. point of view, and is maintained by the U.S. State Department's Counterterrorism Office.

http://www.state.gov/s/ct/

Centre for the Study of Terrorism and Political Violence

The primary aims of the Centre for the Study of Terrorism and Political Violence are to investigate the roots of political violence; to develop a body of theory spanning the various and disparate elements of terrorism; and to recommend policy and organizational initiatives that governments and private sectors might adopt to better predict, detect, and respond to terrorism and terrorist threats.

http://www.st-ANDREWS.ac.uk/academic/intrel/research/cstpv/

Issues about Violence and Arms Control

*W*hatever we may wish, war, terrorism, and other forms of physical coercion are still important elements of international politics. Countries calculate both how to use the instruments of force and how to implement national security. There can be little doubt, however, that significant changes are under way in this realm as part of the changing world system. Strong pressures exist to expand the mission and strengthen the security capabilities of international organizations and to gauge the threat of terrorism. This section examines how countries in the international system are addressing these issues.

- Is Patient Diplomacy the Best Approach to Iran's Nuclear Program?
- Should U.S. Development of a Missile Defense System Continue?

ISSUE 14

Is Patient Diplomacy the Best Approach to Iran's Nuclear Program?

YES: Christopher Hemmer, from "Responding to a Nuclear Iran," *Parameters* (Autumn 2007)

NO: Norman Podhoretz, from "Stopping Iran: Why the Case for Military Action Still Stands," *Commentary* (February 2008)

ISSUE SUMMARY

YES: Christopher Hemmer, an associate professor in the Department of International Security Studies at the Air War College, Maxwell Air Force Base, Montgomery, Alabama, writes that while a nuclear-armed Iran will pose challenges for the United States, they can be met through an active policy of deterrence, containment, engagement, and the reassurance of America's allies in the region.

NO: Norman Podhoretz, editor-at-large of the opinion journal *Commentary*, argues that the consequences of Iran acquiring nuclear weapons will be disastrous and that there is far less risk using whatever measures are necessary, including military force, to prevent that than there is in dealing with a nuclear-armed Iran.

The global effort to control the spread of nuclear weapons centers around the Nuclear Non-Proliferation Treaty (NPT) of 1968. Under it, 85 percent of the world's countries that adhere to the NPT pledge not to transfer nuclear weapons or assist a nonnuclear state to make or otherwise acquire nuclear weapons. Nonnuclear countries also agree not to build or accept nuclear weapons and to allow the UN's International Atomic Energy Agency (IAEA) to monitor their nuclear facilities to ensure their exclusive use for peaceful purposes.

The NPT has not been a complete success. India and Pakistan both tested nuclear weapons in 1998. Israel's possession of nuclear weapons is an open secret. None of them agreed to the treaty. Currently, there are tensions over two countries that have agreed to the NPT. One of those countries is North Korea, which adhered to the NPT in 1970, then violated the treaty in the early

1990s by moving toward building nuclear weapons. Diplomacy failed to halt the development program, and North Korea tested a nuclear weapon in 2006.

Iran, like North Korea, agreed to the NPT in 1970. At that time, Iran was ruled by a pro-Western monarch, Shah Mohammad Reza Pahlavi, who was overthrown in 1979. After the Shah fled, the Ayatollah Ruhollah Khomeini returned from exile and founded a theocratic political system that condemned Western values and influence.

During the 1980s, Iran fought a horrendous eight-year war with Iraq, one in which Iraq used chemical weapons. Partly because of that war and the assumption that Iraq had nuclear weapons ambitions, Iran moved not only to generate enriched uranium and take other steps necessary to generate nuclear fuel for energy, but also to build nuclear weapons. This program also reflected a combination of Iran's desire to become a regional power and its fear of the United States. Among other concerns, President George W. Bush had said Iran was one of the "axis of evil" countries promoting terrorism and had ordered the U.S. invasion of two neighboring Muslim countries, Afghanistan in 2001 and Iraq in 2003. The United States by 2003 was urging international pressure to force Iran to give up its program. Three European Union countries—France, Germany, and Great Britain (the EU-3)—took the lead trying to persuade Iran to end its dual-use efforts. Iran negotiated, but also claimed that its intentions were peaceful and that it had the sovereign right to develop nuclear power. With no progress being made, the council of the International Atomic Energy Agency (IAEA) voted overwhelmingly in February 2006 to refer the matter to the UN Security Council. Since then, the EU-3 have become increasingly critical of Iran, and indications that the country intends to acquire nuclear weapons have grown, but there has been little progress toward persuading Iran to abandon that effort. Christopher Hemmer writes in the first article that moving militarily to disarm Iran would probably damage America's interests in the region so much that the likely costs would far outweigh the benefits. Norman Podhoretz disagrees in the second reading, saying that allowing Iran to acquire nuclear weapons will set the stage for the outbreak of a nuclear war that will become as inescapable then as it is avoidable now.

YES

Christopher Hemmer

Responding to a Nuclear Iran

What should American foreign policy be if current efforts to discourage Iran from developing nuclear weapons fail? Despite the recent resumption of high-level contacts between Iran and the International Atomic Energy Agency, and the potential for stronger action by the United Nations Security Council, an Iranian nuclear weapon remains a distinct possibility. The current debate regarding US policy toward Iran revolves around the relative merits of a preventive military strike, including the possibility of seeking regime change in Tehran, versus a policy that focuses on diplomacy and economic sanctions to dissuade Iran from pursuing a nuclear bomb. This debate, however, risks prematurely foreclosing discussions regarding a wide-range of foreign policy options should diplomacy and sanctions fail to persuade Tehran to limit its nuclear ambitions.

The choices America would face if Iran developed nuclear weapons are not simply between preventive military action and doing nothing. The calculations America would face are not between the costs of action versus the costs of inaction. A nuclear-armed Iran will certainly pose a number of challenges for the United States. Those challenges, however, can be met through an active policy of deterrence, containment, engagement, and the reassurance of America's allies in the region.

American Interests

The United States has three strategic interests in the Persian Gulf: maintaining the flow of oil onto world markets, preventing any hostile state from dominating the region, and minimizing any terrorist threat. Given these interests, the challenges posed by a nuclear-armed Iran need to be addressed by a policy that minimizes the threat to key oil production and transportation infrastructure and negates any Iranian bid for regional hegemony. Additionally, any action taken toward Iran has to be weighed against the potential impact it may have with regard to the global war on terrorism and ongoing US initiatives related to nation-building in Iraq and Afghanistan. Moreover, such a policy needs to be executed in a manner that avoids any nuclear threat to the United States or its allies.

The end-state the United States should be working toward, as a result of these strategic interests, is an Iran that is an integral part of the global economy, at peace with its neighbors, and not supportive of terrorist organizations.

From *Parameters* by Christopher Hemmer, Autumn 2007 (37:3), pp. 42–43. Published by the U.S. Army War College.

While America's strategic interests do not include the proliferation of democracy, any acceptable end-state will likely require some measure of democratic reform. Given the fact that anti-Americanism and anti-Zionism are an integral part of the Islamic Republic's identity, some measure of regime evolution will be required in an effort to advance America's long-term interests.

The Perils of a Preventive Strike

Any attempt to disarm Iran through the use of military options would in all likelihood damage America's interests in the region. While a military option might inflict significant damage on Iran's infrastructure by damaging or destroying its nuclear weapons program, disrupting its regional ambitions, and possibly serving as a deterrent to future proliferators, the likely costs would far outweigh the benefits.

First, any military action against Iran would send seismic shocks through global energy markets at a time when the price of oil is already at record highs. Since Iran relies heavily on the income derived from oil exports, it is unlikely that it would withhold petroleum from global markets. Iran may, however, threaten to disrupt the flow of traffic through the Strait of Hormuz or sponsor attacks on key oil infrastructure on the territory of America's Gulf allies. Such actions could hurt the US economy and potentially bolster Iranian revenue by raising the price of oil. While it is true that the world market would eventually adjust to such actions, as James Fallows has noted, that is a bit like saying eventually the US stock market adjusted to the Great Depression.

Any direct military action against Iran could also have a significant impact on America's war on terrorism. Such action would only serve to confirm many of Osama bin Laden's statements that the United States is at war with the world of Islam. This charge would be difficult to counter, given the fact that the United States has looked the other way for years with regard to Israel's nuclear program, accepted India as a legitimate nuclear-state, and is negotiating with North Korea regarding its nuclear ambitions.

Any military action against Iran would also undermine America's nation-building efforts in Iraq and Afghanistan, due to possible Iranian retaliation in both countries. While Iranian efforts toward stabilizing these two states have been sporadic at best, and purposively obstructive at worst, there is little reason to doubt that Iran could make achieving US objectives in Iraq and Afghanistan far more difficult. Although mostly bluster, there is some truth to former Iranian President Ali Rafsanjani's argument that as long as American troops maintain a formidable presence on Iran's borders, "it is the United States that is besieged by Iran." The same holds true regarding Iran's ties to Hezbollah and its presence in Lebanon. By targeting Iran's nuclear program the United States would unwisely encourage Iranian escalation in a number of these arenas.

Military strikes against Tehran would also undermine Washington's long-term goal of seeing reform movements succeed in Iran. If the history of military incursions and the Iranian nation teach us anything it is the fact that intervention is likely to solidify support for the current regime. The idea that the Iranian people would react to a military strike by advocating the overthrow of the existing regime is delusional. Instead the likely outcome of any direct military incursion would be the bolstering of the current regime.

Moreover, any preventive attack, no matter how effective, is only a temporary fix. First, such a campaign will eliminate only that portion of Iran's nuclear program known to intelligence agencies. Even after the extensive bombing campaign of the 1990–1991 Gulf War, subsequent inspections discovered large parts of Iraq's unconventional weapons programs that were previously unknown. More importantly, even if such an attack succeeded in eliminating significant facets of Iran's nuclear program, it would do little toward discouraging Iran from rebuilding those assets. Thus, even after a fully successful denial campaign, the United States, in a number of years, would likely face the prospect of having to do it all over again.

The Problem with Regime Change

Given the limits of any preventive strike, perhaps the United States should not restrict its goal in Iran to simply nuclear disarmament, but opt instead for the broader objective of regime change. If successful, regime change in Iran could provide for a number of benefits. It may eliminate the Iranian threat of interrupting the flow of oil from the region; it would also send a strong message to potential proliferators about the costs of similar actions; it might diminish Iran's support for terrorism; even possibly eliminate the threat of official Iranian meddling in Iraq and Afghanistan; and could potentially curtail Iran's nuclear ambitions.

The reason a policy advocating regime change is a bad idea, given its potential benefits, is the fact that such a policy is beyond America's means. While the United States certainly possesses the capability to eliminate the regime in Tehran, as the invasion of Iraq has shown, eliminating the present leadership is the easy part of regime change. The more difficult and costly challenge is installing a new government. With America's resources already overly committed in Afghanistan and Iraq, taking on a new nation-building mission in a country far larger and in some ways far more nationalistic than Iraq would be the epitome of strategic overreach.

Additionally, one of the few scenarios where Iran might use its nuclear capability would be if Tehran believed that the United States intended to exercise forcible regime change. A nuclear strike against any American presence in the region might be seen by the leadership in Tehran as its last hope for survival. It goes without saying that once any government has crossed the nuclear threshold, forcible regime change by an external actor is no longer a viable option. The threat of nuclear retaliation would simply be too great. Indeed, this is probably the most important reason why states such as Iran and North Korea desire nuclear weapons. Does this mean that the United States should therefore seek regime change before Iran develops its nuclear capability? No; even without nuclear weapons, forcible regime change in Iran and the ensuing occupation would entail too great a commitment of resources on the part of the United States. Pursuing regime change in Iran as a response to its nuclear program would be akin to treating a brain tumor with a guillotine.

The proposed cure is worse than the disease.

A Better Policy: Deter, Contain, and Engage

Fortunately, US policy options for dealing with a nuclear Iran are not limited to preventive military strikes, regime change, or doing nothing. A more promising option would have four key components. First, deter Iran from ever using its nuclear weapons. Second, prevent Iran from using its nuclear status to increase its influence in the region. Third, engage Iran in a meaningful way that encourages the creation of a government friendly to the United States and its regional allies, one that does not sponsor terrorism. Finally, such a policy should reassure US allies in the region that America's commitment to their security is steadfast. This four-pronged strategy would do a better job of protecting American interests in the region than any military strike or forcible regime change.

Deter

America's overriding concern regarding Iran's nuclear weapons program is that these weapons are never used against the United States or its allies. Fortunately, the strategy of nuclear deterrence can go a long way in resolving this problem. The threat of annihilation as the result of an American retaliatory strike can be a powerful deterrent. As the United States and the Soviet Union discovered during the Cold War and as India and Pakistan have recently learned, the threat of nuclear retaliation makes the use of such weapons problematic.

The central question in any debate over America's policies toward a nuclear Iran is whether or not the regime in Tehran is deterrable. If in fact it is, then deterrence is a less costly and risky strategy than prevention. Proponents of the preventive use of military force argue, as did the alarmists in the late 1940s with regard to the Soviet Union and in the early 1960s about China, that Iran is a revolutionary state seeking to export its destabilizing ideology. For these analysts Iran is often depicted as a regime of religious zealots that cannot be deterred because they are willing to accept an apocalyptic end to any conflict.

While Iran's track record with regard to its foreign policy does indicate a regime that is hostile to America, nothing would indicate that Iran is beyond the realm of nuclear deterrence. The bulk of the revolutionary fervor demonstrated by the Islamic Republic during its infancy died during the long war with Iraq. Moreover, the power of nuclear deterrence lies in the fact that precise calculations and cost and benefit analyses are not needed given the overwhelming costs associated with any nuclear exchange. Iranian leaders are rational enough to understand that any use of nuclear weapons against the United States or its allies would result in an overwhelming and unacceptable response.

What about President Mahmoud Ahmadinejad talking of wiping Israel off the map or the former President Rafsanjani declaring that while Israel could not survive a nuclear war, the Islamic world could survive a nuclear exchange? Fears related to such rhetoric need to be viewed in a historical context. Similar arguments were made about the Soviets and Chinese as they developed their nuclear arsenals. The fear of many Cold War hawks was that the Kremlin was run by ideologues. Wasn't it a fact that they did not shirk while watching 25 million of their own killed in World War II; nor did they flinch while millions more were murdered in internal purges? This demonstrated, many argued, that the Soviet leadership would be impervious to the logic of mutually assured destruction. Indeed, at times Mao Tse-Tung offered strikingly similar rhetoric to that coming out of Tehran today. He also boasted about how China could afford to lose millions in a nuclear exchange and still emerge victorious. Such worries turned out to be baseless with regard to the Soviets and the Chinese, and such rhetoric proved to be just that, rhetoric. While the bizarre views and hostile statements coming from Iran's current President are cause for concern, one must also be cognizant of the fact that the President of Iran is not the commander-in-chief of the armed forces and, in reality, has little influence over the nuclear program. The Supreme Leader does, however, and Ayatollah Ali Khameni has distanced himself from the most bellicose of Ahmadinejad's rhetoric.

To counter these ominous tirades one could look to more reassuring statements, such as Supreme Leader Khameni's argument that nuclear weapons are un-Islamic. More enlightening, however, than comparing dueling quotes, is an examination of what Iran has done in terms of its foreign policy. Iran has shown itself to be pragmatic in its actions to protect national interests, foregoing the activities one associates with a religiously driven revolutionary state.

Following the collapse of the Soviet Union, contrary to expectations, Iran did not seek to export its revolution to parts of the former Soviet Union, understanding that their national interest lay in forging a solid and profitable relationship with Russia. Iran even went so far as to dismiss the war in Chechnya as an internal Russian matter. Similar calculations of national interests led Iran to support Christian Armenia over Muslim Azerbaijan. Following the 1991 Gulf War, Iran did not push for a Shia revolution in Iraq, fearing that the outcome would probably be too dangerous and destabilizing. Following its isolation during the Iran–Iraq War Iran worked vigorously to improve relations with its Gulf neighbors.

But does Tehran's antipathy toward the United States and Israel outweigh its long-term national interests? No; indeed, during the Iran–Iraq War Tehran was willing to engage in arms shipments with the United States and Israel in an effort to further its war against Iraq. Given the difficulties the Iranians had with the Taliban, Tehran has also been fairly supportive of the American intervention in Afghanistan, to include offering the United States the use of its airfields and ports. While Tehran was less supportive of America's subsequent intervention in Iraq, the leadership was astute enough to recognize the benefits associated with the destruction of Saddam Hussein's regime. The point of these examples is not to discount any policy differences that Washington has with Tehran, but to stress that Iran is not run by ideologues, rather by a group of pragmatists devoted to protecting Iranian interests. Leaders who are rational enough to understand that the use of nuclear weapons against America would not be in their national interests.

There has also been a good deal of international media reports related to the fear that Iran might provide nuclear weapons to terrorist organizations. Ironically, the very use by Iran of surrogate terrorist organizations, rather than more overt attacks, is evidence that Tehran is sensitive to the calculations associated with the strategy of deterrence. It is also an affirmation that the Iranian leadership is attempting to minimize the risks to its foreign policy objectives. Such acts argue strongly against any possibility that Iran might provide terrorist organizations with nuclear weapons. Any move of this nature carries with it a great amount of risk; Iranians would lose control over the employment of the weapons while still having to worry that they might be blamed and targeted for response.

Contain

The second pillar of US strategy toward a nuclear Iran should be a policy of containment, to be certain that Iran does not succeed in exercising its nuclear capability as a tool of coercive diplomacy against US or allied interests in the region. Given Iran's perception of itself as the historically preeminent power in the region, Tehran can be expected to continue its policy attempting to increase its regional influence at the expense of the United States.

How would the possession of a deliverable nuclear weapon impact Tehran's foreign policy agenda? One possibility is that a nuclear Iran might be more, rather than less, restrained in its regional agenda. If any of Iran's actions are driven by a sense of insecurity with regard to America's intentions (or the threat created by a nuclear Pakistan or Israel, even the possibility of a resurgent Iraq), the security that Tehran would gain from having its own nuclear deterrent could make the nation's leadership less worried about the regional balance of power. Moreover, possession of a nuclear weapon would certainly increase the attention other world-powers paid Iran. The leadership in Tehran would have to continually worry that if any crisis developed involving another nuclear power the potential foe might opt for a preemptive attack on Iranian nuclear facilities. The fear that even a limited conflict might escalate into a nuclear exchange could make Tehran more cautious across the entire spectrum of conflict.

While such pressures may play a limited role in Iran's decision-making, it would be unwise for the United States to put too much faith in such possibilities. First, Iran's regional behavior is only partially driven by security fears. Even if Iran believed there was no threat from the United States, its status as a potential regional hegemon gives it incentive to increase its role in regional affairs. Second, while a limited amount of learning related to nuclear crisis management did take place during the Cold War, it took the United States and the Soviets a number of crises to fully appreciate these lessons. Although the existence of this Cold War record might enable Iran to learn such lessons more quickly, the limits of vicarious learning offer ample reasons to doubt that Iran will internalize these dictums without experiencing similar crises.

The result is that Iran can probably be expected to continue furthering its regional agenda in an attempt to increase its stature and diminish that of the United States. At least initially, any increased nuclear capability will likely embolden rather than induce caution on the part of Iran's leadership. Having gone to great lengths and paid significant costs to develop its nuclear capabilities, Iran is likely to continue testing the regional and international waters. Such efforts are bound to create challenges for the United States and its allies. The good news is that nuclear weapons have proven to be poor tools for coercive diplomacy, especially against states that already possess nuclear weapons or who may be allied with a nuclear power. Nuclear weapons have proven to be extraordinarily effective at two tasks: deterring the use of such weapons against other nuclear powers or their allies, and deterring states from directly challenging the vital interests of a nuclear power. Beyond these two critical tasks, however, nuclear weapons have not proven particularly useful as diplomatic tools of intimidation. For the United States and its allies, a policy of containment against Iranian attempts to expand its influence in the region is the correct foreign policy strategy. Certainly, such a strategy far outweighs any policy based on preventive war.

Engage

To advance America's long-range goal of an Iran that is part of the global economy, at peace with its neighbors, and not supporting terrorism, Washington would be better served by engaging Iran rather than attempting to isolate it. A policy of engagement could take two forms: the establishment of direct diplomatic relations and the encouragement of Iran's involvement in the global economy.

The United States broke diplomatic ties with Iran in April 1980, during the hostage crisis. The establishment of direct diplomatic ties between the United States and Iran, however, should not be seen as any form of a reward to Iran or as approval of Iranian policies. Nor should the reestablishment of formal relations be seen as the final stage in some sort of grand bargain. Instead, diplomatic relations should be viewed as part of the normal business of conducting America's foreign policy. There is little reason to doubt that Iran would portray any US initiative to reestablish diplomatic relations as a victory, as Tehran did with the recent moves by the Bush Administration to engage in direct talks related to the situation in Iraq. America should not let fear of such a reaction stand in the way of any initiative that would advance America's long-term security interests.

Over the years the United States has found that it needs diplomatic relations with hostile states as well as with allies. Such relationships were maintained throughout the Cold War with the Soviet Union, despite numerous crises and conflicts. In the case of Iran the absence of direct governmental links makes it more difficult to deter and contain Iran. Obviously, Iran would have to concur in the reestablishment of any form of diplomatic relations.

Given the number of domestic challenges the Islamic Republic is facing, most notably a tremendous growth in its youthful population, combined with the incompetence and corruption that has marked its stewardship of the Iranian economy, it is hard to imagine that this regime can continue to avoid collapse without significant reform. At the same time, there is little reason to expect that a democratic revolution is imminent. The reform movements that seemed so promising in the late 1990s have largely been defeated. The best strategy for revitalizing these movements is to encourage Tehran's involvement in the world economy, as opposed to further attempts at isolation. Increasing the Iranian people's exposure to the world economy is much more likely to increase motivation and expand the resources available to any future reform movement. Iran's eventual inclusion in the World Trade Organization is one of the carrots currently being held out to Iran as part of ongoing negotiations regarding its nuclear program. Such incentives may advance America's long-term foreign policy goals in the region even if those efforts fail to negate Iran's development of a nuclear weapon.

Potential economic sanctions against Iran related to its nuclear program need to be carefully addressed. Iran's stagnant economy, as well as its reliance on the international energy market, make it acutely vulnerable to economic sanctions. While the threat of sanctions may be useful in dissuading the development of nuclear weapons, it is less clear that the actual imposition of sanctions would advance US foreign policy interests. While economic sanctions might extract a high toll on the Iranian economy, the reality is that he political effect that accompanies such sanctions often strengthens, rather than undermines, a regime. Sanctions tend to increase a government's control over the country's economic activity, thereby starving potential opponents of resources. Sanctions can also create a "rally round the flag" effect that permits a regime to blame international hostility for the state's internal weaknesses.

In the case of a nuclear Iran, sanctions are only likely to be useful under a fairly stringent set of circumstances. To significantly impact Iran's economy, any sanctions regime would have to be multilateral and include at a minimum the United States, European Union, Russia, and China. Sanctions would also have to be properly targeted against the leadership of the current regime and not structured in such a manner as to inflict indiscriminate damage to Iran's economy. Finally, penalties inflicted by the sanctions need be directly attributable to the regime's development of nuclear weapons.

Creating sanctions that meet these requirements would not be easy. The importance of Iran as a market for Russia and an energy supplier to China makes any sanctions regime a tough sell in Moscow and Beijing. The complicated and often opaque nature of Iranian domestic politics also presents a challenge to the development of "smart sanctions." Finally, given the distrust that exists in Iran regarding the history of external interventions, it is doubtful that any sanctions regime would be interpreted as anything except another attempt to interfere in internal politics. In all likelihood, the United States would be better off by not making sanctions the focal point for its policies regarding a nuclear Iran. Engagement has often proven to be a surer path to regime evolution than economic isolation.

Reassure Iran's Neighbors

The final portion of a US strategy toward a nuclear-armed Iran should focus on convincing Iran's neighbors that the American commitment to their security remains strong. If the United States wants regional powers to resist Iranian attempts at expanding its influence, then Washington needs to bolster security ties in the region. Improving security cooperation with Iran's neighbors could advance a number of American interests beyond simple containment. Such efforts could also help increase the security of the oil infrastructure in the region, as well as expand intelligence cooperation related to international terrorism.

A more definite US security commitment to Iran's neighbors may also decrease the chance that the development of a nuclear weapon would increase the threat of nuclear proliferation in the region. Egypt, Turkey, and Saudi Arabia have been cited as states likely to respond to any Iranian nuclear capability with increased nuclear programs. Egypt, however, has been able to tolerate a nuclear Israel for more than 30 years, as well as accommodate Libya's weapons programs. Given that historical precedent, it is unlikely that an Iranian bomb would dramatically change Cairo's calculations. Similarly, Turkey's membership in the North Atlantic Treaty Organization and its desire to join the European Union are likely to dissuade Ankara from attempting to join the nuclear fraternity. Saudi Arabia and the other members of the Gulf Cooperation Council, however, would more than likely attempt to strengthen security ties with the United States in an effort to bolster their position against a nuclear Iran.

Part of America's strategy regarding regional allies needs to focus on assuring individual states that as long as Iran is contained, the United States will not take any preventive military action. While the Gulf States certainly would prefer that Iran not develop nuclear weapons, it is also important to recognize that they fear any US-Iranian conflict more than they fear the prospect of a nuclear Iran. America's most promising strategy toward a nuclear-armed Iran should be the development of a security architecture based on deterrence and containment.

Conclusion

The United States should be under no illusions regarding the problems that a nuclear-armed Iran would present. The challenges that development would pose for American interests in the region would be monumental and lasting. The strategy of deterrence, containment, engagement, and reassurance provides the framework for achieving America's long-term regional objectives. Such a strategy would minimize disruptions to the international flow of oil, blunt Iran's attempts at regional hegemony, stabilize US efforts in Afghanistan and Iraq, and aid in countering the global war on terrorism. Ultimately, it will provide the time that reformers in Iran need to recast the Iranian government from within. It is this reformation of Iran's government that will offer the best guarantee for preserving America's interests in the region.

When U.S. diplomat George Kennan proposed the doctrine of containment against the Soviet Union at the outset of the Cold War, he argued that Soviet diplomacy was:

> At once easier and more difficult to deal with than the diplomacy of aggressive leaders like Napoleon and Hitler. On the one hand it is more sensitive to contrary force, more ready to yield on individual sectors of the diplomatic front when that force was felt to be too strong, and thus more rational in the logic and rhetoric of power. On the other hand it cannot be easily defeated or discouraged by a single victory on the part of its opponents.... [I]t can be effectively countered not by sporadic acts which represent the momentary whims of democratic opinion, but only by intelligent long-range policies.

Admittedly, the Iran of today is quite different than the Soviet Union of the 1940s. It represents what is at best a regional rather than a global challenge, and its distinctive Persian and Shia ideologies are likely to have limited appeal abroad. These differences aside, Kennan's insight still applies. Iranian nuclear ambitions can best be deterred by means of an intelligent long-range foreign policy, not the threat of military intervention.

 **NO**

Stopping Iran: Why the Case for Military Action Still Stands

Up until a fairly short time ago, scarcely anyone dissented from the assessment offered with "high confidence" by the National Intelligence Estimate [NIE] of 2005 that Iran was "determined to develop nuclear weapons." Correlatively, no one believed the protestations of the mullahs ruling Iran that their nuclear program was designed strictly for peaceful uses.

The reason for this near-universal consensus was that Iran, with its vast reserves of oil and natural gas, had no need for nuclear energy, and that in any case, the very nature of its program contradicted the protestations.

Here is how *Time* magazine put it as early as March 2003—long before, be it noted, the radical Mahmoud Ahmadinejad had replaced the putatively moderate Mohamed Khatami as president:

> On a visit last month to Tehran, International Atomic Energy Agency [IAEA] director Mohamed ElBaradei announced he had discovered that Iran was constructing a facility to enrich uranium—a key component of advanced nuclear weapons—near Natanz. But diplomatic sources tell *Time* the plant is much further along than previously revealed. The sources say work on the plant is "extremely advanced" and involves "hundreds" of gas centrifuges ready to produce enriched uranium and "the parts for a thousand others ready to be assembled."

So, too, the Federation of American Scientists about a year later:

> It is generally believed that Iran's efforts are focused on uranium enrichment, though there are some indications of work on a parallel plutonium effort. Iran claims it is trying to establish a complete nuclear-fuel cycle to support a civilian energy program, but this same fuel cycle would be applicable to a nuclear-weapons development program. Iran appears to have spread their nuclear activities around a number of sites to reduce the risk of detection or attack.

And just as everyone agreed with the American intelligence community that Iran was "determined to develop nuclear weapons," everyone also agreed with President George W. Bush that it must not be permitted to succeed. Here, the reasons were many and various.

To begin with, Iran was (as certified even by the doves of the State Department) the leading sponsor of terrorism in the world, and it was therefore reasonable to fear that it would transfer nuclear technology to terrorists who would be only too happy to use it against us. Moreover, since Iran evidently aspired to become the hegemon of the Middle East, its drive for a nuclear capability could result (as, according to the *New York Times,* no fewer than 21 governments in and around the region were warning) in "a grave and destructive nuclear-arms race." This meant a nightmarish increase in the chances of a nuclear war. An even greater increase in those chances would result from the power that nuclear weapons—and the missiles capable of delivering them, which Iran was also developing and/or buying—would give the mullahs to realize their evil dream of (in the words of Ahmadinejad) "wiping Israel off the map."

Nor, as almost everyone also agreed, were the dangers of a nuclear Iran confined to the Middle East. Dedicated as the mullahs clearly were to furthering the transformation of Europe into a continent where Muslim law and practice would more and more prevail, they were bound to use nuclear intimidation and blackmail in pursuit of this goal as well. Beyond that, nuclear weapons would even serve the purposes of a far more ambitious aim: the creation of what Ahmadinejad called "a world without America." Although, to be sure, no one imagined that Iran would acquire the capability to destroy the United States, it was easy to imagine that the United States would be deterred from standing in Iran's way by the fear of triggering a nuclear war.

Running alongside the near-universal consensus on Iran's nuclear intentions was a commensurately broad agreement that the regime could be stopped from realizing those intentions by a judicious combination of carrots and sticks. The carrots, offered through diplomacy, consisted of promises that if Iran were (in the words of the Security Council) to "suspend all enrichment-related and reprocessing activities, including research and development, to be verified by the IAEA," it would find itself on the receiving end of many benefits. If, however, Iran remained obdurate in refusing to comply with these demands, sticks would come into play in the form of sanctions.

And indeed, in response to continued Iranian defiance, a round of sanctions was approved by the Security Council in December 2006. When these (watered down to buy the support of the Russians and the Chinese) predictably failed to bite, a tougher round was unanimously authorized three months later, in March 2007. When these in turn failed, the United States, realizing that the Russians and the Chinese would veto stronger medicine, unilaterally imposed a new series of economic sanctions—which fared no better than the multilateral measures that had preceded them.

What then to do? President Bush kept declaring that Iran must not be permitted to get the bomb, and he kept warning that the "military option"—by which he meant air strikes, not an invasion on the ground— was still on the table as a last resort. On this issue our Western European allies were divided. To the surprise of many who had ceased thinking of France as an ally because of [President] Jacques Chirac's relentless opposition to the policies of the Bush administration, Nicholas Sarkozy, Chirac's successor as president, echoed Bush's warning in equally unequivocal terms. If, Sarkozy announced, the Iranians pressed on with their nuclear program, the world would be left with a choice between "an Iranian bomb and bombing

Iran"—and he left no doubt as to where his own choice would fall. On the other hand, Gordon Brown, who had followed Tony Blair as prime minister of the UK, seemed less willing than Sarkozy to contemplate military action against Iran's nuclear installations, even as a last resort. Like the new chancellor of Germany, Angela Merkel, Brown remained—or professed to remain—persuaded that more diplomacy and tougher sanctions would eventually work.

This left a great question hanging in the air: when, if ever, would Bush (and/or Sarkozy) conclude that the time had come to resort to the last resort?

Obviously the answer to that question depended on how long it would take for Iran itself to reach the point of no return. According to the NIE of 2005, it was "unlikely . . . that Iran would be able to make a nuclear weapon . . . before early-to-mid next decade"—that is, between 2010 and 2015. If that assessment, offered with "moderate confidence," was correct, Bush would be off the hook, since he would be out of office for two years at the very least by the time the decision on whether or not to order air strikes would have to be made. That being the case, for the remainder of his term he could continue along the carrot-and-stick path, while striving to ratchet up the pressure on Iran with stronger and stronger measures that he could hope against hope might finally do the trick. If he could get these through the Security Council, so much the better; if not, the United States could try to assemble a coalition outside the UN that would be willing to impose really tough sanctions.

Under these circumstances, there would also be enough time to add another arrow to this nonmilitary quiver: a serious program of covert aid to dissident Iranians who dreamed of overthrowing the mullocracy [rule by mullahs, Muslim clerics] and replacing it with a democratic regime. Those who had been urging Bush to launch such a program, and who were confident that it would succeed, pointed to polls showing great dissatisfaction with the mullocracy among the Iranian young, and to the demonstrations against it that kept breaking out all over the country. They also contended that even if a new democratic regime were to be as intent as the old one on developing nuclear weapons, neither it nor they would pose anything like the same kind of threat.

All well and good. The trouble was this: only by relying on the accuracy of the 2005 NIE would Bush be able in all good conscience to pass on to his successor the decision of whether or when to bomb the Iranian nuclear facilities. But that estimate, as he could hardly help knowing from the CIA's not exactly brilliant track record, might easily be too optimistic.

To start with the most spectacular recent instance, the CIA had failed to anticipate 9/11. It then turned out to be wrong in 2002 about Saddam Hussein's possession of weapons of mass destruction, very likely because it was bending over backward to compensate for having been wrong in exactly the opposite direction in 1991, when at the end of the first Gulf war the IAEA discovered that the Iraqi nuclear program was far more advanced than the CIA had estimated. Regarding that by now notorious lapse, Jeffrey T. Richelson, a leading (and devoutly nonpartisan) authority on the American intelligence community, writes in *Spying on the Bomb*:

> The extent that the United States and its allies underestimated and misunderstood the Iraqi program [before 1991] constituted a "colossal international intelligence failure," according to one Israeli expert. [IAEA's chief weapons inspector] Hans Blix acknowledged "that there was suspicion certainly," but "to see the enormity of it is a shock."

And these were only the most recent cases. Gabriel Schoenfeld, a close student of the intelligence community, offers a partial list of earlier mistakes and failures:

> The CIA was established in 1947 in large measure to avoid another surprise attack like the one the U.S. had suffered on December 7, 1941 at Pearl Harbor. But only three years after its founding, the fledgling agency missed the outbreak of the Korean war. It then failed to understand that the Chinese would come to the aid of the North Koreans if American forces crossed the Yalu river. It missed the outbreak of the Suez war in 1956. In September 1962, the CIA issued an NIE which stated that the "Soviets would not introduce offensive missiles in Cuba"; in short order, the USSR did precisely that. In 1968 it failed to foresee the Warsaw Pact invasion of Czechoslovakia. . . . It did not inform Jimmy Carter that the Soviet Union would invade Afghanistan in 1979.

Richelson adds a few more examples of hotly debated issues during the cold war that were wrongly resolved, including "the existence of a missile gap, the capabilities of the Soviet SS-9 intercontinental ballistic missile, [and] Soviet compliance with the test-ban and antiballistic missile treaties." This is not to mention perhaps the most notorious case of all: the fiasco, known as the Bay of Pigs, produced by the CIA's wildly misplaced confidence that an invasion of Cuba by the army of exiles it had assembled and trained would set off a popular uprising against the Castro regime.

On Bush's part, then, deep skepticism was warranted concerning the CIA's estimate of how much time we had before Iran reached the point of no return. As we have seen, Mohamed ElBaradei, the head of the IAEA, had "discovered" in 2003 that the Iranians were constructing facilities to enrich uranium. Still, as late as April 2007 the same ElBaradei was pooh-poohing the claims made by Ahmadinejad that Iran already had 3,000 centrifuges in operation. A month later, we learn from Richelson, ElBaradei changed his mind after a few spot inspections. "We believe," ElBaradei now said, that the Iranians "pretty much have the knowledge about how to enrich. From now on, it is simply a question of perfecting that knowledge."

We also learn from Richelson that another expert, Matthew Bunn of Harvard's Center for Science and International Affairs, interpreted the new information the IAEA came up with in April 2007 as meaning that "whether they're six months or a year away, one can debate. But it's not ten years." This chilling estimate of how little time we had to prevent Iran from getting the bomb was similar to the conclusion reached by several Israeli experts (though the official Israeli estimate put the point of no return in 2009).

Then in a trice, everything changed. Even as Bush must surely have been wrestling with the question of whether it would be on his watch that the decision on bombing the Iranian nuclear facilities would have to be made, the world was hit with a different kind of bomb. This took the form of an unclassified summary of a new NIE, published early last December. Entitled "Iran: Nuclear Intentions and Capabilities," this new document was obviously designed to blow up the near-universal consensus that had flowed from the conclusions reached by the intelligence community in its 2005 NIE. In brief, whereas the NIE of 2005 had assessed "with high confidence that Iran currently is determined to develop nuclear weapons," the new NIE of 2007 did "not know whether [Iran] currently intends to develop nuclear weapons."

This startling 180-degree turn was arrived at from new intelligence, offered by the new NIE with "high confidence": namely, that "in fall 2003 Tehran halted its nuclear-weapons program." The new NIE was also confident—though only moderately so—that "Tehran had not restarted its nuclear-weapons program as of mid-2007." And in the most sweeping of its new conclusions, it was even "moderately confident" that "the halt to those activities represents a halt to Iran's entire nuclear-weapons program."

Whatever else one might say about the new NIE, one point can be made with "high confidence": that by leading with the sensational news that Iran had suspended its nuclear-weapons program in 2003, its authors ensured that their entire document would be interpreted as meaning that there was no longer anything to worry about. Of course, being experienced bureaucrats, they took care to protect themselves from this very accusation. For example, after dropping their own bomb on the fear that Iran was hell-bent on getting the bomb, they immediately added "with moderate-to-high confidence that Tehran at a minimum is keeping open the option to develop nuclear weapons." But as they must have expected, scarcely anyone paid attention to this caveat. And as they must also have expected, even less attention was paid to another self-protective caveat, which—making doubly sure it would pass unnoticed—they relegated to a footnote appended to the lead sentence about the halt:

> For the purposes of this Estimate, by "nuclear-weapons program" we mean Iran's nuclear-weapon design and weaponization work and covert uranium conversion-related and uranium enrichment-related work; we do not mean Iran's declared civil work related to uranium conversion and enrichment.

Since only an expert could grasp the significance of this cunning little masterpiece of incomprehensible jargon, the damage had been done by the time its dishonesty was exposed.

The first such exposure came from John Bolton, who before becoming our ambassador to the UN had served as Under Secretary of State for Arms Control and International Security, with a special responsibility for preventing the proliferation of weapons of mass destruction. Donning this hat once again, Bolton charged that the dishonesty of the footnote lay most egregiously in the sharp distinction it drew between military and civilian programs. For, he said, the enrichment of uranium, which all agree Iran is continuing, is critical to civilian *and* military uses [emphasis added]. Indeed, it has always been Iran's "civilian" program that posed the main risk of a nuclear "breakout."

Two other experts, Valerie Lincy, the editor of Iranwatch.org, writing in collaboration with Gary Milhollin, the director of the Wisconsin Project on Nuclear Arms Control, followed up with an explanation of why the halt of 2003 was much less significant than a layman would inevitably be led to think:

[T]he new report defines "nuclear-weapons program" in a ludicrously narrow way: it confines it to enriching uranium at secret sites or working on a nuclear-weapon design. But the halting of its secret enrichment and weapon-design efforts in 2003 proves only that Iran made a tactical move. It suspended work that, if discovered, would unambiguously reveal intent to build a weapon. It has continued other work, crucial to the ability to make a bomb, that it can pass off as having civilian applications.

Thus, as Lincy and Milhollin went on to write, the main point obfuscated by the footnote was that once Iran accumulated a stockpile of the kind of uranium fit for civilian use, it would "in a matter of months" be able "to convert that uranium . . . , to weapons grade."

Yet, in spite of these efforts to demonstrate that the new NIE did not prove that Iran had given up its pursuit of nuclear weapons, just about everyone in the world immediately concluded otherwise, and further concluded that this meant the military option was off the table. George Bush may or may not have been planning to order air strikes before leaving office, but now that the justification for doing so had been discredited by his own intelligence agencies, it would be politically impossible for him to go on threatening military action, let alone to take it.

But what about sanctions? In the weeks and months before the new NIE was made public, Bush had been working very hard to get a third and tougher round of sanctions approved by the Security Council. In trying to persuade the Russians and the Chinese to sign on, Bush argued that the failure to enact such sanctions would leave war as the only alternative. Yet if war was now out of the question, and if in any case Iran had for all practical purposes given up its pursuit of nuclear weapons for the foreseeable future, what need was there of sanctions?

Anticipating that this objection would be raised, the White House desperately set out to interpret the new NIE as, precisely, offering "grounds for hope that the problem can be solved diplomatically—without the use of force." These words by Stephen Hadley, Bush's National Security Adviser, represented the very first comment on the new NIE to emanate from the White House, and some version of them would be endlessly repeated in the days to come. Joining this campaign of damage control, Sarkozy and Brown issued similar statements, and even Merkel (who had been very reluctant to go along with Bush's push for another round of sanctions) now declared that it was:

dangerous and still grounds for great concern that Iran, in the face of the UN Security Council's resolutions, continues to refuse to suspend uranium enrichment. . . . The Iranian president's intolerable agitation against Israel also speaks volumes. . . . It remains a vital interest of the whole world community to prevent a nuclear-armed Iran.

As it happened, Hadley was right about the new NIE, which executed another 180-degree turn—this one, away from the judgment of the 2005 NIE concerning the ineffectiveness of international pressure. Flatly contradicting its "high confidence" in 2005 that Iran was forging ahead "despite its international obligations and international pressure," the new NIE concluded that the nuclear-weapons program had been halted in 2003 "primarily in response to international pressure." This indicated that "Tehran's decisions are guided by a cost-benefit approach rather than a rush to a weapon irrespective of the political, economic, and military costs."

Never mind that no international pressure to speak of was being exerted on Iran in 2003, and that at that point the mullahs were more likely acting out of fear that the Americans, having just invaded Iraq, might come after them next. Never mind, too, that religious and/or ideological passions, which the new NIE pointedly neglected to mention, have over and over again throughout history proved themselves a more powerful driving force than any "cost-benefit approach." Blithely sweeping aside such considerations, the new NIE was confident that just as the carrot-and-stick approach had allegedly sufficed in the past, so it would suffice in the future to "prompt Tehran to extend the current halt to its nuclear-weapons program."

The worldview implicit here has been described by Richelson (mainly with North Korea in mind) as the idea that "moral suasion and sustained bargaining are the proven mechanisms of nuclear restraint." Such a worldview "may be ill-equipped," he observes delicately:

> to accept the idea that certain regimes are incorrigible and negotiate only as a stalling tactic until they have attained a nuclear capability against the United States and other nations that might act against their nuclear programs.

True, the new NIE did at least acknowledge that it would not be easy to induce Iran to extend the halt, "given the linkage many within the leadership probably see between nuclear-weapons development and Iran's key national-security and foreign-policy objectives." But it still put its money on a:

> combination of threats of intensified international scrutiny and pressures, along with opportunities for Iran to achieve its security, prestige, and goals for regional influence in other ways.

It was this pronouncement, and a few others like it, that gave Stephen Hadley "grounds for hope that the problem can be solved diplomatically." But that it was a false hope was demonstrated by the NIE itself. For if Iran was pursuing nuclear weapons in order to achieve its "key national-security and foreign-policy objectives," and if those objectives explicitly included (for a start) hegemony in the Middle East and the destruction of the state of Israel, what possible "opportunities" could Tehran be offered to achieve them "in other ways"?

So much for the carrot. As for the stick, it was no longer big enough to matter, what with the threat of military action ruled out, and what with the case for a third round of sanctions undermined by the impression stemming from the NIE's main finding that there was nothing left to worry about. Why worry when it was four years since Iran had done any work toward developing the bomb, when the moratorium remained in effect, and when there was no reason to believe that the program would be resumed in the near future?

What is more, in continuing to insist that the Iranians must be stopped from developing the bomb and that this could be done by nonmilitary means, the Bush administration and its European allies were lagging behind a new consensus within the American foreign-policy establishment that had already been forming even before the publication of the new NIE. Whereas the old consensus was based on the proposition that (in Senator John McCain's pungent formulation) "the only thing worse than bombing Iran was letting Iran get the bomb," the emerging new consensus held the opposite—that the only thing worse than letting Iran get the bomb was bombing Iran.

What led to this reversal was a gradual loss of faith in the carrot-and-stick approach. As one who had long since rejected this faith and who had been excoriated for my apostasy by more than one member of the foreign-policy elites, I never thought I would live to see the day when these very elites would come to admit that diplomacy and sanctions had been given a fair chance and that they had accomplished nothing but to buy Iran more time. The lesson drawn from this new revelation was, however, a different matter.

It was in the course of a public debate with one of the younger members of the foreign-policy establishment that I first chanced upon the change in view. Knowing that he never deviated by so much as an inch from the conventional wisdom of the moment within places like the Council on Foreign Relations and the Brookings Institution, I had expected him to defend the carrot-and-stick approach and to attack me as a warmonger for contending that bombing was the only way to stop the mullahs from getting the bomb. Instead, to my great surprise, he took the position that there was really no need to stop them in the first place, since even if they had the bomb they could be deterred from using it, just as effectively as the Soviets and the Chinese had been deterred during the cold war.

Without saying so in so many words, then, my opponent was acknowledging that diplomacy and sanctions had proved to be a failure, and that there was no point in pursuing them any further. But so as to avoid drawing the logical conclusion—namely, that military action had now become necessary—he simply abandoned the old establishment assumption that Iran must at all costs be prevented from developing nuclear weapons, adopting in its place the complacent idea that we could learn to live with an Iranian bomb.

In response, I argued that deterrence could not be relied upon with a regime ruled by Islamofascist revolutionaries who not only were ready to die for their beliefs but cared less about protecting their people than about the spread of their ideology and their power. If the mullahs got the bomb, I said, it was not they who would be deterred, but we.

So little did any of this shake my opponent that I came away from our debate with the grim realization that the President's continued insistence on the dangers posed by an Iranian bomb would more and more fall on deaf ears—ears that would soon be made even deafer by the new NIE's assurance that Iran was no longer hell-bent on acquiring nuclear weapons after all. There might be two different ideas competing here—one, that we could live with an Iranian bomb; the other, that there would be no Iranian bomb to live with—but the widespread acceptance of either would not only preclude the military option but would sooner or later put an end even to the effort to stop the mullahs by nonmilitary means.

And yet there remained something else, or rather someone else, to factor into the equation: the perennially "misunderestimated" George W. Bush, a man who knew evil when he saw it and who had the courage and the determination to do battle against it. This was also a man who, far more than most politicians, said what he meant and meant what he said. And what he had said at least twice before was that if we permitted Iran to build a nuclear arsenal, people fifty years from now would look back and wonder how we of this generation could have allowed such a thing to happen, and they would rightly judge us as harshly as we today judge the British and the French for what they did at Munich in 1938. It was because I had found it hard to understand why Bush would put himself so squarely in the dock of history on this issue if he were resigned to an Iran in possession of nuclear weapons, or even of the ability to build them, that I predicted in these pages, and went on predicting elsewhere, that he would not retire from office before resorting to the military option.

But then came the new NIE. To me it seemed obvious that it represented another ambush by an intelligence community that had consistently tried to sabotage Bush's policies through a series of damaging leaks and was now trying to prevent him from ever taking military action against Iran. To others, however, it seemed equally obvious that Bush, far from being ambushed, had welcomed the new NIE precisely because it provided him with a perfect opportunity to begin distancing himself from the military option.

But I could not for the life of me believe that Bush intended to fly in the face of the solemn promise he had made in his 2002 State of the Union address:

> We'll be deliberate, yet time is not on our side. I will not wait on events, while dangers gather. I will not stand by, as peril draws closer and closer. The United States of America will not permit the world's most dangerous regimes to threaten us with the world's most destructive weapons.

To which he had added shortly afterward in a speech at West Point: "If we wait for threats to fully materialize, we will have waited too long."

How, I wondered, could Bush not know that in the case of Iran he was running a very great risk of waiting too long? And if he was truly ready to run that risk, why, in a press conference the day after the new NIE came out, did he put himself in the historical dock yet again by repeating what he had said several times before about the judgment that would be passed on this generation in the future if Iran were to acquire a nuclear weapon?

If Iran shows up with a nuclear weapon at some point in time, the world is going to say, what happened to them in 2007? How come they couldn't see the impending danger? What caused them not to understand that a country that once had a weapons program could reconstitute the weapons program? How come they couldn't see that the important first step in developing a weapon is the capacity to be able to enrich uranium? How come they didn't know that with that capacity, that knowledge could be passed on to a covert program? What blinded them to the realities of the world? And it's not going to happen on my watch.

"It's not going to happen on my watch." What else could this mean if not that Bush was preparing to meet "the impending danger" in what he must by now have concluded was the only way it could be averted?

The only alternative that seemed even remotely plausible to me was that he might be fixing to outsource the job to the Israelis. After all, even if, by now, it might have become politically impossible for us to take military action, the Israelis could not afford to sit by while a regime pledged to wipe them off the map was equipping itself with nuclear weapons and the missiles to deliver them. For unless Iran could be stopped before acquiring a nuclear capability, the Israelis would be faced with only two choices: either strike first, or pray that the fear of retaliation would deter the Iranians from beating them to the punch. Yet a former president of Iran, Hashemi Rafsanjani, had served notice that his country would not be deterred by the fear of retaliation:

> If a day comes when the world of Islam is duly equipped with the arms Israel has in its possession, . . . application of an atomic bomb would not leave anything in Israel, but the same thing would just produce damages in the Muslim world.

If this was the view of even a supposed moderate like Rafsanjani, how could the Israelis depend upon the mullahs to refrain from launching a first strike? The answer was that they could not. Bernard Lewis, the leading contemporary authority on the culture of the Islamic world, has explained why:

> MAD, mutual assured destruction, [was effective] right through the cold war. Both sides had nuclear weapons. Neither side used them, because both sides knew the other would retaliate in kind. This will not work with a religious fanatic [like Ahmadinejad]. For him, mutual assured destruction is not a deterrent, it is an inducement. We know already that [the mullahs ruling Iran] do not give a damn about killing their own people in great numbers. We have seen it again and again. In the final scenario, and this applies all the more strongly if they kill large numbers of their own people, they are doing them a favor. They are giving them a quick free pass to heaven and all its delights.

Under the aegis of such an attitude, even in the less extreme variant that may have been held by some of Ahmadinejad's colleagues among the regime's rulers, mutual assured destruction would turn into a very weak reed. Understanding that, the Israelis would be presented with an irresistible incentive to preempt—and so, too, would the Iranians. Either way, a nuclear exchange would become inevitable.

What would happen then? In a recently released study, Anthony Cordesman of the Center for Strategic and International Studies argues that Rafsanjani had it wrong. In the grisly scenario Cordesman draws, tens of millions would indeed die, but Israel—despite the decimation of its civilian population and the destruction of its major cities—would survive, even if just barely, as a functioning society. Not so Iran, and not its "key Arab neighbors," particularly Egypt and Syria, which Cordesman thinks Israel would also have to target in order "to ensure that no other power can capitalize on an Iranian strike." Furthermore, Israel might be driven in desperation to go after the oil wells, refineries, and ports in the Gulf.

"Being contained within the region," writes Martin Walker of UPI in his summary of Cordesman's study, "such a nuclear exchange might not be Armageddon for the human race." To me it seems doubtful that it could be confined to the Middle East. But even if it were, the resulting horrors would still be far greater than even the direst consequences that might follow from bombing Iran before it reaches the point of no return.

In the worst case of this latter scenario, Iran would retaliate by increasing the trouble it is already making for us in Iraq and by attacking Israel with missiles armed with non-nuclear warheads but possibly containing biological and/or chemical weapons. There would also be a vast increase in the price of oil, with catastrophic consequences for every economy in the world, very much including our own. And there would be a deafening outcry from one end of the earth to the other against the inescapable civilian casualties. Yet, bad as all this would be, it does not begin to compare with the gruesome consequences of a nuclear exchange between Israel and Iran, even if those consequences were to be far less extensive than Cordesman anticipates.

Which is to say that, as between bombing Iran to prevent it from getting the bomb and letting Iran get the bomb, there is simply no contest.

But this still does not answer the question of who should do the bombing. Tempting as it must be for George Bush to sit back and let the Israelis do the job, there are considerations that should give him pause. One is that no matter what he would say, the whole world would regard the Israelis as a surrogate for the United States, and we would become as much the target of the ensuing recriminations both at home and abroad as we would if we had done the job ourselves.

To make matters worse, the indications are that it would be very hard for the Israeli air force, superb though it is, to pull the mission off. Thus, an analysis by two members of the Security Studies Program at MIT concluded that while "the Israeli air force now possesses the capability to destroy even well-hardened targets in Iran with some degree of confidence," the problem is that for the mission to succeed, all of the many contingencies involved would have to go right. Hence an Israeli attempt could end with the worst of all possible outcomes: retaliatory measures by the Iranians even as their nuclear program remained unscathed. We, on the other hand, would have a much bigger margin of error and a much better chance of setting their program back by a minimum of five or ten years and at best wiping it out altogether.

The upshot is that if Iran is to be prevented from becoming a nuclear power, it is the United States that will have to do the preventing, to do it by means of a bombing campaign, and (because "If we wait for threats to fully materialize, we will have waited too long") to do it soon.

When I first predicted a year or so ago that Bush would bomb Iran's nuclear facilities once he had played out the futile diplomatic string, the obstacles that stood in his way were great but they did not strike me as insurmountable. Now, thanks in large part to the new NIE, they have grown so formidable that I can only stick by my prediction with what the NIE itself would describe as "low-to-moderate confidence." For Bush is right about the resemblance between 2008 and 1938. In 1938, as Winston Churchill later said, Hitler could still have been stopped at a relatively low price and many millions of lives could have been saved if England and France had not deceived themselves about the realities of their situation. Mutatis mutandis, it is the same in 2008, when Iran can still be stopped from getting the bomb and even more millions of lives can be saved—but only provided that we summon up the courage to see what is staring us in the face and then act on what we see.

Unless we do, the forces that are blindly working to ensure that Iran will get the bomb are likely to prevail even against the clear-sighted determination of George W. Bush, just as the forces of appeasement did against Churchill in 1938. In which case, we had all better pray that there will be enough time for the next President to discharge the responsibility that Bush will have been forced to pass on, and that this successor will also have the clarity and the courage to discharge it. If not—God help us all—the stage will have been set for the outbreak of a nuclear war that will become as inescapable then as it is avoidable now.

POSTSCRIPT

Is Patient Diplomacy the Best Approach to Iran's Nuclear Program?

Since the hearings, there has been much ado about Iran's alleged nuclear program, but little has actually changed. Led by the diplomats from the European Union and urged on by the United States, the West has continued to put pressure on Iran to halt all activities that could lead to acquiring nuclear weapons. Iran, for its part, continues to deny a nuclear weapons program or ambitions and to play a cat-and-mouse game with the IAEA by allowing it to inspect some things, sometimes but also being uncooperative at other times in a pattern reminiscent of the on-again-off-again approach of Iraq under Saddam Hussein to IAEA inspectors. General Secretary Mohamed ElBaradei of the IAEA has voiced "serious concern" about Iran's lack of full disclosure in late 2008 and warned, "Unless Iran provides such transparency . . . the agency will not be able to provide credible assurances about the absence of undeclared nuclear material and activities in Iran." Attempts by the West to strengthen UN sanctions on Iran for its lack of full cooperation have been frustrated in the UN Security Council by the resistance of Russia and China, each of which has a veto. The acrimony between Washington and Moscow over Russia's intervention in Georgia in 2008 has made the Security Council even less likely to move firmly against Iran. In any case, Iran pledges not to be moved by any such sanctions. "Whatever they do, Iran will continue its activities. Sanctions are not important. The era of such threats has ended," Ahmadinejad told reporters in late 2008.

Given the virtual stalemate, there appears to be growing possibility that with at least tacit U.S. backing, Israel might launch an attack on Iran's nuclear sites. Israelis are understandably alarmed, given President Ahmadinejad's statement that Israel is a "disgraceful stain on the Islamic world" that should be "wiped away." Israel's concerns were heightened even further in late 2008 by charges that Iran is reconfiguring its Shahab-3 missile to enable it to carry a nuclear warhead. According to Iran, the missile has a range of 1,250 miles, putting Israel well within range. Indeed, in September 2008 former general and Israeli army chief Moshe Ya'alon called war with Iran "inevitable."

Statements by Barack Obama early in his quest for the presidency chastising the Bush administration for being unwilling to talk directly with Iran led some to think a Barack presidency might substantially shift Washington's attitude toward Iran. But as the campaign neared its conclusion, Obama joined John McCain in making veiled threats toward Iran. Speaking on *60 Minutes*, Obama declared that "a nuclear-armed Iran is not just a threat to us, it's a threat to Israel" and a "game-changer in the region" that is "unacceptable." As to what he would do as president, Obama pledged, "I won't take any options off the table, including military, to prevent [Iran] from obtaining a nuclear weapon." In a separate interview on the program, McCain said that if it's a provable direct threat" that Iran had weapons, then "it's obvious that we would have to prevent what we're absolutely certain is a direct threat to the lives of the American people."

To understand Iran better, read Ervand Abrahamian, *A History of Modern Iran* (Cambridge University Press, 2008). For a periodically update background article on this nuclear issue, go to the Council on Foreign Relations' "backgrounder," *Iran's Nuclear Program* at http://www.cfr.org/publication/16811/. The very latest news accounts and an opportunity to join the debate is at the site of Iran Nuclear Watch at http://www.irannuclearwatch.blogspot.com/. The debate over how to deal with Iran continues. For a "soft" approach, see Ray Takeyh, "Time for Détente With Iran," *Foreign Affairs* (March/April 2007). The "hard" option is represented by Norman Podhoretz, "The Case for Bombing Iran," *Commentary* (June 2007).

ISSUE 15

Should U.S. Development of a Missile Defense System Continue?

YES: Jeff Kueter, from Testimony during Hearings on "What Are the Prospects, What Are the Costs? Oversight of Missile Defense (Part 2)," before the Subcommittee on National Security and Foreign Affairs, Committee on Oversight and Government Reform, U.S. House of Representatives (April 16, 2008)

NO: Philip E. Coyle, III, from Testimony during Hearings on "What Are the Prospects, What Are the Costs? Oversight of Missile Defense (Part 2)," before the Subcommittee on National Security and Foreign Affairs, Committee on Oversight and Government Reform, U.S. House of Representatives (April 16, 2008)

ISSUE SUMMARY

YES: Jeff Kueter, President of the George C. Marshall Institute, a conservative think tank in Washington, DC, urges continued support for building a defense against missile attacks because doing so would provide options for addressing a growing threat in an uncertain world.

NO: Philip E. Coyle, III, senior advisor at the Center for Defense Information, a liberal think tank in Washington, DC, and former U.S. assistant secretary of defense, takes the view that trying to build a missile defense system will be very expensive, is unlikely to work, and will reignite a destabilizing nuclear arms race.

$\mathbf{A}$ long-standing controversy in the area of nuclear planning is whether or not to build a ballistic missile defense (BMD) system to attempt to shoot down attacking nuclear-armed missiles. There were some thoughts of mounting such an effort in the 1960s, but high costs and technical unfeasibility led the United States and the Soviet Union to sign the Anti-Ballistic Missile (ABM) Treaty in 1972, largely banning the testing and development of such a system. Ronald Reagan renewed the controversy when he proposed building a BMD system that he called the Strategic Defense Initiative (SDI) but its critics labeled "Star Wars." Yet another name for such an effort is a national missile defense system (NMDS). Whatever it is called, Reagan's vision of a comprehensive shield from missile attack was all but abandoned as too expensive and technically infeasible.

However, as the 1990s progressed, advances in technology and concern about nuclear threats from such "rogue states" as Iran (see Issue 14) and North Korea resurrected the issue of building a BMD system. President Clinton was ambivalent, not willing to kill the idea, but allocating so few funds to it that it progressed only slowly. Among other concerns was that testing a BMD system would violate the ABM Treaty.

Under President Bush, the effort accelerated greatly. Soon after entering office, he gave Moscow the required one-year notice that the United States would withdraw from the ABM Treaty in 2002. He also ordered the Pentagon to make a determined effort to build a BMD system. Annual funding during the Bush administration for the BMD effort has averaged about $9 billion, and the first NMD missile site has been built with some 20 ground-based interceptors at Fort Greely, Alaska, that are meant to physically hit and destroy an incoming warhead. How capable these and other elements of the growing U.S. system are is a matter of some controversy. As you will see in the debate that follows between Jeff Kueter and Philip Coyle, advocates of a BMD system argue that the system's effectiveness is improving substantially, while critics say that even with "rigged" tests, the system is iffy at best.

During your reading of the two articles by Kueter and Coyle, think about what each has to say on four key points. First, what are the odds of either a major nuclear power like Russia or a minor one like Iran launching a nuclear attack on the United States? What might trigger that given the massive nuclear arsenal and an almost certain devastating counterstrike? Second, what are the costs of building a BMD system? No one knows exactly, but "hundreds of billions of dollars" is almost certainly the case. Third, what are the chances that such a system will be effective in defending against a missile strike utilizing warheads traveling through space at 18,000 miles per hour and perhaps using tactics such as deploying numerous decoy warheads? Fourth, what would building a BMD system do to security against a nuclear attack? As you will see critics contend that building a BMD system would make the world more rather than less dangerous by reigniting the nuclear arms race and destabilizing deterrence as other nuclear powers deployed a massive number of delivery devices capable of overwhelming any defensive system.

YES

Jeff Kueter

What Are the Prospects, What Are the Costs? Oversight of Missile Defense

The Importance of Missile Defense

Missile defense provides the United States with options for addressing a growing threat in an uncertain world. During the Cold War, the ballistic missile was an instrument of strategic power, employed by both the U.S. and the Soviet Union as a means to check each other's global power. Through the recognition that use of these capabilities would result in wholesale destruction, a certain macabre stability emerged. Today's security environment is much different and so are the roles that growing ballistic missile arsenals play.

Today, states view the ballistic missile as a relatively cheap way to gain considerable leverage. Through its ability to reliably deliver significant firepower at precise locations, the ballistic missile is assuming strategic roles previously held by fighter and bomber aircraft. The ability to deliver ballistic missiles at long ranges is increasing among nations hostile to the United States. Perhaps because of the ballistic missile's ability to act as an instrument of terror, the pursuit of missiles with ranges in the thousands of kilometers strongly suggests that motives outside of regional concerns are driving the decisions to invest in missiles of longer and longer ranges.

The National Air & Space Intelligence Center concludes its 2006 assessment stating, "Ballistic missiles are already in widespread use and will continue to increase in number and variety. The availability of weapons of mass destruction for use on ballistic missiles vastly increases the significance of this threat."

North Korea already has an arsenal of more than 100 short- and medium-range missiles capable of striking points throughout American allies, South Korea and Japan. Yet, it continues to pursue the longer range Taepodong which is intended to have striking capabilities in the thousands of kilometers. Further, North Korea is working to develop solid fueled intermediate- and short-range missiles, which would provide them with a more accurate and mobile force.

Similarly, Iran is investing in longer-range missiles even though it already possesses a sizeable short- and medium-range arsenal. The extended-range version of the Shahab-3 would give Iran the ability to strike targets in southern

U.S. House of Representatives, April 16, 2008.

and eastern Europe. Like the North Koreans (with whom they share critical technologies, designs, and plans), the Iranians are seeking solid-propellant technology as well as new missile designs.

The emergence of long-range missiles in the arsenals of countries hostile to the United States, our friends, and allies, and the widespread availability of the knowledge and technical capacity to build such arsenals, are cause for concern. Writing in 2001, Michael O'Hanlon and James Lindsay of the Brookings Institution note the consequences:

> The death toll in a biological or nuclear attack from a single missile could easily exceed the total number of U.S. soldiers who died fighting in the Korean War and would probably be comparable to the casualties in Hiroshima and Nagasaki . . . a missile armed with a nuclear warhead that landed on downtown [Los Angeles] at mid-day could kill 250,000 people instantly and tens of thousands more in the days and weeks to follow. The prospect of wholesale slaughter is what gives long-range missiles their coercive power.

A missile defense reduces the coercive power, discourages the acquisition of missiles, deters aggressors from action by reducing the probability of success, and, most importantly, offers the possibility of saving the lives of thousands of people in the event a missile is launched.

Without a defense, the choices available to deter missile proliferators are unpalatable. For instance, Ashton Carter and former Secretary of Defense William Perry, writing in June 2006 as concerns about a North Korean ballistic missile test were at their peak, advocated a pre-emptive strike to prevent the launch of the test missile. They said:

> But intervening before mortal threats to U.S. security can develop is surely a prudent policy. Therefore, if North Korea persists in its launch preparations, the United States should immediately make clear its intention to strike and destroy the North Korean Taepodong missile before it can be launched.

Should the same policy be applied to Iran? What should the United States do when Iran is ready to test its space launch rocket as it has expressed the intention to do? The risks of such a strategy are obvious and the consequences of the war it would start are grim. Even in the case of North Korea, such a provocative use of U.S. offensive military power risks the start of offensive operations against South Korea or Japan as well as widespread international condemnation.

As the aforementioned has illustrated, the end of the Cold War strategic competition has seen important changes in the nature of the ballistic missile threat. The drawdown in the U.S. and former Soviet strategic arsenals may have produced a decline in the aggregate number of ballistic missiles, but the number of states seeking these capabilities is rising, as is the sharing of technical expertise and capabilities. Strengthened enforcement of missile technology control regimes is essential, but not sufficient to deter the existing threat, much less that expected to emerge.

Earlier this month, the Bucharest Summit Communiqué issued by NATO acknowledged the significance of the ballistic missile threat and agreement with the path forward outlined by the United States. It said:

> Ballistic missile proliferation poses an increasing threat to Allies' forces, territory and populations. Missile defense forms part of a broader response to counter this threat. We therefore recognize the substantial contribution to the protection of Allies from long-range ballistic missiles to be provided by the planned deployment of European-based United States missile defense assets. We are exploring ways to link this capability with current NATO missile defense efforts as a way to ensure that it would be an integral part of any future NATO-wide missile defense architecture.

Effectiveness of U.S. Missile Defense Systems

In December 2002, President Bush called for the deployment of missile defense assets capable of providing an initial defense against the rogue state ballistic missile threat. The initial deployment as outlined by the President was expected to be "modest" but available for limited defensive missions beginning in 2004. These efforts were clearly considered just "a starting point" for development and deployment of improved and expanded capabilities in the years that followed.

Today, the United States has twenty-four ground-based midcourse interceptors in missile fields at Fort Greely, Alaska, and Vandenberg Air Force Base, California, with a total of thirty planned for by the end of 2008. Twelve Aegis ships [in the U.S. Navy] are equipped with the long-range surveillance and track capabilities needed to perform ballistic missile defense missions. Conversion of six more is planned by the end of 2008. These vessels are outfitted with Standard Missile Three (SM-3) interceptors. Further expansion of the Navy's capabilities will come with the upgrading of the SM-2 Block IV missile, the goal being to deploy up to 100 interceptors to provide a near-term terminal engagement capability on eighteen Aegis BMD [ballistic missile defense] ships beginning in 2009. The Patriot PAC-3 terminal defensive system [short-range antimissile missiles] was completed and transitioned to the U.S. Army. Work on the Fylingdales Radar in the United Kingdom, the Cobra Dane Radar, the Sea-Based X-Band Radar, and the forward-based transportable X-Band Radar in addition to the development and construction of the communications and battle management systems and software linking the whole system together was completed. The integration of these multiple radars [enlarges] the battlespace, provide overlapping fields of vision to increase the accuracy of tracking data and prevent the creation of blindspots, and ease the transition or "hand-off" of information to the kill vehicle.

The hit-to-kill approach was successfully demonstrated thirty-four times in various systems since 2001. The purpose of tests is to evaluate progress and reveal areas in need of improvement. The "unsuccessful" intercept tests of the ground-based midcourse defense revealed problems with the booster rockets.

Those problems were corrected, as illustrated by the successful functioning of the system in its September 2007 flight test. The Aegis program has had thirteen successful intercept tests, with its two "failures" linked to assembly issues with the divert attitude control (FM-5, June 2003) and an incorrect system setting, a human error (FTM-11, December 2006). The Terminal High Altitude Area Defense (THAAD) is four for four in its intercept tests, with one target malfunction resulting in a canceled test. The failures therefore revealed hardware and engineering issues associated with the boosters and highlighted the importance of investing in a reliable target set. For each of the systems, the test experiences show that, once deployed, the kill vehicle reliably finds and destroys its target.

The realism of the testing program, particularly for the GMD system, is sometimes questioned. The Patriot PAC-3 system was operationally deployed and used during Operation Iraqi Freedom, where it destroyed nine Iraqi missiles in nine attempts. The Aegis BMD, which has successfully destroyed separating and unitary targets and has had a simultaneous interception of two targets, led Dr. Charles McQueary, Director of Operational Test and Evaluation at the Department of Defense, to state before the Senate Armed Services Committee on April 1st that Aegis BMD has "demonstrated the capability to detect, track, and engage short- and medium-range ballistic missile targets in the midcourse phase with Standard Missile-3 missiles."

The GMD [ground-based midcourse defense, a mid-range element of the U.S. missile defense program] strategy program suffers from the perception that its testing program is lacking in "operational realism." It is important to remember that progress in the test program was delayed by failed launches of the booster rocket in 2004–05 and a target failure in 2007. Nevertheless, the September 2007 flight test involved many operational elements, including servicemen and women crewing the interceptors, the radars, and the fire control system and target intercept geometries based on a North Korean launch against the continental United States.

Approximating conditions reminiscent of the summer of 2006, when intelligence reports provided rough estimates of the times when North Korea might test launch its Taepodongs, the September test provided the warfighter with notice that a window for the test was opening and to be on alert, forcing them to react immediately when the target was launched. Similar approaches are taken for the flight tests of the other systems.

General [Henry A.] Obering, the Director of the Missile Defense Agency [MDA], further described the "operational" aspects of the test for the Senate in early April:

> To demonstrate the long-range BMDS capability, for example, we conducted an integrated flight test last September involving a realistic target launched from Alaska and tracked by the operational upgraded early warning radar in northern California. An Aegis ship and the sea-based X-band radar in the North Pacific tracked the target as well. The target was successfully destroyed by a Ground-Based Interceptor (GBI) launched from an operationally configured silo in central California. The data needed to calculate a fire control solution for the interceptor was

provided by the operational system and the operational command and control, battle management and communications system was employed by the warfighting commanders. Overall, this single test included numerous components separated by thousands of miles and managed by four executing organizations within the Missile Defense Agency.

The absence of sufficient flight test data is cited by the Government Accountability Office as well as Dr. McQueary as an impediment to their assessment of the MDA's modeling and simulation efforts. The MDA is presently working to anchor the models with the flight test data to validate the models, which should address these concerns. Dr. McQueary's office is working directly with MDA personnel in the test planning and execution process.

All agree the challenge is continued demonstration of the GMD and other systems against more complex scenarios and in more stressing conditions. We are all anxious to see further demonstrations of the system's abilities, but the pace of the testing schedule is influenced by the costs of the tests ($80–100 million per test for the GMD) and, more importantly, the time it takes to analyze, interpret, and incorporate the results of the terabytes worth of data generated from each past test into a new test process.

Dr. McQueary's concluding comments offer important perspective on how far the program overall has come, however. He stated:

> Hit-to-kill is no longer a technological uncertainty; it is a reality, being successfully demonstrated many times over the past few years. The challenge now is to demonstrate hit-to-kill in more complex target scenes that include not only target deployment artifacts but countermeasures as well. General Obering has this in his future test plans. Individual element successes indicate their growing capabilities. Integrated ground testing of the BMDS continues to demonstrate that the warfighters understand and can operate the system confidently and effectively. There is still a long way to go, but the MDA's disciplined and principled approach to flight and ground tests is continuing to pay real dividends.

It is asserted that the midcourse defense challenge is insurmountable because adversaries can defeat the defense through the use of countermeasures. Successfully developing and using countermeasures requires detailed knowledge of the defensive system they are designed to overcome, exemplary systems engineering so the offensive system and the countermeasure function properly, and flight testing to ensure proper operation. Knowledge of the operational characteristics of the U.S. system are not widely available. Flight tests of countermeasures would allow study of their performance and modification of our own responses accordingly. Should flight tests be foregone so as to avoid such detection, the prospective attacker has introduced significant risk into their missile arsenal. The U.S. GMD system was tested against known countermeasures in seven ground and flight tests between 1997–2002. Since that time, the target acquisition, discrimination, and terminal homing abilities of the kill vehicle are tested on a regular basis with 2008 flight test plans calling for the resumption of active flight testing against countermeasures. Future plans entail the use of ever more advanced sensors and algorithms as well as a volume kill capability.

In summary, the ballistic missile defense today represents significant progress since 2002. The construction and fielding of the initial defensive capability called for by the President is well underway. Future efforts will build on this foundation by engaging missiles in their boost phase of flight, enabling multiple intercept opportunities from the same interceptor, and improving the sensor, tracking, and battle management abilities of the entire system.

Evaluating the Investment in Missile Defense

An examination of expenditures on missile defense efforts since the 1980s reveals short bursts of growth or reductions followed by periods of stability. Missile defense has seen rising shares of total defense research and development (R&D) since the inception of a dedicated effort in the early 1980s. After averaging between 8–10% of the defense R&D budget for most of the FY 1987–2001 period, the share of defense R&D funds allocated to missile defense has fluctuated around 11% since FY 2001. In FY 2008, missile defense accounted for 11% of the defense R&D budget. The FY 2009 budget request maintains that allocation.

While the R&D share has grown, missile defense remains a small element of the overall defense portfolio. Only once in more than 25 years has missile defense's share of total defense budget authority exceeded 2% of the annual budget. That occurred in FY 2002 when it reached exactly 2%. In FY 2008, missile defense activities represented 1.3% of the total defense budget, down from 1.6% in FY 2007. The FY 2009 request would allocate 1.5% of defense budget authority for missile defense R&D.

The growing of share of missile defense in the R&D portfolio is indicative of increased effort and priority, but it is also a function of changes to other elements of the defense R&D portfolio. The Air Force and Navy show generally rising R&D budgets in the most recent fiscal years whereas the Army, the Defense Advanced Research Projects Agency (DARPA) and others all present flat or declining budgets, in inflation-adjusted terms.

Looking over the FY 1982–2009 period, support for missile defense activities shows three distinct phases. In the 1980s, support for missile defense increased rapidly between FY 1984–1987 and then leveled off at approximately $4.5 billion annually before beginning to decline noticeably after FY 1992. Through the 1990s (FY 1990–99), the missile defense R&D budget averaged $3.6 billion with large annual fluctuations, ranging between a low of $2.6 billion in FY 1995 and a high of $4.5 billion in FY 1992. A sharp increase occurred in FY 2002, when the budget jumped from $4.1 to $6.6 billion. From FY 2002–2008, the missile defense R&D budget averaged $7 billion and shows a pattern of slow growth since FY 2002, rising $394 million in inflation-adjusted dollars between FY 2002–2008.

Examining the top-line financial picture reveals how the prioritization of the missile defense mission has changed over time. Much like the top-line Air Force R&D budget, which covers activities as disparate as airframe development, engines, satellites, and rockets and shows changing emphases over time, the total missile defense budget encompasses sensor platforms, communications, software development, kill-vehicles, boosters, and lasers.

Over time, the mix of these priorities has changed substantially. Like any development program, changing priorities and requirements add delays. In the case of missile defense, these changes are substantial. The missile defense envisioned by Presidents [Ronald W.] Reagan and George H.W. Bush is not the defense we are building today. They saw global defense utilizing small hit-to-kill interceptors deployed in space to intercept missiles in the boost phase of flight, supplemented by ground- and sea-based assets to provide interception options in the midcourse and terminal phases of flight.

The [President Bill] Clinton Administration substantially altered the focus of the nation's missile defense effort. Eliminating the space-based efforts, the Clinton program initially emphasized theater defenses. But, by 1997, the Clinton Administration had committed to developing a longer-range limited midcourse defense, along with the theater defenses. That decision laid the groundwork for the base of capabilities being deployed today. Issues arising from the Anti-Ballistic Missile (ABM) Treaty's limitations on the construction of missile defense assets prompted President Clinton in September 2000 to defer decisions about deployment, leaving them for President George W. Bush.

The Bush Administration chose first to withdraw from the ABM Treaty and then commit to the deployment of missile defense assets as they developed. The significance of the June 2002 withdrawal from the ABM Treaty cannot be overlooked when evaluating the recent performance of the missile defense system. The Treaty placed limits on the development and testing of missile defense assets. For example, the Treaty limited the speed and range of target missiles and prevented the use of sea-based radars to support interceptor tests. The Treaty limited construction and deployment activities, including the construction of battle management radars in the Aleutians, deployment of land-based interceptors outside of Grand Forks, ND, and sea-based radars. Finally, the Treaty prohibited the transfer of missile defense components to our allies. As outlined above, our program has taken advantage of being freed from each of these limitations.

In summary, much like the ebb-and-flow of the top-line of the budget, the areas of emphasis within that budget have changed over time. Between 1984–1993, the principal emphasis was the development of space-based systems to provide global defensive capabilities. From 1993–1996, the defense of deployed U.S. forces and allies rose in prominence, leading to the rise in emphasis on terminal phase interceptors. From 1997 to the present, the focus shifted to providing a defense against the emerging long-range ballistic missile threat from North Korea and other so-called "rogue" states. This focus placed prominence on defenses in the midcourse phase of flight as well as continued development of terminal phase defensive systems.

The evaluation of the nation's investments in missile defense must recognize that the change in emphases over time (from global to theater to national) [raises] very different technical challenges and require weapon systems designed to confront those unique conditions. Much as the Air Force deploys different airplanes for different missions, the missile defense mission is met through distinct systems tailored for specific purposes.

Finally, the timelines for developing technically complex weapons systems has increased dramatically. Longer and longer development timelines are the norm, with the many weapon systems averaging more than a decade between system definition and the fielding of initial operational capabilities. For example, between 1950–1970, fighter aircraft and bombers required 4–5 years to complete the development cycle. From the 1980s forward it now takes fourteen years or more to complete the cycle. The reasons for this state of affairs are many. The decline in the technical competence of the government's acquisition system, changing requirements through the design process, uncertainty about acquisition plans, the expense of the planned systems, and the sheer technical complexity are all cited to explain the delays endemic to virtually all major defense systems.

Summary Remarks

The decision to deploy missile defense assets as they mature is driven by the desire to provide the building blocks of a defense against emerging threats. The simple fact is that not all threats are known or will be known and, in the current security climate, many are not deterrable. Even in their current form, the elements of the U.S. missile defense system offer options heretofore unavailable. With further research, development, and testing, the accuracies and capabilities of these systems will only improve. Further improvement of the defense is essential, but the progress is positive.

NATO's recognition of the threat posed to Europe from ballistic missiles is an important recent indicator of the seriousness of the situation. That Japan, the United Kingdom, Australia, Israel, Germany, the Netherlands, Denmark, Italy, France, India and many others are working with the U.S. on missile defense is further evidence that ballistic missiles are recognized as a global security challenge and that the approaches outlined by the United States are valid.

Philip E. Coyle, III  **NO**

What Are the Prospects, What Are the Costs? Oversight of Missile Defense

Introduction

There is a troublesome lack of clarity in public discourse regarding both the rationale for and the technical progress toward a U.S. missile defense network. The reason for this confusion is clear when one examines the historical record. Quite simply, the public statements made by Pentagon officials and contractors are often at variance with all the facts at hand. In the ongoing administration advocacy to ensure continuing support for a missile defense program that is expected to cost hundreds of billions of dollars, it has become difficult to separate programmatic spin from genuine developmental progress, and claimed value from liabilities. In particular, there has been a lack of substantive discussion about the ways in which missile defenses can undermine America's arms control and non-proliferation objectives.

The Pentagon is developing a variety of missile defense systems – land, sea, air, and space-based – but the Ground-based Midcourse Defense system (GMD) – formerly called National Missile Defense (NMD) – attracts the most attention from lawmakers and the media. It is the largest and most complex of the systems, and will be the most costly. It is also the centerpiece in the current Defense Department plan for defending the United States from long-range intercontinental ballistic missiles (ICBMs) fired by a hostile enemy, and for those reasons I will concentrate on that system today.

The Lack of Operational Criteria

In reviewing the status of U.S. missile defense programs, I want to stress at the outset the current programs have no operational criteria for success.

How good is the system supposed to be? Is 10% effectiveness good enough? What about 1%? Can the system handle realistic threats as documented in Intelligence Community threat assessments? How many interceptors should be required to defeat one target?

Without answers to such questions, it is very difficult to evaluate these programs. This also explains why the [military] has been reluctant

U.S. House of Representatives, April 16, 2008.

to say that the United States has an operational capability or whether it would be effective.

Eight years ago President [Bill] Clinton established four criteria against which he would make a deployment decision. The Clinton criteria, announced by the White House in December 1999, a year before he would make a decision, were:

1. "Whether the threat is materializing;
2. the status of the technology based on an initial series of rigorous flight tests, and the proposed system's operational effectiveness;
3. whether the system is affordable; and
4. the implications that going forward with National Missile Defense (NMD) deployment would hold for the overall strategic environment and our arms control objectives."

At that time the goal was to be able to shoot down a single missile due to an accidental or unauthorized launch from Russia or China, not to be able to defend against a deliberate missile attack. But at that time there had been only three NMD flight intercept tests, and because the last two of those three tests failed, the missile defense system clearly was shown not to be effective. As a result, President Clinton did not have to spend much time considering the cost or the international relations aspects of his decision to not deploy the system. The system simply had not been shown to be effective, and that was that.

During the [President Ronald W.] Reagan years, Paul Nitze, the highly regarded scholar and statesman, presented three criteria that any – in those days it was the Strategic Defense Initiative (SDI) – missile defense system must meet before being considered for deployment. The Nitze criteria were shorter and included two important military considerations: that the system be able to survive direct attack, and that the system be cost effective on the margin. Nitze's criteria were formally adopted as National Security Directive No. 172 in 1985. The Nitze criteria were:

1. The system should be effective;
2. be able to survive against direct attack; and
3. be cost effective at the margin – that is, be less costly to increase your defense than it is for your opponent to increase their offense against it.

The Ground-based Missile Defense system being deployed in Alaska and California, and the proposed U.S. missile defense system for Europe, meet *none* of the above criteria, not the Clinton criteria and not the Nitze criteria. And new or different criteria for the system have not been established by the current administration.

Instead the Missile Defense Agency (MDA) is pursuing a path of "spiral development," sometimes called, "Capability Based Acquisition," concepts which have been taken to an unworkable extreme by the MDA. The extreme example is the overall Ballistic Missile Defense System about which the Missile Defense

Agency insists, "There are currently no final or fixed architectures and set of requirements for the proposed BMDS." Under this approach, spiral development or other "dynamic acquisition" concepts become like building a house while the floor plan is constantly changing. It makes for a very expensive house, and if your family ever gets to move in, they find they don't like how their topsy-turvy house turned out. With dynamic acquisition processes, especially capability-based acquisition, there may be no established baseline for even the first increments. In missile defense, and a few other complex DOD programs, the problems with dynamic acquisition stem from a lack of definite requirements.

The Defense Science Board has advised the DOD that "Each spiral should be an enforced baseline," and adds, "There needs to be a careful assessment of technological readiness, with risk reduction activity outside and preceding major program activity where significant technical risks exist." In missile defense, this advice is too often not heeded.

Without an enforced baseline of requirements or other established criteria, the Congress cannot rely on the Pentagon's cost estimates, or know whether an effective system will result. Without established criteria the Congress is buying another Winchester Mystery House, that famous 160-room Victorian mansion in San Jose, California, that was under continuous construction for 38 years without any master building plan. The maze-like house has staircases that lead to nowhere, second floor outside doors that open to nothing except a 10-foot drop, and oddly arranged rooms where you would least expect them. For this reason, the criteria described above, both the Clinton criteria and the Nitze criteria, are still helpful today in helping us to gauge where we stand with missile defense, what we have gotten for the effort, and where we should be going.

In making his decision in December, 2004, to deploy the GMD system in Alaska and at Vandenberg AFB in California, President Bush appears to have had no criteria other than an ideological commitment. Former Senator Sam Nunn [D-GA] has said it best: "National missile defense has become a theology in the United States, not a technology." But when it comes to missile defense, theology is not enough. Missile defense is the most difficult development the Pentagon has ever attempted, beyond any Army tank, Navy ship, high performance jet fighter or helicopter. And those developments often take 20 years or more. Missile defense has been under development in the United States for 60 years. As noted by the Chairman in your first hearing, a conservative estimate is that the U.S. has spent more than $120 billion on missile defense. From looking at figures from the Congressional Budget Office, I would estimate that since President Reagan's famous "Star Wars" speech in 1983, about $150 billion has been spent. And over the next five years, the Pentagon has requested another $62.5 billion for missile defense, with no end in sight. If the Congress supports this spending on missile defense, by the end of 2013 over $110 billion will have been spent just since 2003, not counting the missile defense spending in the previous 20, 40, or 60 years.

The question before you today is what, if anything has really changed in the last eight years? Is the threat worse or less? Is the technology more tractable? Is the cost manageable and affordable in relation to other U.S. priorities?

And is the danger to America growing because of the response of other countries to U.S. missile defenses?

The Threat, or Not

In your March 5, 2008, hearing, [long-time nuclear weapons analyst] Joseph Cirincione testified that since 2001, the threat – especially the threat from intercontinental ballistic missiles that can reach the United States – has gone down, not up. Yet the Missile Defense Agency [MDA] claims that the threat from ballistic missiles is growing.

To motivate the need for missile defenses, the MDA has pointed to missiles in twenty countries. However, all but two of these twenty countries – Iran and North Korea – are either friends, allies, or countries from which we have no missile threat – for example, Israel, India, Pakistan, Vietnam, South Korea, Moldova, Ukraine, Saudi Arabia, and Egypt. Venezuela was recently added to the list. Further, with the exception of Russia and China, none of these twenty countries – including Iran and North Korea – has ballistic missiles that can reach the United States. In October 2007, the White House announced: "America faces a growing ballistic missile threat. In 1972 just nine countries had ballistic missiles. Today, that number has grown to 27 and it includes hostile regimes with ties to terrorists." Vice President [Richard] Cheney reiterated that estimate in a speech on March 11, 2008. The White House has not explained how it came up with twenty-seven countries, rather than MDA's already misleading claim of twenty.

Operationally, such estimates are pointless since the MDA says that it can only handle "an unsophisticated threat," that is, just one or at most two missiles from Iran (or North Korea), with no decoys or countermeasures. This is not because that would be a realistic threat, but because it is the toughest threat that MDA claims to be able to deal with.

It is not credible that Iran (or North Korea) would be reckless enough to attack Europe, or the United States, with a single missile – with no decoys or countermeasures – and then sit back and wait for the consequences? As we know, ballistic missiles have return addresses. Thus, if Iran were reckless enough to attack Europe or the United States, they wouldn't launch just one missile, and if they launched several missiles or used decoys and countermeasures, current U.S. missile defenses would not be effective. Further, if Iran or North Korea were intent on attacking Europe or the United States, and if they believed that U.S. missile defenses worked, they likely would emulate Russia. Against Russian or Chinese ICBMs launched en masse, the most futuristic missile defenses would not be effective. This fact was recognized by Congress in 1974, when lawmakers voted to shutdown the Safeguard system (which relied on nuclear-armed interceptors) almost immediately after it was declared operational. It had become obvious that the system could not defend against an all-out Soviet attack.

We will not have a safer world if U.S. missile defenses cause Iran, North Korea, or other countries to build up vast arsenals of ballistic missiles to overwhelm our defenses. U.S. missile defenses could create new dangers for

America, stimulating a new arms race, and encouraging U.S. adversaries to build more and more missiles so as to overwhelm our defenses. By responding to the perceived "unsophisticated threat," we are motivating new threats for which we do not have technical solutions.

Decoys and Countermeasures

Decoys and countermeasures are the Achilles Heel of missile defense, are the Achilles Heel of the missile defense systems being deployed in Alaska and California, and also of the U.S. missile defense system proposed for Europe.

To use a popular analogy, shooting down an enemy missile going 17,000 mph out in space is like trying to hit a hole-in-one in golf when the hole is going 17,000 mph. If an enemy uses decoys and countermeasures, missile defense is shooting a hole-in-one when the hole is going 17,000 mph and the green is covered with black circles the same size as the hole. The defender doesn't know which target to aim for.

In 1999 and in 2000, the U.S. Intelligence community provided assessments that North Korea or Iran would soon know, if they didn't already, how to field decoys and countermeasures. A September 16, 1999 report by Robert Walpole, National Intelligence Officer for Strategic and Nuclear Programs, stated:

> We assess that countries developing ballistic missiles would also develop various responses to US theater and national defenses. Russia and China each have developed numerous countermeasures and probably are willing to sell the requisite technologies. Many countries, such as North Korea, Iran, and Iraq probably would rely initially on available technology – including separating RVs, spin-stabilized RVs, RV reorientation, radar absorbing material (RAM), booster fragmentation, low-power jammers, chaff, and simple (balloon) decoys – to develop penetration aids and countermeasures. These countries could develop countermeasures based on these technologies by the time they flight test their missiles.

This assessment is not surprising since decoy and countermeasure techniques are described in the public literature and on the Internet.

As Mr. Walpole noted, decoys can include objects that provide a close representation of the attacking enemy missile or its warhead encased in a re-entry vehicle. For example, a simple balloon in the shape of a cone – the shape of a re-entry vehicle – would travel out in space as fast as the RV itself and be confusing to the defender. An enemy missile could carry many of these balloons that are inflated at the time of stage separation and travel along with the re-entry vehicle and other objects, such as the "bus" that first housed all these objects, and debris from stage separation. The debris from stage separation itself could act as a kind of decoy as that debris might reflect, turn, or tumble in a manner resembling the target re-entry vehicle. Countermeasures could include chaff or debris deliberately scattered by the attacker with the target missile or warhead to reflect the search radar of a missile defense system. This might be short metal wires – like paper clips – of the proper length, or bits of metal foil to reflect the radar, or to cloud the view the radar might otherwise have of the target.

For missile defense systems that operate in the infrared, infrared-burning pellets can be released by the attacker to confuse the defender. Even the angle of the sun can be important, heating various objects in the target cluster by different amounts. The five early, successful, GMD flight intercept tests that included simple round balloon decoys were all conducted so that the sun was shining away from the interceptor and "over its shoulder" so that the sun was not shining into the "eyes" of the infrared seeker on the interceptor. As a result, the sun was heating up those balloons and making them hotter and easier to spot than they would have been at other times of the day or at night.

Different missile defense systems prompt the use of different sorts of decoys or countermeasures by the offense. For example, the laser being developed for missile defense, the Airborne Laser, is to be a high power laser carried in a jumbo 747 aircraft. But if the enemy paints their missiles with an ordinary white paint, a white paint that is 90% reflective to the laser, then 90% of the laser energy bounces off. To compensate for this, the Airborne Laser would need to be ten times more powerful and would need an aircraft bigger than a Boeing 747.

For radars, jamming or electronic interference with the radar is another common countermeasure. An enemy also can apply radar-absorbing materials to the attacking missiles or re-entry vehicles to reduce their radar cross-sections and make them "stealthy" and less easily detected by radar. In all out battle, missile defense radar and interceptor sites would be prime targets for an enemy.

The Inadequacy of the U.S. Ballistic Missile Defense System

Some would argue that if not a realistic threat today, North Korea and Iran may become a real threat in the future. However, the MDA FY-2008 budget request contains a remarkably candid statement: "This initial capability is not sufficient to protect the United States from the extant and anticipated rogue nation threat." The full context of this statement is provided below:

Close Gaps and Improve This Capability

This initial capability is not sufficient to protect the United States from the extant and anticipated rogue nation threat. We therefore must close the gaps in the system and improve its capability to keep pace. Three key elements of this effort are additional Aegis BMD sea-based interceptors, the introduction of four transportable Terminal High Altitude Area Defense (THAAD) fire units consisting of radars and interceptors, and the introduction of a land- and sea-based volume kill capability (Multiple Kill Vehicle program) to address potential countermeasures. Additionally, to ensure full coverage of the United States against threats from the Middle East, we will upgrade an Early Warning Radar in Thule, Greenland. This radar, is conjunction with the radar at Fylingdales, U.K. [United Kingdom] provides the ability to track threats to the U.S. and Europe from the Middle East. Because we must protect these radars or risk losing the "eyes" of our system, we are planning to field ground-based interceptors and an associated ground-based midcourse radar site in Europe. This achieves four goals: protecting the foreign-based radars, improving protection of the United States by providing additional and earlier intercept opportunities; extending this protection to our allies and friends; and demonstrating international support of ballistic missile defense.

Clearly, the MDA sees the proposed missile defenses in Europe as a first line of defense to protect existing radar sites in Greenland and the United Kingdom necessary to defend the U.S., not first and foremost to defend Europe. And it certainly confirms the Union of Concerned Scientists report, "Technical Realities," four years ago, which stated, "The ballistic missile defense system that the United States will deploy later this year will have no demonstrated defensive capability and will be ineffective against a real attack by long-range ballistic missiles." Indeed, today the GMD system still has no demonstrated effectiveness to defend the U.S., let alone Europe, against enemy attack under realistic operational conditions.

The MDA budget statement above also shows that an enemy bent on attacking Europe or the United States would attack the "eyes" of the system first. Applying traditional military strategy, an enemy of Europe or the United States would first attack the radar proposed to be built in the Czech Republic as well as the existing radars in the United Kingdom and Greenland.

The Limitations of GMD Flight Intercept Tests

Flight intercept tests with parts of the GMD system have been ongoing for nearly a decade. In 2000, there had been three GMD flight intercept tests; as of today there have been 13. Seven of these 13 tests have been successful, but six have failed. By that measure the system is doing slightly better than 50%. But in the last five years there have only been 5 flight-intercept tests, and three of those have failed, a success rate of only 40%. Two failures occurred when the interceptors failed to get off the ground. Those two failures occurred for different reasons, but twice in a row, GMD interceptors failed to get out of their silos.

Thus, in the past five years there have been just two successful GMD flight intercept tests. At that rate, it would take the Missile Defense Agency 50 years before they could be ready for realistic operational testing. The MDA still must carry out successfully about 20 more flight intercept tests of different types before the system might be ready for realistic operational testing. If they do not improve their rate of success, it could take them 50 years to achieve 20 successful flight intercept tests.

From a target discrimination point of view, during the past five years the flight intercept tests have been simpler and less realistic than the tests in the first five years. None of the GMD flight intercept tests have included decoys or countermeasures during the past five years. In addition, developmental tests also are needed to demonstrate that the system can work at night or in bad weather, can work when the sun is shining in a disadvantageous direction, can work when the enemy re-entry vehicle is spin-stabilized to minimize its radar cross section, and alternatively can work when tumbling and not spinning, can work when multiple attempts are needed to bring down a single target, and can work when more than one missile is launched by an enemy.

Cost and Cost Effectiveness at the Margin

As noted earlier the United States has already spent over a hundred billion dollars on missile defense. In FY-2009 the president's budget request asks for $12.4 billion for DOD spending on missile defense. The Missile Defense Agency itself accounts for $9.4 billion of that total. On top of that, the DOD FY-2009 budget request calls for another $62.5 billion to be spent over the next five years. If the Congress supports this spending on missile defense, by the end of 2013 over $110 billion will have been spent just since 2003, not counting the missile defense spending in the previous 20, 40, or 60 years.

Since there are no criteria established for the system, not even the Missile Defense Agency itself can say what the eventual costs might be. The costs are open ended and there is no end in sight. Indeed, some of the elements of the planned GMD system of systems do not yet exist. For example, SBIRS-High and the Space Tracking and Surveillance System (STSS) are billions of dollars over budget and years behind schedule. If, as the MDA asserts, the system can already defend the United States when two major satellite systems for missile defense – SBIRS-High and STSS – do not exist, why should the Congress appropriate funds for these satellite systems? And if these satellite systems are required, how can the MDA claim that the system defends us today?

While carried in the R&D portion of the DOD budget, the GMD program is one of the biggest procurement programs in history. MDA is planning to buy *hundreds* of new interceptors between now and 2013. This includes 20 more interceptors for the GMD system in Alaska and California, 111 SM-3 interceptors and 100 Terminal Sea-based interceptors for the Aegis BMD system, 96 THAAD interceptors, and about 400 new Patriot PAC-3 interceptors, and 10 new interceptors for the proposed missile defense system in Poland. This adds up to about 635 new interceptors proposed to be bought in the next five years. The cost for these new interceptors does not include new Navy ships to be bought or modified, two dozen new Patriot batteries, new THAAD fire control systems and FBX radars, nor the proposed new satellite systems, nor all the ground support equipment connected to these systems.

However, the threat being used to justify these enormous purchases has been exaggerated, and if it were real the proposed missile defense systems couldn't deal with it anyway. This is an example of what Paul Nitze was talking about when he proposed the criteria of "cost effective at the margin."

It is easier for an enemy to increase its offenses than it is for the defender to increase its defenses against those new offenses. It is cheaper for an enemy to build more missiles as the Soviet Union did during the Cold war, cheaper for an enemy to add decoys or countermeasures, and cheaper to change the nature of an attack by firing many missiles at once or by firing them in unpredictable ways. And if an enemy is going to attack the United States or Europe, the first thing they would attack would be the missile defense radars themselves, as those are the "eyes" of the system. To defend those "eyes" would require building defenses for U.S. defenses, ad infinitum, and would be prohibitively costly.

Incomplete Information for the Congress and the Media

Too often the MDA makes incomplete public statements. Particularly in recent years, both the DOD and the MDA have made statements about GMD effectiveness or capability that are at best inaccurate. At a March 18, 2003, hearing before the Senate Armed Services Committee, Edward "Pete" Aldridge, U.S. Undersecretary of Defense for Acquisition, Technology and Logistics assessed the effectiveness of the deployed GMD system in the event of an actual attack. In that hearing Aldridge was asked by a senator how effective the system to be deployed in 2004 would be against a North Korean missile launched at the United States. Aldridge's response was, "As of today the projected effectiveness would be in the 90 percent range." The senator followed up, "If you're advising the president of the United States, and there is a possibility of the North Koreans hitting Los Angeles or San Francisco with a nuclear warhead, you are advising him that we would have a 90 percent chance of taking that down before it can get there, as early as the end of fiscal year 2004, and if millions of lives depend on it, that's your answer?" "Yes sir," Aldridge responded. Undersecretary Aldridge was mistaken. The United States did not have that capability in 2004 and still doesn't today.

On a more serious matter, the Pentagon may not have given the President accurate information about the capabilities of U.S. missile defenses. In an interview taped at the White House on July 6, 2006, President and Mrs. Bush appeared on *Larry King Live from D.C.* This was two days after North Korea had tested a Taepodong-2 missile which fell apart about 40 seconds into its flight and flopped into the sea. At one point Larry King asked the President what would we do if North Korea launched a missile at the United States. Suggesting we had a missile defense system that could shoot it down, the President replied, "If it headed to the United States we've got a missile defense system that will defend our country." The very next day at his news conference in Chicago, the President was asked the question again, and said, "Yes, I think we had a reasonable chance of shooting it down. At least that's what the military commanders told me."

When the President said that, the ground-based system hadn't had a successful flight intercept test in four years. In the two most recent attempts, the interceptors never got off the ground and failed to leave their silos. And in the only other recent attempt at that time, the kill vehicle failed to separate from its booster and missed its target.

Just last week, in a letter to the *Boston Globe,* the MDA Public Affairs Director overstated GMD target discrimination capabilities. He wrote, "Your conclusion that the current technology cannot discriminate decoys from actual warheads is likely based on the word of so-called experts – people who have no access to information on advances in decoy discrimination technology because of the highly classified nature of such data. Five successful intercept tests from

1999 to 2002 used the type of decoys we would expect from countries such as North Korea and Iran, and future tests will introduce more challenging decoys to keep up with expected threats." I am familiar with those five tests, and the types of decoy balloons used which were not classified. All of those five tests used balloons that did not resemble the target reentry vehicle. [Moreover, i]n those five tests the defender was provided, and used, advanced information about how both the mock enemy target and the balloons would appear to the kill vehicle sensors. A real enemy might do something quite different, as for example, disguising their warheads with decoys that looked similar.

The Ability to Survive Direct Attack

The major elements of the U.S. missile defense systems are vulnerable to direct attack. For example, the floating Sea-based X-band Radar (SBX) is literally a sitting duck. So also are the early-warning radars in Greenland and in England, as would be the radar proposed to be sited in the Czech Republic. Many of the systems of U.S. missile defense program are housed in ordinary buildings providing no more protection that would a common warehouse.

But an enemy needn't bother attacking U.S. missile defense sites with bombs, munitions or improvised explosive devices. According to the DOD Inspector General in a report released on February 24, 2006, "the BMD system may have been left wide open to hackers with such serious security flaws that the MDA and its contractor, Boeing, may not be able to prevent misuse of the system." The report suggested that these security flaws made the system vulnerable to hackers who could cripple the missile defense network.

The Nuclear Environment

The Pentagon does not explain it, but we need to remember that if we ever need to rely on missile defenses against enemy ICBMs it would be in an all out nuclear war. In all out nuclear war some of those enemy missiles will reach their targets, including the ones that U.S. missile defenses miss. Some enemy ICBMs might be equipped with warhead fuses to go off before an approaching interceptor would reach them. Some enemy ICBMs might be deliberately triggered to explode at high altitude, to cause EMP effects and disrupt U.S. military command and control including U.S. missile defense command and control systems. So when we talk about "realistic operational conditions," that includes the effects of the nuclear environment – mushroom clouds, blast, neutrons, x-rays – on U.S. missile defense silos, radars, satellites, and command and control installations. There is no evidence that missile defense could be depended upon under those conditions.

The Role of Diplomacy

In 1999, former Secretary of Defense William Perry made a series of diplomatic trips to convince North Korea to stop developing and testing long-range missiles. He was remarkably successful in encouraging them to enact a missile testing moratorium that held for some time. In fact, as news of his success reached the Pentagon, officials there joked: "There goes the threat!" The Pentagon appreciates a good threat to justify its programs, and the joke underscored that the most effective route in dealing with nuclear and missile proliferation threats can be through creative diplomacy, not military technology. Dollar for dollar, Dr. Perry was the most cost-effective missile defense system the United States ever had, and he showed that effective diplomacy is hard to beat.

Unfortunately, the Bush administration did not sustain and support that agreement, especially that the U.S. would stop threatening North Korea, and so North Korea went back to developing long-range missiles. Now that Ambassador Christopher Hill is achieving diplomatic success with North Korea, not unlike Dr. Perry's success eight years earlier, people in the Pentagon must be saying, "There goes the threat," once again.

If North Korea and the United States continue to make progress in face-to-face negotiations and in the Six Party Talks, there will be little justification for the presumed-to-be-effective missile defense systems in Alaska, California, and Japan. And once again, Ambassador Hill has shown that diplomacy, not technology, is the most cost-effective missile defense system.

Implications for the Overall Strategic Environment and U.S. Arms Control Objectives

At the G-8 Summit in early June, 2007, the strategic implications of proposed U.S. missile defenses in Europe were on full display. In the weeks preceding the G-8 Summit, Russian President Vladimir Putin had set the Bush administration – and the world – back on its heels with talk of Russian missiles aimed at Europe in retaliation for proposed U.S. missile defenses in Poland and the Czech Republic.

From the outset, the Poland/Czech Republic arrangement had raised questions about who exactly it was defending against? Was it really to defend against Iran, as advertised, or was it an attempt by the United States to locate missile defenses close to Russia and to defend the U.S. from Russia? Or was it part of a broader plan to establish U.S. military bases and a U.S. military presence closer to the Russian border?

In October, at a news conference, President Putin drew the analogy with the Cuban missile crisis in 1962 when the Soviet Union based missiles in Cuba that could easily reach the U.S. "The situation is quite similar technologically for us. We have withdrawn the remains of bases from Vietnam and Cuba, but such threats are being created near our borders," Putin said. Just as 46-years ago America saw Russian missiles in Cuba as an alarming threat, Russia clearly feels that the proposed U.S. missile defenses in Poland and the Czech Republic are too close to its territory.

Of course, the Soviet missiles in Cuba were offensive, and the proposed U.S. interceptors in Poland are to be defensive. Nevertheless the U.S. proposal is in direct violation of the Joint Declaration issued in conjunction with the Strategic Offensive Reductions Treaty – also known as the Moscow Treaty – signed by Presidents Bush and Putin on May 24, 2002. That Joint Declaration calls for joint U.S./Russian research and development on missile defense technologies, and U.S./Russian cooperation on missile defense for Europe. The Bush proposal to establish U.S. missile defenses in Europe was neither joint nor cooperative, and was undertaken unilaterally almost before the ink had dried on the Joint Declaration. Putin also noted that the U.S. decision to deploy missile defenses close to Russia was presaged by the unilateral withdrawal in 2002 of the United States from the Anti-Ballistic Missile Treaty, which President Nixon and Soviet Communist Party Secretary Leonid Brezhnev signed together in Moscow in 1972.

Given [U.S.] inconsistency relative to the aforementioned accords, it is not surprising that Russia might regard the proposed U.S. interceptors as potentially offensive. The proposed U.S. interceptor missiles are two-stage variants of a proven launch vehicle, Pegasus missiles, which have enough payload and thrust to carry satellites into low-earth orbit. Accordingly, these missiles could easily carry nuclear warheads aimed at Russia. Russia may not be willing to take the Pentagon's word that these missiles are for defense only, and do not carry a lethal offensive payload. If Russian verification and inspection provisions are to accompany the deployment of U.S. missile defenses in Europe, those agreements themselves could take years.

Also, since the proposed GMD missile defense systems in Poland and the Czech Republic could not cover all of Europe, some members of Congress raised questions about why the United States would choose to "defend" some European countries and not others.

Ever since President Reagan's "Star Wars" speech in 1983, the U.S. has been saying it wants to cooperate with Russia on missile defense but through six administrations under Reagan, Bush [president #] 41, Clinton, and Bush [president #] 43, real cooperation has not been realized. Putin's proposal opened up new avenues for U.S./Russian cooperation.

Perhaps Russia and the United States will cooperate on missile defenses, but if they acknowledge that these missile defenses are not effective under realistic operational conditions, then the real benefit would be to show that Russia and the United States can cooperate closely on a difficult matter, not to actually defend Europe from Iran.

And if the MDA will not acknowledge that missile defenses are not effective under realistic operational conditions, pretending that U.S. missile defenses actually might work in an all-out war, then they are also pretending that those U.S. missile defenses might work against Russian missiles. If those defenses are located where they might be effective against Russia, this is something which Russia cannot accept.

Russia has indicated strongly that it will not accept U.S. missile defenses being deployed in Eastern Europe. Russia has threatened to pull out of the Conventional Forces in Europe (CFE) Treaty, potentially restarting the Cold War; Russia has resumed strategic bomber training flights; Russia has threatened that it may have to aim offensive missiles at Europe; and Russia has announced the successful development of new offensive ICBMs with maneuvering re-entry vehicles that U.S. missile defenses could not stop. Russia has also said they want the U.S. to stop the deployment of attack weapons in space, which they also find threatening.

Will our adversaries just build more and more ballistic missiles to overwhelm our missile defenses? Will they turn instead to cruise missiles, against which our ballistic missile defenses are helpless? Or will they attack us through our ports with containers containing nuclear, chemical or biological weapons? And what about terrorism, against which missile defenses are useless?

By spending such colossal sums on ballistic missile defense it is as if we have defined how our adversaries will attack us. We have declared that our adversaries will use ballistic missiles first and foremost – not cruise missiles, not cargo shipments, not terrorism – even though our ballistic missile defenses are not effective against realistic ballistic missile threats. And we are choosing to ignore the international consequences of that choice, as well as the budgetary and technical consequences.

Just as the United States needs to think through how other countries may react to U.S. missile defenses, so also do NATO, Poland, the Czech Republic, and Japan. For example, one option for the Poland or the Czech Republic is to make a decision similar to that made by Canada in 2005, when Canada decided not to participate in U.S. missile defenses. While still committed to NORAD, Canadians were skeptical that U.S. missile defenses would be effective. Also Canadians did not want to contribute to an arms race in space, and were concerned about the costs.

Interestingly, on January 3, 2008, the South Korean Defense Minister announced that South Korea also will not participate in the overall U.S. missile defense system, preferring to sustain their [nonconfrontational] Sunshine Policy with North Korea.

Poland and the Czech Republic each have their own point of view, but they share some concerns in common. Neither country faces a threat from Iran, but by hosting U.S. missile defenses in their territory they could motivate new animosity in Iran and other Muslim populations towards Poland and the Czech Republic. In an actual ballistic missile defense battle, Poland and the Czech Republic would become the *first* targets that an enemy would attack, as simply a matter of ordinary military tactics. By attacking the proposed Czech radar, an enemy could blind the system so that it could not see attacking missiles, and by attacking the interceptors in their silos, an enemy could disable the interceptors themselves.

Taken more broadly, Europe as a whole also does not face a threat from Iran, but by cooperating with the U.S., Poland and the Czech Republic might cause Europe to become a more frequent target of terrorists or even to be viewed less favorably by Iran. Also, to the extent that Russia sees the proposed U.S. missile defenses as a threat, Russia might retaliate in some ways towards Poland or the Czech Republic, especially if U.S./Russian relations turned unusually sour. For example, President Putin indicated last year that Russia might target Poland and the Czech Republic, and threatened to deploy Russian medium-range offensive missiles in the Russian enclave of Kaliningrad on the Polish border.

Conclusion

The level of debate both in America and in Europe has not been adequate to inform the public about the limitations and liabilities of missile defense. Thanks to belated but successful negotiations with North Korea, and a new National Intelligence Estimate for Iran, there appears to be no urgent threat, and if there were, U.S. missile defenses are not adequate to the task, because of the artificial constraint that an enemy would only attack with one or two missiles, and would use no decoys or countermeasures.

The U.S. proposal to establish missile defense sites in Poland and the Czech Republic has alienated Russia to a degree not seen since the height of the Cold War, and for no good purpose since the proposed U.S. system in Europe has no demonstrated capability to defend the United States, let alone Europe, under realistic operational conditions.

It is a truism that Americans and the U.S. military have a tendency to count on technological breakthroughs to solve thorny national security problems. Many Europeans hope that U.S. technology could be relied upon to solve international conflicts, too. Technology has produced some amazing advances, such as personal computers and the Internet that have changed our lives at home and at work. But too often America relies on technology as the first, best hope to save us from our problems. This is apparent in fields as diverse as defense, medicine, and the environment. By appealing to a single-point technological fix, we hope we can avoid dealing with the long-term problem. In national security, as in other fields, we use our hope for technological relief as an excuse to avoid dealing with our adversaries – sometimes at a very high cost in political and economic terms; sometimes in dangerous self-delusion about our own military capabilities in the global environment in which we all exist.

POSTSCRIPT

Should U.S. Development of a Missile Defense System Continue?

The evolving U.S. BMD system has sparked both international opposition and support. Sharply negative reactions have come from potential opponents such as China and Russia. They see a U.S. BMD system as a threat, worrying that, as a top defense official in China has put it, "Once the United States believes it has both a strong spear and a strong shield, it could lead them to conclude that nobody can harm the United States and they can harm anyone they like anywhere in the world." Even some allies had expressed doubt. For one, French President Jacques Chirac argued that a BMD system "cannot fail but to re-launch the arms race in the world."

Russia has become especially adamant in its opposition since 2007 when plans to deploy U.S. BMD missiles in Poland and control radars in the Czech Republic came to light. Ostensibly the purpose is to defend against a potential threat from Iran, but Moscow suspects a different purpose. In late 2008, Russian Foreign Minister Sergey Lavrov told reporters, "We see a threat to Russian's security as a result of the American [BMD] strategic system drawing closer to our borders. Other than [a focus on] Russia's strategic arsenal, the system for a long time will not have a goal." Russian military officials have also given dire warnings to the Poles and the Czechs. For example, General Anatoly Nogovitsyn, deputy chief of staff of Russia's armed forces, said that Poland "is exposing itself to a [Russian nuclear] strike—100 percent."

If such concern cast on the wisdom of building a BMD system, other recent factors add to the argument for acquiring a BMD. Both Iran and North Korea tested new ballistic missiles in 2008. While neither country can yet strike the United States, their ability to do so is probably just a matter of time and intent. Also Russia is to a degree modernizing its nuclear force, including test firing a new type of submarine-launched ballistic missile, the Bulava, in 2008. This modernization along with declining U.S.–Russia relations could increase the nuclear threat.

As of January 20, 2009, the future of the U.S. BMD program rests substantially in the hands of the new president, Barack Obama. As a candidate, he had pledged to "cut investments in unproven missile defense systems." That sounds anti-BMD, but it is actually a hedged statement given the disagreements about how "unproven" U.S. existing capabilities are. Thus it remains unclear what Obama will do. More pointedly, John McCain's campaign Web site declares that he "strongly supports" a BMD system because, "Effective missile defenses are critical to protect America [and its military forces aboard and allies] from rogue regimes like North Korea. . . . [and] Iran . . . and to hedge against potential threats from possible strategic competitors like Russia and China."

A Web site that backs continued development of a U.S. BMD system is the Claremont Institute's Missilethreat.com Project at http://www.missilethreat.com/. Information from an organization generally opposed to BMD systems is available from the Center for Defense Information at http://www.cdi.org. Select "missile defense" in the program window on the CDI homepage. The U.S. Missile Defense Agency's Webs site is at http://www.mda.mil/. For analyses by the General Accountability Office of the progress of the Missile Defense Agency, go to the GAO's report Web site at http://www.gao.gov/docsearch/repandtest.html and enter "missile defense" in the advanced search window. A critical issue about BMD systems is whether they will enhance or detract of nuclear stability. One of those who thinks security will be diminished is Robert Powell, "Nuclear Deterrence Theory, Nuclear Proliferation, and National Missile Defense," *International Security* (2003). Taking the opposing side is Stephen L. Quacken, "National Missile Defense and Deterrence," *Political Research Quarterly* (2006).

Internet References . . .

The United Nations Department of Peacekeeping Operations

This UN site is the gateway not only to all the functions of the United Nations, but also to many associated agencies.

http://www.un.org/

The International Law Association

The International Law Association, which is currently headquartered in London, was founded in Brussels in 1873. Its objectives, under its constitution, include the "study, elucidation and advancement of international law, public and private, the study of comparative law, the making of proposals for the solution of conflicts of law and for the unification of law, and the furthering of international understanding and goodwill."

http://www.ila-hq.org

United Nations Treaty Collection

The United Nations Treaty Collection is a collection of 30,000 treaties, addenda, and other items related to treaties and international agreements that have been filed with the UN Secretariat since 1946. The collection includes the texts of treaties in their original language(s) and English and French translations.

http://untreaty.un.org

Jurist: Terrorism Law and Policy

This site maintained by the University of Pittsburgh is a good source for the many complex legal issues involved in defining and combating terrorism.

http://jurist.law.pitt.edu/

International Law and Organization Issues

*P*art of the process of globalization is the increase in scope and importance of both international law and international organizations. The issues in this section represent some of the controversies involved with the expansion of international law and organizations into the realm of military security. Issues here relate to increasing international organizations' responsibility for security, the effectiveness of international financial organizations, and the proposal to authorize international courts to judge those who are accused of war crimes.

- Is UN Peacekeeping Seriously Flawed?
- Is U.S. Refusal to Join the International Criminal Court Wise?
- Has the U.S. Detention and Trial of Accused Foreign Terrorists Been Legally Unsound?

ISSUE 16

Is UN Peacekeeping Seriously Flawed?

YES: Brett D. Schaefer, from Testimony during Hearings on "United Nations Peacekeeping: Challenges and Opportunities," before the Subcommittee on International Operations and Organizations, Democracy, and Human Rights, Committee on Foreign Relations, U.S. Senate (July 23, 2008)

NO: William J. Durch, from "Peace and Stability Operations: Challenges and Opportunities for the Next U.S. Administration," Testimony during Hearings on "United Nations Peacekeeping: Challenges and Opportunities," before the Subcommittee on International Operations and Organizations, Committee on Foreign Relations, U.S. Senate (July 23, 2008)

ISSUE SUMMARY

YES: Brett D. Schaefer, the Jay Kingham Fellow in International Regulatory Affairs at the Heritage Foundation, a conservative think tank in Washington, DC, contends that the increased number and size of recent UN deployments have overwhelmed the capabilities of the UN Department of Peacekeeping Operations, leading to problems that make support of UN peacekeeping questionable.

NO: William J. Durch, senior associate at the Henry L. Stimson Center, an internationalist-oriented think tank in Washington, DC, acknowledges that UN peacekeeping has had problems, but argues that the UN is making major reforms and deserves strong support.

The United Nations was established in 1945 as a reaction to World War II with its horrendous destruction of life and property. In an effort to avoid a repeat of that calamity, most of the victorious and neutral countries agreed to a UN Charter that outlined a number of steps to maintain or restore peace. One was a pledge by all member countries not to resort unilaterally to war or other international violence except for self-defense. In all other cases where violence threatened or was occurring, the issue is supposed to be brought to the Security Council for its decision about how to respond.

306

One option involving military force is for the Security Council to authorize member countries to take military action against an aggressor. This has happened only twice: the UN authorized interventions in Korea (1950–1953) and in the Persian Gulf (1990–1991). The United States tried but failed to convince the Security Council in 2003 that the situation in Iraq warranted a third such collective security action.

Peacekeeping is the other military option available to the Security Council. In contrast to option one, which identifies an aggressor authorizes others to defeat it, peacekeeping deploys a military force under UN command that is made up of units contributed by member countries. Since UN forces are traditionally fairly small and lightly armed, the idea of peacekeeping is not to defeat one side or another but to prevent fighting, usually by acting as a buffer.

From 1945 to 2007, the United Nations sent over 9 million soldiers, police officers, and unarmed observers drawn from two-thirds of the world's countries to conduct 61 peacekeeping or truce observation missions. The frequency of such UN missions has risen sharply since the end of the cold war also ended the frequent veto of using peacekeeping forces by the Soviet Union and, to a lesser degree, the United States. To a degree, the difficulty of the missions has grown also as the Security Council has increasingly sent peacekeepers into unstable situations such as the Balkans, Democratic Republic of the Congo, and Darfur in western Sudan where the mission has had to try to establish peace or protect one or more groups.

A candid review of the success of UN peacekeeping missions would give them only mixed reviews. Some have worked well, but others have proven ineffective. There are several reasons for the limited effectiveness of UN forces, and to a degree, the debate in this issue is about relative importance of the problems that beset UN peacekeeping and what to do about them.

Those who support peacekeeping focus on two problems. First, countries frequently do not meet their financial obligation to support UN forces, thereby limiting what they can do. As of late 2007, the UN's members were $3.2 billion behind on their peacekeeping payments. The largest debtor, the United States, owed about a third of this total. Second, it is often difficult to get the self-interested Security Council members, to agree to authorize a UN mission. Even when the mission is authorized, it is often given little authority to act and a troop contingent that is too small and too poorly armed to make a difference. When, for example, the UN initially sent forces to the Balkans in 1992, the secretary-general asked for 35,000 peacekeepers. However, the Security Council authorized only 7,000 troops, with restrictions and limitations. These limits prevented the peacekeepers from being effective and even led, at one point, to UN troops being taken hostage and publicly humiliated.

Those who are skeptical of UN peacekeeping often focus as does Brett D. Schaefer in the first reading, on a third problem that it is the internal problems and scandals that have cast a shadow on the UN's peacekeeping efforts. He responds to these problems by urging the U.S. government to be wary of funding UN peacekeeping and by advocating fewer, less ambitious peacekeeping missions. William J. Durch in the second reading argues that needed reforms are being instituted and that the United States should give strong financial and military support for UN peace operations, thus setting an example for others.

YES

United Nations Peacekeeping: Challenges and Opportunities

UN Peacekeeping

One of the United Nations' primary responsibilities—and the one that Americans most agree with—is to help maintain international peace and security, but the UN has come under increasing criticism, both within the United States and around the world, for its inability to keep the peace where it is asked to do so. The UN Charter places principal responsibility for maintaining international peace and security within the UN system on the Security Council. The Charter gives the Security Council extensive powers to investigate disputes to determine whether they endanger international peace and security; to call on participants in a dispute to settle the conflict through peaceful negotiation; to impose mandatory economic, travel, and diplomatic sanctions; and ultimately to authorize the use of military force. This robust vision of the UN as a key vehicle for maintaining international peace and security quickly ran athwart the interests of the member states, particularly during the Cold War when opposing alliances prevented the UN from taking decisive action except when the interests of the major powers were minimal.

As a result, between 1945 and 1990, the Security Council established only 18 peace operations, despite a multitude of conflicts during that period that threatened international peace and security to greater or lesser degree. Traditionally, Security Council authorizations of military force have involved deployments into relatively low-risk situations such as truce monitoring. The bulk of these peace operations were fact-finding missions, observer missions, and other roles in assisting peace processes in which the parties had agreed to cease hostilities. UN peace operations were rarely authorized with the expectation of the use of force.

Since the end of the Cold War, the UN Security Council has been far more active in establishing peace operations. In the early 1990s, crises in the Balkans, Somalia, and Cambodia led to a dramatic increase in missions. However, the debacle in Somalia and the failure of UN peacekeepers to intervene and prevent the 1994 genocide in Rwanda and or to stop the 1995 massacre in Srebrenica, Bosnia, led to a necessary skepticism about UN peacekeeping. With a number of troubling situations, many in Africa, receiving increasing attention in the media in recent years, however, the Security Council has found itself under pressure to respond and "do something." The

U.S. Senate, July 23, 2008.

response, for better or worse, has often been to establish a new peacekeeping operation.

The Security Council has approved over 40 new peace operations since 1990. Half of all current peacekeeping operations have been authorized by the Security Council since 2000. These post-1990 operations involved a dramatic expansion in scope, purpose, and responsibilities beyond traditional peace operations. Moreover, these missions reflected a change in the nature of conflict from interstate conflict between nations to intrastate conflict within states by authorizing missions focused on quelling civil wars.

This expansion of risk and responsibilities was justified by pointing out the international consequences of the conflict, such as refugees or preventing widespread conflict and instability. While such actions may be justified in some cases, they represent a dramatic shift from earlier doctrine. As a result, from a rather modest history of monitoring cease-fires, demilitarized zones, and post-conflict security, UN peace operations have expanded to include multiple responsibilities including more complex military interventions, civilian police duties, human rights interventions, reconstruction, overseeing elections, and post-conflict reconstruction.

At the end of May 2008, there were 17 active UN peacekeeping operations and another three political or peace-building operations directed and supported by the UN Department of Peacekeeping Operations (UNDPKO). Ten of these operations, including political missions, were in Africa (Burundi, Central African Republic and Chad, Côte d'Ivoire, Darfur, Democratic Republic of Congo, Ethiopia and Eritrea, Liberia, Sierra Leone, Sudan, Western Sahara); one was in the Caribbean (Haiti); three were in Europe (Cyprus, Georgia, and Kosovo); and the remaining six missions were in the Middle East (the Middle East, Lebanon, the Syrian Golan Heights) and in Asia (Afghanistan, East Timor, and India and Pakistan).

The size and expense of UN peace operations have risen to unprecedented levels. The 17 peacekeeping missions cited above involved some 88,000 uniformed personnel from 117 countries, including over 74,000 troops, 2,500 military observers, and 11,000 police personnel. There were also over 19,500 UN volunteers and other international and local civilian personnel employed in these 17 operations. Additionally, over 2,000 military observers, police, international and local civilians, and UN volunteers were involved in the three political or peace-building missions directed and supported by UNDPKO.

All told, including international and local civilian personnel and UN volunteers, the personnel involved in UN peacekeeping, political, or peace-building operations overseen by UNDPKO totaled more than 109,500 at the end of May 2008. These operations involved the deployment of more uniformed personnel than were deployed by any single nation in the world other than the United States.

This activity has also led to a dramatically increased budget. The approved budget for UNDPKO—just one department in the UN Secretariat—from July 1, 2007, to June 30, 2008, was approximately $6.8 billion. The projected budget for UN peacekeeping operations is $7.4 billion for the July 1, 2008, to June 30, 2009, fiscal year. This is a 10 percent increase over the previous budget and nearly a threefold increase in budget and personnel since 2003. By comparison, the annual peacekeeping budget is now triple the size of the annualized UN regular biennial 2008/2009 budget for the rest of the Secretariat.

In general, the U.S. has supported the expansion of UN peacekeeping. Multiple Administrations have concluded that it is in America's interest to support UN operations as a useful, cost-effective way to influence situations that affect the U.S. national interest but do not rise to the level of requiring direct U.S. intervention. Although the UN peacekeeping record includes significant failures, UN peace operations overall have proven to be a convenient multilateral means for addressing humanitarian concerns in situations where conflict or instability makes civilians vulnerable to atrocities, for promoting peace efforts, and for supporting the transition to democracy and post-conflict rebuilding.

The U.S. contributes the greatest share of funding for peacekeeping operations. The U.S. is assessed 22 percent of the UN regular budget, but is assessed over 26 percent of the UN peacekeeping budget. All permanent members of the Security Council—China, France, Russia, the United Kingdom, and the United States—are charged a premium above their regular assessment rate. However, none pay nearly what the U.S. is assessed. In 2008–2009, the UN assessment for the U.S. is just under 26 percent. China is assessed 3.15 percent, France is assessed 7.4 percent, Russia is assessed 1.4 percent, and the U.K. is assessed 7.8 percent. Thus, the U.S. is assessed more than all of the other permanent members combined. Japan and Germany, even though they are not permanent members of the Security Council, rank second and third in assessments at 16.6 percent and 8.6 percent, respectively.

Based on the UN's July 1, 2008, to June 30, 2008, budget projection for peacekeeping, the U.S. will be asked to pay over $1.9 billion for UN peacekeeping activities over that time. As a means of comparison, the 30-plus countries assessed the lowest rate of 0.0001 percent of the peacekeeping budget for 2008–2009 will be assessed $7,352 based on that projection.

Although the U.S. and other developed countries regularly provide lift and logistics support, many developed countries that possess trained personnel and other essential resources are generally reluctant to participate directly in UN peace operations. The five permanent members contribute a total of less than 6 percent of UN uniformed personnel. The U.S. contribution totaled 14 troops, 16 military observers, and 259 police. This is roughly comparable to Russia and the U.K., which contributed 358 and 299 uniformed personnel, respectively. China and France contributed more at 1,977 and 2,090 personnel.

The top 10 contributors of uniformed personnel to UN operations are nearly all developing countries: Pakistan (10,623); Bangladesh (9,037); India (8,862); Nigeria (5,218); Nepal (3,711); Ghana (3,239); Jordan (3,017); Rwanda (3,001); Italy (2,864); and Uruguay (2,617). A number of reasons account for this situation, including the fact that major contributors use UN participation as a form of training and income.

While the U.S. clearly should support UN peacekeeping operations when they support America's national interests, broadening UN peace operations into nontraditional missions like peace enforcement and the inability to garner broad international support in terms of troop contributions, logistics support, and funding raise legitimate questions as to whether or not the UN should be engaged in the current number of missions and whether these situations are best addressed through the UN or through regional, multilateral, or ad hoc efforts with Security Council support. Concerns are growing that the system for assessing the UN peacekeeping budget is inappropriate, given the far larger financial demands of this expanded role for UN peacekeeping. Such questions are primarily political questions that can be resolved only by the member states.

Outside of the political realm, however, is the fundamental question of whether the system as currently structured is capable of meeting its responsibilities. Indisputably, the unprecedented frequency and size of recent UN deployments and the resulting financial demands have challenged and overwhelmed the capabilities of the UN Department of Peacekeeping Operations, leading to serious problems of mismanagement, misconduct, poor planning, corruption, sexual abuse, unclear mandates, and other weaknesses. Let me highlight two notable problems.

Mismanagement, Fraud, and Corruption

The UN, as illustrated by the Oil-for-Food scandals and the more recent instances of mismanagement by UNDP [UN Development Programme] in North Korea, has proven to be susceptible to mismanagement, fraud, and corruption. [The food-for-oil scandal involved UN administrators profiting from the UN's oversight of the use of Iraq's oil revenues to buy food and medicine for Iraq.] This also applies to UN peacekeeping. The Secretariat procured over $1.6 billion in goods and services in 2005, mostly to support peacekeeping, which has more than quadrupled in size since 1999. An Office of Internal Oversight Services (OIOS) audit of $1 billion in DPKO procurement contracts over a six-year period found that at least $265 million was subject to waste, fraud, or abuse. The U.S. Government Accountability Office concluded:

> While the U.N. Department of Management is responsible for U.N. procurement, field procurement staff are instead supervised by the U.N. Department of Peacekeeping Operations, which currently lacks the expertise and capacities needed to manage field procurement activities.

In reaction to the OIOS audit, the Department of Management and the DPKO accepted a majority of the 32 OIOS audit recommendations for addressing the findings. However, a more recent report from earlier this year indicates that these new procedures may not be sufficient to prevent a recurrence of fraud and corruption. Specifically, the OIOS revealed earlier this year that it is investigating about 250 corruption cases ranging from sexual abuse by peacekeepers to financial irregularities. According to Inga-Britt Ahlenius, head of the OIOS, "We can say that we found mismanagement and fraud and corruption to an extent we didn't really expect." According to the report, $1.4 billion worth of peacekeeping contracts turned up "significant" corruption schemes involving more than $619 million, or 44 percent of the total value of the contracts. At the time of the report, the task force had looked at only seven of the 18 UN peacekeeping missions that were operational over the period of the investigation. A 2008 report on the audit of the UN mission in Sudan revealed tens of millions lost to mismanagement and waste and substantial indications of fraud and corruption.

Worse, even the OIOS seems to be susceptible to improper influence. Allegations were made in 2006 that UN peacekeepers had illegal dealings with Congolese militias, including gold smuggling and arms trafficking. According to the lead OIOS investigator in charge of investigating the charges against the UN peacekeepers in the Congo, he had found the allegations of abuses by Pakistani peacekeepers to be "credible," but the "the investigation was taken away from my team after we resisted what we saw as attempts to influence the outcome. My fellow team members and I were appalled to see that the oversight office's final report was little short of a whitewash." The BBC and Human Rights Watch have provided evidence that the UN covered up evidence of wrongdoing by its peacekeepers in Congo.

Sexual Misconduct

In recent years, there have been several harrowing reports of crimes committed by UN personnel, from rape to the forced prostitution of women and young girls, the most notorious of which have involved the UN Mission in the Democratic Republic of Congo. Indeed, allegations and confirmed incidents of sexual exploitation and abuse by UN personnel have become depressingly routine in Bosnia, Burundi, Cambodia, Congo, Guinea, Haiti, Kosovo, Liberia, Sierra Leone, and Sudan.

The alleged perpetrators of these abuses include UN military and civilian personnel from a number of UN member states involved in peace operations and from UN funds and programs. The victims are refugees—many of them children—who have been terrorized by years of war and look to the UN for safety and protection. In addition to the horrible mistreatment of those who are under the protection of the UN, sexual exploitation and abuse undermine the credibility of UN peace operations and must be addressed through an effective plan and commitment to end abuses and ensure accountability.

After intense lobbying by the U.S. Department of State and U.S. Mission to the United Nations since early 2004, as well as pressure from several key Members of Congress, the UN Secretariat agreed to adopt stricter requirements for peacekeeping troops and their contributing countries. The U.S. also helped the DPKO to publish a resource manual on trafficking for UN peacekeepers. In 2005, Prince Zeid Ra'ad Al-Hussein of Jordan, the Secretary-General's adviser on sexual exploitation and abuse by UN peacekeeping personnel, submitted his report to the Secretary-General with recommendations on how to address the sexual abuse problem, including imposing a uniform standard of conduct, conducting professional investigations, and holding troop-contributing countries accountable for the actions of their soldiers and for proper disciplinary action. In June 2005, the General Assembly adopted the recommendations in principle, and some recommendations have been implemented. For instance, contact and discipline teams are now present in most missions, and troops are now required to undergo briefing and training on behavior and conduct. Tragically, this does not seem to have addressed the problem adequately.

Only this past May, Save the Children accused aid workers and peacekeepers of sexually abusing young children in war zones and disaster zones in Ivory Coast, southern Sudan, and Haiti and going largely unpunished. UN peacekeepers were most likely to be responsible for abuse. According to a report by Save the Children, "Children as young as six are trading sex with aid workers and peacekeepers in exchange for food, money, soap and, in very few cases, luxury items such as mobile phones."

However, despite this action and then-Secretary-General Kofi Annan's announcement of a "zero tolerance" policy, the perpetrators of these crimes are very rarely punished, as was revealed in a January 2007 news report on UN abuses in southern Sudan. The standard memorandum of understanding between the UN and troop contributors clearly grants troop-contributing countries jurisdiction over military members participating in UN peace operations, but little is done if these countries fail to investigate, try, and punish those guilty of such crimes.

The problems of mismanagement, corruption, and misconduct cry out for fundamental reform of the UN peacekeeping structure to improve accountability and transparency. However, corruption, mismanagement and sexual misconduct by UN peacekeepers are not the only problems with UN peacekeeping. The other problem is a political problem. The vast expansion of UN peacekeeping—with the possibility of even more operations on the horizon like the proposal for a new Somalia mission with up to 27,000 peacekeepers—has led some to point out that the UN Security Council has gone "mandate crazy" in its attempts to be seen as effective and "doing something." The willingness of the Security Council to approve missions where "there is no peace to keep"—such as Darfur, Somalia, or Chad—violates a dearly learned lesson that UN peacekeepers are not war fighters.

In general, the UN and its member states had accepted the fact—in the wake of the Somalia, Yugoslavia, Rwanda, and Sierra Leone missions in which there was no peace to keep—that UN peace operations should not include a mandate to enforce peace outside of limited circumstances and should focus instead on assisting countries to shift from conflict to a negotiated peace and from peace agreements to legitimate governance and development. As noted in the *Report of the Panel on United Nations Peace Operations* (the Brahimi Report)

> The United Nations does not wage war. Where enforcement action is required, it has consistently been entrusted to coalitions of willing States, with the authorization of the Security Council, acting under Chapter VII of the Charter.

Yet even situations short of war that may require a UN peace operation are still rife with danger, as illustrated by the nearly 2,500 peacekeepers that have been killed in operations since 1948. They also involve great demands in resources, management, and personnel. Indeed, it has increasingly strained the ability of countries willing to provide peacekeepers, especially in Darfur. Worse, this investment may not be helping the situation.

Dr. Greg Mills, Director of the Johannesburg-based Brenthurst Foundation, and Dr. Terence McNamee, Director of Publications at the Royal United Services Institute for Defence and Security Studies (RUSI), have conducted several cases studies of UN peacekeeping operations in a chapter in a forthcoming book. They have concluded that, in the cases of the Democratic Republic of Congo and Lebanon, it is an open question whether the UN peacekeeping mission has contributed to resolving the situation or exacerbating it.

- Mills and McNamee note that a 30-year United Nations presence has failed to resolve the deep-seated problems in Lebanon. The UN operation has failed to prevent a succession of Israeli incursions. Nor was the mission able to stop Hezbollah and other groups from using the Lebanese border to launch raids and rockets into Israel. The 12,000-plus UN troops currently in place following the 2006 Israeli intervention have not been instructed specifically to disarm the group. Ironically, Hezbollah is now in a stronger position, and the UN mission acts as a buffer to prevent any Israeli assault. Mills and McNamee note, "The problem in Lebanon is more profound than any deal-making or UN force can solve however. It goes to the heart of reconfiguring the state and its role in Lebanon."
- The Democratic Republic of Congo [DRC] is a state in name only. Decades of instability and insecurity have entrenched the view in Kinshasa that anything benefiting the periphery of the country is a threat. Instability is viewed as a political advantage in Kinshasa because it keeps potential rivals focused on each other rather than on the central government. As such, Kinshasa does little to aid the UN effort. Despite more than 19,000 UN military and civilian peacekeepers in Congo at an annual cost of over $1 billion, MONUC has not brought peace or stability. Eastern Congo, bordering Rwanda, Burundi, and Uganda, remains violent. According to Mills and McNamee, "Disarmament, pacification, demobilization and repatriation/reintegration programs could help to dilute the extent of the security threat to the civilian population. But this will require holding [DRC President] Kabila to task . . . removing the fig-leaf of respectability to his indecision and weakness in filling the vacuum with UN troops. But it will require fundamental, root-and-branch reform, with decentralization at its core."

In other cases, such as the UN missions in Cyprus and the Western Sahara established in 1964 and 1991, respectively, the UN presence is simply an historical palliative. The peacekeepers perform little in the way of keeping the peace. Nor does their presence seem to have contributed to the process for resolving the decades-long political standoff. Instead, the missions continue out of inertia and requests by parties to the conflict that they remain in place. It is an open question whether the UN presence has actually contributed to the intractability of the situation by providing the excuse not to develop a resolution to what is largely a political problem.

The next Administration should fundamentally re-evaluate all UN operations that date back to the early 1990s or earlier—some, like UNTSO in the Middle East and UNMOGIP in Kashmir, date back to the 1940s—to determine whether the UN is contributing to resolving the situation or retarding that process. These missions are generally small and among the least costly, but such a re-evaluation would send a welcome message of accountability and assessment that too often has been lacking in the rubber-stamp process of reauthorizing peacekeeping operations.

This is not to say that UN missions are never useful and should be rejected out of hand. UN missions have been successful in situations like Cambodia where it helped to restore stability following dictatorship and civil war. Indeed, no one wants another Rwanda, and the consequences of doing nothing may be unpalatable. But a long list of operations that have been less than successful indicates that the Security Council should be far more judicious when adopting decisions to intervene.

The situation in Darfur is particularly relevant. The U.S. has called the situation in Darfur "genocide." The UN did not come to that conclusion, but it did recognize the widespread human rights violations and suffering. After the African Union mission failed to curtail the violence and suffering, the UN adopted a resolution authorizing a joint AU/UN peacekeeping force despite ongoing conflict and considerable evidence that neither the rebels nor the government-backed forces were prepared to abide by a peace agreement. Protected by China's veto, Sudan also demanded that the peacekeepers be African. This has led to a severe constraint of available troops: There simply are not enough trained and capable African troops to meet the demand. As a result, Jan Eliasson, the Secretary-General's Special Envoy for Darfur, told the Security Council that the situation in Darfur had deteriorated despite the efforts of UN and African Union troops. The recent decision of the International Criminal Court to seek an indictment against Sudanese President Omar Al-Bashir may, if approved by the ICC pretrial chamber, lead to further complications.

In Darfur, the UN Security Council yielded to the pressure to act. Massive suffering was occurring and would likely have grown worse without UN backing and support for the AU peacekeeping effort. However, the Council accepted demands from Sudan that vastly complicate their efforts, such as restricting peacekeepers to African nations. It also entered a conflict situation against the lessons of its own experience. It compounded the error by failing to adopt clear objectives, metrics for success, and an exit strategy. Because of these failings, not to mention the potential for deterioration toward broader conflict or a stiffening of resolve by President Bashir if the ICC proceeds with its indictment, Darfur could very easily become the UN's next spectacular failure.

Recommendations

There are a number of steps the UN and the Security Council should adopt to address the weaknesses identified above.

- **Be more judicious in decisions to authorize UN peacekeeping operations.** The pressure to "do something" must not trump sensible consideration of whether a UN presence will improve or destabilize the situation, clearly establishing the objectives of the operations and ensuring that they are achievable, carefully planning the requirements for achieving those objectives and securing pledges for providing them prior to authorizing the operation, and demanding that an exit strategy be included to prevent the "perpetual mission" trap.

  This process should also apply in reauthorization of existing missions where there is often a rubber-stamp approach. If a mission has not achieved its objective or made evident progress toward that end after a lengthy period, the Council should assess whether it is serving a positive function. In its deliberations, however, the Council should recognize that short, easy missions are extremely rare. When authorizing a mission, the Council should recognize that it may be there for a lengthy period. If the Council seems unlikely to persevere, it should consider not approving the mission.

  Critically, this recommendation should not be construed as implying that all UN peacekeeping operations should or can be identical. On the contrary, differing circumstances often require differing approaches. Indeed, if peacekeeping missions are to be successful, the Council must be flexible in the makeup and composition of UN peacekeeping operations or in choosing to stand back in favor of a regional intervention or an ad hoc coalition if those approaches better fit the immediate situation. However, in the process of deciding to authorize a mission, the Council should not let an "emergency" override the prudent evaluation and assessment process necessary to make sure the prospective mission has the largest chance of success.

- **Transform the DPKO organizational structure to enable it to handle increased peace operations demands and plan for future operations more effectively.** This requires more direct involvement of the Security Council; more resources for staff, supplies, and training; and greatly improved oversight by a capable inspector general dedicated to peace operations.

  A key element of this should include transforming the DPKO to incorporate greater flexibility so that it can rapidly expand and contract to meet varying levels of peace operations activity. Current UN rules do not permit the necessary authority and discretion in hiring and shifting resources to meet priorities. A core professional military staff must be maintained and utilized, but the DPKO should also be able to rely on gratis military and other seconded professionals to meet exceptional demands on UN peace operations. This would readily provide the expertise and experience needed to assess the requirements of mandates under consideration, including troop numbers, equipment, timeline, and rules of engagement, both efficiently and realistically.

- **Build up peacekeeping capabilities around the world, particularly in Africa, and further develop a UN database of qualified, trained, pre-screened uniformed and civilian personnel available for UN operations.** The UN has no standing armed forces and is entirely dependent on member states to donate troops and other personnel to fulfill peace operation mandates. This is appropriate. Nations should maintain control of their armed forces and refuse to support the establishment of armed forces outside of direct national oversight and responsibility. However, the current arrangement results in an ad hoc system plagued by delays; inadequately trained personnel; insufficient numbers of military troops, military observers, civilian police, and civilian staff; inadequate planning; inadequate or non-functional equipment; and logistical gaps.

    The UN has established a Stand-by Arrangements System (UNSAS), wherein member states make conditional commitments to prepare and maintain specified resources (military formations, specialized personnel, services, material, and equipment) on "stand-by" in their home countries to fulfill specified tasks or functions for UN peace operations. This is their prerogative, but the resources committed under the UNSAS fall short of needs. To speed up deployment on missions, the UN would be well served to further develop a database of information on individuals' and units' past experience in UN operations; disciplinary issues; performance evaluations; expertise (e.g., language, engineering, and combat skills); and availability for deployment. In addition, U.S. efforts under the Global Peace Operations Initiative (GPOI) contribute significantly to bolstering the capacity and capabilities of regional troops, particularly in Africa, to serve as peacekeepers through the UN or regional organizations like the African Union.
- **Implement a modern logistics system and streamline procurement procedures so that missions receive what they need when they need it.** To be effective, procurement and contracting must "have a formal governance structure responsible for its oversight and direction," as former Under-Secretary-General for Management Catherine Bertini advised Congress in 2005. Critically, the new logistics system and the procurement system must be subject to appropriate transparency, rigorous accountability, and independent oversight accompanied by robust investigatory capabilities and a reliable system of internal justice.

    The new restructuring of UNDPKO into a Department of Peacekeeping Operations and a Department of Field Support, as proposed by Secretary-General Ban Ki-Moon and approved by the General Assembly, does not appear to have substantially improved peacekeeping procurement. This may be due to the fact that the new department did not receive requested positions or budget, but it also appears to be a case of a "paper reform" rather than an actual reform. Most of the same people remain in place, and it is uncertain that tasking or procedures have changed.
- **Implement mandatory, uniform standards of conduct for civilian and military personnel participating in UN peace operations.** If the UN is to take serious steps to end sexual exploitation, abuse, and other misconduct by peacekeepers, it must do more than adopt a UN

code of conduct, issue manuals, and send abusers home. It should not necessarily involve yielding jurisdiction over personnel to the UN or non-national judicial authority, but it should entail commitments by member states to investigate, try, and punish their personnel in cases of misconduct.

Investigators should be granted full cooperation and access to witnesses, records, and sites where alleged crimes occurred so that trials can proceed. Equally important, the UN must be more willing to hold member countries to these standards. States that fail to fulfill their commitments to discipline their troops should be barred from providing troops for peace operations.

Conclusion

Today's hearing is very pertinent. UN peacekeeping is being conducted at unprecedented pace, scope, and ambition. Unsurprisingly, this activity has revealed numerous flaws, limitations, and weaknesses inherent in UN peacekeeping. Problems with UN peacekeeping are serious and need to be addressed, and the Administration and Congress need to consider carefully any requests by the United Nations for additional funding for a system in which procurement problems have wasted millions of dollars and sexual abuse by peacekeepers is still occurring. Without fundamental reform, these problems will likely continue and expand, undermining the UN's credibility and ability to accomplish one of its primary missions—maintaining international peace and security.

UN peacekeeping operations can be useful and successful if entered into with an awareness of the limitations and weaknesses of UN peacekeeping. This awareness is crucial, because there seems little indication that the demand for UN peacekeeping will fall in the foreseeable future.

William J. Durch  **NO**

Peace and Stability Operations: Challenges and Opportunities for the Next U.S. Administration

Introduction

Peace seems like it ought to be self-enforcing, but the most peaceful states are those with effective police—and fair laws, competent courts, and consent of the governed. States emerging from civil war usually have none of these. Sustaining whatever fragile peace they initially achieve may require outside help, and that help may be needed for several years. In 1995, for example, the North Atlantic Treaty Organization (NATO) poured 60,000 troops into Bosnia to cement the Dayton Accords; today, 2,300 troops and police remain, under European Union (EU) command. So the effort is less but the presence remains. Other places where peacekeepers go are much bigger and more dangerous than Bosnia was when NATO deployed there. Bosnia itself was a very dangerous place before U.S. pressure and NATO air strikes brought its own civil war to a halt, a war where UN peacekeepers had earlier been deployed with neither the power nor the mandate to create and sustain peace. Yet that earlier operation was authorized by unanimous votes of the UN Security Council, votes in which the United States participated; votes that helped to discredit UN peacekeeping in the West for the remainder of the 1990s, because they sent UN forces into dangerous combat environments with which the United Nations cannot cope.

In this decade, the UN found its feet once again as major reforms in how peacekeeping is managed and mandated began to take hold. But in recent years, and especially the past twelve months, the Security Council has again begun to overuse its tools, with the result that UN peacekeepers find themselves in situations better suited to combat forces. One of the lessons of the 1990s is that peacekeepers *must* be able to defend themselves and their mandates when subject to violent tactical challenge, but such challenges must be balanced by high-level, political acceptance of the UN's presence. The Democratic Republic of Congo (or DRC) is one such dangerous place where the UN nonetheless has the support of the elected government and works closely with it against various violent opponents of the peace, especially in this large country's lawless east. Darfur, Sudan, on the other hand, is a dangerous place where the government gives little more than lip service to the UN presence and does

U.S. Senate, July 23, 2008.

everything it can to delay and obstruct its deployment, up to the possible use of proxy forces to attack UN personnel.

Most peace operations in difficult places struggle to attract the manpower and funds they need to create real change over time. The United Nations promotes stability in the DRC, for example, with one-third as many troops as NATO started with in Bosnia, spread over an area six times as large that is teeming with well-armed and vicious militias. At the end of May, the UN deployed 88,000 troops and police globally. Few of those deployed in its toughest operations (which are mostly in Africa) come from developed states, which are the UN's major funders. Not only are in-kind contributions to UN operations from these states rather rare but late payments keep UN operations perennially underfunded. At the end of May, 11 months into its peacekeeping fiscal year, the UN was still short $1.6 billion on a $6.8 billion peacekeeping budget. In one of life's greater ironies, the UN may not borrow funds to cover that shortfall, a rule enforced by the most indebted government on the planet: our own.

As imperfect as the United Nations may be, people around the globe understand, accept, and applaud most UN actions. Compared to regional organizations and ad hoc coalitions, the UN has both broader political legitimacy, greater political reach, and a deeper logistics network supporting both humanitarian relief and peace operations—a network that leans heavily on private sector service providers. But the United Nations also needs consistent U.S. political, financial, and material support to make its operations work. Each of these is well worth strengthening.

Early in the next Administration, the President should begin that strengthening process by:

- Affirming that the United States and the United Nations share common goals in expanding the writ of human rights and realizing human dignity, which in turn requires international peace and individual human security.
- Offering strong support—in cash and in kind—to every UN peace operation for which it casts its vote in the Security Council, setting an example for others by promptly contributing the U.S. share of UN peacekeeping costs.
- Supporting the continued restructuring and strengthening of UN headquarters offices that plan and support peace operations.
- Pledging strong and sustained U.S. diplomatic and political support to UN peacekeeping operations, especially in volatile states and regions.
- Promising temporary U.S. military support, in collaboration with its NATO allies, for UN operations that experience trouble from local spoilers or terrorist action.
- Continuing to train foreign peacekeepers, contingent on their governments' willingness to discipline troops who violate international humanitarian law.
- Announcing that the United States will expand its own capacity to contribute to the non-military elements of peace and stability operations.

A Brief History of Peace and Stability Operations

Contemporary peace operations got their start after World War II, when some 200 unarmed military observers wearing UN armbands patrolled cease-fire lines between India and Pakistan and armistice lines around the new state of Israel. Six decades later, 110,000 troops, police, and civilian personnel in 20 UN missions on four continents use presence, persuasion, and modern weapons to support the rebuilding of peace under tough conditions. The African Union-UN "hybrid" mission in Darfur (UNAMID) will, when fully deployed, drive that total near 130,000. NATO manages a further 50,000 peacekeepers in Kosovo and Afghanistan, the EU manages 2,300 in Bosnia, and the African Union (AU) managed about 7,000 in Darfur through the end of 2007, when that force merged into UNAMID. Washington has authorized, endorsed, or supported all of these operations through its votes in the UN Security Council or on NATO's North Atlantic Council.

In the past two years, in fact, the United States has supported a substantial increase in the size, use, and deployment of UN peacekeeping around the globe, including:

- A new peacekeeping mission in Somalia;
- A seven-fold expansion of the UN's peacekeeping mission in Lebanon;
- The four-fold expansion of the peacekeeping mission in Darfur;
- Reauthorization of the UN's large peacekeeping missions in Haiti and Liberia;
- A renewed peacekeeping mission for East Timor; and
- New missions in Chad, the Central African Republic, and Nepal.

Peacekeeping today costs $10 to $12 billion annually, not including counterinsurgency in Iraq or Afghanistan. The UN's peacekeeping budget accounts for just over half of that total and Washington pays for roughly one-quarter of the UN peacekeeping budget.

The costs of UN peacekeeping operations are pro-rated among member states according to a "peacekeeping scale of assessment," which is based on states' shares of the regular UN budget. The five permanent members of the Security Council each pay a 20% larger share of peacekeeping costs than they do of the UN Regular Budget, given their special responsibility under the UN Charter for international peace and security, and because they can veto any operation they dislike. UN operations, as currently conducted, are a relative bargain for their major funders, costing less than one-fifth of what they would cost if conducted exclusively by the funders' own military forces.

The costs of other peacekeeping missions are borne primarily by the troop contributors. NATO and the EU collectively fund mostly minor "common costs" for their missions. Occasional subsidies from wealthy states allow less-wealthy states to send troops to non-UN operations. Substantial outside cash and in-kind support (airlift and civilian contractors) have enabled the AU, for example, to deploy and support its observer force in Darfur.

The Case for International Cooperation

In deciding how best to defend themselves and their interests, all states face tough policy choices. Small, poor states have few options and often find their choices dictated by others. Big, rich states have more choices—but each choice comes with consequences. America can act on its own in many matters of peace and security, but there are times when acting in concert—through coalitions, alliances, regional groupings, or global institutions—is not only useful but necessary, because even a superpower has finite resources, as the US experience in Iraq and Afghanistan continue to demonstrate. And where resources needed to shore up the peace can be found among many implementing partners and organizations, smart engagement argues for leveraging those resources to accomplish common goals and to better manage hard problems multilaterally.

The United States has found it increasingly cost-effective and politically helpful to lean on other states and organizations to help it advance shared strategic interests in international peace, security, justice, and prosperity. The available forms of collaboration have complementary strengths: Coalitions of the willing are better at suppressing violence but typically lack staying power and means of joint finance. Regional organizations have greater legitimacy and cohesion when working within their regions but risk losing both when they venture farther afield. The UN cannot handle full-scale combat since it lacks both full control over the forces it receives and the cohesion of the best alliances and coalitions, but what it lacks in combat power, the UN makes up for in its legitimacy and staying power.

Compared to regional organizations and ad hoc alliances of states, the UN has greater political reach and a deeper network supporting humanitarian relief as well as peace operations. Those who think of the UN system as desk-bound should witness its fieldwork firsthand, since more UN staff members work in field postings than in headquarters. Peacekeeping operations are supported by a global system of financial assessments that enable the UN to tap the strengths of the private sector, with more than 100 "systems contracts" in place for essential mission support. Given the growth in this area, it is a sure bet that the next Administration will face serious questions of resource allocation regarding the UN and global peace and stability operations.

Coping with Growth in Peacekeeping Operations

In the face of explosive growth in UN peacekeeping over the past decade, the first question is whether the world, and the United States in particular, are providing sufficient resources to support this growth—which they have promoted. The answer to this question would have to be "no." The surge in UN peacekeeping has not been met with steady funding, by commensurate increases in the number of staff in the UN Department of Peacekeeping Operations (DPKO), or in the number of troops or police volunteered to the UN by its richest members for the UN's toughest missions. The result has been forces of highly variable professionalism. In the past three years, the UN has asked states to take back hundreds of troops and police as investigations have implicated them in sexual abuse and exploitation of local populations.

The United States chronically under-budgets its share of UN peacekeeping costs, even as it votes for more and expanded peacekeeping missions on the Security Council. As of February 2008, the U.S. had built up $1.2 billion in essentially permanent prior-year debt for UN peacekeeping and was likely to fall at least another $500 million short in its peacekeeping dues for 2007–08.

Beyond this challenge, ever since operations in Somalia (1992–93), the United States has declined to provide troops for the riskier UN peacekeeping forces. The Force Commander and majority of UN forces in Haiti (1995–96) were American but the last U.S. military unit to serve in a UN-led mission came home in 1999. Subsequent U.S. non-participation means that our government has no military commanders in any current UN field missions and dwindling institutional memory of how UN operations work. U.S. contributions of police officers to UN operations also have dwindled in this decade, from 849 in December 2000 to 230 this June. The second big question is whether the world and the United States are lining up the right kinds of capabilities to meet the world's needs in the peace and stability arena. In peace operations, the military's real exit strategy is successful peacebuilding, or "transition and reconstruction." This involves many tasks—from arranging and supervising elections, training novice lawmakers, and jumpstarting economic activity to rebuilding police forces and promoting independent judiciaries—all tasks for which armed forces are poorly suited or totally inappropriate. Successful peacebuilding, and therefore a successful exit strategy, require complementary civilian capacity working alongside the military.

What Washington Should Do: Recommendations for Action

As UN peacekeeping's largest and most influential donor, the U.S. government, under a new Administration, should make it clear, very early on, that it supports an effective UN that, in turn, supports international peace and security in irreplaceable ways—not as a tool of U.S. policy but as a venue for leveraging scarce funds and people toward a just public order that improves people's lives and contributes to our national security. Early in the new term, while the UN Special Committee on Peacekeeping Operations is in session, the President should set out the following principles and policy goals:

- **Affirm that the United States and the United Nations share common goals in expanding the writ of human rights and realizing human dignity, which in turn requires international peace and individual human security.** The majority of UN member states are poor, less than free, and often difficult to deal with. As a global institution, the UN includes the world's worst human rights offenders but also its strongest human rights proponents. Moreover, the UN Charter and the Covenant on Civil and Political Rights reflect Western values on a global stage.

The General Assembly regularly votes budgets for peace operations that Washington sees fit to support in the Security Council, and
those budgets are cleared first by a committee of 16 states on which the
United States has nearly always had a strong voice. The UN system also
provides a wide range of services through its operational agencies that
work beyond the realm of high politics and security, in food aid, refugee support, human rights support, global public health, vaccinations
against childhood diseases, and nuclear non-proliferation.

- **Offer strong support—in cash and in kind—to every UN peace
  operation for which it casts its vote in the Security Council and
  set an example for others by promptly contributing the U.S. share
  of UN peacekeeping costs.** The UN is precluded from borrowing to
  finance its operations, so when the Security Council votes to support
  a mission, the UN must rely on Member States' payments toward the
  mission's "assessed" budget to get things underway. The Administration frequently under-budgets for UN peacekeeping operations, and the
  Office of Management and Budget in recent years has cut State Department requests, making it up later with "supplemental" requests. This
  sleight-of-hand approach means that money shortages have driven
  U.S. dealings with the UN on matters of peace and security that should
  have been driven by U.S. interests. Even UN missions launched with
  urgent U.S. backing may not receive U.S. funds for months unless they
  can hitch a ride on a timely supplemental in the Congress. U.S. delays
  encourage other member nations to hold back funds. The bottom line?
  Mission deployments slow down to match the flow of funds, jeopardizing the people, places, and peace they are intended to protect.
- **Support the continued restructuring and strengthening of the
  UN headquarters offices that plan and support peace operations.**
  Secretary-General Ban-Ki Moon proposed, and the General Assembly approved, splitting the Department of Peacekeeping Operations
  into two parts, one (which keeps the old name) that is focused on
  policy, strategy, and planning, and another (the Department of Field
  Support) that is focused on finance, personnel, logistics, and communications. The General Assembly also agreed to add 287 staff to UN
  Headquarters support of peacekeeping, bringing the total New York
  staff to about 1,200, to manage up to 130,000 personnel in the field. Its
  cost, together with that of the UN's main peacekeeping logistics base
  at Brindisi, Italy, is five percent of the UN's peacekeeping budget. It is
  difficult to find any other agency (or company) in defense and security
  that runs on five percent overhead.
- **Pledge strong and sustained U.S. diplomatic and political support
  to UN peacekeeping operations, especially in volatile states and
  regions.** Every successful peace operation has had the strong support
  of at least one great power. Such support does not guarantee success,
  but its absence is a near guarantee of failure.
- **Promise temporary U.S. military support, in collaboration with
  its NATO allies, for UN operations that experience trouble from
  local spoilers or terrorist activities.** In spring 2000, in Sierra Leone,
  Britain turned a non-combatant evacuation operation into a mini-
  counterinsurgency campaign against the armed gangs who had threatened both the country's fragile peace and a wobbly UN peacekeeping

operation. Most of the British troops withdrew within four months, leaving behind a training mission to rebuild Sierra Leone's army. The UN operation restructured itself and ended up doing a creditable job, withdrawing in 2005. In 2004, in Haiti, U.S. armed forces led a coalition of the willing that preceded a UN operation, instead of serving in parallel. There is no good reason why such U.S. deployments could not be made in parallel, however, as Britain and the EU have done, should a UN operation run into trouble.

- **Continue training foreign peacekeepers, contingent on their governments' willingness to discipline troops who violate international humanitarian law.** The U.S. supports the G8's Global Peace Operations Initiative, which aims to train 75,000 peacekeepers, primarily in Africa, by 2010. This is a valuable program worth sustaining and extending, but it could also be used to give the UN better leverage over troop-contributing states whose troops commit crimes while on UN duty. The U.S. government should tie continued assistance under this and similar initiatives to recipients' demonstrated willingness to discipline troops who violate their own military codes of justice or UN standards of conduct while serving in UN operations.

- **Announce that the United States will expand its own capacity to contribute to the non-military elements of peace and stability operations.** This includes police personnel, political advisors, and civilian substantive experts who specialize, for example, in infrastructure repair, human rights, or de-mining. In the past two years, the US government has taken important steps toward the goal of building its non-military capabilities for stabilization and reconstruction. The next Administration should reinforce this nascent interagency process for recruiting, training, and deploying civilian personnel, acting on the knowledge that effective "transition and reconstruction" programs are the best exit strategy for peacekeepers—our own and everyone else's.

Lives and Leadership: Both on the Line

For nearly half a century, Washington was the recognized leader of the free world, earning that distinction by investing in and protecting the freedom of others. In the new century, as in the last, alternatives to western-style liberty and self rule are being offered to—or forced upon—peoples in Asia, Africa, Latin America, and the borderlands of Europe, especially in countries recently torn apart by war. Preserving liberty and fostering democracy among such countries is critical to America's interests. It is too big a job for any one country to shoulder alone, but by working with allies and institutions like the UN, we can share that burden and earn back the respect of the world.

POSTSCRIPT

Is UN Peacekeeping Seriously Flawed?

The year 2008 marked the 60th anniversary of UN peacekeeping operations. The first UN peacekeepers were sent to the Middle East to monitor the truce between Israel and the Arab countries in 1948, and during the next six decades, 62 more missions were created. These efforts drew more than 9 million troops, police, and other participants from 118 countries. More than 2,400 have been killed during UN service. With 20 missions underway and over 110,000 armed peacekeepers and supporting civilian staff in the field, 2008 was also a record year for the number of UN peacekeeping operations. The UN peacekeeping budget for 2008 was approximately $7 billion. The U.S. assessment according to the UN's formula based on national wealth was 26 percent of that total, or nearly $1.6 billion. However, despite a legal obligation under the UN Charter to pay, Congress caps the U.S. payment at 25 percent and often appropriates less than that. Furthermore, substantial arrears from over the years remain. There are some complaints about the size of the UN peacekeeping budget and the UN contribution. However, the UN peacekeeping budget for 2008 equaled only about 50 cents for every $100 dollars spent that year by countries of their own militaries. As for the U.S. contribution, even if fully funded it would have equaled only as much as Washington spends every 20 hours on the U.S. military.

UN peacekeeping also continues to struggle with the political realities that so often limit its effectiveness. As Issue 10 on Darfur indicates, getting a large enough force with enough weapons and other equipment and a scope of authority to make a difference has been hindered by numerous factors. The reluctance of China and Russia to vote for a large, well-equipped, substantially empowered force is one. The reluctance of countries to contribute troops, financial restraints, and other problems also persist. Although the Security Council in July 2007 authorized a UN force of 26,000 troops and police for Darfur to aid the African Union peacekeeping effort there, as of October 2008, only 11,000 troops and police had arrived. Equipment is especially hard to come by. The UN force is said to need 19 heavy lift helicopters. Not one has been offered by a member country.

What needs to be done continues to be the main UN peacekeeping issue. There are many proposals, but not the political will to implement them. The veto-related difficulty of getting Security Council agreement is one major hurdle, but neither the United States nor any of the other countries with a veto are are willing to give up their veto powers. A permanent UN force is another proposal, but few countries are willing to fund or permanently attach troop units to it. Whatever one thinks of UN peacekeeping, another issue is alternatives. If it is inadequate and substantial improvements are politically impossible, then what? Would the world be better off without UN peacekeepers?

To learn more, one "must" Web site is that of the UN's Department of Peacekeeping Operations at http://www.un.org/Depts/dpko/dpko/. A source of current research is *International Peacekeeping,* a journal published quarterly by Routledge. For Americans, the journal's 2008 symposium issue *The US Role in Contemporary Peace Operations: A Double-Edged Sword?* would be of special interest. Beginning in 2009, the annual, *International Peacekeeping: The Yearbook of International Peace Operations* published by Martinus Mijhoff was transformed into the quarterly *Journal of International Peacekeeping.* Two of the most recent scholarly books on this topic are Donald C. F. Daniel, Patricia Taft, and Sharon Wiharta, eds., *Peace Operations: Trends, Progress, and Prospects* (Georgetown University Press, 2008); and Virginia Page Fortna, *Does Peacekeeping Work?: Shaping Belligerents' Choices after Civil War* (Princeton University Press, 2008), which concludes that indeed peacekeeping does work.

ISSUE 17

Is U.S. Refusal to Join the International Criminal Court Wise?

YES: John R. Bolton, from "The United States and the International Criminal Court," Remarks to the Federalist Society (November 14, 2002)

NO: Jonathan F. Fanton, from "The Challenge of International Justice," Remarks to the U.S. Military Academy at West Point, New York (May 5, 2008)

ISSUE SUMMARY

YES: John R. Bolton, at the time U.S. Under Secretary State for Arms Control and International Security and beginning in 2005, U.S. Ambassador to the United Nations, explains why President George W. Bush had decided to reject membership in the International Criminal Court.

NO: Jonathan F. Fanton, president of the John D. and Catherine T. MacArthur Foundation, which is headquartered in Chicago, IL, and is among the world's largest independent foundations, maintains that creation of the International Court of Justice is an important step toward creating a more just world, and that the fear that many Americans have expressed about the court have not materialized.

Historically, international law has focused primarily on countries. More recently, individuals have increasingly become subject to international law. The first major step in this direction was the convening of the Nuremberg and Tokyo war crimes trials after World War II to try German and Japanese military and civilian leaders charged with various war crimes. There were no subsequent war crimes tribunals until the 1990s when the United Nations established two of them. One sits in The Hague, the Netherlands, and deals with the horrific events in Bosnia. The other tribunal is in Arusha, Tanzania, and provides justice for the genocidal massacres in Rwanda. These tribunals have indicted numerous people for war crimes and have convicted and imprisoned many of them. Nevertheless, there was a widespread feeling that such ad hoc tribunals needed to be replaced by a permanent international criminal tribunal.

In 1996, the UN convened a conference in Rome to do just that. At first the United States was supportive, but it favored a very limited court that could only prosecute and hear cases referred to it by the UN Security Council (where the United States had a veto) and, even then, could only try individuals with the permission of the defendant's home government. Most countries disagreed, but in 1998 the Rome conference voted overwhelmingly to create a relatively strong court. The Rome Statute of the International Criminal Court (ICC) gives the ICC jurisdiction over wars of aggression, genocide, and other crimes, but only if the home country of an alleged perpetrator fails to act.

Although the ICC treaty was open for signature in July 1998, President Bill Clinton showed either ambivalence or a desire not to have it injected as an issue into the 2000 presidential election by waiting until December 31, 2000 to have a U.S. official sign the treaty. If Clinton had his doubts, his successor, George W. Bush, did not. He was adamantly opposed to the treaty. As directed by the White House, State Department official John R. Bolton, the author of the first reading, sent a letter dated May 6, 2002 to UN Secretary General Kofi Annan informing him that "in connection with the Rome Statute of the International Criminal Court . . . , the United States does not intend to become a party to the treaty . . . [and] has no legal obligations arising from its signature on December 31, 2000." The Bush administration also launched an effort to persuade other countries to sign "Article 98" agreements by which countries agree not to surrender U.S. citizens to the ICC.

This letter formally notifying the UN that the United States does not intend to become a party to the Rome Statute also ended any U.S. participation in the workings of the court. In the first reading, Bolton explains just a few months after his letter to the UN why the Bush administration had decided to reject the ICC treaty. The U.S. position did not, however, prevent the ICC from coming into being. That occurred soon after Bolton's letter, when upon ratification by the 60th country, the treaty went into effect on July 1, 2002. Since then, the ICC has begun to function, and in the second reading Jonathan F. Fanton reviews the evolution of the ICC and says he is convinced that the United States and its armed forces have nothing to fear from the ICC and much to both offer to and gain from its success.

YES

John R. Bolton

The United States and the International Criminal Court

I've been asked to [make] remarks about the pressures of national security on American government. With this in mind, I'd like to address the topic of the International Criminal Court [ICC] and detail our [the Bush administration's] reasons for opposing it. As I will explain, the problems inherent in the ICC are more than abstract legal issues—they are matters that touch directly on our national security and our national interests.

For a number of reasons, the United States decided that the ICC had unacceptable consequences for our national sovereignty. Specifically, the ICC is an organization whose precepts go against fundamental American notions of sovereignty, checks and balances, and national independence. It is an agreement that is harmful to the national interests of the United States, and harmful to our presence abroad.

U.S. military forces and civilian personnel and private citizens are currently active in peacekeeping and humanitarian missions in almost 100 countries at any given time. It is essential that we remain steadfast in preserving the independence and flexibility that America needs to defend our national interests around the world. As President Bush said,

> The United States cooperates with many other nations to keep the peace, but we will not submit American troops to prosecutors and judges whose jurisdiction we do not accept. . . . Every person who serves under the American flag will answer to his or her own superiors and to military law, not to the rulings of an unaccountable International Criminal Court.

So in order to protect our citizens, we are in the process of negotiating bilateral agreements with the largest possible number of states, including non-Parties [to the ICC Treaty: countries that have not ratified it]. These Article 98 agreements, as they are called, provide American citizens with essential protection against the Court's purported jurisdiction claims, and allow us to remain engaged internationally with our friends and allies. To date, 14 countries have signed Article 98 agreements with us. It is a misconception that the United States wants to use these Article 98 agreements to undermine the ICC. To the contrary, we are determined to work with States Parties, utilizing a mechanism prescribed within the Rome Statute itself, to find an acceptable solution to one of the main problems posed by the ICC.

From Remarks to the Federalist Society by John R. Bolton, November 14, 2002.

In the eyes of its supporters, the ICC is simply an overdue addition to the family of international organizations, an evolutionary step ahead of the Nuremberg tribunal, and the next logical institutional development over the ad hoc war crimes courts for the Former Yugoslavia and Rwanda. The Statute of Rome establishes both substantive principles of international law and creates new institutions and procedures to adjudicate these principles. The Statute confers jurisdiction on the ICC over four crimes: genocide, crimes against humanity, war crimes, and the crime of aggression. The Court's jurisdiction is "automatic," applicable to covered individuals accused of crimes under the Statute regardless of whether their governments have ratified it or consent to such jurisdiction. Particularly important is the independent Prosecutor, who is responsible for conducting investigations and prosecutions before the Court. The Prosecutor may initiate investigations based on referrals by States Parties, or on the basis of information that he or she otherwise obtains.

So described, one might assume that the ICC is simply a further step in the orderly march toward the peaceful settlement of international disputes, sought since time immemorial. But in several respects, the court is poised to assert authority over nation states, and to promote its prosecution over alternative methods for dealing with the worst criminal offenses.

The Court's flaws are basically two-fold, substantive, and structural. As to the former, the ICC's authority is vague and excessively elastic, and the Court's discretion ranges far beyond normal or acceptable judicial responsibilities, giving it broad and unacceptable powers of interpretation that are essentially political and legislative in nature. This is most emphatically *not* a Court of limited jurisdiction. Crimes can be added subsequently that go beyond those included in the Rome Statute. Parties to the Statute are subject to these subsequently-added crimes only if they affirmatively accept them, but the Statute purports automatically to bind non-parties, such as the United States, to any such new crimes. It is neither reasonable nor fair that these crimes would apply to a greater extent to states that have not agreed to the terms of the Rome Statute than to those that have.

Numerous prospective "crimes" were suggested at Rome and commanded wide support from participating nations, such as the crime of "aggression," which was included in the Statute, but not defined. Although frequently easy to identify, "aggression" can at times be something in the eye of the beholder. For example, Israel justifiably feared in Rome that certain actions, such as its initial use of force in the Six Day War, would be perceived as illegitimate preemptive strikes that almost certainly would have provoked proceedings against top Israeli officials. Moreover, there seems little doubt that Israel will be the target of a complaint in the ICC concerning conditions and practices by the Israeli military in the West Bank and Gaza. Israel recently decided to declare its intention not to become a party to the ICC or to be bound by the Statute's obligations.

A fair reading of the treaty leaves one unable to answer with confidence whether the United States would now be accused of war crimes for legitimate but controversial uses of force to protect world peace. No U.S. Presidents or their advisors could be assured that they would be unequivocally safe from politicized charges of criminal liability.

As troubling as the ICC's substantive and jurisdictional problems are, the problems raised by the Statute's main structures—the Court and the Prosecutor—are still worse. The ICC does not, and cannot, fit into a coherent, international structural "constitutional" design that delineates clearly how laws are made, adjudicated or enforced, subject to popular accountability and structured to protect liberty. There is no such design, nor should there be. Instead, the Court and the Prosecutor are simply "out there" in the international system. Requiring the United States to be bound by this treaty, with its unaccountable Prosecutor and its unchecked judicial power, is clearly inconsistent with American standards of constitutionalism. This is a macro-constitutional issue for us, not simply a narrow, technical point of law.

We are considering, in the Prosecutor, a powerful and necessary element of executive power, the power of law-enforcement. Never before has the United States been asked to place any of that power outside the complete control of our national government without our consent. Our concern goes beyond the possibility that the Prosecutor will target for indictment the isolated U.S. soldier who violates our own laws and values by allegedly committing a war crime. Our principal concern is for our country's top civilian and military leaders, those responsible for our defense and foreign policy. They are the ones potentially at risk at the hands of the ICC's politically unaccountable Prosecutor, as part of an agenda to restrain American discretion, even when our actions are legitimated by the operation of our own constitutional system.

Unfortunately, the United States has had considerable experience in the past two decades with domestic "independent counsels," and that history argues overwhelmingly against international repetition. Simply launching massive criminal investigations has an enormous political impact. Although subsequent indictments and convictions are unquestionably more serious, a zealous independent Prosecutor can make dramatic news just by calling witnesses and gathering documents, without ever bringing formal charges.

Indeed, the supposed "independence" of the Prosecutor and the Court from "political" pressures (such as the Security Council) is more a source of concern than an element of protection. "Independent" bodies in the UN system have often proven themselves more highly politicized than some of the explicitly political organs. True political accountability, by contrast, is almost totally absent from the ICC.

The American concept of separation of powers, imperfect though it is, reflects our settled belief that liberty is best protected when the various authorities legitimately exercised by government are, to the maximum extent possible, placed in separate branches. So structuring the national government, the Framers believed, would prevent the excessive accumulation of power in a limited number of hands, thus providing the greatest protection for individual liberty. Continental European constitutional structures do not, by and large, reflect a similar set of beliefs. They do not so thoroughly separate judicial from executive powers, just as their parliamentary systems do not so thoroughly separate executive from legislative powers. That, of course, is entirely Europe's prerogative, and may help to explain why Europeans appear to be more comfortable with the ICC's structure, which closely melds prosecutorial and judicial functions in the European fashion.

In addition, our Constitution provides that the discharge of executive authority will be rendered accountable to the citizenry in two ways. First, the law-enforcement power is exercised through an elected President. The President is constitutionally charged with the responsibility to "take Care that the Laws be faithfully executed," and the constitutional authority of the actual law-enforcers stems directly from the only elected executive official. Second, Congress, all of whose members are popularly elected, through its statute-making authority, its confirmation authority and through the appropriations process, exercises significant influence and oversight. When necessary, the congressional impeachment power serves as the ultimate safeguard.

In the ICC's central structures, the Court and Prosecutor, these sorts of political checks are either greatly attenuated or entirely absent. They are effectively accountable to no one. The Prosecutor will answer to no superior executive power, elected or unelected. Nor is there any legislature anywhere in sight, elected or unelected, in the Statute of Rome. The Prosecutor is answerable only to the Court, and then only partially, although the Prosecutor may be removed by the Assembly of States Parties. The Europeans may be comfortable with such a system, but Americans are not.

By long-standing American principles, the ICC's structure utterly fails to provide sufficient accountability to warrant vesting the Prosecutor with the Statute's enormous power of law enforcement. Political accountability is utterly different from "politicization," which we can all agree should form no part of the decisions of either Prosecutor or Court. Today, however, precisely contrary to the proper alignment, the ICC has almost no political accountability, *and* carries an enormous risk of politicization. Even at this early stage in the Court's existence, there are concerns that its judicial nomination process is being influenced by quota systems and back-room deals.

Under the UN Charter, the Security Council has primary responsibility for the maintenance of international peace and security. The ICC's efforts could easily conflict with the Council's work. Indeed, the Statute of Rome substantially minimized the Security Council's role in ICC affairs. While the Security Council may refer matters to the ICC, or order it to refrain from commencing or proceeding with an investigation or prosecution, the Council is precluded from a meaningful role in the ICC's work. In requiring an affirmative Council vote to *stop* a case, the Statute shifts the balance of authority from the Council to the ICC. Moreover, a veto by a Permanent Member of such a restraining Council resolution leaves the ICC completely unsupervised. This attempted marginalization of the Security Council is a fundamental *new* problem created by the ICC that will have a tangible and highly detrimental impact on the conduct of U.S. foreign policy. The Council now risks having the ICC interfering in its ongoing work, with all of the attendant confusion between the appropriate roles of law, politics, and power in settling international disputes. The Council already has had to take action to dilute the disincentive the ICC poses to nations considering troop contributions to UN-related peacekeeping operations.

Paradoxically, the danger of the ICC may lie in its potential weakness rather than its potential strength. The most basic error is the belief that the

ICC will have a substantial deterrent effect against the perpetration of crimes against humanity. Behind their optimistic rhetoric, ICC proponents have not a shred of evidence supporting their deterrence theories. In fact, they fundamentally confuse the appropriate roles of political and economic power, diplomatic efforts, military force, and legal procedures. Recent history is filled with cases where even strong military force or the threat of force failed to deter aggression or gross abuses of human rights. ICC proponents concede as much when they cite cases where the "world community" has failed to pay adequate attention, or failed to intervene in time to prevent genocide or other crimes against humanity. The new Court and Prosecutor, it is said, will now guarantee against similar failures.

But deterrence ultimately depends on perceived effectiveness, and the ICC fails badly on that point. The ICC's authority is far too attenuated to make the slightest bit of difference either to the war criminals or to the outside world. In cases where the West in particular has been unwilling to intervene militarily to prevent crimes against humanity as they were happening, why will a potential perpetrator feel deterred by the mere possibility of future legal action? A weak and distant Court will have no deterrent effect on the hard men like Pol Pot most likely to commit crimes against humanity. Why should anyone imagine that bewigged judges in The Hague will succeed where cold steel has failed? Holding out the prospect of ICC deterrence to the weak and vulnerable amounts to a cruel joke.

Beyond the issue of deterrence, it is by no means clear that "justice" as defined by the Court and Prosecutor is always consistent with the attainable political resolution of serious political and military disputes. It may be, or it may not be. Human conflict teaches that, much to the dismay of moralists and legal theoreticians, mortal policy makers often must make tradeoffs among inconsistent objectives. This can be a painful and unpleasant realization, confronting us as it does with the irritating facts of human complexity, contradiction, and imperfection.

Accumulated experience strongly favors a case-by-case approach, politically and legally, rather than the inevitable resort to adjudication. Circumstances differ, and circumstances matter. Atrocities, whether in international wars or in domestic contexts, are by definition uniquely horrible in their own times and places.

For precisely that reason, so too are their resolutions unique. When the time arrives to consider the crimes, that time usually coincides with events of enormous social and political significance: negotiation of a peace treaty, restoration of a "legitimate" political regime, or a similar milestone. At such momentous times, the crucial issues typically transcend those of administering justice to those who committed heinous crimes during the preceding turbulence. The pivotal questions are clearly political, not legal: How shall the formerly warring parties live with each other in the future? What efforts shall be taken to expunge the causes of the previous inhumanity? Can the truth of what actually happened be established so that succeeding generations do not make the same mistakes?

One alternative to the ICC is the kind of Truth and Reconciliation Commission created in South Africa. In the aftermath of apartheid, the new government faced the difficult task of establishing and legitimizing truly democratic governmental institutions while dealing simultaneously with earlier crimes. One option was widespread prosecutions against the perpetrators of human rights abuses, but the new government chose a different model. Under the Commission's charter, alleged offenders came before it and confessed past misdeeds. Assuming they confessed truthfully, the Commission in effect pardoned them from prosecution.

This approach was intended to make public more of the truth of the apartheid regime in the most credible fashion, to elicit admissions of guilt, and then to permit society to move ahead without the prolonged opening of old wounds that trials, appeals, and endless recriminations might bring.

I do not argue that the South African approach should be followed everywhere, or even necessarily that it was correct for South Africa. But it is certainly fair to conclude that that approach is radically different from the ICC, which operates through vindication, punishment, and retribution.

It may be that, in some disputes, neither retribution nor complete truth-telling is the desired outcome. In many former Communist countries, citizens are still wrestling with the handling of secret police activities of the now-defunct regimes. So extensive was the informing, spying, and compromising in some societies that a tacit decision was made that the complete opening of secret police and Communist Party files will either not occur, or will happen with exquisite slowness over a very long period. In effect, these societies have chosen "amnesia" because it is simply too difficult for them to sort out relative degrees of past wrongs, and because of their desire to move ahead.

One need not agree with these decisions to respect the complexity of the moral and political problems they address. Only those completely certain of their own moral standing, and utterly confident in their ability to judge the conduct of others in excruciating circumstances can reject the amnesia alternative out of hand. Invariably insisting on international adjudication is not necessarily preferable to a course that the parties to a dispute might themselves agree upon. Indeed, with a permanent ICC, one can predict that one or more disputants might well invoke its jurisdiction at a selfishly opportune moment, and thus, ironically, make an ultimate settlement of their dispute more complicated or less likely.

Another alternative, of course, is for the parties themselves to try their own alleged war criminals. Indeed, there are substantial arguments that the fullest cathartic impact of the prosecutorial approach to war crimes occurs when the responsible population itself comes to grips with its past and administers appropriate justice. The Rome Statute pays lip service to the doctrine of "complementarity," or deference to national judicial systems, but this is simply an assertion, unproven and untested. It is *within* national judicial systems where the international effort should be to encourage the warring parties to resolve questions of criminality as part of a comprehensive solution to their disagreements. Removing key elements of the dispute to a distant forum, especially the emotional and contentious issues of war crimes and crimes against humanity, undercuts the very progress that these peoples, victims and perpetrators alike, must make if they are ever to live peacefully together.

In the absence of the means or political will to address grave violations, the United States has supported the establishment and operation of ad hoc tribunals such as those in Yugoslavia and Rwanda. Unlike the ICC, these are created and overseen by the UN Security Council, under a UN Charter to which virtually all nations have agreed.

As the ICC comes into being, we will address our concerns about the ICC's jurisdictional claims using the remedy laid out for us by the Rome Statute itself and the UN Security Council in the case of the peacekeeping force in the former Yugoslavia. Using Article 98 of the Rome Statute as a basis, we are negotiating bilateral, legally-binding agreements with individual States Parties to protect our citizens from being handed over to the Court. Since the European Union's decision in September to permit its member states to conclude Article 98 agreements with the United States, our negotiators have been engaged in bilateral discussions with several EU countries. In the near future we will also be holding discussions on the issue with several countries in the Middle East and South Asia. Our ultimate goal is to conclude Article 98 agreements with every country in the world, regardless of whether they have signed or ratified the ICC, regardless of whether they intend to in the future. These agreements will allow us the necessary protections in a manner that is legally permissible and consistent with the letter and spirit of the Rome Statute.

In order to promote justice worldwide, the United States has many foreign policy instruments to utilize that are fully consistent with our values and interests. We will continue to play a worldwide leadership role in strengthening domestic judicial systems and promoting freedom, transparency and the rule of law. As Secretary Powell has said:

We are the leader in the world with respect to bringing people to justice. We have supported a tribunal for Yugoslavia, the tribunal for Rwanda, trying to get the tribunal for Sierra Leone set up. We have the highest standards of accountability of any nation on the face of the earth.

It is important to note that we are not seeking immunity for our citizens, but a simple, non-surrender agreement as contemplated in the Rome Statute. We fully commit ourselves to, where appropriate, investigate and prosecute serious, credible allegations of war crimes, crimes against humanity and genocide that have been made against any of our people.

We respect the decision of States Parties to join the ICC, but they in turn must respect our decision not to be bound by jurisdictional claims to which we have not consented. As President Bush stated in his National Security Strategy,

We will take the actions necessary to ensure that our efforts to meet our global security commitments and protect Americans are not impaired by the potential for investigations, inquiry, or prosecution by the International Criminal Court, whose jurisdiction does not extend to Americans and which we do not accept.

Signatories of the Statute of Rome have created an ICC to their liking, and they should live with it. The United States did not agree to be bound, and must not be held to its terms.

Jonathan F. Fanton

 **NO**

The Challenge of International Justice

I am glad to be here at the U.S. Military Academy, an institution deeply woven into the fabric of this country's history. In 1902, President Theodore Roosevelt said, "No other educational institution in the land has contributed as many names as West Point to the honor roll of the nation's greatest citizens." After more than a century, that statement remains true – a compelling testimony to the enduring value of the Academy and its high ideals.

The John D. and Catherine T. MacArthur Foundation, has a shorter tradition: we were established in 1978. . . . With an endowment of $6.5 billion, MacArthur will give $300 million in grants and program-related investments to individuals and organizations in the U.S. and abroad this year. . . . The Foundation aims to help build a more just, peaceful, and sustainable world. We do so through sponsoring research, educating the public, and supporting organizations that work in fields that range from conservation to international nuclear disarmament, from renewing America's cities to creating high-quality documentaries for public television. In 2006, we made a grant that was unusual for us – $750,000 to West Point's Program in Conflict and Human Security Studies to support coursework and overseas cadet internships with non-governmental organizations (or NGOs).

I have been impressed by the content and quality of the courses offered in Conflict and Human Security Studies – such as "International Conflict and Negotiation," "Winning the Peace," and "International Security Strategy." The breadth of their approach, their awareness of the human dimension of conflict and restoring peace are impressive and encouraging. . . .

There is no shortage of NGOs with which to work – by one count, there are already five million of them, and new organizations are founded each year. The vision and engagement of these groups – together, called "civil society" – is helping to change the world for the better. Many of them concentrate on issues of human rights, justice for all citizens, and the rule of law – causes MacArthur has supported from our very first grant, which went to Amnesty International.

We fund large organizations that monitor abuses around the world, like Human Rights Watch, and small local institutions that tackle issues like child marriage in India, police abuse in Russia, and the rights of prisoners in Nigeria.

MacArthur holds passionately that individuals everywhere have intrinsic rights that should be enshrined in law and defended by due process. The U.S.

Speech by Jonathan F. Fanton, December 10, 2007. Copyright © 2007 by John D. and Catherine T. MacArthur Foundation. Reprinted by permission. http://www.macfound.org

has a Bill of Rights and courts that are responsive to wronged individuals, other countries have similarly clear and effective justice systems – but many nations do not.

Where are individuals to turn when they are denied freedom of speech, beaten by the police, subjected to harsh discrimination, or forcibly conscripted into rebel armies and there are no independent national courts to hear them? And how is the world to deal with genocide, war crimes, and the brutal acts called "crimes against humanity?"

MacArthur believes that the answer lies in an international system of justice that will supplement unresponsive local courts and provide a forum for those who have suffered the worst abuses. The international community has courts for other purposes, for example the International Court of Justice, International Tribunal for the Law of the Sea, or Dispute Settlement System of the World Trade Organization. These bodies have been functioning over many decades and are central to international relations.

But the time has come to develop an international system of justice with the International Criminal Court as the centerpiece. Let me describe the evolution and objectives of this movement.

The first Geneva Conventions of 1864 and the Hague Conventions of 1899 serve as the foundations for modern attempts to stop wartime atrocities. Tribunals for war crimes were proposed, but not effectively implemented, after WWI. The Nuremberg and Far East tribunals after WWII tried and convicted the most prominent Axis leaders, at last holding individuals accountable for their criminal acts – even when following orders.

The WWII tribunals were possible because there was international consensus among the Allied powers. The Cold War ended that consensus. Only when the Soviet Union had collapsed was there a new impetus toward establishing an international system of criminal justice, prompted by the disintegration of Yugoslavia and the infamous "ethnic cleansing" that followed.

NGOs, human rights activists, and diplomats called for a forum to deal specifically with such crimes against humanity when national systems failed to do so. The UN Security Council responded, establishing an ad hoc Criminal Tribunal for Yugoslavia in 1993 and another in response to the Rwandan genocide in 1994.

The results were encouraging. [President] Slobodan Milosovic of Serbia was the first sitting head of state ever indicted; Jean Kambanda, former prime minister of Rwanda, faced charges of genocide, pled guilty, and is now serving a life sentence in Mali. With trials and appeals continuing, 239 people have been indicted and 78 convicted so far. New tribunals are now at work dealing with the atrocities committed in Sierra Leone's civil war and Cambodia's "killing fields."

The early tribunals helped establish the feasibility of a permanent International Criminal Court (ICC). In 1989, preparation and drafting had begun for a Statute that would establish such a Court; it was completed in 1998 and is commonly called "the Rome Statute." States were asked to ratify the Statute individually; by 2002 the required 60 had done so, allowing the Court to have jurisdiction. To date, 106 countries have ratified and joined the Court; the United States has not.

The Court, based in The Hague, is permanent and independent, dedicated to prosecuting only the most serious crimes against humanity. It has jurisdiction over acts committed on the territory, or by nationals, of States Party to the Statute. Also, the UN Security Council may refer a situation to the Court, regardless of the nationality of the accused or the location of their crimes.

The ICC is a "court of last resort," which means that it has authority only when national courts are unable or unwilling to act. All member nations retain the primary right and responsibility to investigate their own citizens – the principle of complementarity, which the U.S. helped embed in the Treaty.

How is the Court performing so far? It issued warrants, beginning in 2005, against Joseph Kony, head of the Lord's Resistance Army in Uganda, for the murder and torture of civilians; against Thomas Lubanga, leader of the UPF militia in the Democratic Republic of the Congo, for kidnapping children to become soldiers; and against Ahmad Mohammad Harun, formerly Sudan's Minister of State for the Interior, and Ali Kushayb, leader of the Janjaweed militia, for their crimes in Darfur – the forced displacement of millions, and a campaign of terror including abduction, rape, and murder.

Lubanga is in custody and his trial expected to begin in June. It will be the first in the Court's history. Two other militia leaders from the Congo are also in The Hague awaiting trial.

The two other cases exemplify the problems of international justice in practice. Joseph Kony of Uganda is still at large and his rebel movement active. The government of Sudan has no incentive to turn over either Kushayb or Harun. Indeed, it has appointed Harun Minister of Humanitarian Affairs, responsible for hearing human rights complaints from the victims of Darfur.

Unless the international community is prepared to act on the Court's warrants, it cannot be effective. More needs to be done to establish responsibility for apprehending and arresting those charged.

There has been debate about whether the threat of prosecution will be an obstacle in negotiating settlements to violent situations. Leaders who fear indictment, it is argued, will be less likely to relinquish power or end conflicts. This is a valid concern. A 2006 peace accord between the Lord's Resistance Army and the Ugandan government rejected the LRA's demand for amnesty. This may explain why Joseph Kony did not appear to sign the treaty earlier this month. But peace and justice, I believe, complement and reinforce one another. Societies that have been torn apart by atrocities are unlikely to heal unless there is resolution for those who have been harmed and some penalty for the perpetrators.

There is evidence also that the Court has a deterrent effect. In late 2004, there was a wave of violence in Côte d'Ivoire, accompanied by radio broadcasts of hate speech reminiscent of the Rwandan genocide. Juan Mendez, the UN's Special Adviser on the Prevention of Genocide, wrote to remind the Security Council that the ICC has jurisdiction over acts that may lead to crimes against humanity. His intervention was widely reported, and the message was heard in Côte d'Ivoire: the hate speech and threats subsided.

I should note that, while the ICC is the centerpiece of the system of international justice, there are other venues for ordinary people to seek redress when they have exhausted remedies in their own countries.

Regional human rights courts and commissions for Africa, Latin America, and Europe deal with cases that range from freedom of speech to discrimination to police brutality. Often, the courts' decisions have the effect of compelling countries to recognize rights that exist under their own laws or in international treaties they have signed. At present, 80,000 such cases from 70 nations are pending. Perhaps the most significant contribution of the regional courts and the ICC will be strengthening national courts and bringing national laws up to international standards.

So far, MacArthur's staff has been impressed with the early record of the ICC, but the Court is not without its critics. The U.S., as I have noted, is not party to the Rome Statute. This broke with America's record of leading the way in international justice since the Nuremberg and Far East tribunals. The U.S. actively supported the tribunals for the former Yugoslavia, Rwanda, and Sierra Leone and assisted in drafting the Rome Statute. But fears that membership in the ICC would expose Americans to politically-motivated cases have persuaded two successive administrations not to ratify.

Opponents of the Court also object that the Rome Statute impinges on U.S. sovereignty, that it overrides the Constitutional due-process protections afforded to U.S. citizens, and that it would limit America's ability to operate abroad – even in joint humanitarian operations.

So far, those fears have not materialized. And I do not believe they are likely to. ICC procedures have all the same due-process protections as U.S. courts, except that of trial by jury. And the Court has been rigorous in pursuing only those cases that are sufficiently grave and over which it clearly has jurisdiction. The Court has received almost 3,000 communications from 140 nations. The vast majority has been rejected outright, only four investigations have been opened by the Prosecutor, and all charges involving Americans have been dismissed.

The Court would certainly be stronger if the U.S. were a member. American legal expertise would strengthen the early cases and shape the Court's future jurisprudence; American intelligence agencies could provide evidence to ensure successful prosecutions.

Many in the U.S. military have concerns about the ICC. In 2006, MacArthur sponsored the Stimson Center to survey and assess how professional officers, some from the military justice system, perceived the Court and its impact.

Stimson found a range of opinion – much of it positive, some strongly negative – but also that many officers knew little about the Court or the Rome Statute. The most common objections were that the Court "second-guessed" decisions taken in action that were thought to fall within the rules of combat, that American service personnel would be unfairly targeted when abroad, that ignorance of the provisions of the Rome Statute would lead to inadvertent infractions, and that field operations and military alliances would be hampered by further layers of legal restrictions. Others felt the Court would simply be ineffective, unable to bring criminals to justice.

Specific problems were cited: Would the U.S.'s deployment of cluster bombs and landmines, outlawed by the 140 countries party to the Ottawa Convention, give grounds for prosecution? Would decisions taken on faulty intelligence, such as the accidental bombing of the Chinese Embassy in Belgrade in 1999, make officers liable?

Officers with legal expertise pointed out gaps between U.S. domestic law and the Uniform Code of Military Justice and the Rome Statute, which they saw opening the possibility of prosecution for offences that were unclearly defined, or not addressed at all, in American legislation.

These are cogent objections, but I believe they are not insurmountable. Most of the acts prohibited by the Rome Statute are already illegal under U.S. military and civilian codes; where there are gaps or more clarity is needed, further legal work could harmonize the legislation and sharpen definitions. A simple program of education would give service personnel adequate working knowledge of the Statute. As there are few areas in which the Statute differs from existing U.S. codes, there would be little practical difference in field operations.

The specific objections may be met by noting that the use of certain weapons and specific operational decisions do not come under the remit of the Court, whose role is to deal with only the most egregious crimes. If the U.S. joined the Court, the principle of complementarity requires that its military personnel charged with misconduct would be subject to existing U.S. laws and procedures, which are robust and high-functioning.

It is worth noting that, between 2003 and 2006, the Prosecutor received almost 250 submissions related to the conflict in Iraq, the majority concerned with military operations by U.S. and allied troops. In his 2006 response, Prosecutor Luis Moreno Ocampo declined to pursue any of them further, ruling that the Court had no jurisdiction in most cases, that the individual instances did not rise to the level of gravity required, and that there were adequate national judicial systems in place to deal with the alleged offences.

Most of those who participated in the Stimson project supported the overall goals of the Court as being consistent with fundamental American values and the legal standards to which U.S. military personnel are already held. Some also saw the advantages for U.S. personnel of an international court that would strengthen the rule of law within countries that, in the past, would have ignored international standards altogether.

The ICC is arguably the most important new international institution since the founding of the United Nations itself. It is destined to have a considerable and lasting impact on how justice and human rights are defined and enforced. I urge you to acquaint yourselves with the Court, to investigate how it works, and to debate its future. How do you, as citizens, evaluate America's relationship to the ICC? How should your training, and your conduct in operations, take account of the Court's mission to protect the world's most vulnerable people and bring perpetrators of atrocities to justice?

MacArthur will continue to educate the public about the Court, fund groups that further its work, and support an integrated system of international justice. We are convinced that America and its armed forces have nothing to fear from such a system, and much to offer to its success. And we are sure that lively and free-ranging discussion of the issues involved will help build a consensus that the world needs clear, universal, and humane standards of justice for all.

POSTSCRIPT

Is U.S. Refusal to Join the International Criminal Court Wise?

With the ICC treaty in effect, the countries that were a party to it met in 2003 and elected the court's 18 judges and its chief prosecutor. The following year the ICC began operations at its seat in The Hague, the Netherlands. Soon thereafter, the ICC prosecutor launched several investigations, mostly focusing on conflicts in central Africa and in the Darfur region of Sudan in northeast Africa. As of late 2008, the ICC indicted nine individuals from Sudan, Uganda, the Democratic Republic of the Congo, and the Central African Republic and had four in custody awaiting trial. Most significantly, the ICC's chief prosecutor, Luis Moreno-Ocampo of Argentina, asked the court in July 2008 to approve the indictment of President Omar al-Bashir of Sudan for 10 counts of genocide, war crimes, and crimes against humanity. The move to indict a sitting head of state was supported by many but also set off a storm of protest. Some believed that the effort to indict Bashir would complicate the search for a solution in Darfur. Others worried about the ICC's focus on Africa. As of October 2008, the judges of the ICC had not decided on Moreno-Ocampo's request for the indictment. The Web site of the ICC at http://www.icc-cpi.int/ is an excellent source of information about its organization, personnel, and activities.

As of October 2008, 108 countries had formally agreed to the Rome Statute and joined the Assembly of State Parties that constitutes the ICC's governing board. Most of the major countries of Western Europe, Africa, and South and Central America are now parties to the ICC, as are Canada and Japan. China, Russia, India, Iran, Israel, and most of the Arab countries are among the prominent nonadherents. The United States has also remained among the absent. It is unlikely that will change quickly, even with the new president beginning term in January 2009. Barack Obama has expressed a guardedly positive attitude toward the ICC, advocating greater cooperation but also saying that much greater protections for U.S. troops abroad would have to be guaranteed before they would support U.S. ratification of the Rome treaty. A way to begin learning more about the ICC is by reading William A. Schabas, *An Introduction to the International Criminal Court* (Cambridge University Press, 2007). Excellent as a general resource is *Journal of International Criminal Justice,* pubished quarterly. On U.S. policy, read the Congressional Research Service report, "U.S. Policy Regarding the International Criminal Court" (June 14, 2006) on the Web at http://fpc.state.gov/documents/organization/68799.pdf. An article critical of U.S. policy is Robert C. Johansen, "The Impact of U.S. Policy toward the International Criminal Court on the Prevention of Genocide, War Crimes, and Crimes Against Humanity," *Human Rights Quarterly* (May 2006). Taking a more skeptical view is Helena Cobban, "International Courts," *Foreign Policy* (April 2006).

Whatever the new U.S. president thinks or wants, American sensitivity to U.S. sovereignty and to the image of an American being tried by an international court will make adherence to the ICC treaty very controversial. When asked a general question about an international criminal court to try war criminals if their home country would not do so, 71 percent of Americans thought the United States should participate. However, a poll that asked Americans "Should the International Criminal Court be allowed to try United States soldiers accused of war crimes if the United States government refuses to try them?" found 50 percent of the respondents replying no, compared with 37 percent saying yes, and 12 percent being unsure.

ISSUE 18

Has the U.S. Detention and Trial of Accused Foreign Terrorists Been Legally Unsound?

YES: Kate Martin, from Testimony during Hearings on "How the Administration's Failed Detainee Policies Have Hurt the Fight against Terrorism: Putting the Fight against Terrorism on Sound Legal Foundations," before the Committee on the Judiciary, U.S. Senate (July 16, 2008)

NO: David B. Rivkin, from Testimony during Hearings on "How the Administration's Failed Detainee Policies Have Hurt the Fight against Terrorism: Putting the Fight against Terrorism on Sound Legal Foundations," before the Committee on the Judiciary, U.S. Senate (July 16, 2008)

ISSUE SUMMARY

YES: Kate Martin, director of the Center for National Security Studies, criticizes what she describes as extraordinary and unsupportable claims by the executive branch that the president is free to ignore statutory law and violate civil rights in order to conduct the war against terror. She also notes that the president's stand has been repeatedly rejected by the courts.

NO: David B. Rivkin, a partner in the law firm of Baker & Hostetler and former deputy director of the Office of Policy Development, U.S. Department of Justice, contends that while some aspects of the treatment of accused foreign terrorists in U.S. custody have not met the civil liberties standards normally enjoyed by Americans, the Bush administration's policies have been indispensable in protecting Americans during the war on terrorism and that the administration's legal positions have generally been upheld by the courts.

U nder the U.S. constitution, citizens and foreigners alike accused of crimes generally have a wide range of protections under the Fourth, Fifth, Sixth, and Eighth Amendments. For prisoners of war, including members of irregular forces, such as guerillas, treatment is governed by four Geneva Conventions (1864, 1929, 1949, and 1949). The United States, like most countries, is a party to these treaties.

The question here is whether and to what degree should the Constitution and the Geneva Conventions apply to foreign terrorists. While this issue is not wholly new, it came into sharp focus in relation to alleged members of al Qaeda captured by the United States in Afghanistan and elsewhere and held largely at the U.S. naval base at Guantánamo Bay, Cuba. The Bush administration eventually classified them "enemy combatants," on the grounds that they were not members of an organized military. Therefore, the administration held that these prisoners would be tried by special military commissions created by the presidents and were not protected by either the Constitution or the Geneva Conventions. As such, the detainees did not, for example, have the right to be given a speedy trial, to always see the evidence against them, or to have a lawyer; and they were subject to coercion to provide incriminating evidence. These issues have come to a head in three cases that have reached the U.S. Supreme Court. The cases and the court's rulings are:

Rasul v. Bush (2004): Shafiq Rasul, a British citizen captured in Afghanistan by U.S. forces and Guantánamo Bay sough a writ of habeas corpus. The Bush administration argued that since Guantánamo Bay was outside the United States, the federal courts had no jurisdiction. The court rejected this argument.

Hamdan v. Rumsfeld (2006): Salim Ahmed Hamdan of Yemen and another alleged al Qaeda fighter captured in Afghanistan sued in U.S. court challenging the legality of trying him before a military commission established by the president rather than a law enacted by Congress. The Supreme Court ruled for him, finding that the president had no authority to unilaterally create special military courts. Subsequently, Congress passed the Military Commissions Act (2005), a law setting up special procedures for the treatment of Hamdan-like prisoners.

Boumediene v. Bush (2008): Lakhdar Boumediene, a Bosnian citizen seized in Bosnia and accused of being part of an al Qaeda plot to bomb the U.S. embassy there, sought a writ of habeas corpus arguing that the limits for habeas corpus under the MCA and some of the acts restrictions on access to evidence and other normal rights of the accused were unconstitutional. For the third time, the Bush administration lost in the Supreme Court.

It is possible to conclude, as Kate Martin does in the first reading, that the courts have thoroughly disagreed with the legal treatment given to accused foreign terrorists by the Bush administrations 0 and 3 record (0 and 4 if *Hamdi v. Rumsfeld* (2004) granting habeas corpus rights to U.S. citizens held as an "enemy combatant" is included). However, it is also the case that the court's rulings have been fairly narrow. None of the decisions ordered a prisoner released; not did any of them say that enemy combatants had to be tried in civilian courts or by normal military courts-martial with all the constitutional rights those courts ensure. This leads David B. Rivkin to argue in the second reading that the Bush administration's policy was on reasonable legal footing.

YES

Kate Martin

How the Administration's Failed Detainee Policies Have Hurt the Fight against Terrorism: Putting the Fight against Terrorism on Sound Legal Foundations

Introduction

After the terrible attacks of September 11, the international community was united in its support for the United States and condemnation of the attacks. Since then, however, the United States has lost much of the goodwill and cooperation of the international community as a result of its flawed detention policies. We welcome this committee's examination of how these failed detention policies have hurt, rather than advanced the national security and what needs to be done now to put detention policy on a sound legal footing consistent with national security interests.

As this committee is well aware, since 2001, the Executive Branch has advanced extraordinary and unsupportable claims that the President is free to ignore and even violate established law in order to conduct the "war against terror." These claims underlie the detention policies and the administration's posture that neither Congress nor the judiciary has any role in legislating or overseeing detentions. While the Supreme Court has rejected that view on four occasions and Congress has since legislated, the administration continues to claim unprecedented authority to create new forms of detention and decide who may be detained without regard to established law or constitutional limits.

On November 13, 2001, the President publicly instituted these policies with the issuance of Military Order No. 1. In addition to establishing military commissions, the Order authorized the military detention of any non-citizen found in the United States without charge solely on suspicion of being involved in terrorist activities. In May 2002, the President directed the military to seize a U.S. citizen in Chicago, who was then held for more than three years incommunicado without charge or access to a lawyer, solely on the say-so of the President. The administration also directed the military to ignore the Geneva Conventions and established military law and regulations when detaining individuals fighting in Afghanistan. It seized individuals in Bosnia,

U.S. Senate, July 16, 2008.

Europe and elsewhere and held them in secret prisons. It built a detention facility at Guantanamo in order to put detainees outside the reach of the law.

The administration still claims the right to seize any individual anywhere in the world, hold him incommunicado in a secret prison indefinitely without trial. It is now clear that its core reason for doing so was to be able to use "enhanced interrogation techniques" that are internationally recognized and outlawed as torture. (In the case of U.S. citizen Jose Padilla who was held incommunicado for more than three years, the government confessed that it did so in order to interrogate him.)

The result of this approach is the international view that the United States is not following the law, but is instead making up rules for detentions and interrogations. Most significantly, the argument that the United States is engaged in a "global war on terror" has been used to justify detentions that violate human rights and constitutional protections. Guantanamo Bay, in particular, has come to be seen by the world as a symbol for lawlessness and abuse.

These detention policies have undermined rather than strengthened U.S. power. They have discouraged and interfered with, rather than advancing international cooperation and have provided fuel to al Qaeda efforts to recruit foreign terrorists. The universal calls to close Guantanamo reflect the recognition that these detention policies that are inconsistent with the U.S. commitment to the rule of law and human rights have also harmed our national security.

This Committee's examination of how to replace these failed policies and undo the damage done to the rule of law and to U.S. standing in the world is most timely and welcome. A new President and a new Congress will have the opportunity to work together to move forward. The Supreme Court's decision in *Boumediene* provides the first step towards restoring the rule of law regarding the detainees held at Guantanamo. While the details of closing Guantanamo and replacing current detention policies will be complex, the established law of war in conjunction with established criminal law provide a straightforward framework for doing so. Using this established framework of military and criminal law side-by-side will enable suspected terrorists to be detained and tried in a way that will advance rather than undercut the effort to win hearts and minds around the world.

War or Crime?

Much of the public debate about treatment of detainees in Guantanamo and elsewhere has turned on questions of whether the law of war or criminal justice rules should apply to counterterrorism operations. But the absolutist positions adopted in this debate obscure more than they clarify.

The Bush Administration has argued that the threat from al Qaeda is unprecedented in magnitude and nature. Accordingly it has claimed a plenary right to use military force without, however, acknowledging any obligation to follow the rules of war as traditionally understood and articulated by the U.S. military. Thus, while the administration claims that being at war justifies its extraordinary and unprecedented detention practices, its adherence to the rules universally acknowledged to be applicable to military conflicts has been at best ad hoc and inconsistent. For example, the administration claimed that the Geneva Conventions had little or no applicability to the fighting in Afghanistan. (That claim was rejected by the Supreme Court in *Hamdan v. Rumsfeld*, when it held that Common Article 3 of the Geneva Conventions applies to all detainees.)

At the same time, policy-makers have been reluctant to adopt the stance that the threat posed by al Qaeda terrorists to the United States and its allies can be addressed by criminal law enforcement alone. This perspective is sometimes articulated as the proposition that all current detainees must either be charged with a crime or released.

Yet, in reality, since September 11, the United States has employed both congressionally authorized military force, including consequent military detention, in foreign armed conflicts such as Afghanistan and Iraq, and also criminal law enforcement tools against alleged al Qaeda terrorists, including prosecutions of Zacharias Moussaiou, the "American Taliban," John Walker Lindh and Richard Reid, the British "shoe bomber."

In particular, there is general agreement that the attacks of September 11, 2001 by al Qaeda rank as an act of war. Congress responded with the Authorization to Use Military Force "as necessary and appropriate" against al Qaeda and the Taliban in Afghanistan as well as those individuals, who "planned, authorized, committed or aided" the 9/11 attacks. The United Nations Security Council recognized the attacks as threats to the peace and security justifying the international use of force in Afghanistan under the United Nations charter. And since 2003, al Qaeda fighters have attacked U.S. and allied troops in Iraq.

At the same time, many individuals suspected of involvement with al Qaeda, who have been seized in the United States, Europe or elsewhere, have been charged with crimes, prosecuted, convicted and sentenced to long imprisonments.

In sum, even this administration has used both military force and criminal law enforcement in the fight against terrorism. As a matter of both common sense and law, detention policy should reflect this complex reality. Not even the most aggressive advocate of the war model claims that we can persuade our allies to abandon their criminal law traditions, to extradite suspects to us for military detention, or to allow open-ended military operations on their soil. Simply put, it is not realistic to claim that the "war on terror" is only, or even mostly, a matter of military force.

Moreover, when Congress authorized the use of military force as "necessary and appropriate," it did not replace the time-tested constitutional requirements of the criminal justice system, due process or military detention authority. Whatever the extent and nature of the "armed conflict with al Qaeda," it differs fundamentally from the traditional wars of the past. Outside the battlefields of Afghanistan and Iraq, apart from the known al Qaeda leaders who have publicly boasted of their participation in these war crimes, there are no enemy soldiers, indisputably identifiable by uniform or nationality, who may be targeted and detained by the military as combatants under the law of war.

New detention policies are needed that recognize that law enforcement and military force are both important tools for counterterrorism. Respect for the rule of law and individual rights is critical to a successful counterterrorism policy by the United States with its commitment to democracy, freedom and the rule of law. The following recommendations take into account the ongoing military operations in Afghanistan and Iraq. They are based on and consistent with the relevant rulings by the Supreme Court in *Hamdi, Rasul, Hamdan,* and *Boumediene* concerning the law of war and the scope of the Authorization to Use Military Force adopted by Congress in September 2001. These recommendations focus on the threat of terrorism posed by al Qaeda because to whatever extent al Qaeda terrorism poses an existential threat to the United States, no other terrorist group does so.

Recommendations

These recommendations and supporting analysis embody the analysis and conclusions of a Working Paper by the Center for National Security Studies being written with the Brennan Center for Justice. The final form of the Working Paper will be available shortly on our websites www.cnss.org and http://www.brennancenter.org.

A. Application of the Law of War or Criminal Law:

- When military force is used consistent with constitutional authorization and international obligations the United States shall follow the traditional understanding of the law of war, including the Geneva Conventions. Individuals seized in a theater of active hostilities are subject to military detention and trial pursuant to the law of war.
- When suspected terrorists are apprehended and seized outside a theater of active hostilities, the criminal law shall be used for detention and trial.

A new detention policy based on these principles would result in a stronger and more effective counterterrorism effort. It would ensure the detention and trial of fighters and terrorists in accordance with recognized bodies of law and fundamental notions of fairness and justice. It would ensure cooperation by key allies in Europe and elsewhere who have insisted that military detention be limited. It would begin to restore the reputation of the U.S. military, damaged by the international condemnation of the abuses of this administration. And it would deprive al Qaeda of the propaganda and recruiting opportunities created by current policies.

The Supreme Court has reaffirmed that under the law of war, when the U.S. military is engaged in active combat, it has the authority to seize fighters on the battlefield and detain them as combatants under the law of war. The traditional law of war, including the Geneva Conventions and Army Regulation 190-8,9 should be followed when capturing and detaining individuals seized on a battlefield/in a theater of armed conflict/during active hostilities, such as Afghanistan or Iraq. Of course, following the traditional rules for detaining battlefield captives would in no way require "Miranda" warnings or other

"Crime Scene Investigation" techniques. Nevertheless, the Bush administration deliberately ignored these military rules – including the requirement for a hearing under Article 5 of the Geneva Conventions – when it seized individuals in Afghanistan who are now held at Guantanamo.

(While some have claimed that the "battlefield" in the "war against terror" is the entire world, that claim is inconsistent with traditional understandings in the law. For example, one characteristic of a battlefield is the existence of Rules of Engagement, which permit the military to use force offensively against an enemy. Military Rules of Engagement for the armed forces stationed in Germany or the United States for example, are quite different from those applicable to troops in Afghanistan or Iraq. Troops in the United States or Germany are not entitled to use deadly force offensively.)

Outside these battlefields, in countries where there is a functioning domestic judiciary and criminal justice system, criminal laws should be used to arrest, detain and try individuals accused of plotting with al Qaeda or associated terrorist organizations. Outside the war theater, criminal law has proved to be successful at preventing and punishing would-be terrorists, protecting national security interests and ensuring due process. Richard B. Zabel and James J. Benjamin, Jr., In Pursuit of Justice, Human Rights First, May 2008, available at . . .

B. The government must distinguish between the different categories of detainees, who are subject to different rules.

One of the key sources of confusion in the debates to date about detention policy has been to speak about "terrorism detainees" in general as if they are all subject to the samel egal regime. Recognizing that the law of war must be followed when seizing individuals on the battlefield and that criminal law must be followed when arresting suspects in Chicago or Italy, makes it clear that there are different categories of detainees.

- The first category includes fighters in Afghanistan or Iraq (or other countries where U.S. military forces are engaged in active hostilities in the future); the second category is Osama bin Laden and the other self-proclaimed planners and organizers of the 9/11 attacks. Pursuant to the congressional authorization, individuals in the first or second categories may be targeted, captured and tried under the law of war.
- The third category includes suspected al Qaeda terrorists seized in the United States or elsewhere, other than Afghanistan or Iraq, who must be treated as suspects under criminal law.
- The last category is current detainees at Guantanamo, which includes individuals alleged to fall within all three categories listed above. The detainees in Guantanamo are sui generis for a number of reasons, including that their treatment has violated military law and traditions and that it has become an international symbol of injustice.

Fighters captured in Afghanistan or Iraq (or other countries where U.S. military forces are engaged in active hostilities in the future) subject to military detention and/or trial:

- Pursuant to the Supreme Court's ruling in *Hamdi*, individuals fighting in the Afghanistan or Iraq hostilities may be captured and detained pursuant to the law of war and may be held until the end of hostilities in the country in which they were captured.
- All such individuals, immediately upon capture, shall be provided a hearing pursuant to Article 5 of the Geneva Conventions and military regulations to determine whether they are entitled to be treated as prisoners of war, should be released as innocent civilians, or may be held as combatants pursuant to the Supreme Court's decision in *Hamdi*.
- Any such individuals who are accused of violations of the law of war shall be subject to trial by a regularly constituted military tribunal following the rules of the Uniform Code of Military Justice as outlined below.

Osama bin Laden and the other planners and organizers of the 9/11 attacks:

- In the September 2001 Authorization for the Use of Military Force, Congress specifically authorized the use of military force as "necessary and appropriate" against those individuals who "planned, authorized, committed or aided" the 9/11 attacks. The administration has identified approximately six individuals detained at Guantanamo as planners of the attacks and a limited number of others, including bin Laden, remain at large.
- If such individuals are captured rather than killed, they shall be treated humanely and protected from torture and cruel, inhumane or degrading treatment.
- They may be held by the military until they are tried by a military tribunal or the end of the conflict with al Qaeda.
- They may be tried by a regularly constituted military tribunal as outlined below.
- Such individuals may also be tried in the federal district courts on criminal charges.
- The best course from the standpoint of discrediting and opposing al Qaeda may be to conduct a fair public trial of these individuals, rather than detain them without trial.

Suspected al Qaeda terrorists seized in the United States or elsewhere other than Afghanistan or Iraq:

- Individuals found in the United States or in other countries with a functioning judicial system (other than Afghanistan and Iraq), who are suspected of terrorist plans or activities, must be detained and charged pursuant to the criminal justice system and/or deported in accordance with due process.
- Any such individuals may be transferred to other countries only in accordance with the rules outlined below. They must be protected against the danger of torture and may only be transferred in accordance with due process and to stand trial on criminal charges.
- Individuals suspected of terrorist plotting may be subject to surveillance in accordance with domestic laws.

Individuals currently held at Guantanamo:

- The United States should begin a process to close the Guantanamo detention facility. There are many difficult questions about how to accomplish this arising in part from the administration's failure to follow the law in detaining and seizing these individuals. The Center for American Progress has recently issued a report detailing an approach in line with these recommendations.
- The government shall expeditiously transfer all those detainees it has determined are eligible for release to their home country or to some other country where they will not be subjected to abuse or torture.
- Those individuals in Guantanamo who are not alleged to have been captured on the battlefields of Afghanistan or Iraq or fleeing therefrom may not be held by the military as combatants, but must be either charged with a crime, transferred to another country for prosecution on criminal charges, or released.
- As recognized in *Boumediene*, all detainees at Guantanamo are also entitled to habeas corpus.
- Those Guantanamo detainees who are alleged to have been captured in Afghanistan or Iraq and been part of al Qaeda or Taliban forces may be detained until the end of hostilities in those countries if the government sustains its burden of proof in a habeas corpus proceeding. Such detentions without charge for the duration of hostilities were approved by the Supreme Court under *Hamdi* as having been authorized by the AUMF. At the same time, there are likely to be counterterrorism benefits to choosing to bring charges against such individuals and providing them with a fair trial.
- Those detainees who are alleged to be planners or organizers of the 9/11 attacks may be detained until the end of the conflict with al Qaeda if the government sustains its burden of proof in a habeas corpus proceeding that they personally participated in the planning of the attacks.
- Those detainees who are subject to military detention as described above and who are also charged with violations of the law of war may be tried by a regularly constituted military tribunal as outlined below.

C. Military tribunals for individuals who are properly held as combatants, either having been captured on the battlefield or having planned or organized the 9/11 attacks:

As recognized by the Supreme Court in *Hamdan*, combatants may be tried by military tribunals for offenses properly triable by such tribunals. Such tribunals must accord due process and be "regularly constituted courts." In addition, such tribunals must be seen by the world as fair and be consistent with the proud history of U.S. military justice in the past 50 years. The military commission system created for Guantanamo will never be seen as legitimate and thus should no longer be used to try detainees.

If military trials are sought for combatant detainees at Guantanamo, they should be conducted pursuant to the United States Uniform Code of Military Justice courts martial rules to the greatest extent possible.

D. End torture and cruel, inhumane and degrading treatment.

As the Supreme Court has made clear, all of these detainees are protected by Common Article 3 of the Geneva Convention and must be treated humanely. In particular:

- All detainees shall be treated humanely and shall be protected from torture and cruel, inhumane or degrading treatment.
- No individual may be detained in secret.
- The government must institute new mechanisms to ensure that no person is transferred to a country where it is reasonably likely that he would be in danger of torture.
- Individuals may only be seized and transferred to other countries in order to stand trial on criminal charges in accordance with due process and the domestic laws of the country they are transferred to.
- The CIA program of secret detention and interrogation of suspected terrorists shall be ended.

The administration shall consider whether any overriding national security reason exists for CIA involvement in terrorism detentions and interrogations, which outweighs the demonstrated harm these activities have caused to the national security. Before determining that the CIA shall again participate in any detention or interrogation activity, the administration shall report to the Congress concerning the national security interests at stake and specifically outline how, if such participation is authorized, it would be conducted with adequate checks to ensure that its operation conforms to law and is fully consistent with the United States' commitment to human rights.

Conclusion

The administration ignored both the law of war and constitutional requirements and established a new detention regime, largely in order to conduct illegal and abusive interrogations. The results have been disastrous. "Guantanamo" has become a symbol throughout the world of U.S. disregard for the rule of law, even though the Afghanistan invasion itself was widely supported as justified and legal, and even though the taking of prisoners is a natural (and humane) consequence of such an invasion. Detention policies have strained relations with allies and may help terrorist recruiting efforts for years to come. Disrespect for the law has harmed, not enhanced, our national security.

The Supreme Court has now taken the first steps in restoring constitutional limits and the rule of law and the lower courts will continue that task in considering the habeas petitions from Guantanamo detainees. A new administration should pledge a return to respect for the rule of law and commit to following the law of war on the battlefield and the criminal law when plotters are found in the United States or elsewhere. Doing so will serve the national security and help restore basic human rights.

David B. Rivkin

 **NO**

How the Administration's Failed Detainee Policies Have Hurt the Fight against Terrorism: Putting the Fight against Terrorism on Sound Legal Foundations

I realize that many legal positions taken by the [Bush] Administration to deal with the post-September 11 national security challenges, laying the fundamental legal architecture of the war on terror, have not found favor with many critics. Indeed, the title of this hearing, referring as it does to the "failed Administration's detainee policies," certainly reflects this critical sentiment. With respect, I disagree with this position. As I elaborate on this point, I will also make a few recommendations for going forward.

I start from the premise that, both as a matter of law and policy, the challenge that confronted the Bush Administration and, indeed the country, after September 11, was to determine how to prosecute successfully a war against al Qaeda, Taliban, and affiliated entities. The successful war prosecution required the choice of an appropriate legal paradigm. And, as in all prior wars in American history, and consistent with both international and constitutional law requirements, this legal paradigm had to be rooted in the laws and customs of war. Moreover, while this paradigm covered a broad range of legal issues, governing the use of force against the enemy – for example, target selection, choice of the rules of engagement – how to deal with captured enemy combatants was a key element.

Behind this fact is a stark reality. In this war against shadowy pan-national terrorist entities, the U.S. must not only attack and defeat enemy forces. It must also anticipate and prevent their deliberate attacks on its civilian population – al Qaeda's preferred target. International law gives the civilian population an indisputable right to that protection. Furthermore, ascertaining whether enemy personnel captured in this conflict ought to be classified as lawful or unlawful combatants, being able to hold them for the duration of hostilities and being able to elicit intelligence information from them, while utilizing legally appropriate and effective procedures, is indispensable in carrying out the key war-related strategic missions, including protecting our civilian population.

U.S. Senate, July 16, 2008.

To be sure, the questions that the Administration's lawyers have sought to address, particularly those dealing with the interrogation of captured enemy combatants, are uncomfortable ones that do not mesh well with our 21st Century sensibilities. Many of the legal conclusions reached have struck critics as being excessively harsh. Some, of course, have since been watered down as a result of internal debates, political and public pressure brought to bear upon the Administration, and by the results of relentless litigation. Though I would not endorse each and every aspect of the Administration's post-September 11 wartime policies, I would vigorously defend the overall exercise of asking difficult legal questions and trying to work through them. To me, the fact that this exercise was undertaken so thoroughly attests to the vigor and strength of our democracy and of the Administration's commitment to the rule of law, even in the most difficult of circumstances.

In this regard, I point out that few of our democratic allies have ever engaged in so probing and searching a legal exegesis in wartime. I also strongly defend the overarching legal framework, featuring the traditional laws of war architecture, chosen by the Administration. I want to emphasize here that, despite all of the criticisms of the various procedural facets of the Administration's detainee policy, detainees in U.S. custody today enjoy the most fulsome due process procedures of any detainees or prisoners of war in human history. Indeed, the much maligned Combatant Status Review Tribunals and Military Commissions, backed up by statutorily-driven judicial review procedures, are unprecedented in the history of warfare.

This, by the way, was the case even before the Supreme Court's recent *Boumediene* decision, which further augmented the judicial review opportunities, available to detainees in U.S. custody. [In *Boumediene v. Bush* (2008), the Supreme Court ruled 5 to 4 that a foreign national being held as a terrorist "enemy combatant" under military jurisdiction could file a writ of habeas corpus with a civil federal court challenging the legality of his detention and trial.]

Meanwhile, the fact that the U.S. has released hundreds of captured enemy combatants from detention, instead of holding them for the duration of hostilities as allowed by international and constitutional law and fully consistent with past state practice, further underscores the extent of moderation of our detainee policy. We also paid a price for this moderation, as dozens of individuals so released have gone back to combat and killed again.

I recognize, of course, that, unfortunately, this is not the way how much of the world sees America's detainee policies in this war. I happen to believe, however, that it is the critics' rejection of the overall laws of war-rooted legal framework, reflecting their underlying view that this is not a real war, that animates most of their criticisms of the Administration's specific legal decisions. Most controversial, of course, was the Bush Administration's insistence that the 1949 Geneva Conventions have limited, if any, application to al Qaeda and its allies (who themselves reject the "Western" concepts behind those treaties); and the Administration's authorization of aggressive interrogation methods, including, in at least three cases, waterboarding or simulated drowning.

Several legal memoranda, particularly 2002 and 2003 opinions written by the Office of Legal Counsel, considered whether such methods can lawfully be used. These memoranda, some of which remain classified, explore the limits imposed on the United States by statute, treaties, and customary international law. The goal clearly was to find a legal means to give U.S. interrogators the maximum flexibility, while defining the point at which lawful interrogation ended and unlawful torture began.

In truth, the critics' fundamental complaint is that the Bush Administration's lawyers measured international law against the U.S. Constitution and domestic statutes. They interpreted the Geneva Conventions, the U.N. Convention forbidding torture, and customary international law, in ways that were often at odds with the prevailing view of international law professors and various activist groups. In doing so, however, they did no more than assert the right of this Nation – as is the right of any sovereign nation – to interpret its own international obligations.

To the extent that international law can be made, it is made through actual state practice – whether in the form of custom, or in the manner states implement treaty obligations. In the areas relevant to the war on terror, there is precious little state practice against the U.S. position, but a very great deal of academic orthodoxy.

For more than 40 years, as part of the post World War II decolonization process, a legal orthodoxy has arisen that supports limiting the ability of nations to use robust armed force against irregular or guerilla fighters. It has also attempted to privilege such guerillas with the rights traditionally reserved to sovereign states. The U.S. has always been skeptical of these notions, and at critical points has flatly refused to be bound by these new rules. Most especially, it refused to join the 1977 Protocol I Additional to the Geneva Conventions, involving the treatment of guerillas, from which many of the "norms" the U.S. has supposedly violated, are drawn.

I would also submit to you that, until very recently, the Administration's legal positions have been substantially upheld by the courts. I know that this flies in the face of public and even elite perceptions that the Administration has been lurching from one legal defeat to another. Yet, in a series of cases beginning with *Hamdi v. Rumsfeld* (2004), the U.S. Supreme Court, while tweaking various elements of the government's legal policies, has upheld many of the Administration's key positions: that the country is engaged in a legally cognizable armed conflict; that captured enemy combatants can be detained without criminal trial during these hostilities; and that (when the time comes) they may be punished through the military, rather than the civilian, justice system.

The [Supreme] Court has also required that detainees be given an administrative hearing to challenge their enemy-combatant classification, ruled that Congress (not the President alone) must establish any military commission system, and made clear that it will in the future exercise some level of judicial scrutiny over the treatment of detainees held at Guantanamo Bay. Overall, the Administration has won the critical points necessary to continue the war against al Qaeda. Indeed, the two political branches – the Executive and Congress – have responded to the Court's decisions with changes in policies, promulgating two major pieces of legislation, the Detainee Treatment Act and the Military Commissions Act.

Regrettably, in the just-decided *Boumediene v. Bush* case, the Supreme Court has abandoned this approach. It has effectively rendered non-viable a major portion of the Administration's wartime legal architecture, even though it itself has helped to shape it for the last several years. Now, the Court has taken a central role in deciding who may be captured and detained as an enemy combatant, ruling that detainees, akin to criminal defendants, are constitutionally entitled to challenge their confinement through "habeas corpus" proceedings in federal district courts. The Court's reasoning extends far beyond how "unlawful enemy combatants" like the Guantanamo detainees are treated. Legitimate prisoners of war in a future conventional conflict – who now receive less legal process than the detainees at Guantanamo – also can demand habeas proceedings. In my view, the *Boumediene* decision is one of the most deplorable examples of judicial overreaching in our history and is inconsistent with the Constitution, historical practice, and settled case law.

However, what is even more important for the purposes of our discussion today is *Boumediene's* operational consequences. The reason I want to stress this point is because for years the Administration's critics have been arguing that there was no real cost to giving additional legal rights, whether procedural or substantive in nature, to the detainees, that it was only the Administration's obstinacy that was the problem. Well, the critics could not have been more wrong, proving, once again, that balancing individual liberty and public safety is never a cost-free exercise, and particularly so in wartime. Granting detainees the right to the traditional style habeas is going to have momentous and grave consequences across a number of fronts.

The most obvious consequence is that, according to the published reports, the Department of Justice is going to dedicate at least fifty and most likely more attorneys full-time to handle the habeas petitions, filed by Guantanamo-based detainees, spending months and months of time preparing the record for the district court, in an effort to develop acceptable "returns." Contrary to what many believe, they would have to deal not only with the basic question of whether the government has sufficient basis to hold individual detainees as enemy combatants, but would also have to handle literally hundreds and hundreds of lawsuits, dealing with numerous collateral issues, including conditions of confinement, whether given detainees can be transferred to a particular country, and such. Discovery [revealing the evidence the government has] would also be a huge issue, since, in the context of a habeas proceeding, once an acceptable return has been filed by the government, the burden shifts and the detainee is entitled to discovery.

To put it mildly, this flurry of litigation, and particularly the opportunity for captured enemy operatives to press discovery against the country that has taken them into custody, is unprecedented in the history of warfare. We can also expect that the habeas proceedings would result in overturning the enemy combatant status classification of at least some of the Guantanamo-based detainees. To emphasize, in at least some cases this would not happen because they were innocent shepherds or aid workers, who should not have been detained in the first place, but rather because the government simply lacks sufficiently fulsome evidence of their combatancy or even if it does have such evidence, it cannot run the risk of disclosing evidence without jeopardizing the war effort. The consequences of such habeas proceedings are a little unclear, but none of them are particularly good. Indeed, the possibility that some of the dangerous detainees would be released into the United States cannot be ruled out, especially since we can expect the courts to block their repatriation to those foreign countries that may be interested in receiving them.

Presented with this habeas-driven detention policy, on a going forward basis, American forces, if they wish to be sufficiently certain of holding enemy prisoners anywhere in the world, must set about securing CSI-style evidence to satisfy the judges that their captives are indeed what they seem to be – enemies in arms against the United States. Collecting this evidence on the battlefield will cost lives and impair combat effectiveness. Moreover, the need to litigate habeas proceedings, particularly when applied to a large body of prisoners, will impose great additional burdens on the U.S. military, which is already stretched thin by the demands of global operations. One example: Operations in Guantanamo had to be fundamentally recast to accommodate hundreds of detainee lawyers and their support personnel. Expanding this approach worldwide is simply untenable.

In my view, it is unprecedented and deplorable that American forces can no longer detain captured enemy combatants without a burdensome judicial process. Until the Supreme Court's balance changes and *Boumediene* is overruled, the U.S. armed forces will likely be driven to a tragic "catch and release" policy. The most senior enemy operatives, assuming enough evidence can be collected, will be tried for war crimes before military commissions. Others will be taken into custody, interrogated, and then transferred to the custody of allied governments – or even set free in the theater of action after they have been disarmed. With respect to the 270 or so Guantanamo detainees, some are being, or will be, tried by military commissions for war crimes.

The Court's *Boumediene* decision should not prevent those trials from going forward. Indeed, they should be accelerated, and all enemy combatants in U.S. custody, against whom sufficient evidence of war crimes exists, should be brought expeditiously to trial. But for many of those not slated for these trials, habeas proceedings may well result in a release order if the government does not have sufficient evidence to satisfy a civilian judge as to their enemy combatant status.

This is the only area where Congress should promptly act. It may be that a handful of detainees deserve "parole" into the United States on humanitarian grounds, but none of them have a right to enter, even if a federal court does order their release. Where such parole is inappropriate, Congress should establish a category of detention that permits aliens not otherwise lawfully admitted to this country to be held until a suitable foreign government can be found to accept them, however long that may be. Under current law, aliens in the U.S. without a lawful basis for being here, and for whom no receiving country can be found, can only be held up to six months. The Constitution grants Congress plenary authority over questions of immigration and nationality and the Supreme Court has – so far – respected that authority.

That leaves the problem of what to do with those Guantanamo detainees who cannot be repatriated, but who a habeas court determines can be properly detained. For all of the real diplomatic costs incurred over Guantanamo, that base was admirably suited to house captured enemy combatants. It is under complete U.S. control, far from any active battlefield, and it is isolated from nearby civilian populations – largely thanks to the surrounding "workers paradise" [Cuba] run by the Castro brothers [Fidel and Raoul]. In short, the base is easily secured and presents no "host nation" or "not in my backyard" issues. It is those issues that make Guantanamo's prompt closure a bigger problem than almost anyone imagines.

Although many members of Congress have decried the detainees' fate at Gitmo, few have offered their states or districts as a suitable alternative, and chances are none will. For example, last July, a Senate resolution opposing transfer of Gitmo detainees "stateside into facilities in American neighborhoods" passed 94-3. Transferring the Guantanamo detainees to the U.S. would create a security problem of unrivaled character. The new location would immediately become a particular target for al Qaeda and other jihadist groups.

The logical place to hold them, of course, would be the Military Disciplinary Barracks at Fort Leavenworth, Kan. But, unlike Guantanamo Bay, Fort Leavenworth is not isolated from the surrounding civilian population. It is very much a part of the communities of eastern Kansas and western Missouri. Other alternatives, such as the old federal prison on Alcatraz Island, are also surrounded by population centers.

For that very reason it is Congress that must make the decision where to put the detainees. If that is to be Fort Leavenworth, then the Kansas and Missouri delegations must have the opportunity to speak on the subject in the House of Representatives and the Senate. Neither President Bush nor his successor, Democrat or Republican, should act without a full and complete congressional debate on the subject, and legislation establishing the new locus for detainee operations.

POSTSCRIPT

Has the U.S. Detention and Trial of Accused Foreign Terrorists Been Legally Unsound?

The Supreme Court's decision in *Boumediene v. Bush* puts the legal ball back in hands of the White House and Congress. They now have to legislate procedures that will satisfy the court's clear view that enemy combatants do have some rights with the widely held view that giving them all the rights normally afforded the accused would be unwarranted and also might endanger national security. Some legislation was introduced in Congress late in 2008, but with the presidential and congressional election in full swing and with the credit crisis dominating political attention in the fall of 2008, it is unlikely that the terrorist issue will be addressed before the new president and Congress take office in 2009. Barack Obama said the decision "ensures that we can protect our nation and bring terrorists to justice, while also protecting our core values." As noted, the decision really did not do that; it left it to Congress and the president to come up with a way to do that. Most Americans support that task and disapprove of the court's decisions. When asked in 2006 if they favored or opposed having suspected foreign terrorists put on trial in front of military commissions and not being allowed to challenge their detention in a civilian court, 63 percent of Americans responded in "favor," only 34 percent were opposed, and 4 percent were unsure.

More on the Geneva Conventions is available at http://www.genevaconventions .org/. As for the *Boumediene v. Bush* case, go to the Oyez Project at http://www .oyez.org/ and enter the case name in the search window. Doing so will take you to the majority, concurring, and dissenting opinion. You can also hear a recording of the oral arguments when the case was argued. Links to all the merit briefs and amicus curiae briefs filed supporting and opposing Boumediene are available on the Web site of Scotus Wiki at http://www.scotuswiki.com/index .php?title=Boumediene/Al-Odah_v._Bush. For an effort to point the way to laws and procedures that will not ignore basic civil liberties while simultaneously recognizing that dealing with foreign terrorists sometimes requires special legal approaches, read Benjamin Wittes, *Law and the Long War: The Future of Justice in the Age of Terror* (Penguin Press, 2008).

Internet References . . .

EarthTrends

An environmental information portal of the World Resources Institute sponsored by such diverse organizations as the Dutch government, the UN Development Programme, and the World Bank.

http://earthtrends.wri.org/

Worldwatch Institute

The environmental-activist Worldwatch Institute offers a range of information and commentary on environmental, social, and economic trends. The institute's work revolves around the transition to an environmentally sustainable and socially just society—and how to achieve it.

http://www.worldwatch.org

The Common-Sense Environmentalist's Suite

The organizations listed on this link page offer research and commentary on environmental topics that take a skeptical view of many projections on looming environmental disaster.

http://www.heartland.org/policybot/results.html?artld=10488

UNIT 6

The Environment

*W*hen *all is said and done, policy is, or at least ought to be, about values. That is, how do we want our world to be? There are choices to make about what to do (and what not to do). It would be easy if these choices were clearly good versus evil. But things are not usually that simple, and the issue in this part shows the disparity of opinions regarding the current state of the environment.*

- Are Warnings about Global Warming Unduly Alarmist?

ISSUE 19

Are Warnings about Global Warming Unduly Alarmist?

YES: **James Inhofe**, from Remarks on the floor of the U.S. Senate, *Congressional Record* (October 26, 2007)

NO: **Barbara Boxer**, from Remarks on the floor of the U.S. Senate, *Congressional Record* (October 29, 2007)

ISSUE SUMMARY

YES: James Inhofe, a Republican member of the U.S. Senate from Oklahoma, tells the Senate that objective, evidence-based science is beginning to show that the predictions of catastrophic human-made global warming are overwought.

NO: Barbara Boxer, a Democratic member of the U.S. Senate from California, responds that Senator Inhofe's is one of the very few isolated and lonely voices that keeps on saying we do not have to worry about global warming, while, in reality, it is a major problem that demands a prompt response.

We live in an era of almost incomprehensible technological boom. In a very short time – less than a long lifetime in many cases – technology has brought some amazing things. But these advances have had negative by-products. A great deal of prosperity has come through industrialization, electrification, the burgeoning of private and commercial vehicles, and a host of other inventions and improvements that, in order to work, consume massive amounts of fossil fuel (mostly coal, petroleum, and natural gas). The burning of fossil fuels gives off carbon dioxide (CO_2) into the atmosphere. The discharge of CO_2 from burning wood, animals exhaling, and some other sources is nearly as old as Earth itself, but the last century's advances have rapidly increased the level of discharge. Since 1950 alone, annual global CO_2 emissions have more than tripled to about 26 billion tons. Much of this is retained in the atmosphere because the ability of nature to cleanse the atmosphere of the CO_2 through plant photosynthesis has been overwhelmed by the vast increases in fossil fuel burning and the simultaneous cutting of vast areas of the world's forests for habitation and agriculture.

Many analysts believe that as a result of this buildup of CO_2, we are experiencing global warming. The reason, they contend, is the greenhouse effect. As CO_2 accumulates in the upper atmosphere, it creates a blanket effect, trapping heat and preventing the nightly cooling of the Earth. Other gases, such as methane, also contribute to creating the thermal blanket. It is estimated that over the last century Earth's average temperature has risen about 1.1 degree Fahrenheit. The 1990s was the warmest decade since temperature records were first kept in 1856, and the first decade of the 2000s is on track to be even warmer. The pattern of global warming over the last millennium or so is sometimes compared to a "hockey stick." Between A.D. 1000 and 1900, the average world temperature pattern was basically flat, resembling the long shaft of a hockey stick. Since 1900, however, the temperature has risen relatively rapidly upward, with the spike compared to the shorter blade of a hockey stick.

This warming of the atmosphere worries many, who believe that rainfall, wind currents, and other climatic patterns are and could be dramatically, and sometimes dangerously, altered. Among other impacts, the polar ice caps will melt more quickly, and sea levels will rise, displacing perhaps over a 100 million people on the continents' coasts during the coming century. Some weather experts also project an increase in the number and intensity of hurricanes and other catastrophic weather events. James Inhofe lays out this argument in the first reading. Those who agree with Inhofe often call for significant changes in the levels of energy use and other changes in human activity that arguably will have a major impact on lifestyle.

As the commentary in the first reading by James Inhofe indicates, not everyone believes that global warming caused by a CO_2 buildup is occurring or worries about it. Some scientists do not believe that future temperature increases will be significant, either because they will not occur or because offsetting factors, such as increased cloudiness, will ease the effect. Others believe that whatever temperature increase is occurring is from natural trends in Earth's warming and cooling process. They point out that the time since 1856 is a mere blip in climatological time and further note that in the last 1,300 years, two marked temperature changes, the Medieval Warm Period (A.D. 800 to 1400) and the Little Ice Age (A.D. 1600 to 1850) have occurred. Another criticism is that there is only mixed scientific evidence of a level of global warming that will have serious negative effects. By contrast, Barbara Boxer depicts grave consequences from global warming in the second reading, and argues that the longer we wait to address global warming, the harder it will be to achieve the emission reductions we know we need to reach.

YES

James Inhofe

Remarks on the Floor
of the U.S. Senate

An abundance of new peer-reviewed studies, analyses, and data-error dis-coveries in the past several months have prompted scientists to declare that fear of catastrophic manmade global warming [are overstated or false]. Objec-tive, evidence-based science is beginning to crush hysteria. Meteorologist Joseph Conklin, who launched the skeptical Web site climatepolice.com in 2007, recently declared the "global warming movement is falling apart."

I will detail how even committed leftwing scientists now believe the envi-ronmental movement has been "co-opted" into promoting global warming as a "crisis," and I will expose the manufactured facade of "consensus." I will also address the economic factors of the so-called solutions to global warming and how they will have no measurable impact on the climate. But these so-called solutions will create huge economic harm for American families and the poor residents of the developing world who may see development hindered by unfounded climate fears.

I am convinced the future climate historians will look back on 2007 as the year the global warming fears began to crumble. Today, the greatest irony is that the U.N. and the media's climate hysteria grows louder as the case for alarmism fades away. While the scientific case grows weaker, the political and rhetorical proponents of climate fear are ramping up to offer hefty tax and regulatory solutions, both internationally and domestically, to solve the so-called crisis.

Those who want to blame man for all of these problems that they try to make us believe are happening are saying anthropogenic gases [generated by human activity] are the problem. Debunking catastrophic manmade global warming fears can be reduced to four essential points. Now, what I am going to do is read these points and go back and elaborate on each one.

1. Recent climate changes on Earth lie well within the bounds of natural climate variability – even the *New York Times* concedes this. U.N. tem-perature data shows that the late 20th century phase of global warming ended in 1998; new data for the Southern Hemisphere shows that a slight cooling is underway.
2. The second thing we will talk about is almost all current public fear of global warming is being driven by unproven and untestable com-puter model fears of the future, which now even the United Nations

U.S. Congressional Record, October 26, 2007.

concedes that the models – these are computer models; that is what all this stuff is based on – they do not account for half of the variability in nature and, thus, their predictions are not reliable. Even the United Nations agrees with that.

3. The third thing is debunking the relationship that the more CO_2 you have, the warmer the world is. That is very simplistic and it is untrue. Scientists are reporting in peer-reviewed literature that increasing CO_2 in the atmosphere will not have the catastrophic impact doomsters have been predicting. In fact, climate experts are discovering that you cannot distinguish the impact of human-produced greenhouse gases from natural climate variability. That is extremely significant and something that has come around in the last 6 or 7 months.

4. The fourth thing we will talk about is consensus. We hear so much about consensus. The more things that come out of science, where the scientists are saying, wait a minute, we were wrong. In a minute, I will be naming names of scientists who were marching the streets with Al Gore 10 years ago who now say they were wrong. When you talk about that today, those who are promoting this type of fear from the left, they use the word "consensus." The climate change "consensus" exists. Well, it does not exist. Instead, the illusion that it does has been carefully manufactured for political, financial, and ideological purposes.

These four basic points form the foundation of the rational, evidence-based approach to climate science that has come to be called global warming skepticism.

Essential point No. 1 is: The Earth's climate is within the natural variability. On April 23, 2006, the article in the *New York Times* stated, "Few scientists agree with the idea that the recent spate of potent hurricanes, European heat waves, African drought and other weather extremes are, in essence, our fault. . . . There is more than enough natural variability in nature to mask a direct connection, scientists say." The *Times* is essentially conceding that no recent weather events fall outside the range of natural climate variability. On a slightly longer time scale, many scientific studies have shown the medieval and earlier warm periods were as warm or warmer than the Earth's current temperature – when there were no influences that were due to manmade gases.

There have been recent studies refuting claims that the 20th century has seen unprecedented warmth. A June 29, 2007, paper by Gerd Burger of Berlin's Institute of Meteorology in the peer-reviewed *Science Magazine* challenged [the notion] that the 20th century had been unusually warm. Dr. Robert Giegengack, the chair of the Department of Earth and Environmental Science at the University of Pennsylvania, noted on May 27, 2007 that extremely long geologic timescales reveal that "only about 5 percent of that time has been characterized by conditions on Earth that were so cold that the poles could support masses of permanent ice." Giegengack added, "For most of Earth's history, the globe has been warmer than it has been for the last 200 years. It has rarely been cooler."

Even though Greenland has been a "poster boy" for climate alarmists, it is now cooler there than the temperatures were in the 1930s and 1940s. Greenland reached its highest temperatures in 1941, according to a peer-reviewed study published in the June 2006 issue of the *Journal of Geophysical Research*. Keep in mind that 80 percent of the manmade CO_2 came after the 1940s. That is a very interesting thing because, if you look at it, you would say if 80 percent of the CO_2 came after the 1940s, would that not precipitate a warming period – if they are right – in terms of CO_2 affecting warmer climate change? That didn't happen. That precipitated a cooler period.

According to a July 2007 survey of peer-reviewed literature on Greenland:

> Research in 2006 found that Greenland has been warming since the 1880s, but since 1955, temperature averages at Greenland stations have been colder than the period of 1881–1955. Another 2006 peer-reviewed study concluded the rate of warming in Greenland from 1920 to 1930 was about 50 percent higher than the warming from 1995 to 2005.

That is the time [alarmists] say this crisis is taking place. One 2005 study found Greenland gaining ice in the interior higher elevations and thinning ice at the lower elevations. In addition, the often media promoted fears of Greenland's ice completely melting and a subsequent catastrophic sea level rise are directly at odds with the latest scientific studies.

These are scientific facts you will not hear from the U.N. scientists, Gore, or the hysterical liberal left. Yet despite all of this evidence, the media and many others still attempt to distort the science in order to create hysterical fears about Greenland.

Scientists monitoring ice in Antarctica reported on October 1 that the ice has grown to record levels since 1979, when satellite monitoring began. So the ice levels have grown to record levels since that time, according to an announcement by the University of Illinois Polar Research Group Web site. The Southern Hemisphere sea ice area has broken the previous maximum of 16.03 million square kilometers and is currently at 16.26 million square kilometers.

There is more. A February 2007 study reveals Antarctica is not following predicted global warming temperature or precipitation models. [According to the study,] temperatures during the late 20th century did not climb as had been predicted by many global climate models. The study was conducted by David Bromwich, professor of atmospheric sciences at Ohio State University. How inconvenient that the two poster children of alarmism – Greenland and Antarctica – trumpeted by Al Gore and the climate fear mongers have decided not to cooperate with the computer models.

There is much more evidence that the Earth is currently well within natural climate variability. The Southern Hemisphere is cooling, according to U.N. scientist, Dr. Madhav Khandekar. He explained this on August 6, 2007, and these are all new scientific findings:

> In the Southern Hemisphere, the land-area mean temperature has slowly but surely declined in the last few years. The city of Buenes Aires

in Argentina received several centimeters of snowfall in early July, and the last time it snowed in Buenos Aires was in 1918. Most of Australia experienced one of its coldest months in June of this year. Several other locations in the Southern Hemisphere have experienced lower temperatures in the last few years. Further, the sea surface temperatures over world oceans are slowly declining since mid-1998, according to a recent worldwide analysis of ocean surface temperatures.

The media would not report on the historical perspective of Greenland, the ice growing in Antarctica, or the Southern Hemisphere cooling. Instead, the media's current fixation is on hyping Arctic sea ice shifts. What the media is refusing to report about the North Pole is that according to a 2003 study by an Arctic scientist, Igor Polyakov, the warmest period in the Arctic during the 20th century was the late 1930s through the early 1940s. We are talking about the Northern Hemisphere now. Many scientists believe if we had satellite monitoring of the Arctic back then, it may have shown less ice than today.

According to a 2005 peer-reviewed study in the Geophysical Research Letters by an astrophysicist, Dr. Willie Soon, solar irradiance appears to be the key to Arctic temperatures. The study found Arctic temperatures follow the pattern of increasing or decreasing energy received from the sun. In another 2005 study published in the *Journal of Climate*, Brian Hartmann and Gerd Wendler linked the 1976 Pacific climate shift to a very significant one-time shift upward in Alaskan temperatures. These evidence-based scientific studies debunk fears of manmade warming in the Arctic and in Alaska.

I have covered the latest science on both poles. In the Southern Hemisphere, scientists are finding nothing to be alarmed about. It is important to point out that the phase of global warming that started in 1979 has itself been halted since 1998, which is nearly a decade. In other words, the warming that took place, which I believe is from natural causes, stopped in 1998. It is not getting warmer anymore. According to paleoclimate scientist Dr. Bob Carter, this is significant:

> The accepted global average temperature statistics used by the Intergovernmental Panel on Climate Change [IPCC] show that no ground-based warming has occurred since 1998. Oddly, this eight-year-long temperature stability has occurred despite an increase over the same period of 15 parts per million (or 4 percent) in atmospheric CO_2. Second, lower atmospheric satellite-based temperature measurements, if corrected for non-greenhouse influences, such as El Nino events and large volcanic eruptions, show little if any global warming since 1979, a period over which atmospheric CO_2 has increased by 55 parts per million (17 percent).

Another key development in 2007 is the research led by meteorologist Anthony Watts of surfacestation.org which has revealed massive U.S. temperature collection data errors biasing thermometers to have warmer readings. Meteorologist [Joseph] Conklin explained on August 10, 2007:

> The (U.S.) National Climate Data Center is in the middle of a scandal. Their global observing network, the heart and soul of surface weather

measurement, is a disaster. Urbanization has placed many [temperature monitoring] sites in unsuitable locations – on hot black asphalt, next to trash burn barrels, beside heat exhaust vents, even attached to hot chimneys and above outdoor grills. The data and approach taken by many global warming alarmists is seriously flawed. If the global data were properly adjusted for urbanization and station siting, and land use change issues were addressed, what would emerge is a cyclical pattern of rises and falls with much less of any background trend.

I now move to central point No. 2, the unproven computer models that are driving climate fears. Anytime you try to make a projection into the future, you try to have a model you can rely on instead of relying on data that is current and accurate. Of course, you can't prove a prediction of the climate in 2100 wrong today, which reduces the models to speculating on what could or might or may happen 50 or 100 years from now. Even the *New York Times* has been forced to acknowledge the overwhelming evidence that the Earth is currently well within natural climate variation. This inconvenient reality means all the climate doomsdayers have to back up their claims, their climate fears are unproven computer models predicting future doom.

But prominent U.N. scientists publicly questioned the reliability of these computer models. Only a few months ago in a candid statement, IPCC scientist Dr. Jim Renwick, a leading author of the U.N. IPCC 4th Assessment Report, publicly admitted "Half of the variability in the climate system is not predictable, so we don't expect to do terrifically well." In June, another high profile IPCC lead author, Dr. Kevin Trenberth, echoed Renwick's sentiments about the climate models by referring to them as nothing more than "story lines."

Dr. Hendrik Tennekes, a former director of research at The Netherlands' Royal National Meteorological Institute, recently took the critique of climate computer models one step further, saying, "I am of the opinion that most scientists engaged in the design, development, and tuning of climate models are, in fact, software engineers. They are unlicensed, hence unqualified to sell their products to society." Meteorologist Augie Auer of the New Zealand Climate Science Coalition, former professor of atmospheric sciences at the University of Wyoming, agreed, describing models this way, "It's virtual science, it's virtual reality." Auer joked, "Most of these climate predictions are models, they are about a half a step ahead of PlayStation." Prominent scientist Professor Nils-Axel Morner also denounced computer models in 2007, saying, "The rapid rise in sea levels predicted by computer models simply cannot happen." Morner is a leading world authority on sea levels and coastal erosion who headed the Department of Paleogeophysics & Geodynamics at Stockholm University. Physicist Dr. Syun-Ichi Akasofu, the former director of both the University of Alaska Fairbanks' Geophysical Institute and International Arctic Research Center, told a congressional hearing in 2006 that highly publicized computer models showing a disappearing Arctic were nothing more than "science fiction." Geologist Morten Hald, an Arctic expert at the University of Tromso in Norway, has also questioned the reliability of computer models that predict a future melting of the Arctic. He says, "The main problem is that these models are often based on relatively new climate data. The thermometer has only been in existence for 150 years and information on temperature which is 150 years old does not capture the large natural changes."

Physicist Freeman Dyson, professor emeritus of the Institute for Advanced Study at Princeton, [who] calls a "heretic" on global warming [has also] slammed computer models as unreliable. "The fuss about global warming is grossly exaggerated," writes Dyson in his 2007 book, *Many Colored Glass: Reflections on the Place of Life in the Universe*. Dyson focuses on debunking climate model predictions of climate doom. He said:

> They do not begin to describe the real world that we live in. The real world is muddy and messy and full of things that we do not yet understand. It is much easier for a scientist to sit in an air-conditioned building and run computer models than to put on winter clothes and measure what is really happening outside in the swamps and the clouds. That is why the climate model experts end up believing their own models.

In fact, so much of climate computer modeling is based on taking temperature data from a very short timeframe and extrapolating it out over 50 or 100 years or more and coming up with terrifying, scary scenarios. There is often no attempt to look at the longer geologic record.

But much of this type of modeling has about as much validity as me taking my 5-year-old granddaughter's growth rate from the last 2 years and using that to project her height when she is 25. My projections may show she will be 12 feet high at that time. Yet that is exactly how many of these computer model fears of the future are generated for sea level rise estimates on ice melt projections in places such as Greenland and the Arctic and other locations.

Earlier this month, yet another report was issued based on future computer models finding that polar bear populations are allegedly going to be devastated by 2050 due to global warming. The report was issued as part of the U.S. Fish and Wildlife Service consideration of listing the polar bear under the Endangered Species Act. This is a classic case of reality versus unproven computer model predictions. The Fish and Wildlife Service estimates that the polar bear population is currently at 20,000 to 25,000 bears, whereas in the fifties and sixties, estimates were as low as 5,000 to 10,000 bears. We also have a 2002 U.S. Geological Survey of wildlife in the Arctic Refuge Coastal Plain that noted the polar bear populations "may now be near historic highs."

The bottom line is that the attempt to list the polar bear under the Endangered Species Act is not based on any evidence that the polar bear populations are declining or in trouble. It is based on computer models fraught with uncertainties.

The third critical point on global warming is to debunk the notion that the more CO_2, the warmer the world, as simplistic. Environmental economist Dennis Avery, co-author with climate scientist Dr. Fred Singer of the new book, *Unstoppable Global Warming Every 1500 Years*, details how solar activity is linked to the Earth's natural temperature cycles. These two scientists argue, "The Earth has warmed only a net of 0.2 degrees centigrade of net warming since 1940. Human-emitted CO_2 gets blamed for only half of that."

Perhaps the most inconvenient fact for the promoters of climate doom is the abundance of new peer-reviewed papers echoing these many more scientists' skeptical views. A new peer-reviewed study by Brookhaven National Lab scientist Stephen Schwartz, accepted for publication in the *Journal of Geophysical Research*, finds that even a doubling of atmospheric carbon dioxide would not have the previous predicted dire impacts on global temperatures. In fact, this paper implies that we have already seen almost all of the warming from CO_2 that mankind has put into the atmosphere.

Astronomer Dr. Ian Wilson proclaimed in August of 2007 that the new Schwartz study means "Anthropogenic – that is manmade global warming – bites the dust." A former Harvard physicist, Dr. Lubos Motl, said the new study has reduced proponents of manmade climate fears to "playing the children's game to scare each other."

Now, just look at a sampling of the recent peer review studies debunking the issues. There are many others I could talk about, but I am just going to name a few here, things all happening this year, 2007. A September peer-reviewed study counters global warming theory, by finding carbon dioxide did not end the last Ice Age. The study found, "Deep-sea temperatures rose 1,300 years before atmospheric CO_2, ruling out the greenhouse gas as driver of meltdown." The lead author geologist Lowell Stott, explained, "The climate dynamic is much more complex than simply saying that CO_2 rises and the temperature warms." An October 2007 study by the Danish National Space Center Study concluded, "The Sun still appears to be the main forcing agent in global climate change." This study was authored by Physicist Henrik Svensmark and Eigil Friis-Christensen. The Belgian weather institute's August 2007 study dismissed the decisive role of CO_2 in warming, saying, "CO_2 is not the big bogeyman of climate change and global warming." Climate scientist Luc Debontridder explained: "Not CO_2, but water vapor is the most important greenhouse gas. It is responsible for at least 75 percent of the greenhouse effect." This is a simple scientific fact, but Al Gore's movie has hyped CO_2 so much that nobody seems to take note of it.

In 2007, even the alarmist IPCC reduced its sea level rise estimates significantly, thus reducing man's estimated impact on the climate by 25 percent. Meanwhile, a separate UN report in late 2006 found that cow emissions are more damaging to the planet than all of the CO_2 emissions from cars and trucks. Stating it in a different way, the gasses released by stock actually exceed the CO_2 in the atmosphere from all the cars and trucks in the transportation sector. Again, I stress that these research studies are but a sampling of the new science flowing in that is starting to overwhelm the fear campaigns of the global warming alarmists.

Geophysicist Dr. David Deming, associate professor of arts and sciences at the University of Oklahoma explained in January of this year, "No one has ever died from global warming. What kills people is cold, not heat. For more than 150 years, it has been documented in the medical literature that human mortality rates are highest in the winter when temperatures are the coldest." Perhaps the most scathing indictment of the "more CO_2 equals a warmer world" simplicity comes from Ivy League geologist Dr. Robert Giegengack, the chair of the Department of Earth and Environmental Science at the University of Pennsylvania. He said, "[Al] Gore claims that temperature increases solely because more CO_2 in the atmosphere traps the sun's heat. That's just wrong. It is a natural interplay. It's hard for us to say that CO_2 drives temperature. It's easier to say temperature drives CO_2." Giegengack continued, "The driving mechanism is exactly the opposite of what Al Gore claims, both in his film and in that book. It's the temperature that, through those 650,000 years, controlled the CO_2; not the CO_2 that controlled the temperature."

The global warming scare machine is now so tenuous that other liberal environmental scientists and activists are now joining Giegengack and condemning the entire basis for manmade global warming concerns. Denis Rancourt, a professor of physics and an environmental science researcher at the University of Ottawa. He believes that the global warming campaign does a disservice to the environmental movement. Rancourt wrote, on February 27, 2007:

> Promoting the global warming myth trains people to accept unverified, remote, and abstract dangers in the place of true problems that they can discover for themselves by becoming directly engaged in their workplace and by doing their own research and observations. It trains people to think lifestyle choices, in relation to CO_2 emission, rather than to think activism in the sense of exerting an influence to change societal structures.

Rancourt believes that global warming, "Will not become humankind's greatest threat until the sun has its next hiccup in a billion years or more in the very unlikely scenario that we are still be around." He also noted that even if CO_2 emissions were a grave threat, government action and political will cannot measurably or significantly ameliorate global climate in the present world. Most significantly, however, Rancourt, a committed leftwing activist and scientist, believes environmentalists have been duped into promoting global warming as a crisis. This is a far leftwing environmentalist type. He said:

> I argue that by far the most destructive force on the planet is profit-driven corporations and their cartels backed by military might; and that the global warming myth is a red herring that contributes to hiding this truth. In my opinion, activists who, using any justification, feed the global warming myth have effectively been co-opted, or at best neutralized. Global warming is strictly an imaginary problem for the First World middleclass.

Perhaps the biggest shock to the global warming debate was the conversion of the renowned French geophysicist Dr. Claude Allegre from a believer in the dangerous manmade warming fears to a skeptic just last year. This is a guy who was one of the first scientists around to sound global warming fears 20 years ago. Now he says the cause of climate change is unknown, and he ridiculed what he termed the "prophets of doom of global warming" in a September 2006 article.

I just say bravo for the growing scientific dissent. It is not easy for these guys who took a hard position just a few years ago to change their minds. In

October, *Washington Post* staff writer Juliet Eilperin conceded the obvious, writing that the climate skeptics "appear to be expanding rather than shrinking."

Significant scientific advances have been made since the Kyoto protocol was created, many of which are taking us away from a concern about increasing greenhouse gases. If, back in the mid 1990s, we knew what we know today about climate, Kyoto would almost certainly not exist, because we would have concluded it is not necessary.

The fourth and final essential point deals with how the media and the climate doomsters insist that there is an overwhelming scientific consensus of manmade global warming. The notion of a consensus is carefully manufactured for political, financial, and ideological purposes. Its proponents never explain fully what consensus they are referring to. Is it a consensus that future computer models will turn out correct? Is it a consensus that the Earth has warmed? Proving that parts of the Earth have been warming doesn't prove that humans are responsible.

While it may appear to the casual observer that scientists promoting climate fears are in the majority, that is because most of the media wants to believe this. By the way, this sells papers; we all know that. Evidence continues to reveal this is an illusion. Climate skeptics, the emerging silent majority of scientists, receive much smaller shares of university funds. They don't get university research funds, foundation funds.

Climate skeptics also receive smaller shares of government grants and are not plugged into the well-heeled special interest lobby. If you are part of that lobby, you get all these funds. If you are not, they will not play with you. On the other side of the climate debate, you have a comparatively well-funded group of scientists, the activists who participate in the U.N. conferences, receiving foundation moneys, international government support, and fawning media treatment. The number of skeptics at first glance may appear smaller, but the skeptics are increasingly becoming vocal and turning the tables on the Goliath that has become the global warming fear industry.

Key components of the manufactured consensus fade under scrutiny. We often hear how the National Academy of Sciences and the American Meteorological Society issued statements endorsing the so-called consensus view that man is driving global warming. What you don't hear is that both the NAS and the AMS never allowed member scientists to vote on these climate statements because they know that if it doesn't come out this way, they will not get the money they would otherwise get. Essentially, only two dozen or so members on the governing boards of these institutions produced the consensus statements. It appears that the governing boards of these organizations caved in to pressure from those promoting the politically correct view of the United Nations and Gore-inspired science. The Canadian Academy of Sciences reportedly endorsed a consensus global warming statement that was never even approved by its governing board.

Rank-and-file scientists are now openly rebelling. James Spann, a certified meteorologist with the AMS, openly defied the organization when he said in January he does not know a single TV meteorologist who buys into the manmade global warming hype. In February, a panel of meteorologists expressed unanimous climate skepticism, and one panelist estimated 95 percent of his profession rejects global warming fears.

In August 2007, a comprehensive study of peer-reviewed scientific literature from 2004 to 2007 revealed less than half of all published scientists endorsed global warming theory. In addition, a 2007, report from the international group Institute of Physics [IOP] finds no consensus on global warming. According to one news report:

> As world leaders gathered in New York for a high-level UN meeting on climate change, a new report by some of the world's most renowned scientists urged policymakers to keep their eyes on the "science grapevine" arguing that the understanding of global warming is still far from complete. The IOP is also urging world leaders to remain alert to the latest scientific thought on climate change.

There are frequently claims that the U.N. IPCC "Summary for Policymakers" is the voice of hundreds or even thousands of the world's top scientists, but such claims do not hold up even to the light of scrutiny. According to the Associated Press, during the IPCC "Summary for Policymakers" meeting in April of 2007, the most recent, only 52 scientists participated. Many of the so-called hundreds of [other] scientists who have been affiliated with the U.N. as expert reviewers are, in fact, climate skeptics, but were not involved in writing the alarmist summary and its key notion that, "it is very highly likely that greenhouse gas forcing has been the dominant cause of the observed global warming over the last 50 years." An analysis [of the IPCC report] by climate data analyst John McLean says, "The IPCC leads us to believe that this statement is very much supported by a majority of reviewers. The reality is that there is surprisingly little explicit support for the key notion." Among the 23 independent reviewers, just 4 explicitly endorsed the statement that manmade gasses are the primary cause of global warming.

Hurricane expert Christopher Landsea of NOAA's National Hurricane Center was both an author and a reviewer of the IPCC's second assessment report back in 1995 and the third assessment report in 2001 but resigned from the fourth assessment report after charging the U.N. with playing politics with hurricane science. Landsea wrote a 2005, public letter detailing his experience with the U.N:

> I am withdrawing [from the U.N.] because I have come to view the part of the IPCC to which my expertise is relevant as having become politicized. In addition, when I have raised my concerns to the IPCC leadership, their response was simply to dismiss my concerns. I personally cannot in good faith continue to contribute to a process that I view as both being motivated by pre-conceived agendas and being scientifically unsound.

As you continue to scratch beneath the surface of the alleged global warming consensus, more discoveries await. Alabama's State climatologist Dr. John Christy of the University of Alabama in Huntsville served as a U.N. IPCC lead author in 2001 for the third assessment report and detailed how he personally witnessed U.N. scientists attempting to distort the science for political purposes. Christy told CNN on May 2, 2007, just this year:

> I was at the table with three Europeans, and we were having lunch. And they were talking about their role as lead authors. And they were talking about how they were trying to make the report dramatic that the United States would just have to sign that Kyoto Protocol.

Former Colorado State climatologist, Dr. Roger Pielke, Sr., also detailed the corruption of the U.N. IPCC process. This is what he said on September 1, 2007:

> The same individuals who are doing primary research in the role of humans on the climate system are then permitted to lead the [IPCC] assessment! There should be an outcry on this obvious conflict of interest, but to date either few recognize this conflict, or see that since the recommendations of the IPCC fit their policy and political agenda, they chose to ignore this conflict. In either case, scientific rigor has been sacrificed and poor policy and political decisions will inevitably follow.

Politics appear to be the fuel that runs this process – the U.N. process we have been talking about – from the scientists to the bureaucrats to the delegates, and all the way to many of the world leaders involved in it.

The hysteria created by the U.N. and by Gore and the media have prompted frustrated scientists to finally fight back in the name of a rational approach to science. Climate rationalists or skeptics do not need to engage in smoke and mirrors to state their case, and we will be offering the world a chance to read and decide for themselves, unfiltered from the increasingly activist and shrill lens of media outlets such as NBC, *Newsweek, Time,* CBS, ABC, and CNN.

I have stood on the floor for years detailing all the unfolding science that has debunked climate alarmism. These scientific developments of 2007 are the result of years or decades of hard work by scientists skeptical of manmade climate fears. Finally reaching the point where we can watch the alarm crumble is very satisfying. All these scientists have come up with the same response.

Despite the massive scientific shift in favor of skeptics, proponents of climate fears are increasingly attempting to suppress dissent by skeptics. During Gore's Live Earth concert – which was a dismal failure, I might add – that he had in July, environmental activist Robert F. Kennedy, Jr., said of climate skeptics, "This is treason. And we need to start treating them as traitors."

I would like now to address a question that I am asked repeatedly: "What if you are wrong and the alarmists are right? Isn't it better to adopt carbon restrictions to stop carbon dioxide emissions, just in case?" Let's assume for a moment that the alarmists are right, which, of course, they are not, but let's assume for the sake of discussion they are. It still makes absolutely no sense to join Kyoto or any successor treaty or to adopt climate restrictions on our own. Not only does it not make economic sense, it does not make environmental sense.

First, going on a carbon diet, for us, would do nothing to avert climate change. Let's assume [the United States] signed on to the Kyoto treaty in 1997 and all other developed nations – not China, not Mexico, just the developed nations – signed on to it and lived by the emission requirements. How much would it lower the temperature in 50 years? His answer was 0.07 degrees Celsius by the year 2050 – 0.07 degrees is not even measurable, and that is if we took all these drastic steps, and we are not going to be doing that.

Now, I think when we come to the significant part of this – and that is the lesson on economics – the high costs that would be borne under carbon constraints are unjustifiable to achieve minuscule temperature reductions, and that is if the alarmists are right about the science. How much more unjustifiable would it be if I and the growing number of skeptical scientists are right, which I believe we are?

Whatever actions we take today, we must safeguard the well-being of America's families now and into the future. The Senate acknowledged this when resolved in 2005 that the United States should address global warming as long as it will not significantly harm the United States economy and encourages comparable action by other nations that are major trading partners and key contributors to global emissions. Neither the Kyoto protocol nor a single bill before Congress meets these criteria. They range from costly to ruinous.

Both the Energy Information Administration – that is the EIA – and the Wharton Econometric Forecasting Associates – that is the Wharton School of Economics – analyzed the cost of Kyoto when it was signed and the costs were staggering. For instance, EIA found that the annual cost would be up to $283 billion a year. That is in 1992 constant dollars. Wharton put the cost even higher – more than $300 billion a year. Now, that equates out to an increase in taxes $2,700 a year for every family of four in the United States.

What few Americans realize is that the impact of these policies would not be evenly distributed. The Congressional Budget Office recently looked at the approach taken by most global warming proposals in Congress, known as cap and trade – cap and trade the CO_2 emissions – that would place a cap on carbon emissions, allocate how much everyone could emit, and then let them trade those emissions. Let me quote from the CBO report:

> Regardless of how the allowances were distributed, most of the cost of meeting a cap on CO_2 emissions would be borne by consumers, who would face persistently higher prices for products such as electric and gasoline. Those price increases would be regressive in that poor households would bear a larger burden relative to their income than wealthier households would.

Think about that. Even relatively modest bills would put enormous burdens on the poor. The poor already face energy costs much higher as a percentage of their income than the wealthy. While most Americans spend about 4 percent of their monthly budget on heating homes and energy needs, the poorest one-fifth of Americans spend 19 percent of their budget on energy. Why would we adopt policies which disproportionately force the poor and working class to shoulder the higher costs?

So what is the path forward? I categorically will oppose legislation or initiatives that will devastate our economy, as well as those that will cost jobs simply to make symbolic gestures. I believe such measures would be defeated because the approach is politically unsustainable. We are seeing the first signs of that in Europe right now. Even if the alarmists were right on the science – which they are not – their command and control approaches sow the seeds of their own failure. As long as their own policies put national economy in the crosshairs, they will stoke the fires of opposition and eventually collapse under their own weight.

Stabilizing emissions cannot happen in 20, 40, 60 years because our world infrastructure is built on fossil fuels and will continue to be so for a long time to come. The power plants and other facilities being built now and in the future will emit carbon for half a century once they are complete. Quite simply, the technology does not exist to cost-effectively power the world without emitting carbon dioxide.

Let me conclude [by pointing] out that climate alarmism has become a cottage industry in this country and many others. But a growing number of scientists and the general public are coming around to the idea that climate change is natural and that there is no reason for alarm. It is time to stop pretending the world around us is headed for certain doom and that Kyoto-style policies would save us – when, in fact, the biggest danger lies in these policies themselves. Again, new studies continue to pile up and debunk alarm and the very foundation for so-called solutions to warming.

Barbara Boxer  **NO**

Remarks on the Floor of the U.S. Senate

I have been waiting to speak to the Senate to place in the [*Congressional*] *Record* the case that we have to make to take action to ease the impact of unfettered global warming. I think most Americans know by now – at least those who follow environmental issues – that on our committee, we have Senator Inhofe, who is the former chairman, in a very different place than the current chairman, myself. Senator Inhofe spoke for a couple of hours on this subject last week, and I told him I would come down and put forward my thoughts. I am sure he will want to respond to what I say. That is what the Senate should be. We should be able to debate. I have been looking forward to this debate because, frankly, there are very few isolated and lonely voices who keep on saying we do not have to worry about global warming. Those voices are getting fewer and fewer.

The reality is that a growing and diverse group of voices has recognized the importance of addressing global warming. Here are a few calls to action. Some might surprise you. For example, President Bush, on September 28, [2007] said, "Years from now our children are going to look back at the choices we make today, at this deciding moment. . . . [It] will be a moment when we turn the tide against greenhouse gas emissions instead of allowing the problem to grow."

Again, some of these voices are surprising as we build our case for action in the Senate. Gov. Charlie Crist, a Republican Governor from Florida, said, "We're all on the same planet. We need to work together to make sure the environment is an issue at the forefront. It shouldn't be a political issue. It's a global issue. It's not bipartisan. It's nonpartisan." Certainly, in my own State [California], Governor [Arnold] Schwarzenegger and the Democrats in the legislature have worked very closely to make sure we move against unfettered global warming.

"Vatican to Become World's First Carbon-Neutral State" – This is very recent, this year: The Vatican is installing solar panels and purchasing greenhouse gas offsets to become the first carbon-neutral sovereign state. We can see that everyone is working together except for a few. It is unfortunate because in the Senate, a few can stop us from doing our work. We already heard about some of the problems we are having getting the Energy bill through. But I am very optimistic because we have had a bipartisan breakthrough in the Environment and Public Works Committee with [senators from both parties] getting together and putting forward a very solid bill which, if it is enacted, will be the most far-reaching global warming bill in the world today.

U.S. Congressional Record, October 29, 2007.

Earlier this year, the U.S. Climate Action Partnership, known as USCAP, which includes major corporations, joined together with environmental groups to issue a call for action on global warming, calling for reductions of 60 to 80 percent in greenhouse gas emissions by 2050. I thought I would go over some of the members of U.S. Climate Action Partnership because, again, there are just a few voices out there saying we are putting our head in the sand, this isn't a problem. But mainstream America is with the program. Let me tell my colleagues who they are. I am just going to read a few: Alcoa, Boston Scientific Corporation, BP America, Caterpillar, Inc., Chrysler, ConocoPhillips, Deere, Duke Energy, DuPont, Environmental Defense, Ford Motor Company, General Electric, General Motors, Johnson & Johnson, National Wildlife Federation, Natural Resources Defense Council, PepsiCo, Pew Center on Global Climate Change, PG&E Corporation, Shell, Siemens Corporation, Dow Chemical Company, the Nature Conservancy, World Resources Institute, and Xerox corporation.

We can see the diverse members of the American family from corporate America to environmental organizations that have gotten together and have urged us to cap greenhouse gas emissions and cut them. It is very important that we think about the amazing coalition that is out there behind us addressing global warming. When we hear some Senators come down to the floor of the Senate and say this is ridiculous, this isn't an issue, just remember this list of mainstream America urging us forward, urging us to act.

Why should so many industries be calling upon us to enact climate legislation? Because they recognize a couple of points. One, the science is strong, it is irrefutable, and a sound business future for America lies in dealing with climate change. We cannot grow, we cannot move forward if we all of a sudden turn around and our planet is under threat. We cannot have a business looking out 50 years that does not think about this. We have to think about our grandkids and our great-grandkids, and corporate America thinks about the people who are going to come forward to continue the work of that corporation. They recognize the threat, but they also recognize the opportunities.

Let's read from USCAP's call for action. It is very clear:

> We believe that a national mandatory policy on climate change will provide the basis for the United States to assert world leadership in environmental and energy technology innovation, a national characteristic for which the United States has no rival. Such leadership will assure U.S. competitiveness in this century and beyond.

This is a very strong call for action from Republicans, from Democrats, from Independents, from corporate America, from the environmental community, and others that have joined together.

All you have to do, is pick up a newspaper, any newspaper – I don't care if it is a Republican editorial board, a Democratic editorial board, or Independent – and you will see an amazing amount of evidence as to global warming and its potential impact. I am going to go through a few recent headlines. I asked my staff – and they do an amazing job for me – to follow the news and let me know what is being written, what the scientists are saying. So I am going to give you just an example of some of these headlines. If we can walk away from this, then it seems to me we are being irresponsible. We have to listen to them.

Early warning signs: "Greenhouse Gases Fueled 2006 U.S. Heat" (Reuters) – According to NOAA – That is the National Oceanic and Atmospheric Administration. That is the Bush administration's NOAA – "the annual average U.S. temperature in 2006 was 2.1 degrees Fahrenheit above the 20th century average and the ninth consecutive year of above-normal U.S. temperatures" and that this was a result of "greenhouse gas emissions – not El Nino or other natural phenomena." This is our American Government under the President who has been very loath to move on global warming, warning us about these high temperatures.

"Scientists Report Severe Retreat of Arctic Ice" – The Cap of floating sea ice on the Arctic Ocean, which retreats under summer's warmth, this year shrank more than one million square miles – or six Californias – below the average minimum area reached in recent decades.

Again, these are scientists from the National Snow and Ice Data Center in Boulder, CO. This is not a matter of opinion; this is fact. They are measuring the ice. I was in Greenland. I saw it myself. Several of us went. It is the most awesome sight to behold, to see these icebergs, the size of a coliseum, bigger than this beautiful Senate floor, taller than this room, floating into the ocean. Each iceberg is an average of 9,000 years old, and they melt within 12 months from the time they get into the ocean. So let's not put our heads in the sand or under the water.

More early warning signs: "China Blames Climate Change for Extreme Weather" – This is China. China doesn't really want to move forward. They have been slow to come to the table. According to an official from Chinese Meteorological Administration's Department of Forecasting Services and Disaster Mitigation, "It should be said that one of the reasons for the weather extremes this year has been unusual atmospheric circulation brought about by global warming." A lot of people around here say: Let's not do anything until the Chinese come to the table. Now the Chinese are telling us we better watch out for this global warming.

"As Sea Level Rises, Disaster Predicted for Va. Wetlands" – My colleague, [Senator] John Warner [R-VA] was present at a very important set of hearings where we looked at the impact of global warming on his State. It says. "At least half, and perhaps as much as 80 percent, of the wetlands would be covered in too much water to survive if sea levels rise 1 1/2 to 2 feet." The analysis was conducted by Wetlands Watch, an environmental group.

"From Greenland to Antarctica, the world is losing its ice faster than anyone thought possible" (*National Geographic*) – Scientists are finding that glaciers and ice sheets are surprisingly touchy. Instead of melting steadily, like an ice cube on a summer day, they are prone to feedbacks, when melting begets more melting and the ice shrinks precipitously.

This is what is happening. You can come down on this floor and you can put a blindfold over your eyes and you can put your hands over your ears and say: I see no problem, I hear no problem. Then you are not really taking in the signs.

"Fires a Consequence of Climate Change" – This is touching my heart because my State has been burning, and all of my colleagues know this and all of them have been most wonderful to us – to Senator Feinstein and to me – about offering help and assistance. In the long run, we need to do something about global warming or we are going to have that horrible combination of drought, low humidity, high temperatures, and terrible winds – weather extremes that you have experienced from time to time. This is what we are going to see. Greek Prime Minister Costas Kerryman said, "The weather phenomena this year favored, as never before, the outbreak of destructive fires. We are already living with the consequences of climate change."

"Climate Change Pollution Rising – Thanks to Overwhelmed Oceans and Plants" (*Scientific American*) – I am not citing articles here to show you where there is bias. The world's oceans and forests are already so full of CO that they are losing their ability to absorb this climate change culprit. This according to the Proceedings of the National Academy of Sciences.

Some come to the floor [of the Senate] and say: Oh, look at this great scientist, Mr. ABC, or whatever his name, and he is challenging this. Well, he is challenging the world's leading scientists. And I think it is very important to say there are always people who will say HIV doesn't cause AIDS; there are always people who will say cigarette smoking doesn't cause cancer; but thank God this government has followed the preponderance of the science and we now are making progress. How sad it would be if America sits on the sidelines while the whole world looks to us for leadership on global warming.

"The Future Is Drying Up" – According to Nobel Laureate Steven Chu, diminished supplies of fresh water might prove a far more serious problem than slowly rising seas. He also remarked, "The most optimistic climate models for the second half of this century suggest that 30 to 70 percent of the snow pack will disappear." No wonder we have people visiting our offices who are already hurting from the recreation industry in this Nation. They see what is happening. They see the handwriting on the wall. We have to act.

"Study Links CO to Demise of Grazing Lands" (*Los Angeles Times*) – Rising levels of carbon dioxide may be contributing to the conversion of the world's grasslands into a landscape of woody shrubs, much less useful for livestock grazing. So this has implications for the very way of life we have here in America.

"Parks Face Climate Threat" – A report shows how climate change could have a huge effect on the Great Smokey Mountains, the Blue Ridge Parkway and other national parks. This according to a new report by the National Parks Conservation Association. Folks, this is mainstream thinking. Mainstream thinking. We have to act.

"Likely Spread of Deserts to Fertile Land Requires Quick Response, U.N. Report Says" (*New York Times*) – Enough fertile land could turn into desert within the next generation to create an "environmental crisis of global proportions" based on a new U.N. report. The report warns of large-scale migrations and political instability in parts of Africa and Central Asia. The report recommends national and international action to address global warming.

Another call to action. And here, from the Intergovernmental Panel on Climate Change [IPC], which just won the Nobel Peace Prize, along with former Vice President Al Gore: "Projected trends in climate-change-related exposures of importance to human health will increase the number of people suffering from death, disease and injury from heat waves, floods, storms, fires, and droughts.

So to come down here and talk about the polar bear and say the polar bear is fine, the polar bear is not fine, and we will talk about it; but this isn't about the polar bear. This is about God's creation that is in jeopardy. We had testimony from scientists that 40 percent of the species that were created are going to be gone. Now, it is our turn to do our part. That is why I have been working so closely with the religious community, the evangelical community. They are concerned about God's creation, and we ought to be. We talk a good game about it. We talk about values. We talk about it, so let us do something to show we are willing to protect this gift from God we have been given.

"Why Frogs Are Dying" (*Newsweek*) – Climate change is no longer merely a matter of numbers from a computer model. With startling swiftness, it is reordering the natural world.

"Global Warming May Be Behind Increases in Insects and Disease-Carrying Animals" (*Newsday*) – Rising global temperatures may be helping to spark a population boom in insects and disease-carrying animals, creating unexpected threats to human populations, a number of scientific reports say. That is not a pretty future for my new grandson, to think about being exposed to all these vectors that have not attacked us, but this is what lies in our future if we do nothing.

"WHO – the World Health Organization – 77,000 People Die Annually in Asia-Pacific Region from Climate Change" and "Pollution Cutting Life Expectancy in Europe" (both [published in] *USA Today*) – According to a Report by the European Environment Agency: "Poor air and water quality, and environmental changes blamed on global warming, have cut Europeans' life expectancy by nearly a year, Europe's environmental agency warned."

"Report Calls on Europe to Move on Global Warming" – The European Commission report warns that unless there is planning, European countries will face "increasingly frequent crises and disasters which will prove much more costly and also threaten Europe's social and economic systems and its security." The point is, when you invest now, you save $5 later.

How about national security? One of the reasons I got so concerned about this is when I learned what our own Pentagon and our own intelligence people are saying to us. And what are they saying to us? A report commissioned by the Department of Defense in 2003 found that the impacts of global warming would cause the U.S. to "find itself in a world where Europe will be struggling internally, with large numbers of refugees washing up on its shores and Asia in serious crisis over food and water. Disruptions and conflict will be endemic features of life." And, of course, our Pentagon and our Department of Defense are very concerned about that happening with our allies in Europe.

"Warming Will Exacerbate Global Water Conflicts" – According to many studies, including the IPCC, changing weather patterns will leave millions of people without dependable supplies of water for drinking, irrigation, and power.

Now, the reason I took so much time is to show the breadth and the depth of the concern in this country, in the world, to make the point that there is a huge movement in this country and in the world to address global warming. We are not going to listen to those who have their heads in the sand or, frankly, have decided they want to leave this for another generation. That would be irresponsible.

When Senator Inhofe came on the floor, he made a number of statements which were not true, and I am going to deal with a couple of them. He used an MIT [Massachusetts Institute of Technology] report in a misleading fashion. Senator Inhofe has frequently claimed an MIT report shows [that my bill to cut carbon emissions] would lead to a $4,500 tax on a family of four. But the author of the MIT report, John Reilly, said:

> Senator Inhofe misread his findings. Rather than impose a tax of $4,500 as Inhofe described it, he said, the study shows the regulation could generate a substantial amount of Federal revenue for the government to give back to Americans. A family of four, Reilly said, could earn an additional $4,500 if the United States adopted a carbon tax or auctioned off carbon credits.

So let us not misquote authors around here, because that is not the right thing to do for them nor is it the right thing to do to mislead our colleagues.

I mentioned the polar bears before, and many of us have been touched to see the polar bears clinging to smaller and smaller pieces of ice in order to survive. Senator Inhofe has claimed – and he claimed it on the floor – that the polar bear populations are increasing. The best-studied population, in Canada's western Hudson Bay, fell by 22 percent from 1,194 animals in 1987 to 935 in 2004, according to the U.S. Fish and Wildlife Service. Our own people are telling us that the polar bear is in trouble. The World Conservation Union projects that the bears' numbers will drop by 30 percent by 2050 due to continued loss of Arctic sea ice.

I think it is important that we talk about facts. Science must dictate what we do, not ideological arguments that don't have any weight behind them. The leading scientists of the world, including the Intergovernmental Panel on Climate Change, which I earlier mentioned, and which won the Nobel prize along with Vice President Gore, and the IPCC included hundreds of scientists, the best scientists from 130 nations – they tell us clearly that global warming is happening now and human activities are the cause. I believe we can meet this challenge, with hope, not fear. I believe when we meet this challenge, we will be stronger as a nation and we will be healthier as a nation.

And, by the way, we will create a whole new array of green-dollar jobs. My own state, a leader in the environment, has proven the point that when you step out and you address the needs of the environment, what comes with it are only good things – prosperity, job creation, and healthier families. We are doing it in our State with global warming and, by the way, many other States are following. If we did nothing, it would be a shame. This is a seminal issue, and we need to do something about it, because doing nothing is not an option we can afford. The potential consequences will be devastating for our families in the future and for the world.

We are seeing the early warning signs. People can come down to this floor and say whatever they want. We have seen melting of snow, we have seen melting of permafrost, increased temperatures, warming of lakes, rivers, oceans, changing in the seasons, shifts in the ranges of plant and animal species, rising sea levels. In the future, we can expect to see more extreme weather events, more severe heat waves, droughts, flooding, increased storm surges and, sadly, an increased incidence of wildfires. We will see extinction of species; we will see freshwater resources at risk. By 2020, between 75 million and 250 million people will be exposed to increased water stress due to climate change in Africa. In Asia there will be problems. Warming in the western mountains of America is projected to cause decreased snow pack and reduced summer flows, resulting in even greater competition for already over allocated water resources.

[During hearings on the environment] we had scientists who were experts on wildlife. I remember sitting there, being so saddened to hear that if we do nothing, 40 percent of God's species on planet Earth could face extinction.

Now we hear our oceans are at risk as well. The British Royal Society projects that progressive acidification of oceans due to increasing carbon dioxide is expected to have terrible impacts on marine life, such as corals and their dependent species. You have heard of coral bleaching. It is caused by increased water temperatures as well as the oceans becoming acidic from storing excess carbon. The water becomes so acidic [that] some marine life, such as shellfish and coral reefs, can no longer form their shell, as it dissolves in the acidic water.

The IPCC found that pests, diseases, and fire are having terrible impacts on forests, with an extended period of high fire risk and large increases in areas burned. Again, I wish to use this moment to thank the firefighters in my State, all of them – local, state, federal – working seamlessly together. We have the most extraordinary heroic firefighters in California, as we do all over this country. Their jobs are becoming more and more dangerous as these fires are so strong and are fueled by droughts, high temperatures, low humidity, and high winds.

I mentioned before that in July, I was in Greenland. I was there with 10 senators and Dr. Richard Alley, an expert on ice from Penn State, who accompanied us on the trip. It was amazing to see this whole situation with him at my side. What I learned from him is Greenland's ice is melting faster than anyone thought. In some places, the glacier ice is moving so quickly, if you stand there you can actually observe it moving. In the past year, new islands were discovered that were previously connected to the main mass of ice. The Greenland ice sheet holds enough ice to raise sea levels globally by 23 feet. Think about 23 feet. Sea level increases of only a few feet will cause major disruptions.

I wish to talk about public health. Public health officials have issued a call to action. We had a hearing the other day and we heard from the Director of the Centers for Disease Control and Prevention. Unfortunately, her testimony was heavily edited by the White House. I am working very hard, with other colleagues, to get her original draft. Let me tell you, we are not going to rest until we get that. But the fact is the public has a right to know everything about global warming and the threat it poses to their families and to their communities.

At the same hearing where we heard from Dr. Gerberding, the Commissioner of the Tennessee Department of Health presented the committee with a position statement from the Association of State and Territorial Health Officials on Climate Change and Public Health. Their statement was adopted unanimously.

According to the IPCC, climate change has already altered the distribution of some infectious disease vectors and the seasonal distribution of some allergenic pollen and increased heat wave-related deaths. We are already seeing and we are already feeling the difference. If trends continue, we could see increased malnutrition and related disorders, including those related to child growth and development. We will see increases in the number of people suffering from disease, injury, and death because of heat waves and because of droughts and fires and all the things we mentioned.

The World Health Organization has estimated that human-induced changes in the Earth's climate lead to at least 5 million cases of illness and more than 150,000 deaths every year already. We saw the European heat wave which caused countless numbers of illnesses and claimed 35,000 lives. That is accurate – 35,000 lives were lost.

We are beginning to see right here in America what happens when the water warms. The Associated Press reported on September 27 that a 14-year-old boy died from an infection caused by an amoeba after swimming in Lake Havasu [Arizona]. According to a CDC official, these amebas thrive in warm water and as water temperatures continue to rise, we can expect to see more cases of these amoeba infections.

We are going to see an increase of ground-level ozone or smog because that is formed at higher temperatures. We know smog damages lungs and can cause asthma in our kids. We already have asthma as the leading cause of school absences in my state. We have major problems with dangerous smog days.

We know about wildlife. We know, as I said, that 40 percent of the species are at risk of extinction if we do nothing to reduce global warming. The U.S. Fish and Wildlife Service concluded that shrinking sea ice is the primary cause for the decline in polar bear populations. Senator Inhofe comes down and says the polar bears are doing great: Wrong. False information. Listen to your own administration's U.S. Fish and Wildlife Service. The shrinking sea ice is the primary cause for the decline in polar bear populations.

This [the Bush] administration – because it was threatened by a lawsuit – proposed listing the polar bear as threatened under the Endangered Species Act. So come down here and show pictures of those magnificent polar bears, saying everything is fine – that is wrong. It is wrong by every measure, by every scientific account, by our own U.S. Fish and Wildlife Service.

Global warming is a national security issue, as I mentioned before. People are telling me this current humanitarian catastrophe in Darfur is already linked to the extended drought in the region. The Secretary General of the United Nations said the Darfur conflict began as an ecological crisis, arising at least in part from climate change. This is happening right under our nose. The Senate and the House have been asleep at the wheel – until recently.

A report commissioned by the Department of Defense found the impacts of global warming would cause the United States to "find itself in a world where Europe would be struggling." Projected global warming "poses a serious threat to America's national security" and "acts as a threat multiplier for instability." This is all from retired admirals and generals. Projected global warming poses a serious threat to America's national security.

The United States, they said, could more frequently be drawn into situations of conflict "to help provide stability before conditions worsen and are exploited by extremists." Such missions could be long and require the United States to remain for "stability and reconstruction efforts . . . to avert further disaster."

That report also warns of "extreme weather events, drought, flooding, sea level rise, retreating glaciers, habitat shifts, the increased spread of life-threatening diseases" and increased scarcity of clean water that could "result in multiple chronic conditions" and "foster the conditions for internal conflicts, extremism, and movement toward increased authoritarianism and radical ideologies."

I have never seen an issue such as this, where we have such a unanimous call for action, a unanimous call for action – from the business community, from environmental organizations, from admirals and generals, from the Department of Defense, from the Wildlife Service – from all over the world. As yet we are nowhere, but we hope to change that.

Addressing global warming has major benefits. I wanted you to hear the truth about the dangers of global warming. Now I want to tell you what gives me hope. When we step up to the plate, we are going to benefit. We cannot only prevent the most dangerous effects of climate change, but we are going to be better off for it. I already mentioned Sir Nicholas Stern, former chief economist of the World Bank. He said: Spend a dollar now, save $5 later. So people are going to come on the floor and they are going to say: Oh my God, they are spending money on this. No, we are going to save money, because if we can avert the worst problems of global warming – you can't build a flood protection tall enough unless we do something now. Do you know what it costs to build that flood protection? We know because we passed the Water Resources Protection Act and we kept our promises to the people of New Orleans and the others from [hurricanes] Katrina and Rita who suffered so much.

Since 1990, Britain has reduced its greenhouse gas emissions by 15 percent. [Meanwhile,] Britain's economy has grown 40 percent. Britain's environmental industries are the fastest growing sector of the country's economy. I was just there a couple of months ago. Their environmental jobs grew to 500,000 from 135,000 in just the last 5 years.

There is a study at University of California, Berkeley [that says] in California, the gross State product, by 2020 will be up by as much as $74 billion, with 89,000 new jobs created because of our work on global warming and our laws. Sun Microsystems is already reaping the benefits of greater efficiency. They made some simple changes in the way they cool their computer servers. They have been able to cut their electrical consumption in half.

Tesla Motors, I would urge all of you to follow that company. They are producing an all-electric car with performance that rivals or even exceeds the world's best sports cars. It is exciting. It is in production. It is all-electric. There is another company, Bloom Energy, in San Jose. They are creating the next generation of fuel cell electrical generation systems. I visited there and the scientists were explaining how all of this works. I can tell you this technology has the potential to revolutionize the way that electricity is generated. It holds the potential to bring clean electricity to parts of the world that have no electricity now.

So what are the benefits, the benefits of new technology? New jobs, cleaner air as we reduce the pollution that causes global warming, by increasing our use of clean, renewable energy sources such as wind and solar, driving more efficiently, less polluting cars and trucks, and increasing efficiency.

We will reduce other forms of air population too: sulfur dioxide, nitrogen oxides, mercury. Those pollutants will be reduced as we cut global warming pollution. And that means cleaner, healthier air for us all to breathe. The IPCC also concluded that household benefits from reduced air pollution as a result of action to reduce greenhouse gas emissions can be substantial. So when I say: I meet this crisis with hope, not fear, I mean it. I think it is going to create jobs. I think it is going to make our communities healthier. I think it is going to make our air healthier. I think it is going to reduce our dependence on foreign countries to supply oil, which is now up to $90 a barrel.

We know oil is a critical strategic interest of America. Our reliance on oil-rich rogue states and unstable regimes has been at the heart of wars and interventions in the Middle East. As we develop these clean, renewable sources of energy, which is all going to be done by the private sector, my venture capitalists at home cannot wait to make these investments, but they will not make them unless we take the lead on a strong anti-global-warming bill.

I also want to express the moral imperative that was really brought to me by the religious community. The most vulnerable here and around the world have to be protected. I know we have colleagues who continue to say we have to do it, and they are absolutely right.

There is no time to waste because the longer we wait, the harder it will be to achieve the goals we have to achieve – before we find we are spending a fortune on flood control and we are spending a fortune to try to mitigate the terrible ravages that global warming will bring.

In every great issues debate, you always have a few people who stand outside the mainstream, and I respect that. I absolutely give the folks who have that point of view all the time they want to express themselves. Some will say this is not an urgent problem. Do nothing. Some have tried to argue that we should not act now.

I say there is no time to waste. Right now, there is unprecedented momentum for change. We must harness that momentum to pass strong global warming legislation. We have a small window of time to get started down this path. The longer we wait to get started, the harder it will be to achieve the emissions reductions we know we need to reach. Starting now will send a signal to the world and the business community as they make their future plans that the United States is serious about its leadership role.

I have a vision for my 11-year-old grandson and for my new grandson who was born a few months ago. My vision is that these children and yours will grow up and be able to know the gifts of nature that we saved for them, that they will understand we made the right choice for them – we protected the planet that is their home – that because of our action they will not be shackled into fighting wars over the last drops of water or oil or remaining acres of arable cropland. They will not have to spend their last treasure building higher floodwalls, bigger levees, and fortified cities to escape rising seas and angrier hurricanes. Their cars will run on clean renewable fuels that do not pollute the air they breathe. The United States will lead in exporting clean technologies and products that are the engine of a new green economy. We will lead the world in showing the way to live well, in a way that respects the Earth. To make this vision a reality, we must face our challenge in a way that overcomes our differences and that defies our party affiliations.

POSTSCRIPT

Are Warnings about Global Warming Unduly Alarmist?

The debate over the causes, extent, and future impact of global warming is momentous. For those who are alarmed by global warming it could have many increasingly serious negative consequences. Then there is the question of what, if anything, to do about global warming. A UN-sponsored treaty called the Kyoto Protocol in 1997 that requires the industrialized countries to significantly cut their CO_2 emissions does not impose limits on developing countries, including China and India. Most countries ratified the treaty, but the United States and a few others did not. The Bush administration objected that evidence of global warming is not sufficiently proven to warrant the kind of harmful economic changes that the administration claims would have to take place to cut CO_2 emissions. For example, cars might have to be much smaller, gasoline prices higher, and electricity production and consumption curtailed. Also, many analysts project enormous costs. One study has concluded that a program to cut CO_2 emissions by 70 percent over a 40-year period would cost the U.S. economy $2.7 trillion. But the economic calculations cut both ways. For instance, there are projections of a $5 trillion savings in fuel costs. Other studies have pointed to the economic stimulus that would be provided by creating alternative energy technologies. Losses from storm damages will also drop, saving, perhaps, the cost of rebuilding many "New Orleans" shattered by storm-driven flooding. Bush also argued that unless China, India, and other developing countries also had to adopt restrictions, cutbacks by the United States and other developed countries would make little long-term difference.

The Kyoto Protocol expires in 2009, and there is a widely supported move to replace it with a new treaty to be negotiated in Copenhagen, Denmark in 2009. There will be many contentious points, such as whether the developing countries have to accept mandated limits to emissions. In the end though, the crucial questions is what the United States will do. "Without the United States, we can never succeed," Norway's Minister of the Environment has said. "If the Americans are not moving, anyone else who does not want to move will hide behind the Americans." Given that, the question is where the new U.S. president will stand. Both Barack Obama and John McCain believe that global warming that is occurring is caused by human activity and that the United States should limit its emissions as part of an international agreement. However, McCain believes a successful treaty requires mandatory participation by China and India. Obama agrees those two countries are important, but has hedged a bit on the treaty, saying their participation should come soon.

The U.S. Environmental Protection Agency has a good site on global warming at http://epa.gov/climatechange/index.html. An Internet site that takes a skeptical view of the alarm over global warming can be found at http://www .globalwarming.org/. Taking the opposite view is the Union of Concerned Scientists at http://www.ucsusa.org/. A warning about global warming and a plea to address the issue is given by former Vice President Al Gore in the documentary, *An Inconvenient Truth* (2006). The film is criticized in, "The *Real* 'Inconvenient Truth'," at http://www.junkscience.com/Greenhouse/.

ISSUE 20

Should the United States Ratify the Convention to Eliminate All Forms of Discrimination Against Women?

YES: Harold Hongju Koh, from Testimony during Hearings on "Ratification of the Convention on the Elimination of All Forms of Discrimination Against Women," before the Committee on Foreign Relations, U.S. Senate (June 13, 2002)

NO: Grace Smith Melton, from "CEDAW: How U.N. Interference Threatens the Rights of American Women," *Heritage Foundation Backgrounder* #2227 (January 9, 2009)

ISSUE SUMMARY

YES: Harold Hongju Koh, the Gerard C. and Bernice Latrobe Smith Professor of International Law at Yale University and former U.S. assistant secretary of state contends that the United States cannot champion progress for women's human rights around the world unless it is also a party to the global women's treaty.

NO: Grace Smith Melton, an associate for social issues at the United Nations with the Richard and Helen DeVos Center for Religion and Civil Society at The Heritage Foundation, contends that ratifying would neither advance women's equality nor serve American foreign policy interests, including the security and advancement of women around the globe.

Females constitute about half the world population, but they are a distinct economic–political–social minority because of the wide gap in societal power and resources between women and men. Women constitute 70 percent of the world's poor and two-thirds of its literates. They occupy only 14 percent of the managerial jobs, are less than 40 percent of the world's professional and technical workers, and garner only 35 percent of the earned income in the world. Women are also disadvantaged politically. In late 2003, only 17 women were serving as presidents or prime ministers of their countries; women make up just 8 percent of all national cabinet officers; and only one of every six national legislators is a woman.

On average, life for women is not only harder and more poorly compensated than it is for men, it is also more dangerous. "The most painful devaluation of women," the United Nations reports, "is the physical and psychological violence that stalks them from cradle to grave." Signs of violence against women include the fact that about 80 percent of the world's refugees are women and their children. Other assaults on women arguably constitute a form of genocide. According to the U.N. Children's Fund, "In many countries, boys get better care and better food than girls. As a result, an estimated one million girls die each year because they were born female." None of these economic, social, and political inequities is new. Indeed, the global pattern of discrimination against women is ancient. What is new is the global effort to recognize the abuses that occur and to ameliorate and someday end them.

To help accomplish that goal, the U.N. General Assembly in 1979 voted by 130 to 0 to put the Convention on the Elimination of All Forms of Discrimination Against Women (CEDAW) before the world's countries for adoption. Supporters hailed the treaty as a path-breaking step on behalf of advancing the status of women. Many countries agreed, and by September 1981 enough countries had signed and ratified CEDAW to put it into effect. This set a record for the speed with which any human rights convention had gone into force.

CEDAW is a women's international bill of rights. Most of these rights are enumerated in various other treaties as applicable to all humans, but women's rights had not been specifically and fully addressed in any other treaty before CEDAW. Countries that legally adhere to the convention agree to undertake measures to end all the various forms of discrimination against women. Doing so entails accepting legal gender equality and ensuring the practice of gender equality by abolishing all discriminatory laws, enacting laws that prohibit discrimination against women, and establishing agencies protect women's rights.

President Jimmy Carter signed CEDAW in 1980 and submitted it to the Senate for ratification. However, he was soon thereafter defeated for reelection, and the treaty languished in legislative limbo through the presidencies of Ronald Reagan and George H. W. Bush. By contrast, President Bill Clinton made an effort to move CEDAW forward. The Senate Committee on Foreign Relations held hearings on the pact in 1994 and recommended ratification. There the effort on behalf of CEDAW stalled. It did not come up for debate or a vote in the Senate. Ratification requires a two-thirds vote by the Senate, and there was little chance that the measure would garner the required votes.

The testimony that constitutes the first reading here came during hearings in 2002 that were part of yet another effort to gain Senate approval of CEDAW. In that reading, Harold Hongju Koh maintains that failure to ratify the treaty will undermine U.S. efforts to fight for human rights around the world. Nevertheless, the measure never came to a vote in the Senate because the strength of the mostly Republican opposition ensured that the necessary two-thirds support needed for ratification was out of reach. With the election of a Democratic president and an Democratic Congress in 2008, those supporting CEDAW see a renewed possibility of its ratification. However, in the second reading, Grace Smith Melton argues that CEDAW remains unnecessary to protect the right of American women and also opens the United States up to interference by the United Nations and international courts.

YES

Harold Hongju Koh

Ratification of the Convention on the Elimination of All Forms of Discrimination Against Women

In his [2002] State of the Union address, President George W. Bush . . . announced that "America will always stand for the non-negotiable demands of human dignity: the rule of law; limits on the power of the state; respect for women; private property; free speech; equal justice; and religious tolerance." I can imagine no more fitting way for this Administration and this Senate to answer that demand than by moving quickly to ratify this treaty for the rights of women. . . .

My main message today is that this commitment should not stop at the water's edge. Particularly after September 11, America cannot be a world leader in guaranteeing progress for women's human rights, whether in Afghanistan, here in the United States, or around the world, unless it is also a party to the global women's treaty.

Let me first review the background and history of CEDAW [Convention to Eliminate All Forms of Discrimination Against Women]; second, explain why ratifying that treaty would further our national commitments to eliminating gender discrimination, without jeopardizing our national interests; and third, explain why some concerns occasionally voiced about our ratification of this treaty are, upon examination, completely unfounded.

First, some history. The United Nations Charter reaffirms both the faith of the peoples of the United Nations "in the equal rights of men and women," [Preamble], and their determination to promote respect for human rights "for all without distinction as to race, sex, language, or religion." In 1948, the Universal Declaration of Human Rights similarly declared that "everyone" is entitled to the rights declared there "without distinction of any kind, such as race, colour, (or) sex . . ." In 1975, a global call for an international convention specifically to implement those commitments emerged from the First World Conference on Women in Mexico City. But until 1979, when the General Assembly adopted the CEDAW, there was no convention that addressed comprehensively women's rights within political, social, economic, cultural, and family life. After years of drafting, the United Nations adopted the Convention on the Elimination of All Forms of Discrimination Against Women on December 18, 1979, and the Convention entered into force in September 1981.

Committee on Foreign Relations, U.S. Senate, June 13, 2002.

In the more than two decades since, 169 nations other than our own have become parties to the Convention. Only nineteen United Nations member states have not. That list includes such countries as Afghanistan, Bahrain, Iran, Somalia, Sudan, Syria, Qatar, and the United Arab Emirates. To put it another way, the United States is now the only established industrialized democracy in the world that has not yet ratified the CEDAW treaty. Frankly, Senators, this is a national disgrace for a country that views itself as a world leader on human rights.

Why should the United States ratify this treaty? For two simple reasons. First, ratification would make an important global statement regarding the seriousness of our national commitment to these issues. Second, ratification would have a major impact in ensuring both the appearance and the reality that our national practices fully satisfy or exceed international standards.

The CEDAW treaty has been accurately described as an international bill of rights for women. The CEDAW simply affirms that women, like the rest of the human race, have an inalienable right to live and work free of discrimination. The Convention affirms the rights of all women to exercise on an equal basis their "human rights and fundamental freedoms in the political, economic, social, cultural, civil or any other field."

The treaty defines and condemns discrimination against women and announces an agenda for national action to end such discrimination. By ratifying the treaty, states do nothing more than commit themselves to undertaking "appropriate measures" toward ending discrimination against women, steps that our country has already begun in numerous walks of life. The CEDAW then lays a foundation for realizing equality between women and men in these countries by ensuring women's equal access to, and equal opportunities in, public and political life—including the right to vote, to stand for election, to represent their governments at an international level, and to enjoy equal rights "before the law" as well as equal rights in education, employment, health care, marriage and family relations, and other areas of economic and social life. The Convention directs State Parties to "take into account the particular problems faced by rural women," and permits parties to take "temporary special measures aimed at accelerating de facto equality" between men and women, a provision analogous to one also found in the Convention on the Elimination of All Forms of Racial Discrimination, which our country has already ratified.

Ratifying this treaty would send the world the message that we consider eradication of these various forms of discrimination to be solemn, universal obligations. The violent human rights abuses we recently witnessed against women in Afghanistan, Bosnia, Haiti, Kosovo, and Rwanda painfully remind us of the need for all nations to join together to intensify efforts to protect women's rights as human rights. At the State Department, where I supervised the production of the annual country reports on human rights conditions worldwide, I found that a country's ratification of the CEDAW is one of the surest indicators of the strength of its commitment to internalize the universal norm of gender equality into its domestic laws.

Let me emphasize that in light of our ongoing national efforts to address gender equality through state and national legislation, executive action, and judicial decisions, the legal requirements imposed by ratifying this treaty would not be burdensome. Numerous countries with far less impressive practices regarding gender equality than the United States have ratified the treaty, including countries whom we would never consider our equals on such matters, including Iraq, Kuwait, North Korea, and Saudi Arabia.

At the same time, from my direct experience as America's chief human rights official, I can testify that our continuing failure to ratify CEDAW has reduced our global standing, damaged our diplomatic relations, and hindered our ability to lead in the international human rights community. Nations that are otherwise our allies, with strong rule-of-law traditions, histories, and political cultures, simply cannot understand why we have failed to take the obvious step of ratifying this convention. In particular, our European and Latin American allies regularly question and criticize our isolation from this treaty framework both in public diplomatic settings and private diplomatic meetings.

Our nonratification has led our allies and adversaries alike to challenge our claim of moral leadership in international human rights, a devastating challenge in this post-September 11 environment. Even more troubling, I have found, our exclusion from this treaty has provided anti-American diplomatic ammunition to countries who have exhibited far worse records on human rights generally, and women's rights in particular. Persisting in the aberrant practice of nonratification will only further our diplomatic isolation and inevitably harm our other United States foreign policy interests.

Treaty ratification would be far more than just a paper act. The treaty has demonstrated its value as an important policy tool to promote equal rights in many of the foreign countries that have ratified the CEDAW. As a recent, comprehensive world survey issued by the United Nations Development Fund for Women chronicles, numerous countries around the world have experienced positive gains directly attributable to their ratification and implementation of the CEDAW. CEDAW has been empowering women around the globe to change constitutions, pass new legislation, and influence court decisions in their countries. Ratification of the CEDAW by the United States would similarly make clear our national commitment to ensure the equal and nondiscriminatory treatment of American women in such areas as civil and political rights, education, employment, and property rights.

Most fundamentally, ratification of CEDAW would further our national interests. Secretary of State Colin Powell put it well when he said earlier this year: "The worldwide advancement of women's issues is not only in keeping with the deeply held values of the American people; it is strongly in our national interest as well. . . . Women's issues affect not only women; they have profound implications for all humankind. Women's issues are human rights issues. . . . We, as a world community, cannot even begin to tackle the array of problems and challenges confronting us without the full and equal participation of women in all aspects of life."

After careful study, I have found nothing in the substantive provisions of this treaty that even arguably jeopardizes our national interests. Those treaty provisions are entirely consistent with the letter and spirit of the United States Constitution and laws, both state and federal. The United States can and should accept virtually all of CEDAW's obligations and undertakings without qualification. Regrettably, the Administration has not provided a witness here today to set forth its views on the ratification of this treaty. Although past Administrations have proposed that ratification be accompanied by certain reservations, declarations, and understandings, only one of those understandings, relating to limitations of free speech, expression and association, seems to me advisable to protect the integrity of our national law.

Finally, let me address some myths and fallacies that have been circulated about the likely impact of United States ratification of the CEDAW. The most common include the following:

First, that CEDAW supports abortion rights by promoting access to "family planning." This is flatly untrue. There is absolutely no provision in CEDAW that mandates abortion or contraceptives on demand, sex education without parental involvement, or other controversial reproductive rights issues. CEDAW does not create any international right to abortion. To the contrary, on its face, the CEDAW treaty itself is neutral on abortion, allowing policies in this area to be set by signatory states and seeking to ensure equal access for men and women to health care services and family planning information. In fact, several countries in which abortion is illegal—among them Ireland, Rwanda, and Burkina Faso—have ratified CEDAW.

A second fallacy is that CEDAW ratification would somehow undermine the American family by redefining traditional gender roles with regard to the upbringing of children. In fact, CEDAW does not contain any provisions seeking to regulate any constitutionally protected interests with respect to family life. The treaty only requires that parties undertake to adopt measures "prohibiting all discrimination against women" and to "embody the principle of the equality of men in women" in national laws "to ensure, through law and other appropriate means, the practical realization of this principle." How best to implement that obligation consistent with existing United States constitutional protections—which as you know, limit the government's power to interfere in family matters, including most parental decisions regarding childrearing—is left for each country to decide for itself.

Third, some have falsely suggested that ratification of CEDAW would require decriminalization of prostitution. Again, the text of the treaty is to the contrary. CEDAW's Article 6 specifically states that countries that have ratified CEDAW "shall take all appropriate measures, including legislation, to suppress all forms of traffic in women and exploitation of prostitution in women."

Fourth, some claim that if CEDAW were U.S. law, it would outlaw single-sex education and require censorship of school textbooks. In fact, nothing in CEDAW mandates abolition of single-sex education. As one way to encourage equal access to quality education for all children, Article 10 requires parties to take all appropriate measures to eliminate "any stereotyped concept of the roles of men and women at all levels and in all forms of education by encouraging [not requiring] coeducation and other types of education which will help to achieve this aim . . .", including, presumably, single-sex education that teaches principles of gender equality. CEDAW also encourages the development of equal education material for students of both genders. This provision is plainly designed not to disrupt educational traditions in countries like ours, but rather, to address those many countries in the world (like Afghanistan during Taliban rule) in which educational facilities for girls are either nonexistent or remain separate and unequal.

Fifth, some have suggested that U.S. ratification of CEDAW would require the legalization of same-sex marriage. Whatever view one may hold regarding the desirability of same-sex marriage, this treaty plainly contains no such requirement. Article 10 of CEDAW requires only elimination of discrimination directed against women "in all matters related to marriage and family relations." Thus, for example, the practice of polygamy is inconsistent with the CEDAW because it undermines women's equality with men and potentially fosters severe financial inequities. Article 10 would neither require nor bar any national laws regarding same-sex marriage, which by their very nature, would apply equally to men and women.

Finally, and most pervasively, opponents of CEDAW have claimed that U.S. ratification would diminish our national sovereignty and states' rights by superseding or overriding our national, state or local laws. Given the broad compatibility between the treaty requirements and our existing national laws, however, very few occasions will arise in which this is even arguably an issue. Moreover, the treaty generally requires States to use "appropriate measures" to implement the nondiscrimination principle, which by its terms accords some discretion to member countries to determine what is "appropriate" under the national circumstances. Finally, the Senate is, of course, free to address any material discrepancies between national law and the treaty by placing understandings upon its advice and consent, along the lines of the "freedom of speech" understanding discussed above, or by the Congress passing implementing legislation—as it has done, for example, to effectuate the Genocide Convention—specifying the precise ways in which the Federal legislature will carry out our international obligations under this treaty.

Ironically, many of the unfounded claims about the likely effects of CEDAW ratification have been asserted by self-proclaimed advocates of states' rights. In fact, within our own country, the emerging trend has been the opposite. Broad sentiment has been emerging at both the state and local level to incorporate the CEDAW requirements into local law. As I speak, governmental bodies in some fifteen states and Guam, sixteen counties and forty-two cities have adopted resolutions or instruments endorsing CEDAW or adopting it on behalf of their jurisdictions. Far from CEDAW imposing unwanted obligations on local governments, local governments are in fact responding to the demands of their citizens, who have become impatient at the lack of federal action to implement these universal norms into American law.

Particularly in a time of terror, promoting human rights and eradicating discrimination should not be partisan issues. As President Bush recently reminded us, the United States cannot fight a war on terrorism alone; it needs cooperation not only from its current allies, but also from the rest of the world. "We have a great opportunity during this time of war," he said, "to lead the world toward the values that will bring lasting peace . . . [such as] the non-negotiable demands of human dignity [that include] respect for women. . . ."

First Lady Laura Bush echoed that sentiment on International Women's Day 2002, when she said, "People around the world are looking closely at the roles that women play in society. And Afghanistan under the Taliban gave the world a sobering example of a country where women were denied their rights and their place in society. . . . Today, the world is helping Afghan women return to the lives that they once knew. . . . Our dedication to respect and protect women's rights in all countries must continue if we are to achieve a peaceful, prosperous world. . . . Together, the United States, the United Nations and all of our allies will prove that the forces of terror can't stop the momentum of freedom."

The world looks to America for leadership on human rights, both in our domestic practices and in our international commitments. Ours is a nation conceived in liberty and dedicated to the proposition that all human beings— not just men—are created equal. Our country has fought a civil war and a centuries-long social struggle to eliminate racial discrimination. It is critically important that we seize this opportunity to announce unequivocally to the world that we, of all nations, insist on the equality of all human beings, regardless of gender.

Senators, in closing let me say how much United States ratification of this important treaty means to every American. My mother, Hesung Chun Koh, came to this country more than fifty years ago from the Republic of Korea and found equal opportunity here as a naturalized American citizen. My wife, Mary-Christy Fisher, is a natural-born American citizen and lawyer of Irish and British heritage. I am the father of a young American, Emily Koh, who will turn sixteen years old in ten days' time.

Although I have tried, I simply cannot give my daughter any good reason why her grandmother and mother would have been protected by CEDAW in their ancestral countries, but that she is not protected by it in the United States, which professes to be a world leader in the promotion of women's rights and gender equality. I cannot explain to her why this country we love, and which I have served as Assistant Secretary of State for Human Rights, has for so long failed to ratify the authoritative human rights treaty that sets the universal standard on women's equality. Finally, I cannot explain why, by not ratifying, the United States chooses to keep company with such countries as Afghanistan, Iran, Sudan, and Syria, in which human rights and women's rights have been brutally repressed.

The choice is simple. Our continuing failure to ratify this treaty will hamper and undermine our efforts to fight for democracy and human rights around the world. Ratification now of the CEDAW treaty would be both prudent foreign policy and simple justice.

Grace Melton Smith  **NO**

CEDAW: How U.N. Interference Threatens the Rights of American Women

Introduction

The Convention on the Elimination of All Forms of Discrimination Against Women (CEDAW) was adopted in 1979 by the United Nations General Assembly and initiated in 1981 after its ratification by 20 member states; today 185 countries are party to CEDAW. The United States Senate—under both Democrat and Republican leadership—has consistently chosen not to ratify it, with good reason.

While women's groups and some politicians have lobbied the Senate to ratify CEDAW, arguing that it would be a useful instrument in championing women's rights at home and abroad, the treaty has rarely made it out of the Senate Foreign Relations Committee for full Senate consideration. The reasons that the Senate has historically rejected CEDAW remain relevant, particularly the challenges it would create for the United States' federalized system of government. Furthermore, the 30 years that have passed since CEDAW's inception continue to illustrate how little the treaty has accomplished to improve women's rights in some of the most oppressive nations that have ratified it, such as Saudi Arabia, and how United Nations "experts" have used the treaty to create new rights and to intimidate countries into adopting radical social policies.

The U.S. Constitution has been a far better protector of women's rights in America than has any international treaty, and the Senate should not subject the Constitution to this one. The Senate Foreign Relations Committee, the full Senate, and the White House must more effectively explain to Americans, particularly women, why CEDAW and the United Nations are not protectors of their interests.

CEDAW's Purpose and Politicization

CEDAW contains many points that mirror America's efforts to promote equal opportunity for women, yet it also poses many problems for America's federalist system of government and the rights established in the U.S. Constitution. Many of the issues with which CEDAW concerns itself, such as access to health care and education, belong under the purview of state or local jurisdiction in the U.S. constitutional order.

From *The Heritage Foundation Backgrounder*, January 9, 2009. Copyright © 2009 by The Heritage Foundation. Reprinted by permission.

CEDAW requires national governments to work toward eliminating gender-based discrimination in every area of life, using this expansive definition of discrimination against women:

> Any distinction, exclusion or restriction made on the basis of sex which has the effect or purpose of impairing or nullifying the recognition, enjoyment or exercise by women, irrespective of their marital status, on a basis of equality of men and women, of human rights and fundamental freedoms in the political, economic, social, cultural, civil or any other field.

Furthermore, countries that have ratified CEDAW are evaluated based on their compliance with CEDAW by the CEDAW Committee, which meets at the United Nations several times a year. The committee consistently oversteps its mandate, acting as a quasi-judicial body issuing forceful instructions to countries that often do not share its radical social agenda, and committee meetings inevitably serve as a forum for reinterpreting the terms agreed upon by the treaty members.

CEDAW is an ineffective and inappropriate instrument for advancing women's rights around the world. In the case of gross abuses of women's rights, such as sex trafficking or female circumcision, it has been less effective than targeted instruments to address them, such as the American led effort to adopt the United Nations Protocol to Prevent, Suppress, and Punish Trafficking in Persons.

In the case of American women, their freedom and personal dignity are best protected by the U.S. Constitution and the rule of law it establishes. The United States should continue to advance the standing of women domestically and abroad by refusing to ratify CEDAW.

The Enforcers: The CEDAW Committee

The CEDAW Committee was created in 1982 to monitor states' implementation of the Convention on the Elimination of All Forms of Discrimination Against Women and issue recommendations for how states can better comply with the treaty. The committee is what is known in U.N. lingo as a "treaty body."

Members of the CEDAW Committee are self-identified gender experts chosen from the various countries that are party to CEDAW—although they serve in their individual capacities, and not as official representatives of their country's governments. Elected by countries participating in CEDAW, they serve terms of four years and are eligible for re-election. Each country that is party to CEDAW must submit written and oral reports to the committee every four years. The committee questions the delegation and issues concluding observations and recommendations for the state party to follow. In practice, the CEDAW Committee habitually bullies the delegations sent to deliver their countries' reports. The committee pressures state parties to change their domestic policies, and most alarmingly, it regularly reads more into the convention than exists in the actual text of the document. Although the committee is not technically a judicial body, its conclusions and recommendations have been cited in court decisions around the world, including the U.S. Supreme Court.

The CEDAW Committee in Session:

A 2008 Example

The committee met for its 41st session from June 30 to July 18, 2008, to review the periodic reports submitted by Yemen, Lithuania, Nigeria, Iceland, Finland, the United Kingdom, Tanzania, and Slovakia. Its questions to the state party delegations generally focused on the following matters: whether national judiciaries are relying on CEDAW to make legislative decisions while bypassing or changing any conflicting domestic law; using quotas and incentives to achieve equal participation of women in business, politics, and academia; the division of labor and domestic responsibilities between men and women in the home; the protection of women's rights from infringement by "conservatives" and "religious people"; and, "sexual and reproductive health."

Domestication of the Convention.   The committee questioned every country under review about the extent to which the convention has been incorporated into the country's domestic law, specifically inquiring about what kind of training is in place for the judiciary about how to refer to CEDAW in its rulings. For example, the committee chair asked the delegation from Slovakia whether there are any cases before Slovak courts in which CEDAW has been invoked. Another committee member asked for proof that the government of Nigeria is taking the convention seriously.

In its concluding observations on Lithuania's report, the committee expressed concern "that the Convention's provisions and the Committee's general recommendations are not sufficiently known by the majority of judges, lawyers, prosecutors [and women] . . . as indicated by the absence of any court decisions that refer to the Convention." Apparently, Lithuania's proof of compliance with CEDAW depends on its judges citing the treaty. A member of the committee asked the Lithuanian representatives whether the Lithuanian constitution has any provisions that would make the application of "temporary special measures" (affirmative action) on behalf of women unconstitutional. If so, she asked, "[Are] there plans to amend the Constitution? In what area [does] Lithuania plan to apply temporary special measures?"

The committee went even further than pushing countries to adopt CEDAW into law, urging them to enact legislation to comply with the committee's "general recommendations." In concluding observations on Tanzania, for example, the committee "call[ed] on the State party to accelerate its law review process and to work effectively with Parliament in ensuring that all discriminatory legislation is amended or repealed to bring it into compliance with the Convention *and the Committee's general recommendations.*" (Emphasis added.) This is an example of the committee behaving as a quasi-judicial body promulgating substantive interpretations of CEDAW, rather than confining itself to the role of a technical body of experts, as was stipulated in the treaty itself.

Quotas and *De Facto* Equality.   Not satisfied with demonstration of equality of the sexes before the law, the CEDAW Committee seeks *de facto* equalization of women's status in every sphere of society, and often advocates quotas or incentives to achieve it. It recommended that Tanzania "pursue sustained policies aimed at the promotion of women's full and equal participation in decisionmaking *as a democratic requirement* in all areas of public and professional life." (Emphasis added.) In its recommendations to Lithuania, the committee urged the government to "systematically adopt such laws on temporary special measures including goals and time-tables or quotas . . . in order to accelerate the realization of women's *de facto* equality with men in the areas of political and public life, education and public and private employment." That is, Lithuania must adopt laws to ensure that the gender of its legislators (and presumably the rest of its government) reflects its population. During the committee review of the United Kingdom's report, one committee member asked the delegation, "how both the equality of opportunity and the equality *of results* would be guaranteed" (emphasis added) for women throughout the country.

While especially interested in achieving gender parity in governing bodies, the committee also monitors women's participation in academia and the private sector. Consider these examples: One committee member praised Iceland for its 30 percent female representation in Parliament, and expressed her disappointment that only 18 percent of the professors at Iceland's largest university are women. Another asked the Finnish delegation whether it had a timeline for increasing the number of women on the governing boards of both private and government-owned companies. Lithuania was asked about what obligations the private sector faced in order to reduce job segregation and the gender pay gap. Another expert voiced her concerns about women's employment in Yemen, telling Yemen's delegation that the government ought "to pursue the equality of results as opposed to the formal equality of laws. Men and women should have the same job security and equal remuneration."

Family Life.   Beyond the public sphere, the committee calls on state parties to enforce CEDAW by intruding into private family and household matters. It aims to modify interactions between spouses and parental decisions regarding children, regardless of how tenuously related such regulation is to the advancement of women's rights. One committee member questioned several country delegations about corporal punishment and the rights of the "girl child." She asked the delegation from Iceland whether the government is "incorporating so-called 'positive disciplining' in its educational booklets on corporal punishment prevention."

Article 5 of CEDAW calls for the elimination of cultural stereotypes that discriminate against women. The CEDAW Committee uses this directive to instruct state parties on such personal matters as the division of domestic responsibilities within the family. The committee called on Yemen "to foster a better understanding of equality between women and men at all levels of society with a view to transforming stereotypical attitudes and negative cultural norms about the responsibilities and roles of women and men in the family and society." It similarly recommended that Finland work "to promote equal sharing of domestic and family tasks between women and men," and that Slovakia strengthen its efforts "to fully sensitize men to their equal participation in family tasks and responsibilities."

Disregard for culturally distinct patterns of pursuing the advancement of women and their preferences for work-life balance was on display in the committee's treatment of Iceland. The country sought to inform the committee about its own societal norms, explaining that women are more likely to seek part-time employment to be able to carry out their family responsibilities. The Icelandic delegation also referenced surveys that revealed that women are more likely than men to take family commitments into account in their decisions on participation in the labor market.

That prompted one committee member to ask the Icelandic delegation what measures the government has taken "to change these patterns of behavior." Her assumption, which the rest of the committee seems to share, is that women do not choose to focus primarily on family responsibilities, and if they do, they must be victims of discrimination.

Sexual Orientation and Nontraditional Families.   The CEDAW Committee also uses its mandate to eliminate gender discrimination as an opportunity to advance the homosexual-lobby agenda. Several members of the committee suggested that the status of women in same-sex relationships or nontraditional families ought to receive greater attention from the state parties. . . .

Religion and Morality.   The Committee regards religious communities and individuals—particularly conservatives—as a threat to women's freedom.

It regularly recommends that state parties to the convention be vigilant in monitoring such threats, instructing Slovakia, for example, to "adequately regulate the invocation of conscientious objection by health professionals so as to ensure that women's access to health and reproductive health is not limited." In other words, if a Slovakian doctor invokes a conscientious objection to performing an abortion or prescribing a contraceptive, the Slovakian government must "regulate" the invocation of such an objection. The committee wants Slovakia to require doctors to perform abortions regardless of their moral or religious beliefs. The committee expects religious principles and cultural values to accommodate the convention—and the committee's recommendations—not vice versa. . . .

Sexual and Reproductive Health.   CEDAW is a much-debated and carefully negotiated document, and access to abortion is not required, nor even mentioned. But the committee's actions are an entirely different matter.

In its discussion of women's health, the committee focuses almost exclusively on contraception and abortion, referencing its own General Recommendation No. 24 to require countries to liberalize their laws regarding abortion. The committee called on Nigeria "to assess the impact of its abortion law on the maternal mortality rate and to give consideration to its reform or modification." Yemen was reminded that "contraceptives should be free or affordable." . . .

Conclusion

Injustice against women around the world is a reality. It is serious and sometimes even life threatening. Regrettably, the Convention on the Elimination of All Forms of Discrimination Against Women and the CEDAW Committee have done a disservice to the cases of abject discrimination against and mistreatment of women, choosing instead to focus on the advancement of a particular radical social agenda.

It is not the responsibility of the United Nations to set social policy for the United States. Americans rely on their elected representatives in state legislatures and Congress to reflect their values and traditions when legislating domestic issues such as health care, education, marriage, and family policy. The American constitutional order protects the sphere of civil society—families, religious organizations, and private associations—from government intrusion, leaving Americans to determine the course of their private lives, including religious expression and family decisions. Other matters that CEDAW addresses, such as gender equality in the workforce and political participation, are generally sorted out in the free market of ideas, without heavy-handed, government-mandated quotas. American women are free, legally and culturally, to pursue opportunities and relationships of their choosing. Americans should continue to fight incidental discrimination, while preserving the security afforded by the U.S. system of rights enshrined in the U.S. Constitution and protected under federal and state laws.

The actions of the CEDAW Committee are a stark reminder of the dangers of being a party to such multilateral treaties. The U.S. Senate should uphold its responsibility to the American people and not subject them to the tyranny of the CEDAW treaty. Ratifying CEDAW, and by extension subjecting the U.S. to the bullying of the CEDAW Committee, would neither advance women's equality nor serve American foreign policy interests, including the security and advancement of women around the globe.

POSTSCRIPT

Should the United States Ratify the Convention to Eliminate All Forms of Discrimination Against Women?

The concentrated effort to promote women's rights internationally within the context of advancing globalism dates back only to 1975, which the United Nations declared the International Women's Year. There have been many changes that benefit women since that time, but those changes have only begun to ease the problems that advocates of women's rights argue need to be addressed. CEDAW has been a keystone of the international effort to promote women's rights. By mid-2009, all but eight (the United States, Iran, Sudan, Somalia, Qatar, Nauru, Palau and Tonga) of the world's nearly 200 countries had formally adhered to CEDAW.

With President Bush opposed to CEDAW and the Republicans controlling the Senate for most of the time during its tenure, there was little chance that the Senate would ratify CEDAW. In 2008, though, the political wheel turned when the Democrats captured the White House and increased the control of the Senate they had gained in the 2006 elections. President Barack Obama, Vice President Joseph Biden, and Secretary of State Hillary Clinton had all advocated ratification of CEDAW during their campaigns for the Democratic presidential nomination. Moreover, once in office, Obama nominated Harold Koh, the author of the first reading, for the post of legal adviser for the State Department.

In the 111th Congress (2009–2011), Representative Lynn C. Woolsey (D-CA) and 124 co-sponsors introduced a House resolution calling on the Senate to ratify CEDAW. In the Senate, Barbara Boxer (D-CA), who chairs the Foreign Relations Committee's Subcommittee on International Operations and Organizations, Human Rights, Democracy, and Global Women's Issues, is reportedly ready to hold new hearings on CEDAW as a step toward its eventual ratification.

Yet for all the improved political climate for CEDAW, its fate in the Senate remains uncertain. When the Senate confirmed Koh in 2009, the vote was 62 to 35. Of the senators opposed to Koh's confirmation, the prime objection was his advocacy of following U.S. treaty obligations even if they conflict with domestic law. The interface with treaty law and other forms of law under the Constitution is complex, but from the view of many conservatives, following CEDAW would be part of what they see as the general diminution of U.S. sovereignty in general, with a particular threat for the United States to determine its own policy in such areas as abortion. Typical of the Republican opposition to Koh's confirmation, Senator Jim DeMint (R-SC) specifically cited Koh's support of CEDAW and argued that the favoring any "international legal regime when it subordinates the interests of the American legal regime should cause all of us to stop and think." DeMint when on to stay that "everything we are as a country depends first on our sovereignty. . . . This idea of a global world order of some kind is frightening to many people, including myself." DeMint's view may be in a minority, but with a two-thirds vote needed for ratification, the 35 senators who voted against Koh would be enough to block ratification.

Expressing the same view as DeMint is Dr. John Fonte, author of "Democracy's Trojan Horse" (*The National Interest*, Summer 2004). Also on this topic, read Sandra F. VanBurkleo, *Belonging to the World: Women's Rights and American Constitutional Culture* (Oxford University Press, 2000).

To further inform your views on this debate, read the text of CEDAW, which can be found on the Web site of the U.N.'s Division for the Advancement of Women (DAW) at http://www.un.org/womenwatch/daw/cedaw/cedaw.htm. DAW favors CEDAW, as does the group Working Group on Ratification of the U.N. Convention on the Elimination of All Forms of Discrimination Against Women, whose Web site is http://www.womenstreaty.org/. A group opposed to CEDAW is Women for Faith and Family at http://www.wf-f.org/CEDAW.html.

ISSUE 21

Is President Barack Obama's Strategic Nuclear Arms Control Policy Sound?

YES: William J. Perry, from Testimony during Hearings on "The July Summit and Beyond: Prospects for U.S.-Russia Nuclear Arms Reductions," before the Committee on Foreign Affairs, U.S. House of Representatives (June 24, 2009)

NO: Keith B. Payne, from Testimony during Hearings on "The July Summit and Beyond: Prospects for U.S.-Russia Nuclear Arms Reductions," before the Committee on Foreign Affairs, U.S. House of Representatives (June 24, 2009)

ISSUE SUMMARY

YES: William J. Perry, former U.S. secretary of defense, reviews and generally supports the statements and early policy moves of the Obama administration with regard to strategic nuclear weapons.

NO: Keith B. Payne, professor in and head of the Department of Defense and Strategic Studies at Missouri State University, outlines "six major concerns" he has with the apparent early direction of the Obama administration's efforts to re-establish strategic arms control as a centerpiece of U.S.-Russian engagement.

$\mathbf{S}$oon after atomic flashes leveled Hiroshima and Nagasaki in 1945, the world's countries began to seek safety from what had been created by devising ways to restrain the number of nuclear weapons and who possessed them. As early as 1946, the organization now called the International Atomic Energy Agency (IAEA) was created to limit the use of nuclear technology to peaceful purposes.

During the 1950s the cold war kept arms control efforts in the deep freezer, but by the early 1960s worries about nuclear weapons began to overcome frosty U.S.-Soviet relations. The first major step toward nuclear arms control came in 1963, when most countries agreed to cease testing nuclear weapons in the atmosphere.

In the 1970s arms control was able to advance. The Antiballistic Missile (ABM) Treaty (1972) constrained U.S. and Soviet efforts to build a ballistic missile defense (BMD) system, which many analysts believed could destabilize nuclear deterrence. During that decade, Washington and Moscow also concluded the

Strategic Arms Limitation Talks I (SALT I) Treaty (1972) and the Strategic Arms Limitation Talks II (SALT II) Treaty (1979). With the about 10,000 strategic range (over 5,500 kilometers) nuclear warheads and bombs each, the two treaties put important limits on the future growth of nuclear weapons.

As the cold war thawed even more during the 1980s and then ended in 1991 with the collapse of the Soviet Union, the pace of arms control sped up even more. The effort now was not to limit the future growth of nuclear arsenals, but to reduce them. Moscow and Washington agreed to the Intermediate-Range Nuclear Forces (INF) Treaty (1987), which banished nuclear-armed missles with ranges between 500 and 5,500 kilometers. Then, the two superpowers agreed in 1991 to the Strategic Arms Reduction Treaty (START I). Each country was required to reduce their nuclear inventories to 1,600 delivery vehicles (missiles and bombers) and 6,000 strategic explosive nuclear devices (warheads and bombs). Two years later, Presidents Boris Yeltsin and George H. W. Bush took a further step when they signed the second Strategic Arms Reduction Treaty (START II). It required that by 2007 the two countries would slash their nuclear warheads and bombs to 3,500 for the United States and 2,997 for Russia.

At this point, the story's progress becomes less straightforward. On the negative track, the U.S. Senate ratified START II in 1996, but Russia's parliament, the Duma, did not. The refusal had to do with U.S. military moves that alarmed Moscow. One was the enlargement of NATO in the late 1990s to include some former Soviet bloc countries and to bring the alliance closer to the Russian border. Then in 1999, the Senate rejected the Comprehensive Test Ban Treaty, creating fears that the United States wished to test new generations of nuclear weapons. The third factor was the beginning of a ballistic missile defense system under President Clinton and its acceleration under President Bush, including his December 1991 decision to withdraw from the ABM Treaty. START II remained unratified by the Duma and, therefore, had no legal standing.

On the positive track, President George W. Bush met with President Vladimir Putin in 2002. The two signed the so-called Moscow Treaty. Under it, the two countries agreed to cut their arsenals of nuclear warheads and bombs to no more than 2,200 by 2012. Experts disagree about the value of the treaty. On the upside, the arsenals have fallen between 2002 and 2009, with the number of deployed U.S. strategic range bombs/warheads dropping from 5,986 to 2,602, and the Russian arsenal declining from 4,951 to 3,496. On the downside, there were no interim deadlines for reductions, no verification procedures, and warheads/bombs taken out of "deployed" status could be stored rather than destroyed.

Now 2012 is drawing close. There is a new president, Dmitry Medvedev in Moscow, and an even newer president, Barack Obama in Washington. These presidents face numerous issues related to nuclear weapons. The issue of a U.S. missile defense system remains a very sore point between the two capitals, and they are not in full agreement on what to do about the existing nuclear weapons in North Korea and the potential of nuclear weapons in Iran. Former Secretary of Defense William Perry reviews Obama's emerging policy in the realm of nuclear weapons arms control and for the most part praises the new president. Professor Payne takes a much dimmer view of the pronouncements and policies of President Obama.

YES

William J. Perry

Strategic National Arms Control

I have been asked to testify to this committee on the future prospects for strategic nuclear arms control. I will do this by summarizing the relevant findings of the Congressional Commission on the Strategic Posture of the United States which I [as a former U.S. secretary of defense] chaired along with Jim Schlesinger [also a former U.S. secretary of defense], the relevant findings of a CFR [Council on Foreign Relations] Task Force, which I co-chaired, along with Brent Scowcroft [former national security adviser to the president], and the conclusions I reached from four different visits to Russia these past six months. I will begin by relating findings of the Commission and the Task Force to the emerging administration policy in this field as expressed by President [Barack] Obama in his April [2009] speech in Prague.

The President said that the US faced growing threats from nuclear proliferation and nuclear terrorism, but that we must continue to hedge against the possibility of a resurgence of old threats. The Commission and the Task Force agreed with that assessment.

The President said that the Nuclear Nonproliferation Treaty (NPT) and the International Atomic Energy Agency (IAEA) would be critical tools in dealing with the emerging threats, and that the US apply more resources to the IAEA, work to strengthen the NPT and prepare carefully for NPT review conference in 2010. With regard to the IAEA, the Commission specifically recommended that the US provide stronger political, financial and technical support to the IAEA to enhance its capabilities to perform its unique and vital mission.

The President said that success in preventing proliferation would require the cooperation of all nations and that getting their full cooperation would entail meaningful progress in nuclear disarmament between the US and Russia. The Commission and Task Force agreed, but some members thought that link was strong and others thought it was relatively weak.

The president said that the US should move forward with the European missile defense system as long as an Iranian missile threat persisted, and that we should seek to find a way of cooperating on missile defense with Russia. The commission agreed. More specifically, the Task Force urged a delay in deploying missile defenses to Europe until the system has been proven but also recommended the system be linked to evolving assessments of the ballistic missile threats from Iran and North Korea.

The president declared that this administration seeks a world without nuclear weapons, and would work for it. He said that it would take a very long

U.S. House of Representatives, June 24, 2009.

time to achieve this goal, but, in the meantime, we should seek to reduce the numbers and the salience of nuclear weapons. He also clearly stated as long as any nation had nuclear weapons the US would maintain safe secure and reliable nuclear forces that provided both deterrence and extended deterrence.

The Commission and the Task Force supported the commitment to maintain deterrence forces as well as the commitment to reduce the salience and numbers of nuclear weapons provided that the reductions were done bilaterally. But about half of the Commission members did not support the nuclear elimination goal. Some thought that such a goal was not feasible. A few thought that even if it was feasible it was not desirable.

The President said that he would seek to have the CTBT [Comprehensive Test Ban Treaty] ratified. I agree with that goal; indeed I believe that if the US does not ratify CTBT that we will be unable to provide the necessary leadership in curbing proliferation. The Task Force also endorsed this goal. However, the Commission members split 50-50 on whether this was desirable. The Commission prepared the pro and con views for ratification in its final report. However, the Commission did agree on steps the Administration should take to prepare the way for Senate re-consideration of the treaty.

The President also said that the US would seek to negotiate a follow-on START [Strategic Arms Reduction Talks] treaty and a Fissile Material Cutoff Treaty. Both the Commission and the Task Force agreed with those goals.

The Commission discussed new strategic arms agreements in some detail, saying that the US should proceed in stages. The first stage could be completed before expiration of the START treaty in December if the US pursued modest objectives and kept it simple. Additional strategic arms treaties would necessarily involve very difficult issues, would take longer, and be much harder to reach agreement.

The Commission was formed by the Congress to inform the administration and the Congress on strategic issues entailed in the NPR [National Posture Review of strategic nuclear weapons and doctrine] now under preparation. Additionally, the NPR should inform the administration and the Congress on the nation's arms control strategy. I believe that this is, in fact, in process. The first phase of the NPR, which focused on actions that would affect the near-term treaty, is essentially finished. The second phase, which will focus on longer term and more difficult arms control issues, is just getting underway. It is also important in considering the more comprehensive arms control strategy, that the US should consult with allies and friends, especially those covered by extended deterrence. The Commission put a major effort in meeting with allies and seeking to understand their views, and their views are clearly reflected in the Commission's report. I understand that the administration already has such consultations underway.

The Commission made a number of substantial recommendations on the programs necessary to maintain safe secure and reliable deterrence forces. I have been briefed by senior officials in the DOD [Department of Defense] and DOE [Department of Energy, which is responsible for nuclear warheads and bombs] and am pleased to hear that the Commission's recommendations in that respect are being received positively by the administration and have been a fundamental input to the NPR.

I have had an excellent opportunity to see how these issues are regarded by the Russians, since I have made 4 trips to Moscow in the last 6 months, the most recent of which I returned from two days ago. I have talked with a number of Russian technical experts, a number of Duma [Russia's national parliament] members, and key government leaders, including the President, Foreign Minister, and National Security Advisor.

Besides these recent meetings, I have maintained a sustained dialog on security issues with Russian colleagues for almost 30 years, and, during the time I was Secretary of Defense, worked very closely with the Russian government in the dismantlement of nuclear weapons in the former Soviet republics under the Nunn-Lugar program.

Nevertheless, I had stopped visiting Russia in 2007 and 2008 because I felt the relations between our two countries had become so strained that a constructive dialog had become impractical. But this February, at a security conference in Munich, Vice President [Joseph] Biden said that it was time to "press the reset button" on US-Russia relations. Many predicted that the Russians would react to that with cynicism or skepticism. But I had an opportunity to test this first hand in March when I visited Moscow for a meeting chaired by former PM [prime minister Yevgeny] Primakov and [former U.S. secretary of state] Henry Kissinger. The highlight of this meeting was a discussion with President [Dmitry] Medvedev. He was preparing for his upcoming London meeting with President Obama, and I had the impression that he used his discussions with us to "test market" what he planned to say to President Obama. He told us that he supported the long-term goal of eliminating nuclear weapons. And he said that Russia was anxious to resume serious arms control discussions with the US, with the immediate goal of negotiating a follow-on treaty to START and SORT. He believed that such a treaty could and should be completed before START expired in December [2009]. Based on these and other comments, I was confident that our two presidents would have a constructive dialog. Indeed, that confidence was justified by the summit meeting that the two leaders had in London in April, and I believe that it will continue to be justified next month at the summit meeting in Moscow.

Nevertheless, there is some reason to be concerned about basically different perspectives between the US with Russia on nuclear arms treaties. They are strongly opposed to our ballistic missile defense system in Eastern Europe; they believe that the counting rules agreed to in SORT are disadvantageous to them, and they have not agreed to include non-strategic nuclear weapons, in which they have a large numerical advantage. I believe that these issues will not prove to be a barrier to the START follow-on treaty being negotiated this year; I can see a suitable compromise being worked out for the counting rules, and I believe that the both sides will agree not to consider non-strategic nuclear weapons this year. However, these will be very difficult issues to resolve in any follow-on agreements. On balance, I believe that we can this year negotiate a START follow-on treaty compatible with our security, but that in doing so both sides will decide to defer to future negotiations issues too difficult to resolve at this time. I believe that is right approach.

Keith B. Payne    **NO**

U.S.-Russian Strategic Arms Control

President Obama has announced that the United States will seek, "a new [post-START] agreement by the end of this year that is legally binding and sufficiently bold." Based on public statements by Russian and U.S. leaders, the basic parameters of an agreement appear to be emerging. I would like to make six short points about the apparent direction of this engagement because some of the early indications are troubling.

First, the discussion of the specific numeric limitations of an agreement should only follow the conclusions of the Nuclear Posture Review just underway at the Pentagon. That review is intended to assess U.S. strategic force requirements. Identifying specific arms control ceilings for agreement prior to its conclusions would be putting the cart before the horse. Our military leaders frequently note that arms control numbers should not drive strategy requirements; rather strategy requirements should drive the numbers. The Obama Administration has assembled a first-rate team in the Pentagon with responsibility to conduct the current Nuclear Posture Review. I have considerable personal experience in conducting a Nuclear Posture Review; my hope is that before specific arms control numbers are set this team will be allowed to complete the time consuming and complex set of analyses necessary to reach even preliminary conclusions about the force requirements of strategy and how to meet those requirements. This would be in keeping with having our strategy drive numbers, and not allowing arms control numbers to drive strategy.

Second, the Russian and U.S. sides have agreed that the post-START [Strategic Arms Reduction Talks] treaty will not reduce only the number of nuclear warheads; it will include reductions in the number of strategic force launchers, i.e., the number of deployed ICBM [intercontinental range ballistic missiles], SLBMs [sea launched ballistic missiles], and strategic bombers. Russian President [Dmitry] Medvedev has said that Russia would like the number of these strategic launchers to be reduced several times below the 1,600 launchers permitted now under START. We should be very careful about moving toward low launcher numbers because it would provide significant advantages for the Russian Federation, but significant disadvantages for U.S. strategy. It is a smart position for Russia, but bad for us.

U.S. House of Representatives, June 24, 2009.

Why so? Because Russian strategic systems have not been designed for long service lives and the number of deployed Russian strategic ICBMs, SLBMs, and bombers will drop dramatically with or without a new arms control agreement. Based solely on Russian sources, it is likely that within 8–9 years the number of Russian strategic launchers will have dropped from approximately 680 launchers today (some of which already are not operational) to approximately 270 launchers simply as a result of the aging of their systems and the pace of their modernization program. In contrast, the service life of existing U.S. systems extends several decades. Russia confronts the dilemma of how to maintain parity with the United States while withdrawing its many aged strategic force launchers. President Medvedev's answer, of course, is to gain comparable reductions in serviceable U.S. systems via arms control negotiations.

In short, the Russians would like to make lemonade out of the lemon of their aging launchers by getting reductions in real U.S. systems without eliminating anything that they would not withdraw in any event. This is not simply my conclusion; it is the conclusion of Russian officials and commentators as expressed in Russian publications. General Nikolay Solovtsov, commander of the Strategic Missile Troops, has recently stated that no Russian missile launchers will be withdrawn "if they have remaining service life. This approach will remain under the new treaty that will be signed with the USA to replace START-1. . . ." Aleksandr Khramchikhin, department chief at the Institute of Political and Military Analysis puts it simply: "America, in proposing radical reduction in the strategic nuclear forces, is doing us a favor. It may allow itself to reduce nothing, while watching with interest as we make cuts without benefit of any treaties."

Gen. Solovtsov has also stated that Russia's Cold War ICBMs will be largely gone by 2016 and completely gone, with the possible exception of 30 SS-19 missiles, by 2017–2019. The Russian SLBM force is in almost as bad a shape. *RIA Novosti*, an official Russian information agency, reports that four of Russian missile submarines are not combat ready even today. The announced ballistic missile submarine force is six-to-eight new Borey class submarines by 2015—eight being very unlikely since only three are being built today. The announced Russian bomber program will involve the retention of 50 Bear H and Blackjack bombers (a few new ones will be produced). Despite spending up to 25% of the Russian military budget on the strategic forces, Russia's strategic nuclear forces will decline steeply with or without arms control.

Beyond the bad negotiating principle of giving up something for nothing, there would serious downsides for the United States in moving to low numbers of strategic launchers, including:

- It would encourage placing more warheads on the remaining launchers, i.e., "MIRVing"—which is precisely what the Russians are doing. [MIRV means multiple independent reentry vehicles, that is, having more than two or more independently targetable war years on a single missile.] Moving away from heavily MIRVed strategic launchers has long been considered a highly stabilizing approach to the deployment of strategic forces and a key U.S. START goal.

- It would likely reduce the survivability and flexibility of our forces—*which is exactly the wrong direction to be taking in the post-Cold War environment.* The report by the bipartisan Congressional Strategic Posture Commission concluded that the United States could make reductions, "if this were done while also preserving the resilience and survivability of U.S. forces." Moving toward very low launcher numbers would violate that good advice.
- It could cause some allies serious concerns. A key ally has strongly stated its view that the United States must not reduce its strategic force levels to numbers so low that they call into question the credibility of the U.S. nuclear umbrella or encourage China to see an opportunity to achieve strategic parity with the United States. Moving toward the very low launcher numbers desired by Russia could contribute to both problems.
- Finally, if the destruction of strategic launchers is required, as reportedly is called for by the Russian side, moving toward low launcher limits could also cut considerably into U.S. conventional force capabilities by requiring the destruction of our multipurpose bombers.

Third, the forthcoming negotiations appear to exclude the entire arena of non-strategic nuclear weapons. Excluding so-called tactical nuclear weapons entirely is an understandable Russian negotiating ploy; it is in this category of weaponry that Russia maintains *most* of its nuclear arsenal. According to Russian sources, Russia has approximately 4,000 deployed tactical nuclear weapons and many thousands more in reserve. These reportedly include nuclear artillery, tactical missile warheads, air-delivered weapons, naval weapons, air defense weapons and possibly the retention of so-called nuclear suitcases. Russia apparently has an astounding 10:1 numeric advantage over the United States in tactical nuclear weapons. The Russians have little incentive to negotiate when the numbers are so asymmetrical.

Yet, these Russian tactical nuclear weapons are of greatest concern with regard to the potential for nuclear war and proliferation; they should be our focus. Russia is engaged in troubling advanced developments of its tactical nuclear arsenal and Russian doctrine highlights war-fighting roles for these weapons. Understandably, some of our key allies have expressed considerable concern about these Russian tactical nuclear capabilities. The Congressional Strategic Posture Commission report identified the Russian tactical nuclear arsenal as an "urgent" problem. Yet, the Obama Administration appears to have agreed to negotiate *only* on strategic forces at this point, and to have excluded Russian tactical nuclear weapons entirely. If this position holds, it will be a serious mistake.

The administration's hope may be that we can negotiate a quick new agreement on strategic forces now, and achieve reductions in Russian tactical nuclear weapons later. If so, it is a vain hope. Russia has repeatedly rejected limitations on tactical nuclear weapons. If we cannot get the Russians to agree to the reduction of tactical nuclear weapons now, what hope can there possibly be for doing so later *after* we have expended negotiating leverage that resides in our serviceable strategic forces? As Russian General Vladimir

Dvorkin of the Russian Academy of Sciences said on this subject recently, "A treaty on the limitation and reduction of tactical nuclear weapons looks absolutely unrealistic."

The notion that the U.S. can succeed in getting tactical nuclear reductions in a second phase of negotiations reminds me of the unmet promise of the [President Richard] Nixon Administration in SALT I [first Strategic Arms Limitations Talks/Treaty] to negotiate useful limits on Soviet countersilo offensive forces [those meant to attack ICBM silos] in a follow-on SALT II agreement. Despite nearly two decades of effort following SALT I, the United States was unsuccessful in securing useful limits on Soviet countersilo offensive forces because the Soviets did not want such limits and the U.S. had expended its major negotiating leverage in SALT I.

Fourth, the Russian side has demanded numerous additional limits on other U.S. capabilities as the price to be paid for an early agreement on strategic nuclear forces. For example, President Medvedev recently said that strategic reductions are only possible if the U.S. alleviates Russian concerns about, "U.S. plans to create a global missile defense."

In fact, no limits on U.S. missile defenses are necessary for significant reductions in Russian strategic force launchers and warheads because, as noted above, the number of Russian strategic launchers will plummet with or without an arms control treaty. The need for U.S. BMD [ballistic missile defense] capabilities could not be clearer given recent North Korean nuclear missile rattling and Iranian political upheaval. U.S. BMD is not about Russia. Yet, the Russians are demanding this linkage. It would seem self-evidently a mistake to include any limits on U.S. BMD as a price to be paid for an agreement that requires nothing of the Russians beyond discarding the aged systems they plan to eliminate in any event and will not touch the real problem of Russian tactical nuclear weapons.

The same caveat is appropriate for the additional Russian demand that the United States meet Russian concerns about U.S. plan's to create *non-nuclear* strategic capabilities. Senior U.S. military officials have long emphasized the U.S. need for non-nuclear strategic capabilities for prompt global strike as a way of reducing reliance on nuclear capabilities. The Russians would like to derail such U.S. capabilities and thus now link them to a post-START agreement. One is forced to wonder how many elements of U.S. military power Russian leaders hope to control or eliminate in exchange for the same strategic force reductions that they will have to make without any agreement. We should not agree to pay Russia many times over with important U.S. capabilities for essentially an empty box.

Fifth, before establishing new nuclear arms control limits, it would seem reasonable to resolve Russian violations of its existing arms control commitments. The entire arms control process is devalued if violations are downplayed or go unchecked. Arms control proponents should be the first to insist on strict compliance with existing agreements. In this regard, the August 2005 State Department Compliance report on *Adherence to and Compliance with Arms Control, Nonproliferation, and Disarmament Agreements and Commitments* reported multiple Russian violations of START verification provisions. Russia also is in violation of other START provisions and other nuclear arms control commitments.

In my opinion, the most important of these violations has been discussed openly in Russian publications. It is the Russian testing of the SS-27 ICBM with MIRVs in direct violation of START. The SS-27 is listed as a single-warhead ICBM and can only be tested and deployed with a single warhead under START. Russian sources place the number of MIRVs on this forthcoming missile at 4 or more. As the Congressional Strategic Posture Commission notes, the Russians also are in violation of their commitments concerning tactical nuclear weapons under the 1990–1991 Presidential Nuclear Initiatives. This is not speculation; Russian officials have openly reported the activities that make up these outstanding arms control violations. Russian noncompliance with existing commitments is not a trivial issue; confidence in Russian compliance should be established prior to or as part of any effort to establish new limitations.

Sixth and finally, President Obama has endorsed the goal of nuclear disarmament and some U.S. senior statesmen have suggested that the post-START re-engagement with Russia should be seen as a useful step toward "nuclear zero." Any new agreement, however, should be judged on its own merit, not on the hope that it constitutes a step toward nuclear zero.

The Congressional Strategic Posture Commission rightly concluded that for nuclear zero to be plausible there would have to be a fundamental transformation of the world order. The transformation required is in the basic nature of states: from a system of self-seeking and competitive sovereign actors with autonomous power and authority to an essentially cooperative world order, or to an international system in which great power and authority are held by a universally trusted international institution. The realization of either system would represent a more dramatic change in the world than the decline and eventual fall of the Western Roman Empire in AD 476.

That such a dramatic transformation would be necessary for nuclear zero to be plausible does not mean that the goal is impossible. It does suggest that taking any steps now ought *not* be predicated on such an elusive goal. Indeed, the unintended consequences of steps taken now in the hopes of fostering nuclear zero are largely unpredictable and as likely to endanger U.S. and allied security as to promote it. It is useful to recall the physician's goal of first doing no harm—in this case harm to the hard-earned conditions and U.S. capabilities that have helped keep the peace.

The burden of proof is on advocates not only to describe the requirements for nuclear zero, which they have done to some extent, but also to explain how and why the fundamental transformation of the world should be considered practicable on any timeline. Proponents have provided no such explanation; instead they use the metaphor of climbing a "mountain top." The route to nuclear disarmament, however, is not akin to climbing a mountain because there is no basis for anticipating that this particular "mountain top" can ever exist or what steps now might be helpful if it ever does exist.

British Prime Minister Winston Churchill once noted along these lines, "Be careful above all things not to let go of the atomic weapon until you are sure and more than sure that other means of preserving peace are in your hands." There is no basis whatsoever for that confidence, and we should not pursue arms control measures as if anyone knows how to get there.

These are the six major concerns I have with regard to the apparent early direction of the administration's efforts to re-establish strategic arms control as a centerpiece of U.S.-Russian engagement. It is important to establish the right agenda at the beginning of negotiations. If not, the results can be unacceptable no matter how well our team negotiates. My concern is that the administration may be in the process of agreeing to an agenda with serious potential problems.

POSTSCRIPT

Is President Barack Obama's Strategic Nuclear Arms Control Policy Sound?

There is an ancient Greek myth in which Prometheus steals fire from the gods. As punishment, Zeus chains Prometheus to a rock, where each day an eagle eviscerates him. There is something in this story that relates to humans unleashing the near divinely awful potential of the atom in 1945 and finding themselves unable to escape the horrendous possibility that evil in the form of an ICBM, rather than an eagle, will be the agent of agony.

As the introduction to this debate indicates, the efforts to constrain nuclear arms that began seriously in the 1960s made progress, even if slowly, for more than thirty years. The number of new countries (apart from the United States, Soviet Union/Russia, Great Britain, France, and China) with nuclear weapons grew by but one: Israel. The Soviets and Americans restrained testing, put caps on their nuclear expansion, and toward the end of the period moved to actually begin to reduce their respective massive arsenals.

Since the mid 1990s, however, progress faltered. It is true that the number of deployed U.S. and Russian warheads and bombs has continued to drop steadily. It is also the case, though, that India, Pakistan, and North Korea joined the ranks of nuclear powers, and Iran seems intent on doing so. Russia's Duma refused to ratify SALT. The U.S. Senate refused to ratify the Comprehensive Test Ban Treaty. The United States withdrew from the ABM Treaty.

Additionally, the era of good relations between Moscow and Washington for a time after the collapse began cool. The Russians were distressed by what they saw as the surge of NATO toward their borders and by the disadvantage they would face if the United States developed a ballistic missile defense system to supplement the U.S. offensive capability. For their part, the Americans worried about the steady diminution of democracy in Russia and by its sale of nuclear technology to Iran.

The collapse of the Soviet Union and end of the cold war in the early 1990s seemed to ease the threat of nuclear war so much that nuclear weapons arms control moved to the back burner of public concern and international diplomacy. The issue played no role in the presidential election of 2008, and press commentary on the nuclear weapons policy orientation of the new president has been nearly nonexistent. That does not mean that important issues, such as proliferation, the CTBT, BMD, and nuclear terrorism, do not remain troublesome. As the preceding readings reveal, there is also controversy about how to proceed.

The first major step by President Obama came in July 2009 when, after negotiations with President Medvedev in Moscow, the two signed an agreement in principle to begin negotiations aimed at cutting their respective nuclear warhead/bomb arsenals to 1,500 each. Obama delivered his first major address on nuclear weapons during a public speech on April 5, 2009, in Prague, the Czech Republic. It is available on the White House Web site at www.whitehouse. gov/the_press_office/Remarks-By-President-Barack-Obama-In-Prague-As-Delivered/. There is also documentation and information on a range of nuclear-related issues on the Web site of the U.S. State Department at www.state.gov/t/isn/. An article that, like President Obama, calls for eliminating all nuclear weapons is Harald Muller's "The Future of Nuclear Weapons in an Interdependent World" (*Washington Quarterly*, 2008).

More information on current developments are available at three defense-oriented think tanks, the Center for Strategic and International Studies (www. csis.org), the Center for Defense Information (www.cdi.org/), and the Center for Security Policy (www.centerforsecuritypolicy.org). For a look at the wisdom of disarmament, including the somewhat unusual argument that more nuclear weapons may be better, see Scott D. Sagan and Kenneth N. Waltz, *The Spread of Nuclear Weapons: A Debate Renewed* (W. W. Norton, 2003).

To learn more about the nuclear weapons of the United States, Russia, and other countries, go the Web site of the *Bulletin of the Atomic Scientists* at http://www.thebulletin.org/. Look in the archives, and toward the end of most issues is a section entitled "Nuclear Notebook," which contains valuable data.

Contributors to This Volume

EDITOR

JOHN T. ROURKE, Ph.D., is a professor of political science at the University of Connecticut. He has written numerous articles, book chapters, and papers, and is also the author of *Congress, the Executive, and U.S. Foreign Policy-making* (Westview Press, 1985); *International Relations on the World Stage*, 11th edition (McGraw-Hill, 1987–2006); *Making Foreign Policy: United States, Soviet Union, China* (Brooks/Cole, 1990); and *Presidential War and American Democracy: Rally Round the Chief* (Paragon House, 1993). Professor Rourke is the co-author of *Direct Democracy and International Politics: Deciding International Issues Through Referendums*, with Richard Hiskes and Cyrus E. Zirakzadeh (Lynne Rienner Publisher, 1992); *Making American Foreign Policy*, with Ralph Carter and Mark Boyer, 2nd edition (Brown & Benchmark, 1994, 1996); and *International Politics on the World Stage: Brief Edition*, with Mark Boyer, 7th edition (McGraw-Hill, 1996–2007). In addition to this 14th edition of *Taking Sides: Clashing Views in World Politics* (McGraw-Hill, 1987–2007), he is the editor of *Taking Sides: Clashing Views on Controversial Issues in American Foreign Policy*, 2nd edition (Dushkin Publishing Group, 2000, 2002) and *You Decide: Current Debates in American Politics*, 4th edition (Longman, 2004–2007). A long career in both the academic and applied sides of politics has convinced the author that politics impacts everyone and that those who become knowledgeable and get active to promote what they believe in, whether that is based on self-interest or altruism, are the single most important driving force in the ultimate contest: politics.

AUTHORS

PETER F. ALLGEIER is deputy U.S. Trade Representative. He has also served as U.S. ambassador to the World Trade Organization (WTO) in Geneva, Switzerland. He has a Ph.D. in international economics from the University of North Carolina at Chapel Hill.

NORMAN A. BAILEY is consulting economist and senior fellow at the Potomac Foundation. He was the senior director of International Economic Affairs at the National Security Council during the Reagan administration, has served on the faculty of City University of New York, and has been the president of an investment banking firm. He holds a Ph.D. from Columbia University.

PATRICIA BERLYN writes on Israelite history and culture and is a former associate editor for the *Jewish Bible Quarterly* in Jerusalem. She has also worked for the Council on Foreign Relations, as well as its journal, *Foreign Affairs*.

NANCY BIRDSALL is the founding president of the Center for Global Development. Prior to that, she served for three years as senior associate and director of the Economic Reform Project at the Carnegie Endowment for International Peace. From 1993 to 1998 as executive vice president of the Inter-American Development Bank, the largest of the regional development banks, she oversaw a US$30 billion public and private loan portfolio. Before joining the Inter-American Development Bank, she spent 14 years in research, policy, and management positions at the World Bank, including as a director of the Policy Research Department. She has a Ph.D. from Yale University.

SAMUEL A. BLEICHER is currently a principal in his consulting firm, The Strategic Path LLC. From 2001 to 2007, he served as chief strategist for New Initiatives in the Overseas Buildings Operations Bureau of the U.S. State Department.

JOHN R. BOLTON is a former U.S. ambassador to the United Nations. Prior to that he served as under secretary of state for arms control and international security, assistant secretary of state for international organization affairs, assistant attorney general in the U.S. Department of Justice, and as assistant administrator for Program and Policy Coordination and as general counsel in U.S. Agency for International Development. He has also been senior vice president of the American Enterprise Institute (AEI). He holds a J.D. from Yale Law School.

BARBARA BOXER is a Democratic member of the U.S. Senate from California. She chairs the Senate's Committee on Environment and Public Works. Earlier she served five terms in the U.S. House of Representatives.

BARRY R. CHISWICK is UIC distinguished professor in and head of the Department of Economics, University of Illinois at Chicago and director of the UIC Center for Economic Education. He holds a Ph.D. in economics from Columbia University.

PHILIP E. COYLE, III, is senior advisor at the Center for Defense Information. He has served as assistant secretary of defense and director, Operational

Test and Evaluation, and has worked at the Lawrence Livermore National Laboratory.

WILLIAM J. DURCH is senior associate at the Henry L. Stimson Center. He has served in the U.S. Arms Control and Disarmament Agency, as a research fellow at the Harvard Center for Science and International Affairs, and as assistant director of the Defense and Arms Control Studies program at the Massachusetts Institute of Technology. He holds a Ph.D. from the Massachusetts Institute of Technology.

MICHAEL EISENSTADT is a senior fellow and director of The Washington Institute's Military and Security Studies Program. In 2002–2003 he served as an advisor to the State Department's Future of Iraq defense policy working group, and in 2006 he was an advisor to the congressionally mandated Iraq Study Group (the Baker-Hamilton Commission). Earlier he worked as a civilian military analyst with the U.S. Army. He has an M.A. in Arab studies from Georgetown University.

STUART E. EIZENSTAT is a partner in the law firm of Covington & Burling. He has served as chief White House domestic policy adviser during the Carter administration, and as ambassador to the European Union, under secretary of Commerce for International Trade, under secretary of state for economic, business and agricultural affairs, and deputy secretary of the treasury in the Clinton Administration. He has a J.D. degree from Harvard University Law School.

IVAN ELAND is a senior fellow at the Independent Institute. He has been director of Defense Policy Studies at the Cato Institute and spent 15 years working for Congress on national security issues, including time as an investigator for the House Foreign Affairs Committee and principal defense analyst at the Congressional Budget Office. He also has served as evaluator-in-charge (national security and intelligence) for what is now the Government Accountability Office. He holds a Ph.D. in public policy from George Washington University.

JONATHAN F. FANTON is president of the John D. and Catherine T. MacArthur Foundation. He has also served as president of the New School for Social Research and vice president for Planning at the University of Chicago. He has a Ph.D. in American history from Yale University.

JULIA GALEOTA was a high school senior at Holton Arms School in McLean, Virginia, at the time she wrote her essay. The essay won first place in the thirteen-to-seventeen-year-old age category of the 2004 *Humanist* Essay Contest for Young Women and Men of North America and was published in the *Humanist*. She has gone on to undergraduate studies at Yale University in New Haven, Connecticut.

TUCKER HERBERT is an undergraduate student at Stanford University and foreign affairs editor of the Stanford Review.

CHRISTOPHER HEMMER is an associate professor in the Department of International Security Studies at the Air War College at Maxwell Air Force Base,

Montgomery, Alabama. He has also taught at Cornell University and Colgate University. He has a Ph.D. in government from Cornell University.

JAMES INHOFE is a Republican member of the U.S. Senate from Oklahoma. He has chaired the Senate's Committee on Environment and Public Works. He has also been a member of the U.S. House of Representatives, Mayor of Tulsa, Oklahoma, a member of both houses of the Oklahoma legislature, and as president of the Quaker Life Insurance Company.

ANTHONY B. KIM is a Policy Analyst for the Center for International Trade and Economics (CITE). Kim researches economic issues with a focus on economic freedom and free trade at The Heritage Foundation.

HAROLD HONGJU KOH is currently legal adviser to the U.S. Department of State. Before that he was Martin R. Flug '55 Professor of International Law at Yale University. His earlier notable appointments include Dean of Yale Law School and U.S. assistant secretary of state for democracy, human rights and labor. He holds 11 honorary doctoral degrees and has received more than thirty awards including the 2005 Louis B. Sohn Award from the American Bar Association International Law Section and the 2003 Wolfgang Friedmann Award from Columbia Law School for lifetime achievements in international law. He is author or co-author of eight books and more than 150 articles. He hold a J.D. from Harvard Law School.

JEFF KUETER is president of the George C. Marshall Institute. He has an M.A. in political science and another M.A. in security policy studies and science and technology studies, both from George Washington University.

PHILIPPE LEGRAIN is chief economist of Britain in Europe. He was previously special adviser to the director-general of the World Trade Organization and the trade and economics correspondent for *The Economist*. He has also written for *The Financial Times, The Wall Street Journal Europe, The Times, The Guardian, The Independent, New Statesman, Prospect,* and *The Ecologist,* as well as *The New Republic, Foreign Policy,* and *The Chronicle Review.* He has a master's degree in economics from the London School of Economics.

KATE MARTIN is director of the Center for National Security Studies. She has a J.D. degree from University of Virginia Law School.

JENNIFER MCCOY is a professor of political science, Georgia State University and director of the Americas Program at the Carter Center. She holds a Ph.D. in political science from the University of Minnesota.

GRACE SMITH MELTON is Associate for Social Issues at the United Nations with the Richard and Helen DeVos Center for Religion and Civil Society at The Heritage Foundation.

PATRICK A. MULLOY is the Washington representative of the Alfred P. Sloan Foundation. He has served on the United States-China Economic and Security Review Commission, on the staff of the Joint Economic Committee of the U.S. Congress, and as assistant secretary of commerce for international trade administration.

BARACK OBAMA is the President of the United States. He has served in the Illinois state senate and has a J.D. from Harvard University.

KEITH B. PAYNE is a professor in and head of the Graduate Department of Defense and Strategic Studies at Missouri State University. He has served as deputy assistant secretary of defense for forces policy and is a member of the Department of Defense's Defense Science Board. He is co-founder and current president of the National Institute for Public Policy, a think tank that focuses on national security policy. He is editor-in-chief of the journal *Comparative Strategy*, and is author or co-author of 16 books and 90 articles. He earned a Ph.D. in international relations from the University of Southern California.

WILLIAM J. PERRY is co-chair of Congressional Commission on the Strategic Posture of the United States. He is a former U.S. secretary of defense. Other earlier notable public posts include deputy secretary of defense and under secretary of defense for research and engineering He was also president of ESL, Inc., an electronics firm that he helped found. Additionally, he has served on the faculty of Stanford University's School of Engineering, where he was co-director of the Preventive Defense Project at Stanford's Center for International Security and Cooperation. Among other awards, he holds a U.S. Presidential Medal of Freedom and is Knight Commander of the British Empire. He earned a Ph.D. in mathematics from Pennsylvania State University.

NORMAN PODHORETZ is the editor-at-large of *Commentary* and widely acknowledged as one of the most influential conservative thinkers of his time. He was awarded the Presidential Medal of Freedom by George W. Bush in 2004.

DIANE RAUB is an undergraduate student at Stanford University and a staff writer for the *Stanford Review*.

ROBERT B. REICH is professor of public policy at the University of California, Berkeley and a former U.S. secretary of labor in the Clinton administration. He has been on the faculty of Brandeis University and the John F. Kennedy School of Government at Harvard University. He was a Rhodes Scholar and has a J.D. from Yale University Law School.

SUSAN E. RICE is a senior fellow in foreign policy and global economy and development at the Brookings Institute. She served as assistant secretary of state for African affairs in the Clinton administration and before that as senior director for African affairs at the National Security Council and director for International Organizations and Peacekeeping at the NSC. She has a D.Phil. (Ph.D.) in international relations from Oxford University.

DAVID B. RIVKIN is a partner in the law firm of Baker & Hostetler. He has also served as associate executive director and counsel of the President's Council on Competitiveness during the Reagan administration, and as associate general counsel, U.S. Department of Energy and deputy director of the Office of Policy Development in the U.S. Department of Justice during the first Bush administration.

EUGENE B. RUMER is a senior fellow in the Institute for National Strategic Studies at the National Defense University. Before that, he was a visiting scholar at the Washington Institute for Near East Policy, a member of the Secretary's Policy Planning Staff at the U.S. Department of State, and director for Russian, Ukrainian, and Eurasian affairs at the National Security Council. He holds a Ph.D. in Russian Studies from Georgetown University.

BRETT D. SCHAEFER is the Jay Kingham Fellow in International Regulatory Affairs at the Heritage Foundation. He has an M.A. degree in international development economics from the School of International Service at American University.

ROSEMARY E. SHINKO is a member of the political science faculty at Bucknell University and former coordinator of academic services at the Stamford Campus of the University of Connecticut. She holds a Ph.D. in political science from the University of Connecticut.

DAN SICILIANO is executive director of the program in law, economics, and business at Stanford Law School, where he teaches corporate law and practice. He has also headed a private law firm and a management consulting firm and practiced immigration law. He holds a J.D. from Stanford University.

JOHN J. TKACIK, JR., is senior research fellow in China Policy in the Asian Studies Center at the Heritage Foundation. He is a retired diplomat who served overseas with the U.S. Foreign Service in Taiwan, Iceland, Hong Kong, and two tours in China as well as in the State Department, where he was chief of China Analysis in its Bureau of Intelligence and Research. He has a master's degree from Harvard University.

ALEX DE WAAL is the program director at the Social Science Research Council and a fellow at the Global Equity Initiative at Harvard University. He has a D.Phil. (Ph.D.) in social anthropology from the Oxford University.

LORI WALLACH is director of Public Citizen's Global Trade Watch, a division of Public Citizen. She is a graduate of Harvard Law School.

LAWRENCE B. WILKERSON is the Pamela C. Harriman visiting professor of Government and Public Policy at the College of William and Mary. He is a retired colonel in the U.S. Army and served as chief of staff to Secretary of State Colin Powell from 2002 to 2005. He has also served as director of the U.S. Marine Corps War College at Quantico, Virginia.